Dictionary of Literary Biography

Documentary Series

Yearbooks

Concise Series

Concise Dictionary of American Literary Biography, 6 volumes (1988-1989): *The New Consciousness, 1941-1968; Colonization to the American Renaissance, 1640-1865; Realism, Naturalism, and Local Color, 1865-1917; The Twenties, 1917-1929; The Age of Maturity, 1929-1941; Broadening Views, 1968-1988.*

Concise Dictionary of British Literary Biography, 8 volumes (1991-1992): *Writers of the Middle Ages and Renaissance Before 1660; Writers of the Restoration and Eighteenth Century, 1660-1789; Writers of the Romantic Period, 1789-1832; Victorian Writers, 1832-1890; Late Victorian and Edwardian Writers, 1890-1914; Modern Writers, 1914-1945; Writers After World War II, 1945-1960; Contemporary Writers, 1960 to Present.*

Dictionary of Literary Biography® • Volume One Hundred Eighty-Eight

American Book and Magazine
Illustrators to 1920

Dictionary of Literary Biography® • Volume One Hundred Eighty-Eight

American Book and Magazine Illustrators to 1920

Edited by
Steven E. Smith
Catherine A. Hastedt
Donald H. Dyal

A Bruccoli Clark Layman Book
Gale Research
Detroit, Washington, D.C., London

The paper used in this publication meets the minimum requirements
of American National Standard for Information Sciences–Permanence
Paper for Printed Library Materials, ANSI Z39.48-1984.∞ ™

Library of Congress Cataloging-in-Publication Data

American book and magazine illustrators to 1920 / edited by Steven E. Smith, Catherine A. Hastedt,
  and Donald H. Dyal.
    p. cm.–(Dictionary of literary biography; v. 188)
"A Bruccoli Clark Layman book."
Includes bibliographical references and index.
ISBN 0-7876-1843-8 (alk. paper)
1. Illustration of books–United States–Bio-bibliography. 2. Magazine illustration–United States–
Bio-bibliography. I. Smith, Steven E. II. Hastedt, Catherine A. III. Dyal, Donald H. IV. Series.
Z5961.U5A515 1998
[NC975]
741.6'4'092273–dc21
[B]
                                                                                    98-42547
                                                                                    CIP

10 9 8 7 6 5 4 3 2 1

Contents

Plan of the Series

The advisory board, the editors, and the publisher of the *Dictionary of Literary Biography* are joined in endorsing Mark Twain's declaration. The literature of a nation provides an inexhaustible resource of permanent worth. We intend to make literature and its creators better understood and more accessible to students and the reading public, while satisfying the standards of teachers and scholars.

To meet these requirements, *literary biography* has been construed in terms of the author's achievement. The most important thing about a writer is his writing. Accordingly, the entries in *DLB* are career biographies, tracing the development of the author's canon and the evolution of his reputation.

The purpose of *DLB* is not only to provide reliable information in a convenient format but also to place the figures in the larger perspective of literary history and to offer appraisals of their accomplishments by qualified scholars.

The publication plan for *DLB* resulted from two years of preparation. The project was proposed to Bruccoli Clark by Frederick C. Ruffner, president of the Gale Research Company, in November 1975. After specimen entries were prepared and typeset, an advisory board was formed to refine the entry format and develop the series rationale. In meetings held during 1976, the publisher, series editors, and advisory board approved the scheme for a comprehensive biographical dictionary of persons who contributed to North American literature. Editorial work on the first volume began in January 1977, and it was published in 1978. In order to make *DLB* more than a reference tool and to compile volumes that individually have claim to status as literary history, it was decided to organize volumes by

topic, period, or genre. Each of these freestanding volumes provides a biographical-bibliographical guide and overview for a particular area of literature. We are convinced that this organization—as opposed to a single alphabet method—constitutes a valuable innovation in the presentation of reference material. The volume plan necessarily requires many decisions for the placement and treatment of authors who might properly be included in two or three volumes. In some instances a major figure will be included in separate volumes, but with different entries emphasizing the aspect of his career appropriate to each volume. Ernest Hemingway, for example, is represented in *American Writers in Paris, 1920–1939* by an entry focusing on his expatriate apprenticeship; he is also in *American Novelists, 1910–1945* with an entry surveying his entire career, as well as in *American Short-Story Writers, 1910–1945, Second Series* with an entry concentrating on his short stories. Each volume includes a cumulative index of the subject authors and articles. Comprehensive indexes to the entire series are planned.

The series has been further augmented by the *DLB Yearbooks* (since 1981) which update published entries and add new entries to keep the *DLB* current with contemporary activity. There have also been *DLB Documentary Series* volumes which provide biographical and critical source materials for figures whose work is judged to have particular interest for students. One of these companion volumes is entirely devoted to Tennessee Williams.

We define literature as the *intellectual commerce of a nation:* not merely as belles lettres but as that ample and complex process by which ideas are generated, shaped, and transmitted. *DLB* entries are not limited to "creative writers" but extend to other figures who in their time and in their way influenced the mind of a people. Thus the series encompasses historians, journalists, publishers, book collectors, and screenwriters. By this means readers of *DLB* may be aided to perceive literature not as cult scripture in the keeping of intellectual high priests but firmly positioned at the center of a nation's life.

DLB includes the major writers appropriate to each volume and those standing in the ranks behind them. Scholarly and critical counsel has been sought in deciding which minor figures to include and how full their entries should be. Wherever possible, useful references are made to figures who do not warrant separate entries.

Each *DLB* volume has an expert volume editor responsible for planning the volume, selecting the figures for inclusion, and assigning the entries. Volume editors are also responsible for preparing, where appropriate, appendices surveying the major periodicals and literary and intellectual movements for their volumes, as well as lists of further readings. Work on the series as a whole is coordinated at the Bruccoli Clark Layman editorial center in Columbia, South Carolina, where the editorial staff is responsible for accuracy and utility of the published volumes.

One feature that distinguishes *DLB* is the illustration policy—its concern with the iconography of literature. Just as an author is influenced by his surroundings, so is the reader's understanding of the author enhanced by a knowledge of his environment. Therefore *DLB* volumes include not only drawings, paintings, and photographs of authors, often depicting them at various stages in their careers, but also illustrations of their families and places where they lived. Title pages are regularly reproduced in facsimile along with dust jackets for modern authors. The dust jackets are a special feature of *DLB* because they often document better than anything else the way in which an author's work was perceived in its own time. Specimens of the writers' manuscripts and letters are included when feasible.

Samuel Johnson rightly decreed that "The chief glory of every people arises from its authors." The purpose of the *Dictionary of Literary Biography* is to compile literary history in the surest way available to us—by accurate and comprehensive treatment of the lives and work of those who contributed to it.

The *DLB* Advisory Board

Introduction

Dictionary of Literary Biography volume 188 *American Book and Magazine Illustrators to 1920* explores the American contribution to illustration through a few dozen of its most noteworthy practitioners. It begins with some of the earliest illustrators in America and continues through the so-called Golden Age of illustration, a period of unprecedented growth and opportunity that lasted from about 1890 until sometime in the 1920s. Although some of the artists treated in this book were active well into the mid twentieth century, their careers were molded in this Golden Age, and they carried the mark of that time throughout their careers. Several now lesser-known illustrators as well as individuals who are better known today as "fine artists" have also been included to provide as full a picture as possible of the profession.

Illustrators are often regarded as second-rate artists. Because they have traditionally worked on commission with little or no say in the selection of subject matter, some critics have seen their work as somehow less pure or less worthy than that of their "fine art" colleagues. The illustrator does work under different constraints than those of other artists. He works for a client (an advertiser, publisher, author, or art editor), and this client determines the audience and the method of reproduction, sets a deadline, and often takes an active part in the creative process. The goal of the client is also commercially oriented. He wants to sell something, whether a book or a soap powder. The profession is thus by necessity collaborative and commercial, and these two characteristics have tended, at least in critical circles, to set the illustrator a notch or two below other artists. The fine artist creates art for its own sake; the illustrator, so the stereotype goes, creates for the sake of the marketplace.

However, the idea that working for hire debases art is a false concept. Throughout history artists have depended on the support of patrons, and to think that the concerns and wishes of the latter have never influenced the products of the former would be naive. Art, in one way or another, has always been beholden, if not to the advertiser or publisher, then to the prince, nobleman, church, wealthy businessman, gallery, or, more recently, the nonprofit foundation or government agency. The illustrator may work with his client more closely than the traditional artist works with his patron, and the constraints under which he works may be more apparent, but the nature of his working conditions and the goal he pursues are more closely allied with that of the fine artist than is often assumed.

The illustrator, nevertheless, has been and continues to be seen as a stepchild of the art family. He has as much claim, however, to the rich heritage of the field as any traditional artist. Illustration descends directly from narrative painting. Narrative, after all, is the essence of illustration, and its antecedents can be found throughout history, from the colored images of animals on cave walls to the pictographic writing found in ancient-Egyptian variations on the Book of the Dead to the mosaics at Pompeii and the frescoes in early Christian churches. In these examples and many others that could be cited the scenes and figures depicted serve decorative and commemorative purposes. Their significance lies elsewhere. As narrative images they also serve to communicate the values, hopes, and traditions of their cultures. Although often in an overtly commercial environment, illustration serves the same ends. J. C. Leyendecker accomplished much more than increased sales of Arrow shirt collars and Kuppenheimer suits; he established an ideal of sartorial excellence that is still impressive after seven decades. Many illustrators, with almost no supporting text, produced an automotive lifestyle through powerful images and stylish statements regarding automobiles like Jordan, Pierce-Arrow, Duesenberg, and others. Alice Roosevelt so clearly personified Charles Dana Gibson's ideal girl in look and demeanor as to become a fashion statement herself. Jessie Willcox Smith defined motherhood for generations through her soft and sensitive illustrations. Frederic Remington, Howard Pyle, James Montgomery Flagg, and hosts of others labored to create an imaginative link between the viewer and history, the viewer and literature, the viewer and a product, or the viewer and an ideal.

In communicating these ideals the illustrator has always been dependent on and to some extent limited by technology. His end product is not the canvas or the sketch pad but the printed page, and thus he is obliged to work within the constraints of the mechanical, photographic, or, more recently, electronic processes that reproduce his art. During the Golden Age there were many significant advances in technology, the earliest and most important of which was the technique of cutting and printing from woodblocks known as wood engraving. Developed in the late eighteenth century by an English artist, Thomas Bewick, this process not only laid the technological groundwork for the boom in illustration that would occur during the nineteenth century but also revived–some would say rescued–the woodblock as a means of producing illustrations and prints.

During the eighteenth century the art of woodcut illustration in Europe had fallen into virtual disuse, surviving only as a means of printing simple and relatively crude ornaments–coats of arms, billing heads, stamps, seals, and other such ordinary uses. The copperplate, due to its superior line, had become the chief medium for the printing of fine illustrations. There were, however, serious drawbacks to printing from copper. Because copperplates do not print in relief as does letterpress, they require a separate printing press. Copperplates also begin to wear and smudge after relatively few impressions. Until a better method was developed the detail that could be achieved from copper compensated for these drawbacks.

Bewick's innovations were brilliant for their simplicity. Woodcuts had traditionally been done on the side or "plank" of a board, with the lines of the illustration produced by cutting away the background with a knife. Bewick chose to cut on the end grain instead of on the plank, which is relatively soft, and thus does not lend itself to very detailed work. Because the endgrain is harder than the plank side, it prints better and lasts longer. Bewick also was the first to use a graver, an engraving tool, instead of a knife. He is also credited with developing the white-line technique, which involves removing the line instead of the background. Together these innovations resulted in a fineness of detail that rivaled that of the copperplate. Wood engraving also had economic advantages over copper. First, wood was cheap. Second, because a wood engraving, like type, works in relief, the woodblock could be set up in the press and printed with the text. This eliminated the cost and labor of operating one press for the text and another for illustrations. Third, a woodblock wears better than copper and thus allows a great many more impressions. The result was a reduction in cost, an increase in the durability of the plate, and no loss–and in some cases an improvement–in quality.

Stereotyping, which had been known as a means of reproducing type pages since before 1700, began to be used to reproduce wood engravings in the early nineteenth century. The process involved making a mold of the original engraving and then filling that mold with hot metal to make a replica. The finished plate was more durable than the woodblock and made impressions virtually indistinguishable from it. In addition to preserving the original engraving, stereotyping also meant that the publisher could make multiple copies of the engraving for use in different publications. Stereotyping boosted the economy of printing wood engravings and thereby greatly contributed to their remarkable popularity.

Wood engravings were first made in America at the end of the eighteenth century. By 1850 they were ubiquitous. On their way to becoming the dominant method for book and magazine illustration, however, an important change took place. In England, Bewick not only drew directly on the block but also cut the image into the wood himself, thus combining the roles of engraver and artist. For Bewick wood engraving was not merely a means of reproduction but a creative endeavor in itself. The first American to practice wood engraving, Alexander Anderson, followed in this tradition, but as time passed, the roles of artist and engraver were separated. By the middle of the century the individuals who made engravings for the large periodical presses and book publishers were not the originating artists but intermediary craftsmen, sometimes called sculptors. The sculptor's job was to transfer the artist's work from paper to the woodblock. Though often highly skilled and capable of producing engravings with an astonishing fidelity to the original, these craftsmen were a source of dissatisfaction for illustrators, who complained that their work was simplified and even distorted in the translation process. An important improvement was brought about with the advent of "photography-on-the-block." In order to cut out the image, the engraver first had to redraw or copy the illustrator's drawing onto the woodblock. Photography-on-the-block meant developing a photograph of the drawing directly on the wood surface, a process that in turn allowed the engraver to cut from lines reproduced with the accuracy of a photograph. Despite this improvement, the interposition of another hand between the original and the printed work continued to frustrate illustrators.

In the last quarter of the century a new method of reproducing illustrations was developed that would revolutionize the industry. Frederick Eugene Ives patented the halftone process in America in 1881 although its widespread use did not occur until a decade later. This invention involved photographing the original image through a fine screen. The screen broke up the image into dots and, when used in printing, allowed continuous tonal gradation; until this time such gradation had been rendered by the engraver with a series of lines known as cross-hatches. Early halftones were sometimes touched up on the plate to increase the definition of the print, but for the most part they did not require any human intervention. Like engravings, halftones could be printed with the text. Now artists were able to work in oils, gouaches, and watercolors with more confidence that their work would be accurately translated to the printing surface. For a time publishers continued to use wood engravings as they perfected and grew accustomed to this new process, but during the 1890s the older method and the tradition of sculptors that had grown up with it was phased out completely.

Around the same time that halftones were being developed the industry was beginning to use another photographic method. First experimented with by Fox Talbot in England in the 1850s but not put into commercial use for another thirty years, the photogravure, like the halftone, allowed the reproduction of tonal values. In fact, the photogravure was considered superior to the halftone in this regard. Its one great disadvantage, however, hearkened back to the copperplate. Because the photogravure does not print in relief, it must be produced separately from the text on a special press. This circumstance limited its use almost exclusively to the most expensive books.

With the refinement of the halftone process also came the capacity to reproduce color illustrations, the first examples of which appear in the last decade of the nineteenth century. Color-process halftones also involved photographing the artwork through a screen to produce photomechanical plates, one for each of the four colors involved. The plates were then printed one after the other to produce the color image. In the beginning the process was used with only one or two colors, the effect being that of a "tinted" illustration. Color halftones were clunky at first and were neither perfected nor economically feasible until the late 1920s. Many artists, N. C. Wyeth perhaps the most notable among them, complained that their original colors were flattened and muted in the process.

The color halftone had its first impact on the covers of illustrated periodicals. Vying for customers in the highly competitive newsstand market of the late 1890s, magazine publishers were quick to exploit color to make the previously monochromatic covers of their magazines more eye-catching. Unfortunately, the expense of color tended to reduce the number of illustrations in books. Instead of several pictures, publishers limited themselves to a frontispiece and the cover or dust jacket, as if one or two key scenes rendered in color made up for the absence of several black-and-white images spaced throughout to help develop the plot. Except for the cover or dust jacket, illustrations were gradually eliminated from books altogether. This development, along with the first uses of color on magazine covers, meant that illustration began to take on the function of advertising in addition to storytelling.

Other methods of reproducing illustrations, such as steel engraving and lithography, existed, but like photogravure their use was limited because of their expense. Wood engraving, the halftone process, and the introduction of color by the halftone were by far the most important technological developments, for these were the processes that fueled the expansion of the industry. The story of illustration, however, is not only about technology but also about people and society. Although illustration began in the United States in the late eighteenth century and was influenced, as were all the early arts in America, by England, most of the early work in America was either imported from England or directly copied from the work of English illustrators. Bewick was the British artist of widest influence, and Anderson was the first illustrator in the United States to adopt his techniques. No less important than Anderson's assimilation of Bewick's style and innovations, though, is the role he played as teacher. He trained many of the illustrators of the postcolonial period—the time when American illustration was beginning to distinguish itself from British influence.

The biggest obstacle for early illustrators in America was the widespread availability of noncopyrighted images from England. Book publishers simply had little incentive to commission original illustrations when ready-made work from England was available for the cost of copying. This difficulty was only overcome as the market for subjects that could not be copied from British artists grew, namely books set in the United States written by its citizens. The first distinctly American illustrations appear in books by such characteristically American authors as Washington Irving and James Fenimore Cooper. The artist to lead in this breakthrough was Felix Octavius Carr Darley, and his success made him the first American illustrator to be recognized by the reading public. At a time when authors were still writing under pseudonyms or otherwise obscuring their identity, Darley's name was appearing on title pages as illustrator. Another important early artist was Hammatt Billings, whose work on books by Nathaniel Hawthorne and Harriet Beecher

Stowe also helped to establish a niche for American illustration. Perhaps the best measure of these pioneer illustrators' achievement is that in time American publishers commissioned them to illustrate books by English writers, among them Charles Dickens, Alfred Tennyson, and Sir Walter Scott.

One of the most important factors influencing the history of illustration in America was the rise of the illustrated periodical in the mid nineteenth century. Up to this point books had been the main medium for illustrations, but magazines soon took their place. Publications such as *Frank Leslie's Illustrated Newspaper* and *Harper's Weekly* fed and whetted the public's appetite for news as well as for leisure reading. The increased demand for graphic material by these and other publications meant that for the next few decades most illustrators derived the majority of their income from magazine work. After the 1860s many artists ceased book illustration altogether. Since most illustrated monographs published from then until after the turn of the century began in serialized-magazine form, the illustrations that accompanied them were simply reprinted for the book. When the late-nineteenth-century illustrator sat down at his easel or drawing board, more often than not he conceived his work in the format and layout of the periodical page. This point may seem insignificant at first, but it becomes more important when one considers that the periodical page was often much larger than the book page. Furthermore, magazine layout and design was oriented toward the graphic—that is what made the magazine appealing, after all. The use of multiple columns, decorative mastheads, ornaments, display type, and varying sizes of type were all employed in much greater abundance in periodicals than in books. When Harper or the Century Company put together a serialized novel or group of articles to make a book, the design of the periodical was either imitated or simplified, and no consideration was given to whether the illustrator thought his work was suited to the new use.

There were exceptions to the periodical-to-book cycle, one of the most important being *The Merry Adventures of Robin Hood,* written and illustrated by Pyle and published by Scribners in 1883. Though an earlier and shorter version of the story was published in *Harper's Young People,* Pyle produced all new illustrations for the book in addition to hand-lettered captions, floral borders, and numerous ornamental head- and tailpieces. In so thoroughly integrating text and pictures, *Robin Hood* was unique for its time. That to create this landmark example of book illustration Pyle not only had to design but also to write the book himself is indicative of the sway periodicals held over the field of illustration.

The success of the illustrated periodical was given a significant boost by the most important event of the century. The Civil War created a demand for news that was unparalleled in this country. Part of that demand was satisfied by illustrators called "special artists" who were sent to the battlefield by the weeklies to record the war firsthand. Winslow Homer and Thomas Nast both started their careers in this manner. Other illustrators of note, such as Alfred Waud, essentially began and ended their careers with the war. But more important than the work of any single illustrator during this period was that a standard in publishing had been set—the American reading public now expected illustrative material in significant quantities to accompany articles in newspapers and magazines. The word and the picture had become linked in the periodical press.

Harper dominated the profession through their magazines for most of the second half of the nineteenth century. Central to this success was Charles Parsons, who joined the firm in 1863. During his twenty-six-year tenure as art editor at Harper, Parsons discovered and guided the careers of some of the most famous illustrators, including Pyle, Remington, Gibson, and Edwin Austin Abbey. Parsons possessed an uncanny ability to spot rough-hewn talent and then guide that talent to mature development. Many of the illustrators he recruited possessed little or no training, and to anyone else but Parsons they would have shown nothing in the way of ability. Parsons's first sight of Remington's work, for example, was a hastily drawn sketch on brown wrapping paper.

The success of *Harper's Weekly* and similar periodicals encouraged other publishers; *Putnam's, The Atlantic Monthly,* and *Scribner's Magazine* are just a few of the periodicals that followed. In addition to a rise in the number of periodicals, the post–Civil War period saw the birth of more narrowly focused titles. In 1867 Harper began publication of *Harper's Bazar,* a women's magazine. In 1879 the same company took aim at the juvenile market with *Harper's Young People.* In 1883 the *Ladies' Home Journal* spun off from the newspaper *The Tribune and Farmer. Puck,* the first successful American humor magazine, was launched in 1877. From these first attempts to reach specific groups of readers there would eventually develop magazines limited to specific genres, such as science fiction and the Western. This trend toward specialization also encouraged illustrators to develop specialties—for example, Joel Chandler Harris, Southern humor; Remington, the West; and Gibson, high society and fashion.

As the nineteenth century turned to the twentieth, the profession found itself in the middle of what has since been termed the Golden Age of illustration. The increased prosperity of the country resulted in an increasingly literate and leisured population. The country's growing rail system coupled with modern postal service opened up markets far beyond city borders. Improvements in the printing press helped supply these new markets by greatly speeding up the printing process. Advances in the technology of illustration helped improve the quality of pictures while reducing the expense. All of these developments contributed to lower prices for the consumer and higher profits for the publisher. The net result was a boom market in which illustrators found greatly enhanced opportunities, and many began to earn incomes and achieve levels of fame that their predecessors never imagined. The most successful became celebrities better known than many of the authors whose books they illustrated. Their private lives were newsworthy, and their opinions on politics and other matters far afield from art were quoted in the press.

During the Golden Age advertising developed as a significant outlet for illustrators and, for the most successful, accounted for a substantial portion of their income. The increased use of the dust jacket and the increased emphasis on decorative magazine covers meant that the illustrator began to take on the role of promoter in addition to that of pictorial storyteller. But the most important factor behind the move of illustrators into advertising was the poster craze of the 1890s. Originating a decade earlier in France with the work of Henri de Toulouse-Lautrec, posters were first used in the United States to advertise magazines, so for illustrators to design them was natural. Soon posters were used to sell other products. Maxfield Parrish, one of the most prolific of the early poster illustrators, worked for the Philadelphia Horse Association, Colgate, the N. K. Fairbank Company (a purveyor of bath soaps), and Adlake Camera, among others. He also went on to work in other advertising media such as billboards, calendars, and box tops. Some illustrators became bankable commodities in their own right. Gibson and Howard Chandler Christy, for example, not only illustrated products but also endorsed them and appeared in advertisements.

The stunning success of a few was just that—the success of a few. Only those at the top of the profession could afford lives of extravagance and luxury. There were many well-known illustra-

tors who were not celebrities and never became rich. Thure de Thulstrup, who worked for all the major periodicals from the 1870s into the 1910s, died forgotten in a home for the elderly in 1930. J. Allen St. John, the most famous illustrator of Edgar Rice Burroughs's Tarzan stories, never rose above the most modest of circumstances. Mary Hallock Foote achieved a measure of financial stability, but even at the height of her career her income was only a fraction of that of her more eminent colleagues. What is remarkable about the Golden Age is not that a few enjoyed great success but that so many merely made a living. Indeed, for every Gibson or Christy there were hundreds of Thulstrups, St. Johns, and Footes.

Despite the growing prestige of illustration, many illustrators were not content with their newfound status. Some saw their work only as a means of paying the bills while they aspired to higher artistic goals, and others openly disparaged the profession. Much of the enmity that exists between illustration and the rest of the art world originated at this time from within its own ranks. Near the end of his life Remington gave up illustration to pursue "fine art." Wyeth thought that magazine and book work hindered his development as an artist. He also complained that publishers and authors had lowered the standards of illustration. The Golden Age was a period of unprecedented growth for the profession, but just as its practitioners were not uniformly successful, neither were they uniform in their feelings over the gains made by illustration or its merits as an art form.

This era of opportunity lasted until the late 1920s and early 1930s, when a shift in tastes and an increased reliance on photographs led to compression in an industry that had only known expansion. The halftone process led to accurate reproductions of tonal values in drawings. Unfortunately for the artist, it also facilitated the reproduction of photographs. Up to this point illustrators had demonstrated an amazing facility for adapting their work to the new printing processes. Now technology contributed to their downfall. The first to feel the effects were the journalistic illustrators, those who covered parades, funerals, campaign speeches, and other public events. The camera could record these events more effectively, and eventually news-oriented magazines such as *Time* and the new *Life,* which relied almost exclusively on photographs, emerged to take the place of the illustrated periodicals such as *Harper's Weekly.*

Financial factors also influenced the publishing industry. A decline in subscriptions and advertising revenues as radio and movies provided alternative sources of entertainment forced publishers to recover their costs by trimming their art departments. Furthermore, during the Great Depression years, romance and adventure, which had been among the dominant themes of illustration since the 1890s, gave way to realism.

The beginning of the Golden Age of American illustration is usually marked at around 1890. In a sense, however, the history of illustration in America had always been golden. The profession had experienced periods of great change, but that change had always been positive. The quality of illustrations improved; the number of outlets multiplied; the ranks of the profession grew; and the pay and status of illustrators rose. There were individual setbacks, particularly for those who would not or could not adapt to technological developments, but progress was the general experience. In the 1920s the situation reversed. Artists such as Norman Rockwell and Parrish prospered beyond the end of the Golden Age, but they were the exceptions. Increasingly, success was individual and setbacks general. In the decades after the 1920s there were new and different opportunities for illustrators, but the widespread and sustained progress which occurred from the late colonial period to the beginning of the Great Depression never returned.

—Steven E. Smith, Catherine A. Hastedt, and Donald H. Dyal

Acknowledgments

This book was produced by Bruccoli Clark Layman, Inc. Karen L. Rood is senior editor for the *Dictionary of Literary Biography* series. Penelope M. Hope and Samuel W. Bruce were the in-house editors. They were aided by Tracy S. Bitonti.

Administrative support was provided by Ann M. Cheschi and Brenda A. Gillie.

Bookkeeper is Joyce Fowler.

Copyediting supervisor is Jeff Miller. The copyediting staff includes Phyllis A. Avant, Patricia Coate, Christine Copeland, Thom Harman, and William L. Thomas Jr. Freelance copyeditor is Rebecca Mayo.

Editorial associate is L. Kay Webster.

Layout and graphics staff includes Janet E. Hill and Mark McEwan.

Office manager is Kathy Lawler Merlette.

Photography editors are Margaret Meriwether and Paul Talbot. Photographic copy work was performed by Joseph M. Bruccoli.

Production manager is Samuel W. Bruce.

Systems manager is Marie L. Parker.

Typesetting supervisor is Kathleen M. Flanagan. The typesetting staff includes Pamela D. Norton and Patricia Flanagan Salisbury. Freelance typesetters include Melody W. Clegg and Delores Plastow.

Walter W. Ross, Steven Gross, and Ronald Aikman did library research. They were assisted by the following librarians at the Thomas Cooper Library of the University of South Carolina: Linda Holderfield and the interlibrary-loan staff; reference-department head Virginia Weathers; reference librarians Marilee Birchfield, Stefanie Buck, Stefanie DuBose, Rebecca Feind, Karen Joseph, Donna Lehman, Charlene Loope, Anthony McKissick, Jean Rhyne, and Kwamine Simpson; circulation-department head Caroline Taylor; and acquisitions-searching supervisor David Haggard.

The editors would especially like to thank the Cushing Memorial Library, Texas A&M University for permitting their extensive use of the Mary and Mavis P. Kelsey and Illustration Collections.

Dictionary of Literary Biography® • Volume One Hundred Eighty-Eight

American Book and Magazine Illustrators to 1920

Dictionary of Literary Biography

Edwin Austin Abbey
(1 April 1852 – 1 August 1911)

Ken Kempcke
Montana State University

SELECTED BOOKS ILLUSTRATED: Dickens, Charles, *Christmas Stories* (New York: Harper's Household Editions, 1875);

Bryant, William Cullen, and Sydney Howard Gay, *Popular History of the United States,* 4 volumes (New York: Scribner, Armstrong, 1876–1878);

Dickens, Charles, *The Uncommercial Traveler* (New York, 1879);

Longfellow, Henry Wadsworth, *The Poetical Works of Henry Wadsworth Longfellow* (Boston: Houghton, Mifflin, 1880);

Herrick, Robert, *Selections from the Poetry of Robert Herrick* (New York: Harper, 1882);

De Mille, James, *A Castle in Spain* (New York: Harper's Library of Select Novels no. 615, 1883);

Sheridan, Richard B., *Sheridan's Comedies: The Rivals and The School for Scandal* (London: Chatto & Windus, 1885);

Boughton, George Henry, *Sketching Rambles in Holland* (New York: Harper, 1885);

Shinn, Earl, and F. Hopkinson Smith, *A Book of the Tile Club* (Boston & New York: Houghton, Mifflin, 1887);

Goldsmith, Oliver, *She Stoops to Conquer* (New York: Harper, 1887; deluxe folio edition, 1892; London: Sampson, Low, Marston, Searle & Rivington, 1888);

Old Songs (New York: Harper, 1889);

The Quiet Life: Certain Verses by Various Hands (New York: Harper, 1890, 1899; London: Sampson, Low, Marston, Searle & Rivington, 1890);

Edwin Austin Abbey (photograph by Bassano)

Shakespeare, William, *The Comedies of William Shakespeare,* 4 volumes (New York: Harper, 1896);

Goldsmith, Oliver, *The Deserted Village* (New York: Harper, 1902);

Malory, Thomas, *King Arthur Stories from Malory: Done from the Text of Sir Thomas Malory's Morte d'Arthur,* edited by Lillion O. Stevens and Edward Frank Allen (Boston: Houghton Mifflin, 1908).

PERIODICALS: *Harper's Weekly,* 1870–1909; *Harper's Monthly,* 1870–1909; *Scribner's Monthly,* 1874–1876; *St. Nicholas,* 1874–1876; *Scribner's Magazine,* 1894–1895.

At a time when the art of book and magazine illustration was at its zenith, Edwin Austin Abbey was recognized as one of its most distinguished masters. Perhaps the most popular and successful artist of his day, Abbey's genius as an illustrator, principally of William Shakespeare's works and English songs and tales, is derived from his crisp and refined pen-and-ink work and from his devotion to historical research and authenticity. The story embellishments he provided through his elegant illustrations were complementary not only because of their charm and beauty but also because of the artist's remarkable compassion and comprehension of their English themes. Abbey was both an illustrator and an artist in the fullest sense. From his small black-and-white illustrations for *Harper's Weekly* and *Harper's Monthly* magazines to his grand mural paintings in the Boston Public Library and Pennsylvania State Capitol, his work was characterized by an exceptional measure of artistic devotion. By the conclusion of the nineteenth century Abbey had become the preeminent artist in English and American pictorial literature and had a profound influence on the illustrators who followed in his footsteps.

Abbey was born in Philadelphia on 1 April 1852. He was the first child of William Maxwell Abbey, who sold wood and tobacco, and Margery Ann Kiple Abbey. The Abbey family grew to include Edwin's brother, William Burling (born in 1854), and a sister, Jane Kiple (born in 1858).

Abbey's mother was well read and early on developed Abbey's literary tastes. The family's home included a modest collection of books. His parents had intended for Edwin to enter the University of Pennsylvania to become a minister in the Episcopalian Church, of which they were members. They enrolled him in Henry D. Gregory's School, one of the leading private secondary schools in Philadelphia, but Abbey admitted in his later years that he was a disappointment as a schoolboy. Despite their disappointment in his academic work, his parents encouraged the artistic talents that he exhibited as a child. In 1866 he began to attend the art studio of Isaac L. Williams, a landscape and portrait painter. This was the first step in Abbey's artistic training. In 1867, at age fourteen, Abbey began to contribute illustra-

tions to William Taylor Adams's magazine, *Our Boys and Girls,* a young people's periodical. He signed his submissions with the pen name "Yorick" in ironic reference to the dead jester in Shakespeare's *Hamlet.*

In 1868, encouraged by his father, Abbey began an apprenticeship at the wood-engraving firm of Van Ingen and Snyder in Philadelphia to learn the art of drawing on wood for illustrating. Abbey excelled at his work and was soon given the responsibility of creating drawings for schoolbooks, geographies, readers, and spellers. He also developed his talents as an art editor by reading galley proofs of books and selecting passages for illustration.

After work Abbey attended art classes at the Pennsylvania Academy of Fine Arts under the guidance of Christian Schussele. Abbey studied what he called "the science of constructive drawing" and produced illustrations based on the stories of Charles Dickens and Shakespeare. As his biographer, E. V. Lucas, points out, Abbey used books as tools to create artwork. He was meticulous in detail, spending hours at his sketchbook creating intricate drawings of sections of furniture and parts of the human anatomy.

Abbey began to follow the developments of the Pre-Raphaelite school in England and the work of the master German pen-and-ink artist Adolph Menzel. While employed at Van Ingen and Snyder, Abbey began to submit some of his drawings to *Harper's Weekly* in New York, the dynamic center of the American illustrated press. Periodicals, especially monthly periodicals, were expanding to include not only news pictorials but also illustrated feature articles on such subjects as history, natural history, travel, local color, and literature. Abbey's first drawing accepted by *Harper's* was a full-page illustration, *The Puritans' First Thanksgiving,* published in *Harper's Weekly* on 3 December 1870 when the artist was eighteen.

Art editor Charles Parsons wrote Abbey's father offering Edwin, or "Ned" as he came to be known, an opportunity to work for Harper and Brothers in Franklin Square (New York City) for fifteen dollars a week. With the support of his father, Abbey joined the illustrators' department of Harper in February 1871 when he was still eighteen. Harper's magazines were the premier illustrated journals of their time and had on staff a venerable group of international artists who greatly influenced Abbey. The well-traveled and prolific artist C. S. Reinhart, a devotee of the current English style, became Abbey's mentor at Harper. Abbey's colleagues also included John Alexander, Howard Pyle, Harry Fenn, and Joseph Pennell. Abbey was associated with Harper for the next thirty-four years, his last illustration for *Harper's Monthly* appearing in 1909.

The American public had a great penchant for
English literature in the late 1800s, and much of
Harper's Monthly was filled with serial reproductions
of great English works. Abbey's major task was to illustrate many of these works, but his work also included a great diversity of subjects. He proved himself to be a tireless, dedicated, and enterprising
worker who often used mail carriers and colleagues
at Harper for models. Often Abbey worked from
photographs to depict travel scenes such as his
sketch *Round by Propeller* in 1872. With his joyous nature and sense of humor, Abbey gained many
friends in New York and became one of Harper's
most prolific illustrators.

In 1874 issues of *Harper's Monthly* Abbey first
provided illustrations to the works of Robert Herrick and Shakespeare, two authors whose works he
became closely associated with in later life. For the
February 1874 issue Abbey supplied a series of cartoons depicting scenes from everyday life humorously captioned with lines from Shakespeare's
plays. Abbey's expert and sprightly style can be
seen in such illustrations as those for Herrick's
poem "Corinna's Going A-Maying," which appeared in May 1874. His drawings were influenced
by English illustrators and their airy pen-and-ink
technique. Over his lifetime Abbey compiled a
scrapbook full of their work. The success of Abbey's
early illustrations prompted Harper to raise his salary to twenty dollars a week at the end of his first
year and to thirty-five at the end of his second.

After Abbey's third year Parsons was unable
to secure another raise for him. In late 1874, believing he would have more flexibility and be able to
make more money freelancing, Abbey left the firm
and became an independent draftsman. Confident
and ambitious, he moved into a studio on Union
Square with the sculptor and illustrator James Edwin Kelly. The studio was soon filled with period
costumes and props that the artists used as models
for their work.

This period of freelance work in Abbey's life
was eventful. Soon after moving in, Abbey was commissioned by Scribners to provide drawings for William Cullen Bryant and Sydney Howard Gay's
Popular History of the United States (1876–1878), a
schoolbook which in its four-volume 1896 edition
includes more than sixteen hundred illustrations
from some of the most prominent illustrators of the
time, including many of Abbey's former associates
at Harper. The publication of these volumes was
not only a great achievement for Abbey's early career but also a milestone in the history of the illus

Illustration by Abbey for George Henry Boughton's Sketching
Rambles in Holland *(1885)*

trated book in America. After its publication Abbey
contributed many illustrations to the magazines
Scribner's Monthly, *St. Nicholas*, and *Century*, including
drawings for Edward Everett Hale's "Philip Nolan's
Friends" (*Scribner's Monthly*, January 1876), which
exhibited his antiquarian style and concern for historical definitude.

Abbey's interests grew to include the painting
of watercolors; he exhibited some of his work in this
medium for the first time at the American Watercolor Society in New York in 1874. The subject matter of his watercolor work, like his illustrations,
tended to the narrative and was well received at the
exhibition. His painting *The Sisters* eventually sold
for $2,000, at that time the largest price ever given
for an American watercolor. In 1876 Abbey was
elected to membership in the American Watercolor
Society and for many years contributed a painting
to its annual exhibition.

Abbey continued his friendship with Charles
Parsons, the kindly, paternalistic editor at Harper,
who contracted with Abbey to produce illustrations
for Harper's Household Edition of Dickens's *Christmas Stories* in 1875. In the same year Abbey attended
an exhibition of Henry Blackburn's English watercolors which, together with Abbey's Pre-Raphaelite

studies, influenced his artistic direction. His illustrations in *Christmas Stories* reveal this influence. As Abbey grew in reputation and expertise, Harper decided that it wanted the artist back in its employ and offered him fifty dollars a week to return to its art department. Abbey accepted the offer in 1876 and soon completed forty-five illustrations for Charles Dickens's *The Uncommercial Traveler* (1879).

To interrupt the monotony of office routine, Abbey would sometimes turn cartwheels and at one time installed a trapeze above his desk on which he would perform gymnastic maneuvers. The trapeze was removed one day after Abbey, during one of his acrobatic spins, knocked off the fine silk hat of Fletcher Harper Jr., one of the Harper partners. Abbey's work had an immediate, positive effect on all the illustrators at Harper, for although still young, his mature skills, generosity, and wise artistic advice were well respected. He became a mentor to many of the new artists at Harper, including William A. Rogers.

Abbey profited greatly from his experience at Harper. He developed a keen sense of narrative composition. His amiability brought him together with other artists who shared his love of European history and art. Abbey, already a committed Anglophile, held the work of William Morris, William Frend De Morgan, and Alma Tadema in particular in high esteem, and their work had a great influence on many other young American artists as well. Along with Abbey, many of these New York artists, influenced by artistic developments in Europe, formed the "Tile Club," an informal and good-humored social group that met once a week in each others' studios to paint pictures on tiles. There were no dues, no officers, no bylaws, no teaching sessions, and no formal exhibitions; the only rule was that the group would not exceed twelve members (later increased to twenty), to insure the intimacy of the association. Abbey, known as "Chestnut" in the group, often played the piano at these merry gatherings—which grew to include many of the most prominent artists, architects, sculptors, and musicians of the day, among them Frederick Dielman (muralist, illustrator, and etcher), Frank Davis Millet (writer and painter), William Chase (painter), and Augustus Saint-Gaudens (sculptor).

Abbey's second term at Harper lasted two years. His diversity of illustrations for the publishing house was enormous. In addition to illustrations for literature and travel narratives, he also produced drawings for poems and children's stories, including a series of drawings for "Fizz and Freeze," "The Old Deacon's Lament," and "The Book of Gold," all appearing in *Harper's Monthly* in 1877. The 1878 Christmas issue of *Harper's Monthly* includes Abbey's illustrations for three Christmas poems, a serious story by Elizabeth Stuart Phillips, and a comic short story by Rose Terry Cooke. Although Abbey's remarkable versatility characterized his early career as an illustrator, his specialty was historical subjects. Also at this time Abbey completed his first mural painting—a vista of red roofs from a window—which adorned a small panel for the reception room at Harper.

The Centennial Exhibition of Art took place in Philadelphia in 1876. At that time Abbey was more impressed with the overwhelming contributions of English artists than with the productions of the American painters. He called the English section "a great eye opener." When, in late 1878, Harper offered Abbey the opportunity to travel to England to make background studies for his ongoing series of illustrations for Herrick's poetry and an article on Stratford-upon-Avon, he was enthusiastic, but he only consented after bargaining for more pay than was originally offered. After a send-off dinner with the Tile Club and an extravagant farewell banquet at Delmonico's restaurant attended by many of Abbey's fellow artists, he left New York in December 1878 on the vessel *Germanic*. While his original mission was only to gather enough material and English atmosphere to make his illustrations authoritative on British themes, he made England his home for the rest of his life, with only occasional visits back to America.

After arriving in Liverpool, Abbey traveled to Stratford-upon-Avon; checked into the Red Horse Hotel, where Washington Irving had slept; and went to work on illustrations for an article by William Winter about Shakespeare's birthplace. The resulting sketches appeared in the May 1879 issue of *Harper's Monthly*. Abbey was moved by the warmth by which he was received in England and intrigued by the new landscapes and people that he encountered. Writing home in a letter reproduced in Lucas's biography of the artist, Abbey wrote, "I've been so touched by the warm-hearted way perfect strangers have treated me here that I don't want any Englishman to go to America and meet with any less cordial reception." The trappings of old England were the foundation for his artistic inspiration. His imagination was invigorated by the quaint villages, gardens, hills, and architecture of rural England. This first English stay lasted three years. Hence, Abbey became a voluntary expatriate, though his American ties remained strong. Two artist predecessors to Abbey, Benjamin West and Charles Robert Leslie, had also come from Pennsylvania to make their careers in England.

In early January 1879 Abbey left Stratford for London. There he began to call on artists whose work he was familiar with through his connections at Harper. Among these artists were George Henry Boughton, Fred Barnard, and the English countryside painter Alfred Parsons, who became one of Abbey's closest friends and collaborators. These comrades were generous with their advice and support. The colorful painter James McNeill Whistler also became a close friend of Abbey.

Abbey continued to send illustrations back to America for Harper publications, which also had an English circulation. A set of nine drawings accompanied John Keats's "The Eve of St. Agnes" (first published in 1820) in the January 1880 issue of *Harper's Monthly*. Abbey's name first appeared in the table of contents of *Harper's Monthly* in May 1881, accompanied by some of his best illustrations for Herrick's poems. A friendship with writer William Black resulted in Abbey's illustrations of Black's *Judith Shakespeare*, which ran in *Harper's Monthly* throughout the year 1884. Despite his many contributions to the journal Abbey still suffered from money difficulties. At Harper illustrators were not paid per drawing but according to the size of the drawing when reproduced. Of course the illustrator had no control over the size that actually appeared in the pages of the magazine, a matter which often disturbed Abbey because diminishment of his drawings often ruined their beauty and effect. An artist could spend days on a particular detail that would later be cut out of the picture by a Harper editor back in the States or clumsily reproduced by an unpolished engraver.

Abbey also continued to contribute to exhibitions back in the States. An offshoot of the American Watercolor Society, the Salmagundi Sketch Club expressed the interests of illustrators, and its exhibitions featured illustrations and printmaking. The club was formed to highlight and gain respect for the work of illustrators. Its success was partly due to the American public's introduction to artwork through the great presses of the day and the technological developments that made art reproductions of respectable quality. The American public were becoming more sophisticated art connoisseurs. Abbey sent pen-and-ink drawings to the exhibition of the Salmagundi Sketch Club in 1880 that were again well received by critics, who admired their invention, range, and strength. After the third Salmagundi exhibition, *Scribner's,* the American publication with the most avant-garde taste in illustration, named Abbey one of the two most promising American figure artists.

During the first months of 1880 Abbey suffered from a serious stomach illness that rendered him bedridden and virtually incapable of any work. He did manage to produce illustrations for Herrick's poetry, his staple work that continued to appear in *Harper's Monthly*. Near the end of the year he continued work on illustrations for James De Mille's novel *A Castle in Spain* (1883), but he was still plagued by illness and money worries. The work on De Mille's book had actually begun in 1878; by 1880 Abbey grew tired of the project. The work was finally published serially in *Harper's Monthly* in 1883 and later in volume form, which included Abbey's illustrations.

In October 1888 Boughton and Abbey traveled to Holland. Their busy three-week journey took them throughout the Dutch countryside and to more than thirty towns, both of the artists making quick sketches along the way. The artists later developed the work from this excursion into *Sketching Rambles in Holland* (1885), a book that includes twenty-seven of Abbey's illustrations and also some from Boughton and John E. Rogers. Boughton's dedication reads "To Edwin A. Abbey, my fellow-rambler and fellow-sketcher, to whose delightful companionship may be set down any extra washes of couleur de rose that may be discovered in these pages by the cold sad cynic whose good fortune it has not been to ramble with such a perfect fellow-traveller this writing is inscribed."

His health improved, Abbey returned to New York in late September 1881. He resumed attendance at Tile Club gatherings and moved into a studio on west Tenth Street. At this time Abbey was working on various watercolors and continuing to submit drawings to Harper, primarily the Herrick illustrations. Along with other Tile Club members, Abbey was instrumental in putting together a successful (both artistically and financially) compilation of poems and illustrations for a Christmas 1882 issue of *Harper's Monthly*. Improvements in photomechanical reproductive techniques gave Abbey more control over the appearance of the final illustration on the page.

Abbey returned to England in May 1882 and traveled to Paris in June to see the Salon des Société des Artistes Français. Near the end of the year *Selections from the Poetry of Robert Herrick* was published. This was the book form of the poems and drawings that had first run in *Harper's Monthly* as a serial; it revealed Abbey's talents to a wide readership in both England and America. Art critic Frank Jewett Mather called it the finest illustrated book that had appeared in America up to its time. It was published in a luxurious art nouveau cloth binding of green,

from SHE STOOPS TO CONQUER

Illustration by Abbey for Oliver Goldsmith's She Stoops to Conquer *(1887)*

gold, and cream. Also at this time Abbey commenced work on illustrations for Oliver Goldsmith's eighteenth-century farce *She Stoops to Conquer,* which began to appear in the pages of *Harper's Monthly* in December 1884 and ran until August 1886. These drawings reflect Abbey's interest in painting and lifelong practice of drawing true to period.

In the summer of 1885 Abbey visited the small village of Broadway in England, where he was to make his home for the next four years. There he shared a house, built in 1563, with Millet and his wife. Having completed drawings for *She Stoops to Conquer,* Abbey turned his concentration to work on *Old Songs,* a collection of seventeenth- and eighteenth-century ballad and folk-song lyrics that first appeared in *Harper's Monthly* in December 1886. He approached the work with firmness and vivacity.

His illustrations for Harper brought Abbey wide acclaim. In an article in *Harper's Weekly* for 4 December 1886, Henry James had high praise for Abbey's work: "His drawing is the drawing of direct, immediate, solicitous study of the particular case, without tricks or affectations or any sort of cheap subterfuge, and nothing can exceed the charm of its delicacy, accuracy and elegance, its variety and freedom, and clear, frank solutions of difficulties. If for the artist it is the foundation of every joy to know exactly what he wants (as I hold it is indeed), Mr. Abbey is, to all appearance, to be constantly congratulated."

James considered Abbey's illustrations for the oversized, richly embellished *She Stoops to Conquer* to be his best to date, and many shared his opinion. Goldsmith's drama was luxuriantly illustrated with sixty-nine of Abbey's black-and-white drawings, in-

cluding ten full-page illustrations reproduced at Abbey's insistence by photogravure. James stated: "No work in black-and-white in our time has been more truly artistic and certainly no success more unqualified. The artist has given us a complete evocation of a social state to its smallest details, and done it with an unsurpassable lightness of touch." The actual drawings for *She Stoops to Conquer* were exhibited at the Grolier's Club in New York from 16 December to 22 December 1886; it was Abbey's first one-man exhibition.

Henry Mills Alden, editor in chief at *Harper's Monthly,* first contacted Abbey about illustrating Shakespeare's plays in 1886. In a letter to Abbey dated 18 February 1886 and reproduced in Lucas's biography, Alden wrote: "We have long had in view some drawings from you illustrating characters and situations in Shakespeare's *Comedies*. The thought first took shape when I saw your drawing of Autolycus. I would like to have your name go down to posterity associated with Shakespeare!" (The illustration that Alden refers to is of the singing peddler-thief from *The Winter's Tale* that accompanied Amelia Barr's article "Ballads and Ballad Music Illustrating Shakespeare." The article appeared in *Harper's Monthly* in June 1881.) In September 1887 Abbey wrote Charles Parsons that he was considering the idea and outlined the time and expenses the work would require. A fanatic for historical accuracy, Abbey often spent the bulk of his commission money on props and research materials. He demanded that books, costumes, and furniture be acquired for the drawings and also that he travel to the settings of the various stories so that he could take in the architectural monuments and landscapes. The contract for the illustrations was signed 17 March 1888. It stipulated that Abbey was to produce an average of seven pages for each of the fourteen comedies, or 132 drawings in all, at $125 per page. Harper retained ownership and copyright of the drawings.

From that point forward Abbey immersed himself in the task. He spent months studying the dress and architecture appropriate to the comedies and accumulated a large library of books by and about Shakespeare and the time periods of the plays. His chief source for costumes and props was Eugène-Emmanuel Viollet-le-Duc's six-volume compendium, *Dictionnaire raisonné du mobilier francais de l'époque carlovingienne à la renaissance,* published between 1858 and 1878 and in later editions. He also carried about with him pocket-sized volumes of the individual plays edited by the Reverend John Hunter and filled them with notes and sketches. Abbey did the vast majority of the illustrations for the comedies in pen and ink. During this same time period Abbey was also working on illustrations for *The Quiet Life,* a group of poems celebrating life in the English countryside, and *Old Songs,* which ran in *Harper's Monthly* from 1886 to 1889. Both serials were later published in book form, *Old Songs* in 1889 and *The Quiet Life* in 1890.

In January 1888 Abbey traveled to Venice and Verona and brought back sketches of Venetian backgrounds for his upcoming work on *The Merchant of Venice.* Traveling through Germany and France, Abbey also purchased books, swords, and costumes in preparation for his Shakespeare illustrations. In June 1888 Abbey had his first exhibition in England at the Fine Art Society showing his drawings for *She Stoops to Conquer.* He also was persuaded to design costumes for a theatrical production of Victorien Sardou's play *La Tosca* staged in November 1889. Theatrical culture had always informed Abbey's work.

The Millets traveled to America in 1887 and brought a guest, Mary Gertrude Mead, back with them to Broadway in May 1888. Miss Mead was of English descent, had a degree from Vassar, and had traveled and studied widely in Europe. Abbey and Mead became close and eventually married. Their relationship remained powerfully strong throughout their lives.

After Mead had returned to America, Abbey left England again to join her in January 1890. They soon after became engaged, and Abbey, wishing to remain in America until his marriage, again took a studio in New York. Throughout the year Abbey worked in oils, watercolors, and pen and ink. He exhibited his work both at the Royal Academy in England and at the spring exhibition of the American Watercolor Society. He completed painting a large panel for the Hotel Imperial in New York, a mural titled "Playing Bowls in New Amsterdam." In addition he completed eight illustrations for *As You Like It,* which appeared in the December 1890 issue of *Harper's Monthly.* Even though the Tile Club had been disbanded, Abbey attended many social gatherings in the spring of 1890 in New York, Boston, and his hometown of Philadelphia. Surrounded by loyal friends, Abbey and Mead were married in the home of Mead's parents on 22 April 1890.

The illustrations for the Harper edition of Shakespeare's *Comedies* were accompanied by commentaries on the plays by Andrew Lang, a poet and recognized authority on the classics. Abbey and Lang, however, did not collaborate on their work. Lang's text was meant to be ancillary to the illustrations but is also a detailed critique of Shakespeare's writing. While most of the illustrations were done in pen and ink, Abbey also experimented with gouache

drawings in grisaille using the photographic halftone process. A small percentage of the illustrations were done in charcoal, crayon, graphite, or a combination of media. Three illustrations for *Measure for Measure* were completed in oil and reproduced in halftone. The drawings appeared in various sizes and often on the same page with text.

Abbey's illustrations for Shakespeare, models of accurate learning and careful research, made his reputation. The illustrations began to appear in the pages of *Harper's Monthly* in November 1889. To herald the start of the series two drawings for *The Merry Wives of Windsor* also appeared in two other house publications, *Harper's Bazar* and *Harper's Weekly,* in November. Abbey became known to many as America's greatest draftsman. In his *Picture and Text* (1893) Henry James stated that "While the superficial qualities of Abbey's work can be imitated by anyone, his rendering of the seventeenth and eighteenth centuries, which he has reconstructed so wonderfully, will never be approached on the lines he is following. His present position as an illustrator has been attained and maintained simply by treating illustration, as it should be treated, as seriously as any other branch of art." Abbey's drawings enhanced the masterpieces through masterful use of light and setting and demonstrated his expert ability to grasp and cultivate the dramatic essence of a scene or situation. In an article for *Scribner's Magazine* in August 1895, F. Hopkinson Smith noted, "Abbey in his art really has done what Wagner has done in music, Tennyson and the poets in verse. He has taken the old, retouched it, and made it new, giving us something infinitely better than the thing he found. An author's noblest work, his truest ideal may indeed be always safely trusted in his hands."

The year 1890 was a year of furious activity for the artist. With the encouragement of his wife and friends, Abbey consented to paint a series of murals for the Boston Public Library, which was then under construction. The trustees of the library took a chance on Abbey since he had little experience in painting murals, but his talent for telling a story recommended him. When Abbey and his wife left again for England in the summer of 1890, he carried with him a commission to provide the "Delivery Room" of the library with a frieze 180 feet long by 8 feet high, to include a series of designs chosen by the artist, and for which he would be paid $15,000, not a great amount of money for so large a project. Abbey settled on the Legend of the Holy Grail as the inspiration for his murals. The task occupied a great deal of his time for the next twelve years. In the end he told the story in a series of fifteen scenes set in the twelfth century.

After traveling to Italy in the spring of 1891, Abbey settled in the vine-clad country estate of Morgan Hall near Fairford, Gloucestershire, and constructed a huge studio in it. There he completed work on many illustrations for the Harper edition of Shakespeare's *Comedies*. Work also began in earnest for the Boston murals. For the next ten years Abbey traveled around Europe studying Romanesque architecture and dress for his Grail murals.

By 1894 half of the mural was complete. At this time Abbey also began to draw in pastels. Since he had completed the illustrations for the *Comedies,* Abbey was no longer under contract with Harper to produce more illustrations. However, he was still much in demand as a magazine illustrator. Edward L. Burlingame, the editor of *Scribner's,* asked Abbey to produce an Easter scene to be run in the April 1895 issue of the magazine, and Abbey acquiesced. Reproductions of some of Abbey's pastels appeared in the August 1895 issue of *Scribner's.* As technological developments in the photomechanical process advanced, so did Abbey's career. With improvements in the photomechanical line block process, an artist's work could be reproduced with little interference from engravers. With his fluid style Abbey was able to fuse his love of painting with his talents as an illustrator.

Abbey enjoyed sports; he spent many days rowing on the rivers of England and cycling. He also had a great enthusiasm for cricket, an outgrowth of his love of American baseball. He established an Artists' Cricket Club in England and often played in matches in the field he created around Morgan Hall. He found that the sport took his mind off painting and models and provided him with joy and relaxation. A Mr. Swinstead, writing of Abbey's love for cricket in a letter quoted in Lucas's biography, stated: "Abbey's enthusiasm for cricket was an outstanding feature in his broad and genial outlook upon life. This enthusiasm was quite in harmony with the intense vitality of his art. Being a man full of life and energy himself, he realized the danger of an artist becoming narrow-minded, rusty, and self-absorbed, and saw in the recreative effect of air and exercise the necessary physical and mental help to creative power." Lucas devotes an entire chapter to Abbey's love for the sport.

In 1896 Abbey was elected to an associateship in the Royal Academy, a great honor, especially for an American-born painter. The Royal Academy was the only art institution in England managed by artists without either government aid or outside help. Abbey was later promoted to Royal Academician in 1898, another rare occurrence for an American. Even though the English art establishment accepted Abbey and he thrived in its atmosphere, his American connections remained strong through both publication and exhibition.

A Paris exhibition of the original drawings for Shakespeare's *Comedies* was held in 1896. It was well received with much fanfare. Also in 1896 Harper published Shakespeare's fourteen comedies including Abbey's illustrations. Published in four large octavo volumes and sold by subscription for $30 per set, only fifteen hundred sets were printed. Abbey's illustrations were reproduced in photogravure, an expensive and opulent method of book illustration. The cost to make and print the engravings was a little more than $4,000. Harper aggressively promoted the book and prominently featured it in the editorial pages of *Publishers' Weekly* and *Book Buyer.* Later, in 1899, Harper again offered for sale by subscription a limited edition of 750 numbered copies. Abbey earned about $34,000 altogether for the reproductions in the magazine and from additional royalty payments from the book.

Abbey returned to America to receive an honorary master of arts degree from Yale University in 1897. He was the first artist Yale had ever recognized by an honorary degree. This honor indicates the high esteem in which he was held by his contemporaries. The citation of the degree reads in part: "[Abbey's] genius as an illustrator . . . is inseparable from the power which enables him in imagination to produce life in past times. . . . But this power would be inadequate were it not allied with cultivation of a high order and patient researches."

On 1 January 1899 Abbey wrote John Hay, U.S. secretary of state and a friend from earlier meetings, protesting the heavy duty on imported works of art in America. Abbey lived in England because he was a student of English history, but his national loyalty remained to the country of his birth. The American tax on imported art made moving artworks into the country difficult for foreign or expatriate artists.

In March 1899 Abbey and his wife moved from Fairfield to Chelsea Lodge in London, where they lived for the rest of Edwin's life. He became somewhat distracted with city life, serving on committees, attending art meetings, and receiving guests such as Arthur Scribner, John Hay, Mark Twain, and his family from America. He also assisted in work on the panels of the House of Lords. In a letter (reproduced in Lucas's biography) to a Mr. Alden at Harper, Abbey stated: "I am asked to do all sorts of things—to serve on committees; to award prizes at schools; to judge Government competitions; preside at meetings; be president of things; and give advice to fond parents who think their children coming

Illustrations by Abbey for Much Ado About Nothing *(1891), from a series on William Shakespeare's comedies and tragedies created for* Harper's Monthly *(1890–1909)*

Raphaels, etc., etc., etc." He was forced to turn down much work because of these demands on his time, all of which he approached, however, with good humor.

Also in 1899 the sixteen illustrations for *Old Songs* won a gold medal at the world exhibition in Paris. Abbey had prepared the illustrations during a six-year period; they displayed moods varying from rapture to playful humor. The work on *Old Songs* was actually a collaboration with Alfred Parsons: in many of the illustrations Abbey drew the figures, and Parsons drew everything else. In all of the pictures Abbey distinguished himself with the exhaustive fineness of his pen and disciplined tonal organization.

Abbey completed the murals for the Boston Library in 1901, and the public flocked to see them in such numbers that the crowds often disrupted the services of the library. These murals remained the most popular ones in America for decades. Free from the responsibility of the Grail paintings, Abbey accepted a new commission from Harper to illustrate the tragedies of Shakespeare and Goldsmith's long poem *The Deserted Village*. The total number of drawings agreed on for the tragedies was one hundred. The contract, signed on 7 August 1901, stated that they were to be completed within six years, and Abbey would receive $50,000. The serialization of the tragedies in *Harper's Monthly* began with *King Lear* in December 1902, a holiday treat for readers.

Abbey had actually begun illustrations for *The Deserted Village* in 1899, but they were not published in *Harper's Monthly* until 1902. *The Deserted Village* was later published in book form, but Abbey was extremely disappointed in the quality of the book. In a letter to the publishers quoted in Lucas's biography, Abbey wrote:

> I must not defer longer in putting in my protest about the way you are treating my work. The get-up and arrangement of *The Deserted Village* book were a shock and a bitter disappointment to me. . . . I never dreamed that you intended to put forth the cheap and vulgar edition that you have published, in type that is simply barbarous, with a cover that is an eyesore, and paper to match—and this *before* a fine edition was done. The pictures were far better printed in the *Magazine* than they were in the book.

Abbey returned to Boston to oversee the final installation of the library murals in late 1901. While in America, Abbey received an honorary doctor of laws degree from the University of Pennsylvania and visited President Theodore Roosevelt in Washington, D.C. While he was in Philadelphia, civic leaders approached Abbey about decorating the state capitol at Harrisburg. Abbey did not accept at first, wanting to rest after just completing the Boston assignment, but this task eventually became the artist's dominating occupation for the rest of his life. He accepted the commission in 1904.

In March 1901 Abbey undertook by command of King Edward VII to paint the official picture of His Majesty's coronation, a great honor for the American artist. The ceremony took place in 1902, and Abbey was constantly busy with the fifteen-by-six-foot painting up until its completion in 1904. The sittings of all the famous people depicted in the painting took up considerable time. The painting was exhibited in various halls around England before it was hung in Buckingham Palace. The king offered Abbey a knighthood, but he declined the honor in order to retain his American citizenship.

A biographical pamphlet about Abbey by Elbert Hubbard was published in 1902. It was titled *Little Journeys to the Homes of Eminent Artists* and was filled with so many falsities that Abbey was often forced to dispel all of the lies that appeared within its pages. Hubbard even claimed that the Abbeys had more than nine children. (The Abbeys were childless.) Another book including biographical information on Abbey, *Famous Painters of America* (1916), written by J. Walker McSpadden, also includes inaccuracies, perhaps based on Hubbard's faulty work. Hubbard later admitted his ignorance of his subject, but *Little Journeys* was circulated widely. Hubbard confessed that he had actually never met Abbey and had made up the story about the Abbey children because the English countryside would seem drab to his readers without a lot of youngsters running around it.

Abbey became sick in May 1906, a sickness which he called "a bad cold on the liver" and which slowed his work on the Harrisburg decorations. Abbey's pressure on himself to create continually added to his illness. His illustrations for Shakespeare's tragedies continued to appear in the pages of *Harper's Monthly* at this time. After recovering, Abbey served as "Visitor" for the School of Painting at the Royal College of Art at South Kensington, where he served on the council from 1907 to 1910. He was a popular teacher and stressed to his students the importance of an education in history and architecture as well as precision and historical accuracy in drawing. Abbey traveled to Athens in 1909 to study for a painting on a Greek subject he had agreed to produce for the walls of the Curtis publishing company in his hometown of Philadelphia. He did not live to complete the project.

Abbey's series of illustrations for Shakespeare's tragedies for Harper came to a close with the publication of *Titus Andronicus* in October 1909. Each of the illustrations filled an entire page, and nine of the illustrations were reproduced in full color from originals in oil and gouaches. Abbey was extremely unhappy with the quality of the reproductions of many of his colored works. The illustrations for the tragedies are accompanied by commentary from many poets, critics, and scholars. Critics considered the commentary dull, lifeless, and full of feeble theories. The series never appeared in book form because of problems with the format, the disappointing text, Abbey's own delays in completing the drawings, and perhaps changing public tastes. All in all, Abbey had produced a total of 71 illustrations for the tragedies and 133 for the comedies, a tremendous achievement. After 1909 Abbey worked almost exclusively on the Harrisburg decorations and a few works on canvas. In May 1910 Abbey played his last game of cricket.

Abbey had a busy social schedule in 1911 but suffered with his ailing liver. On 25 January, Abbey underwent exploratory surgery that revealed his liver had deteriorated. The surgeons could do nothing and gave him only a few months to live. Abbey's bed was moved into his studio, where he continued to direct his assistants until his death on 1 August 1911 at the age of fifty-nine. American ambassador Whitelaw Reid and many American friends represented his native land at his funeral. Members of the Royal Academy were also present to mourn the loss of their distinguished fellow member. Abbey's body was cremated and the ashes buried in the Old Kingsbury churchyard in England. John Singer Sargent, Abbey's close compatriot, supervised the completion of the murals at Harrisburg.

At the time of his death Abbey was a member of an astounding number of prestigious associations both in America and abroad. Among these were the National Academy of Design, American Watercolor Society, Society of Mural Painters of New York, the Royal Academy of London, and the Royal Bavarian Academy. He was a chevalier of the Legion of Honor of France; an associate of the Academie des Beaux Arts; a fellow of the Society of Antiquaries; an associate of the Royal Watercolor Society, London; and a member of the Royal Institute of Architects and the Society of Artists of Madrid, Spain. Abbey was also a member of the Century Club in New York; and in London of the Athenaeum, Reform, Arts, and Beefsteak clubs, and president of the Artists' Cricket Club.

Abbey was the foremost illustrator of the "Golden Age of Illustration" both in Great Britain and America. The reading public mourned the loss of so great an artist. Abbey's life and work were an inspiration to many accomplished artists who came after him. Vincent Van Gogh, Norman Rockwell, Charles Dana Gibson, Fred Pegram, Sidney Paget, and many others claimed that Abbey's illustrations positively influenced their careers. His exhaustive knowledge of legend, literature, history, and fiction, together with the great passion and skill he had for uniting pictures and text, endeared him to professionals and the general public alike. His workmanlike methods and thoroughness of research set the standards by which other artists labored. The range and fertility of his art were marks of his refined genius, for his illustrations, watercolors, pastels, oils, and mural paintings all attained conspicuous success. Abbey was, simply, one of the most talented illustrators who ever lived and a brilliant storytelling painter.

Bibliographies:
Annette Ward, "Abbey's Illustrations of Shakespeare's Comedies," *Bulletin of Bibliography,* 11 (January 1920–April 1932): 141–142;
Theodore Bolton, *American Book Illustrators: Bibliographic Check Lists of 123 Artists* (New York: R. R. Bowker, 1938);
Michael Felmingham, *The Illustrated Gift Book: With a Checklist of 2500 Titles* (Aldershot, Hampshire, U.K.: Wildwood House, 1989).

Biography:
E. V. Lucas, *Edwin Austin Abbey, Royal Academician,* 2 volumes (New York: Scribners, 1921).

References:
Nancy D'Anvers Bell, "The Work of Edwin Austin Abbey, R.A.," *Artist,* 29 (January 1901): 169–181;
"Books and Bookmen," *Harper's Weekly,* 47 (21 February 1903): 313;
Lorinda Munson Bryant, *American Pictures and Their Painters* (New York: John Lane, 1917);
Charles Caffin, *American Master of Painting: Being Brief Appreciations of American Painters; Illustrated with Examples of Their Work* (New York: Doubleday, Page, 1902);
Royal Cortissoz, *American Artists* (New York: Scribners, 1932);
Cortissoz, "The Art of Edwin Austin Abbey," *Scribner's,* 85 (February 1929): 230–238;
Charles DeKay, "Abbey and His Art," *Harper's Weekly,* 55 (12 August 1911): 8–9;
Edwin Austin Abbey, Exhibition Catalogue by Kathleen Foster and Michael Quick (New Haven: Yale University Art Gallery, 1973);
"Edwin Austin Abbey: The Record of His Life and

Work," *Arts & Decoration,* 16 (January 1922): 248–251;

Eugene Exman, *The House of Harper* (New York: Harper & Row, 1967);

Kathleen Adair Foster, "Makers of the American Watercolor Movement: 1860–1890," dissertation, Yale University, 1982;

Arthur Hoeber, "Edwin A. Abbey, N.A., R.A.," *Bookman,* 34 (September 1911): 24–34;

Hoeber, "Edwin Austin Abbey, Illustrator, Painter, Decorator," *International Studio,* 44 (October 1911): 55–62;

A. Holman, "Abbey: The Man and His Work," *Craftsman,* 21 (October 1911): 11–22;

Samuel Isham, *The History of American Painting* (New York: Macmillan, 1905);

Henry James, "Edwin A. Abbey," *Harper's Weekly,* 30 (4 December 1886): 786–787;

James, "Our Artists in Europe," *Harper's Monthly,* 79 (June 1889): 54–57;

James, *Picture and Text* (New York: Harper, 1893);

Frank Jewett Mather, *Estimates in Art: Sixteen Essays on American Painters of the Nineteenth Century* (New York: Holt, 1931);

Robert Mowat, *Americans in England* (Boston: Houghton Mifflin, 1935);

Lucy Oakley, *Unfaded Pageant* (New York: Miriam and Ira D. Wallach Art Gallery, 1994);

Mary Rosetta Parkman, *High Adventurers* (New York: Appleton-Century, 1931);

Walt Reed, "Illustration in America, 1890–1900," *Graphus,* 272 (March–April 1991): 88–91;

W. A. Rogers, "Abbey at Franklin Square," *Colophon,* part 6, no. 2 (1931);

Homer Saint-Gaudens, "Edwin Austin Abbey: The Career of a Great American Artist," *World's Work,* 16 (8 May 1908): 10191–10204;

Marc Simpson, "Reconstructing the Golden Age," dissertation, Yale University, 1993;

Simpson, "Windows on the Past: Edwin Austin Abbey and Francis David Millet in England," *American Art Journal,* 22, no. 3 (1990): 64–89;

F. Hopkinson Smith, *American Illustrators* (New York: Scribners, 1892);

Smith, "The Pastels of Edwin A. Abbey," *Scribner's,* 18 (August 1895): 137–147;

Henry Strachey, "The Art of E. A. Abbey," *Harper's Monthly,* 100 (May 1900): 875–884.

Archives:

The principal collection of Abbey's artwork and correspondence is located in the Abbey Collection at the Yale University Art Gallery. Other public collections include those at the Corcoran Gallery of Art (Washington, D.C.), the Metropolitan Museum of Art (New York), the Boston Public Library, the Liverpool Museum (England), and the Cape Town Museum (South Africa).

Alexander Anderson
(21 April 1775 – 17 January 1870)

Jane R. Pomeroy

SELECTED BOOKS ILLUSTRATED: Dilworth, Thomas, *A New Guide to the English Tongue* (New York: W. Durell, 1791);

Maynard, George Henry, *The Whole Genuine and Complete Works of Flavius Josephus* (New York: W. Durell, 1792);

Gessner, Salomon, *The Death of Abel* (New York: S. Campbell, 1794);

Berquin, Arnaud, *The Looking-Glass for the Mind* (New York: W. Durell, 1795);

Johnson, Richard, *The Blossoms of Morality* (New York: D. Longworth, 1800);

The Holy Bible (New York: Printed for W. Durell by G. F. Hopkins, 1801);

Bloomfield, Robert, *The Farmer's Boy . . . Ornamented with Elegant Wood Engravings by A. Anderson* (New York: G. F. Hopkins, 1801);

Emblems of Mortality (Hartford: J. Babcock, 1801);

Hardie, James, *The New Universal Biographical Dictionary,* 4 volumes (New York: Johnson & Stryker, 1801–1804);

Beattie, James, *The Minstrel* (New York: W. Durell, 1802);

Rogers, Samuel, *The Pleasures of Memory, and Other Poems. And the Pains of Memory by Robert Merry* (New York: D. Longworth, 1802);

Goldsmith, Oliver, *The Vicar of Wakefield* (New York: Printed for C. Brown by J. Oram, 1803);

Bewick, Thomas, *A General History of Quadrupeds. The Figures Engraved on Wood, Chiefly Copied from the Original of T. Bewick, by A. Anderson* (New York: G. & R. Waite, 1804);

Footsteps to the Natural History of Beasts (Philadelphia: J. Johnson, 1804);

Langhorne, John, *The Fables of Flora* (New York: D. Longworth, 1804);

Watts, Isaac, *Divine Songs for Children* (Philadelphia: B. Johnson, 1804);

Webster, Noah, *The American Spelling Book,* third revised edition (Philadelphia: J. Johnson, 1804);

Saint-Pierre, J. H. Bernardin de, *Paul & Virginia . . . With Engravings on Wood, by Anderson* (New York: E. Duyckinck, 1805);

Alexander Anderson in 1867 (drawing by August Will; engraving by Elias J. Whitney)

Bloomfield, Robert, *Wild Flowers* (Philadelphia & Richmond, Va.: J. Johnson, 1806);

Oakman, John, and others, *Moral Songs* (Philadelphia: B. Johnson, 1806);

The Present; a First Book for Children (New York: T. B. Jansen, 1806);

The Young Child's ABC, or, First Book (New York: S. Wood, 1806);

The Holy Bible: Containing the Old and New Testaments (New York: Collins, Perkins, 1807);

Dodsley, Robert, *The Economy of Human Life . . . With Thirty-Two Elegant Cuts, by A. Anderson* (Philadelphia: J. Johnson, 1807);

Irving, Washington, William Irving, and Kirke Paulding, *Salmagundi* (New York: D. Longworth, 1807–1808);

Thomson, James, *The Seasons* (Portland: T. B. Wait, 1807);

Barbauld, Anna Letitia (Aikin), *Hymns in Prose, for the Use of Children* (New York: S. Wood, 1808);

The Cries of New-York (New York: S. Wood, 1808);

Bell, Charles, *The Anatomy of the Human Body,* 2 volumes (New York: Collins & Perkins, 1809);

Goldsmith, Oliver, *The Vicar of Wakefield . . . Ornamented with Wood Cuts by Anderson* (New York: W. Durell, 1809);

Watts, Isaac, *Songs, Divine and Moral, for the Use of Children* (New York: S. Wood, 1809);

MacPherson, James, *The Poems of Ossian . . . With Engravings on Wood by Anderson,* 2 volumes (New York: Printed for E. Sargeant, 1810);

The Works of William Shakspeare, 9 volumes, revised by Isaac Reed (Boston: Munroe, Francis & Parker / New York: E. Sargeant / Philadelphia: Hopkins & Earle, 1810–1812);

Thomson, James, *The Seasons* (Boston: O. C. Greenleaf, 1810);

Godwin, William, *Fables, Ancient and Modern* (Philadelphia: Johnson & Warner, 1811);

Thomson, James, *The Seasons . . . Ornamented with Engravings on Wood, Designed and Executed by Dr. A. Anderson* (New York: T. & J. Swords, 1812);

Aikin, John, and Anna Letitia (Aikin) Barbauld, *Evenings at Home,* 2 volumes (Philadelphia & Richmond, Va.: Johnson & Warner, 1813);

The Holy Bible (New York: E. Duyckinck, J. Tiebout, G. & R. Waite / Albany, N.Y.: Websters & Skinners, 1813);

Edgeworth, Maria, *The Parent's Assistant,* 3 volumes (Boston: W. Wells, T. B. Wait / New York: Kirk Eastburn / Philadelphia: M. Carey, M. Thomas, E. Parker, [1814]);

Irving, Washington, *Salmagundi,* 2 volumes (New York: D. Longworth, 1814);

Aikin, John, *The Calendar of Nature* (New York: S. Wood, 1815);

The History of Alexander Selkirk (New York: S. Wood, 1815);

Thomson, James, *The Seasons* (New York: W. B. Gilley, 1817);

Elliott, Mary, *Simple Truths in Verse* (New York: S. Wood, between 1818 and 1824);

Elliott, *Grateful Tributes* (New York: S. Wood / Baltimore: S. S. Wood, 1819);

Goldsmith, Oliver, *The Traveller, The Deserted Village, and Other Poems* (Philadelphia: M'Carty & Davis, 1819);

Sproat, Nancy, *The Good Girl's Soliloquy* (New York: S. Wood / Baltimore: S. S. Wood, 1819);

Webster, Noah, *The American Spelling Book* (Brattleborough, Vt.: J. Holbrook, 1819);

Sproat, Nancy, *The School of Good Manners* (New York: S. Wood / Baltimore: S. S. Wood, 1822);

Sturm, Christoph Christian, *Reflections on the Works of God in Nature and Providence* (Baltimore: Armstrong & Plaskitt, 1822);

Taylor, Ann and Jane, *Rural Scenes, or, a Peep into the Country, for Children* (New York: S. Wood / Baltimore: S. S. Wood, 1823);

The New-York Cries, in Rhyme (New York: M. Day, 1826);

Howland, Avis C., *Rhode-Island Tales* (New York: M. Day, 1829);

Howell, John, *The Life and Adventures of Alexander Selkirk, the Real Robinson Crusoe* (New York: M. Day, 1830);

The Young Lady's Book, illustrated by Anderson and others (Boston: A. Bowen, Carter & Hendee / Philadelphia: Carey & Lea, [1830]);

Leslie, Eliza, *The American Girl's Book* (Boston: Munroe & Francis, 1831);

Saint-Pierre, J. H. Bernardin de, *Paul and Virginia* (Boston: Lilly, Wait, 1834);

Defoe, Daniel, *Life and Adventures of Robinson Crusoe . . . With New Designs on Wood by Anderson* (Boston: Munroe & Francis, circa 1834);

Mother Goose's Melodies (Boston: Munroe & Francis, 1837);

O'Reilly, Henry, *Settlement in the West. Sketches of Rochester* (Rochester: W. Alling, 1838);

Bentley, Rensselaer, *The Pictorial Spelling Book* (New York: Robinson, Pratt, 1839);

Downing, Andrew Jackson, *Cottage Residences* (New York & London: Wiley & Putnam, 1842);

Webster, Noah, *The Elementary Spelling Book* (New York: G. F. Cooledge, between 1842 and 1845);

Downing, Andrew Jackson, *A Treatise on the Theory and Practice of Landscape Gardening,* revised edition (New York & London: Wiley & Putnam, 1844);

Stephens, John Lloyd, *Incidents of Travel in Central America, Chiapas, and Yucatan,* 2 volumes (New York: Harper, 1841);

Stephens, *Incidents of Travel in Yucatan,* 2 volumes (New York: Harper, 1843);

Bentley, Rensselaer, *The Pictorial Primer: Being an Introduction to the Pictorial Spelling Book* (New York: George F. Cooledge, 1847);

Holley, Orville L., *The Life of Benjamin Franklin* (Boston: Sanborn, Carter & Bazin, 1848);

Downing, Andrew Jackson, *The Architecture of Country Houses* (New York: D. Appleton; Philadelphia: G. S. Appleton, 1850).

PERIODICALS: *Medical Repository,* 1803–1820;
American Medical and Philosophical Register, 1810–1820;
Physico-Medical Society of New York, Transactions, 1817;
Medical and Surgical Register, 1818–1820;
New York Mirror, 1823–1838;
American Tract Magazine, 1824–1836;
Cabinet of Instruction, Literature, and Amusement, 1828–1829;
Family Magazine, or Weekly Abstract of General Knowledge, 1833–1843;
Parley's Magazine, 1833–1844.

Woodcut by Anderson for the 1795 translation of Arnaud Berquin's The Looking-Glass for the Mind

Called the father of American wood engraving, Alexander Anderson was this country's first skilled and sophisticated relief engraver. He was the first documented American artist to use the engraver's burin on end-grain wood, and beginning at a time when relief illustration in American books was either mostly absent or frank but awkward, he produced images that quickly gained critical recognition. Relief engraving entered a new era due not only to Anderson's use of a durable and economical medium but also to the quality of his work.

Alexander Anderson was born on 21 April 1775, the second son of a literate family of moderate means. His father, an immigrant from Aberdeen, Scotland, was a publisher and printer in New York before the Revolution and later was an auctioneer; his mother, Sarah Lockwood, came from Greenwich, Connecticut. The family lived in the hub of the city, on Wall Street, close to the docks, markets, and the publishing trade on nearby Pearl Street.

Anderson's early interest in copying anatomical engravings from books encouraged his parents to apprentice him at the age of fourteen to a doctor, a choice that better reflected their ambitions for him than respected his keen interest in art. According to his biographer, Benson J. Lossing, in the September 1885 London *Art Journal,* Anderson taught himself to engrave by "peeping into the shop windows of silversmiths when they were lettering spoons and other articles," by reading instructions in encyclopedias and books, and by talking to contemporary artists such as Peter Rushton Maverick and particularly Cornelius Tiebout. His affectionate and close-

knit family's social contacts ranged from tradesmen to professors and members of the clergy.

Anderson continued to engrave during his medical apprenticeship, and despite pressure from his parents it is clear that he shied from committing himself permanently to a physician's career. In a brief autobiography written in his seventy-third year Anderson stated, "I soon discovered that the practice of medicine was a different thing from the study of physic. The responsibility appeared too great for the state of my mind." The account is included in Lossing's *A Memorial of Alexander Anderson, M.D.* (1893).

However, Anderson wrote a dissertation for his medical degree, which was awarded in 1796, began a new practice, and cared for his spirited and outspoken mother, of whom he was particularly fond. The family thought that her periodic fits were evidence of madness; the topic of Anderson's dissertation had been insanity, undoubtedly pursued as an attempt to understand his mother's condition. His extant diary, begun in 1793 and continuing with daily entries until the middle of 1799, reveals that Anderson feared that he too was touched by the same weakness. It is no surprise, therefore, that some of his later engravings reflect the chaos he must have witnessed and the fear of instability that he experienced.

Married in 1797 to Ann Van Vleck, the daughter of a Moravian exciseman, Anderson had little time to enjoy his new life with his wife and their infant son. By the autumn of 1798 his wife, son, mother, father, brother, mother-in-law, and sister-in-law had all died in that summer's yellow fever epidemic. Within two weeks after their deaths Anderson abandoned medicine, perhaps in part because of his failure to save those closest to him, but also because he was now free to pursue an interest that had endured since earliest childhood–engraving.

Emotional scars from the loss of his family remained, helping to shape the emotion with which he imbued his engravings. In a letter written to his daughter Julia in November 1857, describing a visit by Washington Irving, whom he had known as a boy, Anderson commented that both he and Irving had "met with severe afflictions in early life, I by the loss of all my near relations, and he by the death of a young lady to whom he was engaged–but he took the wisest course, to mix with the world, while I undertook to shun it and led an almost solitary life, the cause of many evils."

Anderson married again in 1800, to his first wife's sister, Jane, and during the years before her death in 1815, six children were born. Conscripted in the War of 1812 as a soldier–not a physician–he found a replacement, enabling him to return to his family and his wife, who was already ill with tuberculosis. Anderson continued to live in New York City for the rest of his life and would outlive all but three of his children.

By 1800, from evidence in his diary, Anderson had provided illustrations for more than thirty publications. The earliest works that attracted attention were his seven copperplates for an ambitious edition of George Henry Maynard's *The Whole Genuine and Complete Works of Flavius Josephus* (1792). Containing sixty plates copied from the London edition of 1789, it was published by William Durell. Anderson, only seventeen when he began the commission, etched his plates, which was an early use of the technique in American art.

Also notable during this period was a frontispiece to Salomon Gessner's *The Death of Abel,* completed in March 1794. The illustration was roughly engraved on type metal but in technique approached the white-line work that he would successfully use in the future. Despite the assumptions made by Frank Weitenkampf in his *American Graphic Art* (1924), there is no evidence that Anderson had as yet seen any of the work of Thomas Bewick, the great English wood engraver who perfected the use of the white-line technique. Weitenkampf may have misinterpreted a comment made by Anderson in his autobiography.

Equally notable and even surprising so early in his career are Anderson's two extant anatomical engravings, each more than three feet high. The first was completed early in 1798, a wood engraving based on a skeleton from Albinus. It was an impressive feat, especially given the difficulties of printing and engraving so large a figure. William J. Linton, in his *History of Wood-Engraving in America* (1882), called it "a remarkable work, especially for that time."

The following year Anderson completed an etched-line engraving of a male anatomical figure that was reduced from life-size plates by Gautier d'Agoty. It is a startling and impressive figure and convincing proof of his talent. Copying anatomical illustrations was an exercise that he mentioned many times in his diary, and it is clear that from such copying and from his medical studies he learned to know and draw the human form. Later his engravings would be distinguished by good drawing of the human figure.

Although Anderson was certainly capable of engraving on copper, it appears neither to have been his greatest strength nor his primary interest. By far the most important influence on him during these early years was the wood engravings of Thomas and John Bewick. In June 1794 he began working on Durell's edition of Arnaud Berquin's *The Looking-Glass for the Mind,* originally illustrated by John Bewick in the English translation. He had begun the project by using type-metal blocks, the customary material for relief engraving and which he habitually used, but he completed the majority on end-grain boxwood. His familiarity with the use of end-grain wood for tobacco stamps and geometric figures facilitated his move to more-demanding images. However, from testimony in his diary, his first efforts in the medium for *The Looking-Glass for the Mind* were technically difficult for him. He copied Bewick's work closely but in reverse, having transferred the designs onto his own blocks. This is the first documented use of a medium that would revolutionize American illustration, partly due to the durability of end-grain boxwood in comparison to type metal. The book appeared in 1795 and continued to be printed into the 1850s, going through some thirty editions with Anderson's reengravings from his original cuts.

In 1795 he saw Thomas Bewick's *General History of Quadrupeds,* a work that would be one of the greatest influences on his career. The book contains more than three hundred wood engravings. Because of their quality these engravings had been as surprising to English reviewers after its publication in 1790 as they must have been to Anderson. He could now see relief engraving as an art, not merely the craft it had been considered at the time. As he wrote in his diary on 29 July 1797, "The beautifull [*sic*] specimens of Bewick's work have been the means of stimulating me to improve in the art of Engraving

Two of Anderson's woodcuts illustrating Old Testament subjects: the Pharaoh's dream and the baker's dream

on wood." After the spring of 1796 Anderson seems to have abandoned type metal altogether, as thereafter the technical descriptions and references he made in his diary only mention boxwood for relief work.

George Hopkins's publication of Robert Bloomfield's *The Farmer's Boy* (1801) may have been the first American book illustrated by relief engravings to use an illustrator's name on the title page. *The Farmer's Boy* shows a huge advance in Anderson's ability; while the illustrations, which were after those in an English edition, are still hesitant, they doubtless helped establish his reputation. His rendering of some of the faces is expressive, a talent that would become stronger as time passed. A review in the 14 February 1801 issue of the Philadelphia periodical *Port Folio* said the book was "embellished with a variety of appropriate and elegant cuts, executed in a very superior manner on wood."

Despite the general reluctance of printers to handle wood blocks, Anderson's work was already so much more skilled and sophisticated than earlier relief illustration that he created a market for himself. Additionally, books illustrated by the Bewick school had been sold in this country before 1800; American booksellers had not only recognized the excellence of the illustrations but were also well aware of the acclaim they had received in England. With rising pride in the new republic, publishers were eager to turn out a product that, both in printing and in illustration, could vie with the best imported books. These factors combined to Anderson's benefit.

In these early years Anderson usually followed the designs he found in English publications.

As a result his cuts, though popular enough to be traded among publishers in New York and Philadelphia (especially his copies of Bewick tailpieces), were frequently somewhat tentative and stilted. The vigor of his later work, however, is foreshadowed in an engraving of the devil and Minerva he used to advertise his bookstore. In 1797 he opened what was probably the first bookstore in this country devoted exclusively to children's books. He announced this short-lived venture in the *New York Argus,* creating an engraving of Minerva with a book in one hand, and a spear, aimed at the devil, in the other. Between the two figures are four little boys playing marbles, three of them fighting. The image reflects many of Anderson's values. He believed in the civilizing influence of education and abhorred conflict.

Anderson provided four wood engravings for the first American illustrated edition (1803) of Oliver Goldsmith's *The Vicar of Wakefield.* The full-page cuts display a touch of caricature in the large heads and exaggerated expressions on some of the figures. Caricature and satire came naturally to Anderson. As a child he had been delighted by Hogarth's engravings of the idle and the industrious apprentices and stated in his autobiography that they had "made a strong impression" on him. Although sometimes pointed and mixed with the grotesque, his love of caricature is seldom expressed in savage portrayals. At times a tone of sadness prevails, perhaps due to the many adversities in his personal life.

The 1804 edition of *A General History of Quadrupeds,* illustrated by Anderson after Thomas Bewick, was a well-received but painstaking effort. He wrote in his autobiography that the "laborious undertaking" involved "three hundred cuts" for which he was "poorly paid." His engravings follow Bewick's closely, but almost always in reverse. In a few instances Anderson adds foregrounds or backgrounds, giving a more natural and complete picture. Thomas Hugo, in his 1866 edition of *The Bewick Collector*, wrote, "Some of the cuts in this volume are wonderful copies of the originals, and an inspection of them would stagger not a few who are accustomed to attribute to 'Bewick' every engraving of more than ordinary ability produced at the time when these were published." In his *History* Linton called them "tamer certainly than the originals . . . yet showing a real artistic perception of their best qualities." His accomplishment is remarkable, especially coming so early in his career.

Anderson's autobiography mentions by name only two of the more than twenty-five hundred books illustrated during his lifetime with his engravings—the *Quadrupeds* and *The Fables of Flora*—both published in 1804. *The Fables of Flora*, written by John Langhorne, was a well-printed and well-made volume of poetry whose subject was the simple pleasures of nature and flowers. Anderson's delicate and lovingly wood-engraved flowers for this volume are accompanied by his eleven copperplates (after the English illustrator Thomas Stothard) that had appeared earlier in *The American Ladies & Gentlemens Pocket Almanac for 1802*. Anderson felt at home in natural settings and frequently took walks all over Manhattan and into Long Island. As he wrote in his autobiography, he often recalled playing as a boy "on the shores of the Sound, building little huts among the rocks and roofing them with sea weed, delighted in everything around me."

Also among his early work are wood engravings, copied from copperplates in the English volume, for *Paul and Virginia*, published in 1805, and for Robert Bloomfield's *Wild Flowers*, which appeared in 1806, again after the English edition. In 1807 he illustrated Robert Dodsley's *The Economy of Human Life*. The cuts on wood are well engraved and proof of Anderson's growing mastery of the medium. Later that year he provided engravings that depict rural scenes and the simplicity of country life for James Thomson's *The Seasons*. Although less polished than his cuts for *The Economy of Human Life*, they are vigorous. Over the years some of his most finished wood engravings would appear in various editions of *The Seasons*, a book that was enormously popular in the early nineteenth century.

In 1809 Anderson illustrated Durell's New York edition of Goldsmith's *The Vicar of Wakefield*, which includes one of the purest of his white-line engravings. Evert A. Duyckinck, in his *A Brief Cata-logue of Books Illustrated with Engravings by Dr. Alexander Anderson* (1885), stated that the engravings were after the English originals by Robert Branston. The illustration of Mr. Burchell seated under trees, reading to the Primrose girls, displays Anderson's pleasure in the strong contrasts of light and dark. The black shadows under the trees contrast with the white brightness of the sun on the backs of the woman and the lower legs of Mr. Burchell, producing a detailed, vibrant image with good depth.

In the same vein and even more accomplished as a group are Anderson's eight wood engravings for *The Poems of Ossian*, published in 1810. The illustration of Larthmor, a strong, bearded old man, seated with his arms raised at the base of a tree is dramatic and effective. Despite his youth Anderson depicted the old with emotion and sympathy as though he saw himself careworn and his strength already diminished. But sometimes, in this book and others as well, Anderson's drawing of background figures, often partly hidden in shadow, was carelessly handled.

The August 1812 issue of the *Philadelphia Port Folio* reviewed the second annual exhibition of the Society of Artists (precursor to the Pennsylvania Academy of Fine Arts) and commented on Anderson's entry: "Shelric and Venvela [*sic*], from Ossian, engraved on wood, by A. Anderson, of Newyork [*sic*]. We have at all times been delighted in viewing the works of this excellent, useful, and unassuming artist. Engravings on wood, when finely executed, are of great importance, as they are printed with the letter-press, take off a large number of impressions, and are afforded at a low price; but the talents and skill necessary in this truly useful branch of the arts, is not perhaps at present sufficiently appreciated." Weitenkampf, in his *American Graphic Art*, noting the above critique, stated, "The recognition of Anderson and the inclusion of a wood-engraver's work in so early an art exhibition are as noteworthy as is the understanding of both the commercial and artistic possibilities of wood-engraving shown in this notice."

Anderson executed yet another series of wood engravings for Thomson's *The Seasons* in 1810. The illustrations are of a high quality and display his great strength in the use of light and shade. For "Spring" a man is seated under a tree, his fishing pole extended before him. The detailed vegetation catches the light as it comes through the heavy canopy of the large tree above. There is a sense of isolation and peace, of relaxation in the man's pose and in the heavy shadows in the right background where a willow is hanging over the water. Sunlight glances from leaves in the foreground. This design was

Crusoe and His Family; *illustration by Anderson for the* Life and Adventures of
Robinson Crusoe (circa 1834)

reengraved several times by Anderson and to even greater effect in 1822 for *Reflections on the Works of God in Nature and Providence* by Christoph Christian Sturm. His illustration for "Summer," in *The Seasons,* depicts three boys swimming. One boy, naked, his back to the viewer, is about to enter the water, hesitating as though feeling the chill; another is pulling off his shirt in a languid gesture suited to the day's heat; the third is seated, taking off his shoes. The hot summer sun is beating on their backs, and sunlight is reflected on the tree above them and on the shore. The scene may have been drawn from memory, as Anderson often talked of his joy at swimming off the shores around Manhattan.

Also from *The Seasons* is the illustration for "Winter," which depicts a man bent into the wind at the edge of a forest on a stormy evening. Anderson used this composition several times in his illustrations for children's books, possibly identifying with the rigors of the scene. As an old man, when he had to move from a house on Broome Street where he had lived for many years, he inscribed on his new business card, "Flexus non fractus"—bent, not broken. Important as well are different wood engravings for two more editions of *The Seasons,* one published in 1812, the other in 1817, the latter containing some of the most finished cuts in his oeuvre.

Of note among his illustrations for English poetry is a wood engraving for a volume published by M'Carty and Davis in 1819 in Philadelphia, *The Traveller, The Deserted Village, and Other Poems,* by Goldsmith. It is after a copperplate designed by the English artist Richard Westall. An old woman is shown crouching by a stream, gathering cress, the caption below reading, "yon widow'd, solitary thing /. . . . The sad historian of the pensive plain." Using the white-line style that produced some of this best work, the central character is expressed in strong contrasts. The foreground is dark, as are the woman's clothing and the tree above her, while the background is light. Her figure, stooped and resigned to old age, and the use of light help to express her isolation. The cut is a highly successful translation of an intaglio engraving to wood.

In the first two decades of the nineteenth century Anderson provided copperplates for many publications, including several Bibles. The engraving *Jesus Conversing with His Disciples after Supper* was printed in two Bibles published in New York in 1813 and, according to Linton in his *History,* was engraved after Holbein. From 1801 to 1804 Anderson's copperplate portraits of well-known Americans were included in James Hardie's *The New Universal Biographical Dictionary,* published in New York.

Weitenkampf called the portrait of John Carroll of Baltimore "quite delicate" but thought that one of the other portraits was "thin." The comment could rightly be applied to Anderson's intaglio work. His copperplates, whether stipple or line engraving, seem hesitant, unlike the bold forms made from contrasts of dark and light in his wood engravings. Anderson continued to produce copperplate engravings until about 1820 but was never as successful in copper as he was in wood. Copperplate engraving paid far better, however, and the need for money may have compelled him to persist in the medium as long as he did.

Two large wood engravings that can be called Anderson's masterpieces were executed at about this time. *Waterfowl,* after David Teniers, is dated 1818 in the block; *Returning from the Boar-Hunt,* after Johann Elias Ridinger, is undated and measures 12⅛" by 8¾". Linton used this latter print as a folding frontispiece for his *History,* commenting that "No more vigorous piece of white line work has been done outside of the Bewick circle. By pure white line I mean a line drawn with meaning by the graver." Ridinger's original intaglio engraving has not been located, but in other works by him a diffused light blurs the design. Anderson's wood engraving, on the other hand, plays with the light that reflects back and forth off the shapes, giving them body and depth. The different tones and contrasting lights and darks make this a satisfying and almost spiritual image. Unlike the copperplate engraving, Anderson used no crosshatching in his block, a method he seldom employed. The wood engraving was not meant to substitute for intaglio work but rather to exploit the richness of the inked wood surface in order to achieve tone.

The engravings above are some of Anderson's most ambitious work in these early years. In some senses these efforts were a failure. The engravings were generally printed on rough paper; they were muddy and indistinct, the fine lines and careful shading obscured. Those that survived the poor inking and presswork, usually because they were printed on India paper, are superior examples of the wood engraver's art. They helped to secure Anderson's status not as a craftsman but as an artist. Recognized by all the major institutions of his time, he was elected in 1810 to the precursor of the Pennsylvania Academy of Fine Arts and six years later to the American Academy of Fine Arts in New York. Anderson went on to become one of the founding members of the National Academy of Design in 1826 and was elected an honorary member in 1843.

In addition to his work for literary publications Anderson executed humorous caricatures, cartoons, and illustrations for medical texts. Some of the latter are wood engravings, such as those for the two-volume edition of Charles Bell's *The Anatomy of the Human Body* (1809). The cuts are again poorly printed but still notable for their detail and skill. Anderson also supplied copperplates for medical periodicals. One of the editors of the *Medical Repository* was Samuel Latham Mitchill, a scientist in the early republic, who had supervised Anderson's dissertation for his medical degree and had helped him when he was a student by finding him engraving jobs. The *American Medical and Philosophical Register* and the *Medical Repository* contain the last known examples of Anderson's copperplates.

Anderson sometimes ventured into the realm of the comedic or grotesque. Irving's *Salmagundi,* first published between 1807 and 1808, contains a portrait on wood of Langstaff that has been credited to Anderson. The oval bust depicts *Launcelot Langstaff, Esq.,* with a huge, long nose and an oversized head. There is some question whether another wood engraving from this work, *The Little Man in Black,* which was signed by Anderson and shows a figure walking and carrying a large book inscribed "Linkum Fideli[us]," first appeared in the 1814 edition. It is more consistent with Anderson's style in 1808 than in 1814. Both cuts are deliberately crude, their heavy lines and the obvious caricatures meant to reflect the broad humor of the text. James Kirke Paulding, one of the authors in this collection of tales, had objected to the illustrations in the 1814 and 1820 editions, but when Harper published Paulding's works, including *Salmagundi,* in 1835, the *Knickerbocker* magazine in July of that year complained that "We look in vain for the portrait of Will Wizard . . . the two fashionables engaged in the waltz—and the likeness of that mysterious personage, the 'Little Man in Black.' [They] were potent helpers of the imagination." *Langstaff* and *The Little Man in Black* were used as late as 1859 in an edition published by G. P. Putnam.

The engravings *Will Wizard* and *Waltz Dance,* both copperplates, first appeared in the 1814 edition. They are delightful illustrations that poke fun at New York society. Will Wizard, with his clubbed hair, dressed in his China-silk waistcoat, his thick legs planted apart, watch fobs hanging below his waist, is depicted standing foursquare before a fireplace. More amusing and subtle is the depiction of a fashionable couple engaged in the scandalous new dance, the waltz. The young man's fingers hardly touch the young woman's bare back; her stance is impossible—without holding more firmly to her partner's shoulders, she would have fallen. Their bodies are unnaturally elongated to portray ele-

"There were two blind men went to see / Two cripples run a race"; illustration by Anderson for
Mother Goose Melodies (1837)

gance, and their hair is fashionably frizzled, lending the couple an air of insouciance.

Anderson stated in his autobiography that the "grotesque vignettes in old editions of books done when the artist had not the fear of criticism before his eyes had charms for me, and I am not ashamed to say something of that taste still remains with me." It was an unfashionable taste at the time and probably accounts for the limited number of examples in Anderson's work. Two engravings in particular come to mind. One, a full-page wood engraving titled *What He Saw in the Fire,* was published in Lossing's *Memorial.* It was the illustration's only appearance, Lossing stating that it was based on an early drawing by Anderson. The cut depicts monsters with open mouths, devils, animals with human faces, and insects that are half human, all of which fill the space around a huge creature that is devouring a smaller one with human legs. The design's nightmarish fantasy is reminiscent of the work of the sixteenth-century Flemish artist Hieronymus Bosch.

Another pointedly grotesque engraving, found in Anderson's proof books, was probably done on type metal and is certainly much earlier than *What He Saw in the Fire.* It depicts a dwarf with thick lips; a

hideous, demented face; and a huge head. In style, it might be mistaken for a modern illustration by Maurice Sendak. Although Anderson continued to use grotesque images in his later work, none were as pronounced as these early examples.

If Benjamin Franklin's *Join or Die* cut is not counted, Anderson contributed what may be the first cartoon for newspaper publication. Anderson (as the engraver) and the portrait painter John Wesley Jarvis (as the designer) collaborated on an antiembargo cartoon that appeared in the *New York Evening Post* on 25 April 1814. A less well-known embargo cartoon appears in the 1821 New York City directory published by Longworth. It deals with copyright poaching and uses the same caption as the second embargo cartoon, "How he nicks 'em." These cuts were boldly and simply engraved.

Although Anderson provided illustrations for medical works and volumes of poetry as well as prose, the largest number of his wood engravings appeared in children's books. His illustrations for *The Present; a First Book for Children,* published in 1806, are enthusiastic and should be compared to those he provided for *The Looking-Glass for the Mind.* In *The Present* children are seen in a variety of situations: playing, being naughty, in everyday clothes, caught with stolen apples, or with their trousers wet from wading in a pond. These depictions were at odds with the more elegant English models from which he had been working, but it was this kind of representation that would make him the most appealing illustrator of children's books into the 1840s. These were American designs, down to earth, without pretensions in dress or behavior. Clearly observation of his own six children must have educated him in juvenile behavior and physical characteristics.

In the first years of the nineteenth century Anderson was working for the Philadelphia publishers Benjamin Johnson and Jacob Johnson, and the firm of Jacob Johnson and Benjamin Warner. Later, from about 1816, he illustrated books for Benjamin Warner alone. He illustrated adult works for these publishers, but his engravings for children's books are perhaps better known.

Some of the engravings, as well as the text, were after English originals. The London Darton and Harvey publications, for example, which were imported by American firms, were usually executed with more care than Anderson's illustrations for the early Samuel Wood juveniles in New York. Philadelphia had a tradition of books more finely crafted than those printed in New York, and Anderson responded in kind. In 1804 he supplied engravings for *Footsteps to the Natural History of Beasts* and for Isaac Watts's *Divine Songs for Children*. Four of his thirty-seven cuts used in the 1804 *Divine Songs* and in the 1806 edition of *Moral Songs* by John Oakman and others were reengraved by Anderson and were later offered as stereotypes in type-foundry specimen books; by this means they appeared in dozens of publications for juveniles throughout the country. Seventy-one of Anderson's cuts illustrated Johnson and Warner's 1811 edition of *Fables, Ancient and Modern* by William Godwin; he appears to have copied the designs from the copperplates of the 1805 "superior" London edition for Thomas Hodgkins. But his most demanding work for the Philadelphia publishers was for *Evenings at Home* by John Aikin and Anna Letitia (Aikin) Barbauld, published by Johnson and Warner in 1813. The book contains one hundred engravings by Anderson plus a few of his tailpieces that had appeared earlier. As far as can be determined, the work was after his own designs. The illustrations are all in the white-line style, consistent with his technique at this time.

"The late Samuel Wood was one of my most constant employers, I did an infinity of cuts for his excellent set of small books," Anderson wrote in his autobiography. The first book that he illustrated for Wood was *The Young Child's ABC, or, First Book*, published in New York in 1806. It, and the subsequent three readers and spellers that Wood published and probably wrote, all contained Anderson's wood engravings. So popular were these publications that some of them were still being issued as late as 1865.

Of even greater appeal were the dozens of small, paper-wrapped toy books put out by Wood. Almost all used Anderson's work. They presented an open, frank portrayal of children, animals, and nature, such as the illustrations for Barbauld's *Hymns in Prose, for the Use of Children* (1808) and Watts's *Songs, Divine and Moral, for the Use of Children* (1809). The cuts are engaging if often roughly engraved. As it is clear that Anderson could produce superior work, he must have tailored his illustrations to his market—meaning that children's books selling for a few pennies were not considered important enough to make a large effort. However, his cuts for Wood's later books, especially by the 1820s, are of a higher standard and are examples of some of the most winning and delightful work that he did for any children's publisher.

Anderson's diary reveals a keen sympathy for the poverty and disease he saw around him in New York. His artistic comments in Wood's 1808 *The Cries of New-York* are based on what he had experienced as a doctor and as a young man who knew the streets of the city. In *The Cries of New-York* (once again, roughly engraved but expressive) the weariness of the gingerbread boy with a heavy basket on his back and a tired face are eloquently depicted. A well-dressed little boy with a ruffled white collar is shown in the background about to give a piece of his gingerbread to his pet dog begging in front of him. Rosalind Halsey, in her 1911 *Forgotten Books of the American Nursery*, acknowledged that the book was modeled after the English cries of London but noted its American content, saying that "the scenes drawn from the street life of the town gave the old-fashioned child its first distinctly American picture-book." Halsey also correctly suggested that the cuts were designed by Anderson.

In addition to children's books, Wood, who was a Quaker, published antislavery books. Wood's broadside titled *Injured Humanity* (circa 1805–1808) had been illustrated by Anderson with explicit wood engravings that did not spare the viewer the horrors of torture and cruelty committed upon black slaves.

The Calendar of Nature by John Aikin was published by Wood in 1815 and illustrated by Anderson with a cut for each month. These charming, small, rural scenes by Anderson are still used in almanacs today. More ambitious is his work for Ann and Jane Taylor's *Rural Scenes, or, a Peep into the Country, for Children* (1823). The book, showing all types

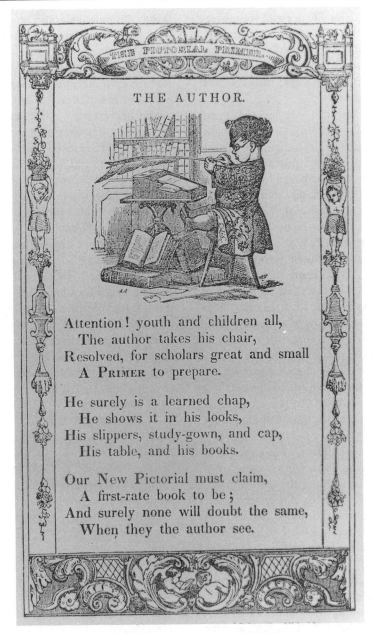

Page from Rensselaer Bentley's The Pictorial Primer: Being an
Introduction to the Pictorial Spelling Book *(1847),*
with engraving by Anderson

of rural pursuits and trades, contains more than ninety cuts by Anderson. They are typical of his illustrations for children, filled with an innocence that is not cloying but straightforward, sturdy, and openly good-natured. Its illustrations were copied from copperplates in the English edition, but Anderson's are more complete and better composed.

Some of Anderson's most successfully illustrated books published by Wood are Mary Elliott's *Grateful Tributes* (1819) and *Simple Truths in Verse* (between 1818 and 1824) and Nancy Sproat's *The Good*

Girl's Soliloquy (1819), *Gift to Good Children* (n.d.), and *The School of Good Manners* (1822). Despite the moralistic tone of the texts, the illustrations are attractive and, at least in the later imprints, well engraved and fairly well printed on uncrowded pages. Many of the books went through multiple editions. Anderson's tiny cuts, such as those in *Simple Truths,* are quick, affectionate, and observant sketches of children in various occupations.

Wood later sold his blocks. Some were used by Edward Livermore in Worcester, Massachusetts; in the same state Elisha Turner and John Metcalf in Northampton in the 1840s published several of the titles originally published by Wood, using the same cuts. The blocks went on to the firm of Merriam and Moore in Troy, New York, in the 1850s and illustrated their toy books.

The New York Religious Tract Society began to illustrate its children's tracts in 1824. Anderson was the major illustrator of their publications, though some engravings were imported from England and a few were by other artists. The cuts were used repeatedly and indiscriminately in different titles, whether related to the text or not. When the society was subsumed into the New York–based American Tract Society in 1825, the stereotypes passed to this organization, which began issuing their children's tracts in 1828. From that date until about 1847 Anderson was almost their only illustrator, providing countless new cuts for their publications. When the format was changed sometime after 1847 stereotypes of his engravings were altered, probably by others in the printing office, to reflect newer styles in clothing. New engravings with refined lines and grayer tones were added. The strong contrast of black and white in Anderson's older, white-line work was often made less pronounced by changes in the stereotypes.

Among publishers of children's books the Babcock firm was one of Anderson's most consistent employers. Beginning in 1795 Anderson supplied wood engravings for many dozens of their juveniles, mostly published as paperbound toy books. In 1801 he produced more than fifty cuts for *Emblems of Mortality* after the illustrations of John and Thomas Bewick's 1789 edition, which were in turn based on the work of Hans Holbein. Although Anderson's results did not approach the technical mastery of the Bewicks', the subjects, including the macabre figure of Death as a skeleton, were of interest to him, and his early effort was vigorous and bold. Unfortunately for Anderson, the Babcock firm's books, especially the later issues that were stereotyped, were often poorly produced. They, like most children's publishers, would use images that did not necessarily illustrate the text. Poor printing on poor paper often obscured Anderson's concise, detailed, and cheerful depictions. His contributions to this firm are best seen in the well-printed impressions in his proof books.

Mahlon Day in New York began employing Anderson about 1820, before Anderson started his work for the American Tract Society. His small relief vignettes for Day, who seemed to like happy children despite the homilies aimed at them in his toy books, are seldom signed, although some of the larger engravings and frontispieces carry the usual "A," "AA," or "Anderson" identification.

Anderson was said to be a modest man. Whether his reluctance to advertise his part in illustrating ephemeral toy books was because of their status or his modesty is not known. When Lossing asked him to have a daguerreotype taken to illustrate an article that he was writing, Anderson was shocked. "He refused," Lossing wrote in the *Memorial,* "because the act would be sheer egotism. Engrave his own portrait!" In the end Anderson agreed and engraved the portrait from a drawing by Samuel Wallin. It accompanied Lossing's article in the London *Art Journal.*

Anderson's illustrations for *The Life and Adventures of Alexander Selkirk, the Real Robinson Crusoe* published by Day in 1830, portray beguiling images of Selkirk and his animals. In one, Selkirk is seated under a tree, holding one cat up by its front paws, with another at his knee and more cats scattered around him. Anderson often included cats in his engravings, and he was adept at depicting their arched backs and round eyes. After his death it is said that his own cat refused to come out from under his bed for several days.

Some of Day's books have American themes, such as his *The New-York Cries, in Rhyme* (1826), *New-York Guide in Miniature* (1827), *Rhode-Island Tales* (1829), and *The True and Wonderful Story of Paul Gasford* (1834). All were illustrated by Anderson, some containing only his work. American content in children's storybooks, which were usually copied from the English, was relatively unusual at this time.

Other popular titles issued by Day and illustrated by Anderson are *The Blackbird's Nest* (1823), whose cuts had been used earlier in New York; *The Two Lambs* (1821); and *Men and Manners in Verse* (1824). Anderson's work for both Day and Wood display the same sturdy, cheerful, and innocent qualities. They are skillful and easily understood portrayals of people, children, and animals.

Day continued to publish Anderson's work until the late 1830s. In 1845 Day's nephew, Stephen Crane, took over the business and reissued many of Day's titles with the same illustrations. The blocks were later sold and reappeared in G. F. Cooledge's primers, as well as in Edward Livermore's juveniles in Worcester and in Degen and Estes's children's books published in Boston in the 1860s.

In addition to illustrating the American Tract Society's children's tracts, Anderson illustrated the vast majority of their adult tracts, reengraving many of the designs by other artists that had been used earlier. Some had been copied from the Religious

Engraved title page for Orville L. Holley's 1848 biography

Tract Society in London, the model for the American institution. However, as he stated in a proof book that contains impressions from more than eight hundred blocks used by the society, many of the images had been designed by him. The proof book can be found today in the Boston Athenaeum.

In the years he worked for the society Anderson supplied it with a total of more than 650 wood engravings. The tracts were printed on a rough, inexpensive paper, and the lines cut in the wood were of necessity stronger and thicker than would

be used for better-quality imprints using a smoother-surfaced paper. The illustrations were supposed to serve an evangelical purpose, therefore the emotions of the characters depicted are transparently displayed, but the work is almost always animated, even striking, such as those used for tracts warning of the evils of drunkenness. Perhaps Anderson drew inspiration from his own past, for during a short period in his youth, having given up engraving for more than a year and depressed by his practice and with money worries, he began to drink too much and take opium.

In the 1840s the American Tract Society switched to a smoother paper, and Anderson's work for them used a finer line, in keeping with the changing styles of wood engraving. In a letter dated 17 August 1865 to his daughter Julia, Anderson noted that for six months he had had no work but that lately the society had asked him for a cut, "probably to ascertain if there was anything of the artist left in me." He was then ninety years old.

The style of Anderson's work began to change in the 1830s. The finer lines with grayer tones and a softer contrast of dark and light were made possible by better paper, presses, and ink. *The Young Lady's Book* published in Boston and Philadelphia in 1830 appears to be a watershed in American wood engraving. It is a well-made book printed on smooth, quality wove paper, and the illustrations by Anderson and two other engravers, as well as by Abel Bowen, one of the publishers, are close copies of an English model. In the introduction Bowen stated that the book might be "considered a perfect facsimile," a judgment echoed by Linton in his *History*. The very fine lines and subtle shading of the cuts were a departure in style. The book, with its examination of hobbies and educated pursuits for the sophisticated young lady, went through many editions.

In the 1830s and 1840s Anderson began to experience competition. Many new engravers had entered the market. In a letter to Julia dated 7 November 1842, Anderson wrote, "As my business is not so profitable as formerly I am oblig'd to work more steady at it—since the first day of this year I have not been idle one day except on Sundays."

Anderson engraved some of his best work for the firm of Munroe and Francis in Boston. The 1837 edition of *Mother Goose's Melodies* contains Anderson's well-known humorous and sometimes grotesque cuts for the nursery rhymes, almost all from his own designs. Done in the style of ironic caricatures, the cuts exhibit a finer line without the sacrifice of dark tones. The illustration for "When good King Arthur ruled this land" is deliberately grotesque: the queen is fat and has heavy features, and the king, squatting in front of the fireplace to add a log, an ax beside him, is decidedly nonregal. The book popularized Mother Goose in America and, with Anderson's engravings, was reprinted by other publishers for decades.

Anderson engraved, and probably designed, thirty illustrations for the same publisher's *Life and Adventures of Robinson Crusoe* (circa 1834). Here his line is sometimes sketchy. Crusoe, shown with a resigned, wondering, and sober expression on his face, is seated in his hut with his animals around him, producing an expressive and amusing portrait.

Also published by the same firm were two books by Eliza Leslie, *The American Girl's Book* (1831) and *The Atlantic Tales* (1833). They are in a more modern style but are humorous and at times gently poke fun at the girls with their fashionable long necks.

All through his career, and especially toward the end of his life, Anderson illustrated school texts. It was often perfunctory work. But probably some of his best-known cuts were executed for Noah Webster's *American Spelling Book* (1804) and his *Elementary Spelling Book* (between 1842 and 1845). Beginning in 1804 Anderson provided several different sets of cuts for the eight fables for some but not all of the distinct editions. His well-known frontispiece of Minerva hand in hand with a boy below a hilltop temple first appeared in 1819. The so-called blue-back speller, *The Elementary Spelling Book,* persisted with Anderson's last group of engravings at least into the 1880s. Many millions were sold, and the book may be the most widely circulated publication with Anderson illustrations.

His engravings for Rensselaer Bentley's *Pictorial Spelling Book* (1839) successfully merged his liking for strong contrasts with a finer, steadier, and more detailed line, especially in the section that includes the seasons. Unfortunately the book was not well printed, and justice was not done to Anderson's affectionate treatment of the rural scenes.

The sketchier, lighter-toned engraving that came into vogue during Anderson's later career did not cater to his strengths. The zest went out of his work when he engraved after designs by such American artists as T. H. Matteson and Edward Purcell. Anderson saw images in terms of shapes formed by dark against light, which created depth and dimension, and not by outline engraving or by fine gradations of tone and color, as favored by the younger artists. His images were created by the rhythm of contrasts of light, not by the depiction of movement. He incorporated all parts of the engraving into his image by manipulating brightness and shadow, encouraging the viewer to take in detail by moving his attention from section to section. He viewed his illustrations as though looking through the wrong end of a telescope, as though the scene were a cameo or static abstraction, however realistic the figures' stances and expressions.

In one of his early notebooks he drew an *S* on its side, the center broken, the end of each hook at the center not touching but adjacent to the other. Incorporating the diagram into his sentence, he stated that the close juxtaposition of curving lines is "absolutely necessary to render a piece of engraving pleasing, and where the drawing and engraving are executed on this principle the performance cannot

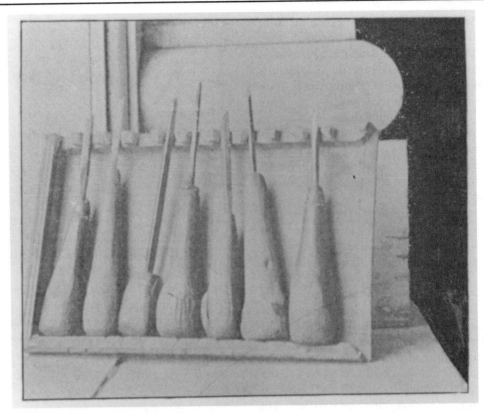

Engraving tools used by Anderson (New-York Historical Society)

fail to delight the eye." His best work delights the eye not only because of a graceful, vibrant line but also due to his skill at drawing, an advantage not shared by many wood engravers.

Anderson had three pupils, the first being Garret Lansing, who came to New York in 1804 and returned to Albany two years later. The second, William P. Morgan, was indentured to Anderson in 1807 to learn wood engraving, but he was said to prefer drawing over wood engraving. Morgan is reputed to have been Anderson's favorite because, writes Lossing, he "caught the spirit of Bewick's style." Very little can be found of his work as he rarely signed engravings, either as designer or engraver. In 1826 John H. Hall from Cooperstown, New York, was apprenticed to Anderson but stayed with him only a short time. After trying various ventures as well as following a career in engraving, in 1849 he joined the gold rush to California, where he died. In addition to Anderson's three pupils, his third daughter, Ann Maverick, was taught by her father and became the first woman in this country to earn her living by wood engraving. Much of her work seems to have been for the New York Protestant Episcopal Sunday School Union publications.

It is sometimes said that Anderson was merely a copier of English illustrators and, specifically, of the work of the Bewick school. Samuel Griswold Goodrich, better known as Peter Parley, stated in the second volume of his 1857 *Recollections of a Lifetime* that the successful booksellers of the country—and he was speaking of the same decades when Anderson was at the height of his career—"were for the most part mere reproducers and sellers of English books." As far as can be discovered, Anderson was not criticized for engraving after others' compositions. Copying the work of others was considered a legitimate method of reproduction and provided more-sophisticated images than were locally available. It was in his work for children's books that Anderson seemed to relax, enjoy, and design composition as he wanted. Not limited by publishers' desires for copies of English images, he produced affectionate and spirited original images. As for the charge that Anderson always copied the Bewicks, a glance at his proof books will serve as a rebuttal.

Alexander Anderson's career spanned seven decades, lasting from 1791, when he first signed an illustration on type metal, until 1868, when he was ninety-three. For all his adult life he lived modestly and, as far as we know, quietly in New York City. He died in the house of his youngest daughter and her husband in Jersey City on 17 January 1870.

Even a preliminary listing of the publications

that contain Anderson's work would include more than twenty-five hundred titles. His proof books, with more than ten thousand wood engravings, apart from book illustrations, include impressions of all types of ephemera, labels, family crests, state seals, and tiny tailpieces. His engravings were printed in every book-publishing center in nineteenth-century America and could be found as far away as the West Indies, Mexico, South America, and in missions in Burma and China. His designs and style were widely copied by early American wood engravers.

Anderson raised the quality of American illustration to a new, high standard. Linton stated that Anderson was one of only two American wood engravers who could "claim place beside the Masters of our art." The strength and assurance of his white-line work has stood the test of time despite a transition to fine-line drawing and criticisms made in the last quarter of the nineteenth century of his engraving as crude and old-fashioned. By introducing the new technique of wood engraving on end-grain wood to this country—with its great artistic and commercial potential—he played an important role in the history of bookmaking and illustration in America.

Bibliography:

Evert A. Duyckinck, *A Brief Catalogue of Books Illustrated with Engravings by Dr. Alexander Anderson with a Biographical Sketch of the Artist* (New York: Privately printed, 1885).

Biography:

Benson J. Lossing, *A Memorial of Alexander Anderson, M.D., the First Engraver on Wood in America* (New York: For the subscribers, 1893).

References:

Sinclair Hamilton, *Early American Book Illustrators and Wood Engravers 1670–1870,* 2 volumes (Princeton: Princeton University Press, 1968);

Helen M. Knubel, "Alexander Anderson and Early American Book Illustration," *Princeton University Library Chronicle,* 1 (April 1940):13–18;

William J. Linton, *The History of Wood-Engraving in America* (Boston: Estes & Lauriat, 1882), pp. 1–9;

Jane R. Pomeroy, "Alexander Anderson's Life and Engravings before 1800, with a Checklist of Publications Drawn from His Diary," *Proceedings of the American Antiquarian Society,* 100, part 1 (1990):137–230.

Archives:

The largest group of Alexander Anderson's papers is at the New-York Historical Society, which also holds 350 of Anderson's blocks. The holograph diary is at Columbia University. The New York Public Library has seventeen volumes of Anderson's proof books of wood engravings, additional portfolios and copperplates, and a small collection of his papers.

Hammatt Billings

(14 June 1818 – 16 November 1874)

John Neal Hoover
Saint Louis Mercantile Library Association

SELECTED BOOKS ILLUSTRATED: Jarvis, James J., *Scenes and Scenery in the Sandwich Islands, and a Trip Through Central America* (Boston: Munroe, 1843);

Chimes, Rhymes, and Jingles: Or Mother Goose's Songs (Boston: Munroe & Francis, 1845);

Lang, William Bailey, *Views, with Ground Plans of the Highland Cottages at Roxbury* (Boston: Bridgham & Felch, 1845);

Frothingham, Richard Jr., *The History of Charlestown, Massachusetts* (Boston: Little, Brown, 1845–1849);

Little, George, *The American Cruiser; or, the Two Messmates. A Tale of the Last War* (Boston: Waite, Peirce, 1846);

Goodrich, Samuel G., *A Pictorial History of America; Embracing Both the Northern and Southern Portions of the New World* (Hartford, Conn.: House & Brown, 1849);

Holmes, Oliver Wendell, *Poems* (Boston: Ticknor, 1849);

Whittier, John Greenleaf, *Poems* (Boston: Mussey, 1849);

Fields, James, ed., *The Boston Book; Being Specimens of Metropolitan Literature* (Boston: Ticknor, Reed & Fields, 1850);

Lippincott, Sara Jane Clarke, as Grace Greenwood, *Greenwood Leaves: A Collection of Sketches and Letters* (Boston: Ticknor, Reed & Fields, 1850);

Hawthorne, Nathaniel, *True Stories from History and Biography* (Boston: Ticknor, Reed & Fields, 1851);

Hawthorne, *A Wonder Book for Boys and Girls* (Boston: Ticknor, Reed & Fields, 1852);

Lippincott, Sara Jane Clarke, as Grace Greenwood, *Recollections of My Childhood* (Boston: Ticknor, Reed & Fields, 1852);

Hildreth, Richard, *The White Slave; or, Memoirs of a Fugitive* (Boston: Tappan & Whittemore, 1852);

Quincy, Josiah, *A Municipal History of the Town and City of Boston* (Boston: Little, Brown, 1852);

Hammatt Billings (courtesy of the American Antiquarian Society)

Stowe, Harriet Beecher, *Uncle Tom's Cabin; or Life among the Lowly* (Boston: Jewett, 1852; republished with additional drawings, 1853);

Hawthorne, Nathaniel, *Tanglewood Tales, for Boys and Girls; Being a Second Wonder Book* (Boston: Ticknor, Reed & Fields, 1853);

Dix, John, *Passages from the History of a Wasted Life* (Boston: Mussey, 1853);

Sumner, Charles, *White Slavery in the Barbary States* (Boston: Jewett, 1853);

Richards, T. Addison, *American Scenery Illustrated* (New York: Leavitt & Allen, 1854);

Whittier, John Greenleaf, *A Sabbath Scene* (Boston: Jewett / Cleveland: Jewett, Proctor & Worthington / London: Low, 1854);

Irving, Washington, *Life of George Washington,* 5 volumes (New York: Putnam, 1855–1859);

Follen, Eliza Lee, *Twilight Stories* (Boston: Wittemore, Niles & Hall, 1856);

Scott, Sir Walter, *Waverly Novels,* 30 volumes (Boston: Ticknor & Fields, 1857–1859);

Dexter, Henry M., *Street Thoughts* (Boston: Crosby, Nichols, 1859);

Lippincott, Sara Jane Clarke, as Grace Greenwood, *Stories from Famous Ballads. For Children* (Boston: Ticknor & Fields, 1860);

Adams, William T., as Oliver Optic, *The Riverdale Story Books* (Boston: Lee & Shepherd, 1862);

Coggeshall, William T., *Stories of Frontier Adventure in the South and West* (New York: Follett, Foster, 1863);

Adams, William T., as Oliver Optic, *Flora Lee Story Books* (Boston: Lee & Shepherd, 1864);

Goldsmith, Oliver, *The Deserted Village* (Boston: Tilton, 1866);

Ingelow, Jean, *Songs of Seven* (Boston: Roberts Brothers, 1866);

Tennyson, Alfred, *Poems of Alfred Tennyson* (Boston: Tilton, 1866);

Ingelow, Jean, *Poems* (Boston: Roberts Brothers, 1867);

Alcott, Louisa May, *Little Women: Or Meg, Jo, Beth, and Amy* (Boston: Roberts Brothers, 1869);

Morris, William, *The Lovers of Gudrun: A Poem* (Boston: Roberts Brothers, 1870);

Dickens, Charles, *A Child's Dream of a Star* (Boston: Fields, Osgood, 1871);

Stowe, Harriet Beecher, *Pink and White Tyranny: A Society Novel* (Boston: Roberts, 1871);

Alcott, Louisa May, *Aunt Jo's Scrap-Bag. My Boys* (Boston: Roberts, 1871);

Phelps, William D., as Webfoot, *Fore and Aft; or Leaves from the Life of an Old Sailor* (Boston: Nichols & Hall, 1871);

Coffin, Charles Carleton, *The Story of the Great Fire, Boston, November 9–10, 1872* (Boston: Shepard & Gill, 1872);

Tennyson, Alfred, *The Last Tournament* (Boston: Tilton, 1872);

Gill, William Fearing, ed., *Laurel Leaves. Original Poems, Stories, and Essays* (Boston: Gill, 1876).

PERIODICALS: *Pictorial National Library,* 1848–1849;
Ballou's Pictorial Drawing Room Companion, 1850–1860;
Boston Almanac, 1850–1860;
Gleason's Pictorial Drawing Room Companion, 1850–1860;
Gleason's Weekly Line-of-Battleship, 1850–1860;
Liberator, 1850–1855;
Lady's Almanac, 1850–1860;
Illustrated News, 1853;
Illustrated Pilgrim Almanac, 1860–1865;
Harper's Weekly, 1866.

Charles Howland Hammatt Billings was a major figure in that group of mid-nineteenth-century artists who developed a native school of American book illustration. Although his designs for a multitude of wood engravings in obscure fiction and regional New England sketches are little known today, he–like F. O. C. Darley, John Sartain, John G. Chapman, and others of his generation–also produced a small but significant body of designs that have become popular archetypes in important works. The modern reader of classic American literature probably subconsciously recognizes these designs.

Young "Charley" Billings was the eldest son of the large family of Ebenezer and Mary D. Janes Billings of Milton, Massachusetts. Hammatt Billings married twice. His first wife, Sarah Mason, died around 1859; shortly thereafter he married Phoebe Warren. Neither marriage produced children.

Billings's interest in drawing and art manifested itself early. He was barely ten when he used paper puppets and silhouettes to give performances of fairy tales for his friends. His family recognized this artistic bent and encouraged him. Billings was receiving formal training in art and drawing by the late 1820s from the German artist Francis Graeter. Sometime before 1834 he was apprenticed to Abel Bowen, one of Boston's pioneer engravers and designers of books for children. Under Bowen's tutelage Billings's training in illustration and graphic design began in earnest. This instruction soon expanded into architectural drafting, which he perfected at the firm of Asher Benjamin. Thus Billings merged the two interests of illustration and architecture into an artistic career of the widest scope available in the 1830s and 1840s for a young man of his training and educational background.

For the next three decades Billings was active in both architectural design and book illustration, his interest and productivity never flagging until his death at the age of fifty-six. Probably his indefatigable willingness to take on any commission and his untiring desire to dedicate himself to many professional associations while trying to make a living contributed to his death at such an early age. By the 1870s, despite an enviable reputation and continued popularity, his work was falling out of favor with authors and publishers. Styles were changing, and

Newspaper flag drawn by Billings (courtesy of the Saint Louis Mercantile Library Association)

younger talents such as Winslow Homer and Thomas Nast were increasingly popular.

As an architect Billings was the designer of many important buildings in New England. His work on Boston churches, famed monuments such as the Pilgrim Fathers at Plymouth and the National Monument to the Forefathers, public buildings, early libraries, schools, and interiors is justifiably famous. His ability as a draftsman in the building arts contributed to his style and ability as an illustrator. His adept handling of landscapes and city views stems from his work as an architect and designer. He gave his energy to many formats, from painting and sculpture to drawing and engraving. A contemporary mid-Victorian analogue in the fields of publishing, illustration, and architecture in Great Britain was the architectural firm of William and George Audsley of Liverpool, which produced illustrations for some of the most elaborately designed plate books. As was Billings in America, the Audsleys were widely read and familiar with the trends in nineteenth-century book design, and they linked architecture and book-design forms firmly together in their work, undertaking many projects and commissions in both fields.

In Billings's productive years as an illustrator, his versatility made his name a household word. The general reader of the day certainly would have known and appreciated his work. In 1860 John Thorndike, writing in his *Dedication of the Mechanic's Hall,* called Billings "a new Michelangelo." In a jour-

nal entry for 11 January 1847 Henry Wadsworth Longfellow described Billings as "the best illustrator of books we have yet had in this country."

Above all else, Billings's early work is of a highly picturesque style. Views, prospects, detailed close-ups of building facades, pleasant vignettes, and decorative set pieces for such works as James J. Jarvis's *Scenes and Scenery in the Sandwich Islands, and a Trip Through Central America* (1843) and Richard Frothingham Jr.'s *History of Charlestown, Massachusetts* (1845–1849) were the building blocks of his reputation. In his early years Billings produced illustrations for books of local history, gift books, textbooks and spellers, and juvenile fiction. *Chimes, Rhymes, and Jingles: Or Mother Goose's Songs* (1845) was one of Billings's most important early commissions; his many nursery rhyme images were highly regarded. Another important early commission was that of the Hartford publisher House and Brown for Samuel G. Goodrich's *Pictorial History of America; Embracing Both the Northern and Southern Portions of the New World* (1849).

In the 1850s Billings was in the spotlight as a major designer for the book trade. He became a regular illustrator for *The Boston Almanac.* He also was called upon increasingly to supply designs for the works of poetry and fiction that were flowing from Boston publishers. Grace Greenwood's *Greenwood Leaves: A Collection of Sketches and Letters* (1850) and *Recollections of My Childhood* (1852) were other popular works that he illustrated. Billings also illus-

Magazine cover illustration by Billings (courtesy of the Saint Louis Mercantile Library Association)

trated Nathaniel Hawthorne's *True Stories from History and Biography* (1851) as well as his *A Wonder Book for Boys and Girls* (1852) and the first edition of *Tanglewood Tales, for Boys and Girls; Being a Second Wonder Book* (1853).

Billings's greatest achievement as an illustrator came when he was given the chance to interpret one of the great best-sellers of the day—Harriet Beecher Stowe's *Uncle Tom's Cabin; or Life among the Lowly* (1852). Six engravings for the first edition were done from drawings by Billings, and he was charged with producing more than one hundred more for the 1853 edition. His design for "Little Eva Reading the Bible to Uncle Tom in the Arbor" was used to illustrate a popular broadside ballad by John Greenleaf Whittier, "Little Eva: Song" (1852), which also helped broadcast Billings's work to the general public of the day.

Although occupied with important architectural commissions throughout the rest of the 1850s and 1860s, Billings, due in large part to his success with Stowe's work, continued to take on a wide range of book-illustration projects. His most prolific illustrations were for entertaining, moral, and educational children's works. In fact, this genre was probably the glue that cemented his entire career as a wood engraver; certainly some of his best work resides in the New England juvenile books of the day: Eliza Lee Follen's *Twilight Stories* (1856), Lippincott's *Stories from Famous Ballads. For Children* (1860), and William T. Adams's *The Riverdale Story Books* (1862), among many others.

After the Civil War, Billings occasionally turned to the illustration of works by English authors. He had earlier produced the illustrations for Sir Walter Scott's *Waverly Novels* (1857–1859) for the Boston publishing firm Ticknor and Fields. In the 1860s and early 1870s he produced illustrations for Oliver Goldsmith's *The Deserted Village* (1866), Tennyson's *Poems* (1866), Tennyson's *The Last Tournament* (1872), and Charles Dickens's *A Child's Dream of a Star* (1871).

Part of Billings's success as an illustrator was due to his location. Living in Boston placed him in the most important publishing city of the day. It also meant that he was well situated for taking advantage of and keeping up with the leading concerns of the day. Movements to ease societal ills, such as the early New England temperance cause, the fight of the abolitionists, questions concerning manifest destiny, and questions about military conquests, were all themes Billings treated. His art became a mirror of society's questions and views, its vices, and its various divisions at a time when America was losing some of its innocence.

Billings was one of the earliest social commentators through American illustration. Perhaps a defining proof of this interest in the great causes of the day is shown by his designing of the third masthead of William Lloyd Garrison's *Liberator* in 1850. In the early and mid 1850s Billings clearly became the philosophical choice to illustrate *Uncle Tom's Cabin* and similar works, such as Richard Hildreth's *The White Slave; or, Memoirs of a Fugitive* (1852), Charles Sumner's *White Slavery in the Barbary States* (1853), and John Greenleaf Whittier's *A Sabbath Scene* (1854).

By the standards of today, Billings's celebration of family life and morality may be considered preachy. Certainly, though, his sentimental illustrations for juvenile books filled the needs of publishers and authors of his own day. His illustrations depicting drunkenness and vice also show how Billings positioned his design work to capitalize on the trends of his time, as did many other illustrators. Hence Darley's masterpiece illustrations to Sylvester Judd's best-selling *Margaret* (1856) can be

THE AUCTION SALE. Page 174.

Illustration by Billings for Harriet Beecher Stowe's Uncle Tom's Cabin *in 1852 (courtesy of the Stratford Lee Morton Collection, Washington University Libraries, Saint Louis)*

compared to Billings's complementary temperance work in John Dix's *Passages from the History of a Wasted Life* (1853).

At the peak of Billings's success in his dual professions came the artist's ironic decline—ironic because of the great praise that had been bestowed upon him from all quarters. Possibly Billings's pioneering works in American illustration were too successful. The praise they won and the insatiable taste they created for more pictures in books encouraged a younger, more experimental group of students. This new generation was quite often better trained, better paid, better equipped technologically, and more focused on work that forced readers, publishers, and critics to acknowledge the truism that illustration was developing into a serious form of art.

The sentimentality, the gentle humanity in the figures, the excited and dramatic expressions in the faces, and the perfected landscapes and backgrounds were seemingly not enough to satisfy Billings's patrons. Louisa May Alcott complained bitterly about Billings's work for the second part of *Little Women* (1869). Her publisher, Roberts Brothers, forced Billings to change the frontispiece. This was a signal moment in Billings's gradual decline.

Between 1870 and 1874 (the year of his death) he produced a few documentary and historical works along with more juvenile books, his mainstay. Two of the more important works he illustrated were William D. Phelps's *Fore and Aft; or Leaves from the Life of an Old Sailor* (1871), an interesting piece of Western Americana, and Charles Carleton Coffin's *The Story of the Great Fire, Boston, November 9–10, 1872* (1872). For these Billings played the role of a graphic reporter in producing excellent illustrations "Taken on the Spot." Many of his last works were relatively uninspired and simply decorative or ornamental, such as that for the anthology *Laurel Leaves. Original Poems, Stories, and Essays* (1876), a collection brought out after Billings's death.

Billings's Boston training in drawing and design in the 1840s commenced and coincided with the rise of a widespread, popular illustrated press on both sides of the Atlantic. His experience in the field of architecture gave him an appreciation for classical and Renaissance principles of design that form the backbone of his composition for illustration.

As the book world suddenly demanded engravings by the dozens for each new title, Billings was ready. His study of art and illustration and his awareness of the work of contemporaries as diversified as

Illustration of Mount Vernon by Billings for T. Addison Richards's American Scenery Illustrated *in 1854 (courtesy of the Saint Louis Mercantile Library Association)*

Thomas Cole, Gustave Dore, George Cruikshank, and fellow American illustrators allowed his versatility to blossom in a prolific array of practical illustrated designs for each new book offered him.

Billings was perhaps the most refined and energetic of all the popular illustrators of the mid nineteenth century. His work was determined by an unemotional sense of order and balance. His illustrations were truly representative of the theme of an author's text. He aimed for a sense of clarity and balance between word and picture. He was careful in his study of what was expected of him as illustrator, perhaps to the point of overconfidence; his illustrations at times seem too mechanical. He was not introspective but direct in his design work. Billings created and sold illustrations according to popular demand. For nearly his entire career he had his finger squarely on the pulse of what would sell, what would have a conventional, immediate impact on the eye of the reader.

His incentive was his living, determined by the vagaries of the Boston economy and the caprices it meted out to artists of any stripe in the mid nineteenth century. Such an illustrator functioned in a world that did not grant the leisure to pursue much individuality.

Billings was a workmanlike illustrator, emulating and expressing his artistic viewpoint within narrow parameters of design. The conventions dictated often gave such an illustrator moments of glory, such as when his vision matched perfectly the voice of the narrator and even more important, the expectations of the reader.

Bibliographies:

Sinclair Hamilton, *Early American Book Illustrators* (Princeton: Princeton University Press, 1958; supplement, 1968);

James F. O'Gorman, *A Billings Bookshelf: An Annotated Bibliography of Works Illustrated by Hammatt Billings (1818–1874)* (Wellesley, Mass.: Wellesley College, 1983).

References:

Ballou's Pictorial Drawing Room Companion, 10 (1856): 252;

Gleason's Pictorial Line-of-Battle Ship, 1 (6 August 1859): 1;

"Hammatt Billings," *Old and New,* 11 (March 1875): 355–357;

Karen Nipps, *Naturally Fond of Pictures: American Illustration of the 1840s and 1850s* (Philadelphia: Library Company of Philadelphia, 1989), pp. 12, 20;

James F. O'Gorman, "H. and J. E. Billings of Boston," *Journal of the Society of Architectural Historians,* 42 (March 1983): 54–73;

Richard Stoddard, "Hammatt Billings, Artist and Architect," *Old-Time New England,* 62 (January–March 1972): 57–79.

Archives:

Few papers and collections of Billings's original art for book illustration have survived. A few letters to Longfellow from Billings exist at Harvard. Some original sketches exist at the Library of Congress, the Boston Public Library, the Massachusetts Historical Society, and the Museum of Fine Arts in Boston. O'Gorman in his *Billings Bookshelf* refers to a large body of architectural drawings. The most important collection of engravings and other book illustrations, the Hammatt Billings Collection, is housed at Wellesley College. Many works, paintings, and sketches once known to exist have long since disappeared. Stoddard cites the location of two oil paintings, of Edward E. Phelps and Albert Smith, at Dartmouth College. Research into the patronage of Billings by various authors and into the illustrator's work in the popular press of his day in other American cities, especially New York, should yield an even larger catalogue of the output of an engraver who typically left his designs unsigned.

Franklin Booth
(8 July 1874 – 28 August 1948)

Laura S. Fuderer
University of Notre Dame

BOOKS: *Franklin Booth: Sixty Reproductions from Original Drawings with an Appreciation by Earnest Elmo Calkins and an Introduction by Meredith Nicholson* (New York: Robert Frank, 1925);

The Buildings; Their Architectural Meaning (Winnetka, Ill.: Book and Print Guild, 1934);

20 Franklin Booth Masterpieces (New York: Frances, 1947).

SELECTED BOOKS ILLUSTRATED: Nicholson, Meredith, *The House of a Thousand Candles* (Indianapolis: Bobbs-Merrill, 1905);

Seawell, Molly Elliot, *The Loves of the Lady Arabella* (Indianapolis: Bobbs-Merrill, 1906);

Metcalfe, Richard Lee, *"Of Such Is the Kingdom": and Other Stories from Life* (Lincoln, Neb.: Woodruff-Collins Press, 1907);

Browning, Elizabeth Barrett, *Lady Geraldine's Courtship: A Romance of the Age* (New York: Appleton, 1907);

Riley, James Whitcomb, *Home Again with Me* (Indianapolis: Bobbs-Merrill, [1908]);

MacGrath, Harold, *The Enchanted Hat* (Indianapolis: Bobbs-Merrill, 1908);

Riley, James Whitcomb, *Riley Roses* (Indianapolis: Bobbs-Merrill, 1909);

Riley, *Old-Fashioned Roses* (Indianapolis: Bobbs-Merrill, [1909]);

Riley, *The Flying Islands of the Night* (Indianapolis: Bobbs-Merrill, 1913);

Riley, *A Discouraging Model* (Indianapolis: Bobbs-Merrill, [1914]);

Nicholson, Meredith, *The Poet* (Boston & New York: Houghton Mifflin, 1914);

Wylie, Ida Alexa Ross, *Five Years to Find Out* (Indianapolis: Bobbs-Merrill, 1914);

Dreiser, Theodore, *A Hoosier Holiday* (New York: Lane, 1916);

Apukhtin, A. N., *From Death to Life* (New York: R. Frank, 1917);

Twain, Mark, *Prince and the Pauper; A Tale for Young People of All Ages* (New York: Harper & Row, 1917);

Franklin Booth

Esarey, Logan, *The Indiana Home* (Bloomington: Indiana University Press, 1953).

PERIODICALS: *Everybody's Magazine,* 1906–1917;
Scribner's Magazine, 1907–1919;
Broadway Magazine, 1909;
Harper's Monthly, 1909–1917;
McClure's, 1909–1917;
Collier's, 1910–1920;
Cosmopolitan, 1911;
American Magazine, 1912–1920;
The Saturday Evening Post, 1913–1928;

Century, 1914–1915;
Good Housekeeping, 1916–1923;
Vanity Fair, 1916–1918.

During his lifetime Jay Franklin Booth was widely known among graphic-arts, advertising, and mass-media circles as one of the preeminent artists in pen and ink. He was admired particularly for his skill at composition, the variety of his pen work, and his capacity for imagination. Born the same year as Joseph Christian Leyendecker, within a year of fellow Hoosier Frederick Coffay Yohn, and within three years of Howard Chandler Christy and Harrison Fisher, Booth, like these other artists, reached his peak during the latter years of America's Golden Age of Illustration. Although eclipsed by names such as James Montgomery Flagg and Charles Dana Gibson, Booth's work deserves the recognition that it has gradually been receiving.

Franklin Booth was born on 8 July 1874 on a forty-acre farm in Clarksville, six miles northeast of Noblesville, Indiana. His father, John Thomas Booth, had migrated to Hamilton County, Indiana, from North Carolina soon after the Civil War. His mother, née Susan Emily Wright, was from Virginia. The third of eight children, Booth grew up on a large farm that his father purchased on the Gray Road southwest of Noblesville.

Early in childhood Booth began drawing farm animals and the scenes around him. Mistaking the engraved illustrations he saw in schoolbooks and weekly magazines for pen-and-ink sketches, he painstakingly copied them line for line. To this childhood experience he attributed his unique pen-and-ink style, which was often mistaken for woodcut. He discovered perspective by himself, coming home from school one day and noticing that the fence did not really form a square but disappeared behind the house.

Hamilton County had been settled in part by Quakers, including several Booth families from North Carolina. As a boy Booth taught Sunday school at the Gray Quaker meetinghouse nearby, and later fondly remembered illustrating lessons on a "roll blackboard" that he carried under his arm.

Never aspiring to attend college, Booth finished high school at the Union Academy, a Quaker school, at Westfield, some miles west of Noblesville. For a while he was content to work on the farm and occupy his leisure time with self-taught drawing, reading, and writing poetry. These early years were the "fair seed-time" in which Booth's mind and soul drank in the beauty of the natural scenery around him when, like William Wordsworth, he observed streams, trees, woodlands, clouds, light, and shad-

ow, sketching them but also storing up visions in his imagination that were to emerge in his art for years to come.

Theodore Dreiser wrote in *A Hoosier Holiday* (1916) that Booth confessed to taking a correspondence course in art. The instructor did not know much but only charged six dollars for fifteen lessons, which was all Booth could afford at the time. Saying, "Art is a matter of feeling, anyhow," Booth confided to Dreiser, "I can't tell you how much feeling I put in those things, either,–the trees, the birds flying, the shocked corn. I used to stop when I was plowing or reaping and stand and look at the sky and the trees and the clouds and wish I could paint them or do something. The big cities seemed so far off. But it's Indiana that seems wonderful to me now."

Booth was twenty-five when his first work was published. In 1899 the *Indianapolis News* paid him five dollars to print one of his decorated poems, "A Thanksgiving Ode." The notion of earning money by writing poetry impressed his father, who up to that point had been less than encouraging of his son's dreamy propensities. Upon meeting the elder Booth years later Dreiser observed that the two men were types not likely to be understanding or sympathetic of each other, the one being a "sensitive, perceptive artist," and the other, "the sheer, aggressive political soldier type." Booth himself was sure that his brother Frederick's penchant for writing and the artistic abilities of his brother Hanson and himself were nurtured by their mother's gentle and poetic nature.

The *Indianapolis News* continued publishing his illustrated verse through 1901. Encouraged by the staff cartoonist, Frank Bowers, to go to art school, Booth enrolled in a three-month course at the Chicago Art Institute. While in Chicago he attempted to sell a full-page pen-and-ink drawing of a country scene, but it was rejected by the smaller newspapers. Deciding to aim for the top, Booth approached one of the larger papers and was rewarded when the art editor promptly offered him fifty dollars for the picture. At the end of the three months he went back to the farm.

In 1901 Booth struck out for New York City, the mecca of American illustration at that time. He attended the Art Students League for three months and was hired for space work at a New York newspaper. About this time he met Theodore Dreiser, who also came from Indiana. Dreiser wrote in *A Hoosier Holiday,* "I was drawn to him then because he had such an air of unsophisticated and genial simplicity while looking so much the artist. I liked his long, strong aquiline nose, and his hair of a fine black and silver, though he was then only twenty-seven or eight." The paper Booth was working on soon failed, however, and he went back to the farm.

Two weeks on the art staff of the *Indianapolis Star* were followed by a position with the *Indianapolis News*. At the *News* his illustration work included line drawings of people and events, feature articles, advertisements, and his own verse. He made friends with humorist Kin Hubbard, cartoonist Frank Bowers, and fellow artists William Heitman and the two Brehm brothers, George and Worth. One spring day in 1903 Hearst cartoonist Homer C. Davenport stopped in to see his cousin, Frank Bowers, and noticed a poster done by Booth. Impressed with his work, Davenport secured for Booth a year's contract with the Frank A. Munsey Company that sent him to work for the *Daily News* in New York. Unfortunately that paper also failed within months, but Booth's contract allowed him to work on the *Journal* in Boston, the *Times* in Washington, and possibly a Munsey paper in Buffalo. After the contract expired in 1904, he did space work on the Sunday *New York Times*. But when summer came he went back to the farm.

After a brief period of illustrating for *Reader* magazine, published by the Indianapolis-based Bobbs-Merrill Company, Booth returned to New York in the fall. When the opportunity arose to travel to Europe with a group of artists in the spring of 1905, he took it. The three months Booth spent in Europe included visits to Rome and Paris, but he spent most of the time in Spain studying under Robert Henri. In a paper read before the Indianapolis Literary Club in 1950, Howard C. Caldwell quoted Booth as saying, "While I did not come back any better artist than I was before I left, my three months in Europe gave me a wonderful talking point. I seemed to impress the magazine editors more when I told them that I had been to Europe studying art than when I told them I came from some newspaper office. In any event, after that trip abroad, I got all the work I could do."

In recounting the early years of his career in a 1912 letter to Eleanor Bernhardt, a Hamilton County resident, Booth said, "I could not write in all the struggle that went with it and the discouragement, and also the delight and the encouragement. These last after all were the main things."

In 1905 Bobbs-Merrill published *The House of a Thousand Candles* by Meredith Nicholson, with illustrations by Howard Chandler Christy and decorations by Booth. Although the decorations amounted to one headpiece and a smaller tailpiece, this assignment was the beginning of a collaboration with Bobbs-Merrill that lasted at least twelve years. From

One of Booth's illustrations for Meredith Nicholson's novel The Poet *(1914)*

1905 to 1917 the publisher involved Booth in fourteen books. Seven used decorations by Booth, and three bore dust jackets designed by him; four were illustrated by Christy and the rest by Clarence F. Underwood, G. C. Wilmshurst, Will Vawter, Will Grefé, Thomas Fogarty, and Arthur I. Keller. Four of the books were entirely illustrated by Booth.

In later years Booth recalled that the way he broke into the big national magazines was once again through an acquaintance. While in New York he had made friends with Thomas S. Jones Jr., whose poetry was being published in the magazines. According to Booth he prevailed on Jones to let him illustrate his next verse, a poem titled "A Deserted Village," which Jones submitted for publication in 1907. In fact, a poem titled "The Winding Brook," written by Jones and illustrated by Booth, appeared in an issue of *Everybody's Magazine* in 1906. The July 1907 issue of *Everybody's* carried a short story, "The

Frontispiece and title page for the first volume Booth illustrated extensively in color, a 1913 gift book that the publisher promoted as much for Booth's art as for Riley's story

New Strong Wine of Spring" by Katharine Holland Brown, with four illustrations by Booth. Booth was popular with the editors at *Everybody's,* and they continued using his illustrations for poems and headpieces for regular features at least through 1917. It was November 1907 before Jones's "The Deserted Village," with Booth's illustration, appeared in *Scribner's.* This appearance meant that Booth had finally broken into the "Big Four," which also included *Century, Harper's,* and *McClure's.*

Also in 1907 appeared the first book wholly illustrated by Franklin Booth: Richard Lee Metcalfe's *"Of Such Is the Kingdom": and Other Stories from Life,* published by the Woodruff-Collins Press in Lincoln, Nebraska. The seven plates accompanying the gently moralizing stories depict children and adults in homey and heartwarming scenes.

Booth's interiors were not always as successful as his landscapes, cityscapes, and depictions of the outdoors. He was at his best when given the chance to let memory evoke natural scenes or imagination invent pure fantasy. The plates for Metcalfe's book fade in comparison to Booth's illustrations for

W. G. FitzGerald's article "War on the Tiger" in the May 1908 *McClure's.* For beauty of design and composition, range of tone in a pen drawing, and dramatic impact of subject, this portrayal of a tiger hunt in tall grass equals the best in American illustration. About forty years later Booth recalled this drawing in a short essay on composition that prefaced *20 Franklin Booth Masterpieces* (1947). Explaining that the focal point of a picture did not have to be large or close-up, he continued, "I first experimented with this thought in a picture of a tiger hunt. The tiger was important but I drew him from the viewpoint of the hunters; you saw him put his head through the grass some distance away. He was vicious and dominated the scene; he was looking at you and you were looking at him; he was compelling in importance but small as a spot. All action was directed toward him. It was not necessary, therefore, to draw attention by using the largest space in the picture."

In 1908 Booth received four more assignments for *Scribner's* and provided poetry illustration for *McClure's* and decorations for two books by Bobbs-Merrill. Booth felt secure enough in 1908 to establish his own studio first on East Fifty-ninth Street and later at 67 West Fifty-seventh Street, where he lived for the remainder of his life.

The following year Booth and Christy were given equal credit for illustrating *Riley Roses* (1909). For this book Booth produced black-line drawings, colored pictures, and decorative borders. Booth's book illustration was confined to the years 1905 to 1917, apart from two collections of his work (1925, 1947) and a book he wrote and illustrated about the World's Fair in 1934, *The Buildings: Their Architectural Meaning*. In that twelve-year period he was involved with twenty books but substantially illustrated only seven. Although he was regarded as almost exclusively a pen-and-ink line artist, five of those seven books were illustrated in color. Beginning in 1905 painting was one of Booth's hobbies, and his watercolors were reproduced quite successfully.

Through the early 1920s Booth was in demand by the magazines to illustrate poems, stories, and articles. Having illustrated his own verse for years, he was adept at conveying the sense of a poem graphically, not only by representing concrete details but also by evoking the tone and spirit of the poet's voice. His illustration for Rosamund Marriott Watson's "The Wind of Dreams" in *Scribner's* (December 1909) is an example. Gigantic, swirling clouds occupy almost four-fifths of the picture; only after close inspection does one see in the outlines of the clouds "Wraiths that the scented breath of summer raises, / Ghosts of dead hours and flowers that once were fair." Left and slightly below center is a towering stand of poplars, typical of Booth's penchant for countering the flatness of a horizon with an extreme vertical in the form of trees, cliffs, or walls. At the foot of the tree appears one of "the harvest-wagons homeward driven." This picture is typical of Booth's masterful landscapes and incidentally reminiscent of the flat, open countryside dotted with groves of trees one sees in north-central Indiana.

Despite his determined attempts to make a living in Manhattan, Booth remained attached to his Indiana roots, and he returned there for a month or so every summer for most of his life. In 1912 he had a studio constructed behind his parents' house in Carmel where they had moved after retiring from the farm. He did much of his work in this studio. This fondness for home was reflected in one of the books written by Riley and published by Bobbs-Merrill, *Home Again with Me* (1908). The dedication page to William C. Bobbs, decorated by Booth with lacey grapevines and scrollwork, included a poem titled "His Love of Home." The last line, "A Hoosier's love is for the old homestead," expressed a sentiment shared by all three men: the poet, the artist, and the publisher. The wooded, rustic homestead Booth designed for the endpaper illustration might have been his own boyhood home.

Booth greatly admired James Whitcomb Riley, and the admiration was mutual. Riley lived in the Lockerbie District near downtown Indianapolis, and Carmel neighbors reported years later that they used to see Riley stroll up the road from the station to the Booth house to spend a lazy summer afternoon under a shady tree chatting with Franklin.

In 1913 Bobbs-Merrill published the first book extensively illustrated in color by Booth, Riley's *The Flying Islands of the Night*. Dubbed a "faery-fantasy" in the advertisements, this work is a peculiar mix of lyrical drama, dark comedy, and fairy tale. In sixteen full-page plates Booth exercised his imagination, portraying medieval costumes, flying green sprites, and clusters of many-towered palaces floating on immense feathered wings above an earthly landscape that looks suspiciously like Indiana. The advertisements for the work promoted it as much for Booth's illustrations as for Riley's text, declaring, "It marks a new page in American art, for this is the first gift book of its splendid sort, wholly the work of native Americans, ever to be published." Described as "7 3/8 x 9 11/16 inches, Cloth, boxed," it sold for three dollars. Booth was dissatisfied with the quality of the color reproduction, which appeared somewhat smudged, and the trimming of the loose plates occasionally cut off parts of the picture.

The middle 1910s were the most productive years of Booth's career. In addition to magazine and advertising work he was involved with the decorations or illustrations of three books in 1914, three books in 1916, and three more works in 1917, including Mark Twain's *The Prince and the Pauper* for Harper and Row and the twenty-volume "Harvard Classics Shelf of Fiction" for Collier. In the midst of this busy period Booth offered to take Theodore Dreiser on an automobile trip back to Indiana. The trip resulted in Dreiser's largely autobiographical book *A Hoosier Holiday*. If Booth's name was not already widely known for his work in the national magazines and the books by Riley, it became well known to all who read this book. Some forty-two reviews were listed in *Theodore Dreiser: the Critical Reception* (1972), and all reviewers who mentioned Booth's thirty-two illustrations were enthusiastic. While Dreiser's friend and champion (and editor of the book) H. L. Mencken observed in his review that Booth remained more shadowy than other individuals Dreiser characterized, Booth's comments and opinions did occasionally emerge.

"Factoryville Bids Us Farewell" and "Vincennes: The Knox County Fair," two of Booth's illustrations for Theodore Dreiser's A Hoosier Holiday *(1916)*

Dreiser thought highly of Booth and introduced him in the book as "an illustrator of repute, a master of pen and ink, what you would call a really successful artist." He was reticent about physical details but informed the reader that Booth's "soft, artistic shock of hair" was now "glistening white." When they went for a swim in a roadside stream in upstate New York, he noted Booth's "strong, lean white body, which showed that it had been shaped in hayfields in his youth. His white hair and straight nose made him look somewhat like an ancient Etruscan, stalking about in the waters." When leaping shocks of grain in a field (testing whether they had been true farmers and would live to be eighty), Booth at age forty-one cleared them "with his coat skirts flying out behind in a most bird-like manner," whereas Dreiser failed miserably.

That Booth could make fast friends with two writers of such opposite temperaments as James Whitcomb Riley (the elderly writer of nostalgic verse) and Theodore Dreiser (the iconoclastic realist) reveals a certain degree of tolerance in Booth's character. Dreiser recognized Booth's tolerance on the first page of the book, observing:

> Franklin is a Christian Scientist, or dreamy metaphysician. . . . He has no hard and fast Christian dogmas in mind. In fact, he is not a Christian at all, in the accepted sense, but a genial, liberal, platonic metaphysician. . . . So-called sin, as something wherewith to reproach one, does not exist for him. He has few complaints to make concerning people's weaknesses or errors. Nearly everything is well. He lives happily along, sketching landscapes and trees and drawing many fine simplicities and perfections. There is about him a soothing repose which is not religious but human, which I felt, during all the two thousand miles we subsequently idled together.

Others who knew Booth over the years universally described him as not only a thorough gentleman but also a truly gentle man.

Because Dreiser was primarily interested in retrieving and in a sense reliving his long-lost youth in Indiana on this automobile trip, he took considerable interest in noting Booth's opinions and impressions about Indiana. When drawing Booth out on what it was about Indiana that produced so many creative people (including themselves, Booth Tarkington, and Riley), Dreiser was somewhat surprised at the metaphysical nature of Booth's response, and he devotes four pages to quoting it, presumably verbatim. Booth attributed the high degree of creativity among some Hoosiers to the magnetism or creative power generated by the soil and light peculiar to the region around Indianapolis. He spoke of the indescribable haze occurring in some July and August days that created a sense of mystery, a spiritual or aesthetic suggestiveness. He related this sense also to the influence of the great forests of maple, beech, poplar, hickory, and oak peculiar to that region. He felt this sense "when the first real summer days begin to take on that wonderful light, and a kind of luminous silence over things suggests growing corn and ripening wheat and quails whistling in the meadows over by the woods." Booth believed that this "soil-generated call" to freedom came to him and to certain other individuals, a freedom not from local experiences but freedom "to achieve a working contact with universal things."

Curiously, it was the Indianapolis Speedway and the possibilities inherent in the automobile that lay at the foundation of Booth's thinking that day. His love affair with the automobile and his passion for the Indianapolis races attracted him back to Indiana year after year perhaps as much as did fondness for home and family. As late as 1941 he informed a journalist that he had missed only three or four races since the Speedway opened. Dreiser apparently shared the admiration for the automobile because Booth's new $3,000, sixty-horsepower Pathfinder becomes almost as much a character in the trip as its four passengers (the artist, the writer, a chauffeur named Speed, and another named Bert). Booth never felt the necessity to learn to drive, however, protesting that one could not watch the countryside while driving.

Booth's illustrations—which he did in Carmel after Dreiser returned to New York by train—probably surprised many who knew his work. Dreiser and the publisher liked the preliminary sketches so much that these were used for the book rather than the pen-and-ink drawings Booth had planned to do. While the sketches reflect his usual fine composition and range of tone, the rough sketches done in charcoal convey a realism and sense of immediacy that are quite different from the polished elegance of Booth's normal medium and technique. The pages about Lake Erie's Cedar Point demonstrate the illustrative abilities of both men: Booth's sketch captures Dreiser's description of "a halcyon evening in which a blood red sun, aided by tattered, wind whipped clouds, combined to give the day's close a fabled, almost Norse aspect" on a long beach where lovers walked hand in hand. In the "curious cloud formations which hung overhead" Dreiser saw "two horsemen riding side by side in the sky."

Two more projects with substantial illustrations by Franklin Booth were published in 1917. One was Mark Twain's *The Prince and the Pauper*, published by Harper and Row with eight full-page illustrations in color. For "The Harvard Classics

Shelf of Fiction," published by Collier, Booth designed the endpapers and the black-and-white frontispiece for each of twenty volumes. Each frontispiece depicted a scene pertaining to the author's life rather than the fictional work. The outdoor scenes far surpass the interiors in quality. The illustration for volume fifteen, *German Fiction,* for example, is "View of Potsdam, Where Storm Lived." In classic Booth style the frontispiece portrays an Old World cityscape viewed from a river, with voluminous clouds rising behind a church steeple. These illustrations may have been copied from photographs, but the influence of Booth's trip to Europe is evident.

Booth continued his magazine and advertising illustration during and after World War I. Many of the poems he illustrated for *Good Housekeeping* in this period are in the form of a prayer, and Booth's idealistic treatment effectively expressed the spiritualism of the subject and the patriotic fervor of the time. One illustration that has subsequently been frequently reproduced was made for Martha Haskell Clark's poem "The Villages." Suggesting "The little, small-town sympathy that steals on neighbor feet / From tiny lamp-lit houses down a maple-shaded street," the illustration shows two tiny figures hurrying across a dirt road below enormous maple trees toward a row of clapboard houses. Typical of the small towns of the Midwest, this drawing is titled "Neighbors" in reproductions. *Good Housekeeping* was so pleased with Booth's work that his name was included in their "Credo," which read in part, "To publish only clean, stirring and inspiring fiction . . . with illustrations of rare, artistic merit by such artists as James Montgomery Flagg, Walter Biggs, Jennie Wilcox Smith, Alonzo Williams, Franklin Booth and Rose O'Neil."

If the 1910s were the peak of Booth's book and magazine illustration, the 1920s may have been the peak of his renown as an important person on the commercial American art scene. He was called upon to endorse products such as Whatman Drawing Paper and India ink for Grumbacher, and in turn he was endorsed by advertisers as "one of the most famous figures in American illustration."

Illustrating advertisements was probably a major source of revenue for Booth. This work alone might have made him a wealthy man—at his peak he was able to charge $500 to $1,500 per drawing. Booth's elegant pen-and-ink technique and idealized, transcendent method of conveying subject matter appealed to advertisers who wanted their products portrayed with a sense of refinement. *The Art of Franklin Booth: Sixty Reproductions from Original Drawings* (1925) includes drawings made for Montgomery Ward, N. W. Ayer and Son, L. Bamberger

and Company, First National Pictures, Paramount Pictures, and Procter and Gamble. The pen-and-ink rendition of Lincoln (after Gutzon Borglum) for Billings and Spencer was also reproduced in Joseph Pennell's book *The Graphic Arts: Modern Men and Modern Methods* (1921). Attacking pervasive imitation among American illustrators, Pennell says of the illustration: "This effective design came out in a daily paper only a week or two ago, and prints remarkably well, and is an example of how one should work for cheap and rapid newspaper and magazine work. He has been successful, and his technique is now imitated by every little thief in the land who can imitate but not invent."

In the preface to Booth's book Elmo Calkins (an advertising agent who commissioned drawings for Estey Organ Company) commended Booth for overcoming the barrier between book and magazine decoration and advertising illustration. He wrote, "Anything undertaken by him is approached in the same creative spirit and executed with the same sure touch. . . . He considers a pipe organ as glorious a subject as an oak tree, and when he has finished with it, it is." In fact, a series of twelve drawings Booth made for the Estey Organ Company in 1922 came to be the artist's favorites among his own work, appealing to the lyrical spirit in his nature. The series included the vaulted interior of a massive cathedral, a radiating citadel upon a hilltop, and a carefree nymph and satyr playing flutes at the foot of a pair of towering arches. The latter was reproduced in Walt Reed's *Great American Illustrators* (1979).

Other advertisers that employed Booth included Wallace Silver, Underwood Typewriters, Victor-Victrola, and the Aeolian Company (maker of phonographs). He also drew album covers for Victor Records. An example of the appeal of Booth's technique is an ad in a 1913 issue of *McClure's* for an electric fan from General Electric Company. The ad begins, "Coolness—that wafts through the warmth of a sultry day like the breaking spray of a wave"; the vertical block of text and picture of a fan are bordered by delicate, swirling lines of waves below innumerable puffs of clouds.

In 1923, when Booth was almost fifty years old, he married for the first time. His wife, Beatrice, was one of his models and the sister of artist Edwin Franklin Wittmack. Booth's parents died in 1921 and 1926, but that did not stop his return trips to Indiana. He continued visiting relatives there, and, having no children of his own, he apparently enjoyed the role of a doting and generous uncle. Besides attending the Indianapolis 500 his activities included golf, horseback riding, and rifle shooting.

Illustration for Martha Haskell Clark's "The Villages," published in Good Housekeeping *during World War I*

His favorite exercise was walking, and he and Dreiser would ferry across the Hudson to walk for miles—as many as twelve or fifteen in a day—along the Palisades.

The year 1925 was an eventful one for Booth as his best work was collected and published in a book and he cofounded the Phoenix Art Institute with Lauros Phoenix, Frank Schoonover, and others. In addition the New York publisher Robert Frank and the Walker Engraving Company produced *The Art of Franklin Booth: Sixty Reproductions from Original Drawings.* Oversize in format, the edition was limited to 210 copies, each signed by Booth. The preface by Calkins praised Booth's dexterity with the pen and his uplifting imagination. The introduction by Meredith Nicholson (a Hoosier author whose books Booth had illustrated) did likewise and identified in the "cobweb fineness" of his work "a consciousness of gracious and beautiful things." The sixty selections ranged from illustrations for poems and fiction in magazines and books to his decorations and advertising work. Although a study in charcoal and one in wash were included, the charcoal sketches from *A Hoosier Holiday* were excluded.

Teaching at the Phoenix Art Institute (later the New York-Phoenix School of Design) established a structure to Booth's routine that lasted the rest of his life. Three times a week he taught classes on composition, life drawing, and illustration. Along with this involvement he began to commit to print his conceptions of the art of illustration. In a series of correspondence courses for the school Booth elaborated on the theories and methods of good composition. Throughout his writings he stressed the primary values of truth (in the sense of learning or observing facts about one's environment, particularly nature) and beauty or the aesthetic (derived from inspiration and feelings). The viewpoint from which the artist conveyed those facts in a picture was determined by his own feelings and imagination, which must be cultivated to add the variety and interest essential to great art.

In 1928 Booth wrote the introduction to Arthur Guptill's book *Drawing with Pen and Ink* (1928), which became a classic on the subject. He published a series of articles on pen-and-ink illustration for the *Professional Art Quarterly* in 1934–1935. Discussing his own technique in these articles, he explained that his intent at times was "to give the pen stroke the quality of the brush stroke" by filling in areas with strokes of the pen in varying, but not opposite, directions. Recognizing that the sky was full of light and color and the air itself conveys a sense of movement, he described his use of the direction and play of lines to capture these elements, including the softening of edges of forms and points of contact between areas of the picture. He described in detail his own unusual method of drawing as follows:

> In doing a drawing, it has been my custom first, of course, to lay in my entire conception with the pencil. This pencilled sketch is not a completed thing, but a generalization. Parts of this I then draw in more fully and follow immediately with the pen. My drawings are usually somewhat involved and a completed pencil drawing to begin with would, in places, become smudged and lost in the process of inking in other parts. So I proceed and complete a part or section at a time and follow through, in this way, to the outer edges of my drawing. At times in the making of my drawings, in one section or more a completed picture will be seen in the midst of white paper and pencilled suggestions.

Apart from his writing and teaching, Booth's fortunes were in decline in the 1930s. He lost heavily in the Crash of 1929, and there was a decline in the popularity of pen-and-ink drawing and in the demand for his own distinctive style of drawing. After more than two decades of success Booth faced a new generation of art editors and directors. He believed he could have responded to the change in taste and styles if given the chance.

In 1934 Booth wrote and illustrated a small book titled *The Buildings: Their Architectural Meaning* about the architectural theory behind the buildings of the Century of Progress International Exposition in Chicago (the World's Fair of 1933–1934). Booth expresses his quiet outrage at the utilitarian values represented in these structures. The metaphors and veiled sarcasm he employs might initially give the reader the impression that the treatise was a defense of, not a diatribe against, the buildings. The writing reflects much of Booth's artistic understanding, including his love of architecture, his roots in the Art Nouveau style, and his veneration for the full range of the cultural past. It also reflects his intense belief in the fundamental position of imagination in the process of producing art.

Booth's appreciation for architecture went back at least to his youthful exposure to the great cities of Europe in 1905; that exposure reappeared in fanciful castles and ornate cathedrals throughout many years of illustration. He once gave directions to his brother Frederick from the studio on Fifty-seventh Street to the office of *Harper's Weekly* according to the facades of buildings along the way. When Frederick asked him how many facades in New York he could describe in detail, Franklin replied, "Hundreds, maybe thousands."

In his book Booth explains that a new country like America is bound to seek new forms of expression, but the theory of "the Modern" underlying the buildings of the exposition reduced architecture to the notion that form must be derived from utility. Beauty and aesthetics, if considered at all, should reside in a building's utility. Booth felt that the ornamentation on some of the buildings, in the form of massive sculptures, was out of all proportion to the six-foot height of a man and resembled a merchandising attraction rather than true ornament. Booth regarded the skyscraper as the solution to a young nation's search for innovation. To him the skyscraper better suited a people whose youth and optimism led them to reach upward where they could look out over vast distances. He had long admired skyscrapers for their tremendous vertical lines and uplifting symbolism, and he incorporated them into many of his cityscapes.

Booth's illustrations of twelve of the buildings almost constitute a deconstruction of his own artistic technique. The same excellent skill at composition remains, but his pen lines, known for their variety in weight and direction, have become heavy and solid. Mass is created by unvarying horizontal lines that are perfectly parallel. Shadows are shown not in shaded tones but in solid black, and highlights appear stark white. Even his characteristic billowing clouds have become heavy masses outlined in solid strokes and completely filled in by parallel horizontal lines.

In 1938 he provided the article on pen drawing for the fourteenth edition of *Encyclopaedia Britannica*. In it Booth observes that the advent of halftone reproduction contributed to the use of photography in publication and the decline of pen-and-ink drawing. The selected illustrations for the article include, besides the work of old masters such as Albrecht Dürer, pictures by Charles Dana Gibson, Edwin Austin Abbey, and one of Booth's series for "The House of Rimmon," published in *Scribner's* in 1908.

Almost ten years later Frances Publishing Company published another, smaller collection of the artist's work, titled *20 Franklin Booth Masterpieces*. The three articles by Booth prefacing the work essentially digest his earlier writings on pen technique and composition but add the confession that "my strong point, and my love, is for the outdoors and the reaches of sky and distance," not for human interest or drama. He summed up much of his life and work when he wrote that "knowing one's weakness is knowing one's strength" and that "one's loves and convictions . . . underlie all individual expression, artistic or otherwise."

Booth continued working and teaching through the 1940s. His entry in *Who's Who in America* at this time identified his politics as Socialist and his religion as Christian Science although no evidence suggests he was active in either. Writing sonnets was a favorite pastime of his later years as it had been in his youth. He sometimes composed while filling in the more tedious parts of a pen drawing. Among his last commissions for illustrations were booklets for the U.S. government and bookplates for institutions in Indiana. The bookplates are still in use at Butler University, the Indiana Historical Society, and the Indiana State Library, all in Indianapolis.

Franklin Booth made a distinct impression on many of his students. Artist John Jellico remembered him as "about six feet tall, broad-shouldered, thick white hair combed to one side." Jellico wrote an enthusiastic article for *American Artist* in 1966 to revive interest in Booth's work. Another student, Walt Reed, commemorated Booth when the Society of Illustrators inducted him into their Hall of Fame in 1983. Reed noted, "As one of his students, I knew him to be guided by the same idealism ['art as truth and beauty'] in his personality. Never dogmatic, he was gentle in his criticism, always encouraging, and he taught most effectively by expecting much of us." Students at the school published an article about Booth in their school journal shortly before his death in 1948, saying, "His grand manner and fine

fellowship endeared him to all with whom he worked." Teaching until a stroke forced his retirement in 1946, Booth died in his studio on 28 August 1948. His ashes were taken by relatives and strewn over the graves of his parents; he had returned home to Indiana for the last time.

References:
Joe Coleman, "Franklin Booth: Artist, Poet, Philosopher," *New York–Phoenix Art Journal* (15 May 1948): 4–6;

John Jellico, "Drawings of Franklin Booth," *American Artist,* 30 (January 1966): 42–46;

Herbert Kerkow, "Franklin Booth: Master of Technique," *Poster,* 20 September 1929, p. 17.

Archives:
The Cooper Union Museum, New York City, possesses ten of Franklin Booth's illustrations that were donated by *Scribner's.* The Brandywine River Museum in Chadds Ford, Pennsylvania, and the Pratt Institute, Brooklyn, each own three illustrations. Other institutions own single items. His papers likewise are scattered; the Dreiser Collection at the Van Pelt Library, University of Pennsylvania, Philadelphia, contains a file titled "Booth/Dreiser Correspondence," and the Indiana Historical Society Library in Indianapolis holds some of Booth's letters.

Howard Chandler Christy

(10 January 1873 – 3 March 1952)

Katherine Kominis
Boston University

BOOKS: *Pastel Portraits from the Romantic Drama* (New York: Scribners, 1899; London: Kegan Paul, Trench & Trübner, 1900);

Men of the Army and Navy: Characteristic Types of Our Fighting Men (New York: Scribners, 1899);

Types of the American Girl (New York: Scribners, 1900);

Music and Life: A Series of Drawings (New York: Scribners, 1904);

Drawings by Howard Chandler Christy (New York: Moffat, Yard, 1905);

The Christy Girl (Indianapolis: Bobbs-Merrill, 1906);

The American Girl as Seen and Portrayed by Howard Chandler Christy (New York: Moffat, Yard, 1906);

Our Girls: Poems in Praise of the American Girl, edited by Christy (New York: Moffat, Yard, 1907);

The Christy Book of Drawings (New York: Moffat, Yard, 1908);

Songs of Sentiment: A Christy Gift Book (New York: Moffat, Yard, 1910);

Liberty Belles: Eight Epochs in the Making of the American Girl (Indianapolis: Bobbs-Merrill, 1912).

SELECTED BOOKS ILLUSTRATED: Woodyear, Rose B., *In Camphor* (New York: Putnam, 1895);

Shakespeare, William, *The Tragedy of Hamlet, Prince of Denmark* (New York: Dodd, Mead, 1897);

Davis, Richard Harding, *The Lion and the Unicorn* (New York: Scribners, 1899);

Page, Thomas Nelson, *The Old Gentleman of the Black Stock* (New York: Scribners, 1900);

Wright, Marcus J., *Official History of the Spanish-American War* (Washington, D.C., 1900);

Churchill, Winston, *The Crisis* (New York: Macmillan, 1901);

Hawkins, Anthony Hope, *The Dolly Dialogues* (New York: Holt, 1901);

Riley, James Whitcomb, *An Old Sweetheart of Mine* (Indianapolis: Bobbs-Merrill, 1902);

Howard Chandler Christy

Longfellow, Henry Wadsworth, *The Courtship of Miles Standish* (Indianapolis: Bobbs-Merrill, 1903);

Riley, James Whitcomb, *Out to Old Aunt Mary's* (Indianapolis: Bobbs-Merrill, 1904);

Longfellow, Henry Wadsworth, *Evangeline* (Indianapolis: Bobbs-Merrill, 1905);

Riley, James Whitcomb, *Home Again With Me* (Indianapolis: Bobbs-Merrill, 1908);

Riley, *Riley Roses* (Indianapolis: Bobbs-Merrill, 1909);

Pulitzer, Ralph, *New York Society on Parade* (New York: Harper, 1910);

Riley, James Whitcomb, *The Girl I Loved* (Indianapolis: Bobbs-Merrill, 1910);

Scott, Sir Walter, *The Lady of the Lake* (Indianapolis: Bobbs-Merrill, 1910);

Riley, James Whitcomb, *When She Was About Sixteen* (Indianapolis: Bobbs-Merrill, 1911);

Tennyson, Alfred, *The Princess* (Indianapolis: Bobbs-Merrill, 1911);

Riley, James Whitcomb, *Good-Bye Jim* (Indianapolis: Bobbs-Merrill, 1913);

Riley, *Complete Works, Including Poems and Prose Sketches,* 10 volumes (Indianapolis: Bobbs-Merrill, 1916).

PERIODICALS: *Leslie's Weekly,* 1895–1898;
Century, 1895–1905;
Life, 1895–1905;
Harper's Monthly, 1898–1912;
Scribner's Magazine, 1898–1920;
Collier's, 1903–1920.

As an illustrator whose work appeared in countless magazines, dozens of books, and on scores of posters, Howard Chandler Christy set his mark on the popular culture of his time. Christy's subjects ranged from romantic interludes in high-society New York to historic battles on the Scottish Highlands, but he was best known for his creation of "the Christy Girl" whose lovely face and form graced magazine covers and stories, sold Christy-style hats and dresses, and convinced young men to join the navy and marines in both world wars. He did most of his book illustrations from 1895 to 1920, worked on posters during the two world wars, and turned almost completely to painting portraits after 1921.

Born on 10 January 1873, Howard Chandler Christy had the kind of childhood that can be thought of with nostalgia as typically American and old-fashioned. Growing up on his parents' farm in Duncan Falls, near Zanesville, Ohio, Christy showed little interest in schoolwork but enjoyed adventures such as hitching rides to school on side- and stern-wheeled riverboats on the Muskingum River, bordering his farm home. Christy's parents had noted his artistic talent by the time he was three and had done all they could to encourage his interest. Francis Christy, his father, took four-year-old Howard to see Zanesville artist Charley Craig. The visit was an inspiration to the young Christy, who immediately insisted that his father buy him a set of watercolors.

At the age of ten Christy had his first commission: he used ordinary house paint on wood from a barn door to create a sign for a butcher shop. Three years later Christy sent to the *Toledo Blade* a drawing of the historic schoolhouse where James Garfield taught. It was published, and the editor offered Christy a job instead of paying for the sketch, not knowing that his potential employee was so young.

Leaving formal schooling at the age of twelve, Christy chose to help his parents on the farm and to use any spare moments to practice drawing and sketching on his own. Determined to go to New York to study art, he did craft work to earn money. His first trip to New York for art studies ended after only a few months due to lack of funds. Christy was determined to return as soon as he could, however. In 1892, only three years later, he was back in New York with more savings and a small loan he reluctantly accepted from a well-to-do cousin. To make sure that his cousin would receive her money in any eventuality, Christy took out a life insurance policy. On this trip Christy carried with him a letter of introduction from Sen. John Sherman, brother of Gen. William T. Sherman, who described Christy as a "young gentleman . . . sober and industrious, the son of a soldier, and worthy of the kind assistance of anyone with whom he comes in contact." This time Christy was able to enroll at the Art Students League and the National Academy of Design to study with some of the best art teachers in the United States.

At the Academy, Christy studied drawing and quickly earned a promotion into an advanced class. At the Art Students League, Christy caught the attention of the well-known instructor and artist, William Merritt Chase, who soon took him on as a private student.

Christy's cousin had lent him enough money for a careful lifestyle in New York, but the loan included the special treat of season tickets to the Metropolitan Opera House. The young artist from Ohio was introduced to the glories of Richard Wagner in the glamour and style of a leading metropolis. The scenes impressed him enough to fill a sketchbook with drawings of the various Wagnerian operas. Learning, under Chase's instruction, to execute sketches with strong lines and to catch the essence of a pose, a gesture, or the drape of a garment, Christy drew fifty-five pages of single figures or parts of operatic scenes, costumes, and staging. Working in charcoal pencil, he sketched loosely drawn, quick impressions of figures as well as more thoroughly lined images of *Frederick Wounded* or *Tristan and Isolde*. Titled *Notes from the Wagner Operas beginning with "Lohengrin," January 9, 1895, Met Opera House,* the sketchbook shows Christy's technical skill close to full maturation. This item is now part of the Harvard Theatre Collection, Houghton Library, Harvard University.

The life of an art student in New York at the turn of the century involved much hard work, and

Illustration by Christy for James Whitcomb Riley's Out to Old
Aunt Mary's *(1904)*

Christy spent two-and-one-half years of intense study at Chase's famous West Tenth Street studio, where he learned to create still lifes from the rich collection of Asian art, antiques, and contemporary European and American works of art that Chase had arranged there. In two summers spent at Chase's school in Shinnecock, Long Island, Christy learned the fundamentals of his art in a rigorous schedule of work, criticism, and revision. As the prototype of open-air art schools in the United States, Chase's summer classes in sketching and painting out-of-doors developed his students' observation and originality in treating natural scenes. The schedule of a day of criticism by Chase of students' work, followed by a day of sketching excursions with Chase to repeat his critique, gave Christy and his one hundred fellow students thorough preparation.

During his third year with Chase, in 1895, Christy heard the newsboys' shouts outside the studio: "Extra! Extra! Wall Street Crash!" Among many other companies, S. V. Whatie and Company, belonging to Christy's cousin's husband, had fallen. Christy immediately moved to an unfurnished apartment on Fourth Street to save money. He had recently sold a painting of the Catskill Mountains for twenty-five dollars, from which he paid rent for the first month.

Faced with the need to earn a living, Christy realized that fine art would not support him. He had admired contemporary magazine illustrators such as Howard Pyle and Edwin Austin Abbey, who were creating a new style of American illustration. New mechanical inventions were reproducing freestyle pen-and-ink drawing without the previous restrictions of transferring the drawing to either metal or wood. Also, new advances in reproduction were making color increasingly viable in mass-media periodicals. Christy decided that illustration provided him the best chance of earning a living. In making this decision Christy, for the first and only time in his career, was joining the forefront of an artistic vanguard.

When Christy announced that he was leaving his formal studies for commercial art, Chase's disappointment caused a rupture between the two that lasted for more than three years. Christy's new venture was financially constrained. He could not even pay the models who posed for him, though he found some who had faith that his drawings would sell. He began to work on a freelance basis, often drawing "he-she" vignettes captioned with a joke. His work began to appear in *Life,* and eventually Christy won his first full manuscript to illustrate—Rose B. Woodyear's novel, *In Camphor* (1895).

Dodd, Mead, and Company gave Christy a commission of $400 to illustrate an edition of William Shakespeare's *Hamlet,* which was published in 1897. Christy had to spend most of the fee on models' charges and costumes. This was the first of many historical works to come, and for it he used his customary media of pencil, pen and ink, and ink wash with Chinese white to portray the brooding prince.

By 1898 newspaper, magazine, and book publishers were regularly commissioning Christy's work, and he had moved to a larger studio on West Twenty-fourth Street. He married one of his models, Maybelle Thompson, with whom he had one daughter, Natalie. It was a crucial year for more than personal reasons. When news reached New York that the U.S. battleship *Maine* had been blown up in Havana harbor, Christy, determined to get into the war, accepted several magazine commissions to sketch and write about the conflict.

Traveling south, Christy camped with the army at Chattanooga and continued on to Tampa and finally to Cuba. Theodore Roosevelt's Rough Riders happened to be Christy's companions on the journey, and Christy and Roosevelt became friends. The artist made many sketches of Roosevelt and his troops, often giving the drawings to the soldiers to send to their families. From quickly made sketches on bivouac and at tentside, Christy created the raw material for the lavishly produced

Men of the Army and Navy: Characteristic Types of Our Fighting Men (1899). Six folio-size pastel drawings of officers of the artillery, navy, infantry, and cavalry, as well as a "Jack Tar" and a "Rough Rider" (modeled after Roosevelt himself), provided the American reading public with visual images of handsome young fighting men ready to do battle with the enemies of their nation. The sketches of soldiers and sailors in full-figure poses, with accurately depicted uniforms, outfitted with headgear, swords, and riding boots, were drawn with Christy's flair for style and gesture. But Christy had the opportunity to draw and paint realistic scenes of the war as well. Reproductions of his sketches at the battle of Santiago and other war scenes were published in Marcus J. Wright's *Official History of the Spanish-American War* (1900).

The reading public had followed Christy's work with approval. Returning to New York, he found himself a celebrated artist, with more commissions for magazine and book illustrations than he could manage. Drawings of servicemen made him famous, and that is what his editors demanded. Typed as a "war illustrator," Christy was given soldier stories until he broke the stereotype by drawing a soldier's sweetheart. It was from this drawing that the "Christy Girl" was born.

Christy's image of the ideal American woman, or "girl," was also the image the public wanted. With lovely features, glowing eyes, and varying expressions denoting a mixture of charm and social grace, innocence and gaiety, the beautiful women Christy drew soon became a composite type. Readers found the Christy Girl such a recognizable image that they often believed her to be a real woman. Men sent her proposals of marriage, and women imitated her style, buying dresses and accessories à la Christy.

In books, in magazines, and later in posters, Christy traced the evolution of the "shy Victorian girl" to the more self-assured modern woman, equally adept at sports, high society, or her studies (the college graduate was an entirely new type of woman for society to assimilate). Although the Christy Girl type did not appreciably change in countless images, her background and social role became more active in depiction. Constantly seen in popular magazines such as *Harper's Monthly* and *Scribner's Magazine,* she was also in demand in gift books and albums, as in *Drawings by Howard Chandler Christy* (1905), *The Christy Girl* (1906), *The American Girl* as Seen and Portrayed by Howard Chandler Christy (1906), *Our Girls: Poems in Praise of the Ameri-*

A 1910 illustration by Christy for Sir Walter Scott's The Lady of the Lake *(courtesy of Special Collections, Mugar Memorial Library, Boston University)*

can Girl (1907), and *Liberty Belles: Eight Epochs in the Making of the American Girl* (1912).

Accepting commissions to illustrate novels and poetry, Christy created frontispieces and fully illustrated editions of works by Henry Wadsworth Longfellow, James Whitcomb Riley, Sir Walter Scott, and Alfred Tennyson, among others. His most enduring partnership was with Riley's literary creations; Christy illustrated seven of his books as well as the Memorial Edition of the *Complete Works* in ten volumes (1916). Riley's stories and characters were perfectly suited to Christy's ability to draw a character or subject with unaffected simplicity. For *Out to Old Aunt Mary's* (1904) Christy drew scenes of the countryside and its denizens perfectly matching Riley's description of a rural childhood.

Although better known for drawing romantic images of women or quiet country scenes, Christy could also produce dramatic vignettes when the literary text demanded them. *The Courtship of Miles Standish* (1903), by Longfellow, gave full scope to Christy's imagination. His rendering of John Alden embracing Priscilla, and of Standish's sudden ap-

Four of Christy's World War I posters, which frequently depicted incarnations of the "Christy Girl" (Library of Congress)

pearance at their wedding, expresses the dramatic plot and the emotions of the characters.

In illustrating Scott's *The Lady of the Lake* (1910) Christy used various methods to depict battles or to portray youth and beauty. Marginal illustrations of tartan-clad Scots are drawn in Conté crayon. For the full-page color plates, among the most lovely Christy produced, he used opaque watercolor and pencil. At their best Christy's historical illustrations carry much of N. C. Wyeth's power to stir the reader's imagination, although they are usually more subtle in style.

After his first marriage ended in separation, Christy returned to his family home in Zanesville, Ohio, bringing with him his daughter, Natalie. He built a new home on his family's land, transforming the second floor of the barn into a studio. The patriotic artist added a cannon to his establishment and played reveille each morning, raising the American flag over his newly christened "Barracks," as he called his home. He established a strict regimen of work from 9:00 to 4:00 each day, working on commissions for book and magazine illustrations that arrived by mail from New York. Women models traveled from New York to pose, and Christy usually relied on local men and boys for his sketches and paintings. Always prolific, Christy was even more productive during this period. He created some of his best work at this time and restored himself to good health and spirits in the process.

On one of Christy's trips to New York, Charles Dana Gibson introduced him to sixteen-year-old Nancy Palmer as a prospective model. Christy agreed to hire her, and she spent three years in Ohio, becoming his chief model. In 1919, upon Christy's divorce from his first wife, he and Palmer were married.

In 1915 Christy up took residence at the Hotel des Artistes on Sixty-seventh Street in New York. He sensed the imminent involvement of the United States in World War I and wanted to assist in the war effort. His portraits of Nancy Palmer for U.S. Navy recruiting posters remain some of the most enduring popular images of World War I. As well as illustrating some forty posters, including the famous *Gee, I Wish I Were a Man* (1917) and *I Want You for the Navy* (1917), Christy donated paintings at public auctions for U.S. Liberty Bonds, victory loans, hospitals, and other groups. In 1921 he became the first civilian to be made an honorary member of the U.S. Naval Academy.

The new decade of the Roaring Twenties marked Christy's return to portraiture as his major artistic activity. Enjoying an elite social life with many of his famous clients, Christy painted por-

Woman and Man, *an illustration by Christy for the June 1925 issue of* Cosmopolitan

traits of President Warren Harding, President and Mrs. Calvin Coolidge, Gen. John J. Pershing, Lillian Russell, and Amelia Earhart, as well as of European leaders and nobility.

Christy now made New York his permanent home, painting in spacious elegance at the Hotel des Artistes, with Nancy Christy giving active encouragement to his work. The Café des Artistes, on the ground floor of the hotel, dedicated a room to Christy, who decorated it with a series of murals. Always fond of social life and his celebrity status, Christy enjoyed these to the fullest in New York, socializing at the Players, Aldine, and Lambs Clubs.

Christy became part of another American tradition when he was asked to be the judge at the first Miss America beauty pageant in Atlantic City. The following year well-known artists such as Norman Rockwell, James Montgomery Flagg, Coles Phillips, and Charles Chambers were asked to be judges as well, but they did not command the attention that Christy did.

Christy's patriotism and love of history inspired him to take up allegorical and historical subjects in murals and paintings. His first depiction of the signing of the Constitution, *We the People,* toured the United States on the Freedom Train. In 1939 Christy took up the subject again, beginning a twenty-foot-by-thirty-foot painting titled *The Signing of the Constitution.* Christy sought models with exact facial resemblances for each of the thirty-nine signers he portrayed. He failed to find reasonable likenesses for only two of his subjects, whom he deliberately left rather sketchy. The only building in Washington large enough for his work was the Navy Sail Loft, and Christy worked there, creating accurate representations of face, physique, clothing, and accessories. Placement of the seventeen-hundred-pound painting for the 29 May 1940 unveiling required twenty men to carry it to the U.S. Capitol. It can be seen there today in its present site above the east Grand Stairway in the Capitol.

During World War II Christy renewed his active work in poster illustration, as in the *Victory Food Specials* and *Fly for Her Liberty–Army Air Force* (1942). These posters conveyed a more serious message than the whimsy of the World War I recruitment posters. Christy painted several more historical murals as well during the 1940s and continued his portraiture. A portrait of Gen. Douglas MacArthur was left unfinished at Christy's death in 1952.

Although Christy received various honors and awards, exhibitions of his portraits and illustration art, and commissions for sculptures and murals, his art was rarely acquired by major art museums. In 1947 the Society of Illustrators made him an honorary member. Christy remained enthusiastic and ac-

tive in his art until his death on 3 March 1952 from ill health resulting from an earlier heart attack. His art was exhibited at the Art Institute of Zanesville in the same year, at the Zanesville Art Center in 1975, and at the Allentown Art Museum in Pennsylvania in 1977. Christy's *New York Times* obituary termed him "an artist of timeless energy, a veritable journalist of the easel and brush" and acknowledged his artistic status to be equivalent to his contemporaries Charles Dana Gibson, James Montgomery Flagg, and Harrison Fisher.

References:

Allentown Art Museum, *Howard Chandler Christy, Artist Illustrator of Style: September 25 through November 6, 1977* (Allentown, Pa.: The Museum, 1977);

Arthur W. Brown, "A Tribute to a Great American on his 80th Birthday," *American Artist,* 16 (January 1952): 50–51, 68;

Susan E. Meyer, *America's Great Illustrators* (New York: Harry N. Abrams, 1978), pp. 232–255;

Walt Reed, *Great American Illustrators* (New York: Crown, 1979), pp. 16–17;

Norris Schneider, *Howard Chandler Christy* (Zanesville, Ohio: Privately printed, 1975);

S. J. Woolf, "Creator of the Christy Girl," *New York Times Magazine,* 18 January 1948, 24–25.

Archives:

Christy materials are included in the Harvard Theatre Collection, Houghton Library, Harvard University.

Joseph Clement Coll

(2 July 1881 – 19 October 1921)

Richard Bleiler
University of Connecticut

SELECTED BOOKS ILLUSTRATED: Dickens,
Charles, *Boys & Girls of Dickens: Twenty of the
Most Famous Children from the Works of Charles
Dickens* (New York: Macaulay, 1910);

Norton, Roy, *The Garden of Fate* (New York: W. J.
Watt, 1910);

Mundy, Talbot, *King—of the Khyber Rifles* (Indianapolis: Bobbs-Merrill, 1916);

Mundy, *The Winds of the World* (Indianapolis:
Bobbs-Merrill, 1917);

Rousseau, Victor, *The Messiah of the Cylinder* (Chicago: McClurg, 1917);

Mundy, Talbot, *Hira Singh: When India Came to Fight
in Flanders* (Indianapolis: Bobbs-Merrill, 1918);

Merritt, Abraham, *The Moon Pool* (New York: Putnam, 1919);

Mundy, Talbot, *The Ivory Trail* (Indianapolis:
Bobbs-Merrill, 1919);

Mundy, *Guns of the Gods* (Indianapolis: Bobbs-
Merrill, 1921).

PERIODICALS: *New York American,* 1898–1900;
Chicago American, 1900–1901;
Philadelphia North American, 1901–1905;
Associated Sunday Magazine, 1903–1913;
Hampton's Magazine, 1910;
Collier's, 1913–1921;
Everybody's Magazine, 1916–1917;
Pictorial Review, 1919–1920;
Redbook Magazine, 1919–1921;
Cosmopolitan, 1920–1921.

Joseph Clement Coll

Joseph Clement Coll was perhaps the finest
commercial artist of the first quarter of the twentieth
century, a pen-and-ink virtuoso whose sophisticated
artwork enthralled readers of the magazines publishing the serializations of best-selling authors such
as Sir Arthur Conan Doyle, Talbot Mundy, Sax
Rohmer, and Edgar Wallace. Coll only occasionally
moved beyond illustrating for magazines, and he
died young without ever having achieved his full potential as a creative artist, but he was nevertheless
remarkably prolific and popular during his lifetime,
and later artists of lesser ability were directly influenced by his style. Coll firmly broke with the traditional nineteenth-century photorealistic, tableau-
style illustrations used by such contemporary artists
as J. Allen St. John; his illustrations blend the ornamented lines and sinuosities associated with the Art
Nouveau movement of the late nineteenth century
with the simplification of form in the Expressionist
movement of the early twentieth century. In Coll's
treatment of his material, however, the sixteenth-

century Italian Mannerists appear to have served as models: his illustrations use such Manneristic devices as crowds, overpowering emotions, strained postures, and chiaroscuro to separate and interrelate his subgroups.

Joseph Clement Coll was born on 2 July 1881 in Philadelphia, the youngest child of a large, lower-middle-class family. His parents were Irish immigrants, and perhaps because his father worked as a bookbinder and his older brothers became printers, Coll developed a love for literature and artwork and was particularly interested in Henry Irving's lectures on drama and the novels of Charles Dickens. He nevertheless graduated from Boys Central High School of Philadelphia having received only minimal formal training in the arts, but his obvious talent got him employed, at the age of seventeen, as an apprentice artist on the *New York American,* a daily newspaper. His artistic style at this time was consciously modeled after (and thus derivative of) the artistic styles of Howard Pyle, Edwin Austin Abbey, Adolph Menzel, and Daniel Vierge, but although Coll's drawings were less polished than those of his mentors, they were also bolder, more forceful, more imaginative, and more extravagant. Coll's drawings were also able to convey a sense of the ineffable and the weird.

Coll began his professional career as a newspaper artist, providing artwork to newspapers in the days before they were technically capable of reproducing halftone photographs. He was thus expected to be able to reproduce a scene or a photograph rapidly, accurately, and as dramatically as possible, and he was expected to be versatile and able to draw (from imagination if necessary) everything from trials to weddings. In all these areas the young Coll excelled, and he was sent to Chicago to serve as a staff artist on the *Chicago American.* He returned to Philadelphia in 1901, invited back to serve as an artist for the newly started *Philadelphia North American,* a newspaper published on Sundays. The majority of his illustrations from this time are typical newspaper artwork, but J. Thomson Willing, the art editor of the Sunday *Philadelphia North American,* recognized Coll's abilities, and the two became lifelong friends. Willing occasionally gave Coll special assignments, one of which, "When Knighthood Was in Flower," was published serially in 1902 and attracted favorable attention.

In a style somewhat reminiscent of the work of Pyle, Coll's pen-and-ink drawings for "When Knighthood Was in Flower" present a romanticized rendition of the events of the later European Middle Ages. The illustrations range from depictions of the crowning of Mary of France to life aboard an En-

glish privateer to a back-alley quarrel between bravos. Where Coll's artwork differs from Pyle's is in its precision and in Coll's sensitive renderings of facial features, for, despite an occasional stiffness in their postures, Coll's figures are drawn with conviction, and evidences of individuality can be found in virtually every figure. The same is true of Coll's settings, which are finely detailed, with careful attention paid to perspectives. Coll's contemporaries also noticed the excellence of his drawings, and in a friendly reminiscence about Coll that appeared in the *Century* of May 1922, his former editor Willing wrote that Coll's illustrations for "When Knighthood Was in Flower" were "done in such forceful lines that bad printing of them was impossible. His technic [*sic*] was suited to its utilization. His design was novel and diversified. He had invention."

Coll left newspaper work in 1905 and went to work as an illustrator for magazines, providing artwork for stories and novels published in the *Associated Sunday Magazine, Collier's,* the *Pictorial Review, Redbook Magazine,* and *Everybody's Magazine.*

Coll, when composing for magazines, used pencil to draw his figures on tracing paper, which enabled him to shift and rearrange the figures until the composition was satisfactory. He would then use pen and ink to redraw the original onto bristol or illustration board, often providing the illustration in a size larger than the final reproduction was to be; this artistic practice, still quite common, enables the published drawings to contain great tonality, depth, and detail. For much of his life, however, Coll did not have models for his art and was forced to draw from his imagination and from his memories of artifacts seen in museums. Furthermore, he was obligated to provide a large drawing and several small drawings for each story during each episode of its serialization. Coll was thus under enormous and constant pressure to produce salable illustrations, but what is remarkable is that his stresses remain invisible to the casual viewer of his art: neither the lack of models nor the pressures necessary to produce this artwork are discernible.

Among Coll's first magazine illustrations was artwork for Sir Arthur Conan Doyle's *Sir Nigel,* which appeared in the *Associated Sunday Magazine* in 1905. Though again in a style slightly reminiscent of Pyle, Coll's illustrations successfully reproduce the pageantry, romance, and dramatic action of Doyle's novel and left no doubt that he was a major illustrator. He would later illustrate the American serialization of Doyle's *The Lost World* (1912), and his illustrations of the characters' deeds of derring-do and their adventures among ape-men and dinosaurs capture perfectly the zest and vitality of Doyle. Coll's

Illustration for the American serialization of Sir Arthur Conan Doyle's The Lost
World *(1912)*

renditions of the toothy, bat-winged, thoroughly menacing pterodactyls found by the explorers on Professor Challenger's expedition are superb even if they are not paleontologically correct.

From 1910 until his untimely death, Coll's artwork frequently appeared as accompaniment to some of the best-selling fiction of the time. The adventures of Sax Rohmer—his stories of the fiendish oriental criminal mastermind Fu-Manchu as well as his exotic, action-oriented tales—were enormously popular with audiences of their day. The stories of Rohmer that Coll illustrated regularly appeared in *Collier's* from 1913 to 1921. Coll's style was by this time completely his own, and his artwork is entirely successful in depicting the fast-paced mystery, violence, and material horrors consistently found in Rohmer's fiction. His illustrations of the fiendish Dr. Fu-Manchu are among the finest of their kind,

conveying the menace and exoticism of Rohmer's criminal mastermind without descending to the use of cultural stereotyping or the employment of racist imagery.

Also enormously popular with contemporary readers were the adventure stories of Talbot Mundy. Unlike Rohmer, whose exotic stories generally had mundane settings, Mundy's adventure fiction generally had exotic settings, for Mundy had traveled widely and was intimately familiar with many areas of India and Africa. Coll provided more than one hundred illustrations for the serialization of Mundy's *King-of the Khyber Rifles* (*Everybody's Magazine,* May 1916–January 1917), as well as providing original illustrations for the book publications of Mundy's *The Winds of the World* (1917), *Hira Singh: When India Came to Fight in Flanders* (1918), *The Ivory Trail* (1919), and *Guns of the Gods* (1921). These

"*Speak!*" *he hissed.* "*You lift up my heart from a dark pit!*" "*I can restore your white peacock,*" *I said*

Coll's rendering of Dr. Fu Manchu for Sax Rohmer's "The White Peacock" (Collier's, 6 March 1915)

illustrations, deservedly considered to be Coll's finest work, depict subjects ranging from studies of skulduggery in the Himalayas to events in an Indian marketplace to well-realized Indian interiors. One of the most elaborate and fascinating of these drawings is set in a castle and portrays an Englishman, face partially shadowed, half-reclining on what appear to be tapestries, intently observing the movements of a beautiful female dancer who is flanked by two menacingly erect hooded cobras. The scene effectively combines action and opulence with a deadly and exotic eroticism.

Well rendered though Coll's action-oriented illustrations were, he was also capable of providing artwork of whimsicality and introspection that was focused on characters rather than events. In 1910 the Macaulay Company commissioned him to provide original illustrations to the works of Dickens. Coll readily complied, and the drawings were published as *Boys & Girls of Dickens: Twenty of the Most Famous Children from the Works of Charles Dickens* (1910). They include renditions of David Copperfield and the Friendly Waiter, Oliver Twist and Fagin, Morleena Kenwigs at the Hairdresser's, Bill Sikes, Uriah Heep and Agnes Wickfield, and Dick Swiveler and the Marchioness, all drawn with care, whimsy, and with little touches that raise them far above the level of mere commercial artwork. Coll remained interested in illustrating the works of Dickens and in 1912 provided the *Associated Sunday Magazine* with a double-page spread containing a mélange of his interpretations of additional Dickens characters. In a similar vein he provided illustrations for the *Hampton's Magazine* publication of an English translation of Edmond Rostand's *Chantecler* (June–September 1910).

By 1920 Coll's artwork could be found illustrating the magazine appearances of writers as diverse and popular as Edgar Wallace, Gouverneur Morris, and Melville Davisson Post. In addition, his illustrations enlivened such early science fiction novels as Victor Rousseau's *The Messiah of the Cylinder* (*Everybody's Magazine,* June–September 1917) and the book publication of A. Merritt's *The Moon Pool* (1919). Coll's illustrations for Rousseau's novel are among his most weird and nightmarish. His backgrounds consist of blasted ruins and exotic structures while in the pictures' foregrounds, perspectives are warped and skewed as oddly contorted characters (often barely recognizable as human) sprawl, writhe, collide with one another, and at times appear ready to climb from the frame of the drawings and do battle with the reader.

During the last years of his life Coll continued to draw as prolifically as ever, but fewer of his illustrations appear with story serializations. Coll had discovered a new market for his illustrations, and he began providing commercial art for the advertisements that appeared in the magazines he regularly illustrated. This art is also of uniformly high quality, for Coll was by then capable of providing everything from simple sketches to exquisitely detailed and shaded drawings reminiscent of photographs. Telling details and perspectives are rendered clearly and concisely, and characterizations are conveyed not only through realistic facial features but also through details in postures and clothing. Willing, in his 1922 reminiscence about Coll, states that "his quality was recognized by advertisers, and he was diverted from featuring fiction and poetry in the body of the magazine to bringing poetry to the advertising pages."

It was at this commercial high point that Coll developed appendicitis and died suddenly in the Presbyterian Hospital in Philadelphia on 19 October 1921, a few months after his fortieth birthday; his wife and a daughter survived him. At the present, some of Coll's artwork is privately held, but most of it is completely inaccessible, buried in newspapers and periodicals that survive only on microfilm when they survive at all. Nevertheless, despite the rarity of his original artwork, Coll's reputation as an illustrator has remained consistently high. His style can be seen as a direct influence on such later magazine artists as J. R. Flanagan, Vincent Napoli, and Charles Schneeman, and several books providing biographical data and reproducing some of his more accessible artwork (including his many illustrations for the serialization of *King–of the Khyber Rifles*) are readily found in most major libraries. Coll will be remembered as the finest pen-and-ink illustrator of the early twentieth century.

References:

Bertha E. Miller, Louise Payson Latimer, and Beulah Folmsbee, *Illustrators of Children's Books, 1744-1945* (Boston: Horn Book, 1947);

Henry C. Pitz, "Joseph Clement Coll: A Master of the Pen," *American Artist,* 14 (December 1950): 38–42, 61–62;

Walt Reed, "Joseph Clement Coll," *The Illustrator in America, 1880–1980* (New York: Madison Press for the Society of Illustrators, 1984), pp. 56–57;

Reed, comp., *The Magic Pen of Joseph Clement Coll* (Westport, Conn.: North Light, 1978);

J. Thomson Willing, "Joseph Clement Coll: Pen Illustrator," *Century,* 104 (May 1922): 117–122.

Felix Octavius Carr Darley

(23 June 1822 – 27 March 1888)

Georgia B. Barnhill
American Antiquarian Society

BOOKS: *Scenes in Indian Life: A Series of Original Designs Etched on Stone* (Philadelphia: Colon, 1843);

Illustrations of Rip Van Winkle (New York: American Art Union, 1848);

Illustrations of The Legend of Sleepy Hollow (New York: American Art Union, 1849);

Compositions in Outline by Felix O. C. Darley from Judd's Margaret (New York: Redfield, 1856);

Darley's Cooper Vignettes (New York: Townsend, 1861);

Sketches Abroad with Pen and Pencil (New York: Hurd & Houghton, 1868; London: Low & Marston, 1868);

Compositions in Outline from Hawthorne's Scarlet Letter (Boston: Houghton, Osgood, 1879);

The Darley Gallery of Shakespearean Illustrations (New York & Philadelphia: Stoddard, 1884);

Character Sketches from the Works of Charles Dickens (Philadelphia: Porter & Coates, 1888).

SELECTED BOOKS ILLUSTRATED: Neal, Joseph C., *In Town & About, or Pencillings & Pennings* (Philadelphia: Gody & McMichael, 1843);

Neal, *Peter Ploddy, and Other Oddities* (Philadelphia: Carey & Hart, 1844);

Thompson, William Tappan, *Major Jones's Courtship,* second edition (Philadelphia: Carey & Hart, 1844);

Thompson, *Chronicles of Pineville: Embracing Sketches of Georgia Scenes, Incidents, and Characters* (Philadelphia: Carey & Hart, 1845);

Hooper, Johnson Jones, *Some Adventures of Captain Simon Suggs, Late of the Tallapoosa Volunteers* (Philadelphia: Carey & Hart, 1845);

Porter, William T., *The Big Bear of Arkansas and Other Tales* (Philadelphia: Carey & Hart, 1845);

Bache, Anna, *Clara's Amusements* (Philadelphia: George S. Appleton; New York: D. Appleton, 1846);

Corcoran, Denis, *Pickings from the Portfolio of the Re-*

Felix Octavius Carr Darley

porter of the New Orleans "Picayune" (Philadelphia: Carey & Hart, 1846);

Hentz, Caroline Lee, *Aunt Patty's Scrap Bag* (Philadelphia: Carey & Hart, 1846);

Johnson, Richard, *The Blossoms of Morality* (Philadelphia: George S. Appleton; New York: D. Appleton, 1846);

Porter, William Trotter, ed., *A Quarter Race in Kentucky, and Other Sketches* (Philadelphia: Carey & Hart, 1846);

Smith, Solomon Franklin, *Ghost Stories; Collected with a Particular View to Counteract the Vulgar Belief in Ghosts and Apparitions* (Philadelphia:

Carey & Hart, 1846);

Smith, *The Theatrical Apprenticeship and Anecdotal Recollections of Sol Smith* (Philadelphia: Carey & Hart, 1846);

Thorpe, Thomas Bangs, *The Mysteries of the Backwoods; or, Sketches of the Southwest* (Philadelphia: Carey & Hart, 1846);

Lovechild, Lawrence, *The Pictorial Primer* (Philadelphia: Zieber, circa 1846–1849);

Lovechild, *Robin Hood* (Philadelphia: Zieber, circa 1846–1849);

Lovechild, *Tom Thumb* (Philadelphia: Zieber, circa 1846–1849);

Field, Joseph M., *The Drama in Pokerville; The Bench and Bar of Jurytown, and Other Stories* (Philadelphia: Carey & Hart, 1847);

Robb, John S., *Streaks of Squatter Life* (Philadelphia: Carey & Hart, 1847);

Lovechild, Lawrence, *Henry Brown* (Philadelphia: Zieber, 1847);

Lovechild, *Fred Fearnought* (Philadelphia: Zieber, 1847);

Lovechild, *Valentine and Orson* (Philadelphia: Zieber, 1847);

Lovechild, *Blue Beard* (Philadelphia: Zieber, circa 1847–1849);

Lovechild, *Cinderella* (Philadelphia: Zieber, circa 1847–1849);

Lovechild, *The Children in the Wood* (Philadelphia: Zieber, circa 1847–1849);

Lovechild, *Guy of Warwick* (Philadelphia: Zieber, circa 1847–1849);

Lovechild, *Jack the Giant Killer* (Philadelphia: Zieber, circa 1847–1849);

Durivage, Francis A., *Stray Subjects, Arrested and Bound Over* (Philadelphia: Carey & Hart, 1848);

Burton, William Evans, *Waggeries and Vagaries* (Philadelphia: Carey & Hart, 1848);

Irving, Washington, *The Sketch Book of Geoffrey Crayon, Gentn.,* revised edition (New York: Putnam, 1848);

Sigourney, Lydia Howard (Huntley), *Illustrated Poems* (Philadelphia: Carey & Hart, 1849);

Headley, Joel T., *Sacred Scenes and Characters* (New York: Baker & Scribner, 1850);

Irving, Washington *A History of New York from the Beginning of the World to the End of the Dutch Dynasty* (New York: Putnam, 1850);

Irving, *Tales of a Traveller* (New York: Putnam, 1850);

Lewis, Henry Clay, *Odd Leaves from the Note Book of a Louisiana "Swamp Doctor"* (Philadelphia: Hart, 1850);

Mitchell, Donald Grant, *The Lorgnette; Or, Studies of the Town* (New York: Stringer & Townsend, 1850);

Sterne, Laurence, *The Works of Laurence Sterne* (Philadelphia: Lippincott, Grambo, 1850);

Irving, Washington, *The Alhambra* (New York: Putnam, 1851);

Mitchell, Donald Grant, *Reveries of a Bachelor; Or A Book of the Heart* (New York: Scribner, 1852);

Wiley, Calvin H., *Life in the South* (Philadelphia: Peterson, 1852);

Morris, George Pope, *The Deserted Bride, and Other Productions* (New York: Scribner, 1853);

Wharton, George M., *The New Orleans Sketch Book* (Philadelphia: Hart, 1853);

Simms, William Gilmore, *The Works of William Gilmore Simms,* 18 volumes (New York: Redfield, 1853–1859);

Lewis, Henry Clay, *Odd Leaves from the Life of a Louisiana "Swamp Doctor"* (Philadelphia: Peterson, 1854–1857);

Shillaber, Benjamin P., *Mrs. Partington's Carpet-Bag of Fun,* illustrated by Darley and others (New York: Dick & Fitzgerald, 1854);

Mathews, Cornelius, *Chanticleer: A Thanksgiving Story of the Peabody Family* (New York: Brown, Loomis, 1856);

Brackenridge, Hugh Henry, *Adventures of Captain Farrago* (Philadelphia: Peterson, 1856);

Brackenridge, *Adventures of Major O'Regan* (Philadelphia: Peterson, 1856);

Herbert, Henry William, as Frank Forester, *The Deerstalkers* (Philadelphia: Peterson, 1856);

Herbert, as Frank Forester, *My Shooting Box* (Philadelphia: Peterson, 1856);

Herbert, as Frank Forester, *The Warwick Woodlands* (Philadelphia: Peterson, 1856);

Willmott, Robert Eldridge Aris, ed., *The Poets of the Nineteenth Century,* illustrated by Darley and others (New York: Harper, 1857);

Irving, Washington, *The Life of George Washington,* 5 volumes, illustrated by Darley and others (New York: Putnam, 1857–1859);

Cooper, James Fenimore, *Cooper's Novels,* 32 volumes (New York: Townsend, 1859–1861);

Willis, Nathaniel Parker, *Sacred Poems* (New York: Clark, Austin & Smith, 1860);

Dickens, Charles, *The Works of Charles Dickens* (New York: Townsend, 1861);

Palmer, John William, ed., *Folk Songs* (New York: Scribner, 1861);

Cooper, James Fenimore, *Pages and Pictures, from the Writings of James Fenimore Cooper, with Notes by Susan Fenimore Cooper* (New York: Townsend, 1861);

Drake, Joseph Rodman, *The American Flag* (New York: Gregory, 1861);

Rymer, James Malcolm, *The Owlet; Or, The Royal Highwayman* (New York: Brady, 1861);

Key, Francis Scott, *The Star Spangled Banner* (New York: Gregory, 1861);

Moore, Clement C., *A Visit from Saint Nicholas* (New York: Hurd & Houghton/Gregory, 1862);

Stockton, Thomas H., *Poems* (Philadelphia: Martien, 1862);

A Selection of War Lyrics, illustrated by Darley and others (New York: Gregory, 1864);

Dodge, Mary Mapes, *The Irvington Stories* (New York: O'Kane, 1865);

Tennyson, Alfred, *Enoch Arden* (Boston: Ticknor & Fields, 1865);

Goodrich, F. B., ed., *The Tribute Book* (New York: Derby & Miller, 1865);

Yankee Doodle (New York: Trent, Filmer, 1865);

Saunders, Frederick, ed., *Festival of Song: A Series of Evenings with the Poets* (New York: Bunce & Huntington, 1866);

Dodge, Mary Mapes, *Hans Brinker,* illustrations by Darley and Thomas Nast (New York: O'Kane, 1866);

Tennyson, Alfred, *Gems of Tennyson* (Boston: Ticknor & Fields, 1866);

Mühlbach, Luise, *Louisa of Prussia and Her Times* (New York: Appleton, 1867);

Longfellow, Henry Wadsworth, *Evangeline, A Tale of Acadie* (Boston: Ticknor & Fields, 1867);

Cooper, James Fenimore, *Stories of the Sea; Being Narratives of Adventure, Selected from the "Sea Tales"* (New York: Hurd & Houghton, 1868);

Whittier, John Greenleaf, *Ballads of New England* (Boston: Fields, Osgood, 1870);

Longfellow, Henry Wadsworth, *The Poetical Works of Henry Wadsworth Longfellow* (Boston: Houghton, Osgood, 1872);

Warner, Charles Dudley, *My Summer in a Garden* (Boston: Osgood, 1872);

Cooper, James Fenimore, *The Leather Stocking Tales* (New York: D. Appleton, 1872–1874);

Bryant, William Cullen, ed., *Picturesque America* (New York: Appleton, 1872–1874);

Cooper, James Fenimore, *The Spy* (New York: D. Appleton, 1873);

Warren, Nathan B., *The Lady of Lawford* (Troy: Nimms, 1873);

Raymond, Rossiter W., as Robertson Gray, *Brave Hearts* (New York: Ford, 1874);

Lossing, Benson J., *Our Country,* 3 volumes (New York: Johnson & Miles, 1875–1879);

Gough, John B., *Sunlight and Shadow; Or, Gleanings from my Life Work* (Hartford, Conn.: Worthington; Chicago: Nettleton, 1880);

Poe, Edgar Allan, *The Bells* (Philadelphia: Porter & Coates, 1881);

Longfellow, Henry Wadsworth, *Longfellow's Evangeline* (Boston: Houghton, Mifflin, 1883);

Gough, John B., *Platform Echoes* (Hartford, Conn.: Worthington, 1885);

Shakespeare, William, *The Complete Works of William Shakespeare,* edited by Bryant (New York: Amies, 1888).

PERIODICALS: *Graham's Lady's and Gentleman's Magazine,* 1841;
Dollar Newspaper, 1843;
United States Democratic Review, 1843;
Godey's Lady's Book, 1846;
Yankee Doodle, 1847;
John Donkey, 1848;
Child's Paper, 1852–1855;
Illustrated News, 1853;
New York Mercury, 1859;
Harper's Weekly, 1860–1870;
Riverside Magazine, 1867;
Appleton's Journal, 1870;
Illustrated Christian Weekly, 1871.

Beginning his career as a book illustrator in 1843, F. O. C. Darley was the most prolific and successful illustrator of his generation. From the time of his earliest work until his death the words "illustrated by Darley" on the title page of a book ensured good sales. Darley was as capable of illustrating humor and books for children as he was works of fiction by authors such as Washington Irving and James Fenimore Cooper. Made a full member of the National Academy of Design in 1853, Darley was the first American to focus his talents on the illustration of American literature.

Felix Octavius Carr Darley was born in Philadelphia on 23 June 1822. His parents, John and Eleanor Westray Darley, were actors who came in about 1800 to the United States, where they were married. Felix Darley grew up in a literate and artistic family. He had at least six siblings, two of whom, Edmund H. and John Clarendon, were artists. A third brother, William Henry W., a music professor, married Jane Cooper Sully, the daughter of the eminent Philadelphia artist Thomas Sully. Jane Darley was a portrait painter in her own right. There were two sisters, Julia and Ellen, who both taught school.

From an early age Darley began to exhibit his talent for drawing. He drew everything around him, and the theatrical background of the parents proba-

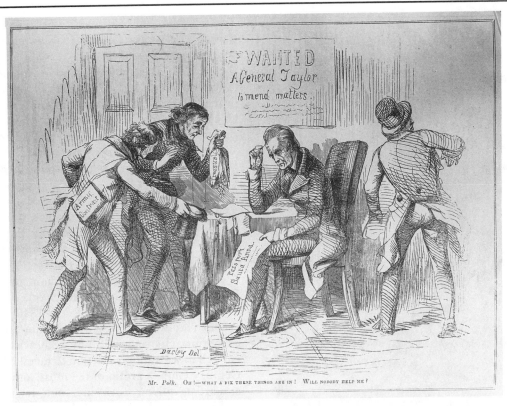

Political cartoon by Darley for the April 1847 issue of Yankee Doodle *(courtesy of the American Antiquarian Society)*

bly fostered the son's ability to depict climactic moments of the stories and novels that he was later commissioned to illustrate. Recalling his childhood in a letter written in 1856, Darley remembered using a chair instead of a table to draw on as a child. In school he drew pictures on his slate, presumably instead of practicing his letters. He also recalled that his parents were proud of his early efforts, considering him a junior Michelangelo.

Rather than being launched by his parents into an artistic, dramatic, or literary career, however, Darley was discovered working in a mercantile house by Thomas Dunn English, American ballad writer and playwright from Philadelphia. English showed Darley's drawings to an editor of the *Saturday Museum,* a Philadelphia publication edited by Edgar Allan Poe. By 1841 Darley was appointed staff illustrator for *Graham's Lady's and Gentleman's Magazine.* His early illustrations appeared in that magazine and in the *United States Democratic Review* in 1843. That same year his illustrations for *Scenes in Indian Life: A Series of Original Designs Etched on Stone* were published by the firm of J. R. Colon in Philadelphia. The volume, which included seventeen pages of text followed by fourteen lithographed plates, won critical acclaim for the young artist. As the reviewer of the *Saturday Museum* commented re-

garding the as yet unpublished sketches in 1842, "We have enjoyed the opportunity of examining these sketches, and do not hesitate to pronounce them more truthful and full of character than anything of a similar kind which we have seen. The lines are strong, bold and masterly—the conception chaste, notwithstanding the humility of the subject." Later in 1843 Darley's designs appeared in *In Town & About, or Pencillings & Pennings* with text by Joseph C. Neal. This early work also received positive critical comments.

Beginning in 1844 the Philadelphia firm of Carey and Hart commissioned Darley to illustrate a collection of humorous works that eventually formed the series known as the Library of Humorous American Works. The final set comprised eighteen volumes and remained in print into the 1880s. It included *The Big Bear of Arkansas and Other Tales* (1845), edited by William T. Porter; Johnson Jones Hooper's *Some Adventures of Captain Simon Suggs* (1845); and Thomas Bangs Thorpe's *The Mysteries of the Backwoods* (1846). Additional titles in the series were published by Hart from 1850 to 1853. Many of these books dealt with frontier life; the authors successfully wrote about incidents that were particularly amusing to urban readers, both men and women. Darley was adept at interpreting the

Illustration by Darley for his 1856 Compositions in Outline
from Judd's Margaret *(courtesy of the American
Antiquarian Society)*

authors' text accurately, a fact that no doubt caught the eye of publisher Edward L. Carey, who was intrigued by the possibilities of American homespun humor. Carey also collected paintings by American artists, including William Sidney Mount. Carey's love of this genre of painting probably influenced the choice of subject matter for his publishing house, which in turn helped to promote Darley's career.

Even as he was producing the illustrations for this series, Darley was working on books for other publishers. He produced many illustrations for at least twenty titles in the children's series Grandfather Lovechild's Nursery Stories for another Philadelphia publisher, George B. Zieber, from 1846 to 1849. In addition Darley was producing illustrations for children's books for the firms of George S. Appleton in Philadelphia and D. Appleton and Company of New York. A prolific artist Darley also produced comic illustrations for the *John Donkey* and

Yankee Doodle and continued to provide designs for *Graham's Lady's and Gentleman's Magazine* and *Godey's Lady's Book.*

In 1848 Darley left his native Philadelphia and moved to New York City. The major publishing firm of George P. Putnam commissioned him to provide illustrations for Washington Irving's *The Sketch Book of Geoffrey Crayon, Gentn.,* published in 1848, and for Irving's *History of New York,* published in 1850. The American Art Union published in quarto volumes Darley's outline drawings in *Illustrations of Rip Van Winkle* in 1848 and *Illustrations of the Legend of Sleepy Hollow* in 1849. These designs, done in larger format plates by the firm of Sarony and Major, attracted attention from abroad and were highly praised in the *London Literary Gazette.*

That the American Art Union commissioned Darley to undertake these two projects is significant. Most illustrators in the 1830s and 1840s lacked any artistic standing. Darley was a major and singular exception. His reputation by 1850 was significant enough to warrant his election to membership in the Century Club, a group of the most eminent writers and artists in New York—including Irving, Cooper, and Henry Wadsworth Longfellow. By 1852 he also was made a member of the National Academy of Design, the Artists' Fund Society, and the American Society of Painters in Watercolor.

Another indication of Darley's success was the increasing amounts of his commissions. In the late 1840s Darley received $7 per illustration for his work for the publisher Carey and Hart. Although this is far below the $200 per painting that artists such as Thomas Sully received in the 1820s and 1830s from Carey and Hart for use in gift books such as the *Atlantic Souvenir,* it was enough for a young, unmarried man to live on. By 1861 Darley's popularity was such that he commanded $45 per design for the illustrations for Dickens's novels, although at this point in his career he was so committed to various projects that he could only promise the publisher two designs per month. Not bound to a single publisher, Darley took on commissions from a variety of sources. During the 1850s he was an active and well-paid designer of banknote engravings in addition to his illustrative work, and near the end of his career he was also receiving royalty payments from Houghton, Mifflin.

Most of the designs published in books in the nineteenth century were reproduced as wood engravings. That his drawings occasionally were published in large format publications, such as the American Art Union projects, or as steel engravings was indicative of Darley's success. Another indication was that at the end of his career some of his drawings were reproduced as photogravures.

During the 1850s Darley was commissioned to illustrate literary works by such authors as Donald Grant Mitchell, Irving, Frances Sargent Osgood, Calvin H. Wiley, Cornelius Mathews, George Pope Morris, and Benjamin P. Shillaber. Darley also provided illustrations for the complete works of William Gilmore Simms, published by J. S. Redfield from 1853 to 1859. Redfield also published in 1856 *Compositions in Outline by Felix O. C. Darley from Judd's Margaret*. This project occupied Darley's attention for a decade: the finished project was well worth the effort.

Darley received additional praise in the December 1856 issue of the *Crayon*. The article included a lengthy essay on illustration in general and Darley's illustrations in particular and commented that "in technical respects we have here the best compositions and the most effective drawing we have ever seen by Darley." Darley's reputation continued on a high plateau throughout the decade. In 1867 Henry Theodore Tuckerman wrote, "We have had nothing in this style of art to compare with the exquisite and impressive drawings in which Darley has embodied his sense of the beauty, power, and truth of that remarkable fiction."

Darley married Jane Colburn of Cambridge, Massachusetts, in 1859. They moved to Claymont, Delaware, after their marriage, where they lived on property owned by his family and were eventually joined there by Darley's two sisters and two of his brothers, Alfred and Edmund.

The move to Claymont did not seem to affect Darley's productivity. Before he was forty years old Darley had become so successful that publishers were commissioning him to illustrate series of novels. A weekly newspaper in New York, the *New York Mercury,* published ten novelettes in 1859–1860, each including from three to twelve illustrations, for a total of sixty-nine illustrations by Darley. They were probably all separately published as well.

Another major project undertaken by Darley was the illustration of Cooper's novels for the New York publisher W. A. Townsend and Company (1859–1861). The prospectus noted that the edition "will derive enhanced interest from being illustrated by Darley, an artist who, for years, has made the pages of Cooper a congenial study. His drawings, conceived in a spirit and with a breadth worthy of the picturesque pages of his author, have been preserved in all their fidelity by the best engravers in the country." Each of the thirty-two volumes included two steel engravings and nine or ten wood engravings designed by the artist. The illustrated novels were reprinted in the 1860s by J. G. Gregory

Illustration by Darley for James Fenimore Cooper's The Pathfinders; *republished in Darley's 1861* The Cooper Vignettes *(courtesy of the American Antiquarian Society)*

and in the 1870s by Hurd and Houghton. The series of novels were so successful that they generated a demand for volumes of Darley's illustrations from the books. In 1861 *Pages and Pictures from the Writings of James Fenimore Cooper,* edited by Susan Fenimore Cooper, was published and included twenty-eight steel engravings after Darley's designs and 120 vignettes reproduced as wood engravings. The Townsend publication of Cooper's works also generated a secondary volume of Darley's steel engravings, and in 1862 James G. Gregory published *The Cooper Vignettes from Drawings by F. O. C. Darley.*

In 1861 Darley completed another significant undertaking—the illustration of the novels of Charles Dickens. The series was first published by Townsend in 1861 and subsequently by Sheldon and Company, 1862–1865, and by Hurd and Houghton in 1866. There were a total of fifty-five volumes in each of these editions, including forty-seven steel engravings after Darley's designs. A popular author for illustration, Dickens would again figure prominently in Darley's later career.

During the Civil War, Darley illustrated several patriotic songs, including Joseph Rodman Drake's *The American Flag* (1861); Francis Scott Key's *The Star Spangled Banner* (1861); *A Selection of War Lyrics* (1864); and *Yankee Doodle* (1865). He also

Illustration by Darley for "The Village Blacksmith" in The Poetical Works of Henry
Wadsworth Longfellow *(1872)*

contributed designs to some of the elegant books of poetry published during the decade, including Nathaniel Parker Willis's *Sacred Poems* (1860); *Folk Songs* (1861), edited by John William Palmer; Thomas H. Stockton's *Poems* (1862); Alfred Tennyson's *Enoch Arden* (1865); *The Tribute Book* (1865), edited by F. B. Goodrich; *Festival of Song* (1866), edited by Frederick Saunders; Tennyson's *Gems of Tennyson* (1866); and John Greenleaf Whittier's *Ballads of New England* (1870). Each of these volumes includes illustrations by several of the most eminent and renowned artists of the era.

In June 1866 Darley and his wife sailed for Europe, spending thirteen months abroad. As did other artists and illustrators, Darley compiled an illustrated journal of his travels, *Sketches Abroad with Pen and Pencil,* which was published in 1868 by Hurd and Houghton in New York and by Low and Marston in London. Some of the illustrations had earlier appeared in the *Riverside Magazine.* Others were later published in *Appleton's Journal.*

During the 1870s Darley remained active, working for publishers in New York and Boston. One major project was providing more than five hundred illustrations for Benson J. Lossing's *Our Country,* a popular history of the United States, published in parts by Johnson and Miles in New York from 1875 to 1879. In the preface Lossing noted that Darley had "consulted the best authorities for portraiture and costume, and followed their teachings."

Other projects included the illustration of additional works by Cooper published by D. Appleton and Company; thirty-two illustrations (out of six hundred) for *The Poetical Works of Henry Wadsworth Longfellow,* published in Boston by Houghton, Osgood and Company in 1872; and twelve plates done in his outline style for Nathaniel Hawthorne's *The Scarlet Letter,* published by Houghton, Osgood and Company in 1879.

In the 1880s Darley continued to publish widely. His designs for Poe's *The Bells* were published in Philadelphia by Porter and Coates (1881). He provided illustrations for two works by John B. Gough, *Sunlight and Shadow; Or, Gleanings from my Life Work* (1880) and *Platform Echoes* (1885). Both were published in Hartford, Connecticut, by Worthington. Darley also took advantage of the new technique of photogravure and produced several series of his wash drawings, which were published in portfolios during this decade. Examples of this lavish form of presentation include *Longfellow's Evangeline* (1883) and *Character Sketches from the Works of Charles Dickens* (1888). Darley was working on the latter series of drawings at the time of his death on 27 March 1888. Up to the time of his death Darley was looking for new projects. In 1887 he had written to Houghton, Mifflin suggesting that they publish an illustrated edition of the poetry of Robert and Elizabeth Barrett Browning, but he died before he could begin this project.

A Darley illustration for the 1883 edition of Henry Wadsworth Longfellow's Evangeline

Darley's career was full and successful. Early in his career he had the good fortune to become allied with one of the leading publishing firms in the United States. This assured wide circulation of his illustrations as well as steady employment. His work received early critical acclaim, and his prolific production enabled him to work for many publishers simultaneously. He viewed himself not only as an illustrator but also as an artist: he participated during his entire career in exhibitions. His watercolors were sold in galleries during the 1870s and could be found in the collections of such notables as Prince Napoleon Bonaparte, who commissioned Darley to paint four works for him. That his designs appeared in publications in the 1880s with those of Winslow Homer, Howard Pyle, Frederic Remington, and A. B. Frost underlines the respect with which he was held by both the public and the publishers. His draftsmanship did not become stale, and he continued to interpret, rather than merely to embellish, texts of poetry, fiction, and non-fiction.

References:

Georgia B. Barnhill, "F. O. C. Darley's Illustrations for Southern Humor," in *Graphic Arts & the South,* edited by Judy L. Larson (Fayetteville: University of Arkansas Press, 1993), pp. 31–63;

Theodore Bolton, "The Book Illustrations of Felix Octavius Carr Darley," *Proceedings of the American Antiquarian Society* (April 1951): 137–182;

Delaware Art Museum, *". . . Illustrated by Darley"* (Wilmington: Delaware Art Museum, 1978), exhibition catalogue;

John C. Ewers, "Not Quite Redmen: The Plains Indian Illustrations of Felix O. C. Darley," *American Art Journal,* 3 (Fall 1971): 88–98;

Sinclair Hamilton, *Early American Book Illustrators and Wood Engravers, 1670–1870,* 2 volumes (Princeton, N.J.: Princeton University Press, 1958);

Sue W. Reed, "F. O. C. Darley's Outline Illustrations," *The American Illustrated Book in the Nineteenth Century,* edited by Gerald W. R. Ward (Winterthur, Del.: Winterthur Museum, 1982), pp. 113–136;

Henry T. Tuckerman, *Book of the Artists* (New York: J. F. Carr, 1867), pp. 471–476;

Frank Weitenkampf, "F. O. C. Darley, American Illustrator," *Art Quarterly,* 10 (Spring 1947): 100–113;

Weitenkampf, "Illustrated by Darley," *International Studio* (March 1925): 445–448.

Archives:

Notable collections of Darley's drawings may be found at the New York Public Library; Henry E. Huntington Library and Art Gallery; Beinecke Library, Yale University; Graphic Arts Collection, Princeton University Library; Library of Congress; Alderman Library, University of Virginia; Sleepy Hollow Restorations; Free Library of Philadelphia; Historical Society of Delaware; Delaware Art Museum; and the Museum of Fine Arts, Boston. Letters from Darley are found in many libraries, including the Henry E. Huntington Library and Art Gallery, the Historical Society of Pennsylvania, the Harry Ransom Humanities Research Center at the University of Texas at Austin, the Houghton Library at Harvard University, the Pierpont Morgan Library, Henry F. DuPont Winterthur Museum, the Alderman Library of the University of Virginia, and the New York Public Library.

W. W. Denslow

(5 May 1856 – 29 March 1915)

Douglas G. Greene
Old Dominion University

BOOKS: *Denslow's Picture Books for Children: Humpty Dumpty; Little Red Riding-Hood; Three Bears; Mary Had a Little Lamb; Old Mother Hubbard; House That Jack Built; One Ring Circus; Zoo; 5 Little Pigs; Tom Thumb; ABC Book;* and *Jack and the Bean-Stalk* (New York: G. W. Dillingham, 1903); republished in two volumes as *Denslow's Humpty Dumpty and Other Stories* and *Denslow's One Ring Circus and Other Stories* (New York: G. W. Dillingham, 1903);

Denslow's New Series of Picture Books: Scarecrow and the Tin-Man; Simple Simon; Animal Fair; Barn-Yard Circus; Mother Goose A. B. C. Book; and *Three Little Kittens* (New York: G. W. Dillingham, 1904); republished in one volume as *Denslow's Scarecrow and the Tin-Man and Other Stories* (New York: G. W. Dillingham, 1904);

The Pearl and the Pumpkin, by Denslow and Paul West (New York: G. W. Dillingham, 1904);

Billy Bounce, by Denslow and Dudley A. Bragdon (New York: G. W. Dillingham, 1906);

When I Grow Up (New York: Century, 1909).

SELECTED BOOKS ILLUSTRATED: M'Cauley, I. H., *Historical Sketch of Franklin County, Pennsylvania* (Chambersburg, Pa.: D. F. Pursel, 1878);

Cowan, John F., *A New Invasion of the South* (New York: Board of Officers, Seventy-first Infantry, 1881);

Johnston, J. P., *Twenty Years of Hus'ling* (Chicago: Hallet, 1888);

Barnum, P. T., *Dollars and Sense: Or, How to Get On* (Chicago: People's Publishing Co., 1890);

Read, Opie, *A Tennessee Judge* (Chicago: Laird & Lee, 1893);

Armstrong, Le Roy, *Byrd Flam in Town* (Chicago: Bearhope, 1894);

Read, Opie, *An Arkansas Planter* (Chicago: Rand, McNally, 1896);

Hooper, Will Phillip, *An Untold Tale* (New York: Home, 1897);

Stoddard, Charles Warren, *A Cruise Under the Crescent* (Chicago & New York: Rand, McNally, 1898);

Coleridge, Samuel Taylor, *Ye Ancient Mariner* (East Aurora, N.Y.: Roycrofters, 1899);

Fitzgerald, Edward, *Rubáiyat of Omar Khayyám* (East Aurora, N.Y.: Roycrofters, 1899);

Baum, L. Frank, *Father Goose: His Book* (Chicago: G. M. Hill, 1899);

Baum, *The Songs of Father Goose* (Chicago: G. M. Hill, 1900);

Baum, *The Wonderful Wizard of Oz* (Chicago & New York: G. M. Hill, 1900);

Baum, *Dot and Tot of Merryland* (Chicago: G. M. Hill, 1900);

Denslow's Mother Goose (New York: McClure, Phillips, 1901);

Moore, Clement C., *Denslow's Night Before Christmas* (New York: G. W. Dillingham, 1902);

Webb, Richard, *Me and Lawson* (New York: G. W. Dillingham, 1905);

Johnston, Isabel M., *The Jeweled Toad* (Indianapolis: Bobbs-Merrill, 1907).

PERIODICALS: *Hearth and Home,* 1872–1873;
St. Nicholas, 1874, 1909;
American Agriculturalist, 1874–1876;
The Theatre, 1886–1888;
The Californian Illustrated Magazine, 1892–1893;
The Philistine, 1896, 1898–1903, 1906–1908;
The Bill Poster, 1896–1897;
The Fra, 1908–1910;
John Martin's Book, 1915.

A hard-drinking, cynical newspaperman, W. W. Denslow is today remembered for his visual creation of the Land of Oz as illustrator of L. Frank Baum's *The Wonderful Wizard of Oz* (1900). The great success of that book and Denslow's definitive picturing of Dorothy, the Scarecrow, the Tin Woodsman, the humbug Wizard, and the Wicked Witch of the West have overshadowed his other contributions to American illustration. Influenced by the

W. W. Denslow at work, 1901. He signed the photograph with his "Hippocampus" trademark.

decorativeness of 1890s posters—to which craze he was a major contributor—and by the work of British illustrators such as Walter Crane and Randolph Caldecott, Denslow was the first American illustrator to design picture books for children as artistic units, with the covers, endpapers, illustrations, typefaces, and general layouts contributing to a carefully organized and decorative effect.

William Wallace Denslow Jr. (called "Wally" by his family and "Will" or "Billie" by his friends) was born on 5 May 1856 in Philadelphia, the son of William W. Denslow Sr. and Jane Evans Denslow. At the age of fourteen, in 1870, he began formal training in art at the Cooper Union in New York City; two years later he studied at the National Academy of Design. During this period he became friends with a group of magazine artists, including Fred Church and Will Low, who frequented the bohemian Salmagundi Club, and it was through these connections that Denslow began to sell illustrations. His still undistinguished work appeared during the 1870s in such journals as *Hearth and Home, American Agriculturist,* and the new magazine *St. Nicholas,* which soon became the most important magazine ever published for children.

During the late 1870s and early 1880s Denslow was a traveling artist, sometimes designing advertising material, sometimes illustrating local histo-

ries. His work was unexceptional, though he occasionally added cynical touches such as including his own name on a tombstone in a local scene. He married Annie McCartney in Philadelphia in November 1882, and they had a son, William Wallace Denslow III. The couple separated within a year, and it is possible that Denslow never even knew of the birth of his child. By 1885 he had settled in New York City doing theatrical work, primarily posters for plays and illustrations for theatrical magazines. In his work for the magazine *The Theatre,* hints of his later style can be found. The drawings are decoratively designed, often with humorous caricatures of theatrical personages and with solid black shadows, rather than cross-hatching, to set off the figures.

In 1888 Denslow left New York for Chicago to work on the *Chicago Herald.* His stay, however, was short as he was fired several times for drunkenness. He went next to Denver, then to San Francisco to continue newspaper work before returning to Chicago in 1893 to take advantage of the boom created by the World's Columbian Exposition. Contemporaries praised his newspaper illustrations for their "clean, sharp lines," but newspapers are ephemeral, and Denslow—himself a book collector—longed for the recognition afforded by book design. By this time he had taken the Keeley Cure for alcoholism (a treatment

A QUEER AQUARIUM.

HERE are some puzzle-fish. They are as strange as the "Curious Fish" in our March number, but those were real, and the appearance of each of these only indicates its name. Who can tell us what they are?

A puzzle Denslow created for the April 1874 issue of St. Nicholas

that involved injections of a form of gold), and for the next decade or so alcohol did not affect his career.

Denslow entered the social life of Chicago, joining the Whitechapel Club—named in macabre fashion after the Whitechapel murders committed by Jack the Ripper—the Bohemian Club, and the more professional Press Club. In these venues he met such writers and artists as Opie Read, Frank and J. C. Leyendecker, John T. McCutcheon, Will Bradley, and George Ade. The founder of the Bohemian Club was "Amber" (Martha Everts Holden), and in 1896 Denslow married her daughter, Ann Waters Holden.

Signing his work with a stylized seahorse and the letters *DEN,* Denslow was known as "Hippocampus Den." By the mid 1890s he was designing costumes for the stage and posters for newspapers, magazines, and books. It was in his posters that his mature style developed. He was influenced by the fashionable Art Nouveau style and by the prints of the French artist Jules Cheret. He was, however, too cynical to accept the extremes of fashion, and he even drew a poster directly satirizing his friend Will Bradley's version of Art Nouveau. The most significant influence on Denslow was probably the Japanese Tokumgawa "Floating World"

print, with its bright, solid colors and little shading. Like the Japanese print, Denslow's posters downplay modeling and instead depict shapes as flat and flooded with artificial light; they rarely include a horizon line. Even the colors on his posters are decorative rather than realistic, and the figures sometimes seem to float within an undefined space. Denslow's posters are striking and colorful, and his work was praised as far away as London. More practically, his illustrations were in demand by publishers, and from 1896 through 1898 he earned a steady living designing more than one hundred book covers for Rand, McNally and other firms.

During the late 1890s Denslow became the first artist employed by Elbert Hubbard's Roycrofters of East Aurora, New York. Influenced by William Morris, Hubbard brought the Arts and Crafts movement to the United States, and his Roycroft community produced many items by hand. Denslow persuaded Hubbard to let him design Roycroft publications. Spending many summers in East Aurora at a salary of fifty dollars per week, Denslow became a regular contributor to Hubbard's magazine *The Philistine* and, later, *The Fra.* He also hand-illuminated several of Hubbard's books and illus-

Dorothy LIVED IN 1
the midst of the
great Kansas
prairies, with Uncle Henry, 2
who was a farmer, and Aunt Em, who was
the farmer's wife. Their house was small,
for the lumber to build it had to be carried by wagon
many miles. There were four walls, a floor
and a roof, which made one room; and this
room contained a rusty looking cooking
stove, a cupboard for the dishes, a table,
three or four chairs, and the beds. Uncle

"You ought to be ashamed of yourself!"

"Exactly so! I am a humbug."

Illustrations by Denslow for L. Frank Baum's The Wonderful Wizard of Oz *(1900)*

trated two of the Roycrofters' most attractive publications, *Ye Ancient Mariner* and the *Rubáiyat of Omar Khayyám*, in 1899. For both books he temporarily deserted his poster style. His pictures for the *Rubáiyat* are simple and delicate rather than broad and farcical like many of his posters; the illustrations in *Ye Ancient Mariner* have a macabre aspect and, with their flowing lines, show that Denslow could use the techniques of Art Nouveau effectively.

In 1896 at the Press Club, regional novelist Read introduced Denslow to L. Frank Baum, at that time a struggling crockery salesman and occasional writer of topical verse. Baum, however, wanted to write books for children, and in 1899 he and Denslow began designing a collection of nonsense verse to be called *Father Goose: His Book*. Denslow conceived of each page as a miniature poster, with solid, flat colors and bold calligraphy. The borders do not limit the space in Denslow's pictures, as he allowed figures to break through the borders or even sit upon them. He excelled in decorative friezes in which several characters, differing only in tiny details from each other, march across the page. *Father Goose* was a surprise best-seller of 1899, and artist and author began work on the book that would make them famous, *The Wonderful Wizard of Oz,* published in 1900. Denslow contributed to the development of Baum's characters, and the final product integrated text and illustration as no earlier American children's book had done. Denslow's more than one hundred illustrations often cut into the words, and sometimes they were even printed over the type. The full-color plates seem flooded with light, and the entire effect is garish and otherworldly—a perfect fairy-tale world.

Denslow and Baum collaborated on only one more book, *Dot and Tot of Merryland* (1900), perhaps the most purely decorative of all Denslow's works, before personal differences led them to a bitter separation. Baum and Denslow had long clashed over who deserved more credit for their books, and these debates reached a height when they turned *The Wonderful Wizard of Oz* into an immensely popular musical extravaganza premiering in 1902. Baum and his publishers found new illustrators for his books, and Denslow, who had left Chicago for New York, illustrated classic children's works which his publishers sold on his name alone. *Denslow's Mother Goose* (1901) and *Denslow's Night Before Christmas* (1902) are both well-designed quarto picture books that remained in print for many years, but when Denslow tried to write his own stories and verses, he was far less successful. In 1903 and 1904 he illustrated eighteen pamphlets (collected into three volumes) called *Denslow's Picture Books,* each of which included the artist's original verse or his bowdlerized versions of classic nursery rhymes. Denslow had no sense of poetry, and his lines limp

along. Interesting among his work during these years were three projects that indicated his claim as the creator of the characters in *The Wonderful Wizard of Oz.* Around 1903 a pamphlet titled *Pictures from the Wonderful Wizard of Oz* included Denslow's color plates from Baum's books but had no mention of the author. One of his picture books published in 1904 was *Denslow's Scarecrow and the Tin-Man,* again with no acknowledgment to Baum. He followed with a charmingly illustrated newspaper series with the same title.

Meanwhile, Denslow's personal life was unsettled. In September 1903 Ann Waters Holden divorced him on the charge of desertion, and at the end of the year Denslow married his third wife, a widow named Frances Golsen Doolittle. But the money kept coming in from the books and from the *Wizard of Oz* musical extravaganza, and Denslow purchased an island in Bermuda, which, tongue in cheek, he proclaimed a sovereign kingdom.

Denslow's career, nevertheless, was gradually being damaged because he thought himself not only an illustrator but also an author of children's books and a playwright. In 1904 he collaborated with Paul West on *The Pearl and the Pumpkin* both as a children's book and as a musical extravaganza much like the successful *Wizard of Oz.* Though the illustrations for the book are charming, neither it nor the play was popular. Even worse was *Billy Bounce,* written with Dudley A. Bragdon in 1906. A play was written though never produced, but unfortunately the book was published. It is a senseless mishmash of only vaguely connected episodes, and the illustrations are surprisingly clumsy. Denslow had not lost his talent as an artist, however, as demonstrated in his work for a 1907 book, *The Jeweled Toad,* written by Isabel M. Johnston. Except for decorations on the preliminary pages, the book is illustrated only with tightly designed chapter headings in a long, narrow rectangle that create an entrancing rhythm from chapter to chapter.

Denslow followed *The Jeweled Toad* with *When I Grow Up,* a series published in *St. Nicholas* and collected in book form in 1909. The series features Denslow's clumsy but pleasant doggerel about the daydreams of a boy, set off by illustrations that showed the artist neither at his best nor his worst.

From this point Denslow's career began a rapid descent. He was unable to sell his work to major publishers, and he succumbed again to the temptations of drink. His wife Frances divorced him because of alcoholism, and Denslow moved to Buffalo to begin a new career as a commercial artist. Buffalo was a major center for advertising art, and Denslow worked for the Niagara Lithograph Company designing pamphlets that promoted projects ranging from shoes to farm machinery. Many of the pamphlets are attractive. In *Through*

Foreign Lands with "Sunny Jim" (1910) Denslow set off colorful illustrations with a strong gray line, and he showed that people all around the world, no matter their cultural differences, gain strength through Force Malt Wheat Flakes. In *Fairbank's Juvenile History of the United States* (1911) he drew pictures of Fairbank's Fairy Soap playing an integral part in American history. For example, he depicted the Pilgrims floating ashore on a bar of the product.

Around 1913 Denslow returned to New York City, where he was reduced to working for a salary of twenty-five dollars per week at the Rosenbaum Studios, another advertising agency. The amount did not cover his expenses, and to survive he pawned his book collection. He told the other employees that he had once been wealthy and owned a Bermuda island, but when they did not believe him, he refused to speak to anyone at the studios. During his final months, however, he began to sell a few illustrations—some poems and pictures to the children's magazine *John Martin's Book* and a full-color cover to the humor magazine *Life.* The drawing, as Michael Patrick Hearn has pointed out, is a burlesque of Erté's covers for *Harper's Bazaar* and is both humorous and elegant. Denslow was elated by the sale, and he celebrated bibulously for two days. The binge resulted in pneumonia, and he was taken to the Knickerbocker Hospital, where he died on 29 March 1915 at the age of fifty-eight.

The obscurity of Denslow's last years was almost total. No major newspaper or magazine published his obituary, and his grave remained unmarked until a few years ago when the International Wizard of Oz Club had a stone erected. For many years there were no remarks about him at all in studies of American illustration. Part of the reason for this silence was Denslow's fault. His irregular life and prickly personality, exacerbated by drink, meant that he left no friends to preserve his artistic reputation. Moreover, many of his books, especially the ones he wrote himself, had stories that were not the equal of his pictures, and few people would buy such books as *Billy Bounce* solely because Denslow illustrated them. Most important, artistic developments had passed him by. Printing processes using complex shades and reproducing tiny details were suited to glazed oil paintings by Maxfield Parrish and transparent washes by Arthur Rackham, not to the bold and somewhat garish designs of Denslow. It is only within the past two decades that Denslow's work has been reevaluated, and the judgment of critics from the turn of the century has been confirmed by modern scholars. Not only was Denslow a skilled creator of fairyland, but his ideas about artistic book design helped to develop twentieth-century American illustration.

Denslow painting the Scarecrow, a self-caricature drawn for Townsend Walsh, publicity manager for the 1902 musical version of The Wizard of Oz *(Theatre Collection, New York Public Library, Astor, Lenox and Tilden Foundations)*

Bibliography:

Douglas G. Greene, "W. W. Denslow, A Checklist," *Baum Bugle,* 16 (Autumn 1992): 16–24.

Biography:

Douglas G. Greene and Michael Patrick Hearn, *W. W. Denslow* (Mount Pleasant: Clarke Historical Library, Central Michigan University, 1976).

References:

Michael Patrick Hearn, *The Annotated Wizard of Oz* (New York: Clarkson N. Potter, 1973);

Ernest Norcia, "An Artist's Appreciation of W. W. Denslow," *Baum Bugle,* 16 (Autumn 1992): 9–15.

Archives:

The Chicago Historical Society holds an important collection of Denslow's artwork. Other major collections are at the Prints Division of the New York Public Library and at Columbia University Libraries. Some original Denslow illustrations are part of the de Grummond Children's Literature Collection in the McCain Library and Archives, University of Southern Mississippi. The Lilly Library, Indiana University, has some of Denslow's papers.

Arthur G. Dove
(2 August 1880 – 22 November 1946)

Phyllis Peet
Monterey Peninsula College

SELECTED BOOKS ILLUSTRATED: Butler, El-
lis Parker, *Jibby Jones: A Story of Mississippi
River Adventure for Boys* (Boston: Houghton
Mifflin, 1923);
Butler, *Jibby Jones and the Alligator: The Story of the
Young Alligator-hunters of the Upper Mississippi
Valley* (Boston: Houghton Mifflin, 1924).

PERIODICALS: *Century Magazine,* 1903–1908,
1919–1921;
Illustrated Sporting News, 1903–1907;
McClure's, 1903–1910, 1929;
The Saturday Evening Post, 1903–1909;
Evening Mail, 1904;
Pearson's Magazine, 1905;
St. Nicolas, 1905–1908, 1920;
Collier's, 1907–1908, 1928;
Cosmopolitan, 1907–1908;
Harper's Weekly, 1913;
Country Gentleman, 1919–1921;
American Boy, 1920–1925;
Fore and Aft, 1920–1921;
Ladies' Home Journal, 1921;
Elk's Magazine, 1922–1930;
Pictorial Review (1924–1928);
Success (1924);
Scribner's Magazine (1926–1927);
Everybody's (1927);
Youth's Companion (1927–1928);
Liberty (1930).

Arthur G. Dove was a prolific illustrator for
many of America's most popular magazines between
1903 and 1910 and during the 1920s. By that decade
his drawings for illustration had helped to form his
Modernist painting style, for which he is best
known. One of America's earliest abstract painters and a member of the group of avant-garde artists who were in the intimate circle of Alfred
Stieglitz, Dove combined in his career the cultur-
ally conflicting realms of art for art's sake and
commercial illustration.

Arthur G. Dove (photograph by Alfred Stieglitz)

Arthur Garfield Dove was born on 2 August
1880 to prosperous, conservative parents, Anna Elizabeth and William George Dove, in Canandai-
gua, New York, where his father was serving a two-
year term as county clerk. The Doves named their
son after the Republican vice-presidential and presidential candidates of that year. William George
Dove was a building contractor and manufacturer of
bricks in Geneva, New York, where the family returned at the end of his term. Geneva was a small
town of several hundred inhabitants in the center of a
farming community where Dove's father built many
of the buildings, including several at Geneva's Hobart College. Arthur Dove had a conventional up-
bringing and education in local private and public
schools. Except for a sister, Mary Marguerite, who

was born in 1883 and died in infancy, he was an only child until he was twelve years old. His brother, Paul, was born in 1892.

With his father distracted by a busy career as a businessman and politician, Dove developed a surrogate father-son relationship with a close neighbor, Newton Weatherly. A naturalist, truck farmer, amateur painter, and musician, Weatherly had a great influence on Dove's choices of career and lifestyle. Weatherly took Dove fishing and hunting and, most important, inspired him to draw and paint. Dove reportedly accompanied Weatherly on his outdoor painting trips, sitting down to paint beside him, getting pointers as he went. As an adult Dove attempted several times to farm as Weatherly had done in order to earn a living so he could devote his creative energy to painting instead of illustration.

Weatherly's encouragement, as well as that of a neighborhood schoolteacher, supplemented by instruction books, enabled Dove, as a student at Hobart College, to draw illustrations in 1899 and 1900 for the school yearbook, *The Echo of the Seneca* (the annuals for 1901 and 1902). These early drawings show the strong influence of the popular English illustrator Philip William May, whose work appeared frequently in American magazines. Dove was influenced by many different artists, and he particularly studied the work of George Cruikshank, Thomas Rowlandson, Théophile-Alexandre Steinlen, Honoré Daumier, and other contemporary English and French artists. But it was the simplicity and the strong, sinuous line of May's work, which was closely related to the Poster style, that appealed to Dove most. Cartoon and caricature were an important part of May's work, and Dove's drawings for *The Echo,* which include a caricature of Hobart's golf coach called "The Golf Club," demonstrate how Dove borrowed directly from May for the 1900 Hobart College yearbook. Like May, Dove used an economical pen-and-ink style that relied on outline and a spare use of modeling, textures, and dark tonalities articulated with hatching lines. Dove's full-length profile "Golf Club" figure, with his hand in his pocket, smoke in his mouth, crumpled clothing, and hat on his head, is a frequent image in May's drawings.

Dove also drew illustrations for *The Cornellian,* the yearbook of Cornell University, where he completed his junior and senior years and graduated with a bachelor of arts degree in 1903. His course work was about half in art and—following the wishes of his father that he become a lawyer—half in law, politics, and economics. Dove's art professor at Cornell was the illustrator, writer, explorer, and lecturer Charles Wellington Furlong, who encouraged

Dove to become an illustrator. Furlong was a skilled draftsman with a tight, realistic, finished style. Dove's exposure to Furlong's more disciplined style provided him the opportunity to refine and polish his technical skills. In 1903, however, it was still May's style that was clearly the dominating influence on Dove's drawings for *The Cornellian.*

After Dove graduated, he moved to New York City. He worked for a few months in advertising while he built a reputation as a freelance illustrator. He soon began to receive commissions for illustrations from popular magazines and from Frederick A. Stokes Lithographic Company. Eager for work, Dove took an active part in the illustrators' circle, joining the Society of Illustrators and the Players' Club. He appeared at well-known artists' meeting places such as Mouquin's Restaurant, Café Francis, and Petit Pas. He soon came to know John Sloan, William Glackens, and James and May Wilson Preston. Dove became a particularly close friend of the Prestons, and May Wilson Preston, who was also influenced by Phil May and English pen-and-ink drawing, was to provide inspiration and significantly influence Dove's drawing style. Dove and his new wife, Florence Dorsey, whom he married and brought to New York City from Geneva in 1904, were able to live comfortably on his income as an illustrator.

Dove's 1903 commissions for the covers of *The Illustrated Sporting News* demonstrate his skill in the pen-and-ink style inspired by May, in which a monumental figure depicted mostly by strong, fluid outlines is the predominant subject. The single figures engaged in a variety of popular sports such as ice skating, tennis, and skiing are set on blank grounds with detail kept to a minimum and shading and volume implied with the curve and undulation of the pen line. Other more tightly, realistically drawn illustrations in these editions of *The Illustrated Sporting News,* such as that for "A Sin of My Youth" by Clara Morris in the 12 December 1903 edition, recall Dove's contact with Weatherly and Furlong and suggest how Dove would use these contrasting styles to solve a variety of design problems in his illustration commissions throughout the years. Dove's drawings for "The Coasting Killiwogs" by H. M. Kieffer in the December 1905 *St. Nicholas* demonstrate how he often combined the two approaches. He created forms using strong outlines similar to May's style and drew details more carefully, as in Furlong's style. The title characters are featured sliding diagonally down the center of the page with columns of the text broken up on each side of the drawing, creating an attractive page. Designs he made for the Frederick A. Stokes Compa-

Drawn by Arthur G. Dove

"AND REACHED OVER AND JUST TETCHED THAT BILL"

Illustration for Rosa Kellen Hallett's humorous story "Mrs. Tyman Passes the Contribution Box" (Century Magazine, April 1907)

ny's 1906 lithographic "Calendar of Birds and Beasts" exhibit further assimilation of the bold, linear approach of May with a more realistic approach. Here Dove uses the quick, sketchier, lighter, broken-line work to create the details and textures that he learned from May Wilson Preston and the other Philadelphia realists.

By 1907 Dove had developed a consistency in style and an excellence in technical ability. In his title-page drawing for "Mrs. Tyman Passes the Contribution Box" by Rosa Kellen Hallett in the April 1907 *Century,* Dove combined the May-type monumental, humorous figure with a facile, spontaneous, sketchlike drawing style, using the white of the paper as well as lines to indicate form. This drawing represents the style—inspired by May and Preston—Dove continued to develop when he turned to illustration again in the 1920s.

Dove was often commissioned to draw for humorous stories, such as those by Ellis Parker Butler. Some of his earliest illustrations for Butler's work

appear in "Mosby's Depilitator," published in the 13 July 1907 *Collier's.* They are composed of groups of figures reminiscent of May's *Gutter-snipes.* Similar figures appear in Dove's illustrations for "The Americanizing of André Francois" by Stella Wynne Herron in *McClure's* for September 1908 and for his featured drawing, "A Christmas Offering," in the 14 December 1907 *Collier's.* Thus, he was not only receiving unsolicited commissions to illustrate stories, but he had also achieved the status of an illustrator who is featured for his own work alone.

Perhaps inspired by painter-illustrator friends such as John Sloan to study contemporary painting trends, Dove went to Europe in late May or early June 1908 for fourteen months, using the $4,000 he had saved from illustration commissions plus some financial help from his father. In France the Fauvist movement was at its height, and the Cézanne Memorial Exhibition had just been held. Dove became friends with other American artists in Paris, including painter Alfred Maurer, who had been there for ten years. The two remained close friends until Maurer's suicide in 1932. Dove also became acquainted with the avant-garde artists Max Weber, Patrick Henry Bruce, Arthur Carles, and Jo Davidson. He exhibited paintings in the 1908 and 1909 Salon d'Automne. He spent a large amount of time in the countryside, painting in southern France near Cages. Maurer arranged for him to show his paintings to Alfred Stieglitz at the "291" Gallery when Dove returned to New York City. Dove had embarked upon his abstract painting career, and for the remainder of his life he would be closely associated with and supported by Stieglitz.

Dove reportedly worked on illustration commissions after he and his wife returned from Paris, but the only published examples that have been found to date are in the May 1910 *McClure's* and in the 22 March 1913 *Harper's Weekly.* Over the years Dove occasionally wrote in letters or in his diary about how he found it difficult to divide his time and attention between painting and illustration. The two distinct styles he used were based on opposing modes of thought: one realistic, literal, and commercial; the other representing what Modernists had come to call "pure" art: individual, personal expression, stressing a unique interpretation of reality that emphasized the formal qualities of painting.

When their son, William, was born on 4 July 1910, the Doves moved to a farm in Westport, Connecticut, where Dove anticipated supporting his family by farming and painting. Within two years they moved to a second farm, Beldon Pond, near Westport, where he raised chickens, grew vegetables, and eventually fished for lobsters in an attempt to make ends meet. During these years Dove reportedly did occasional illustration jobs, but none dating between 1913 and 1919 have yet been found. He maintained close friendships with his Westport neighbors, Henry Raleigh, Ernest Fuhr, and Clive Weed, all illustrators.

Although Dove was honored by the Farm Board of the State of Connecticut for an efficiently run farm, it was small and low-profit and took long hours to maintain. He found that he had little time and energy left for painting. He asked for and was denied financial help from his father, who did not understand Dove's desire to paint or the abstract paintings he produced. Dove nevertheless continued to paint when he could, and by 1912 he had developed the style that was to place him in the forefront of modern painting in America. Stieglitz gave Dove his first solo painting exhibition at "291" in 1912, which was appropriately titled "Arthur G. Dove, First Exhibition Anywhere." Dove accompanied the exhibition when it traveled to Chicago. He was included in the 1916 "Forum Exhibition of Modern American Painters" at the Anderson Galleries in New York, a show designed to challenge the Armory Show of 1913. Stieglitz closed "291" in 1917. Dove did not exhibit his paintings again until 1924, when he participated in the "Beginnings and Landmarks of 291" exhibition at the Anderson Galleries.

In the winter of 1918–1919 Dove rented his Westport farmhouse to artist Robert L. Lambdin. Dove could find no market for his paintings at the time, and thus he chose to move back to New York City to take up illustration again, though he hoped only temporarily. Arthur and Florence Dove separated in 1920. So did their friends Clive and Helen Torr (Reds) Weed. Soon Dove bought a boat, and he and Helen Torr took up residence aboard it. They were to remain inseparable until Dove's death. Florence never gave Dove a divorce, but after she died Arthur and Reds married, on 22 April 1932.

On their forty-two-foot yawl, *Mona,* Dove again began to illustrate regularly. After years of resisting advertising and magazine work, he recommitted himself to illustration even though deep down he still regarded illustration as something to fall back on rather than his main artistic devotion. He also commented that his years of painting had influenced his illustration work for the better. Indeed, there is a strong relationship between the two. Like his paintings, his illustrations contain fluid and dynamic abstract patterns. The realistic forms in his narrative drawings are done in a manneristic style, using slightly elongated and curvilinear forms that

seem to vibrate and stretch like the forms in his paintings. This fluidity and urge to elongate especially express themselves in his drawings that employ crayon or pencil in rapid, flowing, parallel strokes.

His drawings from this time also reflect his early influences. The large, central figures of May continue to appear in much of his work. His relationship to Preston is also often visible in his quick and free strokes, especially when working in crayon or pencil.

Dove and Reds lived on the *Mona* for more than seven years, cruising Long Island Sound and mooring at Ketewomoke Yacht Club in Halesite near Huntington Harbor during the winters. The space in which they lived was small and cramped, and they were often exposed to harsh weather. It took a great deal of work to maintain the boat, but Dove loved boats and water (they appear as the inspiration for most of his paintings of this period) and felt the hardship was worth the less expensive lifestyle.

Dove regularly worked on his abstract paintings and provided illustrations for more than twenty magazines during the 1920s. He was often solicited by editors to do the work, with one job leading to another, so that he seldom had to go into New York City to seek commissions. Dove often used Reds as a model, placing her in the setting he wanted, or he drew backgrounds from his clipping file. He often traveled miles in search of material to draw for an illustration. He once made a trip to Fire Island for subject matter for a Jibby Jones story in the March 1925 issue of *The American Boy.*

Dove departed from May's strict use of pen and ink early in his career, employing a great variety of other media, depending upon the commission. After sketching from life he would make a preliminary drawing on tissue or thin paper for transfer to illustration board in thin outline. He finished the drawing in pen and ink, pencil and wash, charcoal, or grease crayon, depending upon the reproduction specifications. Dove's sinuous line and heightened color washes gave his illustrations an extraordinarily fluid effect that set his work apart from that of most other illustrators. When reproduced in black and white, these washes enhance the range of grays, giving many of them a soft, warm, translucent quality. Drawings for "Ski" by L. Cabon Hearn in the May 1919 *Century* show this fluidity of line and his elongation of figures.

Some of Dove's most humorous drawings were executed for juvenile periodicals, especially for *The American Boy* between 1920 and 1925. These must have been Dove's favorites, for his sample

Dove in France, circa 1907

Alligator-hunters of the Upper Mississippi Valley (1924).

While *The American Boy* stressed humor, *The Youth's Companion,* another juvenile magazine for which Dove drew, stuck to serious adventure stories. Dove's illustrations for these stories stressed a moment of excitement—usually a tense, dramatic one. He attained much of the feeling of suspense through his use of contrasting lights and darks. Demonstrating how he used variety in his style appropriate to his subject matter, much of this work relies more on a quick sketching style similar to Preston and the Philadelphia realists than it does on abstract shapes and ranges of gray produced through color washes.

Throughout the 1920s Dove illustrated regularly for the weekly magazine *Life.* These drawings are similar in style to those Dove did for other periodicals, but, unlike those for *The American Boy,* they do not usually reveal a sense of humor in themselves. They are vignettes of situations in which people set the stage for the jokes in the captions. The fluid, dynamic forms that make up Dove's abstract paintings sometimes appear exceptionally distinct in these illustrations, such as that for the 17 May 1923 issue of *Life,* in which the arms of a chaise lounge undulate in contrast to the rest of the composition and make the drawing appear highly stylized.

Even more notable than the influence of his abstract painting forms on his illustrations is that Dove's painting style benefited greatly from his experience as an illustrator. The sinuous line he learned to draw so well from the pen-and-ink artists appears in many of his oil and watercolor paintings, such as "River Bottom" (1923) and "Cars in Sleet Storm" (1925). The line is often drawn in black, contrasting with the paint colors and outlining the forms Dove created as he abstracted nature. This specific line is even more predominant in Dove's work of the 1930s when his illustration career had come to an end. It appears in paintings where the subject is still slightly recognizable in the image, for instance in "Below the Flood Gates" (1930), as well as in highly abstract work such as "Graphite and Blue" (1936).

In addition to the common sense of line and form, Dove's sense of rhythm and humor and his use of the anecdotal are clearly visible in many of his paintings and drawings. The placement of common objects in his paintings often provides humor that can be compared to his illustrations. These qualities can by seen in paintings such as "Fog Horns" (1929) and "Bessie of New York" (1932) and in his collages "Goin' Fishin'" (1926) and "Hand Sewing Machine" (1927).

Beginning in 1926, art collector Duncan

book had more examples from this magazine than from others. They are witty in the attitude and expression of the figures, in their compositions, in the free and flowing line, in the slight distortion of the characters, and often even in the settings. Dove's slight tendency toward caricature was just enough to accentuate the point of the humor. There is in these drawings a great deal of the kind of calligraphic vitality that recalls French drawing, for instance in the headpiece and that of the row of caged cats for the serial "The Rose-Colored Cat" in the January 1921 *The American Boy.* Dove illustrated serialized Jibby Jones stories by Ellis Parker Butler in *The American Boy* for several years. In one depicting a group of boys fishing off the limb of a tree, he provided a touch of humor to a classic American theme made famous by Winslow Homer's 1874 wood engraving "Waiting for a Bite." Dove's covers for *The American Boy* were strikingly designed, witty, and often full of action. During this time he also illustrated two of Ellis Parker Butler's books, *Jibby Jones: A Story of Mississippi River Adventure for Boys* (1923) and *Jibby Jones and the Alligator: The Story of the Young*

Phillips bought $1,000 worth of paintings each year from Dove. The money was paid in monthly installments of $75. For the stipend Phillips chose several paintings from Dove's annual exhibition at Stieglitz's gallery. In addition, when Stieglitz opened The Intimate Gallery in 1925, he sold a few of Dove's paintings a year to other clients.

In the winter of 1928–1929 Dove and Reds accepted an offer to be winter caretakers of property on Pratt's Islands across Long Island Sound. The following spring they moved permanently from the boat and took a thirty-by-forty-foot space on the second floor of Halesite's Ketewomoke Yacht Club, which had a view of the harbor. In lieu of paying rent Dove acted as caretaker for the moored boats, and he and Reds threw an annual party for the club members. Dove was able to be more productive in this period because living was easier and because he had more space in which to work. Reds continued to pose for his illustrations and helped him prepare his paintings for the annual exhibitions at Stieglitz's gallery. She also continued to work on her own paintings.

In the 1920s and 1930s photography increasingly replaced drawing in advertisements, covers of magazines, and nonfiction articles. Opportunities for illustration commissions were also adversely affected by the stock market crash of 1929. In September, Dove received one of his last large commissions, a $1,000 job from *Liberty* to illustrate a five-part story. Only a few unsolicited jobs were offered to him in 1930 and 1931, including four advertisements for Squibbs. Commissions were so few that Dove no longer even made the rounds of magazine offices in New York to look for jobs. Except for one unpublished series of drawings, Dove did not illustrate after 1931. He and Reds supported themselves by the sale of a few paintings each year to Duncan Phillips and with odd handcraft jobs Reds obtained. They married in 1932 while living at the Yacht Club.

Dove and his brother, Paul, inherited the family holdings in Geneva when their mother died in 1933. The estate had been poorly managed since their father's death in 1921 and was close to bankruptcy. The brick factory was closed; taxes had not been paid on any of the property for some time; and debts had accrued from the costs of their mother's illness. The Doves sold the *Mona* and in July moved into and renovated a small farmhouse on the family property in Geneva in an attempt to straighten things out. They and Paul tried to raise money to pay

debts and taxes by renting and selling what they could of the family estate, which consisted of two farmhouses, two houses in town, the land, the Dove Block building, and the factory. Because they were cash poor at the height of the Depression, one piece of land after another had to be sold for taxes. Dove also tried to farm the land he did not rent out. They even turned the large family home into apartments. In May 1934 they sold the small farmhouse and moved into the larger house on the farm. They again had to do major renovations to make it livable. This second house was sold for taxes in 1937, so they moved to the top floor of Dove Block. The sixty-by-seventy-foot space had originally been an armory, then an auditorium, and just before their occupancy a skating rink. They had to work hard to make it livable.

Dove spent much of his time trying to settle the estate, and this distracted him from his art. He made one attempt to illustrate during these years. The offer came unsolicited by mail, but the drawings he produced in response were rejected as being too "literal." There is no record that Dove tried to get an illustration job again. He did continue to work at his painting, however. When he made his annual trek to his exhibition at The Intimate Gallery in New York City in 1938, he never returned to Geneva. With $980 from a sale to Duncan Phillips he bought an old post office building in Centerport, New York. It was a twenty-foot-square, one-room structure that jutted into an outlet on Long Island Sound.

Dove and Reds immediately moved in and began to adapt it for living. Dove had taken ill with pneumonia while he was in New York City, however. In January 1939 he had a severe heart atttack. Subsequently, Bright's disease, a serious kidney disorder, incapacitated him for a year. In spite of poor health, he continued to paint. Sales were increasing, and he had fewer financial worries than he had had since his early years as an illustrator in New York. Around the time Alfred Stieglitz died in 1946, Dove had another heart attack. One side of his body was paralyzed, and he could paint only with help from Reds, who steadied his hand and moved it as he directed. He died on 22 November 1946 in a hospital in Huntington.

The standards of the Modernist movement and the notion of art for art's sake resulted in the opinion that commercial art was void of "pure" meaning and thus was of lower status. Dove, who practiced illustration, therefore came under suspicion as one whose paintings could not possibly

" 'An officer is not allowed to strike us drafted
men. I know the law. I shall report you to my
uncle' "

*Illustration by Dove for Howard H. Brown's "A Casual Affair," published in the
February 1920 issue of* Century Magazine

be of high quality or intellectual value. This hierarchy formed Dove's attitude toward illustration. In the 1920s he did not participate in the illustrators' community. He was only minimally active in seeking commissions and did not seek recognition or participate in exhibitions. His professional focus was on his abstract painting; illustration served only to support his efforts to succeed financially in painting. Thus, Dove's illustration work was not reviewed by contemporary critics, and this part of his career was not reported.

Yet Dove's career as an illustrator was not only rich and long, but it also formed his abstract painting style. He developed a distinctive, individual style of drawing that lent to his abstract paintings their calligraphic lines, simplified shapes, spontaneity, rhythm, fluidity, sense of anecdote, and humor. As Dove's illustration style evolved, he gradually incorporated these elements into his abstract painting, transforming the Fauvist-inspired style of his early painting into an abstract style distinctly his own. Illustration, the "inferior aesthetic," provided Dove with inspiration and technique for his avant-garde painting.

References:

Abraham Davidson, *Early American Modernist Painting 1910–1935* (New York: Harper & Row, 1981);

Barbara Haskell, *Arthur Dove* (Boston: New York Graphic Society, 1974);

Jim Jordan, "Arthur G. Dove and the Nature of the Image," *Arts Magazine,* 50 (February 1976): 89–91;

Ann Lee Morgan, *Arthur Dove: Life and Work, with a Catalogue Raisonne* (Newark: University of Delaware Press, 1984);

Sasha H. Newman, *Arthur Dove and Duncan Phillips: Artist and Patron* (New York: Braziller, 1981);

Frederick S. Wight, *Arthur G. Dove* (Berkeley: University of California Press, 1958);

Susan Fillin Yeh, "Innovative Moderns: Arthur G. Dove and Georgia O'Keeffe," *Arts Magazine,* 56 (June 1982): 68–72.

Archives:

Collections of Arthur G. Dove's papers are held by the Alfred Stieglitz Archive, Collection of American Literature, Beinecke Library, Yale University; the Archives of American Art, Smithsonian Institution, Washington, D.C.; and the Van Wyck Brooks Collection, University of Pennsylvania Library, Philadelphia.

Harvey Thomas Dunn

(8 March 1884 – 29 October 1952)

Jackie R. Esposito
Pennsylvania State University

SELECTED BOOKS ILLUSTRATED: Hornung, E. W., *Dead Men Tell No Tales* (New York: Scribners, 1906);

Hornung, *The Shadow of the Rope* (New York: Scribners, 1906);

Parker, Gilbert, *Northern Lights* (New York & London: Harper, 1909);

Beach, Rex, *The Silver Horde: A Novel* (New York & London: Harper, 1909);

Rhodes, Eugene M., *Good Men and True* (New York: Holt, 1910);

Greene, Harry I., *Barbara of the Snows* (New York: Moffat, Yard, 1911);

Wister, Owen, *Members of the Family* (New York: Macmillan, 1911);

London, Jack, *John Barleycorn* (New York: Century, 1913);

Brooks, Noah, *The Boy Emigrants* (New York: Scribners, 1914);

Stringer, Arthur, *The Prairie Wife: A Novel* (Indianapolis: Bobbs-Merrill, 1915);

Kyne, Peter B., *Cappy Ricks; or, The Subjugation of Matt Peasley* (New York: H. K. Fly, 1916);

Rhodes, Eugene M., *The Desire of the Moth* (New York: Holt, 1916);

Grimshaw, Beatrice Ethel, *My Lady of the Island: A Tale of the South Seas* (Chicago: McClurg, 1916);

Irwin, Inez Haynes, *The Happy Years* (New York: Holt, 1919);

Dickens, Charles, *A Tale of Two Cities* (New York: Cosmopolitan, 1921);

Advertising Arts and Crafts, Volume 1, National Edition (New York: Lee & Kirby, 1926);

Wood, William, and Ralph H. Gabriel, *In Defense of Liberty* (New Haven: Yale University Press, 1928);

Dunn, and others, *The Howard Pyle Brandywine Edition: 1853–1933* (New York: Scribners, 1933);

Pyle, Howard, *The Story of Sir Launcelot and His Companions,* Howard Pyle Brandywine Edition, 1853–1933 (New York: Scribners, 1933);

Harvey Dunn in his studio, Tenafly, New Jersey

Hydeman, Sid, *How to Illustrate for Money* (New York & London: Harper, 1936);

Peattie, Donald C., *Jedediah Smith–Trailmaker Extraordinary* (Stockton, Cal.: Jedediah Smith Society, n.d.).

PERIODICALS: *Harper's Weekly,* 1904–1916;
Collier's, 1904–1920;
Century Magazine, 1906–1913;
Scribner's Magazine, 1906–1930;
The Saturday Evening Post, 1906–1939;
Outing, 1909–1923;
Cosmopolitan, 1919–1929;
American Legion Monthly, 1928–1938.

Harvey Thomas Dunn ranks as one of the greatest teachers of American illustration in the early twentieth century. Known for his bold colors and dramatic style as well as for his championing of the art of the pioneer Midwest, Dunn's tremendous output of illustrative work in periodicals, advertising, and books helped make him one of the most popular and influential artists in the field of American illustration.

Born on 8 March 1884 near Manchester and De Smet, Kingsbury County, Dakota Territory (South Dakota), Harvey Dunn was the second child of three born to homesteaders Thomas and Bersha Dow Dunn. His parents came to Dakota from Wisconsin in 1882 to farm a quarter section of land that Thomas had claimed in 1880. The farm was along Redstone Creek, a tributary of the James River, parallel to a buffalo trail. Because the country was going through a period of economic recession and several memorable droughts, the Dunn family was forced to move their homestead (including the house) to Esmond Township when young Harvey was only four. For nine years he attended a single-room schoolhouse in the township.

At a young age Dunn exhibited an eagerness for drawing; in fact, his propensity for sketching in class caused his teacher to hide her chalk from the avid young artist to preserve it. By the age of fourteen he was capable of taking over some of the farmwork–plowing, planting, cultivating, and traversing the family's farmland–but he still pursued his art, drawing by the light of a kerosene lamp in the evenings.

In 1901 at the age of seventeen Dunn, already a huge man physically, left the farm and entered the South Dakota Agriculture College in Brookings as a student in the preparatory course. During his second term he met a young art teacher, Ada B. Caldwell, who was to become his first true artistic inspiration. Edgar M. Howell quotes Dunn's recollections: "Ada Caldwell opened vistas for me. For the first time I had found a serious, loving, and intelligent interest in what I was vaguely searching for. She seemed to dig out talent where none had been and she prayed for genius. She was tolerant and the seal of goodness. With my eyes on the horizon, she taught me where to put my feet."

Caldwell encouraged Dunn's fledgling talent and prompted his 1902 move to the Chicago Art Institute, where he stayed until 1904. His first year in Chicago proved to be memorable for Dunn's family as well; his parents sold their South Dakota homestead and moved to the plains of central Saskatchewan, Canada. Although the departures physically separated the family from South Dakota, they never quite severed Dunn's ties with his birthplace.

Dunn's years at the institute were not particularly noteworthy; nevertheless, they marked Dunn's transition from farm boy to man. He worked hard to develop his drawing skills and to support himself, and he held a variety of odd jobs including work as an artist's model. The requirements of the institute provided Dunn with the opportunity to express himself on paper and canvas as never before, and his talents were encouraged by the staff.

In 1904 Dunn was chosen to join the ranks of students instructed by the noted illustrator and teacher Howard Pyle. Hundreds of art students applied to study under Pyle, who has been acknowledged as the father of modern illustration, but fewer than six were chosen each year. Dunn joined such promising talents as William Henry Koerner, Frank Schoonover, and N. C. Wyeth at Pyle's Brandywine studio in Delaware. He eagerly absorbed his new mentor's message and thoroughly embraced the concepts that Henry C. Pitz, writing about Pyle's students in the January 1969 issue of *American Artist,* described as "masculine vigor, shining color, and ample design" in his work. Dunn remained with Pyle until 1906 when the teacher said the young artist was ready to start his own career. Dunn's affection for Pyle would continue throughout his entire life and would culminate in the compilation of a memorial volume as part of the Howard Pyle Brandywine Edition, 1853–1933, which was published by Scribners in 1933.

During his years with Pyle, Dunn sold his first illustration, a drawing of a railway locomotive, for the "princely" sum of fifty dollars. He also began his artistic association with *The Saturday Evening Post* when his illustration for Rupert Hughes's "Mabel's Choice of Cowards" was published in June 1906. His association with this magazine comprised more than 250 illustrations and lasted until 1939, when Dunn ended the relationship in a dispute over the accuracy of an illustration.

After leaving Pyle, Dunn set up his own studio in Delaware and began work as a commercial illustrator. His first commercial contract was an illustration produced for Kieffel and Esser of New York. That same year he received commissions to illustrate two mystery books by E. W. Hornung: *Dead Men Tell No Tales* and *The Shadow of the Rope.* Dunn's dramatic style was perfectly suited to this genre of literature, and he found almost instant success creating book and magazine illustrations for mysteries, Westerns, romance stories, and other kinds of popular fiction. In the eight years that followed he illustrated books for many authors, including Eugene

Frontispiece for E. W. Hornung's The Shadow of the Rope
(1906), one of Dunn's earliest book illustrations

M. Rhodes's *Good Men and True* (1910) and Jack London's *John Barleycorn* (1913), and worked for several prominent publishing houses including Holt, Scribners, and Harper.

In addition to his book illustrations, Dunn regularly contributed to *Century, Collier's, Cosmopolitan, Harper's Weekly, Outing,* and *Scribner's Magazine,* as well as the *Post.* He was equally comfortable creating images for advertisements, and he quickly developed an audience for his unique, bold style. He drew illustrations for Coca-Cola, Steinway and Sons, Maxwell House Coffee, Texaco, Sinclair, and John Hancock Mutual Life Insurance, among others.

Dunn's reputation for prompt delivery combined with his voluminous output led him to characterize himself as a businessman-artist, but he never allowed the business side to overshadow his artwork. He believed that an artist must be a part of his picture and that no matter what the subject, the artist should inject a lifelike quality into it. His vigorous and painterly approach to color was modified

by the sympathy and perception he had for his subjects.

While apprenticing in Delaware, Dunn met and courted his wife, Johanne "Tulla" Louise Krebs. Her father, a manufacturer of paint pigments in Wilmington, had started as a chemist for DuPont and had made a fortune accepting payment from DuPont in stock. Dunn and Tulla were married on 12 March 1908 in the Unitarian Church, although later they both became followers of Christian Science. The wedding was attended by many of Dunn's fellow-artist friends, with N. C. Wyeth serving as his best man. The Dunns had two children: Robert, born 3 July 1911, and Louise, born 3 November 1912. A third child, another son, died in infancy.

By 1909 Dunn's rich painting, muted colors, and mood-charged pictures were attracting a great deal of attention. His production was monumental; a favorite story about Dunn recounts his producing fifty-five illustrations in eleven weeks for various clients. Due to the demand for his work he decided to move his young family closer to the art markets and relocated from Wilmington to Leonia, New Jersey, directly across the Hudson River from New York City.

The sudden death of Pyle in 1911 in Italy, the influence of Caldwell, and popular demand all spurred Dunn to establish his own art school in 1915. With Charles S. Chapman, Dunn established the Leonia School of Illustration, which would eventually evolve into the Dunn School of Illustration. Among his pupils were Art Mitchell, Grant Reynard, Dean Cornwell, Steven Kidd, Rico Tomaso, Harold Von Schmidt, Mario Cooper, and Dwight Franklin. He also taught at the Art Students League and the Grand Central School of Art in New York, and in the Tenafly, New Jersey, public schools.

Of all the contributions Dunn made to the art world in his long and distinguished career, he himself believed that teaching was the most important. Emulating the style of his mentor Pyle, Dunn tried to instill his idealism and artistic principles into his students. His teaching philosophy focused on his belief that an artist should emphasize the drama within his art, painting the epic rather than the commonplace. Dunn promoted an artistic tradition centered on a concern with human values and a delight in pictorial imagination. Dunn also believed that, properly done, an artist's work should need no explanation; he did not care for titling his pictures and only did so for purposes of identification.

In early 1918 Dunn completed a series of paintings commemorating Hector Berlioz's *Fantastic*

Symphony, Franz Schubert's *The Erl King,* and Richard Wagner's *Tristan and Isolde* for Steinway and Sons. These were the last fanciful images Dunn produced for some time; soon after, an event occurred that profoundly affected his outlook on life.

After the United States became actively involved in World War I, the U.S. government created a Division of Pictorial Publicity as part of the Office of Public Information. The task of the division was to rally support (by means of posters and other forms of publicity) for the American involvement in the war. Headed by Charles Dana Gibson, the division included such artists as Dunn, William Aylward, George Harding, Ernest Peixotto, and Harry Townsend (all former students of Pyle), along with Walter Duncan, James Montgomery Flagg, Wallace Morgan, and J. Andre Smith. In addition to their public-relations work on the home front, the artists were charged with chronicling the American Expeditionary Force (AEF) in action in Europe. Dunn was commissioned as a captain of engineers in March 1918 and spent most of his time painting and sketching the AEF in France until his discharge in April 1919. His objective portrayal of the effects of the war on civilians and servicemen created a valuable visual record although Dunn disliked depicting the despair and violence he witnessed. His *American Machine Gunner* (1918) is the most often reproduced image depicting the war. The strapping, square-jawed soldier seemed the archetypal doughboy. This image, along with his portfolio of sketches from the war, made him one of the best known and most popular of American combat artists of this period.

After the war Dunn had hoped to spend three months to a year reworking his battlefield sketches and even traveling back to France to refresh his memory. However, his discharge from the army, which he considered premature (only two months after returning from France), discouraged him from devoting the time he felt he needed to further develop his war work. A long period of soul-searching and anguish followed his return home. In 1925 he returned to Europe to tour the battlefields with his son, Robert, in an effort to reconcile himself with his feelings about the devastation caused by the war. Three years later his paintings and drawings of the war began to appear on the covers of the *American Legion Monthly,* providing Dunn with enough exposure to reinforce his position as a premier World War I artist.

In 1919 Dunn moved the family and his studio to Tenafly, New Jersey, where he lived until his death in 1952. Teaching became the center of his life after the war. One of Dunn's students, Dean Cornwell (who would go on to become a leading illustrator for *Red Book*), remembered that Dunn was hardest on his best students. Despite his sometimes strict attitude toward them, many of his students would become lifelong friends. They encouraged him to publish his teachings, and in 1934 *An Evening in the Classroom* appeared as a privately printed limited edition of one thousand copies. This slim volume of notes taken by students outlined Dunn's teaching advice, counsel, witticisms, and comments. In it Dunn reasserted his basic philosophy that as artists his students "had to become the character they were trying to visualize . . . the expression of any character was really only the expression of themselves."

Dunn became more introspective after the war. He began a series of annual visits to South Dakota for the Kingsbury County Old Settlers' Day celebrations and focused his art on depicting the life he remembered in South Dakota. Dunn often spoke of his attachment to his roots, and it is no surprise that his natural talents gravitated toward illustrations of the pioneer country of the West. He dedi-

THE GIRL STOOD BAREHEADED UNDER THE WINTRY SKY

Frontispiece by Dunn for Rex Beach's The Silver Horde *(1909)*

In Search of an Eldorado *(1938), illustration by Dunn for* The Saturday Evening Post

cated himself to portraying the life of prairie pioneers and what Pitz called the "unending mystery of just ordinary people." He celebrated the grandeur of the land and the sturdy, self-reliant men and women who endured hard labor to tame it. Ever the perfectionist, Dunn insisted on sketching subjects from real life with a straightforward and honest approach.

In 1938 his original mentor Caldwell died. Dunn was commissioned to paint her portrait for the South Dakota State College yearbook, *Jack Rabbit,* and this event signaled the beginning of his long association with and devotion to bringing South Dakota art back to the people of that state. For twenty-five years Dunn continued to make his annual summer visits, although none was more satisfying than his 1950 trip to display forty-two of his paintings in his hometown of De Smet. Instigated by old friend and publisher Aubrey Sherwood, the exhibit created overwhelming local response. More than five thousand visitors registered at the exhibition, and Dunn talked to many of them personally. In the final week of the exhibit, the president of South Da-

kota State College, Dr. Fred H. Leinbach, persuaded Dunn to leave the paintings to the people of South Dakota. In August 1950 the college (now university) accepted permanent custodianship of the collection, which was subsequently augmented.

Dunn also created murals, including an expansive five-panel mural of the Lord and Taylor department store of New York for its centennial. Dunn won recognition among his peers as well, becoming an associate member of the National Academy of Design in 1935 and a National Academician in 1945. He served as president of the Society of Illustrators from 1948 to 1951 and was a member of the Salmagundi Club and the Artists' Guild; he was also a Freemason. In 1952 South Dakota State College conferred an honorary Doctor of Fine Arts degree on Dunn. The official citation read:

South Dakota can be thankful that our homesteader stock and our prairies produced such a man as Harvey Dunn—painter, illustrator, philosopher, and American . . . his love for the prairies and their people has brought him to depict them for generations to appreciate . . . for his contributions as painter and teacher; for the color, character, honesty and historical merit of his art in preserving the recollections of prairie settlement . . . we can take pleasure and pride in honoring him.

Unfortunately, the artist who had done so much to raise awareness of the art of South Dakota was too ill to attend the ceremony. Dunn died soon after of cancer at his Tenafly home on 29 October 1952. He was survived by his wife; children; brother, Roy; sister, Caroline; and five grandchildren.

A memorial service was held for Dunn in his studio on 8 November 1952. Nearly two hundred people attended, including family members, acclaimed artists, and former students. Von Schmidt gave the eulogy, holding Dunn's artist palette. As recorded in Robert F. Karolevitz's 1970 biography of Dunn, Von Schmidt spoke movingly of his former teacher, remembering him as "Harvey Dunn—illustrator, teacher, poet, man. It was my privilege to know him as all four. . . . He gave freely of himself. . . . His high intolerance [of mediocrity or laziness] matched his honesty in the keeping of his code. This code was service—service as he saw and knew it. Gentle as only a big man can be, he could use both quirt and spur when needed. . . . Not only did he make us [his students] better illustrators—he made us better men."

Bibliography:

Jeff Dykes, "Harvey Thomas Dunn, 1884–1952," in his *Fifty Great Western Illustrators: A Bibliographic Checklist* (Flagstaff, Ariz.: Northland Press, 1975), pp. 109–115.

Biography:

Robert F. Karolevitz, *The Prairie Is My Garden: The Story of Harvey Dunn, Artist* (Aberdeen, S.D.: North Plains Press, 1969); expanded as *Where Your Heart Is: The Story of Harvey Dunn, Artist* (Aberdeen, S.D.: North Plains Press, 1970).

References:

William T. Anderson, "Plowing & Painting the Prairie: Dakota Farm Boy Harvey Dunn Portrayed Brave Pioneers in a Harsh Land," *American West,* 22 (May/June 1985): 38–43;

Patricia J. Broder, *Dean Cornwell: Dean of Illustrators* (New York: Watson-Guptill, 1978);

Alfred Emile Cornebise, *Art From the Trenches: America's Uniformed Artists in World War I* (College Station: Texas A&M University Press, 1991);

An Evening in the Classroom: Being Notes Taken by Miss Taylor in One of the Classes in Painting Conducted by Harvey Dunn and Printed at the Instigation of Mario Cooper (Tenafly, N.J.: Privately printed, 1934);

Charles W. Ferguson, "Americans Not Everybody Knows: Harvey Dunn," *PTA Magazine,* 62 (January 1968): 10–12;

Harvey Dunn, Son of the Middle Border (Brookings, S.D.: South Dakota Memorial Art Center, 1984);

Edgar M. Howell, *Harvey Dunn: Painter of Pioneers,* Montana Heritage Series, no. 15 (Helena: Montana Historical Society, 1968);

Howell, "The Look of the Last Frontier," *American Heritage,* 9 (June 1961): 41;

John E. Miller, "Manchester: Harvey Dunn Country," in his *Looking for History on Highway 14* (Ames: Iowa State University Press, 1993), pp. 64–76;

Ruth G. Patterson, *The Influence of Howard Pyle on American Illustration* (Rochester, N.Y.: University of Rochester Press for ACRL, 1955);

Henry C. Pitz, *The Brandywine Tradition* (Boston: Houghton Mifflin, 1969);

Pitz, "Four Disciples of Howard Pyle," *American Artist,* 33 (January 1969): 38–43;

Mari Sandoz, "Dakota Country," *American Heritage,* 9 (June 1961): 43–53.

Archives:

Dunn's papers and the largest collection of his art are located at the South Dakota Memorial Art Center, South Dakota State University, Brookings, South Dakota. Significant collections of original art can also be found at the Smithsonian Institution; the Brandywine River Museum, Chadds Ford, Pennsylvania; the U.S. Military Academy at West Point; and the Steinway Collection of Paintings, Metropolitan Museum of Art, New York.

W. Herbert Dunton
(28 August 1878 – 18 March 1936)

Michael R. Grauer
Panhandle-Plains Historical Museum

WRITINGS: "A Suburban Grouse Hunt," *Amateur Sportsman,* 21 (May 1899): 14–15;

"A Day's Trouting," *Amateur Sportsman,* 21 (July 1899): 3–5;

"A Day with the Ducks," *Amateur Sportsman,* 21 (October 1899): 5–8;

"Bill Leavitt's B'ar," *Amateur Sportsman,* 22 (November 1899): 4–7;

"Madge at Limpid River," *National Sportsman,* 5 (November 1900): 441–448;

"One Christmas of Ye Olden Time," *National Sportsman,* 5 (December 1900): 533–539;

"An August Trouting Trip," *Amateur Sportsman,* 24 (January 1901): 7–10;

"Our First Fox Hunt," *National Sportsman,* 6 (January 1901): 31–36;

"A Real Hero, a Story of the Plains," *National Sportsman,* 6 (February 1901): 132–137;

"Ducks from Temple Lake Blinds," *Field and Stream,* 6 (March 1901): 461–465;

"Sam Nelson's First Grizzly," *National Sportsman,* 6 (March 1901): 235–240;

"A Week in Winter's Camp," *National Sportsman,* 6 (April 1901): 296–302;

"Brook Trouting," *National Sportsman,* 6 (May 1901): 425–430;

"A Joke on the Joker: The Singular Result of a Bass Fishing Trip," *National Sportsman,* 6 (June 1901): 410–417;

"The Fish-Pole Girl," *National Sportsman,* 7 (July 1901): 35–40;

"The Witch Hollow Hold-Up—A Christmas Tale," *Brown Book of Boston,* 4 (December 1901): 43–44, 60;

"The Fair in the Cow Country," *Scribner's Magazine,* 55 (April 1914): 454–465.

SELECTED BOOKS ILLUSTRATED: Potter, Mary Knight, *Councils of Croesus* (Boston: L. C. Page, 1902);

Braden, James A., *Connecticut Boys in the Western Reserve* (Akron, Chicago & New York: Saalfield, 1903);

W. Herbert Dunton in 1932 (photograph by Will Connell)

Thwing, Eugene, *The Red-Keggers* (New York: Book-Lover Press, 1903);

Ogden, G. W., *Tennessee Todd* (New York: A. S. Barnes, 1903);

Hains, Thornton Jenkins, *The Black Barque* (Boston: L. C. Page, 1905);

Wilson, Bingham Thoburn, *The Village of Hide and Seek* (New York: Consolidated Retail Booksellers, 1905);

Bindloss, Harold, *Winston of the Prairie* (New York: Stokes, 1907);

Lewis, Alfred Henry, *Wolfville Folks* (New York: Appleton, 1908);

Bronson, Edgar Beecher, *Reminiscences of a Ranchman* (Chicago: McClurg, 1910); republished as

Cowboy Life on the Western Plains (New York: Doran, 1910);

Parrish, Randall, *Keith of the Border: A Tale of the Plains* (Chicago: McClurg, 1910);

Grey, Zane, *The Young Forester* (New York: Grosset & Dunlap, 1910);

Lewis, Alfred Henry, *Faro Nell and Her Friends,* illustrated by Dunton and J. N. Marchand (New York: G. W. Dillingham, 1913);

Grey, Zane, *The Light of Western Stars* (New York & London: Harper, 1914);

Burt, Maxwell Strothers, *John O'May and Other Stories* (New York: Scribners, 1918);

Gregory, Jackson, *Judith of Blue Lake Ranch* (New York: Scribners, 1919);

Gregory, *Ladyfingers* (New York: Scribners, 1920);

Grey, Zane, *Riders of the Purple Sage* (New York & London: Harper, 1921);

Grey, *Wanderer of the Wasteland* (New York & London: Harper, 1923).

PERIODICALS: *Amateur Sportsman,* 1899–1902;
Household, 1900–1901;
Brown Book of Boston, 1900–1904;
National Sportsman, 1900–1904;
Field and Stream, 1901;
Everybody's, 1906–1910, 1912, 1914;
Munsey's, 1906, 1911–1914;
Popular Magazine, 1906–1915;
Associated Sunday Magazine, 1907–1912;
Cosmopolitan, 1907–1912, 1914;
Scribner's Magazine, 1908, 1910–1916;
Harper's Monthly, 1909–1910, 1912–1914, 1917;
Collier's, 1910–1915, 1917, 1920;
Woman's Home Companion, 1911–1913, 1919, 1921;
McClure's, 1913, 1920–1921.

When W. Herbert "Buck" Dunton moved from New York to Taos, New Mexico, in 1914, he was one of the best-known Western illustrators in the United States. His paintings of the American West had graced the pages of periodicals such as *Harper's Monthly, Popular Magazine,* and *Scribner's Magazine* as well as books by Harold Bindloss, Zane Grey, and Alfred Henry Lewis. In fact, his reputation as an illustrator and his knowledge of the West prompted the view of Dunton as the successor to Frederic Remington.

Born on 28 August 1878 in Augusta, Maine, William Herbert Dunton was the first son of William Henry Dunton and Anna Katherine Pillsbury Dunton. The elder Dunton was an amateur actor and a photographer who worked for the *Kennebec Journal* in Augusta, but little is known of the mother's occupation. Dunton grew up on a trotting-horse farm owned by his maternal grandfather, John Currier Pillsbury, and on his maternal great-grandmother's farm. Bert, as he was then called, became attracted to the outdoors at an early age, often accompanying his grandfather on explorations of the New England countryside. These early excursions formed the foundation of Dunton's love of big-game hunting and of chronicling North American wildlife. Young Dunton was different from other outdoorsmen because he often carried a sketch pad along with his rod or rifle during his outings.

Along with the outdoors, the American West gripped the imagination of the budding artist. He listened to stories and yarns about the West at his grandfather's knee and was exposed to the Western dime novels that inundated the East in the 1880s and 1890s. He spent much of his youth playing cowboy, discussing grizzly bears and Indians, and making a fantasy frontier out of a nearby pasture.

When he was sixteen his yearning to see the West became too great, and he quit school to earn money for the trip by working in a men's clothing store. In 1896 Dunton's opportunity finally arrived, and he headed west. After a brief stop at Broken Bow, Nebraska, where he sketched at the fair, he traveled until his money ran out in Livingston, Montana, although he had hoped to go farther. He soon made the acquaintance of a bear hunter with whom he hunted for nearly two years, supplying meat to ranches in Montana.

In 1897, while working as a cowboy north of Billings, Dunton may have met Western painter Charles M. Russell, who had just settled in Great Falls. Dunton idolized Russell and emulated him in some of his early work. The artists would later become good friends.

Although Dunton made several trips west between 1896 and 1911, the specific details of his travels remain ambiguous. However, he worked as a cowboy in Wyoming, Oregon, Colorado, Nebraska, New Mexico, and Mexico in addition to Montana. He confined these trips to summers and returned east to paint and study during the rest of the year.

Dunton moved to Boston in 1897 and enrolled at the Cowles Art School. He also studied with Andreas M. Andersen, William Ladd Taylor, and Joseph Rodefer DeCamp. During this time he began to pursue his illustrating career in earnest and started to receive commissions from small publishers around Boston. There Dunton met and married Nellie Hartley in 1900; three years later the couple moved to New York City searching for a larger market for his illustrations. In spite of modest success with Boston publishers, Dunton found New York

Dunton's cover for the May 1906 issue of Popular Magazine, *one of the illustrations that helped his career as a Western artist*

hard going during his first years there, and he provided illustrations for a plethora of non-Western themes such as seafaring, the Civil War, and high-society romance. He and his wife had two surviving children, Vivian and Ivan, though the marriage later ended in divorce.

Dunton's first illustrations had appeared in the May 1899 issue of the *Amateur Sportsman* accompanying an article he had written on grouse hunting. He also wrote and illustrated articles for the October and November issues, and the next year he placed illustrations in the *Brown Book of Boston* and the *National Sportsman*. Dunton's first Western illustrations appeared with stories he wrote for *National Sportsman* in 1901. His color illustrations for the covers of the May 1906 issue of *Popular Magazine* and the June 1906 issue of *Munsey's* magazine gave him important exposure. Thereafter, his stock as a Western illustrator skyrocketed, resulting in commissions from *Collier's, Cosmopolitan, Harper's Monthly,* and *Scribner's*

Magazine, and from publishers for books by Bindloss, Grey, and Lewis.

Dunton was in such demand in 1911 that *Cosmopolitan* asked him to continue illustrating the serialized autobiography of Gen. Nelson A. Miles, begun by Remington but halted by the artist's unexpected death in 1909. In May 1913 a critic for the *Los Angeles Times* wrote that Dunton was "regarded as one of the most brilliant of the younger illustrators." When Dunton completed his last commercial work in 1923 he had illustrated at least fifty-three books and nearly four hundred covers or articles for thirty-five magazines.

Dunton's career as an illustrator of Western subjects coincided with the cowboy craze that swept the country following the publication of Owen Wister's *The Virginian* in 1902. While Western dime novels had been circulating since the 1870s and Buffalo Bill's Wild West show had been touring since the early 1880s, it was *The Virginian* that gave rise to the mythological character of the great Cowboy Hero who was "young, heroic, independent, and relentlessly Anglo Saxon," as historian Lonn Taylor has written in *The American Cowboy* (1983). This genre also grew to include Western women who embodied these same traits. Dunton was the ideal man to lend authenticity to illustrations for stories that focused on the Cowboy Hero and Cowgirl Heroine.

Dunton's popularity as an illustrator of Western stories stemmed from his intimate knowledge of the subject. The majority of artists who went west to glean material for their canvases only played at being cowboys for relatively short periods of time. Although Remington boasted of his life on the range, his days as a cowboy were limited to a short period of sheep ranching in 1883 in Kansas. Perhaps second only to Remington in today's perception of illustrators of the American West, N. C. Wyeth took three trips to the West before returning to Pennsylvania with sketches from which he made many of his well-known Western paintings. Dunton worked as a cowboy and hunter in the West intermittently for fifteen years before moving there permanently in 1914. In fact, according to an unpublished biography written by his son, Ivan H. Dunton, he probably turned to painting only after cowboy work and hunting proved nonlucrative.

Besides Russell, only Dunton had experienced and made his living in the Old West, albeit as it was passing away. Like many others he was a great collector of Western garb and weapons. Yet, whether the pictures were en grisaille or in color, Dunton was never compelled to disguise a lack of knowledge of the West behind gear and trappings. Instead, his Western

Whooping It Up, illustration by Dunton for Marion Sherrard's "A Big Breezes Kaleidoscope: The Montana Schoolmarm's View of Daily Life in a Town That's Still Wild," in the 5 October 1912 issue of Collier's

experiences spawned authentic Western figures, characters, and situations. Unlike Wyeth, for example, Dunton never exaggerated poses or distorted facial expressions to the point of caricature.

The figures in Dunton's Western illustrations are cut from the Cowboy Hero mold, but they are nevertheless believable; this quality is what separates Dunton from his illustrator peers. Dunton's illustrations rarely display the air of artificiality or fantasy integral to the work of most illustrators. Dunton allowed the dirt and grit of the West to seep into his pictures; his West was not a dream, but real.

Dunton obviously scrutinized the work of his peers, and he owed his greatest debt to Remington. In terms of solutions to ideas for illustrations, Dunton looked to Remington as an example more often than to any other artist. For *The Breed Trapper, 1830* (1913), frontispiece for the July 1914 issue of *Scribner's Magazine,* Dunton clearly paid homage to Remington's well-known *Indian Trapper* (1889), first reproduced in *Harper's New Monthly Magazine* in 1891. Similarly, some Dunton titles are virtually identical to some of Remington's, and the paintings to which these titles were applied are quite similar to those of Remington. Dunton's *The First Lesson,* used for the April 1911 cover of *Popular Magazine* and painted from sketches made in Mexico, harkens back to Remington's *His First Lesson,* first reproduced in color in *Collier's* (16 September 1903).

However, Dunton did not merely copy Remington. Rather, in pursuing a similar subject Dunton, like all artists throughout history, looked to a recognized master of a certain genre for possible approaches. Consequently, Dunton was compared favorably to Remington in the press and was often called the "Southwestern Remington" or "Remington of the Southwest."

Although he was considered a "mere illustrator," by 1908 Dunton had made important inroads with the New York art establishment to the extent that he was elected to the exclusive social fraternity of artists, the Salmagundi Club. About this time he began studies at the Art Students League under illustrators Frederick C. Yohn, Frank V. DuMond, and Ernest L. Blumenschein.

Dunton divulged to Blumenschein his growing dissatisfaction with the grind of commercial illustration. Blumenschein then encouraged Dunton to visit Taos, New Mexico, and paint the spirit of the West rather than simply the West of cowboys and Indians. Dunton decided to take his teacher's advice; his June 1912 visit to the New Mexico village was followed by visits the next summer and a permanent move there in 1914. Thus began the second phase of his career, although he did not give up illustration completely until 1923. In 1915 Dunton became one of the founding members of the Taos Society of Artists and remained a member until 1922.

The consequences of Dunton's move were dire. Relinquishing the financial security of illustration commissions, Dunton lived in near poverty for much of the rest of his life. Moreover, not only did he fall from grace as an illustrator, with his accomplishments in that arena now largely forgotten, but also ironically many of his easel paintings are dismissed from serious consideration by American art historians today because they are too "illustrative" or "literal."

Dunton initially saw Taos and the surrounding landscape through the eyes of an illustrator—as a background for paintings of the Old West. In a 10 May 1913 article for the *Los Angeles Times* Dunton said:

> This is the ideal place for me because there are more varieties of atmosphere than I have found in any other place. Up in the high hills one can get the right setting for old trapper pictures. There are several varieties of sage and cactus for backgrounds, according to the elevation you choose. The Taos Indians are as fine types as I have ever seen and if one wants to paint a Mexican picture he can get a background almost anywhere near Taos that you would swear was a transplanted bit of Old Mexico.

Dunton's first paintings in Taos, such as *The Breed Trapper, 1830,* demonstrate his use of the Taos area as settings for Old West compositions.

Northern New Mexico, with its strange, clear atmosphere and intense light, stunned Dunton as it did many artists. This environment may have hastened his interest in the effects of outdoor painting as opposed to studio compositions, denoting a marked shift in his work.

A brightening of palette and a slight loosening of brushwork are characteristic of Dunton's work between 1912 and 1920, and these qualities align him with other American artists who were showing the effects of French Impressionism in their own work. American Impressionists—such as Childe Hassam, John H. Twachtman, and J. Alden Weir—were an integral part of the conservative milieu in the United States. However, American Impressionism never took the dissolution of forms to the extent of French Impressionism. Dunton's paintings during this phase show his sensitivity to different light effects on a variety of surfaces at different times of the year and place him in the category with his contemporaries back east.

Although dressing as a cowboy made Dunton an anomaly among his gentlemen-painter *compadres* in Taos, his work shared characteristics with many of his fellow artists there. His interest in light effects aligned him with such Taos painters as Walter Ufer

and Victor Higgins. His preoccupation with the Old West of cowboys also found a kindred spirit in Oscar Berninghaus. Though much of Dunton's work focused on Anglos or wildlife of the Taos area, he periodically turned to the Taos Indians as subjects, certainly more often than is usually considered. Like E. Irving Couse and Joseph Henry Sharp, Dunton clothed his models in the garb of the Northern Plains Indians, a stereotype left over from nineteenth-century American art. However, Dunton broke with that tradition in the late 1920s with a series of portrait drawings of Taos Indians. Yet Dunton's work in Taos shows the greatest formal similarity with that of his former teacher Blumenschein.

Dunton's dire financial straits were relieved somewhat in 1920 when he was asked to provide illustrations for two Zane Grey masterpieces. Grey's *Wanderer of the Wasteland* was serialized in *McClure's* from June 1920 through May 1921, and Dunton created twenty-one paintings en grisaille for the commission.

In 1921 a special edition of Grey's *Riders of the Purple Sage* was published by Harper and Brothers with eleven freshly painted Dunton illustrations. Dunton reached his zenith as an illustrator with the *Riders of the Purple Sage* commission. While augmenting the story, his paintings for the commission are consistent with contemporaneous works in their palette, and the early stylization and repetition of forms are characteristic of and integral to Dunton's mature style.

In 1923 Harper published Grey's *Wanderer of the Wasteland* with three of the *McClure's* illustrations by Dunton. Unfortunately—and disappointingly after the beauty of *Riders of the Purple Sage*—the illustrations in the latter book were reproduced en grisaille. Nevertheless, *McClure's* and Harper clearly saw Dunton as the only painter of the time capable of handling their commission even though he had left the commercial art field some years before. Dunton's status as a premier Western illustrator and painter remained intact.

Dunton resigned from the Taos Society of Artists in 1922, either because he protested an insult by Ufer to Blumenschein or because he was reluctant to serve his turn as secretary of the society. Although he retained his associations with most of the members, his resignation forced him to market his own paintings. While he continued to send paintings to the annuals in Chicago, Philadelphia, and New York, he also arranged and accompanied traveling exhibitions of his work in the Midwest, Texas, and Oklahoma. He exhibited in Kansas City, Missouri; Tulsa and Ponca City, Oklahoma; and the major cities in Texas—Amarillo, Dallas, El Paso,

Fort Worth, Galveston, Houston, and San Antonio–between 1922 and the early 1930s.

In the early 1920s Dunton's easel work shifted again, both stylistically and philosophically, into what can be called his mature style. The stylistic shift was probably due, at least partially, to instruction he received from Russian artist Leon Gaspard, who had moved to Taos in 1918. Although the effects of Gaspard are difficult to discern in Dunton's work after 1918, the emotive power of the brushstroke and an even richer palette are perhaps the clearest influences. His work of this period exhibits a marked use of organized brushstrokes, in some cases resulting in almost mosaic-like areas in his paintings.

Dunton's subject emphasis also shifted again. Instead of concentrating solely on the Old West (which by then had virtually disappeared), he turned to subjects of contemporary Western life in Taos. He chose to paint and draw these subjects as they existed in the present rather than as they had been. Dunton was determined to render contemporary life and characters in the Southwest although assuredly it was a selective contemporary life.

The major portraits he painted in the 1920s and 1930s are distinctly different from similar images of a decade earlier: the later portraits no longer have the feeling of spontaneity or of having been painted outdoors. Instead they are rigidly controlled compositions, in everything from the lighting to the poses of the figures. Rather than attempting to re-create images of an Old West that was almost gone, Dunton began to render the visages of old-timers or types who had participated in the Old West, perhaps to suggest the changes wrought in Old West occupations and how these changes surfaced in the New West.

Dunton probably intended for these figure paintings to stand the test of time and somehow to act as icons or reminders of how the West was once uncomplicated by the influence of an all-too-commercial world. By carefully composing these paintings Dunton may have been indicating that he was not attempting photographic images of the Old West. Instead he put down on canvas, and thereby saved, his interpretations of the West and the values of which he was then a part before they too disappeared. He recognized that art was the ideal medium for this effort, as he was quoted in the *Pawhuska (Oklahoma) Daily Journal* in January 1925: "What is needed most now art will do. It will combat commercialism."

The third phase of Dunton's career is also marked by an emphasis on nature. While his frequent packhorse trips into the Sangre de Cristos are well known, he began to "dry-fish" and "dry-hunt"

Illustration by Dunton for Zane Grey's Wanderer of the Wasteland *(1923)*

more often, "taking" his quarry with brush or pencil rather than with rod or rifle, and his interest in pure landscape was coupled with a focus on wildlife.

For much of his life he had sketched and painted animals in the wild and in zoos. During the third phase of his career he began to integrate animals, particularly elk, deer, and bear, into simplified, stylized landscapes characterized by rich color; examples include *Black Tails (Black Tails and Aspen)* (1922), *Sunset in the Foothills* (circa 1930), and *Aspens in Autumn* (circa 1930). He also made several landscape sketches abstract in feel, such as *Sketch #6 (Ledge Pine)* (circa 1930).

Dunton achieved his compositions at this time through increased simplification and stylization of form, resulting in highly decorative canvases reflective of the Art Nouveau and Art Deco movements. However, it was with the Midwest Regionalists, especially the work of Grant Wood and certain Texas Regionalists, that Dunton has the closest associations.

While Taos has been called a Regionalist center, of the artists who worked there only Blumenschein and Dunton are truly aligned with Regionalist styles and philosophies. Dunton's acknowledged interest in contemporary life in the Southwest, and specifically around Taos, places him within the tenets of Regionalism. Further, the stylization of forms in his canvases of the late 1920s and 1930s is consistent with the highly decorative paintings of Wood, who is regarded by some as the quintessential Regionalist. Like Wood, who depicted farms and farmers indigenous to his beloved Iowa, Dunton painted the surrounding landscapes and character types—such as trappers, big-game hunters, and even cowboys—present in Taos in the 1920s and 1930s.

During his tours of Texas at this same time, Dunton became acquainted with the *Southwest Review,* a publication that extolled the virtues of Regionalism, and with the work of the Dallas Nine, a cadre of artists whose work reflected Regionalist ideals. Dunton became a close friend of Alexandre Hogue, one of the more vocal members of the Dallas group, who wrote in 1927 that Dunton's work placed him "in the front rank of living American painters."

In the early 1930s, with the Depression greatly affecting sales of paintings, Dunton turned to lithography in order to make art that was more affordable during lean times. He also painted *Fall in the Foothills* for the Public Works of Art Project in 1934, and the painting was chosen by President Franklin D. Roosevelt to hang in the White House. This was one of Dunton's last artistic successes as hard financial times were coupled with failing health. In 1935 doctors diagnosed Dunton with prostate cancer, followed by diagnoses of stomach and lung cancer in 1936. On 18 March 1936 Dunton died at the age of fifty-seven.

Dunton was at the fore of American Western illustration from 1906 until 1923 and was a tangential member of American Impressionism. His work is also allied with other Regionalist works of the late 1920s and early 1930s. Dunton was more than a cowboy painter or mere illustrator. Clearly his work ranks as some of the best figurative art produced in the United States in the first third of this century. In terms of Western illustration Dunton's skill as a painter, coupled with his firsthand knowledge of his subjects, places him near the top of the field.

Bibliography:

Jeff Dykes, "W. Herbert (Buck) Dunton, 1878–1936," in his *Fifty Great Western Illustrators: A Bibliographic Checklist* (Flagstaff, Ariz.: Northland Press, 1975), pp. 117–121.

Biography:

Julie Schimmel, *The Art and Life of W. Herbert Dunton, 1878–1936* (Austin: Published for the Stark Museum of Art by the University of Texas Press, 1984).

References:

Michael R. Grauer, "Dear Bill: The Letters of W. Herbert Dunton to Harold D. Bugbee," *Panhandle-Plains Historical Review,* 64 (1991): 1–52;

Grauer, *W. Herbert Dunton: A Retrospective* (Canyon, Tex.: Panhandle-Plains Historical Museum, 1991);

Alexandre Hogue, "W. Herbert Dunton: An Appreciation," *Southwest Review,* 13 (October 1927): 48–59;

Lonn Taylor and Ingrid Maar, comps., *The American Cowboy* (Washington, D.C.: American Folklife Center, Library of Congress / New York: Harper & Row, 1983).

Archives:

Notable collections of original art for Dunton's illustrations, as well as copies of Dunton manuscripts, are at the Stark Museum of Art, Orange, Texas; the Panhandle-Plains Historical Museum, Canyon, Texas; and the Museum of New Mexico, Santa Fe. Original manuscripts are at the Barker History Center, University of Texas at Austin. The Research Center of the Panhandle-Plains Historical museum also has more than seventy of Dunton's letters to fellow artist and illustrator Harold D. Bugbee, written between 1922 and 1935, in the Harold Dow Bugbee Collection. The unpublished biography by Ivan Dunton is in the possession of his widow.

Harry Fenn

(14? September 1837 – 21 April 1911)

Sue Rainey

WRITINGS: "The Story of Whittier's *Snow-Bound*,"
St. Nicholas, 22, no. 6 (April 1893): 427–430;
"Silk & Cedars: A Scramble in the Lebanons," *St.
Nicholas* (April 1897): 467–471;
"The Bishop and the Boy," *St. Nicholas*, 37 (June
1910): 705–706.

SELECTED BOOKS ILLUSTRATED: Goodrich,
Frank B., *The Tribute Book: A Record of the Munificence, Self-Sacrifice, and Patriotism of the American People During the War for the Union,* illustrated by Fenn and others (New York: Derby
& Miller, 1865);
Willis, Nathaniel P., *Trenton Falls,* illustrated by
Fenn and others (New York: Orr, 1865);
Whittier, John Greenleaf, *National Lyrics,* illustrated
by Fenn and others (Boston: Ticknor & Fields,
1865);
Barnard, Henry, ed., *Armsmear: The Home, the Arm,
and the Armory of Samuel Colt: A Memorial,* illustrated by Fenn and others (New York: Printed
by Alvord, 1866);
Longfellow, Henry Wadsworth, *Flower-de-Luce,* illustrated by Fenn and others (Boston: Ticknor
& Fields, 1867);
Stowe, Harriet Beecher, *Religious Poems,* illustrated
by Fenn and others (Boston: Ticknor & Fields,
1867);
Richardson, Albert D., *Beyond the Mississippi,* illustrated by Fenn and others (Hartford: National,
1867);
Holmes, Oliver Wendell, and Donald G. Mitchell,
eds., *The Atlantic Almanac,* illustrated by Fenn
and others (Boston: Ticknor & Fields, 1868);
Agassiz, Louis and Elizabeth, *A Journey in Brazil,* il-
lustrated by Fenn and others (Boston: Ticknor
& Fields, 1868);
Whittier, John Greenleaf, *Snow-Bound: A Winter Idyl*
(Boston: Ticknor & Fields, 1868);
Murray, William H. H., *Adventures in the Wilderness or
Camp-Life in the Adirondacks,* illustrated by Fenn
and others (Boston: Fields, Osgood, 1869);

Harry Fenn

New York Illustrated, illustrated by Fenn and others
(New York: Appleton, 1869);
Whittier, Greenleaf, *Ballads of New England,* illus-
trated by Fenn and others (Boston: Fields, Os-
good, 1870);
Stowe, Harriet Beecher, *Little Pussy Willow,* illus-
trated by Fenn and others (Boston: Fields, Os-
good, 1870);
Beecher, Henry Ward, *The Life of Jesus, the Christ*
(New York: Ford / Edinburgh & London: Nel-
son, 1871);
Winter Poems; by Favorite American Poets, illustrated by
Fenn and others (Boston: Fields, Osgood,
1871);

Bryant, William Cullen, *The Song of the Sower,* illustrated by Fenn and others (New York: Appleton, 1871);

Bryant, *The Story of the Fountain,* illustrated by Fenn and others (New York: Appleton, 1872);

Bryant, ed., *Picturesque America,* 2 volumes, illustrated by Fenn and others (New York: Appleton, 1872–1874);

Holland, J. G., ed., *Illustrated Library of Favorite Song,* illustrated by Fenn and others (New York: Scribner, Armstrong / Chicago: Hadley & Kane, 1873?);

Taylor, Bayard, ed., *Picturesque Europe,* 3 volumes, illustrated by Fenn and others (New York: Appleton, 1875–1879);

Bryant, William Cullen, *Poetical Works of William Cullen Bryant,* illustrated by Fenn and others (New York: Appleton, 1878);

Wilson, Charles W., ed., *Picturesque Palestine, Sinai, and Egypt,* illustrated by Fenn and John Douglas Woodward (New York: Appleton, 1881–1883; London: Virtue, 1884);

Read, T. Buchanan, *Poetical Works of T. Buchanan Read,* illustrated by Fenn and others (Philadelphia: Lippincott, 1883);

Tennyson, Alfred, *The Lady of the Lake,* illustrated by Fenn and others (Boston: Osgood, 1884);

Gray, Thomas, *Elegy Written in a Country Churchyard,* Harry Fenn Edition (Boston: Roberts, 1884);

Read, T. Buchanan, *The Wagoner of the Alleghanies,* illustrated by Fenn and others (Philadelphia: Lippincott, 1885);

Carleton, Will, *City Ballads,* illustrated by Fenn and others (New York: Harper, 1886);

Tennyson, Alfred, *The Day Dream,* illustrated by Fenn and others (New York: Dutton, 1886);

The Sermon on the Mount, illustrated by Fenn and others (Boston: Roberts, 1886);

Harrison, Constance, *Bar Harbor Days,* illustrated by Fenn and W. H. Hyde (New York: Harper, 1887);

Scott, Sir Walter, *Christmas in the Olden Time,* illustrated by Fenn and others (New York: Casswell, 1887);

Holmes, Georgiana Klingle as George Klingle, *Bethlehem to Jerusalem: A New Poem* (New York: Stokes, 1888);

Battles and Leaders of the Civil War, illustrated by Fenn and others (New York: Century, 1888);

Muir, John, *Picturesque California,* illustrated by Fenn and others (New York: Dewing, 1888);

Wilson, Edward L., *In Scripture Lands,* illustrated by Fenn and others (New York: Scribners, 1890);

I'Anson, Miles, *The Vision of Misery Hill: A Legend of the Sierra Nevada and Miscellaneous Verse,* illustrated by Fenn and others (New York: Putnam, 1891);

Conway, Moncure D., *Barons of the Potomac and the Rappahannock* (New York: Grolier Club, 1893);

Howells, William Dean, Mark Twain, and others, *The Niagara Book* (Buffalo: Underhill & Nichols, 1893);

Newkirk, Garrett, *Rhymes of the States* (New York: Century, 1896);

Tennyson, Alfred, *In Memoriam* (New York: Fords, Howard & Hulbert, 1897);

Wilson, Woodrow, *George Washington,* illustrated by Fenn and others (New York: Harper, 1897);

Wilson, *History of the American People,* 5 volumes, illustrated by Fenn and others (New York: Harper, 1902);

Shackelton, Robert and Elizabeth, *The Quest of the Colonial* (New York: Century, 1907);

Van Dyke, Henry, *Out-of-Doors in the Holy Land; Impressions of Travel in Body and Spirit* (New York: Scribners, 1908);

Schauffler, Robert Haven, *Romantic America,* illustrated by Fenn and others (New York: Century, 1913).

PERIODICALS: *Frank Leslie's Illustrated Newspaper,* 1857–1858;

Our Young Folks, 1865–1869;

Harper's Monthly, 1868–1869, 1882–1908;

Harper's Weekly, 1868–1869, 1882–1883, 1886–1890, 1894, 1896–1901;

Appletons' Journal, 1869–1872;

Hearth and Home, 1869–1870;

Every Saturday, 1871;

Illustrated Christian Weekly, 1871–1873;

Century, 1882–1911;

Youth's Companion, 1884;

St. Nicholas, 1886–1888, 1891–1903, 1910;

Scribner's Magazine, 1888, 1890–1891, 1893, 1895;

Cosmopolitan, 1891–1895;

Harper's Young People, 1891, 1896;

McClure's, 1901, 1903.

Harry Fenn was a prominent and highly prolific artist/illustrator whose images of landscape achieved great popularity in the latter half of the nineteenth century for their combination of fidelity to nature and sentiment. Reproduced primarily as wood or steel engravings through the mid 1880s and thereafter as photomechanical engravings or halftones, his works reached a wide public in books such as *Snow-Bound* (1868) and *Picturesque America* (1872–1874) and such popular magazines as *Harper's Monthly, Century,* and *St. Nicholas.* His renderings of both landscapes and architectural fea-

Scene by Fenn for Appleton's Journal *(9 October 1869)*

tures were characterized by fluidity and variety of line—delicate as well as bold; dramatically high or low viewpoints; dynamic, often diagonal, compositions; and striking contrasts of light and dark. Joseph Pennell in *Modern Illustration* counted Fenn along with Thomas Moran and John Douglas Woodward "among the pioneers of American landscape illustration." Pennell, writing in his *Pen and Ink Drawing,* also considered that Fenn "might almost be said to have invented the artistic illustration of architecture in America." Others in the generation that followed Fenn gave him credit for helping to establish and promote the use of illustrations in books and magazines. Francis Hopkinson Smith, in the persona of the Doctor in *American Illustrators,* called Fenn "the Nestor of his guild" because the great financial success of *Picturesque America* led to a prolif-

eration of illustrated publications and made the way smoother for many who came after him. In addition to his successful activity as an illustrator Fenn was a founding member of the American Watercolor Society and participated regularly in the exhibitions of that society as well as those of other organizations and institutions.

Henry Fenn, later known as Harry, was born near London in Richmond, Surrey, probably on 14 September 1837 (biographical records vary), the son of James R. Fenn, a dry-goods merchant, and Alice C. Gibbs Fenn. Fenn's interest in art was evident from an early age, as an extant sketchbook attests. A story he wrote for the June 1910 *St. Nicholas* recounted how the gift of a box of paints and brushes from a stranger who happened upon the twelve-year-old Fenn painting an old oak in Richmond Park changed his destiny. The stranger turned out to be the bishop of New Zealand, and Fenn recalled: "At home I was only a little chap who liked to amuse himself with paints. After the bishop laid his hands upon me I felt myself dedicated to the work of transcribing the beauties of the world."

Acknowledging his son's interest in art but aware of the need for practicality, Fenn's father apprenticed him to the prominent London wood-engraving firm of the Dalziel Brothers. In the 1850s, when Fenn served his term there, the Dalziels were engraving for the finest English illustrators, including Richard Doyle, John Gilbert, John Everett Millais, John Tenniel, and Birket Foster. In *The Brothers Dalziel: A Record of Fifty Years' Work 1840–1890*, George and Edward Dalziel recounted that Fenn was one of their "earliest and very cleverest pupils." While at the firm he almost certainly spent time copying some of the landscape illustrations of Foster, for the Dalziels urged their apprentices who wanted to learn drawing on wood as well as engraving to copy the landscapes of Foster and the figures of John Gilbert "as the best models for style and manner." Some of Fenn's later works clearly seem to be modeled on Foster's, especially on those in the highly acclaimed *Pictures of English Landscape* (1862). Interestingly, Fenn was described as "a pupil of Birket Foster" by the writer of "Art and Artists" in the Boston *Daily Evening Transcript* of 22 March 1887. Like Foster, Fenn became adept at depicting ordinary bits of landscape and rural life in ways that appealed to the growing nostalgia for a simpler past and the self-sufficient family farm.

In 1856 or 1857 Fenn and Charles Kingdon, who had also served his apprenticeship at the Dalziel firm, sailed for the United States, purportedly with the primary goal of seeing Niagara Falls. They stayed on, however, and, according to Budd L. Gambee in his dissertation "*Frank Leslie's Illustrated Newspaper,* 1855–1860," Fenn soon found work as a wood engraver for *Frank Leslie's Illustrated Newspaper,* contributing engravings to volumes four through six in 1857 and 1858. He may have engraved for other firms as well, in particular Nathaniel Orr and Company of New York, the firm that prepared wood engravings to illustrate the early Beadle's Dime Novels beginning in 1860. Some of Fenn's earliest designs may have been for these popular novels, for Fenn was one of the Beadle illustrators. He also attended the Graham Art School in Brooklyn, according to *A History of the Brooklyn Art Association* (1970).

In 1862 Fenn married Marian Thompson, daughter of William Thompson, a Brooklyn silver chaser, or engraver. They eventually had six chil-

dren: twin sons, one of whom died in infancy, and four daughters. The surviving son, Walter J. Fenn (1863–1961), also became an artist/illustrator. Soon after their marriage the couple sailed for England. By this time Fenn was determined to abandon wood engraving for drawing and painting. According to a September 1889 article in the *American Bookmaker,* before sailing he "gave away all his gravers, informing his fellow workers that he intended thereafter to use only pencil and brush." Fenn apparently spent some time in Italy studying painting, returning to the United States by 1863. At first he and his family lived in Brooklyn; they then moved to Montclair, New Jersey.

In the post–Civil War years Fenn was able to establish himself as a sought-after illustrator. At the same time he produced watercolors for the exhibitions of the American Watercolor Society—of English and Italian subjects from 1867 through 1869, and primarily of American landscapes from 1870 through 1874. Among his early commissions for illustrations, those in 1865 were representative of the range of subjects he would treat throughout his career: views of Trenton Falls for a guidebook; illustrations for poems of John Greenleaf Whittier; images of ships and sites connected with the Civil War for *The Tribute Book;* and depictions of plants, birds, and farm life for *Our Young Folks.* From 1865 to 1868 his design work was done either for the Nathaniel Orr firm or for Ticknor and Fields, the Boston firm that published *Our Young Folks* and many gift books of poetry, including Henry Wadsworth Longfellow's *Flower-de-Luce* (1867). Harriet Beecher Stowe must have liked his work, for he produced illustrations to accompany several of her pieces for *Our Young Folks* and a poem in *Religious Poems* (1867). Even in these early years Fenn sometimes worked from photographs as he did for *Beyond the Mississippi* (1867) by Albert D. Richardson and *A Journey in Brazil* (1868) by Louis and Elizabeth Agassiz.

By 1868 Fenn expanded his professional relationships to include New York's largest publishing firm, Harper and Brothers, where fellow Montclair resident Charles Parsons was art director. Fenn provided illustrations for both *Harper's Monthly* and *Harper's Weekly.* The same year he also undertook an assignment for Ticknor and Fields that allowed him to illustrate an entire book himself—a special illustrated edition of *Snow-Bound,* Whittier's greatest popular success, first published in 1866. This work led to Fenn's first widespread recognition. Fenn's thirty-nine designs, in formats varying from sharp rectangles to irregular vignettes, were interspersed throughout the lines of poetry and expertly engraved in wood by A. V. S. Anthony and W. J. Lin-

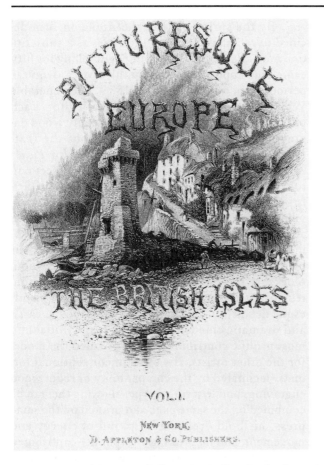

Title page and illustration by Fenn for the three-volume travelogue edited by Bayard Taylor (1875–1879)

ton. His designs achieved harmony with variety, considered a hallmark of the picturesque. In a prefatory note Whittier commended Fenn's illustrations for their "faithfulness" to "the spirit and the details of the passages and places" in his ballad. Indeed, Fenn had gone to considerable lengths to achieve this faithfulness. He related in the April 1893 *St. Nicholas* that by 1868 Whittier's boyhood home was so changed that the sixty-year-old poet did not even want him to see it. Fenn insisted, claiming that Ticknor and Fields had ordered him to go there. He eventually persuaded the immigrant woman renting the house to let him retrieve the old crane and some old furniture from the attic and produced drawings so appropriate they brought tears to Whittier's eyes. This edition of *Snow-Bound* was so successful and highly acclaimed that it is often credited as being the first illustrated gift book published in the United States. Although incorrect, the claim suggests the impact of the book.

In subsequent years many gift books of poetry were published by American firms. Most were illustrated with original designs by American artists reproduced as wood engravings rather than with re-

used steel plates imported from England as had been common earlier. Fenn contributed to many of these. In 1870 Fields, Osgood, and Company (the successors to Ticknor and Fields) followed up the success of *Snow-Bound* with Whittier's *Ballads of New England,* featuring Fenn's landscape settings as headpieces and tailpieces for each ballad. Although the book included illustrations by other artists whose subsequent reputations have surpassed Fenn's—including Winslow Homer, Felix Octavius Carr Darley, and Sol Eytinge Jr.—at least one critic, in the December 1869 *Atlantic Monthly,* found Fenn's work the most appealing:

> The most charming illustrations in this beautiful book are the pictures of Mr. Fenn, who in studies of the very scenes described by the poet has reproduced all the moods and sentiments of the New England landscape: the pathos of the rainy and cloudy coasts, the tender serenity of the river-bordered fields, the life and brightness of the villages, the sadness of the lonely farm, the solemnity of the hill-side graveyard.

In the next three years Fenn contributed to illustrated editions of William Cullen Bryant's *The Song of the Sower* (1871), the anthology *Songs of Home* (1871), and Bryant's *The Story of the Fountain* (1872).

During the decade of 1870 to 1880 Fenn's major commissions were from D. Appleton and Company, the second largest publishing firm in New York. His first assignments were to prepare landscape illustrations for the new weekly magazine *Appletons' Journal,* which used high-quality wood and steel engravings as a selling point. His contributions to a series called "New York Illustrated" beginning in April 1869 were much more striking than the primarily frontal views of buildings by other artists, as were his foldout *View of Castle Garden and New York Bay* (15 May 1869) and full-page *Cape Ann Cedar Tree* and *Star Island, Isles of Shoals* (9 October 1869).

By the summer of 1870 the Appleton firm commissioned Fenn to travel to the South to make drawings for a new *Appletons' Journal* series to be called "Picturesque America," which would feature "splendidly-executed views of the most unfamiliar and novel features of American scenery accompanied with suitable letter-press." Fenn had sparked the idea for this series by his response to a visiting Englishman who, in a gathering including some of the Appletons, said there was nothing picturesque about American scenery. Fenn, as reported in *The National Cyclopedia of American Biography,* countered with, "If they will make it worth my while, we will show the young man if there is any thing picturesque in America."

The choice of the South in 1870 as the first region to receive attention was significant: by featuring it as appealing to tourists, *Appletons' Journal* promoted sectional reconciliation, satisfied curiosity, and attempted to expand the market of the magazine. The "Picturesque America" series opened on 12 November 1870 with views along the Saint John's and Ocklawaha Rivers in Florida, vivid depictions of swamp life that were different from the more familiar picturesque scenery typical of the Northeast and England. Images of the French Broad River in North Carolina were next, followed in early 1871 by views of the coal-mining transportation center in Mauch Chunk, Pennsylvania, and the Natural Bridge in Virginia. After a brief defection to illustrate Pittsburgh and the Pennsylvania oil fields for *Every Saturday* (published by James R. Osgood, successor to Fields, Osgood and Company), Fenn returned to *Appletons' Journal.* He prepared more illustrations for the Picturesque America series throughout 1871, including East Hampton; Charleston, South Carolina; Saint Augustine; Lookout Mountain; and Chattanooga. The series was popular enough to inspire competitors, most notably the *Aldine,* to initiate similar series.

By the spring of 1872 the Appleton firm decided to recast and expand the series as a subscription book. Parts of twenty-four pages selling for fifty cents each appeared twice monthly over a two-year period, from mid 1872 to mid 1874. The venerable William Cullen Bryant was named as editor. Each part included a steel engraving, and many wood engravings were interspersed throughout the text. Fenn continued to prepare illustrations for *Picturesque America* throughout 1872, but the project editor, Oliver Bell Bunce, commissioned other artists—including Woodward, Alfred R. Waud, Granville Perkins, James D. Smillie, and Moran—to cover additional regions. In preparing the wood engravings Fenn and most of the other artists redrew their own preliminary sketches on the whitened woodblocks; to make the images more appealing to contemporary audiences, they added all sorts of picturesque details, such as figures, animals, boats, carts, and dramatic clouds or sunsets. As the initial and most prolific contributor Fenn provided the model for the other artists. His often unconventional formats—facilitated by the compatibility of relief wood engravings and letterpress type, allowing them to be combined on the same page and printed on the same press; his bold draftsmanship, full of energy and movement; and his striking viewpoints—contributed to the perception that the book was one of the finest productions of American publishers. It was recognized as such at the Centennial Exposition of 1876. The other artists varied in their ability to match Fenn's standard. Some of the works of those who lacked Fenn's familiarity with how to draw on the block in such a way as to facilitate an attractive engraving were characterized by an overall grayness and ineffective use of line.

Picturesque America was so successful that the Appleton firm decided to prepare a similar work about Europe. They sent Fenn and his family to England in 1873. From there Fenn traveled widely to prepare drawings for *Picturesque Europe,* published in parts from 1875 to 1879 by D. Appleton in New York and Cassell, Petter, and Galpin in London. Once again Fenn was the primary contributor, in this case joined by many British artists as well as Woodward, sent to England by the Appletons in 1876. Fenn covered parts of the British Isles, Spain, Italy, Germany, France, Belgium, and Switzerland for this publication. The London *Art Journal* for January 1877 praised Fenn's contributions to *Picturesque Europe* for their "force and beauty" and continued: "Mr. Fenn has a very happy faculty of seizing upon unconventional points of view in a scene, and always succeeds in giving great freshness to the most familiar places."

A third Appleton project occupied Fenn from 1878 through about 1882: *Picturesque Palestine, Sinai, and Egypt,* published serially from 1881 to 1883, with the London edition published by James S. Virtue. There was great interest at the time, especially among American Protestants and British Anglicans, in exploring the Bible lands and determining the actual sites of biblical events. Such a book had long been a goal of George S. Appleton, who died before its completion. To make drawings for this book Fenn and Woodward made two extensive trips to the Near East in 1878 and 1879. Even with arrangements provided by Thomas Cook, travel in Palestine and Sinai was still quite strenuous and adventuresome, involving many days on horseback and nights in tents. Sometimes the artists needed guards to fend off hostile Moslems or opportunistic Bedouins, and they became tired of trying to create interesting compositions from historic piles of rubble. The two men came to be fast friends and despite the hardships were glad to have made these trips. Woodward's letters of 22 March and 21 June 1878 recount their sitting together on the Mount of Olives across from Jerusalem reading to each other the biblical passages related to that spot and taking evening strolls among the ruins at Baalbek. Woodward wrote, "After working all day, Fenn and I would take our Arab cloaks and long pipe and wander through the ruins, or sit for hours on some fragment of former grandeur and enjoy the marvelous effects of light and shade, or pass the time telling yarns."

Fenn and Woodward contributed approximately equal numbers of the more than six hundred wood engravings and thirty-eight steel engravings in *Picturesque Palestine, Sinai, and Egypt.* The book provided the most comprehensive visual survey of the Holy Land available to that point, and the text was eventually provided by many prominent experts on the topography and history of the region, with Col. Charles W. Wilson of the British Palestine Exploration Society serving as editor. The compositions and formats of the wood engravings were similar to those of *Picturesque America* and *Picturesque Europe* with one addition: juxtapositions of close-ups of flowers with landscape scenes in primarily rectangular viewing boxes, a style that became popular in the following decade.

The work Fenn and Woodward did for *Picturesque Palestine, Sinai, and Egypt* established them as experts in depicting the region, and often in future years they were commissioned to provide images of the Holy Land and Egypt. Fenn did many such illustrations for *Century* based on the photographs of Edward L. Wilson and probably reused some of his own sketches to prepare the illustrations for *The Ser-*

mon on the Mount (1886), and the watercolors reproduced in *Bethlehem to Jerusalem* (1888) and *Out-of-Doors in the Holy Land* (1908). He also reportedly lectured on Oriental subjects.

Fenn spent the remainder of 1879 and 1880 in England, presumably selecting and reworking his drawings for *Picturesque Palestine.* His last child was born in September 1880 at Haslemere, where Alfred Tennyson lived. Fenn reportedly became acquainted with Tennyson, and in the 1880s and 1890s he illustrated several American editions of Tennyson's poems, including *In Memoriam* (1897).

Fenn and his family returned to the United States in 1881, again settling first in Brooklyn and then moving by 1885 to Montclair. The painter George Inness moved to Montclair about the same time and became acquainted with Fenn. The Fenns built on Orange Mountain a rambling sixteen-room shingle-and-half-timbered house called The Cedars with many gables, turrets, and piazzas. Fenn's well-lighted studio was in one of the gables. That this house was featured in several magazine articles attested to Fenn's prominence and his prospering career. Fenn's income during this period was substantial for the time. A brief article concerning "the earnings of the best artists" in the 22 March 1887 Boston *Daily Evening Transcript* claimed that Fenn had earned $10,000 a year for his work on *Picturesque America* and was probably earning that much for his "general work" in 1887.

During the 1880s and 1890s Fenn remained extremely prolific as an illustrator while he continued to produce, exhibit, and sell watercolor paintings and, from around 1888, some etchings. Probably the largest number of commissions during this period came from *Century* magazine, the successor to the original *Scribner's Monthly,* which under the editorship of Richard Watson Gilder—with Arthur Drake as head of the art department and master printer Theodore L. De Vinne in charge of production—was much admired both in the United States and England for the high quality of its articles and illustrations. From 1882 to his death in 1911 Fenn contributed many illustrations to almost every volume. In addition, correspondence with Gilder reveals that he sometimes proposed articles with an eye to the potential market. For example, on 22 March 1895 Fenn suggested an article about the literary figures of Essex County, Massachusetts, pointing out that many from that area had migrated to the Far West and would be interested in the piece if they "could make it *smell* strong *enough* of the *soil.*" He may well have also proposed to Gilder several articles by his oldest daughter, Alice Maude, that he illustrated. He also wrote three articles for the popu-

Illustration by Fenn for Will Carleton's City Ballads *(1886)*

lar children's magazine *St. Nicholas,* published by the Century Company.

The first *Century* article illustrated entirely by Fenn appeared in August 1882; "The Borderlands of Surrey" dealt with the region where the family had lived and was written by Alice Maude. Among the illustrations was one of Tennyson's home. In 1883 Fenn resumed work for the Harper firm, contributing views of American scenic areas to both *Harper's Monthly* and *Harper's Weekly.* By this time the usual procedure was to photograph the artist's drawing on the block to guide the wood engraver. But Fenn sometimes still made changes on the block, as is shown by his notation on a wash drawing of Haine's Falls in the Catskills now at the Library of Congress; he instructed that it be photographed on a block an extra half-inch long so he could add more water at the bottom.

By 1884 Fenn was among the most active contributors to *Century.* Volume twenty-eight, May through October, includes fifty-four works by him,

identifiable either in the index or by his distinctive monogram combining *H* and *F.* He illustrated such articles as "Recent Architecture in America" by Mrs. Schuyler van Rensselaer, in which his renderings are noticeably more interesting than the flat, frontal ones of the other artists—*The Salem of Hawthorne, On the Track of Ulysses,* and *Social Conditions in the Colonies.* With this level of activity for *Century* and commissions completed for *Harper's Monthly* and books of poetry, Fenn could well afford his new house.

Fenn's contributions to *Century* continued at a high level with the launching in November 1884 of the celebrated "Battles and Leaders of the Civil War" series, which engaged generals from both sides to recount their experiences. Many artists were employed to depict the events and sites connected with the battles either on the scene or from old photographs or drawings. Fenn was a primary contributor; others were Theodore R. Davis, Edwin Forbes, Edwin J. Meeker, William Ludwell Sheppard, Homer, Pennell, Walton Taber, Waud, and Woodward. Some of these specialized in drawing figures, others in landscapes. The series ran in the magazine through 1887 and was published in expanded form in four volumes in 1888. Stephen Sears, the editor of a 1983 book reproducing many of the original drawings for the series, which were owned at the time by American Heritage, thought highly of Fenn's work: "He is the most skilled of the artists represented in this collection; of the entire corps of artists who worked on *Battles and Leaders,* only Winslow Homer and Joseph Pennell would outrank him."

For this series Fenn made both ink drawings, reproduced by the relatively new photoengraving process, and wash drawings, reproduced as tonal wood engravings. The development of photoengraving was a boon to Fenn as well as many other illustrators, for it enabled ink drawings to be reproduced exactly, in whatever size was appropriate for the page, without the intervention of an engraver. Through his skillful use of the pen Fenn could produce lively images full of detail, texture, and contrasts, even from photographs.

During his period of great productivity in magazine illustration in the 1880s and 1890s, Fenn increasingly worked from photographs. He did undertake another major journey, however, from July to October 1890 to southern California. This trip allowed him to sketch firsthand an area that was of great interest to the American public for its mild climate and agricultural productivity and for its history of early Spanish settlement and the Gold Rush. After this trip *Century* viewed him as a California expert, engaging him to illustrate many articles about the state, including in 1891 and 1892, among others, "Pioneer Spanish Families in California," "The Missions of Alta California," "Across the Plains in the Donner Party," and "Picturesque Plant Life of California." He also produced fanciful illustrations for a poem about the Sierra Nevada by Miles I'Anson, *The Vision of Misery Hill* (1891).

In this period Fenn experimented with a more impressionistic style in both his ink drawings and his watercolors—more white space, sparer use of line, and less precise forms. Younger illustrators such as Pennell, André Castaigne, and later Jules Guerin, Ernest Peixotto, and many others used such approaches. Yet Fenn remained most comfortable with bold line drawings and precise renderings. As the aesthetic movement influenced book design, he sometimes designed decorative borders for blocks of text or poetry as well as decorative titles combining hand lettering with pen or wash drawings. Fenn was one of twenty-one American artists awarded a

medal for "Works in Black and White" at the World's Columbian Exposition in Chicago in 1893.

In addition to his work for magazines, Fenn contributed to many books in his last three decades, including poetry and travel accounts. Some of the more notable ones were illustrated solely by him. In 1884 Roberts Brothers in Boston published what they labeled the "Harry Fenn Edition" of Thomas Gray's *Elegy Written in a Country Churchyard.* A note in the book claimed many of the illustrations were "from sketches taken at Stoke Pogis, the scene of the poem, by Mr. Fenn." In 1897 Fords, Howard, and Hulbert published a new edition of Tennyson's *In Memoriam* illustrated by Fenn, with elaborate decorative initials embellishing each canto. And in 1908 Charles Scribner's Sons reproduced Fenn's watercolors of the Holy Land as color halftones in *Out-of-Doors in the Holy Land* by Henry Van Dyke. The halftone process at last allowed the reproduction of Fenn's watercolors without the intervention of an engraver.

During the last twenty years of his life, from about 1890 to 1911, Fenn remained active, but his prestige gradually diminished as more-impressionistic styles gained in popularity and as publishers increasingly relied on photographs reproduced as halftones to illustrate their works. A March 1892 letter to a staff member at Harper (now at the Pierpont Morgan Library, New York, MA 1950) reveals some pique at his treatment: "I wonder if I shall ever again get a batch from Harpers that I can 'do myself proud' on. . . . It's hard to 'make a silk purse out of a sow's ear.'" He must have found similar challenges in the series of illustrations of insects he did for *Harper's Monthly* from 1904 to 1907.

Fenn continued to be engaged by *Century* magazine until his death, most often illustrating plants and trees or architecture, the types of subjects he excelled at rendering. Two late assignments for which he produced noteworthy illustrations and received the credit line "Illustrated by Harry Fenn" were "Art in Modern Bridges" in May 1900 and "Suburban Gardening" in April 1911, the month of his death.

By all accounts Fenn was a genial person with a zest for life and a generosity of spirit. His willingness to help a young, aspiring illustrator is evident in the remembrances of Will H. Low, recorded in the DeWitt McClellan Lockman Papers (Archives of American Art, mfm roll 503). Low, who admired Fenn's work, wrote to ask him how he drew moonlight. Fenn responded in a long letter and invited Low to visit him in Montclair, which Low did. Fenn remained active in the American Watercolor Society throughout his life and was also a member of the

Salmagundi Club from 1891 and of the Society of Illustrators, organized in 1901 to enhance the status of the profession. Fenn moved from the large house on Orange Mountain after his children were grown to a smaller house on Park Street in Montclair, where he died on 21 April 1911.

Fenn deserves recognition for his widely acclaimed and emulated landscape and architectural images. He is also important for the impact that the success of his works had on American publishing and on the "Golden Age of American Illustration" that followed him. Although F. Hopkinson Smith may have somewhat overstated the case in *American Illustrators,* his viewpoint is instructive: "but for Harry Fenn this present school of American illustrators would not exist."

References:

Anderson Auction Company, *A Collection of Water Color Drawings by Harry Fenn . . . will be sold Nov. 9, 1911* (New York: Anderson Auction, 1911);

Sydney Brooks, "Harry Fenn: An Appreciation," *Harper's Weekly* (13 May 1911): 10;

George and Edward Dalziel, *The Brothers Dalziel: A Record of Work, 1840–1890* (London: Batsford, 1978);

Budd Leslie Gambee Jr., "*Frank Leslie's Illustrated Newspaper,* 1855–1860: Artistic and Technical Operations of a Pioneer Pictorial News Weekly in America," dissertation, University of Michigan, 1963;

"Harry Fenn," *American Bookmaker,* 9, no. 3 (September 1889): 1;

George Parsons Lathrop, "Glimpses of Picturesque Places," *Quarterly Illustrator,* 1 (January 1893): 166–169;

Clark S. Marlor, *A History of the Brooklyn Art Association* (New York: Carr, 1970);

The Montclair Art Colony Past and Present (Montclair, N.J.: The Montclair Museum of Art, 1997);

Sue Rainey, "Images of the South in *Picturesque America* and *The Great South,*" in *Graphic Arts & the South,* edited by Judy L. Larson, Proceedings of the 1990 North American Print Conference (Fayetteville: University of Arkansas Press, 1993);

Rainey, *Creating Picturesque America: Monument to the Natural and Cultural Landscape* (Nashville, Tenn.: Vanderbilt University Press, 1994);

Rainey and Roger B. Stein, *Shaping the Landscape Image, 1865–1910: John Douglas Woodward* (Charlottesville, Va.: Bayly Art Museum of the University of Virginia, 1997);

R. Riordan, "Artists' Homes: Mr. Harry Fenn's, at Montclair, New Jersey," *Magazine of Art,* 9 (1886);

Stephen W. Sears, ed., *The American Heritage Century Collection of Civil War Art* (New York: American Heritage, 1983);

John Douglas Woodward, "An Artist Abroad in the Seventies," typed transcript of letters, Virginia State Library, Richmond.

Archives:

Among the institutions owning artworks by Fenn are the Bancroft Library, University of California, Berkeley; Boston Museum of Fine Arts; Cleveland Museum of Art; Cooper-Hewitt Museum; the Library Company of Philadelphia; the Library of Congress; the Delaware Art Museum; the Metropolitan Museum of Art; Montclair Museum of Art; Oakland Museum of Art; New York Historical Society; National Museum of American Art; New York Public Library; Pasadena Historical Society; Royal Ontario Museum; San Diego Museum of Art; and the Wadsworth Atheneum. The few Fenn letters that have been located are available through the Archives of American Art. The originals are in the following collections: *Century* Magazine Collection, Manuscripts Division, New York Public Library; and the Harper Collection, Pierpont Morgan Library. The letters of John Douglas Woodward, which describe his travels with Fenn for *Picturesque Palestine, Sinai, and Egypt,* are in the Woodward Family Papers, Ms/c/38, Valentine Museum, Richmond, Virginia.

James Montgomery Flagg

(18 June 1877 – 27 May 1960)

Susan Thach Dean
University of Colorado at Boulder Libraries

BOOKS: *Yankee Girls Abroad* (London: Sands, 1900);

Tomfoolery (New York: Life, 1904);

"If": A Guide to Bad Manners (New York: Life, 1905);

Why They Married (New York: Life, 1906);

Yours Truly and One Hundred Other Original Drawings, by Flagg and others (New York: Judge, 1907);

All in the Same Boat (New York: Life, 1908);

Nervy Nat: His Adventures; From Originals in "Judge" (New York: Judge, 1908);

City People (New York: Scribners, 1909);

The Adventures of Kitty Cobb (New York: Doran, 1912; London: Heinemann, 1912);

I Should Say So (New York: Doran, 1914);

The Well-Knowns (New York: Doran, 1914);

The Mystery of the Hated Man, and Then Some (New York: Doran, 1916);

Boulevards All the Way—Maybe; Being an Artist's Truthful Impression of the U.S. from New York to California and Return, by Motor (New York: Doran, 1925);

Roses and Buckshot (New York: Putnam, 1946);

Celebrities: A Half-Century of Caricature and Portraiture, With Comments by the Artist (Watkins Glen, N.Y.: Century House, 1951); republished as *Celebrity-Artist, with Biographical Portrait by G. L. Freeman* (Watkins Glen, N.Y.: Century House, 1960);

The James Montgomery Flagg Poster Book (New York: Watson Guptill, 1975).

MOTION PICTURES: *The Adventures of Kitty Cobb,* book by Flagg, Warner's Features, 1914;

His Wife Knew All About It, screenplay by Flagg, Vitagraph, 1915;

Is Christmas a Bore, screenplay by Flagg, Vitagraph, 1915;

Miss Sticky-Moufie Kiss, screenplay by Flagg, Vitagraph, 1915;

The Art Bug, screenplay by Flagg, 1918;

The Artist's Model, screenplay by Flagg, Edison, 1918;

The Bride, screenplay by Flagg, Edison, 1918;

The Good Sport, screenplay by Flagg, Edison, 1918;

Hick Manhattan, screenplay by Flagg, Paramount, 1918;

Independence, B'Gosh, screenplay by Flagg, Paramount, 1918;

The Lonesome Girl, screenplay by Flagg, Edison, 1918;

The Man-Eater, screenplay by Flagg, Edison, 1918;

The Matinee Girl, screenplay by Flagg, Edison, 1918;

Perfectly Fiendish Flanagan; or, The Hart of the Dreadful West, screenplay by Flagg, Paramount, 1918;

Romance and Brass Tacks, screenplay by Flagg, Paramount, 1918;

The Screen Fan, screenplay by Flagg, 1918;

The Spirit of the Red Cross, screenplay by Flagg, Committee of the National Association of the Motion Picture Industry, 1918;

The Spoiled Girl, screenplay by Flagg, Edison, 1918;

The Starter, screenplay by Flagg, Edison, 1918;

The Stenog, screenplay by Flagg, 1918;

The Superstitious Girl, screenplay by Flagg, 1918;

Tell That to the Marines, screenplay by Flagg, Paramount, 1918;

One Every Minute, screenplay by Flagg, Paramount, 1919;

Beresford of the Baboons, screenplay by Flagg, Paramount, 1919;

The "Con" in Economy, screenplay by Flagg, Paramount, 1919;

The Immovable Guest, screenplay by Flagg, Paramount, 1919;

Impropaganda, screenplay by Flagg, Paramount, 1919;

The Last Bottle, screenplay by Flagg, 1919;

Welcome, Little Stranger, screenplay by Flagg, Paramount, 1919;

Pride and Po'k Chops, screenplay by Flagg, 1920.

SELECTED BOOKS ILLUSTRATED: Barbour, Ralph Henry, *An Orchard Princess* (Philadelphia & London: Lippincott, 1905);

Crawford, F. Marion, *The Diva's Ruby* (New York: Macmillan, 1908);

Nicholson, Meredith, *The Little Brown Jug at Kildare* (Indianapolis: Bobbs-Merrill, 1908);

Chester, George Randolph, *The Making of Bobby Burnit* (Indianapolis: Bobbs-Merrill, 1909);

Page, Thomas Nelson, *John Marvel, Assistant* (New York: Scribners, 1909);

Brennan, George H., *Bill Truetell: A Story of Theatrical Life* (Chicago: McClurg, 1909);

Locke, William J., *Septimus* (New York: John Lane, 1909);

Street, Julian, *The Need of Change* (New York: Dodd, Mead, 1909);

Porter, William Sydney, as O. Henry, *Options* (New York & London: Harper, 1909);

Locke, William J., *Simon the Jester* (New York: John Lane, 1910);

Dorset, G., *A Successful Wife: A Story* (New York & London: Harper, 1910);

Bennett, Arnold, *What the Public Wants: A Play in Four Acts* (New York: S. S. McClure, 1910);

Brown, Katharine Holland, *White Roses* (New York: Duffield, 1910);

Codman, Anna Kneeland Crafts, *An Ardent American* (New York: Century, 1911);

Hughes, Rupert, *Excuse Me!* (New York: H. K. Fly, 1911);

Bausman, Frederick, *Thieves* (New York: Duffield, 1911);

Mighels, Philip Verrill, *Thurley Ruxton* (New York: Desmond FitzGerald, 1911);

Ingram, Eleanor M., *From the Car Behind* (Philadelphia & London: Lippincott, 1912);

Janvier, Thomas A., *From the South of France* (New York & London: Harper, 1912);

Gerry, Margarita Spalding, *As Caesar's Wife: A Novel* (New York & London: Harper, 1912);

Scott, John Reed, *The First Hurdle* (Philadelphia & London: Lippincott, 1912);

Ferber, Edna, *Roast Beef, Medium: The Business Adventures of Emma McChesney* (New York: Stokes, 1913);

Jenks, George C., and Carlyle Moore, *Stop Thief!* (New York: H. K. Fly, 1913);

Irwin, Violet Mary, *The Human Desire* (Boston: Small, Maynard, 1913);

Street, Julian, *Welcome to Our City* (New York: John Lane, 1913);

Ferber, Edna, *Personality Plus: Some Experiences of Emma McChesney and Her Son, Jock* (New York: Stokes, 1914);

Hughes, Rupert, *Empty Pockets* (New York & London: Harper, 1915);

Johnson, Owen, *Making Money* (New York: Stokes, 1915);

Vance, Louis Joseph, *Sheep's Clothing* (Boston: Little, Brown, 1915);

McCutcheon, George Barr, *Mr. Bingle* (New York: Dodd, Mead, 1915);

Irwin, Inez Haynes, *The Ollivant Orphans* (New York: Holt, 1915);

Prouty, Olive Higgins, *The Fifth Wheel* (New York: Stokes, 1916);

Hughes, Rupert, *The Thirteenth Commandment: A Novel* (New York & London: Harper, 1916);

Hughes, *We Can't Have Everything: A Novel* (New York: Burt, 1917);

King, Basil, *The Lifted Veil* (New York & London: Harper, 1917);

Towne, Charles Hanson, ed., *For France* (Garden City, N.Y.: Doubleday, Page, 1917);

Luther, Mark Lee, *The Hope Chest* (Boston: Little, Brown, 1918);

Hughes, Rupert, *The Unpardonable Sin: A Novel* (New York & London: Harper, 1918);

Browne, Porter Emerson, *A Liberty Loan Primer* (New York: Liberty Loan Committee, Second Federal Reserve District, 1918);

Luther, Mark Lee, *Presenting Jane McRae* (Boston: Little, Brown, 1920);

Roche, Arthur Somers, *Uneasy Street* (New York: Cosmopolitan Book Corporation, 1920);

Hart, William S., *Told Under a White Oak Tree* (Boston & New York: Houghton Mifflin, 1922);

Dawson, Coningsby, *The Vanishing Point* (New York & London: Cosmopolitan Book Corporation, 1922);

Baxter, John E., *Locker Room Ballads* (New York & London: Appleton, 1923);

Hart, William S., *A Lighter of Flames* (New York: Crowell, 1923);

Ade, George, *The Old-Time Saloon: Not Wet—Not Dry, Just History* (New York: R. Long & R. R. Smith, 1931);

Hooper, Bett, *Virgins in Cellophane: From Maker to Consumer Untouched by Human Hand* (New York: R. Long & R. R. Smith, 1932);

Flagg, Elisha Jr., *Rookie* (Chicago: Whitman, 1940);

Washburn, C. M., *Honeymoon Isle, Florida* (New York: Honeymoon Isle, 1941);

Fay, Frank, *How to Be Poor* (New York: Prentice-Hall, 1945).

PERIODICALS: *St. Nicholas,* 1890–1898;
Judge, 1891–1924;
Life, 1891–1929;
Atlantic, 1895;
Bookman, 1896, 1924;
Scribner's Magazine, 1906–1919;
Harper's Weekly, 1907–1910;

James Montgomery Flagg (photograph by Percy Rainford)

Woman's Home Companion, 1908–1919;
American Magazine, 1910–1917;
Cosmopolitan, 1910–1939;
Century, 1915–1916;
Everybody's Magazine, 1915–1916;
Leslie's Weekly, 1917;
Hearst's Magazine, 1920–1921;
Good Housekeeping, 1923–1934;
McCall's, 1926;
McClure's, 1926;
Liberty, 1926, 1928;
Photoplay, circa 1927–1951;
Golden Book Magazine, 1929, 1936;
Delineator Magazine, 1935;
Red Book, 1935–1936.

James Montgomery Flagg is best remembered as the creator of the most famous recruiting poster of all time, the commanding figure of Uncle Sam pointing his finger and declaring, "I Want You!" Effective as this poster was in two world wars, and as frequently as it has been adapted or parodied since, it represents only a minuscule portion of Flagg's enormous output and shows only one aspect of his versatility as an artist. A painter and prolific illustra-

tor, as well as a poster artist, Flagg was also a well-known bon vivant and intimate of celebrities. His outspokenness and flair for publicity kept him in the limelight, and the eagerness with which he embraced and recorded the changing interests of the times makes him one of the great chroniclers of early-twentieth-century America.

James Montgomery Flagg was born on 18 June 1877 in Pelham Manor, New York, and spent most of his childhood in New York City. He began drawing as a young child, and at the age of twelve he took the unusual step of bringing samples of his work to the offices of *St. Nicholas* magazine and asking to see an editor. Tudor Jenks, the assistant editor to whom Flagg was referred, later recalled in a June 1915 *Century* article that "there was something in those easy, unstudied lines that breathed ability and capacity so great that words of praise and encouragement seemed only a duty." Jenks discussed the young artist's talent with his parents, declaring that "the rarity of the boy's gift entitled him to give his life to art work." Flagg's drawings were published in the September 1890 issue of *St. Nicholas* as "A Page of Sketches by a Young Contributor," and his career was launched.

"I DON'T WANT ANY MODELS AT PRESENT," SAID THE BRUTE.
"LEAVE YOUR CARD ON THE TABLE."

Illustration by Flagg for P. G. Wodehouse's "The Man Up-stairs," in the March 1910 issue of Cosmopolitan

At the age of fourteen Flagg sold an illustration to *Life,* a humorous magazine in the style of *Punch,* and became a regular member of the staff. Soon he was also on the staff of rival periodical *Judge,* for which he created the character "Nervy Nat," an impudent tramp whose adventures were published in book form in 1908. Flagg was now financially independent and felt able to dispense with further conventional schooling. Instead, he began studying at the Art Students League, where he formed close friendships with John Wolcott Adams and Walter Appleton Clark, both of whom also became illustrators. Later in his life Flagg disparaged art schools, declaring in a 9 September 1938 letter to the *New York Herald Tribune,* "There are no art teachers. Art cannot be taught. Artists are born that way." In 1898 Flagg traveled to England, ostensibly to study at Hubert von Herkomer's school in Hertfordshire, but he spent much of his time in London, enjoying the theaters and an active social life. He returned to the United States in 1899, and his first book, *Yankee Girls Abroad,* was published in London the following year.

On his return Flagg went to Saint Louis, as he would later recall in his memoir, *Roses and Buckshot* (1946), "to do the silliest thing an artist can do—get married." He had fallen in love with Nellie McCormick, his "idea of Beauty," two years earlier in Maine, despite the fact that she was a wealthy socialite eleven years his senior. Although the marriage was a stormy one, marked by occasional separations and Flagg's frequent affairs, it lasted until Nellie's death in 1923. In *Roses and Buckshot* Flagg describes her as "the finest woman I ever knew. She helped me unselfishly through those first years of finding myself. She had beauty, great beauty, taste, and was a gentlewoman."

After their marriage the Flaggs traveled extensively for several years. Flagg briefly studied painting in Paris, received several commissions for watercolor portraits, and had a painting exhibited in the Paris Salon of 1900. For the next four years the couple spent winters in the United States and summers in Europe. In 1904 they settled in New York in an apartment and studio on West Sixty-seventh Street.

Although Flagg had no definitive plans for his career, he continued to produce illustrations, usually at the rate of one a day. In addition to drawing for periodicals, Flagg also wrote and illustrated books of comic verse, beginning in 1904 with *Tomfoolery,* followed by *"If": A Guide to Bad Manners* (1905), *Why They Married* (1906), and *All in the Same Boat* (1908). From 1907 to 1910 his pen-and-ink drawings frequently appeared in the center double-page spread of *Harper's Weekly.* These humorous sketches depicted life in New York, often satirizing the romantic foibles of youth; a selection of them was published under the title *City People* in 1909.

In 1906, after several attempts, Flagg's work was accepted by *Scribner's Magazine.* As he wrote in *Roses and Buckshot,* "To be reproduced in *Scribner's . . .* meant you had arrived." He was a regular contributor thereafter, illustrating stories by such popular authors as Henry Blake Fuller, whose tales of society life in the capitals of America and Europe were especially suited to Flagg's style. In 1908, while traveling in Europe, he not only illustrated an article on musical-instrument making in a Bavarian village but also wrote the text when the prospective author was unable to fulfill his commitment. Flagg worked for *Scribner's* for more than a decade, and in his memoir he later described the editor, Joseph Chapin, as "the *beau ideal* of art editors."

In the first decade of the century Flagg established a distinctive style in his pen-and-ink illustrations which makes them easily recognizable. Crisp, angular, and with an engaging air of spontaneity, they are composed almost entirely of parallel lines

You Would, Would You?, *illustration by Flagg for his 1912 book,* The Adventures of Kitty Cobb, *which depicts a typical Flagg Girl*

with virtually no cross-hatching. In addition to using pen and ink, he filled in some areas with a brush and left the broad pencil outline of the subject as an integral part of the finished work. Flagg's original sketches were many times larger than they eventually appeared in print, but he visualized his final product so well that each drawing attained a remarkable resolution when reduced. He used watercolor and oil for halftone or color reproduction, and sometimes a combination of pen and ink and watercolor, as in his covers for *Life* and *Judge;* but his illustrations in pen and ink alone are his most characteristic work.

During this period Flagg also perfected the representation of his ideal of feminine beauty, who became known as the "Flagg Girl." While the Gibson Girl, created in the previous decade by Charles Dana Gibson, was the epitome of aristocratic elegance, the Flagg Girl radiated health, good humor, and uncomplicated sensuality. Tall and shapely, with wavy hair and full lips, her physical beauty was matched by her quick-wittedness and ability to rise to any occasion. The Flagg Girl figured in the artist's work throughout his life; exuberant and fun loving in peacetime, she became a nurse during both world wars, and she appears repeatedly in the faces of the movie stars Flagg sketched for *Photoplay.* In 1912 he chronicled the escapades of a quintessential

Flagg Girl in *The Adventures of Kitty Cobb,* a novel in pictures with captions, published in both New York and London. A rural innocent who seeks her fortune in the city, Kitty narrowly avoids the traditional pitfalls and marries a rich man, then rescues her marriage from predictable disillusionment. In *Kitty Cobb,* Flagg both satirizes the sentimental "fallen woman" novel and celebrates his heroine's pluck.

In the years before World War I Flagg illustrated many books and magazine stories, in some cases establishing relationships with authors such as Rupert Hughes and Julian Street, whose books he would continue to illustrate throughout his career. Most of these authors, although popular in their day, have faded into obscurity, but Flagg's depictions of scenes and characters still enliven the text and pique the potential reader's curiosity. Some of his most delightful illustrations were for Edna Ferber's Emma McChesney stories, first published in *American Magazine* and later in book form as *Roast Beef, Medium: The Business Adventures of Emma McChesney* (1913) and *Personality Plus: Some Experiences of Emma McChesney and Her Son, Jock* (1914). Emma was an unusual character for the time, a mature divorced woman with a teenaged son, making an arduous living as a traveling salesperson. Flagg clearly appreciated her good humor, good sense, and the

Four of Flagg's covers for Life *and* Judge

warmth with which she responded to those in need; in his illustrations Emma became a typical Flagg Girl, despite her age and occasionally caustic tongue.

At this time Flagg became established not only as a famous artist but also as a well-known man-about-town, the friend of John Barrymore and other celebrities, and a prominent member of several New York clubs. He had gained admission to the Lotos Club at the age of twenty-one after painting a portrait of Mark Twain, and in 1911 he founded the Dutch Treat Club with a group of writers and artists, including Street, Hughes, and Gibson. The club put on annual shows, written by Flagg, that were legendary for their ribald humor. The annual shows that he wrote, produced, and acted in for the Society of Illustrators were equally successful, until their reputation attracted the interest of brothers Lee, Samuel, and Jacob Shubert, theatrical entrepreneurs who produced what Flagg called a "Shubertized Broadway version" of one of the shows; Flagg, in disgust, ceased to participate. He was also a member of the Lambs Club, the Artists and Writers Club, and the Players Club. *Roses and Buckshot* includes many references to "our gang," "the mob," and "the crowd." He clearly relished his association with this highly creative, if sometimes rowdy, coterie, and the pleasure he took in his friends' company lends an added poignancy to the loneliness of his final years.

While he was already famous and financially successful, Flagg's role as a poster artist in World War I made him immortal. He later declared in *Roses and Buckshot* that he was "glad [he] was beyond the age to get into the trenches" and complained that "sentiment was rampant" during the war; but his skill in evoking sentiment was precisely what made his posters so powerful. Flagg's first poster of the war, done while he was a member of the New York Civilian Preparedness Committee, was titled *Storm Coming* (circa 1916) and was in pen and ink; he later expressed dissatisfaction with it, calling it "not so hot." His lithograph poster *Wake Up, America* (circa 1918) had a similar theme, showing "Columbia asleep on a porch with a terrific thunderstorm coming along in the background." This was a much more successful work and showed the Flagg Girl in a new incarnation, representing America itself. In 1917 Flagg was appointed the State Military Artist of New York and was also a member of an artists' committee, chaired by Charles Dana Gibson, that worked in cooperation with the Division of Pictorial Publicity in Washington. The formalities of the committee bored Flagg, however, and he declared that he

Illustration by Flagg for Edna Ferber's Roast Beef, Medium: The Business Adventures of Emma McChesney *(1913)*

"functioned alone, for [he] was not herd-conscious."

Flagg's famous depiction of Uncle Sam reflected this rugged individualism. Previously Uncle Sam had been a stock comic character, a gangling figure in stars and stripes representing a raw and unsophisticated country. In Flagg's hands he became a compelling symbol of national resolution, his call to action affirming the value of each individual's contribution to the common cause. Flagg's painting, for which he used himself as a model, originally appeared on the cover of *Leslie's Weekly* (6 July 1916). It may have been based on Alfred Leete's British recruiting poster of 1914, depicting Lord Kitchener pointing his finger and declaring, "Your Country Needs You," but Flagg's Uncle Sam was a uniquely American figure, craggy and indomitable. He appealed to the American sense of individualism, in contrast to the uniformed image of Kitchener, which seems to have been designed to evoke loyalty to the group. Approximately four million copies of Flagg's poster

Flagg's best-known World War I poster and one of his World War II posters

were printed during the war, and he himself called it "the most famous poster in the world."

Flagg not only painted for the war effort, he performed. The steps of the New York Public Library became a center for war publicity, and the artist was often seen there. He drew portraits of those who pledged to buy a $1,000 Liberty Bond and even re-created his famous poster *Tell That to the Marines* as he perched on a ladder and painted on an enormous canvas from a live model while a platoon of marines with bayonets marched around him.

In the 1920s and 1930s Flagg resumed illustrating books and magazines, although his output was not as great as it had been prior to the war. Some of his liveliest work during this period was for the stories of P. G. Wodehouse. Flagg had illustrated an early Wodehouse story, "The Man Upstairs," for *Cosmopolitan* in 1910, and starting in 1926 he frequently illustrated Wodehouse's work in *Liberty* and *Red Book* as well as in *Cosmopolitan*. Although other artists, particularly Wallace Morgan, more frequently illustrated this popular author's stories, Flagg's conceptions of Wodehouse's characters rank with the best. Done both in pen and ink and in

watercolor, his depictions brought the vapid and chinless Bertie Wooster, the impeccable Jeeves, and the dotty but unmistakably aristocratic Lord Emsworth vividly to life. Wodehouse's irrepressible female characters were especially suited to Flagg's style, and they became British versions of the Flagg Girl, spirited, saucy, and irresistible.

As a natural outgrowth of his interest in the theater Flagg was fascinated by motion pictures. During World War I he was involved in making films for both the Red Cross and the Marine Corps. But Flagg could not be serious for long, and he soon turned to more frivolous subjects. With the backing of Eltinge Warner he wrote twelve one-reel comedies based on the Flagg Girl under the collective title "Girls You Know." These were so successful that he progressed to two-reelers; one of the first was *Perfectly Fiendish Flanagan; or, The Hart of the Dreadful West* (1918), a burlesque of the westerns of William S. Hart. Flagg both wrote and acted in this satire which ridiculed the formula of the outlaw reformed by the love of a pure woman. Flagg, who later became a close friend of Hart, reported that the author had "nearly ruptured himself laughing" on first viewing the film. Other films included *Beresford of the Baboons* (1919), a satire on Tarzan; *The Last Bottle* (1919), which lampooned Prohibition; and films mocking conventional love stories, including *The Bride* (1918) and *Hick Manhattan* (1918). After writing some two dozen films Flagg lost interest in making them himself, but he continued to be a well-known Hollywood figure. His charcoal sketches of film stars appeared regularly in *Photoplay* until the 1950s, and being the subject of one of those sketches was considered an essential step in any actor's career.

The decades between the wars were less productive for Flagg in part because of difficulties in his personal life. After Nellie's death in 1923 he married one of his models, Dorothy Wadman. Shortly after giving birth to their daughter, Faith, she suffered a mental breakdown, and Flagg supported her in an institution for the remainder of his life. An intense nine-year relationship with a German model, Ilse Hoffman, ended tragically when she committed suicide in 1937. During these years Flagg kept his private life separate from his public persona, but his output declined sharply. Nonetheless, one of the few books that he illustrated in the 1930s, Bett Hooper's *Virgins in Cellophane: From Maker to Consumer Untouched by Human Hand* (1932), includes drawings that are as lively and funny as any he produced.

The familiar figure of Uncle Sam appeared in many of Flagg's posters for World War II, recalling the energy and optimism of an earlier period. Despite the forcefulness of these works and the skill with which they were executed, the artist was showing signs of exhaustion and disillusionment. He described the mood of the times as "the capitulation of the Decent Man. . . . It is all so terrible, so impossible, so horrifying and beyond his ken, that he passes the buck to God. . . . It is unconditional surrender to Fate."

Flagg's last years were painful ones. *Roses and Buckshot* is a cheerful, if cantankerous, description of his eventful life, but a few years later he was more candid. G. L. Freeman, in a biographical portrait included with *Celebrity-Artist* (1960), quoted Flagg as saying that "even the recall of a gay past gives an unbeautiful picture and a nauseating smell." With most of his erstwhile cronies dead, Flagg complained, "All my life I have associated with the clever and witty. . . . Is it any wonder I don't like to look at the physical mess and mental dullness that

has set in for me. As far back as I can remember, I've been in the lime-light; now I'd rather be dead than be passed by ignored." He did take comfort in the companionship of a few young friends, particularly the portrait painter Everett Raymond Kinstler. When Flagg died in 1960, Kinstler delivered the eulogy at his funeral.

Flagg chronicled the fun and foibles of an optimistic America, a country where anything was possible. Julian Street described Flagg's sense of humor in a February 1912 *American Magazine* article as an "inexhaustible, bubbling spring," and Street quoted Charles Dana Gibson as saying that he knew of no one "with a greater gift of humor." Flagg was a keen and tireless observer of the life around him, recording details that those less attentive might miss. Some aspects of Flagg's work seem dated today; his attitudes toward other nationalities, nonwhite races, and women, as displayed in his writing, sometimes grate on late-twentieth-century readers. But his energy and inventiveness never fail to delight. Flagg himself best exemplified the qualities he once declared were those of the ideal woman: "courage, humor, and passion."

Biography:
Susan E. Meyer, *James Montgomery Flagg* (New York: Watson Guptill, 1974).

References:
Louis H. Frohman, "Flagg, Born Illustrator," *International Studio,* 77 (August 1923): 396–400;

Tudor Jenks, "Current Comment: James Montgomery Flagg," *Century,* 90 (June 1915): 320–320A;

Everett Raymond Kinstler, "Artists of Note: James Montgomery Flagg," *Artist,* 55 (July 1958): 87;

Susan E. Meyer, "James Montgomery Flagg: A Portrait of America," *American Artist,* 38 (November 1974): 40–47, 102–104;

Julian Street, "James Montgomery Flagg," *American Magazine,* 73 (February 1912): 417–419;

Frederic B. Taraba, "Celebrity Virtuoso: James Montgomery Flagg," *Step-By-Step Graphics,* 5 (November–December 1989): 116–123.

Archives:
A large collection of Flagg's original art was donated to the Society of Illustrators by Everett Raymond Kinstler and is now part of the Museum of American Illustration run by the Society in New York City.

Mary Hallock Foote

(19 November 1847 – 25 June 1938)

Carrie L. Marsh
Claremont Colleges

See also the Foote entry in *DLB 186: Nineteenth-Century American Western Writers.*

BOOKS: *The Led-Horse Claim* (Boston: J. R. Osgood, 1883);

John Bodewin's Testimony (Boston: Ticknor, 1886);

The Last Assembly Ball, and the Tale of a Voice (Boston & New York: Houghton, Mifflin, 1889);

The Chosen Valley (Boston & New York: Houghton, Mifflin, 1892);

Coeur d'Alene (Boston & New York: Houghton, Mifflin, 1894);

In Exile, and Other Stories (Boston & New York: Houghton, Mifflin, 1894);

The Cup of Trembling, and Other Stories (Boston & New York: Houghton, Mifflin, 1895);

The Little Fig-Tree Stories (Boston & New York: Houghton, Mifflin, 1899);

The Prodigal (Boston & New York: Houghton, Mifflin, 1900);

The Desert and the Sown (Boston & New York: Houghton, Mifflin, 1902);

A Touch of the Sun, and Other Stories (Boston & New York: Houghton, Mifflin, 1903);

The Royal Americans (Boston & New York: Houghton Mifflin, 1910);

A Picked Company: A Novel (Boston & New York: Houghton Mifflin, 1912);

The Valley Road (Boston & New York: Houghton Mifflin, 1915);

Edith Bonham (Boston & New York: Houghton Mifflin, 1917);

The Ground-Swell (Boston & New York: Houghton Mifflin, 1919);

A Victorian Gentlewoman in the Far West, edited by Rodman Paul (San Marino, Cal.: Huntington Library, 1972);

Idaho Stories and Far West Illustrations of Mary Hallock Foote, compiled by Barbara Taylor Cragg, Dennis M. Walsh, and Mary Ellen Williams Walsh (Pocatello: Idaho State University Press, 1988).

Mary Hallock Foote

SELECTED BOOKS ILLUSTRATED: Richardson, A. D., *Beyond the Mississippi* (Hartford, Conn.: American Publishing, 1867);

Longfellow, Henry Wadsworth, *The Hanging of the Crane* (Boston: J. R. Osgood, 1874);

Whittier, John Greenleaf, *Hazel Blossoms* (Boston: J. R. Osgood, 1875);

Whittier, *Mabel Martin: A Harvest Idyl* (New York: Houghton, Mifflin, 1876);

Longfellow, Henry Wadsworth, *Skeleton in Armor* (Boston: J. R. Osgood, 1876);

Hawthorne, Nathaniel, *The Scarlet Letter* (Boston: J. R. Osgood, 1876);

Tennyson, Alfred, *A Dream of Fair Women* (Boston: J. R. Osgood, 1879);

Bulwer-Lytton, Edward, as Owen Meredith, *Lucile* (Boston: Houghton, Osgood, 1879);

Foster, Stephen C., *My Old Kentucky Home* (Boston: Ticknor, 1888);

Foster, *Old Plantation Melodies* (Boston: Ticknor, 1890).

PERIODICALS: *Scribner's Monthly*, 1870–1880;
St. Nicholas, 1875–1897;
Century, 1881–1906.

Mary Hallock Foote was one of the leading women illustrators of her day in America. Perhaps best remembered as a novelist and short-story writer of the American West, in the late nineteenth century she enjoyed equal fame in art and publishing circles for her black-and-white woodcut illustrations, especially of local-color western life and scenery.

Mary Anna Hallock was born on 19 November 1847 on a remote farm on the Hudson River near Milton, New York, the youngest of the four children of Nathaniel and Ann Burling Hallock. The family, devout Quakers, were loving and close. Molly, as she was called, learned gentility and refinement from her mother; from her father she gained her lifelong love of literature. The Hallocks were learned, serious people. Various relatives were involved in social causes—abolition, woman suffrage, and the like—so while family life was insular, for Molly it was also nurturing and stimulating. Because an old dispute concerning her uncle Nicholas Hallock's forceful antislavery sermons separated the Hallock family from local Quaker fellowships, they turned to each other for support and companionship. Their ability to close ranks and their deep Quaker beliefs served perhaps to prepare Molly to endure the isolation she would often experience after her marriage and move west.

Hallock's talent for drawing was recognized when she was a child, and it was fostered by her family. Her older sister, Bessie, served often as her model for school assignments. When Molly expressed her desire to attend art school and her parents balked, her sister-in-law intervened on her behalf. In 1864, determined to be an artist, Hallock left her family for the first time to begin three years of study at the School of Design at the Cooper Union in New York City. She perfected the difficult techniques of woodcut illustration under the tutelage of William James Linton and William Rimmer. For most of her career she drew directly on the woodblocks, and another artist engraved them in preparation for the printing process. Even when she lived in the West, she had the blocks sent to her from back east.

Her first commission as a professional artist came in 1867 when she published four black-and-white drawings in A. D. Richardson's *Beyond the Mississippi*. More commissions soon followed. In the 1870s she contributed illustrations for stories and poems in such prominent magazines as *Scribner's Monthly* and *St. Nicholas*. The typical subjects of these illustrations are rural landscapes and tranquil domestic scenes inspired in large part by life at the Hallock farm. She often recruited relatives who happened to be close at hand to model. Once when in need of a "wassailer" Hallock used a male cousin who happened to be close by, roughing him up as best she could to fit the type.

In the early 1870s Hallock's illustrations gained the attention of Henry Wadsworth Longfellow. He invited her to collaborate on a deluxe gift-book edition of his *The Hanging of the Crane* (1874). Longfellow highly praised her illustrations for his book, inviting her to visit him in Boston. William Dean Howells in the December 1874 *Atlantic Monthly* also praised her work: "Every picture indeed is suffused with the light of a quick and refined sympathy; and this is reinforced by a skillful pencil which has, so far as we can observe, no unpleasant tricks or mannerisms." Indeed, contemporary reviews of Hallock's works comment on the accomplishment of her style and her ability to capture precisely a variety of subjects—scenery, domestic scenes, and figures—and infuse them with her own sensibility. Regina Armstrong in *The Critic* (August 1900) quotes Edwin Austin Abbey: "I'm trying to get the feeling that Mary Hallock Foote puts into her work—and I can't." Other notable accomplishments of Hallock's early career include collaborations with John Greenleaf Whittier on two works, *Hazel Blossoms* (1875) and *Mabel Martin: A Harvest Idyl* (1876).

Though she returned to her family after art school, Hallock did not altogether lead the quiet, rural life in which she had been raised. Early success encouraged an independence in her that was unusual for a young woman of the time, or at least a young woman of her social standing and community. Her career kept her traveling to New York and Boston to meet with the publishers and writers who commissioned her work, and she took advantage of these trips to socialize with the friends she had made while a student. Helena de Kay (who later married Richard Watson Gilder, the editor of *Scribner's Monthly* and later *Century*) was her closest friend and confidante. De Kay introduced Hallock to New York's prominent intellectuals, artists, and writers. Richard Watson Gilder helped to launch the young

One of Foote's illustrations for John Greenleaf Whittier's Mabel Martin: A Harvest Idyl *(1876)*

artist by publishing some of her earliest illustrations in his magazines. After her marriage and move west they were her link to the East and the intellectual and artistic society she had left behind. Particularly delighted by the western letters and sketches she sent them after her marriage, the Gilders persuaded her to submit pieces about her western experiences for publication. The rich correspondence between Hallock and the Gilders continued through several decades.

During one of her visits to New York in 1873, Hallock met a young mining engineer bound for the West. Arthur DeWint Foote came from an upper-class Connecticut family (his father was a member of the Connecticut legislature). He was ambitious and fiercely driven to make his mark on the new frontier. After a long-distance courtship they were married on 9 February 1876. In the midst of wedding preparations Hallock strove to finish the illustrations to accompany Longfellow's story of Viking life, *Skeleton in Armor* (1876). After the wedding her husband traveled alone to his job in California so that she could finish the commission. The difficulties of balancing a career and married life were apparent to her from the first. The publishers of *Skeleton in Armor* had prepared their advertising posters for the book reading "illustrated by Miss Mary A.

Hallock," and they were not pleased when her name changed in the middle of the contract. They then made it plain that wedding or not, they still expected her work on time.

Now Mary Hallock Foote, she traveled across the country, away from family, friends, and career in the East, and arrived at the mining camp in New Almaden, California, where her husband had built a large redwood cabin for them. She was unprepared for camp life. Left alone much of the time, Foote occupied herself with her art. She had arrived in California with a young female maid who had a small child, and they served as models for Hester Prynne and baby, respectively, in her illustrations of an 1876 gift-book edition of Nathaniel Hawthorne's *The Scarlet Letter* (commissioned before she had left the East). She produced twenty-nine drawings in a few months, though she struggled to keep up the quality of her work in such rural living conditions. Nevertheless, her work for the project was a success. The ability to convey a particular mood or emotion expressively was always important to her as an illustrator. She attempted to go beyond the textual description and evoke the highly intense emotion of the characters, especially Hester Prynne. The poignant *Scarlet Letter* engravings were enthusiastically reviewed by Howells in the *Atlantic Monthly*

(December 1877), and he singled Foote out as "the artist who perhaps unites more fine qualities than any other."

Life in a western mining camp was lonely and strange for Foote. She was the only woman at the New Almaden mine (aside from her servant) and socialized mainly with the engineers and with James D. and Mary Foote Hague (sister and brother-in-law of Arthur), who lived in San Francisco, more than fifty miles away.

Northern California was different from upstate New York. The land was dry and, to Foote, barren, and the days were long and monotonous. She observed the economic and social stratification of the camp's Mexican and Chinese workers, and her drawings of New Almaden reveal her ambivalence toward the community. She depicts the poverty in which the Mexican laborers worked, but she also conveys the dignity of the water carrier and the innocence of a child with his pet lizard. Her talent for expression of emotion through detail is clear in these works.

After a year in New Almaden, Arthur resigned his job and moved his family (their son was a few months old) to Santa Cruz, California. Confronted with financial insecurity (Arthur wanted to try freelance engineering work), the family lived off of the commission from Mary's *Scarlet Letter* work. *Scribner's Monthly* published a few of her western drawings along with short articles in 1878, and this began her career as an author-illustrator of the West. Encouraged by the Gilders to try her hand at fiction with a western setting but too shy and self-deprecating to trust their flattery, Foote submitted a short story about New Almaden, "In Exile," to Howells at the *Atlantic Monthly,* and it was published in 1881.

The Footes' married life was often unsettled because Arthur frequently changed jobs. Mary eventually took her son home to Milton in March 1878 for a year's stay. Being with her family helped to free her from the anxiety and loneliness she often felt in California. This was also a prolific period for Foote professionally—she produced drawings for *Scribner's Monthly* and short stories mostly set in the West, which were received with approval.

In 1879 Foote joined her husband at a new job in Leadville, Colorado. After a few months rivalry between two of the mines caused Arthur to lose another position. This incident proved advantageous in one way: it inspired Mary's first novel, *The Led-Horse Claim,* published by J. R. Osgood in 1883. However, the instability of their lives caused her to reassess her ability to complete commissions. Her artwork was much in demand by publishers in the

AWAY FROM HOME ON CHRISTMAS-DAY.
Drawn by Mary Hallock Foote.

Frontispiece for the January 1884 issue of St. Nicholas

late 1870s, and because this meant added income for the family, Foote did not like to turn down new commissions. She accepted two in 1879, one for an illustration for Alfred Tennyson's *A Dream of Fair Women* and another for Edward Bulwer-Lytton's *Lucile.* Both commissions required period detail. Because she knew her life was to be in the West (and thus isolated from fellow artists, libraries, and other sources of inspiration and historical detail), she worried about her ability to execute authentic drawings for works with non-Western themes. In *A Victorian Gentlewoman in the Far West* (1972) she recounts: "I ventured to take on myself another book contract, the most preposterous one yet. Imagine illustrating *Lucile* for an edition de luxe in Leadville—I who had never been abroad in my life and didn't know even what sort of chairs they sat on at European watering places! . . . But it wasn't so ingenuous of me as it was sheer commercial."

Another lost engineering position by Arthur meant that Mary was the sole wage-earner for the family. Concerned with meeting difficult deadlines and rendering period authenticity, she determined

The Sheriff's Posse *and* The Last Trip In, *two 1889 illustrations of the Old West that Foote drew for* Century Magazine

that she would accept no more commissions for other writers' works but instead would devote her time to illustrating her own literary efforts.

Foote traveled to Mexico with her husband on a mine-inspection job in the summer of 1881, and she agreed to record her experiences for *Century*. She was enthralled by the romance of the trip and recorded what fascinated her. Her character studies and depictions of Mexican houses and landscapes were well received. By 1884 Arthur had moved his family again, this time to Idaho. Mary uncomplainingly settled her family in the new place, and she greatly appreciated the beauty of the mountains and canyons. In a June 1887 letter she wrote to Helena Gilder, Foote describes her feelings toward the Idaho frontier: "There is something terribly sobering about these solitudes, these waste places of the Earth. They belittle everything one is, or tries to do. The vast wonderful sunsets, the solemn moonlights, and the noise the river makes on dark nights. The wash of water and of land and the immense dignity of it all!"

Her time in Idaho was both rewarding and difficult. The isolation of their mountain cabin, economic instability (the serialization rights of her novels to date helped to support the family), and plaguing doubts over her work placed a terrific strain on Foote. She produced a few illustrations for such magazines as *St. Nicholas* (using her children as models) during this period as well as some Western romance-adventure stories. One bright spot for the entire family during this time was Rudyard Kipling's correspondence. He wrote to Foote, complimented her on her work, and asked her to supply two drawings for *The Naulahka* (1892).

Yet the milestone of Foote's artistic career was achieved during this difficult time. By the late 1880s she had gained prominence, according to Alpheus S. Cody in *Outlook* (26 May 1894), as the "best known woman illustrator" for her frontier landscapes and character studies. Richard Watson Gilder urged her to submit a collection of drawings of the West for a series to run in *Century*. Her *Pictures of the Far West* series appeared in 1888 and 1889 to enthusiastic praise. She produced eleven drawings for the series, using her own house and children as models, and these illustrations rival the best work of her peers. The subjects of her series are the rivers, canyons, deserts, ranchers, miners, and families of Idaho. The West in these drawings is nearly tamed, and many of the woodcuts reveal a pastoral ideal. *The Orchard Windbreak* and *The Irrigating Ditch* are quiet, picturesque depictions of women seemingly unthreatened by the frontier. In *Afternoon at a Ranch* and *The Pretty Girls in the West* the sweetness and nor-

malcy of the settled frontier are shown in a small child sleeping on a ranch-house porch and a young man courting a pretty girl. A rougher aspect of frontier life is conveyed in Foote's drawings of a wagon train moving west across a barren land in *The Last Trip In*. A man protects his young family against an unseen foe in *The Coming of Winter*. The nearly treeless land, vast sky, and limitless view contribute a sense of solitude and melancholy in many of the illustrations. Of this series and other drawings William Allen Rogers wrote in *A World Worth While: A Record of 'Auld Acquaintance'* (1922), "There is a charm about her black-and-white drawings which cannot be described, but it may be accounted for by the fact that, more than any other American illustrator, she lived the pictures from day to day which she drew so sympathetically."

Though Foote often expressed doubts about her talent as an illustrator, her peers recognized her by selecting her as an art juror for the World's Columbian Exposition (Chicago World's Fair) in 1893. She served on the awards jury for etching. She was included in "The Century Series of American Artists" tribute in *Century*. In addition she was invited to accept the principalship of the Cooper Union, her alma mater (which she declined). In 1895 the Footes settled in Grass Valley, California, where they lived for the following thirty years. By the late 1890s, at the height of her popularity as an illustrator, Foote stopped illustrating altogether in favor of her writing career. Her retirement from illustrating provoked many tributes from her contemporaries. In his autobiography, *The Adventures of an Illustrator* (1925), Joseph Pennell calls Foote "one of our best illustrators." Regina Armstrong in the *Critic* (August 1900) evaluates Foote's contribution to the art of illustration, asserting that it "possesses that intrinsic quality that we would least part with; its intimacy is appealing, and it has strength and vigor. Pastoral, elemental, with the earth-feeling throbbing through it, but essentially poetic and spiritual, it is more the psychic expression of force and delicacy." In a letter to William Dean Howells (29 August 1906) Samuel Clemens has nothing but admiration for her: "My idea is this: that I send this letter of yours to Clara & let her submit it to her dear & valued & level-headed friend & mine, Mary Foote. . . . Never mind the rest of the Feet, Mary Foote is a fine human being, of full age, & has more sense than you & me (damn the I), put together." Of her Western stories and illustrations Rogers wrote in *A World Worth While*, "Somehow she and Owen Wister, two products of the most refined culture of the East, got closer to the rough frontier character than any writers I know, and Mrs. Foote supplemented this with pictures that one feels were made while looking from the rim of some deep canyon or by the light of a lantern in a lonesome cabin."

Prospering quietly with her family in northern California, Foote found much success writing novels and stories based on her experiences and observations of life in the American western frontier. In 1922 she began her "Reminiscences," edited by Rodman Paul and published as *A Victorian Gentlewoman in the Far West*. In 1932 she moved east with her husband to Hingham, Massachusetts, where she died on 25 June 1938.

Changing aesthetic attitudes in writing and art, in part, caused Foote's life and work to fall into obscurity until she was rediscovered by Wallace Stegner, who in his prizewinning novel *Angle of Repose* (1971) dramatizes her life and career. An operatic version of the book was produced in 1976.

During her life Foote produced many illustrations, both for the literary efforts of others and for her own novels and stories. Almost all were received with critical acclaim, and she enjoyed the high esteem of her contemporaries. She started her art career in a field dominated by men, and she succeeded beyond even her own expectations. A gentle, refined woman, Foote followed her husband west and endured both disappointment and contentment, all the while producing a body of work, artistic and literary, that distinguishes her among her peers. Though today she is best known as a writer of Western stories, her wood engravings, especially those depicting life in the American West, are among the best of the "Golden Age" of American illustration.

References:

Regina Armstrong, "Representative American Women Illustrators," *Critic,* 37 (August 1900): 131–141;

Lee Ann Johnson, *Mary Hallock Foote* (Boston: Twayne, 1980);

William Allen Rogers, *A World Worth While: A Record of 'Auld Acquaintance'* (New York: Harper, 1922).

Archives:

Mary Hallock Foote's papers can be found in two major repositories: the Huntington Library in San Marino, California; and the Stanford University Library. The Library of Congress; the Bancroft Library at the University of California, Berkeley; Harvard University; the New York Public Library; and the Wisconsin Historical Society also hold Mary Hallock Foote manuscript materials.

A. B. Frost
(17 January 1851 – 22 June 1928)

Catherine A. Hastedt
Texas A&M University

BOOKS: *Stuff & Nonsense* (New York: Scribners, 1884);

The Bull Calf and Other Tales (New York: Scribners, 1892);

Shooting Pictures, by Frost and Charles D. Lanier (New York: Scribners, 1895);

The Golpher's Alphabet, by Frost and William Gilbert van Tassel Sutphen (New York & London: Harper, 1898);

Sports and Games in the Open (New York & London: Harper, 1899);

The A. B. Frost Portfolio (New York: Collier, 1903);

A Day's Shooting (New York: Scribners, 1903);

A Book of Drawings (New York: Collier, 1904);

A Portfolio of Twelve Original Illustrations Reproduced from Drawings to Illustrate The Pickwick Papers (London: A. J. Slater, 1908);

Carlo (Garden City, N.Y.: Doubleday, Page, 1913).

SELECTED BOOKS ILLUSTRATED: Adeler, Max [C. H. Clarke], *Out of the Hurly Burly* (New York: P. Garret, 1874);

Clarke, Charles Heber, *Elbow Room* (Philadelphia: Cowperthwait, 1876);

Shortcut, Daisy, and Arry O'Pagus, *One Hundred Years a Republic: Our Show* (Philadelphia: Claxton, Remsen & Haffelfinger, 1876);

Frost, S. Annie, *Almost a Man* (New York: American Tract Society, 1877);

Dickens, Charles, *Pictures from Italy, Sketches by Boz and American Notes* (New York: Harper, 1877);

Dickens, *The Posthumous Papers of the Pickwick Club* (London: Ward, Lock, 1881);

Clarke, Charles Heber, *An Old Fogey and Other Stories* (London: Ward, Lock, 1881);

Tourgée, Albion W., *Hot Plowshares* (New York: Fords, Howard & Hulbert, 1883);

Carroll, Lewis, *Rhyme? & Reason?* (London: Macmillan, 1883);

Carroll, *A Tangled Tale* (London: Macmillan, 1885);

Roosevelt, Theodore, *Hunting Trips of a Ranchman* (New York: Putnam, 1885);

Arthur B. Frost

Stockton, Frank R., *Rudder Grange* (New York: Scribners, 1885);

Harris, Joel Chandler, *Free Joe and Other Georgian Sketches* (New York: Collier, 1887);

Brunner, H. C., *The Story of a New York House* (New York: Scribners, 1887);

Stockton, Frank R., *The Squirrel Inn* (New York: Century, 1891);

Munkittrick, Richard Kendall, *Farming* (New York: Harper, 1891);

Harris, Joel Chandler, *Uncle Remus and His Friends* (Boston: Houghton, Mifflin, 1892);

Davis, Richard Harding, and others, *The Great Streets of the World* (New York: Scribners, 1892);

Thanet, Octave, *Stories of a Western Town* (New York: Scribners, 1893);

Page, Thomas Nelson, *Pastime Stories* (New York: Harper, 1894; New York: Scribners, 1898);

Aldrich, Thomas Bailey, *The Story of a Bad Boy* (Boston: Houghton, Mifflin, 1895);

Harris, Joel Chandler, *Uncle Remus: His Songs and His Sayings* (New York: Appleton, 1895);

Bunner, Henry Cuyler, *Jersey Street and Jersey Lane* (New York: Scribners, 1896);

Twain, Mark, *Tom Sawyer Abroad, Tom Sawyer Detective, and Other Stories* (New York: Harper, 1896);

Bangs, John Kendrick, *Ghosts I Have Met and Some Others* (New York: Harper, 1898);

Harris, Joel Chandler, *The Chronicles of Aunt Minervy Ann* (New York: Scribners, 1899);

Carruth, Hayden, *Milo Bush and Other Worthies* (New York: Harper, 1899);

Boyle, Virginia Frazer, *Devil Tales* (New York & London: Harper, 1900);

Major, Charles, *The Bears of Blue River* (New York: Doubleday & McClure, 1901);

Harris, Joel Chandler, *The Tar Baby and Other Rhymes of Uncle Remus* (New York: Appleton, 1904);

Harris, *Told by Uncle Remus: New Stories of the Old Plantation* (New York: McClure Phillips, 1905);

Wood, Eugene, *Back Home* (New York: McClure Phillips, 1905);

Philips, Henry Wallace, *Red Saunders' Pets and Other Critters* (New York: McClure Phillips, 1906);

Philips, *The Pets* (New York: McClure Phillips, 1906);

Dickens, Charles, *The Pickwick Papers* (London: A. J. Slater, 1908);

Carroll, Lewis, *Phantasmagoria and Other Poems* (London: Macmillan, 1911);

Harris, Joel Chandler, *Uncle Remus Returns* (Boston: Houghton Mifflin, 1918).

PERIODICALS: *New York Daily Graphic,* 1875–1876;
Harper's Weekly, 1876–1906;
Century, 1886–1906, 1914–1920;
Collier's, 1887–1905;
Scribner's, 1887–1906, 1915–1927;
Sporting Pictures, 1895–1896;
McClure's, 1904–1905;
Life, 1920–1926.

Called the dean of American illustrators by critics and contemporaries, A. B. Frost has been described as the most American of the American illustrators of the turn of the century. Throughout his fifty-year career as an illustrator he displayed an un-

paralleled ability to capture the essence of the rural America of his time. His skill in portraying humorous situations set the standard for comedic art, and his characterizations of Joel Chandler Harris's Uncle Remus and Brer Rabbit have become inseparable from those stories.

Born in Philadelphia, Pennsylvania, on 17 January 1851, Arthur Burdett Frost was the youngest child of the three surviving from ten born to John Frost and Sarah Ann Burdett Frost. Like most young boys, Frost liked to while away the hours drawing, and his family would often come upon him sprawled on the floor happily doodling pictures of Indians. His early childhood was happy, but when Frost was only eight years old, his father died. Although John Frost had earned a reputation as a prolific author of books on the military and other subjects, he was unable to pass on a more tangible legacy to his children. The family was left in poor financial shape.

At the age of fifteen Arthur took his first job as an apprentice and delivery boy to a wood engraver. He hated the menial nature of the job and bemoaned the dull, mechanical drawing that came with it. After six months his employer fired him, declaring that Frost was "without talent as draftsman or messenger." Despite the tediousness of the work, Frost did come away from his first job with the one skill he would need to start him on his chosen career as an artist-illustrator: he had learned to draw on wood.

Reproducing illustrations by wood engraving was the method of choice for all the major publishing houses of the second half of the nineteenth century. Illustrations could be reproduced more quickly and cheaply than with metal engravings, and the results were just as clean and crisp. Artists would either draw directly on the fine wood blocks or would provide drawings that would be transferred to the wood. The engravers, who were amazingly skilled (but usually uncredited), would then transform the drawings into the finished product. Both black-line and white-line engraving methods were used, although Frost preferred the black-line method.

Frost's next job was with the Ketterlinus lithography shop. He worked there for several years, learning all aspects of the printing process: from transforming original drawings to printing plates to the intricacies of wood engraving and the kinds of illustration and drawing techniques that reproduced the best. Frost found the work discouraging because it, like his previous job, was commercial in nature and did not allow him freedom of expression. It did, however, teach Frost to develop the habit of making quick sketches of what interested him, and he rapidly filled several sketchbooks with his work. Frost would continue this habit for the rest of his life despite the fact that he did not use any of his thousands of sketches for his final illustrations.

Work was not the only thing that occupied the young man's time, however. Frost was athletically inclined and frequently participated in sporting activities. As befitted a young man of his shy and retiring nature, he was drawn to more-restrained rather than combative athletics. One of his favorite sports was rowing. He was a member of the Undine Barge Club and acquired the habit of rowing early in the morning before work. He joined the Philadelphia Fencing and Sparring Club and also enjoyed going on shooting parties with his friends in the country. It is no surprise, therefore, that many of his early drawings are of a sporting nature or that he would display such an intimate knowledge and feel for hunting and shooting scenes later in his career. In addition to sports, Frost actively pursued his art. He would often spend his after-work hours at the Philadelphia Sketch Club absorbing everything that he could learn from its instructors. In 1873 he contributed several line drawings to the Philadelphia Sketch Club Portfolio.

At the age of twenty-three Frost had his first real break. He became friends with William J. Clarke, an artist and critic, who examined Frost's sketchbooks and admired the warmth and humor he saw in the lines. Clarke was the brother of Charles Heber Clarke, who wrote humorous novels under the pseudonym Max Adeler. William convinced his brother to let Frost produce a few of the illustrations needed for Charles's new book, *Out of the Hurly Burly* (1874). Frost quickly produced more than four hundred illustrations and was delighted when most of them were used in the final publication.

The author prophesied a bright future for the young artist. In the preface to *Out of the Hurly Burly* Clarke complimented the versatility and originality of the sketches and the "genial humor, with so little extravagance and exaggeration" of Frost's concepts. The book was an immediate and international success. Newspaper reviews at the time were universally complimentary; in fact, the critic for the *Philadelphia Evening Bulletin* hailed the drawings as "much the best that have ever been given in any American book of humor." The publication went on to sell more than a million copies and was translated into almost every European language.

The success of *Out of the Hurly Burly* brought Frost additional commissions. By 1877 he had illustrated three more books, including another novel by Charles Heber Clarke, *Elbow Room* (1876); *One Hun-*

Cover for Frost's first book (1884)

dred Years a Republic: Our Show (1876) by Daisy Shortcut and Arry O'Pagus; and a book by his sister, S. Annie Frost, *Almost a Man* (1877). All were well received and helped alleviate some of the chronic doubts Frost had about his work.

In 1875 Frost, through the influence of Clarke, got a job with the *New York Daily Graphic,* where he worked for several years producing comic illustrations and political cartoons. His good draftsmanship, combined with a nascent talent for humor ranging from gentle satire to slapstick, soon caught the eye of Charles Parsons, the head of the art department at Harper and Brothers. Parsons had an innate ability to spot budding talent and had already assembled one of the most impressive rosters of illustrators ever to work for a major publisher, including Howard Pyle, E. W. Kemble, Charles S. Reinhardt, Frederic Remington, and Edwin Austin Abbey. In 1876 Frost joined the team and was quickly accepted by the others for his talent and geniality. Frost liked working in the friendly atmosphere at Harper. He was closest to Pyle and would later be best man at Pyle's wedding. The two would remain friends for the rest of their lives and would often go on sketching trips together along Pyle's beloved Brandywine River.

As a staff artist Frost was required to produce work rapidly, often averaging two to three drawings a week. The assignments were interesting, however, and he was allowed to indulge his imagination. Parsons thought highly of Frost's work, and under his leadership and guidance Frost perfected his command of the comic genre. Within seven years he was one of the most popular artists at Harper, producing many illustrations and cartoons and earning over a hundred dollars a week, which, as Frost excitedly wrote in an 11 July 1883 letter to his fiancée, was a "mighty good price."

Although Frost would eventually go on to great success with this publisher, he decided after a year to take a hiatus and travel abroad. Like most young artists of the time, Frost felt the necessity of making a pilgrimage to London. This great metropolis was considered the mecca of all aspiring illustrators, where they could meet and learn from such greats as George Cruikshank and John Leech. Some modern-day critics compare Frost's early illustrations to those of Cruikshank, but although the two artists undoubtedly share a talent for comic exaggeration, Frost, unlike Cruikshank, was able to give his characters humanity as well as humor. His gift was making both his figures and his settings real.

During his year in London, Frost quickly gained a wide circle of friends and acquaintances and published a few illustrations, including those for an 1877 edition of Charles Dickens's *Pictures from Italy, Sketches by Boz and American Notes*. Frost was generally disappointed in his trip, however, and returned with little regret to Philadelphia. The trip was to have one unexpected benefit for Frost: it brought him to the attention of Charles Lutwidge Dodgson, better known as Lewis Carroll, the author of the Alice books.

Carroll wrote to Frost in 1878, asking if he would be interested in illustrating a new book called "Rhyme? & Reason?" Carroll had been impressed by a few Frost cartoons he had seen and thought that Frost had the comic genius necessary to undertake his new book. The author's long-standing association with the English illustrator John Tenniel, who thirteen years earlier had brilliantly created the drawings of Alice and the denizens of Wonderland, had been severed. Tenniel no longer worked in woodcut illustrations, which were required by Carroll, and he had refused to undertake the job.

Frost agreed to the commission, and five years later, in 1883, *Rhyme? & Reason?* was published. It was a long and grueling project for Frost. Carroll had definite ideas about the book's appearance. Not only did he minutely criticize and revise each drawing, he also fancied himself an amateur illustrator and would sometimes make preliminary sketches for Frost to copy. Frost knew that this commission, his first for such an internationally known author, would be the making of his career, so he persevered despite the constraints put upon him.

Rhyme? & Reason? owes much to the work of Tenniel, whose dry, shaded-outline technique clearly influenced Frost's illustrations. It is not clear how much this influence is due to the exacting requirements of Carroll and how much is due to Frost's assiduous studying of Tenniel's techniques, but the work is vastly different from his cartoons for *Out of the Hurly Burly*.

Although Frost absorbed much from Cruikshank and Tenniel, he came back from England aware of his shortcomings in drawing the human form. He decided he needed to pursue academic training and immediately began his studies under Thomas Eakins at the Philadelphia Academy of Fine Arts. Frost eagerly absorbed the teachings of Eakins in his evenings at the academy (1878–1881), and the influence of Eakins on Frost's early work, particularly in the delineation of his lines and the articulation of body movement, is easily recognized. Frost and Eakins also shared the same artistic vision: they both advocated truth and realism in their art as well as a naturalistic approach to their subject that rejected affectation. The two men became close friends, and Eakins would produce two portraits of the redheaded, bearded Frost.

Frost met another of his lifelong friends in Eakins's class, the painter Augustus S. Daggy. Daggy remembered their time at the academy as an intense one for Frost: "I never saw a man study so hard. Anatomy, photographs, everything he could get that would satisfy his consuming passion to know it all. He took such pains I really felt he would kill himself with overwork."

Frost was an extremely self-critical artist and would often destroy dozens of drawings, convinced that he would never get it right. Despite his quick temper and self-doubts, his intimate friends knew him as warmhearted, generous, and entertaining. Full of nervous energy, he felt the need to be constantly active.

Frost had returned from England determined to work. He rejoined the staff at Harper and continued his studies at the Philadelphia Academy of Fine Arts. There he met his future wife, Emily Louise Levis Phillips. An accomplished artist in her own right, she was also studying at the academy under Eakins and is considered by many to be the model for Eakins's 1877 painting *Young Girl Meditating*. The Frosts

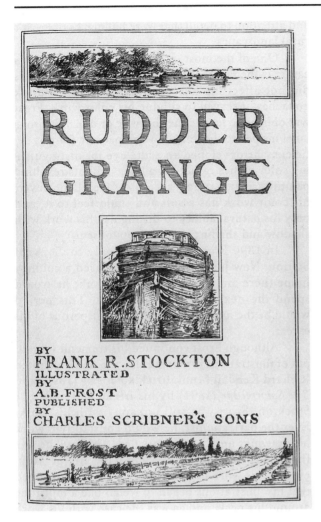

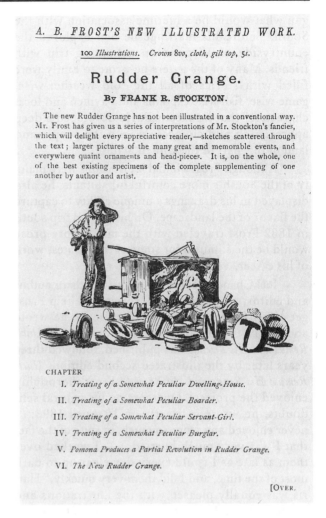

A. B. FROST'S NEW ILLUSTRATED WORK.

100 Illustrations.   Crown 8vo, cloth, gilt top, 5s.

Rudder Grange.

By FRANK R. STOCKTON.

The new Rudder Grange has not been illustrated in a conventional way. Mr. Frost has given us a series of interpretations of Mr. Stockton's fancies, which will delight every appreciative reader,—sketches scattered through the text; larger pictures of the many great and memorable events, and everywhere quaint ornaments and head-pieces. It is, on the whole, one of the best existing specimens of the complete supplementing of one another by author and artist.

CHAPTER
    I. *Treating of a Somewhat Peculiar Dwelling-House.*
   II. *Treating of a Somewhat Peculiar Boarder.*
  III. *Treating of a Somewhat Peculiar Servant-Girl.*
  IV. *Treating of a Somewhat Peculiar Burglar.*
   V. *Pomona Produces a Partial Revolution in Rudder Grange.*
  VI. *The New Rudder Grange.*

[OVER.

Title page and advertisement for the first book by another author to be illustrated solely by Frost

were married on 19 October 1883 and had two children, Arthur Jr. (born in 1887) and John (born in 1890).

By the mid 1880s Frost's illustrations were appearing regularly in *Scribner's Magazine* and *Century*. In 1885 he illustrated another book by Carroll titled *A Tangled Tale* as well as Frank R. Stockton's *Rudder Grange* and Theodore Roosevelt's *Hunting Trips of a Ranchman*. Although critics lamented that Frost's work suffered in the reduction process, they applauded his easy humor, which did not rely on exaggerated caricatures to provoke laughter.

In addition to his regular illustration work, 1884 also marked the publication of Frost's first collection of comic illustrations, *Stuff & Nonsense*. Although Frost had by no means originated the idea of the comic strip, he was the one who laid the groundwork for such classic comedic forms as the "double take," the "slow burn," and, as was later popularized by Stan Laurel and Oliver Hardy, the series of mishaps that slowly build to a major disaster. One

of the best examples of Frost's sharp comedic sense is the series of illustrations in *Stuff & Nonsense* called *The Fatal Mistake—A Tale of a Cat*. It tells of a cat who, after accidentally consuming rat poison, rampages through a house and out into the street trying to outrun his fate. With a few masterful strokes of the pen, the artist conveys the wide-eyed, dismayed expression on the cat's face when he realizes what he has done. After the second frame the cat never touches the ground again, spooking butlers, invalids, dogs, and fish.

Stuff & Nonsense was enthusiastically received by the public. Although later contemporaries would disparage the grotesque humor of the sketches when compared to the more-subtle work in his illustrations for the Uncle Remus tales, they could not deny the widespread appeal of the drawings, which were readily understood and appreciated by Americans. Frost had a tolerant and sympathetic eye for the foibles of his fellowman, and his drawings reflect it.

Shortly after his return to America, Frost began what would be a lifetime association with the South. Before his marriage he had explored the countryside of Virginia on a hunting trip with friends. Many of the letters he wrote to Emily were filled with stories of all the "old weather-wise, game-wise, fish-wise captains and baymen and local characters" that he sketched. He developed a deep appreciation and connection with the people and land of this part of the United States.

Although Frost's initial impressions were mainly of the South's more colorful inhabitants, he also displayed in his drawings a unique ability to capture the flavor of the landscape. On his second trip south in 1882 Frost traveled with the man whose prose would be the stimulus for some of the greatest work of his career.

Joel Chandler Harris, the great Southern author and editor, agreed to tour Georgia and help Frost get a feel for the people and landscape he wrote about. The two became close friends. In 1892 *Uncle Remus and His Friends* was published, followed three years later by the illustrated second edition, *Uncle Remus: His Songs and His Sayings.* Frost thoroughly enjoyed the projects. Overcoming his natural self-doubts, he wrote to Harris on 10 April 1893, "I never enjoyed any work so much, in spite of the fact that I was very much hurried. . . . I worked over them as late as I could every day clear up to dark most of the time, and I did them very quickly." Harris was equally pleased with the illustrations and wrote in the preface to the 1895 edition of Uncle Remus, "it would be no mystery at all if this edition were to be more popular than the old one. Because, by a stroke here and a touch there, you have conveyed into their quaint antics the illumination of your own inimitable humor. . . . The book was mine, but now you have made it yours, both sap and pith."

The critics were wholeheartedly in agreement. The art critic for *The New York Times* wrote in a 13 November 1895 review of an exhibition of Frost's Uncle Remus drawings that "the humanity that the artist has infused into the beasts, the absurdity of costume, and the subtle, delicate touches that everywhere abound are irresistible. They show, too, an able grasp of the most minute detail, the thousand and one nothings that stamp the efforts of the truly artistic."

Frost became the preeminent artist of those of the so-called homespun school, who made rural America and particularly Negro life their specialty. Although other artists such as E. W. Kemble, Alice Barber Stevens, and Thomas Fogarty drew the same subjects, they could not approach the naturalness

and attention to detail that were hallmarks of Frost's rural landscapes.

One of the most interesting aspects of Frost's career is the fact that he was color-blind. While this did not affect his line drawings and pen-and-ink gouaches, it served to subdue his color work. Frost was obliged to have either his wife or one of his sons label his palette for him. To compensate for this deficiency he developed an acute eye for distinguishing color values rather than hues, and his resulting paintings are amazingly accurate. Overall, however, his color work has a soft and timid feel to it, and only his natural ability to distinguish his work with shadow and shading saves it from obscurity.

In 1890 Frost moved his family to Convent Station, New Jersey. He had purchased a country home there and dubbed it Moneysunk; he would spend the next sixteen years there. This period would be the most productive and prosperous of his career.

Although Frost continued his tremendous output of illustrations for magazines and had illustrated Richard Kendall Munkittrick's *Farming* (1891) and *The Squirrel Inn* (1891) by his friend and neighbor Stockton, Frost was still unhappy with his work. Ever the perfectionist, he would constantly rework his drawings until he was satisfied. Although he was financially stable and was enjoying life at Moneysunk, his work began to suffer. Frost complained that his illustrations began to weigh like a millstone around his neck, and as was the case with his work for *Collier's,* he became more and more pedantic, exhibiting hard-edged lines and tight, literal compositions. Frost himself referred to this time as his "Cast Iron Period."

Frost knew he needed help, and in 1891 he turned to the American impressionist William Merritt Chase for instruction. Frost immediately began to benefit from Chase's tutelage. He wrote in a January 1891 letter to his friend Augustus Daggy, "I have started painting with Chase and I think he will do me a power of good. He will get me to loosen up my blamed tight fist, and get some go into my work." Frost did, in fact, lose some of the telltale signs of the illustrator in his work. His style became more free flowing, and he did not rely so heavily on minute details in his compositions. The still lifes and outdoor scenes Frost produced during this period show his renewed excitement for his work and the fun he was having with his changed style.

By 1896 the distinctive signature of "A. B. Frost" could be found in all the major magazines—*Harper's Weekly, Scribner's Magazine, Century,* and *Collier's.* Wanting to do more than just the cartoon-style illustrations for which he was known, he began pro-

Brer Bear Acts Frightening, *one of Frost's illustrations for Joel Chandler Harris's* Uncle Remus: His Songs and His Sayings *(1895)*

ducing paintings of outdoor sporting scenes. His love for the sport and for nature in general is revealed in the hunting scenes he did for *Scribner's* and in the portfolio of twelve lithographs and forty line drawings he did for *Sporting Pictures,* published in 1895–1896. The prints were extremely popular and became prized collectibles, decorating salons and men's clubs alike. These carefully composed illustrations are notable for their tranquility and attention to detail. After years of study with Eakins and Chase, Frost's easy handling of the anatomy of the animals and the posture of the hunters was now second nature. The action in the paintings is simply stated but powerful. In 1896 Frost illustrated another classic tale of Americana, Mark Twain's *Tom Sawyer Abroad, Tom Sawyer Detective, and Other Stories.* His characterizations of Tom Sawyer and Huck Finn again demonstrated his sensitivity to the Southern landscape and his facility for portraying the author's intent, so that when illustrations were needed for the spooky tales of the Negro South written by Virginia Frazer Boyle, Frost was the obvious choice. His drawings for *Devil Tales* (1900) are classic examples of his talent for drawing characters true to their environment. As Harris later wrote in

the introduction to Frost's *A Book of Drawings* (1904), "they belong to the time and the place, and could belong nowhere else; and they all show the influence of the American spirit and breathe in an atmosphere of American humor."

In 1900 Frost also exhibited some of his works at the Paris Exposition. The French critics were enthusiastic and praised his paintings of American rural life. The continued success of the Uncle Remus books and Frost's assured popularity at home and abroad provided the impetus for the artist to return to his earlier success with *Stuff & Nonsense* and produce his second book of comedic illustrations. *The Bull Calf and Other Tales* (1892) emphasizes Frost's natural ability for comic exaggeration and satire.

The book was a widespread success. Frost understood the tastes of the American people, giving them completely natural drawings with a generous portion of satire and keen observation. In *A Tale of Two Tails,* which chronicles the meeting between a gentleman and a monkey, Frost uses a minimal background and triangular form to focus on the action. The disgruntled expressions on both the monkey and the man—the result of one having burned his coat and the other his tail—are priceless. Rendered with deft strokes and few lines, the cartoon is a perfect example of how Frost's humor focused on the foibles of the common man. Readers were able to identify the characters he drew with people that they themselves knew.

Like many of his contemporaries, Frost was drawn to further his career doing "serious painting" rather than illustration. Although his *Book of Drawings* was widely praised and he had illustrated more than seventy books since he began his career, Frost could not rid himself of his nagging doubts about his talent. By this time his eyesight was failing, but he nevertheless decided that he needed to go to Europe to pursue his art.

In 1906 Frost severed all his business relationships, packed up his family, and moved to Paris. The city was not what he had expected, however, and he soon moved to Giverny to be near the place where Monet had worked. Frost's two sons, who were following in their father's footsteps and learning to paint, remained in Paris. The boys would study at the Academie Julian while Frost and his wife dabbled in impressionist landscapes.

Fate was not kind to the Frost family. Both sons contracted tuberculosis in Paris and were forced to enter a sanatorium. This additional expense compelled Frost to return to illustration to pay for their care. He contacted some publishers back home and soon was commissioned to produce *Carlo* (1913), a story of a boy and his dog. The American public, starved for Frost's work, enthusiastically received the book. Its success, combined with Frost's concern for his family, finally convinced him to give up his painting and return to America. His sons, having sufficiently recovered, went to New York to study, and Frost and his wife settled in Wayne, Pennsylvania.

There was no lack of work waiting for him. He was again drawing for *Scribner's Magazine* and *Century,* and he provided illustrations for Carroll's *Phantasmagoria and Other Poems* (1911) and Harris's *Uncle Remus Returns* (1918). His life seemed on an even keel. Then tragedy struck. His eldest son, Arthur Jr., died unexpectedly from complications with influenza. The death of his son devastated the elder Frost. For nearly a year there is little information about his activities.

In 1918 Frost began to put his life back together. He picked up his audience again with his caricatures of rural bumpkins and assorted odd characters. Barely a year after his first son's death, his son John became ill again. Alarmed, Frost quickly acted on a doctor's advice and moved his family to the drier climate of California, where he was to spend the rest of his days.

In 1920 the renowned "American Beauty" illustrator Charles Dana Gibson approached Frost to contribute to *Life* magazine, which Gibson had recently purchased. Frost's first illustrations for the periodical were happily received by Gibson, and the two men would collaborate for the next six years. In addition to his magazine work, Frost resumed producing book illustrations. His illustrations were still highly sought after by other editors who realized that illustrations by an artist of Frost's stature could enormously increase the sales of a book. Frost was thus able to command top wages. In 1920 he was paid $200 for four illustrations he had done for "The Trials of Jonathon Goode," which appeared in the December 1920 issue of *Scribner's Magazine.* Frost continued to contribute comic vignettes and sporting scenes to *Life* and *Scribner's Magazine* until his death after a short illness on 22 June 1928. So deeply connected with the American psyche was Frost that his death was deeply mourned across the country.

Although present-day critics may view Frost's work as solid and homespun rather than brilliant, they still acknowledge that he was a master at reaching the audience of his time. A character artist rather than a caricaturist, Frost was a close and sympathetic observer of everyday life. He accurately recorded the manners and dress of rural America of the 1880s and 1890s. For his skill with the pen Frost will remain an icon of American illustration of the turn of the century. His illustrations have sustained their appeal through time and will continue to delight new generations.

Biographies:

Henry Wysham Lanier, *A. B. Frost: The American Sportsman's Artist* (New York: Derrydale Press, 1933);

Henry M. Reed, *The A. B. Frost Book* (Charleston, S.C.: Wyrick, 1993).

References:

Gene E. Harris, *Arthur Burdett Frost 1851–1928 Artist and Humorist* (Chadds Ford, Pa.: Brandywine River Museum, 1986);

Henry M. Reed, *The World of A. B. Frost: His Family and Their Circle* (Montclair, N.J.: Montclair Art Museum, 1983);

Frank Weitenkampf, "A. B. Frost," *Arts,* 15 (March 1929): 168–172.

Archives:

Original artwork by A. B. Frost can be found in the collections of the Robert W. Woodruff Library, Emory University; the New York Public Library; the Library of Congress, Division of Prints and Photographs; and the Brandywine River Museum.

Charles Dana Gibson
(14 September 1867 – 23 December 1944)

Catherine A. Hastedt
Texas A&M University

See also the Gibson entry in *DS 13: The House of Scribner, 1846–1904.*

BOOKS: *Drawings* (New York: Russell, 1894);
Pictures of People (New York: Russell, 1896);
People of Dickens (New York: Russell, 1897);
London as Seen by Charles Dana Gibson (New York: Scribners, 1897);
Sketches in Egypt (New York: Doubleday & McClure, 1899);
The Education of Mr. Pipp of New York (New York: Russell, 1899);
The Americans (New York: Russell / London: John Lane, 1900);
A Widow and Her Friends (New York: Russell / London: Lane, 1901);
The Social Ladder (New York: Russell, 1902);
Eighty Drawings, Including The Weaker Sex. The Story of a Susceptible Bachelor (New York: Scribners, 1903);
Everyday People (New York: Scribners, 1904);
Our Neighbors (New York: Scribners, 1905);
Charles Dana Gibson: Four Pictures in Color, portfolio of prints published with *Frederic Remington: Four Pictures in Color* (New York: Collier, 1906);
The Gibson Book: A Collection of the Published Works of Charles Dana Gibson, 2 volumes (New York: Scribners, 1906);
Other People (New York: Scribners, 1911);
Gibson New Cartoons: A Book of Charles Dana Gibson's Latest Drawings (New York: Scribners, 1916);
Cartoons and Cartoonists (Springfield, Ohio: Crowell, 1923).

SELECTED BOOKS ILLUSTRATED: Stockton, Frank R., *The Merry Chanter* (New York: Century, 1890);
Davis, Richard Harding, *Van Bibber and Others* (New York: Harper, 1892);
Davis, *The Exiles, and Other Stories* (New York: Scribners, 1894);
Davis, *About Paris* (New York: Harper, 1895);

Charles Dana Gibson

Davis, *The Princess Aline* (New York: Harper, 1895);
Goodloe, Abbe Carter, *College Girls* (New York: Scribners, 1895);
Magruder, Julia, *The Violet* (New York: Longmans, Green, 1896);
Life's Comedy (New York: Scribners, 1897);
Wheeler, Post, *Reflections of a Bachelor* (New York: Ogilvie, 1897);
Davis, Richard Harding, *Soldiers of Fortune* (New York: Scribners, 1897);
Hope, Anthony, *Prisoner of Zenda: Being the History of Three Months in the Life of an English Gentleman* (New York: Holt, 1898);
Hope, *Rupert of Hentzau: From the Memoirs of Fritz von Tarleuheim* (London: Macmillan, 1898);
Bangs, John Kendrick, *The Booming of Acre Hill and Other Stories of Urban and Suburban Life* (New York: Harper, 1900);

The Gibson Girl

Davis, Richard Harding, *Her First Appearance* (New York: Harper, 1901);

Davis, *The King's Jackal* (New York: Scribners, 1903);

Addison, Julia de W. G., *Mrs. John Vernon: A Study of a Social Situation,* frontispiece by Gibson (Boston: Gorham, 1909);

Davis, Richard Harding, *Gallegher and Other Stories* (New York: Scribners, 1910);

Chambers, Robert W., *Blue-Bird Weather* (New York & London: Appleton, 1912);

Deland, Margaret, *Partners* (New York & London: Harper, l913);

Beach, Rex, *The Auction Block: A Novel of New York Life* (New York: Burt, 1914);

Culter, Richard V., *The Gay Nineties,* foreword by Gibson (Garden City: Doubleday, Page, 1927).

PERIODICALS: *Life,* 1886–1932;
Puck, 1886–1888;
Tid-Bits, 1886–1888;
Scribner's Magazine, 1889–1897;
Century, 1889–1890;
Harper's Magazine, 1889–1903;
Harper's Weekly, 1889–1903;
McClure's, 1897–1898;
Collier's, 1900–1914;
Cosmopolitan, 1907–1913, 1927–1929.

No other American illustrator has had such a profound and direct influence on the American people as Charles Dana Gibson. His creation, the "Gibson Girl," dictated the style, life, and dress of American men and women for nearly two decades. He was the first American illustrator to earn a fortune by his work and is ranked as an excellent pen-and-ink artist.

Born in Roxbury, Massachusetts, in 1867, Charles Dana Gibson was the second of three sons and second of the six children of Charles DeWolf Gibson and Josephine Elizabeth Lovett Gibson. When Gibson was still a small child, the family moved to Flushing, Long Island, where his father, a salesman for the National Car Spring Company, had been transferred. The Flushing neighborhood, as yet undeveloped, was ideal for a growing boy. Woodlands beckoned from the back door of his house; Gibson, his brother Langdon, and Dan Beard, the future leader of the Boy Scouts movement, spent hours exploring together and collecting specimens. These early experiences molded Charles Dana Gibson into the keen observer of life he remained throughout his career.

At an early age Dana, as he was called, manifested a marked faculty for art. Once when he was ill as a small child, his father amused him by teaching him to cut silhouettes out of paper. Instantly fascinated, the child grabbed the scissors from his father's hand and began making them on his own. Young Gibson spent hours diligently practicing, creating amusing little vignettes for his family and friends. Encouraged by their son's innate sense of design, the parents apprenticed him at the age of thirteen to the sculptor Augustus Saint-Gaudens. Gibson showed no aptitude for rendering in three dimensions. Having concentrated so hard on producing perfect silhouettes, he had trouble interpreting an object from more than one perspective. Discouraged, he gave up and returned home to finish high school. Gibson was an indifferent scholar, preferring instead to spend his time participating in the sports of rowing, swimming, and putting the shot. Even so, he kept at his art, for at some point during his high-school years he discovered a talent for drawing that was encouraged by his teachers. Gibson graduated from Flushing High School in 1884.

Despite being descended from a well-connected New England family (Gibson's maternal grandfather was assistant secretary of state for Massachusetts for forty years), the Gibsons were often financially strapped. Gibson knew that if he was going to make a living by his art, he would have to do so as quickly as possible. Ever supportive, his parents had sacrificed in order to enroll him in the Art Students League after he graduated from high school. He studied there for two years under such instructors as Kenyon Cox, William Merritt Chase, and Thomas Eakins. (At one point Gibson had studied alongside Frederic Remington, who left after a few weeks to head west.) Gibson's work upon leaving the Art Students League was, as he himself put it in a 29 November 1902 interview for *Collier's*, "no better . . . than when I went in–at any rate, my work wasn't a bit more salable."

But Gibson was ambitious, and he began a campaign to present his portfolio to all the publishing houses and printers in New York. Not surprisingly his reception was poor. For more than a year Gibson continued to approach art editors and publishers hoping to sell even a single drawing. Not until 1886 did the sharp-eyed editor of *Life*, John Ames Mitchell, detect the traces of Gibson's hidden talent in his work. Mitchell, who was an illustrator himself, thought the work was "reasonably bad" but saw "courage and honesty" in the lines. For four dollars he purchased a small drawing to illustrate the song "The Moon and I" from the *Mikado*, which was then the rage on Broadway. The drawing appeared unsigned in the 25 March 1886 issue of the magazine; it is one of only a few Gibson works without the distinctive "C. D. Gibson" signature scrawled beneath it.

Encouraged by his first sale, Gibson hurriedly produced additional work. He became known to publishing houses as being able to meet a two-hour deadline without faltering under pressure, and his commissions steadily increased. The weekly *Tid-Bits* enabled him truly to establish himself. In this publication Gibson's work progressed from spot drawings to single- and double-page spreads, and his illustrations displayed the artist's increased self-assurance. Gibson's success enabled him to move from Flushing to his first studio in the Alpine Building on Thirty-third Street and Broadway.

Not until he made a pilgrimage to Europe did Gibson develop the style that made him famous. With a modest income garnered from steadily increasing sales, he was finally able to afford to travel and study in the art meccas of London and Paris. While in London he met George Du Maurier, the famous British illustrator of *Punch*, who had a great influence on Gibson's drawing style. Up to this point Gibson's work had been restrained and resembled more the satiric drawings of Thomas Nast, the popular political cartoonist. As work of this period reveals, Gibson quickly emulated Du Maurier's drawing style of fine-lined details. Gibson next became interested in the artwork of Phil May, the English artist whose specialty was rendering his subjects with the fewest possible lines. Gibson adopted May's long, flowing lines and limited backgrounds; they later became Gibson's trademark. After leaving London, Gibson went to Paris where he studied for two months at the Academie Julien until his funds ran out and he was forced to return to America.

Prosperity awaited his return. His earlier success opened doors at all the big magazines–*Century*, *Harper's Weekly*, and *Scribner's Magazine*. He also illustrated books, including several by his close friend Richard Harding Davis: *Van Bibber and Others* (1892), *The Princess Aline* (1895), and *Soldiers of Fortune* (1897) as well as books by other authors such as *The Merry Chanter* (1890) by Frank R. Stockton. His revised pen-and-ink technique, while evocative of the crosshatching of Du Maurier and the flowing lines of May, was transformed by the verve, dash, and assertiveness that was uniquely Gibson. He was well on the way to becoming one of the foremost black-and-white illustrators of his day.

By 1890 he was earning $600 to $800 per month for his artwork. As Davis remembered in *Current Literature* (December 1905), "Where a book of mine without illustrations would sell ten copies, if

AT MONTE CARLO

MR. PIPP'S LUCK HAS CHANGED. HE BREAKS THE BANK.

Illustration from Gibson's The Education of Mr. Pipp of New York *(1899)*

Dana put a few pictures of long-legged men in it it would sell twenty." In fact, Davis often modeled for the dapper hero in Gibson's illustrations although Gibson himself, handsome, well over six feet tall, and broad shouldered, could easily have done so.

An additional stimulus to Gibson's output was the lessening dependence on woodblock printing. The introduction in the 1880s of zinc-block plates and the photographic halftone process enabled a crisper, more finely detailed reproduction of an artist's original. This innovation suited Gibson's newly refined style perfectly.

In 1893 Gibson exhibited thirty-nine drawings at the Chicago World's Fair and received critical acclaim. He continued to work steadily, contributing to *Life, Scribner's Magazine, Harper's Weekly,* and *Harper's Monthly* regularly. He was pioneering in the advertising field with his work for the Chicago, Burlington, and Quincy Railroad. For these accomplishments he might well have been remembered, but the 1894 publication of his first folio book, *Drawings,* truly marked his place in history.

During the early 1890s Gibson began to draw his most famous creation, the Gibson Girl. Tall, athletic, and beautiful, she epitomized the characteristics of the ideal woman for America and answered American society's yearning for an aristocracy. First

appearing in *Drawings,* the Gibson Girl was an overnight sensation, so much a phenomenon that the name Gibson became synonymous with the Gay Nineties. Images of his eponymous creation soon appeared on dishes, pillows, shirtwaists, shoes, dressing-table sets, folio books, and even wallpaper. When the Gibson Girl changed her hairstyle or dress, millions of American women rushed to salons and dressmakers to imitate her. Plays were written about her and hit songs like "Why Do They Call Me a Gibson Girl?" were penned. Her fame quickly spread around the world, attracting notable collectors such as Czar Nicholas II of Russia and Kaiser Wilhelm II of Germany. Her image appeared in shop windows as far away as Tokyo. Sinclair Lewis called her "the Helen of Troy and Cleopatra of her day." There were in fact seven different Gibson Girls: the Beauty, the Boy-Girl, the Flirt, the Sentimental, the Convinced, the Ambitious, and the Well-Balanced. The last was the artist's favorite, for he thought her closest to the ideal. He also created a "Gibson Man" to be her perfect escort.

With Harrison Fisher, Howard Chandler Christy, Coles Phillips, and James Montgomery Flagg, Gibson joined a group known as the "American Beauty" illustrators. Unlike the maternal and Victorian "Brandywine School" girls drawn by

Howard Pyle and his followers, the "American Beauty" was single, liberated, and modern.

Scores of young society girls presented themselves to Gibson as models for his Gibson Girl and appeared anonymously in his illustrations. While he enjoyed the impromptu visits of these lovely young ladies, he often found working with them difficult, and he preferred to use professional models when he could afford them. In turn, the professionals liked to work for Gibson. He was invariably considerate of them; in fact, he was one of the first artists to pay a model, once engaged, regardless of the outcome of the drawing. But in 1895 he met the ideal model for his Gibson Girl. She was Irene Langhorne, one of the five beautiful Langhorne sisters of Virginia. (Another became Lady Astor.) Gibson and Irene Langhorne were married on 7 November 1895 and had two children, Irene (1897) and Langhorne (1899).

Despite the financial success that the frenzy over the Gibson Girl brought to him, Gibson resented the predominance the critics accorded her over his other work. He preferred that the critics pay equal attention to work that he felt was perhaps better. Unfortunately, the popularity of the "Girl" was such that Gibson could not afford to give her up; in lieu of that he began manipulating her for his own purposes. Through her he commented on the foibles of modern society, especially the behavior of the elite Four Hundred—the so-called aristocracy of America. He bitterly decried their loveless marriages to the English nobility to gain titles and their snobbery even though he was now a part of that group. Again and again he penned his stock characters: the fickle young woman, the lovelorn youth, the dissolute nobleman, and the tasteless nouveau riche. The cartoon situations were sometimes comical, sometimes pathetic, but inevitably keenly observed. Always gently satiric, he had the happy ability of making the subjects of his satire, from politicians to society figures, laugh along with him.

Gibson's career flourished. He continued to publish a drawing a week for *Life;* produced another book, *Pictures of People,* in 1896; and contributed countless illustrations to novels, including Davis's *Soldiers of Fortune* and Anthony Hope's *Rupert of Hentzau* (1898). He managed to provide drawings for exhibitions as well. In a review of his 1897 exhibition of forty-one original drawings at the Keppell Gallery in New York, critics were equivocal. While they deemed some works better in the original, they said others "felt the lack of reproduction." Nonetheless, on the whole they praised the strength and delicacy of his art.

Gibson and his newlywed wife set off on an extended honeymoon trip abroad. The result of his observations in England was two volumes: *People of Dickens* and *London as Seen by Charles Dana Gibson,* published in 1897. Despite his enormous popularity back home, his London drawings were not well received in England. As *The New York Times* reported on 12 December 1897, "The general objection to them is that they only here and there catch the truth about the lower classes, while the upper class ladies and gentlemen are not characteristically English at all, but are Americans in London clothes."

There was no doubt, however, that Gibson could capture the essence of American society. Although his London series was perhaps not his best work, he was soon to produce just that. *The Education of Mr. Pipp of New York* (1899) is often hailed as Gibson's best series of illustrations. It chronicles the adventures of the wealthy but downtrodden Mr. Pipp, a small, measly man who with his large, overbearing wife and two beautiful daughters makes a tour of the Continent. In the series, *At the Ambassador's The Order of Precedence as Heretofore Observed by the Pipps Holds Good While the Family Is Abroad* is a masterful example of Gibson's ability to create areas of light and shade; it is also an amusing commentary on the innocent American abroad. The expressions on the faces of Mr. Pipp and his domineering wife, rendered with a minimum of line, are priceless.

Nowhere is Gibson's skill in composition more evident than in *At Monte Carlo Mr. Pipp's Luck Has Changed. He Breaks The Bank.* The entire background of the illustration is a mosaic of different faces peering over Mr. Pipp's shoulder at the huge pile of winnings in front of him. Each line is crisply laid out and the composition reinforced by the obvious diagonals of the dealers' rakes. At the center is Mr. Pipp, his puckish delight at his good fortune radiating from the page.

Soon after the success of *Mr. Pipp* came *A Widow and Her Friends* (1901), *The Social Ladder* (1902), and *Eighty Drawings, Including The Weaker Sex. The Story of a Susceptible Bachelor* (1903). Of these, *The Social Ladder* includes some of the funniest work Gibson did, save perhaps the Mr. Pipp series. As the critic for *Collier's* wrote in the 29 November 1902 issue, "Mr. Gibson's cartoons fairly crackle with spontaneous mirth. The comic situation is there exactly as nature prepared it, not as laboriously contrived by the conscious artist. It never occurs to you that Gibson invented the joke; only that he saw and recorded it." Gibson was unquestionably the most popular artist in America at this point, and the inclusion of his drawings could often make a magazine.

STUDIES IN EXPRESSION
AN IMITATION OF THE LADY OF THE HOUSE.

A satiric cartoon by Gibson, published in a 1902 issue of the humor magazine Life

In 1903 *Collier's* began a campaign to attract the top illustrators of the day to the magazine, promising exclusive contracts, larger format illustrations, and exorbitant salaries. Howard Pyle, Remington, Maxfield Parrish, and others were already part of their staff of illustrators, and inevitably they approached Gibson. Despite an offer of a four-year contract to produce one thousand drawings at $1,000 apiece, the highest salary yet offered an illustrator, Gibson balked at the exclusivity clause. He was unwilling to leave *Life* and Mitchell, who had given Gibson his start. Faced with ultimate rejection, *Collier's* compromised and agreed to share Gibson with *Life,* but only with *Life.* When the *Ladies' Home Journal* subsequently published a Gibson illustration in the midst of the publicity campaign at *Collier's* to announce their new artist, a scandal erupted. *Life* and *Collier's* immediately published refutations. After the ensuing investigation determined that *Ladies' Home Journal* had merely picked up an already-published Gibson work, *Collier's* sales soared.

Gibson's continued popularity seemed assured. He was making a fantastic salary of more than $65,000 a year, almost twice that of his nearest competitor, Pyle. He moved among the highest echelons of society, traveled widely on assignments, and had a happy and healthy home life. But Gibson was not satisfied: he felt that he had reached his limit in black and white. Robert W. Chambers in a *New York Times* article (17 October 1905) recorded Gibson as saying that "while he might continue to make money he would do so at a sacrifice of his artistic self-respect." He yearned to expand his horizons and experiment in colors as other illustrators were doing. Thus, in 1905 he made a public announcement that he was giving up drawing to take up painting in Europe. Before Gibson left for Europe he exhibited three oil portraits to a curious crowd at the American Art Galleries in the Collier's Public Art Show. The critics agreed that the only comparison to his drawing was in his bold brush strokes; some thought this an eccentric whim while others lauded him for turning away from the lure of money and following his heart.

For three years Gibson studied oil painting in Spain, Italy, and France. The Panic of 1907 and the collapse of the Knickerbocker Trust Company dealt Gibson a major financial blow and forced him to return to his lucrative career in drawing. Gibson was unhappy, however, and longed for the day when he could return to painting.

Upon his return to America he began illustrating again for *Life, Collier's,* and *Cosmopolitan,* but times were changing, and a fickle public was beginning to turn its eyes elsewhere. The Gibson Girl was slowly being replaced by the Flapper, and black-and-white illustrations were giving way to photography. Gibson continued to work, however, and his name occasionally brought him commissions to paint and draw portraits of important people. But despite his attempts to evolve with a changing society, he could not seem to catch the more flippant spirit of the times. His drawings were beginning to be regarded as relics of the past.

As World War I approached, Gibson's cartoons became increasingly militant. His early career as a political cartoonist in *Tid-Bits* enabled him to lampoon with ease, and his attacks on the kaiser grew more and more frequent. In 1917 Gibson was asked to head the Division of Pictorial Publicity, the aim of which was to dramatize "Why We Fight." Gibson gathered around him all the top illustrators of the day, and at weekly meetings at Keene's Chop House on Thirty-sixth Street in New York, assignments were passed out with sketches often being made right at the table. The Gibson Girl was transformed into "Miss Columbia," urging Americans to buy Liberty Bonds and defend Europe. So successful was this program that Gibson was honored for his contributions to the war effort, receiving the Order of the Crown of Belgium and being made a chevalier in the Legion of Honor of France in 1923.

After the war Gibson returned to illustration. He continued to work for *Life* despite the death of his friend Mitchell in 1918. When Mitchell's estate came up for auction in 1920, Gibson and a syndicate of friends purchased the magazine, outbidding Doubleday, Page. Unfortunately, Gibson had no talent for running a magazine. The country had changed after the war, and the popularity of humor magazines was waning. *Life* went into a steady decline. Gibson was unable to cope with bickering editors and unhappy staff members; he escaped responsibility as often as he could at his Seven Hundred Acre Island summer home in Penobscot Bay near Isleboro, Maine. The inevitable happened, and in 1925 the disgruntled widow of a former major stockholder sued Gibson. In the lawsuit he was accused of being "recklessly extravagant" in managing the affairs of *Life* and charged with employing "incompetent assistants" and paying them "excessive sala-

Miss Columbia, *the character Gibson created for the Liberty Bond campaign during World War I*

ries." He was also accused of paying himself $30,000 annually for his drawings on top of his base salary of $20,000 as president of the company. The lawsuit was dropped almost immediately "due to a misapprehension on the part of the plaintiff," but the damage was done. Besieged by unhappy employees and by continual losses, Gibson finally gave up and sold the magazine in 1932.

Throughout this period Gibson had continued to pursue his painting career. In 1934 he held his first major exhibition of more than one hundred paintings at the American Academy of Arts and Letters. The exhibition was a resounding success; the art critic for *The New York Times* (8 November 1934), Edward Alden Jewell, wrote, "Make no mistake about it, Charles Dana Gibson is a painter. He proves it again and again in a way the visitor is not likely soon to forget." Gibson continued to pursue his new career steadfastly but away from the public until his death of myocarditis at his home in New York in 1944.

Charles Dana Gibson was a director of the American Institute of Arts and Letters and a member of the National Academy of Design; he also served as president of the Society of Illustrators from 1904 to 1907 and from 1909 to 1921. He received an honorary doctorate in fine arts in 1931 from Syracuse University. A staunch supporter of representative art, Gibson, unlike Pyle, did not believe that a solid background in art education was necessary. Life, according to Gibson, was the best teacher. He never worked from photographs, denouncing those illustrators as mere "copyists" and not true artists. He abhorred modern art. As he said in an interview in *The New York Times* (12 September 1937),

> I've always believed that no one could really accomplish anything in art without enjoying it. I do not believe that any man can force himself to paint a good picture. He must feel an uncontrollable urge. While he is working he may suffer from the knowledge of his inability to express what he wants to; nevertheless, he must be getting fun out of what he is doing. What I can't understand is how any one can get any fun out of turning out some of the pictures that today pass as art.

Looked at in retrospect, the work of Charles Dana Gibson is entirely a product of his time. His sentimental approach to his subject and his gentle satire are a record of a time more useful to historians than art critics. He has been criticized for his limited repertoire of characters and for the unreality of his situations, but even his detractors admit to his careful, elaborate, and well-balanced compositions. His book illustrations are generally held to be not as good as his cartoons. Gibson found the limitations put on him by the text too restricting; they were what the author wanted and not his own observations. Nevertheless, while Gibson's skill with pen and ink may have been approached or copied by other illustrators, his unique ability to observe his subjects and to get them to look at themselves will never be surpassed.

Biography:
Fairfax Downey, *Portrait of an Era as Drawn by C. D. Gibson* (New York & London: Scribners, 1936).

References:
J. M. Bulloch, "Charles Dana Gibson," *Studio International,* 8 (June–September 1896): 75–81;

Woody Gelman, ed., *The Best of Charles Dana Gibson* (New York: Crown, 1969);

Susan E. Meyer, *America's Great Illustrators* (New York: Abrams, 1978), pp. 208–231;

Frederick W. Morton, "Charles Dana Gibson, Illustrator," *Brush & Pencil,* 7 (February 1901): 277–293;

J. A. Reid, "Charles Dana Gibson and His Work," *Art Journal* (1900): 39–44.

Archives:
Notable collections of original Gibson illustrations are held by the New York Public Library; the Society of Illustrators; and the Library of Congress, Division of Prints and Photographs.

William J. Glackens

(13 March 1870 – 22 May 1938)

Nancy Allyn Jarzombek

SELECTED BOOKS ILLUSTRATED: McCain, George Nox, *Through the Great Campaign with Hastings and His Spellbinders* (Philadelphia: Historical Publishing, 1895);

Page, Thomas Nelson, *Santa Claus's Partner* (New York: Scribners, 1899);

Gaboriau, Emile, *File No. 113* (New York: Scribners, 1900);

Seawell, Molly Elliot, *Papa Bouchard* (New York: Scribners, 1901);

Kock, Charles Paul de, *Monsieur Dupont* (Boston: Quinby, 1902);

Williams, Jesse Lynch, *New York Sketches* (New York: Scribners, 1902);

Kock, *The Barber of Paris* (Boston: Quinby, 1903);

Kock, *Frere Jacques* (Boston: Quinby, 1903);

Kock, *Jean* (Boston: Quinby, 1903);

Ford, James B., *The Brazen Calf* (New York: Dodd, Mead, 1903);

Friedman, Isaac Kahn, *The Autobiography of a Beggar: Prefaced by Some of the Humorous Adventures and Incidents Related in The Beggars' Club* (Boston: Small, Maynard, 1903);

Lewis, Alfred Henry, *The Boss and How He Came to Rule New York* (New York: A. S. Barnes, 1903);

Ford, James B., *Edmond and His Cousin, etc.* (Boston: Quinby, 1904);

Ford, *Little Lise* (Boston: Quinby, 1904);

White, William Allen, *In Our Town* (New York: McClure, Phillips, 1906);

Irwin, Will, *Confessions of a Con Man* (New York: Huebsch, 1909);

Dreiser, Theodore, *A Traveler at Forty* (New York: Century, 1913);

Towne, Charles Hanson, ed., *For France* (New York: Doubleday, 1917).

PERIODICALS: *McClure's,* 1897–1904, 1906–1907, 1909–1910;

Munsey's, 1898–1899;

Ainslee's Magazine, 1899;

Scribner's Magazine, 1899–1902, 1905–1906, 1909;

Harper's Bazar, 1900;

William J. Glackens in 1898

Everybody's, 1901, 1912–1915;

Harper's Weekly, 1900–1901, 1903, 1913–1914;

Frank Leslie's Popular Monthly, 1901–1904, 1906, 1908;

Collier's, 1901–1907, 1910–1914, 1918–1919;

Century Magazine, 1902, 1913;

The Saturday Evening Post, 1902–1910, 1912;

Metropolitan Magazine, 1903–1904;

Cosmopolitan, 1905–1906, 1909;

Putnam's, 1908–1910;

Masses, 1913.

William J. Glackens was a distinguished American artist. His contributions to the history of

Glackens's illustration for McClure's *of preparations for the Battle of San Juan Hill, 1 July 1898*

American art include his participation in the exhibition of "The Eight," the group of artists also known as the Ashcan School for their realistic portrayals of city life and their opposition to the American art establishment; his organization of American paintings for the Armory Show of 1913; and his important acquisitions for the collection of Albert C. Barnes. Although best known as a painter, Glackens was also an illustrator, and his vigorous, humorous drawings represent a vital aspect of the graphic tradition in American art.

William Glackens was born in Philadelphia on 13 March 1870, the third and youngest child of Samuel and Elizabeth Finn Glackens. He attended Central High School in Philadelphia, where he met John Sloan and Barnes. With his brother, Louis, who became an illustrator and cartoonist, he exhibited his wit and artistic talent early, entertaining classmates with comical sketches.

From 1891 to 1894 Glackens worked as an artist-reporter for the *Philadelphia Record,* the *Philadelphia Press,* and the *Philadelphia Public Ledger* alongside Sloan, Everett Shinn, George Luks, James Preston, and Frederic Gruger. His fellow reporter-artists considered him skillful and marveled at his ability to recall details. Glackens attended classes at the Pennsylvania Academy of the Fine Arts. There he met Robert Henri, who encouraged him to apply skills he was perfecting as an artist-reporter—drawing city scenes he observed—to easel painting. Glackens shared a studio with Henri in 1894, and the following year the two artists traveled through France and Belgium together.

In 1896 Glackens returned to the United States, settled in New York City, and began working for the *New York Sunday World* and the *New York Herald.* In 1898 *McClure's* sent him to Cuba to make illustrations of the Spanish-American War. He traveled to Tampa, Florida, and managed to get passage to Cuba to cover the events leading up to the celebrated charge up San Juan Hill. At least forty-three drawings survive from this trip, twenty-two of which were published in *McClure's* and *Munsey's.* Glackens worked directly in the field, making drawings as horses and men charged by; he also worked on drawings well after the events took place, using field notes, memory, and photographs.

After Glackens returned to New York, he received commissions from popular magazines such as *McClure's, Scribner's Magazine,* and *Collier's.* He continued in the artist-reporter vein, drawing scenes of New York for stories such as "The New Wall Street" (*Munsey's,* April 1899) and "New York's Charm in Summer" (*Harper's Bazar,* August 1900).

A Football Game (Collier's, *11 November 1911), one of a series of city-street scenes by Glackens*

At the same time he branched out to illustrate adventure stories and romances. In 1902 the *Saturday Evening Post* engaged him to illustrate "The Beggars' Club," a four-part comedy by Isaac Kahn Friedman, and thus began a productive association during which illustrations by Glackens appeared regularly through 1906. After that his contributions became less frequent, and his last drawings for the *Post* were published in 1912.

The *Post* typically gave Glackens urban working-class subjects, especially the comic adventures of big shots (such as "The Boss" by Alfred Henry Lewis in 1903), mischievous kids (for example, "Sequil, or Things Which Ain't Finished in the First" by Henry H. Shute in 1904), and social misfits (such as "Confessions of a Con Man" by Will Irwin in 1909). At the same time Glackens worked on more-serious stories such as Mrs. John Van Vorst's "The Cry of the Children: Human Documents in the Case of the New Slavery," a moving, five-part exposé of child labor that appeared in 1906.

Glackens was part of a convivial circle of artists, many of whom worked as illustrators while pursuing ambitions of becoming painters. He remained close to his Philadelphia friends Sloan, Henri, and Preston. In 1901 he met Edith Dimock, a young art student who lived in the Sherwood Building, where Henri also had a studio. Dimock's apartment, shared by Lou Seymes and the illustrator May Wilson, who married James Preston in 1903, was a lively meeting place for artists. Glackens and Dimock married in 1904. A son, Ira, was born in 1907 and a daughter, Lenna, in 1913.

Glackens's most active years as an illustrator were from 1902 to 1907. During this time he perfected his style. He would make many sketches for each drawing until he got the composition the way he wanted it. He worked with line and wash combined, heavily outlining the figures and using rough hatch work to shade and enliven the drawings. He used charcoal or carbon pencils and ink with a pen or small brush to make the hatched areas. He made the washed areas by dragging a wet brush over the charcoal lines or by applying ink washes, and he would use white paint and an eraser to highlight areas.

Glackens's style was distinctive, but it was not unique. George Luks, Everett Shinn, Florence Scovell Shinn, Frederick Gruger, Wallace Morgan, May Wilson Preston, and other illustrators also made humorous drawings in a quick and spontaneous style. In fact, Gruger and Glackens were particularly close in style for a time. In 1903 Gruger, filling in for his friend, illustrated an installment of "The Boss" for the *Saturday Evening Post* in a style almost identical to that of Glackens. Glackens and Gruger also jointly illustrated several stories by William Allen White for the *Saturday Evening Post.*

Critics were enthusiastic about Glackens's work. As early as 1901 John R. Neil, a critic for the *North American Book Supplement,* called him a "comet flashing into prominence," and Regina Armstrong in the May 1900 *Bookman* praised him as an "eternal pioneer in art who transcribes the life about him in his own particular and definite way." Later critics continued to laud his work. In 1909 the *Bookman* called him one of America's foremost illustrators, and by 1915 he achieved master status when *Vanity Fair* named him one of a dozen of the best illustrators in the world, proclaiming, "he observes the life around him with truly baffling keenness, and draws it with masterful directness and simplicity. If Glackens would only give up painting (and fishing) he would become one of the best illustrators alive."

Despite his success Glackens felt that illustration work took time away from painting. Influenced by Henri's philosophy on art and life, Glackens looked to the world around him for his subjects, painting interior scenes peopled with his family and friends, nearby landscapes, and views of urban life. He regularly entered the annual juried exhibitions at the National Academy of Design, the Society of American Artists, and the Pennsylvania Academy of the Fine Arts. In 1908 he took part in the famous exhibition of The Eight at the Macbeth Gallery in New York. The exhibition was a sensation and raised a furor in the press, who labeled the group a "revolutionary black gang" and criticized the paintings for being coarse and vulgar. Many critics saw elements of modernism, socialism, and anarchism in their work. The organization of the show also went against convention: the group rejected the principle of juried exhibition, adopting instead a process by which the participating artists rather than an outside committee determined the content of the exhibit.

After the Macbeth show Glackens accepted fewer illustration jobs, but he nonetheless produced important pieces, such as the series of full-page views of city streets for *Collier's* published between 1911 and 1913. In 1913 *Century* used his drawings to accompany three stories by Theodore Dreiser, published later that year in the book *A Traveler at Forty,* and from 1913 to 1914 Glackens illustrated the "Denny Nolan" stories by E. R. Lipsett. After 1914 Glackens virtually stopped illustrating. His last drawings were published in *Collier's* in 1918 and 1919 to accompany four stories set on American destroyers during World War I.

During the next two decades Glackens devoted his time to painting and his other great love, fishing. He maintained his studio and home in New York City although he and his family spent summers in Bellport, Long Island, and traveled frequently to Europe. In 1937 Glackens's health began to fail, and he was no longer able to paint. He died of a cerebral hemorrhage on 22 May 1938.

References:

Nancy E. Allyn, *William Glackens: Illustrator in New York 1897–1919* (Wilmington: Delaware Art Museum, 1985);

Allyn and Elizabeth H. Hawkes, *William Glackens: A Catalogue of His Book and Magazine Illustrations* (Wilmington: Delaware Art Museum, 1987);

Ira Glackens, *William Glackens and The Eight* (New York: Horizon, 1957);

Rebecca Zurier, "Picturing the City: New York in the Press and the Art of the Ashcan School, 1890–1917," dissertation, Yale University, 1989.

Elizabeth Shippen Green

(1 September 1871 – 29 May 1954)

Susan Hamburger
Pennsylvania State University

SELECTED BOOKS ILLUSTRATED: Le Galli-enne, Richard, *An Old Country House* (New York: Harper, 1902);

Humphrey, Mabel, *The Book of the Child,* illustrated by Green and Jesse Willcox Smith (New York: Stokes, 1903);

Songs of Bryn Mawr College (Philadelphia: Bryn Mawr College, 1903);

Buchanan, Thompson, *The Castle Comedy* (New York: Harper, 1904);

Chambers, Robert W., *River-Land; a Story for Children* (New York: Harper, 1904);

Donnell, Annie Hamilton, *Rebecca Mary* (New York: Harper, 1905);

Donnell, *The Very Small Person* (New York: Harper, 1906);

Peabody, Josephine Preston, *The Book of the Little Past* (Boston: Houghton Mifflin, 1908);

Cabell, James Branch, *Chivalry,* illustrated by Green, Howard Pyle, and William Hurd Lawrence (New York: Harper, 1909);

Duncan, Norman, *The Suitable Child* (New York: Fleming H. Revell, 1909);

Gerry, Margarita Spalding, *The Flowers* (New York: Harper, 1910);

Van Dyke, Henry, *The Mansion* (New York: Harper, 1911);

Hardy, Arthur Sherburne, *Aurelie* (New York: Harper, 1912);

Janvier, Thomas A., *From the South of France* (New York: Harper, 1912);

Le Gallienne, Richard, *The Maker of Rainbows, and Other Fairy-Tales and Fables* (New York: Harper, 1912);

Tomlinson, Everett T., *The Boys of the Revolution,* illus-trated by Green, Alonzo Chappel, F. G. Cooper, and Walter Bobbett (Boston: Silver, Burdett, 1913);

Ward, Mrs. Humphry, *The Coryston Family* (New York: Harper, 1913);

Hardy, Arthur Sherburne, *Diane and Her Friends* (Bos-ton: Houghton Mifflin, 1914);

King, Basil, *The Side of the Angels* (New York: Harper, 1916);

Elizabeth Shippen Green (courtesy of the American Antiquarian Society)

Burnett, Frances Hodgson, *The White People* (New York: Harper, 1917);

Meiklejohn, Nannine La Villa, *The Coat of Many Colors; a Story of Italy* (New York: Dutton, 1919);

Lamb, Charles and Mary, *Tales from Shakespeare* (Phila-delphia: David McKay, 1922);

Waller, Mary E., *A Daughter of the Rich* (Boston: Little, Brown, 1924);

Willcox, Louise, *The Torch, a Book of Poems for Boys,* il-lustrated by Green and others (New York: Harper, 1924);

Singmaster, Elsie, *Bred in the Bone and Other Stories* (Bos-ton: Houghton Mifflin, 1925);

Malloch, Douglas, *Little Hop-Skipper* (New York: Doran, 1926);

Richardson, Dorothy Hardy, and Arthur Sherburne Hardy, *A May and November Correspondence* (New York: Harper, 1928);

Order of the Pageant–May Day (Philadelphia: Bryn Mawr College, 1928);

Davis, William Stearns, *Life in Elizabethan Days* (New York: Harper, 1930);

Wiggin, Kate Douglas, *Mother Carey's Chickens* (Boston: Houghton Mifflin, 1930);

Chambers, Robert W., *Outdoorland,* illustrated by Green and Reginald Birch (New York: D. Appleton, 1931);

Ballard, Ellis Ames, *Catalogue Intimate and Descriptive of My Kipling Collection* (Philadelphia: Privately printed, 1935);

Elliott, Elizabeth Shippen Green, and Huger Elliott, *An Alliterative Alphabet Aimed at Adult Abecedarians* (Philadelphia: David McKay, 1947).

PERIODICALS: *Philadelphia Times,* 1889–1890;
Jester, 1890;
Lancaster Life, 1890;
Harper's Monthly, 1892–1923;
Philadelphia Public Ledger, 1893;
Sunbeams, 1894, 1897;
Ladies' Home Journal, 1895–1927;
Confectioner's Journal, 1897–1898;
Forward: A Weekly Illustrated Paper for Young People, 1898–1901;
St. Nicholas, 1898–1901;
Scholar's Magazine, 1898–1900;
New York Press Sunday Magazine, 1898;
Saturday Evening Post, 1899–1931;
Woman's Home Companion, 1899–1925;
Critic, 1900;
Sunday School Times, 1900;
Harper's Weekly, 1901–1911;
Delineator, 1902;
Youth's Companion, 1902;
Harper's Bazaar, 1903;
Century, 1904;
Collier's, 1906;
Country Life in America, 1906;
Good Housekeeping, 1906–1933;
McCall's, 1918;
Sunset, the Pacific Monthly, 1918;
American Magazine, 1919;
Pictorial Review, 1919;
American Junior Red Cross News, 1929;
McClure's, 1940.

OTHER: *Report of the Private View of the Exhibition of Works by Howard Pyle at the Art Alliance Philadel-phia, January 22, 1923,* with an essay by Green (Philadelphia: Ad Service Printing, 1923).

Elizabeth Shippen Green was a prolific illustrator with a keen sense of composition, decoration, use of color, and attention to historical detail whose work appeared in books and magazines for almost sixty years. Green was born on 1 September 1871 in Philadelphia, Pennsylvania. Her parents, Jasper and Elizabeth Shippen Boude Green, loved art and encouraged their daughter to pursue it as a career. Green attended Miss Mary Hough's School and Miss Gordon's School, where she soon exhibited artistic talent. At the age of seven Green drew flowers in her notebook and labeled the picture "From Natural Flowers, by Bessie Green, Ralston, Pennsylvania, August 15, 1879." In 1887 Green enrolled in the Pennsylvania Academy of the Fine Arts, where she studied with Thomas Eakins, Thomas Anshutz, and Robert Vonnoh. Along with the other female art students, Green took one year of drawing, working from plaster casts of ancient Greek and Roman statues whose private parts were modestly covered by the instructor.

Eakins insisted his female students have the opportunity to draw from live models, shifting the emphasis away from casts to the human body. He initiated the most intensive study of anatomy offered in any art school at that time. Green spent two years in Eakins's life classes perfecting her technique and surviving his demanding tutelage. After graduation Green prepared to earn a living as an illustrator.

She published her first illustration, *Naughty Mary Jane,* at the age of eighteen in the *Philadelphia Times* on 1 September 1889. Green earned fifty cents for one-column and one dollar for two-column illustrations and up to three dollars for larger ones. She broadened her clientele to include the *Philadelphia Public Ledger* in 1893 and the department store Strawbridge and Clothier, for whose advertising department she prepared fashion drawings. Green's bold confidence won her the advertising job; when asked if she could duplicate an example of their usual advertising design work, she unhesitatingly said yes. Ever eager to expand, she left Strawbridge and Clothier in 1895 for the *Ladies' Home Journal,* where she continued her fashion illustrations, but she needed more challenges and wider contacts in publishing to become successful.

Green found what she needed in Howard Pyle's illustration classes at the Drexel Institute. His arrival in 1894 brought a fresh perspective from a successful, working artist. In *Report of the Private View of the Exhibition of Works by Howard Pyle at the Art Alli-*

ance Philadelphia, January 22, 1923 (1923) Green describes Pyle's impact on her art: "It seems to me he did not so much teach me how to draw but he taught me how to interpret life. He taught me, I might say, what philosophy of life I may possess." When Green enrolled in his afternoon and evening classes, she met two other women illustrators with whom she would form lifelong friendships and working relationships—Jessie Willcox Smith and Violet Oakley.

Smith and Oakley already lived together in an apartment-studio with a third classmate, Jessie H. Dowd. When Dowd returned to her native Ohio, Green joined the others in creating a Friendship Calendar for their departing friend, adding an invented authoritative quote from Pyle: "Now, Miss Dowd, don't you see, just as soon as I touch my brush to your drawing, how much better it becomes?"

In 1897 Green sailed for a tour of London, Stratford-upon-Avon, Brussels, Paris, Antwerp, and Amsterdam. She visited historic and literary sites, art museums, and expositions, sketching much of what she saw. She incorporated the influences of Pyle and Anshutz with her European trip to enhance her skill with decoration and to reaffirm her love of the relics of antiquity. Upon her return Green left her parents' house and moved in with her new friends. With contacts through Pyle and confident that she could earn her living independent of a nine-to-five job, Green left the *Ladies' Home Journal* in 1898 to freelance for a variety of childrens', general interest, and women's magazines, still working occasionally for the *Ladies' Home Journal*.

The three illustrators moved from downtown Philadelphia to Bryn Mawr for the summer of 1900, falling in love with the idea of living and working in the country. They rented the Red Rose Inn in 1902 until the owner sold it in 1905. Their patrons, Mr. and Mrs. George Woodward, subsequently rented a house and studio on their vast property in Germantown to the three women, who named it Cogslea. In addition to the artists, the extended family included Green's ailing parents, whom she supported, and her close friend Henrietta Cozens, who would become the artists' gardener and household manager. The Woodwards introduced the women to architect Huger Elliott, whom they expected would be interested in the youngest, Oakley. Instead Elliott was drawn to Green. Her ready smile, quick wit, and seriousness about her work captivated him. He called her "the Greatest Illustrator of the Age" and courted her intensely. They soon began a five-year engagement. She accepted his marriage proposal on the condition that they wait until her parents died before marrying so that Elliott would not be burdened

Frontispiece for Richard Le Gallienne's An Old Country House *(1902), the first book illustrated by Green*

with their support. In 1911, at the age of forty, Green married Elliott.

Her marriage broke up the fourteen-year Cozens-Oakley-Green-Smith household. Muralist Edith Emerson moved into Cogslea; Smith purchased one acre from the Woodwards and built Cogshill nearby. In 1912 Green accompanied her husband to the Rhode Island School of Design and then to the Boston Museum of Fine Arts before they returned to Philadelphia in 1920. The Woodwards remodeled additional property near Cogslea and Cogshill for the Elliotts which they named Little Garth after their small garden. Green finally had ample space for her work even though she shared her studio space with Elliott. Elliott received another employment call, and the couple moved to Manhattan in July 1925 but retained Little Garth. When Elliott died in 1951, Green returned to Little Garth to be near her old friends until her death in 1954.

Early in their careers Green and Smith shared a similar illustrating style in their use of decoration

A 1916 illustration by Green for Harper's Monthly, *where she worked from 1901 to 1924*

and color. They collaboratively designed and illustrated two calendars for Bryn Mawr College in 1901 and 1902 that became the basis for their acclaimed and successful book with poems by Mabel Humphrey, *The Book of the Child* (1903).

Firmly established as a professional illustrator, Green accepted a long-term contract with Harper and Brothers, for whom she would work from August 1901 until October 1924. While she freelanced for fewer periodicals during this time, Green increased the number of illustrations she provided for books aimed at children and young adults.

Contrary to Pyle's belief that marriage ruined women artists, Green continued illustrating after her marriage and actually produced more work than before. Green was one of Pyle's most prolific female students and the one most influenced by him. She shared his sense of composition, drawing the viewer into the scene from an unexpected area. Her use of rich colors and attention to historically accurate details characterized the medieval subjects in which she specialized. Early in Green's career the critic Harrison S. Morris, writing in the *Book Buyer* for 1902, stated that "the instinct for line which she got from the earliest essays in

pen and ink has controlled and advanced her development, and that what refreshes and renews the half-tone reproductions of her drawings, gives them unaccustomed angles of vision and unusual aspects, is this feeling for the beauty of line showing through the denser masses."

Noted for her pen-and-ink work, Green acknowledged her debt to Pyle in the *Report of the Private View of the Exhibition of Works by Howard Pyle*:

> Mr. Pyle gave us, in addition to the fact—the wonderful fact—that drawing is so easy, three rules. These three rules, if followed out, make the painting of any picture, I think, absolutely simple. There is no question about it. The first rule of all was to realize just as hard as you possibly could the situation that you are about to depict, to make the person or persons in that picture act as they would under those circumstances, in the manner proper to the circumstances—and then the second rule was to realize just as hard as you possibly could; and when you had accomplished that the third and last rule was—to realize!

Green's distinctive and highly regarded work bears the influence of Pyle and of Eakins. Her readings of the text produced interpretive scenes marked by elegance, quiet activity, and dignity. She consistently produced high-quality work in charcoal and watercolor. Green's black-and-white drawings contain heavy outlines and flat shadings for the primary characters. To reproduce these drawings in color she sprayed them with a fixative and applied transparent watercolor washes and touched up with body color.

Undaunted by the succession of moves following her husband's career, Green turned the relocations into opportunities to develop contacts with book publishers in the northeast and mid-Atlantic regions. When Elliott served as the director of educational work at the Metropolitan Museum of Art in New York, Green produced posters and advertisements for the Met's story hour for members' children and illustrated occasional issues of the *Bulletin of the Metropolitan Museum of Art* and its *Children's Bulletin* from 1926 to 1941. Green continued to exhibit her artwork at the Pennsylvania Academy of the Fine Arts. In 1924 she showed four pen-and-ink drawings, each titled *Decoration for Poem.* After moving to New York City she exhibited the watercolors *Rhododendrons* in 1927 and *Helen and Jane; Aetatum 2* in 1930. In 1947 the Elliotts collaborated on *An Alliterative Alphabet Aimed at Adult Abecedarians,* her last book.

Green became the first woman staff artist for *Harper's Weekly* and in her years there produced illustrations that captured the poetic feeling of the stories. Her period-costumed characters were historically accurate, and her depictions of middle-class family life matched the ideals of the magazine and those of its female audience. The high quality of Green's artistry not only garnered her contracts to illustrate thirty books but also earned her the prestigious Mary Smith Prize from the Pennsylvania Academy of the Fine Arts in 1905. As one of the most successful illustrators of her time, Green's commercial appeal and prodigious creative output set a high standard for the following generation of women artists.

References:

Regina Armstrong, "Representative American Women Illustrators: The Decorative Workers," *Critic,* 36 (June 1900): 520–529;

Alice Carter, "The Cogs of Red Rose Inn," *Print,* 51 (January/February 1997): 42–51;

Charlotte Herzog, "A Rose by Any Other Name; Violet Oakley, Jessie Willcox Smith, and Elizabeth Shippen Green," *Woman's Art Journal,* 14 (Fall 1993/Winter 1994): 11–16;

Harrison S. Morris, "Elizabeth Shippen Green," *Book Buyer,* 24 (March 1902): 111–115;

Edward D. Nudelman, *Jessie Willcox Smith: A Bibliography* (Gretna, La.: Pelican, 1980);

S. Michael Schnessel, *Jessie Willcox Smith* (New York: Crowell, 1977);

Catherine Connell Stryker, *The Studios at Cogslea, Delaware Art Museum, February 20–March 28, 1976* (Wilmington: Delaware Art Museum, 1976).

Archives:

Elizabeth Shippen Green Elliott's papers are located in the Free Library of Philadelphia. More than one hundred of her illustrations can be found in the Elizabeth Shippen Green Elliott Collection, Cabinet of American Illustration, Division of Prints and Photographs, Library of Congress. The Delaware Art Museum owns several of her paintings.

Frank B. Hoffman
(28 August 1888 – 11 March 1958)

Stephen Zimmer
Philmont Museum

PERIODICALS: *Redbook,* 1913–1916;
Country Gentleman, 1919–1927;
Liberty, 1925–1927;
Cosmopolitan, 1926–1930;
Ladies' Home Journal, 1926–1935;
Shrine Magazine, 1926–1927;
Scribner's Magazine, 1927;
Woman's Home Companion, 1927;
McCall's, 1928–1930;
American Magazine, 1929–1930;
Collier's, 1930;
The Saturday Evening Post, 1932–1939.

Frank B. Hoffman was a prolific illustrator of popular short fiction during the 1920s and 1930s. His authentic portrayals of Western themes in such periodicals as the *Ladies' Home Journal,* the *Saturday Evening Post,* and *Country Gentleman* won him a national reputation. From 1940 to his death in 1958 he painted Western and outdoor subjects exclusively for the Brown and Bigelow Calendar Company.

Frank B. Hoffman was born in Chicago on 28 August 1888. As a boy he showed little interest in school, being more inclined to spend time drawing animals than in study. After Hoffman took two years to finish the fourth grade, his father sent him to some racing stables the family owned in Ohio. According to the unpublished biography by his wife, Hazel, Hoffman later said that he had been glad to go because he believed he could "see more of the world from the middle of a horse's back than from a school seat."

For the next several years Hoffman exercised horses and rode races on the flat and over jumps on tracks throughout much of the South, the Midwest, and Canada. Along the way he acquired an education, albeit one different from that of other young men his age. He continued drawing and sketching, taking as subjects the horses he rode and cared for. He rode until he was nineteen, when he grew too heavy to make racing weights.

Hoffman then returned to Chicago and went looking for other work. In a steel mill in nearby Gary, Indiana, he found a job that consisted of swinging a sledgehammer ten hours a day, six days a week. Although Hoffman developed physically, the work held little attraction for him. He soon quit and decided to take up boxing, a sport he had pursued during his racetrack days to the extent of winning several Golden Glove bouts. With his newly developed strength he thought he could make it as a professional fighter although while training he was forced to support himself by running a dice box at a southside Chicago saloon.

Hoffman proved good enough to become a sparring partner of Joe Gans, the reigning world lightweight champion. However, he gradually grew disillusioned with the sport after realizing how poorly most boxers were treated and how only a few of the best fighters received a just portion of the gate receipts from their bouts.

One day on a visit to see his mother Hoffman was introduced to Joseph E. J. Ryan, a family friend and the editor of the Chicago *American Weekly.* Ryan saw some of Hoffman's horse drawings during the visit and told Hoffman about a job in his newspaper's art department. Although Hoffman had never considered drawing for a living, he decided that he preferred it over boxing.

Hoffman got the job at the paper, without pay at first. Once he proved he could draw, he was sent with city reporters to make on-the-scene pencil sketches at such varied events as prizefights, jury trials, matinees, fires, and operas. Late into the night he worked his sketches into ink drawings, often using a brush instead of a pen–an idea he got from studying Chinese lettering on advertisements he saw on the streetcars. The technique reproduced well, and Hoffman was to use it extensively for much of his career.

Nevertheless, he felt handicapped in that he had not had formal training in painting with oils, which magazine art editors required for story illustrations. Therefore, he arranged to study drawing and portrait painting with J. Wellington Reynolds, an in-

Frank B. Hoffman (photograph by Will Connell)

structor at the Art Institute of Chicago. For the next five years Hoffman sandwiched art classes between newspaper assignments.

In 1913 Hoffman was asked by Ray Long, the editor of *Redbook,* to illustrate a dog story by James Oliver Curwood; the story appeared in the May issue. Hoffman illustrated other stories for Curwood as well as other *Redbook* authors. The experience greatly boosted his confidence.

In the spring of 1916 Hoffman was rejected for military service in World War I due to a slight eye defect. He traveled to northern Montana after being hired by the Great Northern Railroad to paint wildlife for promotions of Glacier National Park. For the next year he painted elk, deer, buffalo, and moose in the mountains and on the nearby plains, often traveling on horseback leading a packhorse. Hoffman met and sketched many Indians, cowboys, miners, and other frontiersmen and used them for subject matter for the rest of his life.

In Montana he also became acquainted with John Singer Sargent, who was painting portraits of older members of the Blackfoot tribe on their reservation. Hoffman learned much from the hours spent

talking to Sargent and watching him paint, and the association inspired Hoffman to work harder on his own painting.

In the summer of 1918 Hoffman attended a Leon Gaspard one-man show at the Art Institute of Chicago. He came away impressed with the Russian's colorful palette and the loose style in which he painted. They later met and talked at length, especially about Taos, where Gaspard had been painting for several years.

The following winter Hoffman suffered from a severe case of pneumonia and was urged by his doctor to spend the summer in a drier climate. Because of Gaspard's vivid description of Taos, he decided to go there. After arriving, Hoffman arranged to pay Gaspard twenty-five dollars for each criticism of his work. They painted and sketched outdoors together all summer, often using the same models, including Gaspard's personal horses, some Indian ponies, and a few burros. Thereafter Hoffman's work reflected Gaspard's influence, particularly in his use of heavy pigment in an impressionistic manner.

Taos stood in sharp contrast to bustling Chicago, where Hoffman had been studying art and doing advertising and magazine illustrations. There were only a few automobiles in the little village. Instead, there were all sorts of saddle horses, wagons and teams, cowboys, Mexicans, and Indians for him to use as subjects. As others had before him, Hoffman found the mountains and deserts, clean dry air, and bright sun an ideal setting for painting, and a few years later he decided to make Taos his home.

After painting in Taos in 1919 Hoffman returned the following two summers to study with Gaspard. He became friends with Walter Ufer and Herbert Dunton, who encouraged him to apply for membership in the Taos Society of Artists. Although flattered by their praise of his work, Hoffman felt he could not financially afford to paint solely for exhibition. He instead adopted a routine of spending summers in New Mexico painting for pleasure and winters in Chicago working on the increasing number of advertising commissions he had been receiving. Among his clients were Cream of Wheat, General Electric, and Montgomery Ward, whose ads with Hoffman's paintings appeared in many popular magazines. The exposure was important in that it led to more short-story assignments.

In the early summer of 1923 Hoffman hired a young woman named Hazel Nelson to pose for an ad he was doing for Cream of Wheat. She later sat for other work, and their relationship eventually grew beyond a professional one. They fell in love and were married in May 1925.

The following July the Hoffmans left Chicago to spend the remainder of the summer in Taos. Upon arrival they moved into a house on Kit Carson Street, where they frequently bought turquoise and silver jewelry, pottery, and saddle blankets from Indian traders traveling by wagon and team. The summer was spent going to nearby pueblos for dances, riding horseback in the mountains, watching rodeos, and completing painting projects scheduled for delivery in the fall.

On his return to Chicago, Hoffman worked at a furious pace to complete a heavy load of advertising and magazine assignments. His output that fall and the following year was phenomenal, as evidenced by the number of times his work appeared in magazines during 1926.

Beginning in February and continuing through May, Hoffman's illustrations accompanied Zane Grey's serialized Western "Forlorn River," published in the *Ladies' Home Journal*. Before the year was over he had illustrated stories written by Peter B. Kyne, Mary Heaton Vorse, Lucia Zora, Florence Dorsey Welch, Guy Fletcher, and Zack Cartwright (in various issues of *Ladies' Home Journal, Liberty, Shrine Magazine, Country Gentleman, Cosmopolitan,* and

Woman's Home Companion). In addition, five of his paintings appeared in full-page magazine ads.

Most of these stories were of Western themes, although two dealt with horse racing and another two with prizefights. They were all subjects about which Hoffman had personal knowledge, a situation in which he differed from many of his contemporaries, who frequently had to rely on book research to carry out their assignments. Hoffman is quoted in the unpublished biography as saying that his illustrations resulted from what he knew, saw, and felt. Moreover, his popularity with editors and writers stemmed from his ability to embellish a story rather than simply illustrating scenes described within.

The majority of his story illustrations up to that time had been done for the *Ladies' Home Journal*. Due to favorable reader response to his work, he was interviewed by the magazine's editors on their November 1926 "Our Family Album" page. When asked about his background and his talent in painting animals, especially horses, Hoffman replied, "I never said that I'd been a cowboy . . . but you can tell anyone that I sure like to draw a 'hawss.'"

He continued, "A lot of folks figure that because I draw cowpunchers and cowponies, I am, or have been, a cowboy. That isn't true. I've knocked about different camps a lot, but that's all. I can rope my horse, and I've broken a few broncs, too. I reckon I've been thrown more times than the Prince of Wales. They'll tell you that in Taos. I own two of the best cowponies in New Mexico, two that have worked at their trade. The horses I draw and paint are what I call typical cow horses, big enough and strong enough to carry a man and hold a steer after he's down. It's a great country, the West. I love it. All I yearn for is a place on the side of a mountain–about one hundred acres. That will do me for the rest of my life."

In the fall of 1928 Hoffman found in Taos the place he was looking for. It was a sprawling adobe ranch house and two hundred acres of sagebrush located two miles from the Taos plaza. The nearest neighbors lived more than a mile away. He named it Hobby Horse Ranch and, with the help of two Taos Indians, made alterations to the house to make it more livable, the most important of which was an enlarged living room that allowed space for his studio. Once the house was ready, his first project was a set of illustrations for "Desert Bloom," a Vingie Roe story that later appeared in the August 1929 issue of *McCall's*. The story was a Western romance set in Arizona, and Hoffman's pictures were some of the best he had ever done for a magazine.

By 1931 Hoffman had painted dozens of oil paintings to illustrate either short fiction or magazine ads. His work had brought him financial security and a popular following, but like so many illustrators, he was continually burdened with the stress of having to meet deadlines. He was sometimes late with paintings, often because he scraped down canvases that were not to his satisfaction. He said in defense of his work that "an artist should be judged by the best he produces. Especially . . . in judging work where delivery dates were often a deciding factor."

Consequently, at the end of 1931 Hoffman decided to take what he considered to be a well-deserved break from illustrating. He and his wife had for several years been training thoroughbreds at the Hobby Horse Ranch, and they decided to take six of their best two-year-olds to southern California for the winter racing season at Agua Caliente. The colts developed colds in California and were unable to start any races, but Hoffman returned to Taos charged with the idea of devoting his artistic efforts to painting pictures of thoroughbreds, the horses that had been so much a part of his early life.

Over the next year Hoffman completed three paintings of his own horses, works that brought him immense satisfaction, primarily because he was painting for himself and not for art editors. The major painting was of a bright chestnut horse the Hoffmans owned named Quidado Amigo (Lookout Friend) parading to the post at Agua Caliente. It demonstrated not only his knowledge of thoroughbred anatomy but also his ability to handle color in order to capture the play of light on a horse's neck and hips.

The next spring Hoffman went to Chicago and made arrangements to hang the three paintings and some others in a friend's gallery. He had hopes of either selling them or obtaining commissions from interested owners to paint their favorite horses. Over the next few months he discussed the possibility with several horsemen, but nothing concrete came of the effort.

During the summer Hoffman frequently attended horse races, rodeos, and other sporting events and made pencil sketches of the action, much as he had done in his newspaper days. Later he finished them as dry-brush inks and sent them to the *Chicago Tribune* to illustrate the sportswriter's account of the event. Probably the best of these were of the hard-riding players and horses who participated in the much heralded East-West Polo Match held on 7 August 1933.

Finding little success in Chicago, Hoffman decided to go to Long Island, New York, and spend the fall with his friend Louis Stoddard, who was chairman of the United States Polo Association and was familiar with the area's horse owners. The horsemen Hoffman met expressed interest in his work, but the discussions went no further. Disheartened, he wrote his wife in Taos, explaining that his failure was due not only to the economic conditions of the Depression but also to the fact that there was "no tradition in America for the painting of horses, especially Thoroughbreds" by artists trained in the traditional school of fine art. He further commented that tinted photographs seemed to satisfy most owners' need for pictures of their prized horses. Hoffman was forced to return to illustrating, knowing his services were still in demand. He worked first from the ranch in Taos and then a studio in Chicago where he moved in 1937 to be closer to clients.

In December 1939, at the age of fifty-one, Hoffman conceived an idea as a new avenue for his work, one that eventually led to the most satisfying and lucrative time of his career. Early in the month he wrote the Brown and Bigelow Calendar Company of Saint Paul, Minnesota, requesting the opportunity to submit some Western sketches for potential calendar pictures.

Brown and Bigelow was at the time the largest calendar house in the United States. Their devotion to high artistic standards clearly set them apart from their competitors. Norman Rockwell, Maxfield Parrish, Dick Bishop, and R. H. Palenske were among the artists who painted for the company and helped it attain prominence in the field of advertising. Some years earlier they had used paintings by Frederic Remington, Charles Russell, and other Western artists for calendar illustrations, but at the time they did not offer a line of Western subjects. Assuming they were familiar with his years as a Western illustrator, Hoffman hoped he might interest them in using his work.

Shortly after sending the letter Hoffman was contacted by Orion Winford, head of the company's art department. They made arrangements to meet in Hoffman's studio and discuss the proposal further. After viewing some paintings and drawings Hoffman had done for the meeting, Winford asked him to send several to the Saint Paul office for approval.

In January, Hoffman received word that one of his sketches had been selected for a finished painting. It was of a rider in a bright red shirt leading a white packhorse at the point of meeting a mother bear and two cubs on a narrow mountain trail. Hoffman had titled it *Trouble on the Trail* and was informed that its human interest and storytel-

First page of a short story illustrated by Hoffman

ling quality coupled with its rich color made it exactly the type of picture the company sought. He was to receive $750 for the completed painting and was urged to send ideas for others.

With the prospect of selling more work to Brown and Bigelow, Hoffman returned to Taos and the New Mexico sunshine, happy to be home and away from the stress of city life. He finished *Trouble on the Trail* at the ranch, and it appeared in 1942 as the first of more than 150 Brown and Bigelow calendar pictures he would complete before failing eyesight forced him to give up painting in 1953.

As a result of their satisfaction with the painting, Brown and Bigelow asked Hoffman the following May to submit sketches for a twelve-part mailing-card outdoor series of hunters and fishermen pictured in the field. He accepted the assignment, pleased with the opportunity to develop paintings based on his own imagination and experience in the outdoors and not the dictates of a scene from a story. He was offered $200 per finished picture, substantially less than he was receiving for magazine illustrations but sufficient given the possibility for more work and future increases.

Working steadily, Hoffman completed the series and sent it to the Saint Paul office in early November. The response was gratifying for him in several ways. Brown and Bigelow's vice president, Harry Huse, wrote that three of the paintings were worthy of being feature calendar subjects and, therefore, asked for replacements. In addition, because the possibility existed that the company's competitors might contact Hoffman for pictures after the series appeared, Huse requested that he not enter into an agreement with another company without notifying him. He made clear the importance to the company of having exclusive rights to Hoffman's work.

Huse also asked Hoffman for biographical material and photographs the company might use in promoting the series. He wrote in his letter of 6 November that "the story we have in mind . . . in this promotion is . . . of your prominence as an American illustrator, especially as an illustrator of outdoor life and action, the story of the wide range of your activities and of your actual participation in the type of activity which you have illustrated for us."

Over the years that Hoffman painted for Brown and Bigelow, they developed several sales promotions for calendars featuring his paintings. A typical one read:

> Frank Hoffman is America's premier adventure artist. His knowledge of the great outdoors is unparalleled among modern painters, his skill is as great with a brush as it is with a rifle or a paddle. Wild turkeys in the mountains near his New Mexico ranch home are his favorite game, a corral is a good place to work, and an Indian is a mighty good critic of the scenes Hoffman paints exclusively for you through Brown & Bigelow.

Another one, for the 1946 sales year, read:

> There's corral dust on his overalls, echoes of horseman's talk in his speech, the squint that comes from looking at far horizons under a blazing sun in his eye—and in his artist's hands the ability to recapture all the work, hardship and joy of his far adventuring and put it on canvas for wall-bound men to see. That's Frank Hoffman, the rancher artist.

Although more artist than true rancher, Hoffman did keep several saddle horses and a herd of Hereford cows on the Hobby Horse Ranch primarily to serve as models. Continuing his interest in horse racing, he bought some quarter horses soon after returning to the ranch and put them into training for the track. In order to feed his livestock, he spent much of each summer and early fall cutting hay in the fields that surrounded the ranch. Only when not occupied with chores or painting could he go riding or hunting in the nearby mountains for a welcome change and the possibility of chancing upon an idea for a future painting.

In 1944 Hoffman agreed to send Brown and Bigelow twelve hunting, fishing, or wildlife paintings for multisheet calendars and an additional cowboy or ranch scene for a poster calendar each year, an arrangement he maintained with them for the following ten years. He was given the latitude to determine the subject and situation in each and to make them as colorful as he liked. A survey of the completed paintings reveals his familiarity with a wide variety of animals and confirms that he could paint more than just horses. In both contemporary and historical portrayals he painted Indian or white hunters pursuing deer, elk, buffalo, moose, antelope, bighorn sheep, mountain lions, Canada geese, ducks, quail, prairie chickens, and wild turkeys, whereas his fishermen angled for salmon, trout, muskie, and bass.

His ranch-work paintings were popular with cowboys because of their realistic action and accurate detail. The authenticity of clothing, saddles, and equipment received high marks, a fact important to Hoffman, who knew how quick cowboys were to point out inaccuracies found in art pertaining to their work. Many cowboys collected his calendars and used them to decorate the walls of their bunkhouses and cow camps—such collections can sometimes still be found where they were originally hung, still appreciated by today's ranch cowboys.

Because Brown and Bigelow marketed their calendars nationwide, Hoffman gained exposure that exceeded even that of his magazine illustrations. The company kept many of the originals to decorate offices, returning the rest to Hoffman, who sold them only when contacted by a collector whom he knew and liked.

The strain on his eyes of painting over his long career caused Hoffman to put down his brushes for the last time in the fall of 1953. He spent the next four years with his wife at racetracks in Tucson and Raton, where she trained many of their horses to several successful outings. Disappointed over the loss of his eyesight for painting, Hoffman nevertheless enjoyed those years, watching his horses train and race.

Finally his health failed, and he died at his beloved Hobby Horse Ranch on 11 March 1958. He was buried on the ranch between two juniper trees in a grave that faced the mountains to the North. In spite of the popularity of his work during his lifetime, Hoffman has received little scholarly attention, largely because the majority of his work was commissioned and not done for exhibition. As a result, little of it has found its way into museum collections (a retrospective of his work was exhibited at the Panhandle-Plains Historical Museum and the Philmont Museum in 1990). Perhaps that is as Hoffman would have wished, for he never sought critical review. He was content to satisfy his clients, trusting that his work would afterward speak for itself.

References:

Ed Ainsworth, *The Cowboy in Art* (New York: World, 1968), pp. 83–84;

"Frank Hoffman, Artist and Illustrator, " *Quarter Horse Journal,* 22 (December 1969): 82–89, 456–461;

Dorothy Harmsen, *Harmsen's Western Americana* (Flagstaff, Ariz.: Northland, 1971), pp. 102–103;

Betty Harvey, "Frank B. Hoffman," *Artists of the Rockies and the Golden West,* 9 (Summer 1982), pp. 14–21;

John Jellico, "Frank Hoffman," *Southwestern Art,* 7 (Fall 1978);

Mabel Dodge Luhan, *Taos and Its Artists* (New York: Duell, Sloan & Pearce, 1947), p. 34;

Peggy Samuels and Harold Samuels, *Illustrated Biographical Encyclopedia of Artists of the American West* (Garden City, N.Y.: Doubleday, 1976), pp. 229–230.

Archives:

A biographical file on Frank B. Hoffman is held by the Philmont Museum, Cimarron, New Mexico, as is Hazel Hoffman Sanders's unpublished manuscript "An American Artist."

Winslow Homer
(24 February 1836 – 29 September 1910)

David Tatham
Syracuse University

SELECTED BOOKS ILLUSTRATED: Hunter, William S. Jr., *Ottawa Scenery* (Ottawa City: Privately printed, 1855; revised and enlarged, Ottawa City: Privately printed, 1856);

Morse, Abner C., *A Genealogical Register of the Descendants of Several Ancient Puritans by the Names of Adams, Bullard, Holbrook, Phipps, Rockwood, Sanger, and Wood* (Boston: Damrell & Moore, 1855);

Morse, *A Genealogical Register of the Early Planters of Sherborn, Holliston, and Medway* (Boston: Privately printed, 1855);

Morse, *A Genealogical Register of the Inhabitants and History of the Towns of Sherborn and Holliston* (Boston: Jewett, 1856);

Proceedings at the Reception and Dinner in Honor of George Peabody, Esq., of London, by the Citizens of the Old Town of Danvers, October 9, 1856 (Boston: Dutton, 1856);

Woodbridge, Timothy, *The Autobiography of a Blind Minister* (Boston: Jewett, 1856);

Edwards, Catherine M., *The Careless Girl Reformed, and Other Stories* (Boston: Sabbath School Society, 1857);

Morse, Abner C., *A Genealogy of the Descendants of Several Ancient Puritans by the Names of Adams, Bullard, Holbrook, Rockwood, Sanger, Wood, Grout, Goulding, and Twitchell* (Boston: Privately printed, 1857);

The Eventful History of Three Little Mice and How They Became Blind (Boston: Libby, 1858);

Cabot, Eliza Lee, as Mrs. Follen, *Travellers' Stories* (Boston: Whittemore, Niles & Hall, 1858);

Cabot, as Mrs. Follen, *What the Animals Do and Say* (Boston: Whittemore, Niles & Hall, 1858);

Cabot, as Mrs. Follen, *May Morning and New Year's Eve* (Boston: Whittemore, Niles & Hall, 1858);

Cabot, as Mrs. Follen, *Conscience* (Boston: Whittemore, Niles & Hall, 1858);

Cabot, as Mrs. Follen, *Piccolissima* (Boston: Whittemore, Niles & Hall, 1858);

Johnston, Olivia, *Hillside Farm; or, Some Influences and Their Results* (Boston: Hoyt, 1858);

Winslow Homer in 1866 or 1867

Johnston, *Sophie DeBrentz; or The Sword of Truth. A Story of Italy and Switzerland* (Boston: Hoyt, 1858);

Morse, Abner C., *A Genealogy of the Descendants of Lawrence Litchfield, the Puritan* (Boston: Privately printed, 1858);

Eddy, Daniel C., *The Percy Family: A Visit to Ireland* (Boston: Graves, 1859);

Anderson, Isaac H., as Willis Loveyouth, *Fred Freeland; or The Chain of Circumstances* (Boston: Libby, 1859);

"Aunt Dora," *Bassle Grant's Treasure* (Boston: Walker & Wise, 1860);

Cooke, John Esten, *Surry of Eagle's Nest* (New York: Bunce & Huntington, 1866);

Tennyson, Alfred, *Gems from Tennyson,* illustrated by Homer and others (Boston: Ticknor & Fields, 1866);

Saunders, Frederick, *Festival of Song: A Series of Evenings with the Poets,* illustrated by Homer and others (New York: Bunce & Huntington, 1866);

Gordon, Clarence, as Vieux Moustache, *That Good Old Time; or, Our Fresh and Salt Tutors,* illustrated by Homer and Mauritz de Haas (New York: Hurd & Houghton, 1867 [1866]);

Barnes, William, *Rural Poems,* illustrated by Homer and Hammatt Billings (Boston: Roberts, 1869);

Cooke, John Esten, *Mohun,* illustrated by Homer and others (New York: Huntington, 1869);

Whittier, John Greenleaf, *Ballads of New England,* illustrated by Homer and others (Boston: Fields, Osgood, 1870 [i.e., 1869]);

Edwards, Annie, *Susan Fielding,* illustrated by Homer and Solomon Eytinge Jr. (New York: Sheldon, 1870);

Bryant, William Cullen, *The Song of the Sower,* illustrated by Homer and others (New York: Appleton, 1871);

Winter Poems by Favorite American Poets, illustrated by Homer and Harry Fenn (Boston: Fields, Osgood, 1871);

Bryant, William Cullen, *The Story of the Fountain,* illustrated by Homer and others (New York: Appleton, 1872);

Lowell, James Russell, *The Courtin'* (Boston: Osgood, 1874 [1873]);

Bryant, William Cullen, and Sydney H. Gay, *A Popular History of the United States,* illustrated by Homer and others (New York: Scribner, Armstrong, 1876–1881);

Christmastide, illustrated by Homer and others (Boston: Osgood, 1878);

Cusins, W. G., ed., *Songs from the Published Writings of Alfred Tennyson,* illustrated by Homer and others (New York: Harper, 1880);

Roe, Edward Payson, *Success with Small Fruits,* illustrated by Homer and others (New York: Dodd, Mead, 1880);

Johnson, Robert Underwood, and Clarence Clough Buel, eds., *Battles and Leaders of the Civil War,* illustrated by Homer and others (New York: Century, 1887–1888).

PERIODICALS: *Ballou's Pictorial Drawing-Room Companion,* 1857–1859;

Journal of Missions and Youth's Dayspring, 1858;

Harper's Weekly, 1857–1876;

Frank Leslie's Chimney Corner, 1865;

Frank Leslie's Illustrated Newspaper, 1866–1867;

The Riverside Magazine for Young People, 1867;

Good Stories, 1868;

Harper's Bazar, 1868;

Appleton's Journal, 1868–1870;

Galaxy: An Illustrated Magazine of Entertaining Reading, 1868–1869;

Our Young Folks, 1868–1869;

Hearth and Home, 1869;

Every Saturday, 1871;

Scribner's Monthly, 1878–1880;

Century, 1886–1887.

Between 1855 and 1887 Winslow Homer made more than 160 drawings to illustrate prose and poetry published in books and popular literary journals. These illustrations constitute a little-known but significant aspect of the career of one of the most distinguished artists in America. Though he established his lasting reputation through his work as a painter in oil and watercolor and as a graphic artist who contributed highly original depictions of American life to *Harper's Weekly* and other magazines, Homer's illustrations of literature nonetheless hold a distinct place within his oeuvre. Only in his pictorializations of passages from fiction and verse did he depict a truly wide range of emotional states or concern himself with the problems of narrative in visual art, and in these things he proved himself, whenever his texts possessed real substance, to be a master interpreter of literature. He achieved this mastery within the severe constraints that governed processes of pictorial reproduction during his era, constraints that were loosened for the generation that followed him by advances in the technology of pictorial printing. Nearly all of his work as an illustrator reached print before the advent of photographic reproduction in large-run books and magazines; color printing on high-speed presses arrived after he had completed his career as an illustrator. Though the best of his illustrations of literature reached an artistic level rarely attained by other American graphic artists of his generation, his interest in pictorializing texts was never more than sporadic. Painting remained his primary interest, and when his work in oil and watercolor at last assured him of a steady and substantial income, he abandoned illustration altogether.

Homer was born in Boston on 24 February 1836, the second son (of three) of Charles Savage Homer, a merchant of Boston who was a native of the city, and Henrietta Benson Homer, an able amateur watercolorist who was a native of Searsport,

A Homer illustration for The Eventful History of Three Little Mice and How They Became Blind *(1858)*

Maine. Homer spent most of his childhood with his family near Harvard University. While his formal education did not extend beyond the Cambridge public schools, his sensitivity to literary texts probably owes something to the early years he spent in a setting imbued with the values of books and learning.

His mother instructed him in drawing. His father encouraged this interest by apprenticing him as a draftsman at the relatively late age of eighteen or nineteen to Boston pictorial lithographer John H. Bufford. Beyond the training he gained from 1855 to 1857 from Bufford and the graphic artists associated with his shop and in 1860 from a few classes in figure drawing at the National Academy of Design in New York, Homer had no formal art education.

He undoubtedly learned much about painting informally from the other aspiring young artists with whom he associated, including John La Farge. Throughout his long career as a painter, which began in 1862 and continued to 1910, the year of his death, he proved himself to be the most consistently original, perceptive, and "American" of American artists.

By nature Homer was reserved and quietly dignified. In his later years after he had settled at Prout's Neck on the coast of Maine just south of Portland, he gained the exaggerated reputation of being an austere and reclusive Yankee. This image was largely the creation of journalists and early biographers who had failed in their attempts to persuade him to talk about his art. His work was his

A Pass Time: Cavalry Rest *(1863), a lithograph by Homer for Louis Prang of Boston*

life. He never married but maintained lifelong, close ties to his two brothers and their wives.

Homer's illustrations of literature fall chronologically into four groups. In each of these he responded to a different set of circumstances. The first group consists of those illustrations he drew on lithographic stone during his apprentice years, from 1855 through early 1857. While essentially copy work, they show his early development as a draftsman and the first hints of an original style. The second group includes the illustrations he drew on woodblocks for publication as wood engravings in thirteen children's books published in Boston between 1857 and 1859. As products of the Sunday School Movement, the texts of these publications conveyed a moralistic tone which Homer occasionally managed to lighten in his treatments of them. The largest and most varied group of illustrations are those he drew, after moving to New York late in 1859, for a variety of books and literary journals published in New York and Boston between 1856 and 1888. Most were reproduced as wood engravings, a few as heliotypes. In some of these Homer had an opportunity to respond to literary texts of genuine merit, and these led to his finest work as an illustrator. The last group includes illustrations he adapted from his wartime sketches for a large-scale

history of the Civil War. This work was first serialized in *Century* magazine in the mid 1880s and later published as a set of books. The drawings he made for this project are his only illustrations reproduced by photomechanical means. In all four groups most of the books to which he contributed illustrations include work by one or more other artists as well. The best of his illustrations distinguish themselves from the work of others not only in style but also through his superior mastery of the challenges inherent in the pictorial interpretation of literature.

Intimations of his originality began to appear even during his apprenticeship to Bufford. His first book illustrations amounted to little more than straightforward copy work. They include some of the scenic views for the Canadian writer William S. Hunter Jr.'s *Ottawa Scenery* in 1855 and some of the portraits for Abner C. Morse's genealogical works. In these instances Homer hand copied onto lithographic stone drawings and photographs that had been supplied by the authors. He adapted the scale and tonal values of the originals as necessary but otherwise added nothing of note to them. By the last months of his apprentice term, however, he had begun to embellish his sources with original details. He enlivened the photographs and drawings that served as the basis for his illustrations to the *Proceedings at the Reception and Dinner in Honor of George Peabody, Esq., of London* (1856) with active figures and colorful street life. These details offer the earliest evidence of his frequently cited skills as an acute observer of the daily events of the world he lived in.

Though he had now mastered the techniques of lithographic drawing, he rarely returned to the medium after leaving Bufford. He preferred the less time-consuming task of making drawings for reproduction as wood engravings. In this process he drew on woodblocks, which were then engraved by teams of artisans. Because the woodblock itself was incapable of withstanding the pressure of high-speed, large-run printing presses, replicas of its engraved surface were made by electrolysis and then steel-faced for durability. Since an unlimited number of these electrotypes could be made from a single engraved woodblock and fitted to multiple presses, a run of many thousand impressions of an illustration could be completed in a matter of hours. The wood-engraved, electrotype-printed illustrations that Homer drew for large-circulation magazines such as *Harper's Weekly* reached a much greater audience than did any of his paintings.

In the 1850s when illustration by wood engraving had come into near-universal use by the publishers of pictorial magazines and had also become the preferred medium of most book publishers, a demand arose for artists skilled in drawing on woodblocks, with the particular needs of engravers and the electrotype in mind. Probably for this reason, when he was freed from his apprenticeship on his twenty-first birthday in February 1857, he chose to establish himself as a freelance woodblock artist in Boston, the home of many publishing houses, rather than to become an employee of a single publisher. In freelancing he enjoyed a greater freedom in selecting subjects. The demand for his work assured him a steady income.

He became a frequent contributor of woodblock drawings to two large circulation magazines, *Ballou's Pictorial Drawing-Room Companion* in Boston and *Harper's Weekly* in New York. These wood engravings have often been called illustrations, but with few exceptions they illustrate no text other than Homer's own observations of the world he lived in. They have little of the dramatic, emotional, and narrative qualities that entered his work when he pictorialized other people's words. He continued to contribute drawings to pictorial weeklies until 1876. Those he drew in the 1870s were often adaptations of his recent paintings carefully reconsidered and recomposed for a different medium and a different audience.

During the two and one-half years that he spent as a freelance artist in Boston, he contributed illustrations to thirteen books of children's literature. Most of these include only one or two pictures by him. All were products of the effort of the Sunday School Movement to popularize moral tales for young readers, set, in most cases, in contemporary America. The moral questions they addressed to children were largely religious and domestic, though they occasionally touched on such difficult topical issues as slavery. Some were published by denominational presses; others were published by trade publishers who entered this often lucrative market.

These earliest of Homer's original illustrations are, for the most part, skillful but conventional drawings. In style they at first reflected the influence of Hammatt Billings, an older Boston illustrator. By 1859, however, Homer's more individual manner had begun to emerge, one that was increasingly economical in line and dynamic in composition. At the same time Homer showed a growing tendency to amplify and elaborate his authors' texts in ways that added interest to the books. No evidence seems to have survived to indicate whether he dealt with anyone other than publishers in choosing the passages to illustrate in these books. The frontispieces he drew for Eliza Lee Cabot's *Twilight Stories* of 1858 were republished as late as the 1880s.

Not Far to Go, *an illustration by Homer for*
William Barnes's Rural Poems *(1869)*

The most extensively illustrated of the juveniles on which Homer worked in these years was *The Eventful History of Three Little Mice and How They Became Blind* (1858), for which he was the sole artist. His seventeen drawings inject an element of humor into this otherwise didactically moralistic prose retelling of a traditional nursery rhyme. In giving human attributes to the three mice children and their mother, he revealed a talent for fantasy that appears nowhere else in his work. It allowed him to indulge a sense of playfulness that the Sunday School Movement publishers would have found of doubtful appropriateness in depictions of and for children. Except for his work in this book, Homer produced little that was memorable in his first years as an illustrator, but he was, of course, operating under the distinct disadvantage of having no literature of real substance to respond to.

His move to New York in October 1859 marked the opening of a new period in his career as an illustrator. It did not begin auspiciously. Soon after his arrival *Harper's Weekly* commissioned from him a set of eight illustrations for its serialization of Ella Rodman's sentimental novella *The Mistress of the Parsonage*. This story ran in five successive issues in February and March 1860. Though these were

A Homer wood engraving of the death of J. E. B. Stuart for John Esten Cooke's Mohun (1869)

Homer's first illustrations of literature for adults rather than children, he had, of course, been depicting adult life in his textless drawings for pictorial weeklies since 1857. There is a notable disparity between the postured theatricalism of his work for *The Mistress* and the greater naturalism of his work for the weeklies. The difference suggests that at this point in his life he was not really at home with sentimental fiction, or at least not with fiction as uninspiring as Rodman's. In retrospect this set of illustrations can be seen as a false start.

For reasons that are unclear, Homer was inactive as an illustrator of literature for the next five years. In 1862 he began his professional career as a painter, and in the same year he took the first of his trips to Civil War battlegrounds as a "special artist" for *Harper's Weekly*. He returned to drawing on stone briefly to make two sets of Civil War prints for his friend the Boston lithographer Louis Prang. While these activities made new demands on his time, they scarcely slowed his contributions on a variety of subjects to pictorial weeklies and could hardly have prevented him from accepting an offer to contribute drawings to a book project. Other factors now lost to the historical record may have played a part in bringing about this apparent hiatus in his activity as an illustrator of texts.

When he resumed work in the field in 1866, both his drawing style and his approach to interpretation of an author's words demonstrated a newfound maturity. He contributed single illustrations to Frederick Saunders's anthology of British and American verse, *Festival of Song* (1866) to accompany a passage of verse by the Anglo-Irish poet George Darley, and *Gems from Tennyson* (1866) to accompany "The Charge of the Light Brigade." Both of these volumes were specimens of a genre of elaborately produced gift books published for the holiday trade. Printed on heavy stock, gilt-edged, bound in decoratively blocked, bevel-edged boards, and copiously illustrated by many notable artists, each book manifested a spirit of plenitude. *Festival* sported more than seventy illustrations drawn by thirty-one members of the National Academy of Design. *Gems* reprinted illustrations by several Pre-Raphaelite artists from a London (Moxon) edition of Tennyson while adding new illustrations by nine American artists. None of these artists seems to have consulted with any of the others about the project, however, nor did the publisher of either book encourage a unity of style among the several contributors. While the wealth of talent was meant to enrich the volume, it resulted instead in something close to stylistic and interpretive incoherence. Despite the lack of a single controlling intellect in the illustration of *Festival* and *Gems,* in 1866 Homer's two contributions placed him in the ranks of the major American painter-illustrators of his time. Had his paintings begun to sell well at this point, his work for these books might have been among his last as a pictorializer of texts, but despite the critical praise they earned, his oils in the 1860s and for many years thereafter realized only modest prices, and some found no buyers at all.

His more important illustrations of 1866 were for John Esten Cooke's Civil War novel, *Surry of Eagle's Nest* (1866). This was a substantial work of popular fiction by a Virginia writer whose sympathies had been with the Confederacy and who had in fact served as an officer in its armies. Homer's election in 1865 as an associate of the National Academy of Design and his reputation as a Civil War artist-reporter for the weeklies made him both an obvious and a distinguished choice to illustrate the book. As the sole illustrator of the volume, Homer's name appeared prominently on its title page. His four full-page pictures capture the chivalrous manner of the book's hero and the melodramatic spirit of the often implausible plot. The book became a best-seller. Three years later in 1869 Cooke produced a sequel, *Mohun,* but it met with disappointing sales. Homer contributed two illustrations in the manner of his *Surry* work, but his name appears nowhere in the book. The volume included illustrations by other graphic artists, also, none in a style consistent with the others. It would be interesting to know whether Homer, the North's leading war artist, and Cooke, the South's leading novelist of the conflict, ever met or otherwise communicated about these books.

Following the practice of the day in categorizing artists, Homer's Civil War paintings had established him as a figure painter. Accordingly, late in 1866, when he was invited to contribute illustrations to *That Good Old Time; or, Our Fresh and Salt Tutors,* he was assigned figure subjects while the sea subjects in the book went to a fellow New York artist, Mauritz de Haas, who was known as a marine artist. This division of responsibility by subject specialty typified the thinking of publishers of multiple-illustrator books at the time. Ironically, before the end of the century Homer, rather than de Haas, was celebrated as a marine painter.

Published late in 1866, but with the year 1867 on its title page, this book by Vieux Moustache, the pseudonym of Clarence Gordon, included believable characters of psychological complexity. Two of the characters are elderly African Americans. Homer's sympathetic renderings of them precede most of his painted depictions of blacks as dignified individuals. "Clump in Uniform Tells His Story" is the most complex of these illustrations compositionally and emotionally. Clump, the former servant of a Revolutionary War hero, points to a bullet hole in the sleeve of his former master's coat and silences the men and boys he now serves, who unwittingly had laughed at his ill-fitting costume.

The illustrations for this book were among the last Homer completed before sailing for France in

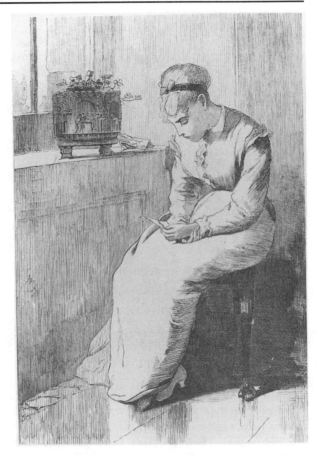

George Blake's Letter, *a wood engraving by Homer for the* Galaxy *magazine serialization of Annie Edwards's* Susan Fielding *(1869)*

the fall of 1866. He went in part because two of his Civil War paintings had been selected for inclusion in the American section of the fine arts pavilion of the Exposition Universelle in Paris, but he seems certain also to have been motivated by an interest in seeing more contemporary French painting than he had access to in the United States. The currents of vital artistic thought that he is bound to have encountered in Second Empire Paris centered on the realism of Gustavé Courbet and Edouard Manet, which had supplanted the landscape and figural paintings of the Barbizon School as the new, provocatively antiacademic, and deeply influential art of the times.

The precise effect of modern French art of the 1860s on his painting style has long been debated, but the impact of his French experience on his work as an illustrator is somewhat clearer, though hardly dramatic. It resulted in a greater naturalism, an increased complexity in composition, a richer tonal range (achieved within the limits of the purely linear process of wood engraving), and, when a passage of text allowed it, more subtle renderings of human

The Playmates, *an illustration by Homer for "My Playmate"
in John Greenleaf Whittier's* Ballads of
New England *(1869)*

feeling. These advances are evident in the first of
the five drawings, *She Turned Her Face to the Window,*
which he made on his return for the serialization in
Galaxy magazine between May and September 1868
of Marion Harland's novel *Beechdale.* Retitled *Jessamine,* Harland's novel later reached publication as
a book but in a format too small to allow the reuse of
Homer's illustrations. That not all of his suite of five
illustrations is as successful as the first suggests that
the publisher or the author selected the passages to
be pictorialized and that Homer warmed to some
more than others.

Another change that occurred in Homer's
work as an illustrator during the years immediately
following his return from France was an enlarged
virtuosity of style. He developed a distinct pictorial
manner for each work that warranted it, responding
to the varieties of literary style present in the texts
that came his way. The extent of the differences can
be seen by comparing his *Beechdale* illustrations with
another set from the same year. Having used a
richly tonal, well-detailed style for Harland's discursive prose and complex plot, he turned to a sparer,
understated style for the concise verse of the Dorset
poet William Barnes. The illustrations Homer prepared for Barnes's *Rural Poems* (1869) are, with a single exception, among his most quietly lyrical. They
possess a sense of simplicity quite in harmony with
Barnes's short forms and seemingly artless style.
Yet in both *Beechdale* and *Rural Poems* one in the series of illustrations fails to meet the high level of

achievement of the others. Faulty perspective and
awkward anatomical drawing undermine these
drawings. Homer's attempt to work from the imagination rather than from models–to minimize expenses–is probably partly to blame for these faults.
Homer shared the illustration of *Rural Poems* with
Hammatt Billings, in whose style he had begun his
career as an original illustrator almost a decade earlier. Homer's style had evolved greatly in the intervening years; Billings's had not. This difference resulted in a pictorial inconsistency in a book of great
literary consistency.

Soon after sharing the assignment to illustrate
Rural Poems with Billings, Homer shared a commission with yet another artist, but in different circumstances. He provided five drawings in 1869 to accompany the serialization in *Galaxy* magazine of Annie Edwards's romance, *Susan Fielding.* The first installments of this English novel had been illustrated
by the New York artist Solomon Eytinge Jr. Then,
for a few months the serial continued without pictures. When Homer took up the task of illustrating
the novel in its final months, he worked directly
from Edwards's text without regard to the likenesses and other details that Eytinge had already established in the early installments. Homer presented
a different and more attractive image of the heroine.
His five contributions are again an uneven group,
but the last of them, *George Blake's Letter,* published
in 1870, is among the more touching of his graphic
works. It reflects the mood of a moving moment
when Susan learns that her beloved suitor, for reasons beyond their control, must resolve never to see
her again. Homer's understatement is quite in accord with the author's at this point in the story.

During the years from 1866 to 1869 Homer
also drew illustrations for a few popular periodicals,
though whether his drawing or the text associated
with it came first is not always clear. His five oftenreproduced depictions of children in bucolic settings, first published in 1868 and 1869 in *Our Young
Folks* magazine and later reused as book illustrations, are among the best-known of these. Their titles–*Swinging on a Birch-Tree, The Bird Catchers, Watching the Crows, The Strawberry Bed,* and *Green Apples*–suggest subjects of rural life that typify one of
Homer's interests as a painter a few years later in
the 1870s. His depictions of American youth in serene natural surroundings may well have carried
symbolic content, showing a nation that, having survived a dreadful storm, now made a new beginning.
Homer apparently made these drawings without reference to any literary text. The magazine solicited
poems to accompany them from Lucy Larcom, R.
H. Stoddard, and John T. Trowbridge, but the fit of

text and image is far from perfect. Each of the poets imposes on Homer's picture a narrative of thought or action for which there is little or no basis in the image and which seems slightly foreign to the viewer.

By 1869 Homer had been an illustrator for more than a decade and had produced many individually fine illustrations, but with the exception of a drawing for a poem by Tennyson and his work in Barnes's *Rural Poems*—both slightly exotic subjects for this distinctly "American" artist—he had illustrated no text likely to be of lasting literary value. If at this point he had ceased to work as an illustrator, he would not have created his most impressive achievements in the field. A group of books to which he contributed drawings between 1869 and 1871 are, however, of a different order. These were collections of poems by several of the most distinguished literary figures in the nation, including William Cullen Bryant, Henry Wadsworth Longfellow, James Russell Lowell, and John Greenleaf Whittier. They allied Homer for the first time with works of American literature that possessed a stature equivalent to his own. The poets were all of an older generation, and the poems had previously been published without illustrations, but these facts seem only to have enhanced their worthiness, judging by Homer's response to them.

His illustrations for these authors appeared in gift books of poetry published in Boston and New York. In each of them an art editor attempted to impose a consistent logic on the relationship between text and image. Most of the books demonstrate a coherence of graphic design that can be seen as a step toward the reform of the gift-book genre. Though no evidence survives to document how their illustrators were chosen, perhaps Homer's thoughtful work in *Rural Poems* and elsewhere commended him to the publishers of the books as an artist whose sensibilities supported the reforms they had in mind. They probably also realized that this American artist might succeed best with distinctly American literature.

The key figure in the move toward reform was Andrew V. S. Anthony, a master wood engraver who had assumed responsibilities approximating those of the modern art editor for the Boston firm of Ticknor and Fields, later Fields, Osgood and Company. The first of his reform books to include work by Homer was *Ballads of New England,* a collection of John Greenleaf Whittier's poems published late in 1869. Anthony's concept seems simple enough now, but it was remarkable in its time. Though he continued to use several artists, he marshaled their talents differently. To one landscape artist, Harry Fenn, he

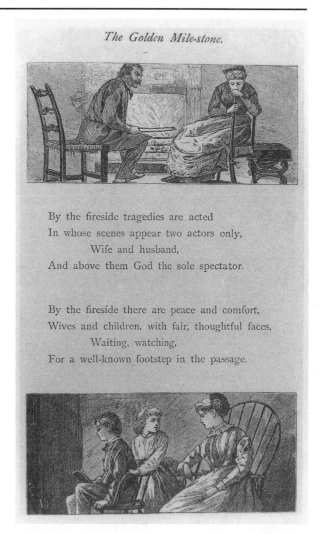

Illustrations by Homer for a Henry Wadsworth Longfellow poem in Winter Poems by Favorite American Poets *(1871)*

gave the task of providing each of the book's ten poems with scenic headpiece and tailpiece vignettes. These little views of the New England landscape opening and closing each poem set the stage for the narrative of each ballad and offered an epilogue to it. Bracketed thus, the content of each poem was illustrated by a single figure artist—two in the case of a long poem. Fenn's vignettes—all similar in size, style, and tonality—recurred every few pages and unified the design of the book. The differing styles of the figure artists, consistent within each poem, provide visual variety. Homer's contribution amounted to two drawings for Whittier's "My Playmate," which in their simplicity of concept and execution capture the spirit of innocence that in the poem pervades the language, ballad meter, and (as a memory of childhood) naiveté of sentiment.

For the next holiday season Anthony followed this gift book with *Winter Poems by Favorite American*

A Homer illustration for William Cullen Bryant's
The Song of the Sower *(1871)*

Poets (1871). His plan for its illustration was simplicity itself. Each of the nine poems in the book was illustrated by a single artist who was left to find his way in both figure and landscape subjects. Homer contributed six drawings to Longfellow's "The Golden Mile-stone." They are among the artist's most sensitive and successful interpretive works and among the most effective of any nineteenth-century illustrations of poetry. Homer began with a head-piece depicting a bleak New England village in winter, in which every detail comes from Longfellow's first three (of twelve) stanzas. The heart of the poem consists of its four central stanzas, all of which open with the words "By the fireplace. . . ." For each, Homer provides an illustration of a domestic scene. The room differs in each case, as does the angle of vision in relation to a fireplace. The mood, ages, and nature of the persons gathered near the hearth change from picture to picture. The first two scenes treat the disillusions of maturity and the overreaching aspirations of youth. The third concerns marital strife. The fourth concerns the quiet anxiety, even in a setting of apparent peace and comfort, of a mother and her children "waiting, waiting" for the arrival of a loved one. Homer configured these four illustrations in oblong compositions that echo the forms of the blocks of verse as they are set on the page.

The scene of marital discord is unique in Homer's work. Nowhere else did he portray realistically such emotions as the rage of the scowling hus-band or the suppressed feelings of the wife who turns away from him. Of the four illustrations, only in this one do his figures turn their backs to the hearth, an ages-old symbol of domesticity and comfort. The facial expressions here, as in the other illustrations, are Homer's inventions; Longfellow presents no such detail in his verse. Homer moved in tandem with Longfellow in these stanzas, elaborating on the poet's images without overburdening them.

In the year in which *Winter Poems* reached publication, Homer also contributed drawings to the gift book published in New York by D. Appleton and Company, Bryant's *Song of the Sower* (1871). Including the work of several artists, this volume had little of Anthony's logic in design, but it included many individually strong illustrations. In subject Homer's three pictures ranged widely. He depicted a Civil War camp, cattle grazing by a stream including the residue of military strife, and the interior of a textile mill with a young woman operative hard at work. Each of these illustrations reflects a serious and subtle response to a brief line or two from Bryant's long poem.

Appleton followed the success of this book with another of Bryant's long poems, now titled *The Story of the Fountain* (1872). Many illustrators were involved, but perhaps in an attempt to achieve a degree of stylistic consistency among them, the engraver imposed on their work a common tonality and eliminated whatever was distinctive in anyone's draftsmanship. As a result Homer's three depictions in this book of children and adolescents in bucolic settings have little of his energy or the highly personal articulation of light that contributed so much to the success of his earlier treatment of similar subjects for *Our Young Folks*.

Anthony's third reform gift book, an edition of Lowell's Yankee dialect poem, *The Courtin'*, was announced by its publisher for the fall of 1872. It was delayed for a year undoubtedly as a result of the Boston Fire of November 1872, a disaster that ravaged the printing and paper trades in that city. Finally published in the fall of 1873, with 1874 on its title page, it was one of the most distinctively designed and produced American books of its decade. Homer illustrated Lowell's humorous verse with seven silhouettes drawn with razor-sharp outlines. They were reproduced as heliotypes. This protomechanical process, which was then new in the United States, printed the silhouettes in deep black on heavy stock. Each full-page illustration faced a page of text. The title page vignette and decorative extratitle are probably also by Homer.

In using "shadow pictures," as Homer called these silhouettes, to illustrate this book, Anthony exploited the popularity of a series of volumes brought out in the late 1860s by Boston publisher Roberts Brothers that reproduced silhouette illustrations by the Polish-born German artist Paul Konewka. Though Homer's work for *The Courtin'* owes something in concept and style to Konewka, it possesses a distinctive spirit. It also reflects a keen appreciation of Lowell's poem, which recounts the culminating episode of a rural Yankee courtship. Homer's own Yankee background made him an ideal choice for this assignment. *An' Wal, He Up an' Kist Her* characterizes the series. The warm-hearted humor of the poem was a far cry from the somber mood of Longfellow's "Golden Mile-stone" or the quiet regret of Whittier's "My Playmate." It is to Homer's credit that he moved with such convincing virtuosity of expression through such a variety of poems.

Lowell was abroad when this edition of his poem reached publication, and he may not have seen a copy of the book until his return to the United States in the spring of 1875. He then made clear in a letter to a colleague that he disapproved of the illustrations. His response to them may well have been colored by the fact that Homer's work, counting the decorative title page, occupies more pages than do Lowell's stanzas. Indeed, Homer's name has a greater prominence than Lowell's in the blocked design on the front cover of the book. Despite Lowell's pique, the Homer-decorated edition of *The Courtin'* stands as one of the few American illustrated books of the nineteenth century in which text and images, both of great substance, are in near-perfect concert.

The Courtin' represents the high point of Homer's work as an illustrator of imaginative literature. Later in the 1880s he returned to the gift-book genre twice but with less satisfactory results. In 1878 he contributed four drawings to *Christmastide,* published by Osgood and Company. His drawings, reproduced as wood engravings, were part of a suite of fourteen by a total of six artists. This suite illustrates Longfellow's poem "Excelsior." There is little evidence of the consistency of style and the thoughtful balancing of parts that Anthony had brought to his gift books at the beginning of the decade. For reasons that can only be speculated upon, Anthony's reform was short-lived. Homer's work for "Excelsior" has some merit, though it shows little special sympathy for the poet's allegory on the man of genius.

Homer's final connection with a gift book occurred in 1879 when he contributed two drawings to

"An' Wal, He Up an' Kist Her," an illustration by Homer for James Russell Lowell's The Courtin' *(1874)*

the small folio *Songs from the Published Writings of Alfred Tennyson* published by Harper and Brothers. This was a book of forty-five songs for voice and piano including full-page, wood-engraved illustrations by three other artists as well. His drawings of young women are full of feeling and typical of the images he painted in the mid and late 1870s, but they have no particular relevance to the texts of the songs that they accompany. He may have presented Harper with drawings already in hand instead of creating new ones with Tennyson's texts in mind.

During the decade of the 1870s Homer's reputation as a painter had grown steadily, aided in part by the watercolors he had begun to paint in 1874. If his income as a painter did not yet match his critical success, it at least freed him from dependence on *Harper's Weekly* for necessary supplemental income. The last of his large format drawings for that publication appeared in 1876, marking the end of an association of nineteen years. In 1878 and 1880 he contributed a few small drawings—five in all—to *Scribner's Monthly.* They were engraved by members of a younger generation of wood engravers who specialized in capturing the feel and tonal nuances of artists' drawings and were printed with greater care than had earlier been the practice in the field.

In 1881 to 1882 Homer spent eighteen months in England, painting in watercolor and oils in Cullercoats, a fishing village on the North Sea. On his return to America he began a series of large oils depicting men and women working on or threatened by the sea. The seriousness and dramatic force of these paintings added greatly to his stature. In 1884 he moved his residence and studio from New York to his family's recently acquired property on the edge of the rockbound coast of Maine, and there he lived Spartanly for the rest of his life. Though Prout's Neck was his residence, he traveled much, including annual excursions to the Caribbean, where the brilliant light and color of the region added striking new qualities to his already-accomplished watercolor style.

Removed from the centers of book and magazine publication that had once been useful to him, Homer may well have assumed in the mid 1880s that his career as an illustrator was behind him. Yet all that changed in 1886 when he was persuaded to participate in a grand-scale history of the Civil War. This project was first conceived by the editors of *Century* as a series of several articles by prominent military figures from both the North and the South giving different points of view on major incidents of the war. It grew prodigiously from the beginning, culminating in the publication of a four-volume, extensively illustrated set of some three thousand pages, *Battles and Leaders of the Civil War* (1887–1888), edited by Robert Underwood Johnson and Clarence Clough Buel. The set sold well and steadily and was reprinted as late as 1914.

Homer made at least seventeen drawings especially for the project, two of which did not reach publication. Of the fifteen published drawings, three appeared only in serialized parts of the series in *Century;* ten appeared only in the four-volume set; and two appeared in both the magazine and the books.

These illustrations differ from all of Homer's earlier book illustrations in several ways. All but one are photomechanical reproductions apparently by the swelled gelatine process, of drawings that Homer had made specifically for that purpose. As such they convey better than any of his earlier illustrations a genuinely autographic sense, even though the published reproductions are considerably reduced in size from his originals. Though Homer probably made these new drawings in 1886 and 1887–and certainly not before 1885–he dated some of them "62" or "65" to indicate the year of the subject. For this series he selected many wartime eyewitness sketches that he had made more than twenty years earlier and used them as bases for new compositions. He combined figures and other details, recomposed settings, and in countless other ways made new works out of old. Of necessity he sacrificed the spontaneity and vigor of his early sketches, which could not have been reproduced by any process of pictorial reproduction of his time, for carefully constructed compositions with great

economy of means distill much of the emotional power of the earlier works.

In this series Homer offered what amounted to an autobiographical report on his part in the war. His drawings are the equivalents of the retrospective reconsiderations and polished prose of the writers who contributed to the *Century* project. His drawings only rarely illustrate a specific text, but the editors placed them near texts with which their subjects had some connection. He made the drawings in a format that extended across the printed page, serving well as a heading or tailpiece to an article. His achievement was impressive, but it has been little noticed, chiefly perhaps because his illustrations lie buried within four hefty volumes. Unlike his woodblock drawings, the originals of his *Century* series were not destroyed in the process of creating a printing matrix. Many of the originals exist in research library and museum collections, notably at the Addison Gallery of American Art at Andover Academy, Massachusetts, the Museum of the Carnegie Institute, the Princeton University Library, and the Yale University Art Gallery.

These drawings concluded Homer's career as a book illustrator. He made them concurrently with another project in the graphic arts, the creation of his etchings, but the two share nothing in subject, medium, or aim. After the 1880s his work consisted only of oils and watercolors, and in these he showed ever greater prowess in every aspect of his enterprise. By 1900 he was widely celebrated as America's greatest painter.

Homer's career unfolded from its beginning in ways that had no real counterpart among other American artists, ways that no one could have predicted. Keenly aware of what others were doing, he set his own course and followed his own instincts. Though his illustrations of literature now seem to be distinctly minor works, compared especially to the great paintings of his later years, the best of them merit great respect within the context of American illustration of the time. They illuminate his sensibilities and reveal much about his patterns of thought. In the energy and clarity of his approach to his literary subjects can be found the germ of the great paintings of his maturity in which the eternal struggle between ocean and land tells a story of a new kind.

Biographies:

William Howe Downes, *The Life and Works of Winslow Homer* (Boston: Houghton Mifflin, 1911);

Lloyd Goodrich, *Winslow Homer* (New York: Macmillan, 1944);

Albert Ten Eyck Gardner, *Winslow Homer: American Artist* (New York: Clarkson, Potter, 1961);

Gordon Hendricks, *The Life and Work of Winslow Homer* (New York: Abrams, 1979);

Nicolai Cikovsky Jr., *Winslow Homer* (New York: Abrams, 1990).

References:

Lloyd Goodrich, *The Graphic Art of Winslow Homer* (New York: Museum of Graphic Art, 1968);

David Tatham, *Winslow Homer and the Illustrated Book* (Syracuse, N.Y.: Syracuse University Press, 1992);

Tatham, *Winslow Homer and the New England Poets* (Worcester, Mass.: American Antiquarian Society, 1979).

Archives:

The Archives of American Arts, Smithsonian Institution, Washington, D.C., holds on microfilm an extensive collection of papers relating to Homer's life and work, but it includes only a few items pertaining directly to Homer's work as a book illustrator. The Ticknor Firm Cost Books in Harvard University's Houghton Library specify payments to Homer for drawings used in a few of that firm's books. Other important collections of Homer papers are at Bowdoin College, Brunswick, Maine, and Colby College, Waterville, Maine. Major collections of books and magazines illustrated by Homer are in the American Antiquarian Society, Worcester, Massachusetts; the Boston Public Library; the Princeton University Library; and the Mary and Mavis P. Kelsey Collection, Cushing Memorial Library, Texas A&M University.

Augustus Hoppin
(13 July 1828 – 1 April 1896)

Georgia B. Barnhill
American Antiquarian Society

BOOKS: *Carrot-Pomade* (New York: Gregory, 1864);

Ups and Downs on Land and Water (Boston: Osgood, 1871);

Crossing the Atlantic (Boston: Osgood, 1872);

Jubilee Days (Boston: Osgood, 1872);

Hay Fever (Boston: Osgood, 1873);

On the Nile (Boston: Osgood, 1874);

Recollections of Auton House (Boston: Houghton, Mifflin, 1881);

A Fashionable Sufferer (Boston: Houghton, Mifflin, 1883);

Two Compton Boys (Boston: Houghton, Mifflin, 1884);

Married for Fun (Boston: Houghton, Mifflin, 1885).

SELECTED BOOKS ILLUSTRATED: Haven, Alice B., *Contentment Better than Wealth* (New York: Appleton, 1853);

Phelps, Elizabeth Stuart, *The Tell Tale* (Boston: Phillips, Sampson, 1853);

Curtis, George William, *Potiphar Papers* (New York: Putnam, 1853);

Bartlett, John Russell, *Personal Narratives of Explorations and Incidents in Texas, New Mexico, California . . .* , 2 volumes (New York: Appleton, 1854);

Judson, Emily, *My Two Sisters* (Boston: Ticknor, Reed & Fields, 1854);

Butler, William Allen, *Nothing to Wear* (New York: Rudd & Carlton, 1857);

Wilmott, Robert Aris, *The Poets of the Nineteenth Century* (London & New York: Routledge, 1857);

Holmes, Oliver Wendell, *The Autocrat of the Breakfast Table* (Boston: Phillips, Sampson, 1858);

Hauff, Wilhelm, *Arabian Days' Entertainment,* translated from the German by Herbert P. Curtis (Boston: Phillips, Sampson, 1858);

Avery, Samuel Putnam, ed., *The Harp of a Thousand Strings; or Laughter for a Life Time,* illus-

Augustus Hoppin (courtesy of the American Antiquarian Society)

trated by Hoppin and others (New York: Dick & Fitzgerald, 1858);

Crowquill, Alfred, *The Giant Hands; or, The Reward of Industry* (New York: Dinsmore, 1858);

Forester, Frank, *Tricks and Traps of Horsedealers* (New York: Dinsmore, 1858);

Clapp, Henry, *Husband vs. Wife* (New York: Rudd & Carlton, 1858);

Craik, D. M., *John Halifax, Gentleman* (New York: Harper, 1859);

Oldfellah, Klaver, *The Discontented Monkey: A Tale of a Tail* (Boston: Brainard, 1859);

Shillaber, Benjamin Penhallow, *Knitting Work, by Ruth Partington* (Boston: Brown, Taggard & Chase, 1859);

Trowbridge, J. T., *The Old Battleground* (New York: Sheldon, 1860);

Palmer, John Williamson, *Folk Songs* (New York: Scribner, 1861);

Curtis, George William, *Trumps, A Novel* (New York: Harper, 1861);

Stockton, Thomas Hewlings, *Poems; with Autobiographic and Other Notes* (Philadelphia: Martien, 1862);

Irving, Washington, *Hudson Legends, Rip Van Winkle and Sleepy Hollow from The Sketch Book* (New York: Putnam, 1864);

Irving, *Legend of Sleepy Hollow* (New York: Putnam, 1864);

Root, N. W. T., *Contraband Christmas* (New York: Dutton, 1864);

Scudder, Horace E., *The Game of Croquet: Its Appointment and Laws* (New York: Hurd & Houghton, 1864);

Sperry, Henry T., *Country Love vs. City Flirtation* (New York: Carleton, 1865);

Goodrich, Frank B., *The Tribute Book, A Record of the Munificence, Self-Sacrifice, and Patriotism of the American People during the War for the Union* (New York: Derby & Miller, 1865);

Greene, Albert C., *Old Grimes* (Providence: Rider, 1867);

Whitney, Adeline Dutton Train, *A Summer in Leslie Goldthwaite's Life* (Boston: Ticknor & Fields, 1867);

Irving, Washington, *Christmas in England* (New York: Putnam/Hurd & Houghton, 1867);

Saint-Pierre, J. H. Bernadine de, *Paul and Virginia* (Boston: Hurd & Houghton, 1867);

Clift, William, as Timothy Bunker, *The Tim Bunker Papers; or, Yankee Farming* (New York: Judd, 1868);

Alcott, Louisa May, *Kitty's Class-Day* (Boston: Loring, 1868);

Alcott, *Aunt Kipp* (Boston: Loring, 1868);

Alcott, *Psyche's Art* (Boston: Loring, 1868);

Seymour, Mary H., *Posy Vinton's Picnic and Other Stories* (New York: Dutton, 1869);

Palmer, John Williamson, ed., *Songs of Life Selected from Many Sources* (New York: Scribner, 1870);

Irving, Washington, *Rip Van Winkle, a Legend of the Kaatskill Mountains* (New York: Putnam, 1870);

Whitney, Adeline Dutton Train, *Mother Goose for Grown Folks* (Boston: Loring, 1870);

Alcott, Louisa May, *Three Proverb Stories* (Boston: Loring, 1871);

Geegee, Mama, *Houses Not Made with Hands* (New York: Carleton / London: Low, 1871);

Johnson, Virginia W., *Travels of an American Owl* (Philadelphia: Claxton, Remsen & Haffelfiner, 1871);

Lowell, James Russell, *The Poetical Works of James Russell Lowell* (Boston: Osgood, 1871);

Howells, William Dean, *Their Wedding Journey* (Boston: Osgood, 1872);

Palmer, John Williamson, ed., *Songs of the Heart, Selected from Many Sources* (New York: Scribner, 1872);

Howells, William Dean, *Suburban Sketches* (Boston: Osgood, 1872);

Stowe, Harriet Beecher, illustrated by Hoppin and John J. Harley, *Oldtown Fireside Stories* (Boston: Osgood, 1872);

Warner, Charles Dudley, *Backlog Studies* (Boston: Osgood, 1873);

Warner, and Mark Twain, *The Gilded Age* (Hartford: American, 1873);

Gould, Jeanie T., *Marjorie's Quest* (Boston: Osgood, 1873);

Holland, Josiah Gilbert, ed., *Illustrated Library of Favorite Song* (New York: Scribner, Armstrong / Chicago: Hadley & Kine, 1873);

Phelps, Elizabeth S., *Trotty's Wedding Tour* (Boston: Osgood, 1874);

Saxe, John G., *The Proud Miss McBride* (Boston: Osgood, 1874);

Whittier, John Greenleaf, *Child Life in Prose* (Boston: Osgood, 1874);

Irving, Washington, *Christmas Stories* (Philadelphia: Lippincott, 1875);

Irving, *The Legend of Sleepy Hollow* (Philadelphia: Lippincott, 1875);

Teuffel, Blanche Willis Howard von, *One Summer* (Boston: Osgood, 1878);

Longfellow, Henry Wadsworth, *The Poetical Works of Henry Wadsworth Longfellow* (Boston: Houghton, Osgood, 1879);

Niebuhr, Barthold Georg, *Greek Hero-Stories* (New York: Dodd, Mead, 1879);

Baker, Virginia, *Prince Carrotte* (Boston: Rockwell & Churchill, 1881);

O'Brien, Fitz-James, *Life, Poems and Stories* (Boston: Osgood, 1881);

Scudder, Horace Elisha, *The Bodley Grandchildren* (Boston: Houghton, Mifflin, 1882);

Irving, Washington, *The Sketch Book of Geoffrey Crayon* (Philadelphia: Lippincott, 1882).

PERIODICALS: *Illustrated American News*, 1851;

An 1852 magazine cover by Hoppin (courtesy of the American Antiquarian Society)

Yankee Notions, 1852–1855;
Putnam's Monthly, 1857;
Harper's Monthly, 1858;
Spirit of the Fair, 1864;
Jolly Joker, 1865;
Mrs. Grundy, 1865;
Our Young Folks, 1865–1873;
Atlantic Almanac, 1868–1870, 1873;
Punchinello, 1870;
Every Saturday, 1871;
Jubilee Days, 1872;
The Pomfret Prattler, 1882.

Born into an eminent family, Augustus Hoppin trained for a legal career but left that field to become an illustrator of adult fiction and children's books. His skillful draftsmanship and lively use of line served his subjects well, and he excelled at social satire. Perhaps his financial independence prevented him from being as prolific as Felix Octavius Carr Darley, his better-known contemporary, but his work was well regarded by nineteenth-century critics.

Hoppin was born in Providence, Rhode Island, on 13 July 1828. The son of Thomas Coles Hoppin and Harriet D. Jones Hoppin, Augustus was one of twelve children, one of whom died in infancy. Hoppin's father, descended from Thomas Hoppin, who came to Massachusetts about 1635, was a successful merchant in the China and West Indies trade until his death in 1850. His widow lived until 1874. In the nineteenth century several members of the extended Hoppin family were prominent. One of Augustus Hoppin's cousins, William Warner Hoppin, was Rhode Island's governor from 1854 through 1856 and held many other political posts. Another cousin, James Mason Hoppin, was a professor of religion and later of art at Yale University. Augustus's brother Thomas Frederick Hoppin, was a painter, sculptor, and etcher. William James Hoppin, another of Augustus's brothers, was a lawyer in New York and was instrumental in founding the Century Association and the Metropolitan Museum of Art. This brother served as first secretary of the legation at the Court of Saint James from 1873 to 1885. A nephew, Joseph Clark Hoppin, became a noted archaeologist. Hoppin's social background is reflected in his easy ability to portray many facets of American society through his illustrations.

Hoppin, along with ten other members of his family, was educated at Brown University; he graduated in 1848. He went on to train as a lawyer at Harvard and received his degree in 1850. After practicing law in Providence for a few years he abandoned that vocation for a career as an illustrator. In 1854 and 1855 he traveled in Europe and Egypt to study the works of the masters. Either before or after this trip he was made treasurer and executive officer of the estate of his mother's family, the Joneses, for which he received a stipend. This was enough to liberate him from the legal profession. After his return from Europe the Providence city directory listed him as an artist.

Hoppin never married, and he made his home with various family members in Providence. After the death of his brother William in 1867, his widowed sister-in-law, Louise Clare Vinton Hoppin, moved to Pomfret, Connecticut, where other relatives lived, and Augustus moved there as well. According to one family memoir, "Uncle Gus was always in love, after his brother's death, with his sister-in-law, and wanted to marry her." Apparently he never did.

Hoppin's earliest magazine illustrations appeared beginning in 1851, and books that he illustrated were published from the early 1850s until 1887. In the 1870s and 1880s he illustrated some of his own texts, including accounts of his trips to

Europe, a book based on his childhood in Providence, and two spoofs on hay fever and nervous exhaustion.

Even at the beginning of his career Hoppin chose not to become affiliated with a single publisher. Apparently in 1857 the Harper firm approached Hoppin in an attempt to forge such a relationship, but Hoppin preferred the freedom to choose his commissions. "This kind of an arrangement would only hamper me, and would soon become disagreeable," he wrote to a friend.

Hoppin's earliest illustrations were published in the popular press. The *Illustrated American News,* published in New York, includes *The Rochester Knockings,* an illustration that satirizes the new vogue for communicating with the spirit world that sprang up in a village near Rochester, New York, in 1848. It shows a group of people seated at a table during a séance and a small boy rapping on a hat while concealed by the medium's coat.

In January 1852 Hoppin began providing many designs for *Yankee Notions,* an illustrated magazine published in New York by Thomas W. Strong. Hoppin designed the frontispiece to volume two and the covers for most of the monthly parts that year. Over the next few years Hoppin's trademark signature—a circle incorporating a man hopping—could frequently be found on everything from social and political cartoons to a series of sketches for "Our Boarding House." Beginning in August 1854 a new feature, "Jonathan Abroad," appeared, with sketches by "Our Artist" which were signed by Hoppin. These were published irregularly over the next year during the period that Hoppin was in Europe. About thirty sketches from that trip survive in the collections of the American Antiquarian Society.

Prior to his trip to Europe, Hoppin's illustrations appeared in five books published by firms in New York and Boston. One of the titles was John Russell Bartlett's *Personal Narratives of Explorations and Incidents in Texas, New Mexico, California . . .* (1854). Hoppin might have traveled to the West on this expedition, but there is no indication from the lists of names in the volume that Hoppin was on the trip, at least in an official position.

Upon his return from Europe, Hoppin's first success was his series of eight illustrations for a satiric, witty poem by William Allen Butler, *Nothing to Wear,* first published in New York in *Harper's Weekly* (without illustrations) and shortly thereafter by Rudd and Carlton in 1857. Hoppin's linear, sketchy style was well suited to the text. His illustrations add to the humor of the poem concerning a shopping spree of a young woman with her father. Hoppin was pleased with the results. In a letter dated 22

THE LANDLADY'S DAUGHTER.

Hoppin's illustration for the first edition (1858) of Oliver Wendell Holmes's The Autocrat of the Breakfast Table *(courtesy of the American Antiquarian Society)*

June 1857 to his childhood friend George William Curtis, whose *Potiphar Papers* he had illustrated in 1853, Hoppin declared that the "cuts appear respectably." The book, widely advertised and reviewed, brought great acclaim to Hoppin. One reviewer in *Putnam's Monthly* (August 1857) wrote that the "book is also remarkable for the singular felicity of its illustrations. . . . It certainly is doing no one injustice to say that, in a department of social humor and poetic fancy, he [Hoppin] is unsurpassed. . . . Mr. Hoppin has a rare union of imagination with his humor—a fine flavor of allegory in his best things, which gives them a peculiar completeness. He is destined, it seems to us, to great distinction in his career." Following this success Hoppin received commissions for many other books. Another review in the *Boston Courier* commented that the "illustrations of this little book are even more than worthy of the text. Nothing of the kind that we know of has ever been produced in America, within a long way of the

Illustration by Hoppin for the first edition (1857) of William Allen Butler's Nothing to Wear *(courtesy of the American Antiquarian Society)*

excellence of these eight wood cuts." Following this success Hoppin received commissions for many other books.

Like many other well-known illustrators of his generation, Hoppin was commissioned to contribute designs for compilations of poetry illustrated by several artists. These volumes lack the cohesion and uniform style of those illustrated by a single hand, but they were elegantly produced and were a means for illustrators to receive challenging commissions from leading publishers. Some artists waited for years before being invited to illustrate such works. In 1857 and 1858 two works of this type appeared that incorporated designs by Hoppin: *The Poets of the Nineteenth Century* and *The Harp of a Thousand Strings; or Laughter for a Life Time,* edited by Samuel Putnam Avery, a wood engraver and eventually an art dealer. John Williamson Palmer's *Folk Songs* (1861) and Thomas Hewlings Stockton's *Poems* (1862) also include several illustrations by Hoppin. Other similar commissions followed throughout his career.

One of Hoppin's most demanding commissions was Oliver Wendell Holmes's *Autocrat of the*

Breakfast Table, published by Phillips, Sampson in 1858. In a letter to Holmes located at the Library of Congress, Hoppin alluded to two sets of drawings for this work, the first of which did not meet with Holmes's approval. Hoppin drew a second set, which was published, but Holmes removed them from copies that he presented to friends. Hoppin defended himself by writing to Holmes, "I am entirely convinced that if the *ideas illustrated* are not the embodiment of the ideas *written,* they only hinder the reader and both ideas are weakened. The 'Autocrat papers' are hardly *illustratable*. There are so many *shades* of ideas, so much that is merely suggested, that it is next to an impossibility to bring them into existence by the pencil." On 10 January 1859 Hoppin wrote Holmes again thanking him for a "beautiful copy of the 'Autocrat'" just received from Phillips, Sampson. "I shall value it exceedingly as well for the complimentary act of courtesy which prompted the gift, as also for the autograph which it contains. Believe me, my dear Sir, (that although from circumstances over which I had no control, my portion of the work has only been an incubus upon it) I still shall always feel happy for the lucky day which afforded me an opportunity of your acquaintance."

Hoppin's illustrations were not of situations or moments in a story but of embodiments of American types. The text was actually of little assistance to the illustrator, and that aspect of the commission caused Hoppin the difficulties that aroused Holmes's disapproval. A review in the *Boston Transcript,* however, praised the illustrations, concluding that "Hoppin in his drawings has done justice to the humor and pathos of the author."

Hoppin illustrated a second work by Curtis, *Trumps,* serialized in *Harper's Weekly* in 1859 and 1860 and published as a book by Harper and Brothers in 1861. The range of situations and characters shows that Hoppin was able to be convincing as an illustrator of sentiment as well as of character. His illustrations of society, such as the one of Aunt Dagon surveying the ballroom, are convincing partly because he was so familiar with such a social setting.

Hoppin's range of ability is also seen in his drawings for *Knitting Work, by Ruth Partington* (1859) by Benjamin Penhallow Shillaber. This Boston author and printer created a humorous female figure, Mrs. Ruth Partington, and Ike, her nephew, who animated a series of tales about small-town New England life. First appearing in a newspaper in 1847, Mrs. Partington's adventures had already been illustrated by another artist in *Life and Sayings of Mrs. Partington,* published in 1854. Five years later Hoppin brought them to life again in *Knitting Work.*

One of the stories describes Ike's mischievous behavior in church. Hoppin depicts him on the church steps after the service with a gay, high step and a broad smile indicating Ike's role as prankster. Hoppin was himself surrounded by a large family that included countless nieces and nephews. There must have been at least one "Ike" within the family circle.

Hoppin's love of children is expressed in the large number of children's books that he illustrated beginning in 1853. They include Alice B. Haven's *Contentment Better than Wealth* (1853), Alfred Crowquill's *The Giant Hands: or, The Reward of Industry* (1858), Klaver Oldfellah's *The Discontented Monkey: a Tale of a Tail* (1859), *Learning to Count: or, "One, Two, Buckle My Shoe"* (1866–1870), and Louisa May Alcott's *Three Proverb Stories* (1871). Hoppin illustrated relatively little during the Civil War. He served in Providence as assistant adjutant general beginning in 1861. After his brother's death he acted as a surrogate father to his nephews and nieces. Possibly during his brother William's absence at the front during the war Hoppin took on some familial responsibilities that further diminished his time for art. The market for work done in Hoppin's style during wartime was also limited. He did find time in 1864 to write the first of his books, *Carrot-Pomade,* a witty alphabet book on the creation of a pomade made out of carrots that cured baldness. That same year he illustrated a children's book, *Karl Kiegler;* stories by Washington Irving; and N. W. T. Root's *Contraband Christmas.* Hoppin's work must have been agreeable to the authors and publishers because he frequently illustrated more than one work by a single author. In 1872 two novels by William Dean Howells were published with illustrations by Hoppin—*Suburban Sketches* and *Their Wedding Journey.*

Hoppin probably became acquainted with Howells in the fall of 1868; that year Hoppin was commissioned to provide illustrations for the *Atlantic Almanac.* Howells had grown up in Ohio and was rewarded with an ambassadorship to Venice after he wrote a campaign biography of Abraham Lincoln for the 1860 presidential election. Upon his return he worked briefly for *The Nation* before becoming an editor at the *Atlantic Monthly.*

Hoppin followed Howells's text closely, for it provided excellent descriptions of people and places. In one letter to Howells, Hoppin expressed the wish that he could see some views of Quebec. He apparently wanted to be as accurate as possible in his settings. While writing to the author, the illustrator offered some advice: "The allegorical ideas, perhaps, are a 'thought too subtle.' I think it would be as well to deal in these sparingly—as the general reader might not at first sight understand them.

How the Pig and Crow Enjoyed Themselves.

Illustration by Hoppin for the first edition (1871) of Virginia W. Johnson's Travels of an American Owl *(courtesy of the American Antiquarian Society)*

There is this to be said regarding such things—If they *attract,* they sometimes afford amusement in the endeavors put forth to discover their meaning."

Hoppin prepared these illustrations on glass with an etching needle. Apparently the glass plates were prepared with an opaque etching ground on which Hoppin drew with the needle, piercing the ground. When the drawing was completed, the glass plates could be used as photographic negatives.

One reason that Hoppin was such a prolific illustrator late in his life was his use of the latest developments in technology. For his own *Ups and Downs on Land and Water* (1871), a collection of humorous sketches made while on a European trip, Hoppin's illustrations were photographed onto lithographic stones by the Chemical Engraving Company. The stones subsequently were printed lithographically by the firm of John H. Bufford in Boston. *Ups and Downs on Land and Water* was published in an edition of one thousand copies. A year later Hoppin's *Crossing the Atlantic* was produced using similar technology. Creating plates from drawings photographically was a distinct improvement over the traditional creation of plates from drawings that were transferred to woodblocks, engraved, stereotyped, and then printed. The process was quicker and did not involve the hand of a wood engraver.

The plates for another work, *Jubilee Days* (1872), may have been made by a more efficient process. Boston was the host city for a popular event in the summer of 1872, the World Peace Jubilee. Hoppin illustrated a daily record of the Jubilee for the publisher James R. Osgood. His designs were reproduced in just hours by the Chemical Engraving Company, which advertised "By uniting and practically applying the various arts of Photography, Transfer-Etching, Zincography, Albumen Printing, Lithography, Heliography, each of which has its separate use, this Company is able to produce artistic and commercial results in illustration, which, for Quality, Rapidity, and Economy, are unequalled." Of course, no details are revealed, but the illustrations could be printed with the text, a great savings of time. Illustrations done by lithography took much longer. Sinclair Hamilton, in his *Early American Book Illustrators and Wood Engravers, 1670–1870* (1958), suggests that *Jubilee Days* was the "beginning of illustrated journalism in the United States."

Possibly, illustrations for books such as *One Summer* by Blanche Willis Howard von Teuffel (1878) and Hoppin's *Two Compton Boys* (1884) likewise were reproduced by the technique described in the advertisement in *Jubilee Days*. The illustrations are interspersed throughout the text.

Henry T. Tuckerman wrote briefly about Hoppin in his *Book of the Artists* (1867). Tuckerman commented that Hoppin's illustrations "are full of character and graceful execution. Some of the elaborate pen-and-ink drawings of this artist surpass in finish, force, and beauty, anything of the kind produced in this country."

In 1937 one of Hoppin's nieces wrote a memoir of the Hoppin family. Of her "Uncle Gus" she wrote: "Augustus was the best-known and best-loved Hoppin of his day. His tall and slender figure, his flowing yellow Dundreary whiskers and his hu-

morous speech gave him a special personality. The world of Society loved and sought him, his family adored him and all hirelings that came within his sphere waited, giggling, upon his lightest wish." She went on to describe him as being "extremely well-informed and an intelligent, though not a fluent, talker. He was a rabid Republican and used to say that he had never met a decent Democrat, except, possibly, Grover Cleveland." Children "swarmed about him like flies, climbing up every available part of his body, clamoring for pictures and shrieking with joy at his funniness." His abundant intelligence, wit, sense of humor, and playfulness found expression in his illustrations of all types. By the end of his thirty-five-year career more than ninety publications included illustrations by Hoppin. The books were of several genres, including juvenile stories, poetry, fiction, and essays. They were published in Boston, New York, and Philadelphia by several of the most prominent publishing firms of the time, and they mark Augustus Hoppin as one of the most amusing and wittiest illustrators of his age.

References:

Theodore Bolton, "American Book Illustrators: A Checklist, Augustus Hoppin," *Publishers' Weekly* (20 September 1941): 1162–1163;

Representative Men and Old Families of Rhode Island, volume 1 (Chicago: J. H. Beers, 1908), pp. 8–11.

Archives:

There are a few of Hoppin's letters in various repositories, including the Library of Congress, the Henry E. Huntington Library, the Providence Public Library, and the Houghton Library of Harvard University. The American Antiquarian Society has a volume of sketches. Other drawings and sketches are located at the Providence Public Library, the Princeton University Library, and the Rhode Island Historical Society. Copies of "The Hoppin Family" by Louise Clare Vinton (October 1937) and "Recollections of the Hoppin Family" by Mary Chapin Smith (1944) are located in the Manuscript Department of the American Antiquarian Society. A scrapbook with newspaper clippings, several drawings, and other family memorabilia is privately owned.

David Claypoole Johnston

(March 1798? – 8 November 1865)

David Tatham
Syracuse University

BOOKS: *Scraps and Sketches, Part 1* (Boston: The author, 1828);

Scraps No. 2, for the Year 1830 (Boston: The author, 1830);

Scraps No. 3, 1832 (Boston: The author, 1832);

Scraps for the Year 1833, in Which Is Included Trollopania (Boston: The author, 1833);

Scraps for the Year 1834, in Which Is Included Fiddle-D.D. (Boston: The author, 1834);

Scraps for the Year 1835 (Boston: The author, 1835);

Outlines Illustrative of the Journal of F. A. K. (Boston: The author, 1836);

Phrenology Exemplified and Illustrated, Being Scraps No. 7 for the Year 1837 (Boston: The author, 1837);

Scraps No. 8 (Boston: The author, 1840);

Scraps No. 1, 1849, New Series (Boston: The author, 1849).

SELECTED BOOKS ILLUSTRATED: Shakespeare, William, *The Dramatic Works of William Shakespeare,* 10 volumes (New York: Durell, 1817–1818);

Buzz, Bumberly, pseudonym, *Ephemera, or the History of Cockney Dandies: A Poem in One Canto* (Philadelphia: Desilver, 1819);

Hawkins, Micah, *Mynhieur Herrick von Heimelman, the Dancing-Master; and The Big Red Nose* (New York: The author, 1824);

Mack, Ebenezer, *The Cat-Fight: A Mock Heroic Poem* (New York, 1824);

Anonymous, *Eccentric Biography, or Sketches of Remarkable Characters, Ancient and Modern* (Boston: Balch, 1825);

Anonymous, *The Laughing Philosopher: or, Fun, Humor and Wit* (Boston, 1825);

Milton, John, *Paradise Lost* (Boston: Bedlington, 1825);

Bancroft, Aaron, *The Life of George Washington,* 2 volumes (Boston: Bedlington, 1826);

Emmons, William, *An Oration and Poem Delivered July 4, 1826* (Boston: The author, 1826);

Anonymous, *The Galaxy of Wit; or Laughing Philosopher,* 2 volumes (Boston, 1826);

David Claypoole Johnston, self-portrait in 1837

Anonymous, *The Letters of Junius,* 2 volumes (Boston: Whitaker, 1826);

Cobb, Enos, as Lord Hail-fair, *Fame and Fancy, or Voltaire Improved* (Boston, 1826);

Anonymous, *Le Souvenir, a Picturesque Pocket Diary for 1827* (Philadelphia: Poole, 1826);

Dorothea Dix, as A Teacher. Conversations on Common Things; or Guide to Knowledge with Questions (Boston: Munroe & Francis, 1826);

Hill, Frederic S., ed., *Memorial. A Christmas and New Year's Offering* (Boston: True & Greene, 1826);

Young, Edward, *The Complaint, or Night Thoughts, and the Force of Religion* (Boston: Bedlington, 1826);

Paxton, James, *Illustrations of Paley's Natural Theology* (Boston: Hilliard, Gray, Little & Wilkins, 1827);

Calef, Robert, *The Wonders of the Invisible World Displayed* (Boston: Bedlington, 1828);

Anonymous, *P's and Q's* (Boston: Bowles & Dearborn, 1828);

Paltock, Robert, *The Life and Adventures of Peter Wilkins,* 2 volumes (Boston: Baker & Alexander, 1828);

Thacher, James, *American Medical Biography*, 2 volumes (Boston: Richardson & Lord/Coltons & Barnard, 1828);

Morgan, William, *Illustrations of Masonry* (Boston: Sumner & Marsh, 1829);

Willis, Nathaniel P., ed., *The Token; A Christmas and New Year's Present* (Boston: Goodrich, 1829);

Russell, William, *Rudiments of Gesture* (Boston: Carter & Hendlee, 1830);

Allyn, Avery, *A Ritual of Freemasonry* (Boston: Marsh, 1831);

Finn, Henry J., *American Comic Annual* (Boston: Richardson, Lord & Holbrook, 1831);

Anonymous, *The Aurora Borealis, or Flashes of Wit; Calculated to Drown out Care and Eradicate the Blue Devils* (Boston, 1831);

Finn, Henry J., ed., *American Comic Annual* (Boston: Richardson, Lord & Holbrook, 1831);

Goodrich, E. G., *A Child's History of the United States* (Boston, 1831);

Pickering, Henry, *The Buckwheat Cake. A Poem* (Boston: Carter, Hendee & Babcock, 1831);

Scott, Walter, *Kenilworth* (Boston: Parker, 1831);

St. Clair, Henry, *The United Criminal Calendar* (Boston: Gaylord, 1832);

Burroughs, Stephen, *Memoirs of the Notorious Stephen Burroughs* (Boston: Gaylord, 1832);

Smith, Thomas, and John Choules, *Origin and History of Missions* (Boston: Walker, 1832);

Smith, Seba, as Jack Downing, *The Life and Writings of Major Jack Downing of Downingville* (Boston: Lilly, Wait, Colman & Holden, 1833);

Felton, Cornelius C., ed., *The Iliad of Homer* (Boston: Hilliard, Gray, 1833);

Malte-Brun, Conrad, *System of Geography*, 3 volumes (Boston: Walker, 1834);

Child, Lydia Maria, ed., *The Oasis* (Boston: Bacon, 1834);

Anonymous, *The Campaigns of Napoleon Buonoparte* (Boston: Gaylord, 1835);

Greenwood, Francis W. P., *Lives of the Twelve Apostles* (Boston: Hilliard, Gray, 1835);

St. Clair, Henry, *Tales of Terror or the Mysteries of Magic* (Boston: Gaylord, 1835);

Cervantes Saavedra, Miguel de, *Don Quixote* (Boston, 1836);

Fessenden, Thomas, as Christopher Caustic, M.D., *The Terrible Tractoration, and Other Poems* (Boston, 1836);

Tanner, Henry S., *The American Traveller* (Philadelphia: The author, 1836);

Weld, H. Hastings, *Corrected Proofs* (Boston: Russell, Shattuck, 1836);

Von Miltitz, C. B., *The Game of Life, a Drawing by Moritz Retzch, Explained* (Boston, 1837);

Warren, John C., M.D., *Surgical Observations on Tumors, with Cases and Operations* (Boston: Crocker & Brewster, 1837);

Kettell, Samuel, as Timo. Titterwell, Esq., *Yankee Notions. A Medley* (Boston: Otis, Broaders, 1838);

Neal, Joseph C., *Charcoal Sketches; or, Scenes in a Metropolis* (Philadelphia: Carey & Hart, 1838);

Osborne, Laughton, *The Vision of Rubeta, an Epic Story of the Island of Manhattan* (Boston: Weeks, Jordan, 1838);

Peabody, Joel R., *A World of Wonders; or Divers Developments, Showing the Thorough Triumph of Animal Magnetism in New England* (Boston: Davis, 1838);

Morris, George P., *The Little Frenchman and His Water-Lots* (Philadelphia: Lea & Blanchard, 1839);

Read, J., *Child Martin, an Epic Poem* (New York, 1840);

Rogers, John G., *Specimens of Modern Printing Types, Cast at the Letter Foundry of the Boston Type and Stereotype Company* (Boston, 1841);

Cooley, James E., *The American in Egypt* (New York: Appleton, 1842);

Gliddon, George R., *Appendix to "The American in Egypt"* (Philadelphia: Merrihew & Thompson, 1842);

Moore, John McDermott, *The Adventures of Tom Stapleton* (New York: Wilson, 1842);

Kettell, Samuel, as Sampson Short-and-Fat, *Daw's Doings; or, The History of the Late War in the Plantations* (Boston: White & Lewis, 1842);

Parsons, Thomas W., trans., *The First Ten Cantos of the Inferno of Dante Alighieri* (Boston: Ticknor, 1843);

Warland, John, *The Plume* (Boston: Mussey, 1847);

Boyce, John, as Paul Peppergrass, *Shady M'Guire; or, Tricks on Travellers: Being a Story of the North of Ireland* (New York: Edward Dunigan, 1848);

Sargent, Lucius M., *The Legal Remedy* (Boston: Redding, 1849);

The Thousand and One Nights, or the Arabian Nights' Entertainments (Boston: Phillips, Sampson, 1852);

Trask, George, as Uncle Toby, *Thoughts and Stories on Tobacco for American Lads* (Boston: The author, 1852);

Curtis, Mary, *Memoirs of a Country Doll Written by Herself* (Boston: Munroe, 1853);

Adams, William Taylor, as Oliver Optic, *The Boat Club; or The Bunkers of Rippleton* (Boston: Lea & Shepard, 1855);

Anonymous, *Winter Sermon for Christmas and New Year* (Boston: Brown, Bazin, 1856);

Burton, William, ed., *The Cyclopedia of Wit and Humor* (New York: Appleton, 1858);

Sargent, Lucius M., *The Ballad of the Abolition Blunder-buss* (Boston, 1861).

PERIODICALS: *Boston Monthly Magazine,* 1825;

Athenaeum, 1826;

American Journal of Science and Arts, 1830;

Liberator, 1831;

People's Magazine, 1833–1834;

Pioneer, 1834;

New York Mirror, 1837–1838;

Boston Notion, 1841;

Brother Jonathan: A Weekly Compend of Belles Lettres, 1842–1843;

New Mirror, 1843;

Ballou's Pictorial, 1855;

Gleason's Weekly Line-of-Battleship, 1858.

Frontispiece by Johnston for William Emmons's An Oration and Poem Delivered July 4, 1826

David Claypoole Johnston was the earliest American artist to create a substantial body of original book illustration in a distinctive style. Between the mid 1820s and the early 1860s he contributed illustrations to at least seventy books, as well as many periodicals. He illustrated many kinds of books, including medical, historical, and dramatic subjects, but his most original and interesting work was as an illustrator of humorous fiction. As an admirer and follower in his early career of the amiably satiric work of his British contemporary George Cruikshank, Johnston gained the sobriquet "the American Cruikshank," but as his career progressed, his own style and artistic persona emerged. In his best work Johnston captured better perhaps than any other graphic artist of his era the good-humored optimism and robustly democratic spirit of Jacksonian America. Late in his career his work also reflected the more somber ethos of the national issues that led to the Civil War. Though he illustrated no American literary works of enduring importance, his amiable, ebullient, sometimes farcical treatment of many now-forgotten works of fiction has supplied these books with a level of interest they would otherwise lack.

David Claypoole Johnston (he consistently used only the initials of his first and middle names) was born in Philadelphia to a family of modest means but notable theatrical and literary interests. His obituary places his birth in March 1798, though other accounts of no better authority give the year as 1797 or 1799. His father, William P. Johnston—at various times a bookkeeper, storekeeper, and printer—was long associated with the Chestnut Street Theatre in Philadelphia as its box-office manager and treasurer. His mother, Charlotte Rowson

Johnston, had been an actress in her native England. Her sister-in-law, the English actress Susanna Haswell Rowson, who had written the best-selling novel *Charlotte Temple* (1791) based on her childhood years in America, settled in the United States a few years before her nephew's birth and in time probably contributed to his avid lifelong interest in literature and the stage. When Johnston attempted a career as an actor in Philadelphia and Boston between 1821 and 1825, he followed a family tradition. His first and more serious interest, however, lay with art rather than acting. After spending the 1825–1826 season at the Federal Street Theatre in Boston while concurrently establishing himself as a pictorial artist, he acted no more. Nevertheless, his work as an artist frequently dealt with the theater as a subject, and he often took theatrical approaches to other subjects.

Having settled in Boston, Johnston made that city and its environs his home for the rest of his life. In 1830 he married Sarah Murphy, a native of Concord, Massachusetts. By 1832 he had converted from his family's Protestant faith to his wife's Roman Catholicism. That this act, in an age of widespread religious bigotry, deprived him of few commissions as an illustrator except among Protestant-affiliated denominational publishers of religious books perhaps testifies to the affection that Bostonians felt for him. Five of Johnston's children survived to maturity. His two sons, Thomas Murphy

'Stop Major! I'll give you a ride.' —
'Cant stop; got an express for the Gineral.'

An illustration by Johnston for Seba Smith's The Life and Writings of
Major Jack Downing of Downingville *(1833)*

(1836–1869) and John B. (1848–1886), became successful painters. His three daughters—Mary Priscilla, Charlotte, and Sarah—were skillful amateur artists, and Charlotte also enjoyed a modestly successful career as a dramatic reader, musician, and translator of French literature.

Johnston's career in Boston was many-faceted. In addition to working as a painter and book and magazine illustrator, he made numerous separate etchings and lithographs. For some years he conducted a small but respected academy of art—Louisa May Alcott was one of his pupils—in which he taught mechanical drawing as well. His richly deserved reputation as a humorist notwithstanding, he also engaged the serious issues of his day in his work, taking strong stands against slavery and religious intolerance. As early as 1831, his pictorial masthead for *The Liberator* allied him with the abolitionist movement.

His initial training in art had begun at age fifteen through an apprenticeship to Francis Kearney, a leading Philadelphia engraver. From Kearney he learned the intaglio techniques of copperplate etching, line engraving, and aquatint. By 1818, nearing the end of his term of apprenticeship, he signed

seven of the frontispiece plates that he had engraved after designs by others for the multivolume *Dramatic Works of William Shakespeare* (1817–1818), published in New York by Henry Durell. While he never became a virtuoso draftsman, he soon developed a distinctive graphic style. Around 1825 he learned the techniques of lithographic drawing, and in this medium, then new to the United States, he became one of the earliest masters in America. His best work as a lithographic artist is found in his broadside prints. Most of his book illustrations are copperplate etchings and engravings by his own hand or wood engravings in which others cut what he drew on woodblocks.

Having etched several satiric broadside prints and theatrical portraits in Philadelphia in the early 1820s, in 1824 he gained his first opportunities to illustrate books during an acting season in New York. For the merchant and playwright Micah Hawkins, he made six etchings to embellish the comic *Mynhieur Herrick von Heimelman, the Dancing-Master; and The Big Red Nose* (1824). For Ebenezer Mack he contributed five etchings to that author's mock-heroic poem *The Cat-Fight* (1824). Both of these sets of illustrations seem hastily conceived and roughly exe-

The Poet Emerson strives to start up his Pegasus. Pegasus is indulging in "Leaves of Grass," by Walt. Whitman.

One of Johnston's illustrations for Lucius M. Sargent's The Ballad of the Abolition Blunder-buss *(1861)*

cuted compared to the portrait prints of actors in character that he had made in Philadelphia, but they are full of an energetic liveliness of a kind rarely seen in earlier American illustration.

By comparison, the book illustrations of his first two years in Boston were more restrained, in concert with the serious subjects of the books they illustrated. Among them were frontispieces adapted from English sources for Boston editions of John Milton's *Paradise Lost* (1825) and *The Letters of Junius* (1826). More interesting, and wholly original, were the two etched groups of English and American actors in character and the ten wood-engraved comic vignettes that he provided for the two volumes of *The Galaxy of Wit* (1826) and the full-length portrait of William Emmons delivering a speech that serves as the frontispiece for that author's *Oration and Poem Delivered July 4, 1826* (1826).

By this time Johnston was a moderately busy book illustrator and printmaker. In 1825 he had advertised his availability as a portrait painter in newspapers but evidently got few, if any, commissions. No painted portrait by him from these years is known, though he exhibited a view of Boston Common in oils (now lost). He painted in watercolor for most of his life and exhibited often at the Boston Athenaeum. He took the subjects for many of his paintings from literature, often from Shakespeare and Sir Walter Scott. These choices enabled him to pictorialize characters and passages from texts of far greater substance than those he typically dealt with for publishers and allowed him to execute them in color and at a larger scale than book illustration permitted. After 1826 painting became a secondary interest for him as his work as a graphic artist began to provide him with a dependable income.

Most of his assignments for book publishers in the late 1820s called for high seriousness; a few, gentle humor. The only truly satiric volume of these years to include his work was *Fame and Fancy, or Voltaire Improved* (1826) by Enos Cobb writing as Lord Hail-fair. These unsigned illustrations can be attributed to Johnston on grounds of style. His bent for satire and burlesque found its outlet in the late 1820s not so much in book illustration as in his original prints, which include many etched or litho-

Frontispiece by Johnston for Samuel Kettell's 1842 book Daw's Doings; or, The History of the Late War in the Plantations
(courtesy of the American Antiquarian Society)

graphed cartoons on political and other topical matters.

Johnston occasionally indulged in comic writing to accompany his own comic art. His first major effort to include an original humorous text as part of his work came with the publication of his *Scraps and Sketches, Part 1* (1828). This was a set of four plates of original etched comic vignettes bound in wrappers. Johnston's legends and captions for these vignettes, full of puns and drolleries, constitute a skeletal literary program. In format and spirit Johnston modeled this publication on Cruikshank's six-plate *Phrenological Illustrations* (1826), published in London, and its successors, *Illustrations of Time* (1827) and *Scraps and Sketches, Part 1.* Johnston published eight further numbers of *Scraps,* variously titled, for the years 1830, 1832, 1833, 1834, 1835, 1837, 1840, and 1849. Three of these include, in addition to the usual four plates of etched vignettes with captions, two or more pages of Johnston's own satiric text printed in letterpress, for which some or all of the vignettes serve as illustrations.

The nine numbers of *Scraps* document the steady advance of Johnston's skills as a draftsman over two decades, as well as the sharpening of his wit and the broadening of his interests. The objects of his satire range from the decline of state militia systems in the late 1820s to the rise of the women's rights movement in the late 1840s and touch on political and social issues of many stripes. His treatment of these topics rose above political rancor to become portrayals of more universal human foibles. In his texts he often cited or alluded to Shakespeare, whose works he knew intimately from his years on the stage and his omnivorous reading. Johnston's *Scraps* remain valuable not only for their intrinsic humor but also for the light they shed on the development of American manners, vernacular speech, and regional dress, and the emergence of such purely American types as the Yankee and the Mississippi riverboat man. In ridiculing vanity and pretense, and poking fun at the beef-witted and pea-brained among us, Johnston delineated not only the democratic character of Jacksonian society but also the more general foibles of humanity. His best satiric work seems ever pertinent and continues to bring forth smiles. When on rare occasions he treated topical events that allowed no humor—such as the burning of the Ursuline Convent in Charlestown, Massachusetts, in his *Scraps for the*

My purchase P. 9

An illustration by Johnston for Mary Curtis's 1853 book Memoirs of a Country Doll
(courtesy of the American Antiquarian Society)

Year 1835–his pictorial response was unyielding in its condemnation.

As was true of Cruikshank, John Leech, and the other major British comic illustrators of the day, caricature was a major component of Johnston's style. He was a master of subtle as well as broad exaggeration and at times approached the grotesque without offending the tastes of his times. His comic sense commended him to the leading humorous writers of the period, and their publishers frequently commissioned illustrations from him. He made fourteen etchings and seventeen wood engravings for *American Comic Annual* (1831), a book by his friend and fellow Bostonian, the actor Henry J. Finn. The same year he etched fourteen plates for a collection of comic pieces titled *The Aurora Borealis, or Flashes of Wit*. Perhaps the most enduring of the comic texts he illustrated in the 1830s was Seba Smith's satiric *The Life and Writings of Major Jack*

Downing of Downingville (1833), an epistolary novel written in Yankee dialect, published originally as a series of letters in newspapers and then in book form in Boston with six wood engravings designed by Johnston. The book's popularity occasioned several reprintings.

In the late 1830s he contributed four etchings to Joseph C. Neal's *Charcoal Sketches; or, Scenes in a Metropolis* (1838), published in Philadelphia, a book that also went through several printings. An indication of the attractiveness of Johnston's work within the profession at this point in his career is that three years later the English illustrator Hablot K. Brown ("Phiz") adapted, apparently without permission, two of Johnston's etchings from *Charcoal Sketches* for use in *The Pic-Nic Papers* (1841), edited by Charles Dickens. Though Johnston worked primarily for Boston publishers throughout his career, he occasionally received commissions from Philadelphia publishers in the 1830s and 1840s, perhaps in part through the offices of his relatives in that city. In a single year in the late 1830s Johnston illustrated three works of fiction in which he demonstrated a growing capacity to modify his comic style to suit the tenor of the texts he illustrated. The four lithographs that he contributed to Laughton Osborne's historical romance *The Vision of Rubeta, an Epic Story of the Island of Manhattan* (1838) include affectionately humorous rather than satiric depictions of Roman Catholic nuns and are invested with suggestions of natural dignity hitherto unseen in his work. By contrast, his eight etchings for Joel R. Peabody's *A World of Wonders* (1838) gently burlesque the voguish interest of the day in the pseudoscience of animal magnetism without depriving the characters in the book of sympathy. His six etchings for Samuel Kettell's *Yankee Notions. A Medley* (1838) display to even better effect his penchant for caricature and give needed vitality to the author's relatively placid characterizations of New England types.

During all of these years Boston publishers also called on Johnston to provide illustrative matter for books of more serious kinds. These include learned and technical volumes, and occasionally American editions of European literature. He designed and engraved on copper elaborate frontispieces for two of the three quarto volumes of the Boston edition of Conrad Malte-Brun's *System of Geography* (1834). For a Spanish-language edition of Cervantes's *Don Quixote* published in Boston (1836), he adapted seven of the fifteen illustrations that Cruikshank had etched three years earlier for a London edition of this masterpiece and added four of his own. The next year he drew sixteen original lithographs for inclusion in John C. Warren's *Surgical Observations on Tumors, with Cases and Operations* (1837). These hand-colored specimens of medical illustration are a world apart from Johnston's more typical sallies into the world around him, and they attest both to his versatility and to the scarcity in Boston of other able graphic artists equally at home in etching, line engraving, lithography, and drawing for wood engravers.

While the number of books that Johnston illustrated declined gradually during the decade of the 1840s, the variety of his subjects was greater. His numerous illustrations for James E. Cooley's *American in Egypt* (1842) are among his most subtle; the sense of Americans making their way in an exotic culture comes through effectively. In the same year he completed another large commission for wood-engraved illustrations to John McDermott Moore's novel *The Adventures of Tom Stapleton*. In both of these projects Johnston strove for a more serious tone, but

he rarely achieved more than postured melodrama. While this fault did not impede him in comic subjects, it limited his range. His dependence on caricature prevented him from being persuasive when he attempted to depict serious emotion. Compared to such contemporaries as F. O. C. Darley, he seemed constitutionally unable to keep a smile from breaking through.

In Samuel Kettell's *Daw's Doings, or The History of the Late War in the Plantations* (1842) he returned to the ludicrously comic manner in which he had no equal in those years in America. Later in the decade he brought a gentler humor to *Shandy M'Guire; or, Tricks on Travellers: Being a Story of the North of Ireland* (1848), an amusing Irish tale by Paul Peppergrass, the pseudonym of the Reverend John Boyce. If Boyce sought Johnston as an illustrator because of their shared religion, it was one of the few known instances in which the artist's faith brought him a commission.

In the 1850s the rapid expansion of children's literature as a major genre for trade publishers brought Johnston a few commissions. For Mary Curtis's *Memoirs of a Country Doll Written by Herself* (1853) he made four etchings that in their simplicity and quietude perfectly suit the author's tone and are at some distance from the theatrical display of most of his earlier work. For the first of William Taylor Adams's Oliver Optic tales, *The Boat Club; or The Bunkers of Rippleton* (1855), Johnston drew some serviceable but uninspired illustrations that played only a brief role in the long history of this book. Johnston's wood-engraved illustrations were dropped from later editions undoubtedly because they were soon out of date in style. To conform to the graphic style of the succeeding volumes in the Oliver Optic series they were replaced by the work of younger artists.

After the late 1840s the graphic arts that served the world of publishing entered a period of major change, and Johnston found himself less in demand as an illustrator. Immigrants from England, France, and Germany, well trained in all aspects of the art and craft of illustration, arrived in Boston and other publishing centers in increasing numbers. Standards of draftsmanship in the graphic arts rose sharply nationwide. The technologies of book manufacture and pictorial reproduction moved steadily toward mechanization. In this context Johnston by the 1850s had begun to seem quaintly old-fashioned in both his style and his production methods.

Another factor that undoubtedly contributed to the diminution of his commissions in the 1850s was a change in the mood of the nation. The antic comic sense that distinguished so much of Johnston's work in the 1820s and 1830s had been part and parcel of Jacksonian culture. It flourished in the theater in such plays as James Kirke Paulding's highly popular *Lion of the West* (1831) and in much popular literature, including the plethora of comic Crockett almanacs published throughout the nation in the mid and late 1830s. Visitors from England in the 1820s and 1830s as varied as the actor Charles Mathews, the author Frances Milton Trollope, the naval officer and travel writer Basil Hall, and the actress Frances Ann Kemble remarked in their accounts and memoirs not only on the energy, vigor, and optimism of the new democratic society but also on its ubiquitous vulgarities and pretense to refinement. These disparities in American manners constituted Johnston's great subject and the foundation blocks of his best humorous illustrations. But by 1850 the ungainly roughness of Jacksonian society had lost its novelty as a source of amusement. The mood of the nation became anxious as the issues of slavery and states' rights increasingly seemed incapable of peaceful resolution. Johnston's distinctive sense of humor began to seem out of sync with the times.

With the outbreak of the Civil War in 1861 Johnston made many spirited broadside cartoons directed against the Confederacy. And so it is ironic that his last book illustrations, which were completed just prior to the beginning of hostilities, decorate a satiric pamphlet in doggerel verse by Lucius M. Sargent, *The Ballad of the Abolition Blunder-buss* (1861). Sargent ridicules the governor and legislature of Massachusetts for their manner in pressing for the immediate abolition of slavery, and he lampoons a few local nonpoliticians as well. Sargent's sour verse has lost whatever humor it once had, but Johnston's amusing wood-engraved illustrations show his powers undiminished. They include two caricatures of Ralph Waldo Emerson, one of them chiding his praise of the first edition of Walt Whitman's *Leaves of Grass* (1855).

Within a generation of his death Johnston and his work were largely forgotten. Only with the revival of interest in Jacksonian culture and antebellum American graphic art that began in the early decades of the twentieth century was his historical role assured. Because he left no record of his life's work, the compilation of checklists of his book illus-

trations have depended on widespread searching and chance encounters. Most of the books that he illustrated are of small format, products of an age of handpresses and small publishing houses. The present-day scarcity of most of the titles suggests that many of them were published in editions of no more than a few hundred copies and, considered purely ephemeral in their own time, were often soon discarded. Rare as they are, these books as a group attest to a distinctive talent that served an irrepressible comic spirit. It grew steadily for nearly half a century and continues to amuse readers sympathetic to the human condition.

References:
Clarence Brigham, "David Claypoole Johnston: The American Cruikshank," *Proceedings of the American Antiquarian Society,* 50 (April 1940): 98–110;
Malcolm Johnson, *David Claypool [sic] Johnston* (Worcester & Boston: American Antiquarian Society & Boston Public Library, 1970);
David Tatham, "A Note about David Claypoole Johnston with a Check List of his Book Illustrations," *Courier, of the Syracuse University Library Associates,* no. 34 (Spring 1970): 11–17; and no. 35 (Summer 1970): 26–31;
Tatham, "D. C. Johnston's Satiric Views of Art in Boston, 1825–1850," *Art and Commerce: American Prints of the Nineteenth Century* (Charlottesville: University Press of Virginia, 1978), pp. 9–24;
Tatham, "David Claypoole Johnston's *Militia Muster,*" *American Art Journal,* 19, no. 2 (1987): 4–15.

Archives:
The most extensive collection of Johnston's papers is owned by the American Antiquarian Society in Worcester, Massachusetts. That institution also holds virtually all of Johnston's published book and periodical illustrations, as well as numerous original drawings and watercolors. A few Johnston letters are in the collections of the Pierpont Morgan Library, New York, the Boston Public Library, and the Houghton Library of Harvard University, Cambridge, Massachusetts. The Houghton Library also has some original drawings by Johnston relating to his book illustrations.

E. W. Kemble
(18 January 1861 – 19 September 1933)

Francis Martin Jr.
University of Central Florida

BOOKS: *Kemble's Coons: Drawings Of Colored Children and Southern Scenes* (New York: Russell, 1896);
The Blackberries and Their Adventures (New York: Russell, 1897);
A Coon Alphabet (New York: Russell, 1898);
Comical Coons (New York: Russell, 1898);
The Billy Goat and Other Comicalities (New York: Scribners, 1898);
Coontown's 400 (New York: Life Publishing, 1899);
Kemble's Sketch Book (New York: Russell, 1899);
Kemble's Pickaninnies (New York: Russell, 1901).

SELECTED BOOKS ILLUSTRATED: Twain, Mark, *Adventures of Huckleberry Finn* (New York: Webster, 1884);
Twain, *Mark Twain's Library of Humor* (New York: Webster, 1888);
Page, Thomas Nelson, *Two Little Confederates* (New York: Scribners, 1888);
Edwards, Harry Stillwell, *Two Runaways and Other Stories* (New York: Century, circa 1889);
Pendleton, Louis Beauregard, *King Tom and the Runaways* (New York: Appleton, 1890);
Smith, Francis Hopkinson, *Colonel Carter of Cartersville* (Boston: Houghton, Mifflin, 1891);
Stowe, Harriet Beecher, *Uncle Tom at Home in Kentucky*, 2 volumes (Boston: Houghton, Mifflin, 1892);
Harris, Joel Chandler, *On the Plantation* (New York: Appleton, 1892);
Riley, James Whitcomb, *Poems Here at Home* (New York: Century, 1893);
Irving, Washington, *Knickerbocker's History of New York* (New York: Putnam, 1894);
Dodge, Mary Mapes, *The Land of Puck* (New York: Century, 1894);
Jacobs, W. W., *Many Cargoes* (New York: Stokes, 1895);
Harris, Joel Chandler, *Daddy Jake. The Runaway* (New York: Century, 1896);
Stuart, Ruth McEnery, *Solomon Crow's Christmas Pockets and Other Tales* (New York: Harper, 1896);

Stockton, Frank R., *A Story-Teller's Pack* (New York: Scribners, 1897);
Stuart, Ruth McEnery, *Moriah's Mourning* (New York: Harper, 1898);
Page, Thomas Nelson, *Two Prisoners* (New York: Russell, 1898);
Dunbar, Paul Laurence, *Folks from Dixie* (New York: Dodd, Mead, 1898);
Twain, Mark, *Pudd'nhead Wilson and Those Extraordinary Twins* (New York: Harper, 1899);
Dunbar, Paul Laurence, *The Strength of Gideon. And Other Stories* (New York: Dodd, Mead, circa 1900);
Phoenix, John [George Horatio Derby], *Phoenixianna: Or Sketches and Burlesques* (New York: Appleton, 1903);
Dunbar, Paul Laurence, *The Heart of Happy Hollow* (New York: Dodd, Mead, 1904);
Harris, Joel Chandler, *The Tar-Baby. And Other Rhymes of Uncle Remus* (New York: Appleton, 1904);
Irwin, Wallace, *At the Sign of the Dollar* (New York: Duffield, 1905);
Marquis, Don, *Danny's Own Story* (Garden City, N.Y.: Doubleday, 1912);
Stuart, Ruth McEnery, *Plantation Songs and Other Verses* (New York: Appleton, 1916);
Russell, Irwin, *Christmas Night in the Quarters. And Other Poems* (New York: Century, 1917);
Harris, Joel Chandler, *Uncle Remus: His Songs and His Sayings* (New York: Appleton, 1920);
Brown, Kenneth, *Putter Perkins* (Boston & New York: Houghton Mifflin, 1923);
McNeill, John C., *Lyrics from Cotton Land* (Charlotte, N.C.: Stone & Barringer, 1927);
Lincoln, Joseph, *Cape Cod Ballads. And Other Verses* (Trenton, N.J.: Albert Brandt, 1929).

PERIODICALS: *Harper's Bazar,* 1880–1900;
Harper's Young People, 1881–1893;
Harper's Weekly, 1882–1913;
Life, 1883–1922;
St. Nicholas, 1883–1925;

Century, 1884–1921;
Harper's Monthly, 1886-1903;
Youth's Companion, 1889–1920;
Ladies' Home Journal, 1890–1919;
Cosmopolitan, 1892–1914;
Harper's Round Table, 1894–1896;
Leslie's Weekly, 1898–1918;
Collier's, 1901–1925;
Good Housekeeping, 1911–1920;
Judge, 1914–1916.

One of the most admired illustrators and cartoonists of the late nineteenth century, E. W. Kemble dominated what some historians have termed "the genial school of American caricature." His illustrations for Southern authors and his cartoons were pervasive in the books and illustrated journals of his day.

Born in Sacramento, California, on 18 January 1861, Edward Windsor Kemble was the second son of Edward Cleveland Kemble, a newspaper publisher in the early years of California journalism who was descended from William Whipple, a general in George Washington's army and a signer of the Declaration of Independence; his mother, Cecilia Amanda Windsor, was the daughter of a respected New York family with its own prominent lineage. The Kembles and Windsors descended from English stock who had settled in the New York area generations earlier; they were Republican and Episcopalian. Apparently there were no artists in either family line, but both parents encouraged young Kemble's fondness of drawing; perhaps because of his own journalistic involvements, the senior Kemble took a special interest in his son's artistic inclinations. From his father Kemble inherited a capacity for seeing the humorous side of life, and he learned to make his pen tell the story. In 1872 Colonel Kemble left publishing to become an inspector of Indian affairs for the government, an appointment he received from President Ulysses S. Grant.

While accompanying his father on a trip to relocate Sioux Indians from the Dakotas to a reservation in Oklahoma, Kemble produced a series of character sketches of Indians. Four years later, in 1877, while attending a Philadelphia boarding school, his letters home were filled with sketches. Humorous characterization would become his specialty. A few years later, when Kemble was working for Western Union, his father encouraged him to take some of his best pen-and-ink comics to Harper and Brothers Publishers in New York City. Kemble, only nineteen, nervously presented them to Charles Parsons, the art editor, who asked that he leave them and return the following day. When Kemble

returned, Parsons offered him seventy dollars in gold for the lot. The four drawings, Kemble's first published works, appeared in the September and October 1880 issues of *Harper's Bazar.*

Having decided on an art career, Kemble joined the sketch class at the Art Students League in New York City. The tuition was five dollars per month. Although the league was run cooperatively and managed by the students themselves, the foremost artists of the day, such as William Merritt Chase and Carroll Beckwith, presided over the classes. It was more than a school, however; it was a gathering of eager students who shared ideas on art, technique, and methods of marketing. Kemble remained for about a year; he later complained that the class did nothing for him, as no one ever looked at his work. However, he returned occasionally and on one such visit took up with Frederic Remington, who would become Kemble's closest friend. Both men were the same age, quick to learn, essentially self-taught, and drawn to the pen-and-ink style of illustration.

Although Kemble's experience at the league was his only formal training, in 1881 he became a staff cartoonist on the *Daily Graphic,* which was at the time the only illustrated daily in New York. The position required him to draw whatever came his way and demanded a spontaneity that did not allow for much refinement. As Kemble plunged into his many assignments this spontaneity helped him develop a quickness of touch, but in many ways it discouraged careful draftsmanship. As a result, his drawing occasionally displayed inconsistencies, a fault some of his contemporaries noted. Yet this approach made Kemble quick to seize the graphic point in what he saw and encouraged the quality of expressiveness in his work. At times his style manifested an eclecticism, reflecting various stylistic and technical influences. Like many of the illustrators of his day, Kemble owed something to earlier English illustrators such as George Cruikshank and John Leech, yet his humor—in its degree of exaggeration, observation, and wit—is thoroughly American.

Another influence on Kemble's style was A. B. Frost. Both men worked for the same editors and authors and shared a similar pen style. Although the stylistic relationship between Kemble and Frost is one of the most complex and significant factors in the evolution of Kemble's mature style, he was never at any time Frost's pupil. He was inspired by Frost, learned something of his technique, shared with him a similar taste for humor, and used many of the same standard comic techniques, but Kemble without question remained his own man.

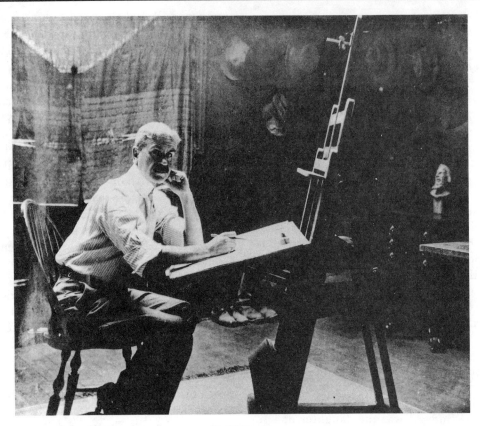

E. W. Kemble

When *Life* came into being in 1883, Kemble joined its staff as a regular contributor. Over the years he did more illustrations for *Life* than for any other magazine. It was one of his early drawings for this periodical, "Some Uses for Electricity" (13 March 1884), that caught the eye of Mark Twain and ultimately led to his receiving the assignment for the illustrations to Twain's *The Adventures of Huckleberry Finn* (1884), although one wonders if Twain's association with E. C. Kemble on the *Alta California,* a newspaper Kemble's father had established, also had something to do with it. At any rate, Kemble did 175 pen-and-ink drawings for Twain's novel and received the sum of $1,200. He was in his early twenties, relatively unknown, and still struggling with his technique. It was his first illustrated book and certainly a plum for such a young and inexperienced artist, but it proved to be a plum with a few pits, not the least of which was Twain himself.

Twain and Kemble never met. The artist dealt with Charles L. Webster, Twain's publisher. Twain was being rushed by his English publishers, Chatto and Windus, who were eager for proofs so they could start early canvasing in time for the 1884 Christmas sales, something that Twain's American publishers also hoped to do. In his efforts to speed things up, Twain hurried Kemble, who at times had to work without a completed manuscript, and the initial drawings displeased Twain. Kemble must have been exasperated to find his drawings rejected, but he completed a new set, which were then sent on to Twain, who received them enthusiastically.

This was the first time Twain had been in a position to select his own illustrator; previously it had always been the responsibility of his publisher. He must have found it personally rewarding to see his faith in Kemble justified. The illustrations were a critical success and are in many ways the perfect visual counterpart to Twain's great novel, and they certainly made Kemble's reputation as one of the most recognized illustrators of his day.

In fact the first publication of *The Adventures of Huckleberry Finn* was delayed until after the Christmas buying season, finally appearing in February 1885. At a late time—shortly after the book had gone to press—it was discovered that one of the plates for the book had been altered to a sexually offensive picture of Uncle Silas. Because the book was heavily aimed at a largely juvenile audience and because of Twain's reputation, the implications were considerable. Many commentators have tried unsuccessfully to explain the mutilated condition of the plate; a few

Kemble's portrayal of the title character of Mark Twain's Adventures of
Huckleberry Finn *(1884), the artist's first book assignment*

have proposed Kemble as the culprit, but the evidence is slight and the cause or causes remain purely conjectural.

In 1899 Kemble produced four more pen-and-wash illustrations for the standard Autograph Edition of *The Adventures of Huckleberry Finn* in Mark Twain's collected works; and for a special Mark Twain number of the colored comic section "The Funny Side" of the *New York World* (10 December 1899), he contributed three new pen-and-ink sketches of incidents from the novel. His last drawing for *The Adventures of Huckleberry Finn* was produced in 1932, when George Macy, publisher of the Limited Editions Club, commissioned Kemble to add something to a 1933 edition.

Three excerpts from the novel, along with Kemble's illustrations, had been serialized between December 1884 and February 1885 in the newly established magazine *Century*. It was the beginning of a long and successful association between Kemble and the magazine's editor, Richard Watson Gilder. Through *Century* Kemble's reputation as an illustrator of Southern themes and humor was established. Whenever an editor needed an artist for a piece about the South, Kemble's name came up.

In March 1885 Gilder sent Kemble to New Orleans to illustrate two articles on the New Orleans Exposition by Eugene V. Smalley. Kemble's twenty-two illustrations appeared in the

May and June issues of *Century* and greatly pleased Gilder. During the next few years Gilder offered Kemble assignments to illustrate stories by Richard Malcolm Johnston, Frank R. Stockton, Joel Chandler Harris, George W. Cable, Maurice Thompson, Thomas Nelson Page, James Whitcomb Riley, and Twain. In September 1887 Gilder sent Kemble to Kentucky to research James Allen's story "Mrs. Stowe's 'Uncle Tom' at Home in Kentucky" (October 1887) and Allen's "Two Kentucky Gentlemen of the Old School" (April 1888). Kemble produced twenty illustrations for these two pieces. Kemble had become Gilder's choice for illustrating stories on Southern rural life, but authors also approved. He was widely respected among the best writers of Southern life. Harriet Beecher Stowe, Ruth McEnery Stuart, Riley, and Twain all praised his work.

The accolades were not unanimous, however. Harris preferred the work of A. B. Frost, a rival illustrator of Southern life. In time Twain also criticized Kemble's work; in a 24 May 1884 letter to his publisher Charles L. Webster, he called Kemble's illustrations for *Mark Twain's Library of Humor* (1888) "blackboard outlines and charcoal sketches." He added, "If Kemble's illustrations for my last book were handed me today, I would understand how tiresome to me the sameness would get to be, when distributed through a whole book, and I would put them promptly in the fire."

Despite Harris's and Twain's reservations, many editors, who were demanding when it came to the illustrations they selected for publication, were delighted with Kemble's work. One of these was the editor of the successful children's magazine *St. Nicholas;* Mary Mapes Dodge thought that Kemble's style and humor perfectly suited her publication. Kemble began illustrating for *St. Nicholas* in 1883, and he continued to work for the magazine for forty years. Toward the end of this period Kemble also wrote and illustrated some of his own poetry, such as "Playin' Bride" (June 1913).

By 1885, with his career well underway, Kemble's thoughts turned to marriage. In May, Kemble married Sarah Briggs, daughter of Capt. George and Julia Elizabeth Brewster Briggs, in New York City. The following year they rented a house in Mott Haven on Mott Avenue in the upper city near 140th Street, which was then still like the country in northern Manhattan, with vistas running to the Harlem River. In a makeshift studio in the back of the house Kemble set up his drawing table, a sheaf of Bristol boards, different pens and inks, and various props. There, with his characteristic quick, vigorous, impressionistic line, he drew his "fun in ink."

Kemble's next-door neighbor on Mott Avenue was his close friend Remington. Both men spent a good deal of time together and were members of the Manhattan Athletic Club, where Kemble, light and lean, won many trophies for the hundred-yard dash. Although Remington was considerably heavier and less fit, they shared an interest in the outdoors: skating, swimming, tennis, and evening walks. They enjoyed the all-male dinners on Saturday nights at The Players, with celebrated actors, authors, and artists, and they were members of The Lambs, another supper club whose members were famous for their camaraderie, conviviality, and startling tales. The Lambs' Star Minstrel often featured Kemble as the end man. When the Remingtons moved from Mott Avenue to New Rochelle, the Kembles followed, and the friendship continued.

Mott Avenue was a convenient location, since the nearby New York Central Railroad meant that the city was only nine minutes away, putting editors and publishers within convenient reach and making accessible the clubs where Kemble liked to drink with "the boys." On 10 February 1886 Kemble's father died in Mott Haven, where he had been convalescing. Four months later, on 6 June, Kemble's first son, Edward "Ned" Brewster, was born.

In 1888 Kemble illustrated Thomas Nelson Page's *Two Little Confederates.* First serialized in *Century,* then published in hardcover, the illustrations greatly pleased Page. Twain agreed to Kemble's illustrating his latest book, *Mark Twain's Library of Humor,* a representative cross section of nineteenth-century American humor containing 145 works by 54 authors. Kemble completed 253 pen-and-ink drawings for it. As already noted, Twain was not pleased with the drawings. It was the last time he offered Kemble a commission, although he never voiced his disapproval to Kemble. On 13 April 1888 the Kembles celebrated the birth of their first daughter, Beth Elsie.

In 1890 Kemble made a trip to Georgia and Florida to do research on Southern life and rural locales. He admitted that this experience sharpened his eye for characterizations. On this trip he documented with an almost Dickensian quality the working conditions in a Georgia cotton mill in which workers, especially children, labored under the worst of circumstances. Kemble's on-the-spot illustrations were published with "The Georgia Cracker in the Cotton Mill" (*Century*

Magazine, February 1891) by Miss de Graffenreid. De Graffenreid deals with the working conditions that existed in the Southern cotton mills around Macon, Georgia, an area in which she had grown up. When the article appeared, it created a controversy, and the *Atlanta Constitution* carried several letters to the editor in which *Century,* the author, and Kemble were severely criticized for presenting what was seen as an inaccurate view of mill conditions. Kemble received the most criticism, and his illustrations were labeled and dismissed by the letters appearing in the *Constitution* as distortions. The artist—never slow to respond to a challenge—wrote a lengthy letter to the editor on the accuracy of his illustrations; it was published on 10 June 1891.

On 22 October 1891 a second son, Schuyler (Sky), was born to the Kembles. Six years later, on 24 April 1897, Kemble's last child, a daughter named Frances Gail, was born in New Rochelle, New York. With a growing family, Kemble was eager to supplement his income. While a staff artist on the *Daily Graphic* he had done some advertising work, drawing the famous "Gold Dust Twins," which became the popular image in selling the then well-known soap powder. When the manufacturers of the soap, N. K. Fairbank Company of Chicago, invited him to do a booklet on the "Twins," Kemble accepted.

In 1892 Kemble made another trip south to study and sketch the region. This time, however, he took a camera, which he concealed in a briefcase. It was set up in such a way that he could photograph people without their knowledge. He was delighted with these candid shots.

Kemble's production soared in the 1890s. His reputation grew among editors. In addition to illustrating books, including Francis Hopkinson Smith's *Colonel Carter of Cartersville* (1891), Harriet Beecher Stowe's *Uncle Tom at Home in Kentucky* (1892), James Whitcomb Riley's *Poems Here at Home* (1893), Washington Irving's *Knickerbocker's History of New York* (1894), Joel Chandler Harris's *Daddy Jake. The Runaway* (1896), and Mark Twain's *Pudd'nhead Wilson and Those Extraordinary Twins* (1899), he worked for practically all the illustrated periodicals of the day. In the late 1890s he also worked for several New York newspapers, which ran a colored comic supplement in their Sunday editions. The *New York World* and the *New York Journal* ran Kemble's "comicalities."

Although a prolific book illustrator, Kemble's major production was for the magazines. Among his work in this media were his social car-

A VISIT FROM UNCLE EBEN.

Illustration by Kemble for Paul Laurence Dunbar's Folks from Dixie *(1898)*

toons. During the 1890s there was a type of cartoon developing in the illustrated press based on a close observation of life. It had no relation to politics or public affairs but illustrated some phase of life with either satire or sympathy. For Kemble it was frequently coupled with humor—his unrelenting characteristic. The subjects that attracted him were varied and multiple and included such themes as the changing role of women in society, conditions of city life, rural life, housing conditions, fire safety, police protection, the treatment of animals, the power of the press, and the syndicate theater; he also drew attention to such relatively new inventions as the airplane, the blimp, the cable car, and the automobile, the last of which received more of his attention than any other single theme. He was particularly interested in the effect cars were having on the pattern of daily life. Many of these social cartoons appeared in the pages of *Harper's Weekly* and *Life.*

Despite Kemble's interest in the social and political cartoon, he continued to produce humorous cartoons and series for the pictorial press. One of his most popular series was for *Life,* a weekly piece titled "Frogville Frolics." Anthropomorphism was common in the illus-

Kemble's 11 November 1905 cover satirizing editor and publisher
William D'Alton Mann

trated comic press of the day, but Kemble's frogs seemed to leap off the page with their playful antics.

In 1898 Kemble illustrated Paul Laurence Dunbar's *Folks from Dixie*. Dunbar was the first black poet after Phillis Wheatley to gain anything approaching a national reputation in the United States. Kemble illustrated other books by Dunbar, and the two men remained friends; Dunbar even collected a few original pen-and-ink drawings by Kemble. Once the editor of *Century* sought Dunbar's judgment on whether the magazine overemphasized the comic character of the

black man, something Kemble had significantly helped to create. The poet responded that a laugh could not hurt the black man. Both Kemble and Dunbar were criticized for perpetuating an unfavorable stereotype of blacks. Kemble was not insensitive to the implications contained in his caricatures—his drawings expressed those particular qualities which were thought to characterize black people at the turn of the century, qualities that existed in the minds of a major part of the reading public. They were meant to entertain in a period when racial themes formed a large part of the humor found in many of the leading magazines and newspapers; however, Kemble drew them with more sympathy and understanding than many artists.

Realizing the market potential of Kemble's black "comicalities," H. H. Russell and Sons published in the 1890s a series of year-end gift books based on them. These picture books, with such unfortunate titles as *Kemble's Coons* (1896), *The Blackberries and Their Adventures* (1897), and *Kemble's Pickaninnies* (1901), were produced essentially for a children's audience and published in time for the holiday season. From 1896 to 1901 eight such picture books were produced.

Kemble began his career in a period of specialties and specialists, such as Remington's scenes of the West, Charles Dana Gibson's views of high society, and Kemble's own rustic humor and black comicalities. In fact, Kemble is so identified with these comicalities that there is often the erroneous impression that he worked exclusively with this theme. He often complained about this perception and was fond of saying that the theme had pursued him and that he had not pursued it.

After the turn of the century Kemble turned more frequently to the political cartoon. It was a field for which he was well suited because he understood that the humor of satire is not the humor of burlesque (although the two can have an affinity) and that exaggeration for the purpose of ridicule differs from exaggeration intended simply for entertainment. It was a period of great social and political change, and it was only natural that much of its humor was bound to be political, or to have political overtones, as humor is often used to bring about change and reform. Kemble used humor and wit for this purpose and did so with skill and vigor. Periodical humor in general tends to be ephemeral and topical, however—political cartoons only a few years old lose an astonishing amount of their impact, something Kemble's cartoons have not completely escaped.

Much of Kemble's political style seems to have been derived from Thomas Nast. In fact, Nast worked on the *Daily Graphic* when Kemble joined the daily in 1881, and it is possible that Kemble knew Nast personally. Kemble's cartoons antagonized many a prominent figure, including President William Taft, who once remarked that he feared no political weapon so much as Kemble's sketched irony.

Kemble's political and social cartoons had already appeared in several leading magazines when in 1903 *Collier's* hired him to draw exclusively for them as their political cartoonist. The art staff at *Collier's*, a magazine that aimed at printing only the best, consisted of several outstanding artists, including Maxfield Parrish, Frederic Remington, and Charles Dana Gibson. In one of his cartoons, "Sewage" (11 November 1905), Kemble sketched Colonel Mann, a prominent figure and editor of *Town Topics*, as a large, grotesque frog sitting over a sewer while copies of his magazine float in the sewage below. The cartoon so inflamed Mann that he threatened to bring criminal action against *Collier's* if they allowed the issue to circulate on the newsstands of New York. As a result the magazine removed the offending work but offered to mail a copy to anyone requesting one. In 1907 Kemble left *Collier's* to become a political cartoonist for *Harper's Weekly*.

During the 1910s Kemble's career was robust. Magazines solicited his work. As a humorist skilled in the art of satire, his cartoons—social, political, and humorous—appeared in most of the leading magazines of the day. He had an apartment on Washington Square South (next to Rose O'Neill, the designer of the Kewpie Doll). He was as solvent as he would ever be when he purchased a large estate in Towners, Putnam County, New York, one of the original Dutch estates still intact at that time. Kemble, who was known affectionately in the family as "Gippy," fancied himself a gentleman farmer and took pleasure in planting fruit trees and inviting weekend guests to "help out." He had a studio built in back of the house. In 1910 he gave his son Edward Brewster and his bride five acres on which to construct their first home. Kemble was active and maintained his membership in the Lambs Club and the Salmagundi Club and was involved in the Seventh Regular New York National Guard.

But during the 1920s Kemble's career and finances were in decline. He gave up the apartment on Washington Square and sold the estate in Towners. By 1930 his vision had deteriorated. With cataracts in both eyes, he drew with the aid of a magnifying glass. However, his humor was still strong. Coming home from the eye doctor one afternoon, he told his young grandson, Brewster "Bo" Kemble, that he expected his eyes to improve since they had just been removed, pressed, and put back. He continued to work in a detached studio constructed in the backyard of his daughter's home; at one point this studio had an eighty-pound trunk filled with Kemble's original work. It was a lifetime of work collected over the years from his editors and publishers. Its destruction in an accidental fire devastated Kemble, who perhaps saw the nearness of his own end reflected in the ashes.

Until his death on 19 September 1933 Kemble and his wife lived in Ridgefield, Connecticut, with their daughter Beth. The day before his death Kemble finished his last sketch, a "character study" of a black man that he signed and dated "E. W. Kemble 1933." He was buried at Maple Shade Cemetery in Ridgefield. Sarah Kemble lived with her daughter until her death in 1935.

Even before his death Kemble and his brand of pen-and-ink humor were losing popularity. Except among a few enthusiasts, Kemble was forgotten. Only lately have scholars and collectors reassessed his significant contribution to American illustration and graphic humor. Kemble was one of the men and women who created an image of his time; he was an artist of monumental stature in an age of great competition.

References:

Michael Patrick Hearn, *The Annotated Huckleberry Finn* (New York: Clarkson N. Potter, 1981), p. 15;

Francis Martin Jr., "Edward Windsor Kemble, a Master of Pen and Ink," *American Art Review,* 3 (January–February 1976): 54–67;

James A. Porter, "Four Problems in History of Negro Art," *Journal of Negro History,* 27 (January 1942): 9–36;

Darwin Turner, "Paul Lawrence Dunbar: The Rejected Symbol," *Journal of Negro History,* 52 (January 1967): 3;

Samuel Webster, *Mark Twain: Business Man* (Boston: Little, Brown, 1946), p. 248.

W. R. Leigh

(23 September 1866 – 11 March 1955)

Michael R. Grauer
Panhandle-Plains Historical Museum

BOOKS: *Clipt Wings: A Drama in Five Acts* (New York: Thornton W. Allen, 1930);

The Western Pony (New York & London: Harper, 1933);

Frontiers of Enchantment: An Artist's Adventures in Africa (New York: Simon & Schuster, 1938).

SELECTED BOOKS ILLUSTRATED: Andrews, Elisha Benjamin, *The History of the Last Quarter-Century in the United States, 1870–1895* (New York: Scribners, 1896);

King, William Nephew, *The Story of the War of 1898* (New York: Collier, 1898);

Wyckoff, Walter A., *The Workers: An Experiment in Reality (The West)* (New York: Scribners, 1898);

Camp, Walter, *Authors and Inventors* (New York: Collier, 1903);

Camp, *Travellers and Explorers* (New York: Collier, 1903);

Andrews, Elisha Benjamin, *The United States in Our Own Times: A History from Reconstruction to Expansion* (New York: Scribners, 1903);

Lefevre, Edwin, *The Golden Flood* (New York: McClure, Phillips, 1905);

Quick, Herbert, *Virginia of the Air Lanes* (Indianapolis: Bobbs-Merrill, 1909);

London, Jack, *When God Laughs, and Other Stories* (New York: Macmillan, 1911);

Grey, Zane, *The Vanishing American* (New York: Harper, 1925);

Bryant, Lorinda Munson, *The Children's Book of Animal Pictures* (New York: Century, 1931).

PERIODICALS: *Scribner's Magazine,* 1896–1906, 1922;

McClure's, 1900;

Collier's, 1900–1915;

Munsey's, 1922;

Mentor, 1924.

W. R. Leigh

For some ten years beginning in 1896, W. R. Leigh worked as a commercial illustrator based in New York. His illustrations appeared in popular magazines of that time, as well as in several books. Leigh's genius in both visual arts and writing came together in his masterpiece of the two arts, *The Western Pony,* published in 1933.

William Robinson Leigh was the fifth of seven children born to William Leigh and Mary White Colston Leigh at Maidstone, the family estate in Berkeley County, West Virginia. Leigh's father sailed for twenty years on a man-of-war in the United States Navy before retiring in 1854 in favor of agricultural pursuits. Leigh's mother was de-

191

Illustration by Leigh for Walter A. Wyckoff's The Workers: An Experiment in Reality *(1898)*

scended from colonial Virginians, and Leigh counted Thomas Jefferson and John Marshall as maternal relatives. Jefferson was a distant cousin, and Marshall was the brother of Leigh's great-grandmother. Leigh often included Pocahontas and Sir Walter Raleigh in his family tree although the former claim was erroneous and the latter a possible distant relation by marriage.

Both of Leigh's grandfathers were well-respected statesmen. His maternal grandfather, Edward Colston, was elected to the Virginia House of Delegates and the United States Congress; his paternal grandfather, Benjamin Watkins Leigh, was also elected to the Virginia House of Delegates and later became a United States senator. Leigh's grandfathers were also brothers-in-law, as B. W. Leigh married Colston's sister.

During Reconstruction in West Virginia, where home schooling was considered better than integrated schools with poor teachers, Leigh's mother taught him at home. A lover of all wildlife, Leigh spent much of his childhood playing with and studying animals on the family farm. As he grew older he frequently sketched and made paper cut-outs of animals, winning a prize for one at a local county fair. As a student of animal life and lore

Leigh often read from the four-volume *Cassell's Popular Natural History* (1865–1866).

Seeking to become an artist, Leigh moved to Baltimore in 1880 to live with relatives and study at the Maryland Institute of Arts. A newly arrived instructor at the school, Hugh Newell, was a former student of British animal painter Sir Edwin Landseer. Well grounded in the academic tradition, Newell passed on his knowledge to the young Leigh, beginning with elementary drawing of simple geometric forms and shapes. For three years Leigh studied under Newell, earning high marks for his drawings and eventually landing a teaching position at the institute during his third term.

Through a cousin in Washington, D.C., Leigh's high marks caught the attention of Washington art collector and philanthropist William W. Corcoran. Corcoran sponsored the artist's studies at the institute. In 1883 Newell encouraged Leigh to further his studies in Europe since his work had surpassed the capabilities of the instructors at the Maryland Institute.

Hoping to study in Paris as was then considered an essential part of any artist's education, Leigh was forced by limited finances to accept a much less expensive educational path in Munich.

Sponsored by two uncles, Charles Fry and Chapman Leigh, Leigh sailed for Germany in July 1883 and won admittance to the Royal Academy in Munich on the strength of his drawing of a death mask. After studying exclusively in Munich from 1883 to 1896 with a short return to the United States from August 1887 to July 1888, Leigh still hoped to move on to Paris.

Following the academic tradition preached by the Royal Academy in Munich, Leigh began his studies in Karl Raupp's antique class, where each day he drew from plaster casts of Greek and Roman sculpture from eight o'clock in the morning until four o'clock in the afternoon. Lectures in art history and related topics followed from four o'clock until seven o'clock. A night drawing class was conducted by lamplight from seven o'clock to nine o'clock. Ignorant of the German language in which all classes were conducted, Leigh began studying German grammar almost immediately upon his arrival. Leigh had ascended to Nicolas Gysis's nature class by the fall of 1884 and by the spring of 1886 was accepted in Ludwig Loefftz's painting class. Leigh supplemented his formal curriculum by studying paintings at the Alte Pinakothek and frequently sketching in the surrounding countryside. In 1885 he took a side trip to Venice to sketch and study paintings by Titian, Tintoretto, and Paolo Veronese.

Because Leigh spent his sponsorship monies with abandon, the support from home was withdrawn. In spite of another gift of $200 from Corcoran, Leigh was forced to return to the United States in August 1887. Pleas with his former benefactor and uncle, New York banker Fry, fell on deaf ears, and he denied Leigh's request for a loan to continue his European studies. Leigh returned first to the new family home near Martinsburg, West Virginia; then he moved to Baltimore, where he taught an art class for young women. Leigh augmented his teaching salary with occasional painting sales and by the summer of 1888 had earned enough to return to Munich.

Throughout the fall of 1888 and the winter of 1888–1889 Leigh lived on his meager savings and funds secured from the infrequent sales of paintings sent from Munich back to Baltimore, where his uncle Alfred Williams peddled them. Too poor to hire models for his works, Leigh began using photographs as studies for paintings, a practice he continued throughout his career. He eventually amassed an enormous collection of photographs.

In the summer of 1889 Leigh was admitted to Wilhelm von Lindenschmidt's composition class at the Royal Academy. Under Lindenschmidt, Leigh learned to plan carefully each part of a painting, us-

ing sketches from live models as well as photographs. His painting for the term received a silver medal and an honorable mention at a Paris exhibition.

The same summer Leigh was also hired to assist in painting a panorama, *The Battle of Waterloo,* the first of many such projects on which he would work during his European sojourn. Two additional panorama projects soon followed, and Leigh's monthly earnings more than doubled. In 1892 he began work on *The Crucifixion of Christ,* a panorama for the pilgrimage resort at Einsiedeln, Switzerland. Leigh painted the figures while two other artists painted the architecture and landscape. The following year he began considering illustration as a possible avenue for earning enough to work as a professional easel painter. However, not until the 1896 sale of a painting did he have enough funds to return to the United States.

Arriving in the United States destitute, Leigh attempted to find a sponsor for his easel painting efforts but met with no success. Leigh later recalled, "At all costs I had hoped to avoid illustrating, yet it seemed as if I were doomed to do it." Even while a student in Munich he purposely did not attend the receptions sponsored by *Harper's Magazine,* whose representatives came to Munich searching for new talent.

Finally acknowledging his dire straits in 1896, Leigh interviewed with *Scribner's Magazine,* which hired him at $100 per drawing. His early assignments ranged from drawing a wheat harvest in North Dakota on his first trip to the West to sketching campus scenes at Princeton University–the alma mater of the Scribner family–later presented to the university by the Scribners.

Sketching for a series of articles in *Scribner's Magazine* by Walter A. Wyckoff on the conditions for workers in Chicago, Leigh claimed a constant need for a revolver for his own safety. He combined depictions of the sordid conditions and employers portrayed as corrupt characters, with a clear nod to the caricatures of Thomas Nast. Illustration historians consider the Wyckoff articles, including Leigh's illustrations, as integral to the growing social awareness in the United States at the turn of the century.

While Leigh's attention to detail in his illustrations earned him the nickname Buttons and Shoestrings, he was recognized as an important illustrator by 1900. In addition to *Scribner's Magazine,* his work appeared in *McClure's, Collier's,* and *Harper's Weekly.*

His trip to North Dakota and an introduction three years later in 1900 to the great Western landscape painter Thomas Moran whetted Leigh's appe-

Read the words on the white slip and knit his brows.—Page 728

A Leigh illustration for William Allen White's "A Victory for the People" in Scribner's Magazine
(June 1899)

tite for the West. Finally in 1906 he accompanied Albert Groll, a landscape painter and fellow student at the Royal Academy in Munich, to Laguna, New Mexico. This trip–which also took Leigh to Zuni, Acoma, and encounters with Navajos–spawned a lifelong interest in Native American life, its cultures, and its surroundings. While at Laguna, Leigh encountered another fellow Royal Academy alumnus, Joseph Henry Sharp, then an illustrator for *Harper's Weekly*.

The Santa Fe Railroad provided Leigh's 1906 passage to the Southwest in exchange for one painting of the Grand Canyon. (The Santa Fe Railroad often sponsored artists in exchange for paintings to be used to promote the Southwest and, they hoped, encourage tourists to use rail service to see the places and peoples depicted in the canvases.) Along with Leigh the Santa Fe Railroad hired Moran, Groll, E. Irving Couse, W. Herbert Dunton, and many other well-known painters of the Southwest.

Leigh did illustrations in New York during the winters and painted in the Southwest during the summers for the next three years. In 1908 the Santa

Fe Railroad hired Leigh to create two more paintings of the Grand Canyon. For this commission he spent two weeks alone sketching near the south rim of the canyon. In 1910 Leigh accompanied a hunting party to the Grand Teton Range, and in the following two summers he traveled in the Yellowstone region and the Rocky Mountains.

By 1913 Leigh began to consider a career as a full-time easel painter and secured the interest of Babcock Galleries in New York to represent him. That same year, hoping to gain the respect of his peers and recognition by critics, he submitted his work to the annual exhibition at the National Academy of Design, then the arbiter of an artist's success.

The beginning of World War I spelled hard economic times for artists. Leigh also recognized that photoreproductions and photographs had all but replaced engravings as the preferred reproduction method for illustrations. Full-color paintings were usually reproduced only on front covers of magazines and dust jackets for books. Consequently, Leigh nearly gave up painting completely and even tried his hand at acting. He eventually

THE WATER HOLE

LURE OF THE DESERT, BY VAN DYKE
PARK TO PARK HIGHWAY ILLUSTRATED

Cover illustrated by Leigh

joined the scene-painters' union in 1915 to paint theatrical backdrops. Leigh's previous work on panoramas prepared him well for such work, which in turn may have dovetailed into his later natural-history dioramas.

In 1916 Leigh again traveled to the Southwest, this time to Arizona, where he used the Hubbell Trading Post near Ganado as his base. He traveled to Canyon de Chelly and various places on the Navajo reservation and visited the Hopi villages of Walpi, Shipaulovi, and Oraibi. According to Leigh biographer D. Duane Cummins, this trip provided material for Leigh's paintings for the next five years.

Leigh returned to New York to produce paintings from his trip for spring and fall exhibitions at Babcock Galleries in 1917. The following two years Leigh exhibited at the gallery with other Western painters, including members of the Taos Society of Artists.

Married in 1899 and divorced by 1906, Leigh married again in 1921 at age fifty-five. His new wife, Ethel Traphagen, directed the Traphagen School of Fashion and Design in New York. Leigh and his bride honeymooned in the Kayenta region of Arizona and Yellowstone in Wyoming before returning to their respective New York studios.

By 1926 Leigh was teaching illustration at the New York School of Industrial Art. He was also asked to accompany a safari sponsored by the American Museum of Natural History to secure specimens for its planned African Hall. The museum hired Leigh to paint the dioramic backgrounds for the proposed habitats. The trip lasted more than a year and was followed by a second trip in 1928. The African Hall project was suspended for four years during the Great Depression but was finally completed in 1936, despite Leigh's abrupt resignation from the project in 1935. Before his resignation Leigh directed a staff of artists to paint the backgrounds and wrote of his adventures in the museum's journal, *Natural History,* in 1927 and 1929.

Leigh and his wife traveled through the Southwest, Mexico, Panama, and Cuba in 1931. Following his resignation from the African Hall project, they sailed around the world in 1936. In the 1930s Leigh focused on writing. His most acclaimed book, *The Western Pony,* was followed by *Frontiers of Enchantment: An Artist's Adventures in Africa* in 1938. Leigh also dabbled in writing for the theater, with little success: his play, *Clipt Wings,* published in 1930 and based on a premise that all William Shakespeare's plays were actually written by Sir Francis Bacon, never reached the production stage.

After 1938 Leigh again devoted his energies to painting and was rewarded with a major exhibition at the Grand Central Art Galleries in New York during the 1939 World's Fair. He also taught at the Art Students League and the New York School of Industrial Art, and he returned to the Southwest to sketch again at the end of 1939.

Through the 1940s Leigh's work was recognized widely; exhibitions throughout the United States culminated in the 1944 Grand Central exhibition, *Cowboys and Indians: Paintings of the Old West,* all by Leigh. Reviewers pointed to Leigh as the remaining member of a media-created and mythical triumvirate of Western painters, also including Charles M. Russell and Frederic Remington. The 1944 exhibitions were followed by an exhibition of one hundred paintings four years later when Leigh was eighty-two.

Leigh received many awards during the twilight of his life and career, including election to the National Academy of Design as an associate member in 1953 and as a full academician in March 1955. Nine days after receiving the latter award, and following a full day of painting, Leigh died in his sleep. While his work as an illustrator was not as extensive as that of Russell or Remington, he was classed among them by many critics, and he contributed a great many works to the Western genre throughout his long and illustrious career.

References:

D. Duane Cummins, *William Robinson Leigh: Western Artist* (Norman: University of Oklahoma Press, 1980);

June Du Bois, *W. R. Leigh: The Definitive Illustrated Biography* (Kansas City: Lowell, 1977);

Jeff Dykes, *Fifty Great Western Illustrators* (Flagstaff, Ariz.: Northland Press, 1975).

Archives:

Notable collections of original art by W. R. Leigh are found in the Gilcrease Museum in Tulsa, Oklahoma, and the Woolaroc Museum in Bartlesville, Oklahoma. An extensive archive of personal papers, diaries, memoirs, and unpublished manuscripts is also housed at the Gilcrease Museum along with Leigh's studio collection.

J. C. Leyendecker

(23 March 1874 – 25 July 1951)

Susan Thach Dean
University of Colorado at Boulder Libraries

BOOK: *An Exhibition of Original Poster Designs by J. C. Leyendecker* (Chicago: Inland Printer, 1898).

SELECTED BOOKS ILLUSTRATED: *Bible* (Chicago: Powers, 1894);

Moore, Frank, *One Fair Daughter* (Chicago: Weeks, 1895);

Catherwood, Mary Hartwell, *Spanish Peggy* (Chicago: Stone, 1899);

Morris, Margaretta, and Louise Buffum Congdon, eds., *A Book of Bryn Mawr Stories* (Philadelphia: Jacobs, 1901);

Boyland, Grace Duffie, *The Kiss of Glory* (New York: G. W. Dillingham, 1902);

Norris, Frank, *A Deal in Wheat and Other Stories of the New and Old West* (New York: Doubleday, Page, 1903);

Chambers, Robert W., *Iole* (New York: Appleton, 1905);

Harland, Marion, and others, *365 Breads and Biscuits: A Bread or Biscuit for Every Day in the Year* (Philadelphia: Jacobs, 1905);

Lorimer, George Horace, *The False Gods* (New York: Appleton, 1906);

Paine, Ralph D., *The Praying Skipper and Other Stories* (New York: Outing, 1906);

Williams, Egerton R. Jr., *Ridolfo: The Coming of the Dawn* (Chicago: McClurg, 1906);

Hudson, Charles Bradford, *The Crimson Conquest: A Romance of Pizarro and Peru* (Chicago: McClurg, 1907);

Chester, George Randolph, *Get-Rich-Quick Wallingford: A Cheerful Account of the Rise and Fall of an American Business Buccaneer* (Philadelphia: Altemus, 1908);

Innes, Norman, *The Lonely Guard* (Philadelphia: Jacobs, n.d.);

Morris, Gouverneur, *The Voice in the Rice* (New York: Dodd, Mead, 1910);

New Rochelle Chamber of Commerce, *New Rochelle: The City of the Huguenots* (New Rochelle, N.Y.: Knickerbocker, 1926).

PERIODICALS: *Interion,* 1894;
Inland Printer, 1895–1899;
Century, 1896, 1905–1910;
Collier's, 1898–1918;
Up to Date, 1899;
The Saturday Evening Post, 1899–1943;
Success, 1900–1908;
Delineator Magazine, 1901–1905;
Scribner's Magazine, 1905;
Popular Magazine, 1909;
Judge, 1911;
American Weekly Magazine, 1945–1951.

For more than forty years J. C. Leyendecker created the prototype of American elegance and style. Leyendecker's "Arrow Collar Man" became the masculine counterpart of the "Gibson Girl," embodying the fantasies of millions. His advertising art, book illustrations, and hundreds of covers for *The Saturday Evening Post* and other magazines enabled America to visualize itself and influenced the tastes and attitudes of two generations.

Joseph Christian Leyendecker was born at Montabaur in western Germany on 23 March 1874. His brother and close companion for most of his life, Frank Xavier, was born three years later. In 1882 the family emigrated to the United States, settling in Chicago, where a daughter, Augusta, was born.

Leyendecker was already demonstrating artistic talent. In a rare interview in *The Saturday Evening Post* (15 October 1938) he describes his early work, with typical self-deprecation, as "pretentious paintings which, for want of canvas, were done on oilcloth of the common kitchen variety. Whatever their faults, these pictures lacked nothing in size. They were all dutifully presented to long-suffering friends and relatives." At age sixteen Leyendecker "decided to find a job and gain some practical experience in the profession of being an artist." He took samples of his work to a Chicago engraving house, J. Manz and Company. "The boss inspected a stag at bay, a chariot race, and a Biblical subject, with amusement, but he did tell me to report for work."

J. C. Leyendecker, circa 1940

Leyendecker became an apprentice without pay; in less than a year he began making a salary, starting at two dollars a week, and was able to enroll in the evening drawing class at the Art Institute of Chicago. From 1889 to 1894 he took many classes, primarily from John H. Vanderpoel, whom he credited with helping him to develop his abilities as a draftsman. During this period Leyendecker was promoted to illustrator at Manz and was able to take day as well as evening classes. His brother, Frank, who had left school at the age of thirteen to apprentice to a stained-glass maker, also began taking evening classes.

Although Frank also exhibited artistic talent early, Joe apparently received more encouragement and practical help from their parents. Norman

Rockwell, who knew both brothers at the height of their careers, theorized in his memoirs that "the family had decided that Joe was a genius and, like many immigrant families, had henceforth concentrated all their efforts on helping him to fulfill himself." Joe, however, seems to have believed in Frank's abilities and urged him to develop them.

Leyendecker's earliest major work was a set of illustrations for the Manz edition of the Bible, published by the Powers Brothers Company in 1894. The approximately sixty illustrations depict familiar scenes in conventional Victorian style, revealing no trace of Leyendecker's later distinctive technique. That a work of this scope was entrusted to a boy not yet twenty shows the confidence his employers must have had in his industry and talent. In pronounced

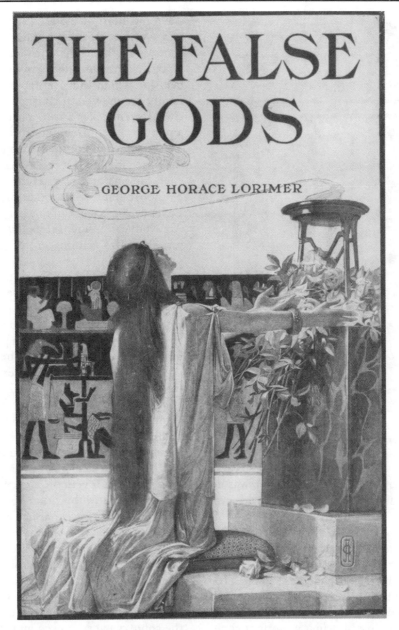

Leyendecker's cover for a 1906 book by the editor of The Saturday Evening Post

contrast his three covers for the Chicago magazine *The Interior,* published the same year, display some of the crispness and sharp planes characteristic of his mature style. In 1895 Leyendecker designed posters for the novels *One Fair Daughter* (which he also illustrated) by Frank Moore and an edition of the popular *Dolly Dialogues* by Anthony Hope, both published by the Chicago publisher E. A. Weeks.

The turning point in Leyendecker's early career came in 1896 when he won the *Century* magazine poster contest with a striking green, red, and gold Art Nouveau design. This recognition of his talent (Maxfield Parrish took second place) and the small cash prize spurred him to fulfill his dream of

studying at the Academie Julian in Paris, where two of his teachers at the Art Institute had been pupils. Joe and Frank left Chicago in September 1896 and enrolled at both the Julian and the Colarossi, studying under Benjamin Constant and Jean-Paul Laurens. The traditional techniques taught at the Julian were congenial to the brothers, and they employed them so well that the monthly prize for the best student work, given by the director, Adolphe Bouguereau, was invariably awarded to one or the other. Several of Joe's drawings remained on permanent exhibition at the Julian until they were destroyed in a World War II bombing raid. In April 1897 he had a one-man show at the Salon Champs du Mars.

Leyendecker's first New Year cherub cover for The Saturday Evening Post. *He designed a New Year baby cover for the magazine every year until 1943.*

Although Leyendecker's Paris education was in conventional academic painting, he clearly seems to have been influenced by the flourishing popular art of the city. The financial success of the great French poster artists demonstrated that commercial art could be both profitable and aesthetically pleasing. Throughout most of his life Leyendecker showed a remarkable ability to make money without compromising his artistic integrity.

Leyendecker received his first important commercial assignment even before he left Paris. A Chicago trade magazine, *The Inland Printer,* which had published one of Leyendecker's illustrations in September 1895, commissioned a cover illustration and poster for the November 1896 issue. This venture was such a success that commissions for the succeeding eleven months followed. Covers for *The Inland Printer* utilize a variety of styles; some show Art Nouveau influence while others are more traditional. In January 1898 an exhibit of the original posters for the 1896–1897 covers was held at the Kimball Cafetier, a Chicago restaurant. The last page of the catalogue of the exhibit is a photograph of the young artist surrounded by his designs.

The Leyendecker brothers returned to Chicago in August 1897 and opened a joint studio on the tenth floor of the Fine Arts Building on Michigan Avenue. Both had many advertising commissions. Joe's clients included Carson, Pirie and Scott; A. B. Kirschbaum Clothiers, and the McAvoy Brewery, for which their father had worked since the family first moved to Chicago.

Leyendecker's 1897 poster for *The Chap-Book,* a popular and influential little magazine published by the Chicago company Stone and Kimball, was the sixteenth and last of a series commissioned from such famous artists as Henri-Marie-Raymond de Toulouse-Lautrec and Will Bradley. Like much of Leyendecker's work of this period, it shows a strong Art Nouveau influence; its flat planes and bold patterns are also reminiscent of Japanese woodblock prints.

In 1899 Herbert S. Stone and Company, the successor to Stone and Kimball, published *Spanish Peggy* by the regional author Mary Hartwell Catherwood. This fictionalized account of the young Abraham Lincoln was illustrated in part by Leyendecker; he also designed the cover. The crisp brush strokes and sharp planes of the figures, as well as the relative lack of background detail, presage Leyendecker's mature style. His popular Ivory Soap advertisement, commissioned the same year but published in 1900, utilizes a typical Art Nouveau line, in the steam rising from the tub, combined with medieval and Byzantine elements.

A major event in Leyendecker's career occurred with the publication of his first cover illustration for *The Saturday Evening Post* on 20 May 1899. His long association with *The Saturday Evening Post,* for which he produced 322 covers over a span of forty-four years, not only brought him considerable fame but also created American traditions. His New Year's baby first appeared on the cover of the 29 December 1906 issue and chronicled the vicissitudes of the country every subsequent year until 1943. Leyendecker's holiday covers embodied a vision of American life that Rockwell developed into popular mythology but without the elements of caricature that Rockwell introduced into some of his subjects.

The Leyendecker brothers closed their Chicago studio in 1900 and moved to New York, where they opened a studio at 7 East Thirty-second Street. Joe continued to illustrate books and magazines. His first cover for *Collier's* had appeared on the Thanksgiving issue of 1898; he did forty-seven additional covers during the next twenty years. *The Rubaiyat of Omar Khayyam,* with portions of the text integrated into the illustrations, appeared in *Delineator Magazine* in 1901. Commissions for similar work followed from *Century* and *Scribner's Magazine,* as well as *Delineator Magazine.* The variety of styles that Leyen-

A World War I poster by Leyendecker, 1917

decker employed for these illustrations is remarkable, ranging from a combination of medieval and Renaissance elements in *A Christmas Hymn* in *Century* (December 1905) to a striking use of Egyptian motifs in *A Song of Faith* for *Delineator Magazine* (December 1905).

Virtually all of Leyendecker's book illustrations were produced in the first decade of the century. He designed a charming Art Nouveau cover, unfortunately marred by a Gothic typeface, for *A Book of Bryn Mawr Stories* in 1901. In contrast, his cover for *The Kiss of Glory*, published the following year, is an Egyptian design similar to those in *A Song of Faith*. The frontispiece for *A Deal in Wheat and Other Stories of the New and Old West* (1903) by Frank Norris is reminiscent of the illustrations for *Spanish Peggy*, but the modeling of the figures is more solid and three-dimensional. Egyptian motifs return in several of his drawings for *The False Gods* (first published in *The Saturday Evening Post* on 27 January and 6 February 1906 and published as a book the same

year) by George Horace Lorimer, editor of *The Saturday Evening Post*.

Ridolfo: The Coming of the Dawn (1906) includes some of the most beautiful, if uncharacteristic, illustrations produced by Leyendecker for a book. The elaborate detail and rich, jewel-like tones resemble the Shakespearean paintings of E. A. Abbey. Both the colors and the composition of Leyendecker's *In the Banquet Hall* parallel those of Abbey's painting *King Henry IV and Prince Henry,* reproduced in the March 1906 issue of *Harper's Monthly*. Leyendecker's frontispiece for *The Crimson Conquest: A Romance of Pizarro and Peru,* published the following year, is also a richly colored, romanticized vision of the past.

Leyendecker's drawings for the short story "A Victory Unforeseen," first published in *Scribner's* (July 1905) and later reprinted in *The Praying Skipper and Other Stories* (1906), are similar to the frontispiece for *A Deal in Wheat* although there is much more background detail, and the versions in *Scribner's* are delicately colored. The illustration ti-

A Leyendecker advertisement for Arrow shirt collars, 1929

tled *You are a disgrace to Yale, all of you,* however, is markedly different from the rest. In it the figures of the rowers stand out starkly against the stylized pattern of the water, recalling Japanese prints and anticipating Leyendecker's later technique of setting figures off against a flat or patterned background. The cover illustrations for *365 Breads and Biscuits: A Bread or Biscuit for Every Day in the Year* (1905) and *Get-Rich-Quick Wallingford: A Cheerful Account of the Rise and Fall of an American Business Buccaneer* (1908), as well as the two illustrations for *Iole* (1905), are more typical of Leyendecker's later style. Printed in black and red, they have little or no background detail and emphasize the planes and angles of the figures.

In the middle of this decade Leyendecker's style underwent a pronounced change. The angles of his figures, always well defined, become even sharper, until each image seems to be composed of planes like the facets of a crystal. The background is often filled in with sharply angled brushstrokes in white or grey. A poster done in 1906 for the University of Pennsylvania is a striking early example of this style. In it a football player is seen in isolation, surrounded by a background of brushstrokes that reflect the acute angles composing his figure. This image was later reproduced on the cover of the 14 November 1908 issue of *The Saturday Evening Post.* Leyendecker did not use this style exclusively, but after 1906 it, or elements of it, become increasingly common. The crisp appearance that this technique gives to the artist's work is a major component of the characteristic Leyendecker look and contributes to the grace and sophistication so prominent in his clothing advertisements.

Leyendecker's distinctive style is the result of his rigorous classical training and is based on an extensive knowledge of anatomy. He is known to have sketched constantly, recording anything that caught his eye; many of his finished works are composites of these sketches. He was adamant about always drawing from a model, eschewing the use of photographs. Leyendecker enlarged his sketches by the traditional method of "squaring up," superimposing a grid on them and then copying them onto a grid the size of the finished piece. Instead of blending colors, he often used brushstrokes of contrasting colors. This technique, combined with his use of a medium that made the oil paint fluid so that it dried without showing the brushstrokes, gave his paintings their dazzling, reflective surfaces.

The Voice in the Rice (1910) is the only book completely illustrated in Leyendecker's mature style. Each of the six plates exhibits his characteristic brushwork and eloquently conveys the steamy atmosphere of this tale of intrigue in the bayous.

Leyendecker's most significant commercial work began in 1905 when he was commissioned by Cluett, Peabody, and Company to do advertisements for their Arrow shirt collars. His style proved ideal for the subject, and soon the debonair Arrow Collar Man became the paragon American men strove to emulate—and American women swooned over. Thousands of letters addressed to the "Arrow Man" poured into the offices of Cluett, Peabody each month, including proposals of marriage and threats of suicide. Other clothing manufacturers, such as Interwoven Socks, B. Kuppenheimer, and Hart, Schaffner and Marx, hired Leyendecker to give their products the same aura of elegance. The urbane sophisticates that he created were such powerful images that Leyendecker's clothing advertisements have even been credited with establishing the convention of a clean-shaven face. They may have influenced hairstyles as well, for in F. Scott Fitzgerald's 1929 story "The Last of the Belles" the heroine's brother has "a handsome, earnest face with a Leyendecker forelock." Leyendecker also designed advertisements for Pierce Arrow and Overland automobiles, Chesterfield cigarettes, and Kellogg's Corn Flakes, but it is through his clothing advertisements that he shaped the taste of three decades.

One of Leyendecker's most frequent models for his early Arrow ads was Charles Beach. The two probably met around the turn of the century, but virtually nothing is known about Beach's background or about the circumstances of their nearly fifty-year relationship. Beach eventually became Leyendecker's business manager, handling many of the details of his work, including hiring models and delivering finished pictures. In 1914 Joe and Frank, who had been living with their sister, Augusta, in suburban New Rochelle since 1910, built a luxurious mansion there on Mount Tom Road. Designed in the style of a French château, it had a large formal garden and a studio wing for Frank; Joe commuted to New York, where he had a studio in the Beaux Arts Building. Beach lived in the mansion as well and assumed much of the responsibility for running the house.

Rockwell, who also lived in New Rochelle, became acquainted with the brothers at this time. He recalled in his memoirs that they "were both very handsome—dark-complexioned with high cheekbones and straight, delicately molded noses. Like Spaniards. And trim, well built, the line of their jackets falling straight from shoulder to hip." While Rockwell greatly admired Joe's work, believing that "there wasn't an illustrator in the country who could draw better," he deplored Joe's insistence on always living slightly beyond his means. While Leyendecker felt that constant financial pressure motivated him to work, Rockwell regretted the fact that he declined commissions that would have "raise[d] his stature as an artist" in favor of those that paid better. During his career Leyendecker had the opportunity to do murals for several public buildings, including the Boston Public Library and the New York Public Library, but he always refused such offers in favor of the immediate financial rewards of magazine and advertising work.

During World War I, Leyendecker, along with many other famous American illustrators, created posters for the U.S. Navy and for the Fuel Administration. His advertising art of this period also had a patriotic slant: dashing pilots and doughboys smoke Chesterfield cigarettes, and demobilized soldiers are measured for new Kuppenheimer suits under the watchful eyes of their proud parents.

In 1920 Leyendecker gave up his New York studio and began working at home, where his domestic situation was increasingly tense. Continual friction between Frank and Beach eventually caused the former and Augusta, who sided with him, to move out of the mansion in 1923. Joe continued to support Augusta, but Frank, who would accept no money from him, lived alone in a garage apartment. Heavy drinking, perhaps combined with drug use, contributed to Frank's death in 1924 at the age of forty-seven.

Although Joe was deeply distressed by Frank's death, the 1920s and 1930s were some of his most productive years. His style was ideally suited to portray the Jazz Age, and during the Depression his elegant images provided a valuable escape into fantasy for a beleaguered America. The 1940s proved a more difficult time. The years took their toll on Leyendecker's inventiveness, and changes in fashion, combined with a change in editorship at *The Saturday Evening Post,* caused a decline in the demand for his work. He continued to receive commissions, however, and he was designing the 1952 New Year's cover for *American Weekly Magazine* when he died of a heart attack on 25 July 1951 at the age of seventy-seven.

Despite, or perhaps because of, his great success Leyendecker's work has had few emulators. His style was so unique and easily identified that any adaptation of it verges on parody. His greatest influence may have been on Rockwell, who depicted small-town America with the same acute eye for detail that Leyendecker applied to urban life. The world of Leyendecker's art vanished with World War II, but his images still evoke an era that was both sophisticated and innocent, when the talented son of immigrant parents could make a fortune portraying the fantasies of his adopted country.

Interview:

"Keeping Posted," *Saturday Evening Post,* 211 (15 October 1938): 108–109.

Biography:

Michael Schau, *J. C. Leyendecker* (New York: Watson-Guptill, 1974).

References:

"The *Century* Prize Posters," *Critic,* 28, new series 25 (16 May 1896): 357;

"J. C. Leyendecker, Artist," *Inland Printer,* 15 (September 1895): 620;

Herbert Kerkow, "Leyendecker–Creator of an American Type," *Commercial Art,* 7 (July 1929): 18–21;

J. C. Leyendecker, *The J .C. Leyendecker Poster Book* (New York: Watson-Guptill, 1975);

"A Leyendecker Exhibition," *Brush and Pencil,* 1 (January 1898): 109–110;

Louis R. Metcalf, "The Home of Messieurs J. C. and F. X. Leyendecker," *Country Life,* 36 (June 1919): 52–53;

Susan R. Meyer, *America's Great Illustrators* (New York: Abrams, 1978);

Steven C. Pettinga, "In Celebration of Cherubs," *Saturday Evening Post,* 267 (January/February 1995): 56–61;

Frank B. Rae Jr., "J. C. Leyendecker, Illustrator," *Brush and Pencil,* 1 (September 1897): 15–16;

Walt and Roger Reed, "Learning from Masters of the Past," *Step by Step Graphics* (January/February 1987): 86–93;

Norman Rockwell, *Norman Rockwell: My Adventures as an Illustrator* (Garden City, N.Y.: Doubleday, 1960);

"The Rose Garden of Two Popular Artists," *House and Garden,* 34 (November 1918): 34;

Wesley Stout, "Yes, We Read the Story," *Saturday Evening Post,* 204 (25 June 1932): 8–9, 34–40;

Harold R. Willoughby, "The Leyendecker Brothers," *Poster,* 14 (March 1923): 5–8, 22.

Archives:

The original oil paintings for Leyendecker's illustrations were left to his sister, Augusta, and to Charles Beach. Most were sold after his death and are primarily located in private collections. The Society of Illustrators in New York has some of the originals; the Haggin Museum in Stockton, California, also has original art, including Leyendecker's portrait of his brother, Frank.

Thomas Nast

(26 September 1840 – 7 December 1902)

Felicia A. Piscitelli
Texas A&M University

BOOKS: *Nast's Illustrated Almanac, 1871–1875,* 5 volumes (New York: McLoughlin, 1870; New York: Harper, 1871–1874);

Christmas Drawings for the Human Race (New York: Harper, 1890); republished as *Thomas Nast's Christmas Drawing for the Human Race* (New York: Dover, 1978).

SELECTED BOOKS ILLUSTRATED: Haven, Alice B., *Loss and Gain: or, Margaret's Home* (New York: Appleton, 1860);

Amusing Stories for Young Folks (Boston: Cyrus G. Cooke, 1861);

Duyckinck, Evert Augustus, *National History of the War for the Union: Civil, Military and Naval,* 3 volumes (New York: Johnson, Fry, 1861–1865);

Palmer, John Williamson, ed., *Folk Songs* (New York: Scribners, 1861);

Goodrich, Frank Booth, *The Tribute Book: A Record of the Munificence, Self-Sacrifice and Patriotism of the American People during the War for the Union* (New York: Derby & Miller, 1865);

Clarke, Rebecca Sophia, as Sophie May, *Dotty Dimple* (Boston: Lee & Shepard, 1865 / New York: Lee, Shepard & Dillingham, 1865);

Dodge, Mary Mapes, *Hans Brinker: or, The Silver Skates* (New York: James O'Kane, 1866);

Edwards, Richard, *Analytical First Reader* (New York: Taintor Bros., 1866);

Goss, Warren Lee, *The Soldier's Story of His Captivity at Andersonville, Belle Isle, and Other Rebel Prisons* (Boston: Lee & Shepard, 1866);

Baker, William Mumford, as George F. Harrington, *Inside: A Chronicle of Secession* (New York: Harper, 1866);

Dickens, Charles, *Dickens' Christmas Story of the Goblins Who Stole a Sexton* (New York: McLoughlin, 1867);

Locke, David R., as Petroleum V. Nasby, *Swinging Round the Cirkle* (Boston: Lee & Shepard, 1867);

Thomas Nast

O'Connor, William Douglas, *The Ghost* (New York: Putnam, 1867);

Defoe, Daniel, *The Life and Strange Surprising Adventures of Robinson Crusoe* (New York: Hurd & Houghton, 1868);

Clarke, Rebecca Sophia, as Sophie May, *Dotty Dimple at Home* (Boston: Lee & Shepard, 1868)

Locke, David R., as Petroleum V. Nasby, *Ekkoes from Kentucky. . . : Being a Perfect Record uv the*

Ups, Downs and Experiences uv the Dimocrisy (Boston: Lee & Shepard, 1868);

Adams, William Taylor, as Oliver Optic, *Our Standard Bearer: or, The Life of General Ulysses S. Grant* (Boston: Lee & Shepard, 1868);

Winter, William, *Wonderful Adventures of Humpty Dumpty* (New York: McLoughlin, 1868);

Moore, Clement Clarke, *A Visit from St. Nicholas* (New York: McLoughlin, 1869);

The Story of Yankee Doodle (New York: McLoughlin, 1869);

Webster, George P., *Rip Van Winkle* (New York: McLoughlin, 1869);

Swinton, William, *History of the Seventh Regiment, National Guard, State of New York, During the War of the Rebellion* (New York: Fields, Osgood, 1870);

Webster, George P., *Santa Claus and His Works* (New York: McLoughlin, 1870);

Pullen, Charles Henry, *The Fight at Dame Europa's School* (New York: Francis B. Felt, 1871);

Pullen, *Miss Columbia's Private School: or, Will It Blow Over?* (New York: Putnam, 1871);

Dickens, Charles, *The Posthumous Papers of the Pickwick Club* (New York: Harper, 1873);

Moustache, Vieux, *Boarding-School Days* (New York: Hurd & Houghton, 1873);

Shaw, Henry W., as Josh Billings, *Everybody's Friend: or Josh Billing's Proverbial Philosophy of Wit and Humor* (Hartford, Conn.: American Publishing, 1874);

Shaw, *Josh Billings: His Works Complete* (New York: G. W. Charleton, 1876);

Wells, David Ames, *Robinson Crusoe's Money: or Remarkable Financial Fortunes of Remote Island Community* (New York: Harper, 1876);

Dickens, Charles, *Pictures from Italy, Sketches by Boz, and American Notes,* illustrated by Nast and Arthur B. Frost (New York: Harper, 1877);

Pictorial War Record, volume 1 (New York: Stearns, 1881–1882);

Coffin, Charles Carleton, *The Boys of '61: or, Four Years of Fighting* (Boston: Estes & Lauriat, 1882);

Saunders, Frederick, *Salad for the Solitary and the Social* (London: Robert Bentley, 1885; New York: Thomas Whittaker, 1886);

Cleveland, Grover, *The President's Message: 1887* (New York & London: Putnam, 1888);

Shapley, Rufus E., *Solid for Mulhooly: A Political Satire* (Philadelphia: Gebbie, 1889);

Fawcett, Edgar, *A New York Family* (New York: Cassell, 1891);

Wright, General Marcus, ed., *Official and Illustrated War Record* (Washington, D.C., 1899);

The Stock Exchange in Caricature, volume 1 (New York: Abram Stone, 1904).

PERIODICALS: *Frank Leslie's Illustrated Weekly Newspaper,* 1855–1858, 1862;
Harper's Weekly, 1859, 1862–1887;
Vanity Fair, 1859–1860, 1872;
London Illustrated News, 1860–1861, 1866;
New York Illustrated News, 1860–1862;
Harper's Bazaar, 1867–1885;
Riverside Magazine for Young People, 1867–1869;
Harper's Young People, 1879–1885;
Collier's, 1888, 1890–1893;
Time, 1889–1891;
New York Herald, 1890–1891, 1894–1895, 1897;
Nast's Weekly, 1892–1893;
New York Recorder, 1895–1896;
Insurance Observer, 1896–1902.

Thomas Nast's life and work as an illustrator, cartoonist, and painter exemplify two familiar maxims: "A picture is worth a thousand words" and "The pen is mightier than the sword." Regarded as America's greatest caricaturist, Nast's more than three thousand cartoons and illustrations brought freshness and originality as well as political relevance to the American art scene. He created the symbols of the Tammany tiger, the Republican elephant, and the Democratic donkey, and he popularized the images of Santa Claus, Uncle Sam, and Miss Columbia. His journalistic work for illustrated current-affairs magazines placed him in contact with the most important social and political figures of his time. Nast's witty, often scathing political cartoons helped to sway public opinion in presidential campaigns from 1864 through 1884. They were instrumental in exposing corruption, notably the "Boss" Tweed-Tammany Hall scandal, and other social ills of the Gilded Age. However, detractors decried his work as mean-spirited, vulgar, and one-sided. Some of his pictures exhibit a nineteenth-century sentimentality whose appeal has diminished over the years. Nevertheless, the foreign-born Nast embraced and expressed what he believed to be wholesome American values and beliefs.

Thomas Nast was born on 26 September 1840 in Landau, Bavaria, to Joseph Thomas and Apollonia Abriss Nast. His family was imbued with the liberal, anticlerical, romantic, and nationalistic attitudes prevalent in Germany during much of the nineteenth century. Apparently Nast's father, a trombonist with the Ninth Regiment Bavarian Band, was outspoken in his political opinions and decided that America would provide a better environment for his family. Nast, his mother, and an older sister named Caterina immigrated to the United States in 1846 and settled in New York City; his father finished his term of service and arrived in 1850. At first young Nast did not speak any English, so he attended schools where German was an accepted language. While still a child his exceptional artistic talent came to light. In *Th. Nast, His Period and His Pictures* (1967) his biographer, Albert Bigelow Paine, relates that when the artist was about thirteen years old, he made a drawing of Louis Kossuth, the Hungarian revolutionary; the drawing was praised by his teacher and hung near the principal's desk. Nast would sketch and draw almost anyone or anything that interested him—scenes from plays, actors and singers, soldiers, ships, or fires. He was fascinated by the volunteer firefighters of the Big Six Precinct, whose chief at the time was William M. Tweed and whose logo was a fierce-looking tiger. Years later Nast, Tweed, and Americus the tiger would come together again in an ironic way that would change both men's lives.

Nast's parents wanted him to learn a trade or become a musician like his father, but clearly he was more interested in art than in anything else. He was still in his teens when he quit school and began formal art study with Theodore Kaufmann, a German-born historical painter. Kaufmann's studio was in the same building as that of Alfred Fredericks, who became a valuable friend and mentor. A fire destroyed the old building, and Nast had to study on his own for a time, copying works exhibited at museums and art galleries. Through Fredericks's guidance Nast was admitted to the Academy of Design, where he met other artists.

His artistic career began in earnest when he presented samples of his work to Frank Leslie, the English-born founder and publisher of a new periodical, *Frank Leslie's Illustrated Weekly Newspaper* (1855–1922), in the hope of finding remunerative employment. Leslie ordered him to make a picture of a crowd boarding the ferry at Christopher Street, which Nast did. A running boy and an energetic white dog in the foreground add to the picture's realism. Leslie then sent Nast to his staff artist, Alfred Berghaus, to learn the technique of drawing on a woodblock for engraving. Photography was still a new technology at that time and was not yet employed in newspaper or periodical illustration. When the fifteen-year-old had successfully redrawn his picture on the block, Leslie hired him for four dollars a week. Nast memorialized this interview with a caricature reproduced in the Paine biography showing himself—a short, pudgy, round-faced boy—looking up to a demanding and much taller Leslie. The three years he worked for *Frank Leslie's*

"The Gallant Color Bearer," Nast's first Civil War cover

Illustrated Weekly Newspaper were practically a paid apprenticeship in the field of pictorial journalism. Nast befriended and worked with comic illustrator Sol Eytinge and studied cartoons from the British magazine *Punch* by John Leech, John Gilbert, and John Tenniel, particularly their use of such symbols as the British Lion, John Bull, and Brother Jonathan (Uncle Sam's predecessor as an emblem for the United States). From Tenniel especially, Nast learned the line-drawing technique he used in his best cartoons. He discovered how art could be used to combat societal evils when he took part in Leslie's protracted assault on the "swill milk" disgrace, in which unsafe milk from sick cows fed on swill from distilleries was sold with the sanction of city officials.

In 1858 Nast went to Long Point, Canada, to report in pictures on a prizefight between "the Benicia boy," John C. Heenan, and John Morrissey, a noted politician as well as a boxer. He went to England the following year on a similar assignment for the *New York Illustrated News* to cover the controver-

"Hilda and Gretel," one of Nast's illustrations for Mary Mapes Dodge's Hans Brinker: or, The Silver Skates *(1866)*

sial prizefight between Heenan and the lighterweight British champion Thomas Sayers. Nast also had drawn pictures of the funeral of the abolitionist John Brown and depictions of squalid tenement life for the *New York Illustrated News.*

Eager to participate in a struggle for freedom, Nast went to Italy in May 1860 to join the Italian patriot Giuseppe Garibaldi in his battle against the Kingdom of the Two Sicilies. This was Garibaldi's most crucial campaign in forming a united kingdom of Italy under Victor Emmanuel II, proclaimed in 1861 after Nast had returned to the United States. The artist drew vivid pictures of the expedition for both the *New York Illustrated News* and the *London Illustrated News.* The latter paper even offered him employment, but the pay was less than Nast desired. Moreover, the artist had fallen in love with a young woman in New York and intended to return there and marry her. While in Rome he made sketches of the Coliseum that presaged later cartoons. Always able to combine work and pleasure, Nast visited art galleries and journeyed through Italy, Switzerland, and Germany, even going to Landau, the Bavarian town of his birth.

On 19 February 1861, only days after his return to America, Nast covered the reception of

newly elected President Abraham Lincoln in New York and went on to Philadelphia and Washington, D.C., for the inauguration. According to Philip van Doren Stern in *They Were There: The Civil War in Action as Seen by Its Combat Artists* (1961), Nast based a sketch of Lincoln disembarking a train in Baltimore on incorrect information; the president would have avoided that city due to a rumor that he might be assassinated there. Lincoln's presidency was fraught with danger from the beginning, for tensions between North and South had been mounting. By the time of his inauguration South Carolina, Mississippi, Florida, Alabama, Georgia, Texas, and Louisiana had seceded from the Union. On 12 April the shot was fired at Fort Sumter, South Carolina, that plunged the nation into bloody civil war for four years. One week later the New York Seventh Regiment marched down Broadway; Nast drew a picture of this scene, which he later portrayed in a painting that would hang in the regiment's armory for years. The Civil War period was important in Nast's development: while he worked toward greater artistic maturity, his inner moral convictions grew along the lines espoused by the Republicanism and Unionism of Lincoln and Ulysses S. Grant. Basically the Republicans, especially the Radical wing, supported preserving the Union, freeing the slaves and extending civil rights to them, and punishing the South for its intransigence. The ethics of Protestantism and temperance tinged the party's outlook. Northerners who sympathized with the South or who desired conciliation with it were perceived as dangerous to the Union and called Copperheads, hence their recurrent representation by a snake, the classic symbol of evil, in certain cartoons. Nast incorporated these ideas into his own moral perspective and came to see them as representing the good while viewing opposing perspectives, such as Southern or Democrat, as inimical to it. He was uncompromising in his beliefs. The formation of attitudes that took place during the Civil War and Reconstruction eras profoundly influenced his art, and later, when he modified some of his views, his work started to lose its sharp edge.

On 26 September 1861 Nast married Sarah Edwards, a cousin of biographer and author James Parton; the pair went to Niagara Falls for their honeymoon. Their mutual love of music is apparent in their first major expenditure, which was for a piano. Sarah had more formal education than her husband, and she often read to him while he worked. She also helped with some of his written captions. When she was too busy with their children or with household tasks, Nast hired college students to read for a dollar an hour. This enabled the artist to make many literary allusions in his works and to keep up with current events. The Nasts had five children: Julia, Thomas Jr., Edith, Mabel, and Cyril, who served as models for their father's Christmas pictures.

From 1859 through the mid 1860s Nast contributed caricatures to an obscure paper called *Phunny Phellow.* After a brief return to the financially struggling *Leslie's,* in 1862 Nast began a relationship that was to last twenty-five years when he joined the artistic staff of *Harper's Weekly.* Showing both industry and competence, he contributed six pictures to the popular periodical in his first year. The artist found an ally in Fletcher Harper, the editor, who valued his work and shared his Republican views. As Nast's fame increased, *Harper's Weekly* rewarded him with excellent pay and nearly ideal working conditions. However, over the years Nast would frequently clash with George William Curtis, the managing editor, even when both men were on the same political side. Their disagreements were due largely to differences in personality and style. Curtis, an urbane man of letters, preferred to use subtle persuasion and appeals to reason in his editorials whereas Nast aimed "to hit the enemy between the eyes and knock him down." Nast had dreamed of working for *Harper's Weekly* since its introduction in 1857, and in fact he published a page of nine drawings with captions dealing with police corruption, "The New York Metropolitan Police, a Pictorial Analysis of the Report to the Legislature," which appeared in the 19 March 1859 issue, before his European tour. Necessity played a part in his good fortune, for Civil War coverage increased the periodical's need for illustrators. Nast's first Civil War drawing for *Harper's Weekly,* "John Morgan's Highwaymen," appeared in the 30 August 1862 issue, bearing his characteristic signature, Th:Nast. A front cover, "The Gallant Color-Bearer," appeared on 20 September. Nast's early Civil War pictures were fairly conventional in form and style, similar to illustrations by other artists working for *Harper's Weekly,* but already they revealed a realism and an emotional intensity that appealed greatly to viewers. "The Battle of Fredericksburg" (27 December 1862) is noteworthy for its detail. One of his earliest Christmas pictures, "Christmas Eve 1862," published 3 January 1863, enclosed two vignettes in wreaths: a mother praying or gazing longingly out of a window while her children sleep, and a Union soldier looking at a picture of his family by campfire light. Miniature views of Santa Claus and his reindeer at the top of the picture contrast with war scenes below. Its obvious sentimentality touched readers experiencing the ravages of the Civil War. Nast used the same structural framework for "The War in the Border States" two weeks later in the 17 January 1863 issue.

The artist contributed thirty-two pictures to *Harper's Weekly* in 1863. On 1 January of that year the Emancipation Proclamation was issued. Nast commemorated the event with a picture, "Emancipation," dated 24 January 1863, contrasting the horrors of slavery on the left side with the prosperity of freedom on the right; a warm family scene dominates the center. That summer he started sketching from the battlefield. He introduced Miss Columbia, a resolute, robust, long-haired woman in Greco-Roman costume symbolizing the Union, Liberty, or Justice. He also began to use transparent wraiths and skeletons to represent real or imaginary threats. War casualties were high, and on 3 March 1863 Congress passed an act subjecting all men twenty to forty-five years of age to conscription. One could avoid service by paying $300 or hiring a substitute, however; such exemptions obviously favored the well-to-do. On 13 July the conscription act, racial hatred, and general malaise touched off the four-day Draft Riots in New York City. Gov. Horatio Seymour, who opposed the act, tried unsuccessfully to appease the mobs. Nast attempted to make sketches of the disaster but decided to return home for his and his family's safety.

By 1864 Nast was clearly articulating his views in his illustrations. He supported Lincoln and castigated the Democrats for capitulating to Southern demands. His pictures "Compromise with the South" of 5 September 1864—wherein a haughty Jefferson Davis extends a hand to a wounded and humiliated Northern soldier while Columbia weeps—and "The Chicago Platform" of 15 October with its running text created extra demand for those issues of *Harper's Weekly.* They were also used as campaign documents. In 1865 Nast won a $100 prize for the first front cover of *Mrs. Grundy,* a weekly magazine that was published for only two months. The faces of nearly a hundred persons could be recognized in this picture, which was only six by eight inches in size.

While Lincoln's assassination on 14 April 1865 caused Nast grief, the ascendancy of Andrew Johnson to the presidency created consternation in him. Johnson's Reconstruction policies and political motives made enemies among the Radical Republicans, who demanded impeachment. By this time the artist's talent for portraiture and caricature had developed considerably, and in Johnson, with his strong facial features and antagonistic demeanor, he found an appropriate target. The strongly Unionist Nast portrayed the president as a treacherous Iago pretending to befriend blacks, personified by

Nast's illustration for the 12 January 1867 issue of Harper's Weekly, *one of many drawings in which he championed the rights of African Americans*

Othello, in "Andrew Johnson's Reconstruction and How It Works" in the 3 September 1866 issue of *Harper's Weekly*. In the 3 November 1866 issue he characterized Johnson as a tyrant, "King Andy I," curiously effete looking with his thin, bare legs. Next to him William H. Seward, the lanky, long-nosed secretary of state, and the bearded secretary of war, Edwin M. Stanton, looks on while Radical Republicans await execution, including Sen. Charles Sumner on the chopping block and Nast at the end of the line; Liberty is in chains. Nast reacted bitterly to the killing of participants in a Republican convention in New Orleans, many of them blacks, on 30 July 1866. He created a double-page spread, "Amphitheatrum Johnsonianum," for the 30 March 1867 issue, wherein Johnson, Seward, Stanton, Secretary of the Navy Gideon Welles, and others observe the carnage in a Roman arena; a centurion, Ulysses S. Grant, restrains the sword of Gen. Philip Sheridan. The Roman setting hearkened back to Nast's Italian tour and looked forward to his famous "Tammany Tiger Loose" cartoon, another double-page feature. This size is noteworthy: since *Harper's Weekly* was more than thirty centimeters in height, a picture taking up two pages was forceful by its very dimensions.

Nast's illustrations for books are a relatively little-known aspect of his work. In 1866 he created pictures for the first edition of Mary Mapes Dodge's *Hans Brinker: or, The Silver Skates.* He also illustrated *The Life and Strange Surprising Adventures of Robinson*

Crusoe (1868) by Daniel Defoe, from which he received inspiration for a few of his later cartoons; Clement Clarke Moore's *A Visit from St. Nicholas* (1869), which figured in many Christmas drawings; and several Little Prudy books by Rebecca Sophia Clarke, who also wrote under the pseudonym Sophie May. Many of the pictures Nast contributed to *Harper's Weekly* in 1866 were illustrations for *Inside: A Chronicle of Secession* by George F. Harrington (pseudonym of William Mumford Baker), a story serialized in the magazine and then published by Harper's as a book. In 1867 he contributed illustrations to the *Riverside Magazine for Young People;* this magazine's editor, Horace Scudder, selected pictures showing perception in rendering children's faces and figures. In that same year Nast met David R. Locke, known by his pseudonym Petroleum V. Nasby, whose political satire written in dialect delighted Lincoln and Sumner as well as Nast. The artist illustrated Nasby's *Ekkoes from Kentucky . . . : Being a Perfect Record uv the Ups, Downs and Experiences uv the Dimocrisy* (1868) and *The Struggles (Social, Financial and Political) of Petroleum V. Nasby* (1872), with an introduction by Sumner. He also provided illustrations for another humorist, Josh Billings (pseudonym of Henry W. Shaw), who, like Nasby, wrote in dialect. On 18 April 1868 Nast, along with Curtis, James Parton, Horace Greeley, and other journalistic and literary notables, attended a dinner at Delmonico's restaurant given by the New York Press Club for Charles Dickens, who was in America for his second and last time. Nast occasionally alluded to Dickens's plots or characters in his cartoons and illustrated several of the renowned English author's works.

With the recent war, Johnson's impeachment and acquittal, and the issue of voting rights for blacks and former rebels in the air, the election of 1868 inspired both fear and hope. From Nast's point of view the Democratic nominee, Horatio Seymour, resembled a devil, for he had opposed both the Emancipation Proclamation and the conscription act. The cartoonist acted on the analogy by shaping tufts of Seymour's hair into horns. Nast pictured Seymour as Lady Macbeth trying to remove the stain left by the Draft Riots in "Time, Midnight.–Scene, New York City Hall" on the back page of the 5 September 1868 *Harper's Weekly*. Nast staunchly supported the Republican candidate, Ulysses S. Grant, in the election campaigns of 1868 and 1872 and throughout both of his presidential terms. His admiration for Grant apparently blinded him to the former general's scandal-ridden administration. Grant was said to have credited his election in large part to General Sheridan's sword and Nast's cartoons.

Though he championed the rights of blacks, Chinese, and other minorities, Nast had such antipathy for the Catholic Church in general and for Irish Catholics in particular that he has been accused of bigotry. Except for individuals whom he assailed personally, he regularly depicted the Irish as hideous, heavy-jowled, grinning apes. To his credit he did include a human-looking Irishman among the guests at "Uncle Sam's Thanksgiving Dinner" (*Harper's Weekly*, 20 November 1869), and he occasionally reminded fellow German as well as Irish immigrants that they were now Americans. His prejudices were probably due partly to childhood experiences and his later association with the anticlerical Garibaldi but more importantly to his internalization of the Radical Republican viewpoint and the general American social temper of the time, both of which included separation of church and state, a Protestant outlook, and anti-Catholic and anti-Irish biases as strong components. It was commonly feared that Catholics would swear greater allegiance to a foreign pope than to their own nation. These feelings intensified with the huge influx of Catholic Irish (and others) during the nineteenth century and persisted even until the 1960s, when John F. Kennedy had to confront them. The Catholic Church was viewed as alien and antithetical to progress. Pope Pius IX's reactionary 1864 encyclical *Quanta cura* with its accompanying "Syllabus of Errors" and the declaration of papal infallibility promulgated by the First Vatican Council of 1869–1870 did nothing to moderate that view. At the same time many Catholics displayed their own ignorance and intolerance, thereby reinforcing the malice directed at them. Religious enmity erupted in violence in New York City on Saint Patrick's Day in 1867 and again on 11–12 July 1871, when Protestant Orangemen staged a parade. Mismanagement by the Tammany-controlled city government under Mayor Abraham Oakey Hall contributed to the mayhem. Both riots inspired bitter cartoons from Nast. His defenders point out that the artist did not object to Catholic rites or practices and that his contention against church-sponsored schools extended to all denominations, as illustrated on the bottom panel of "Our Common Schools As They Are and As They May Be" (*Harper's Weekly*, 26 February 1870). Rather, he opposed the position of the church in political affairs–specifically the prominence of Catholics in the Democratic Party and in Tammany Hall, government support of religion-affiliated schools, the power of the church's hierarchy over individuals, and the idea of infallibility. These last three problems continue to be debated today.

The artist's opinions on these issues are clear in his illustrations for an allegory of American politics by Charles Henry Pullen, *Miss Columbia's Private School* (1871), and in cartoons in *Harper's Weekly*. In a cartoon of 19 March 1870 Nast likened the menace of the "ecclesiastical canon" toward public schools to the cannon that fired on Fort Sumter–both divided the nation. "The American River Ganges" (20 September 1871) is an imaginative and lurid depiction of Catholic bishops as crocodiles, their miters forming the animals' toothy mouths, coming across the water to threaten public-school children. Members of the "Tweed Ring" and a gallows loom in the background. The First Vatican Council furnished imagery for other pictures.

Nast's crowning accomplishment, for which he achieved enduring fame, was his ruthless ridicule of the Tweed Ring, or the Tammany Hall affair, which furnished real issues for the cartoonist to attack and enemies on which to practice his brand of pictorial psychology. Only a few years after the scandal Charles F. Wingate hailed Nast as a genius in "An Episode in Municipal Government," a three-part article in the *North American Review*. The Tweed Ring consisted of a handful of unscrupulous politicians–Tweed, Peter B. Sweeny, Hall, and Richard B. Connolly–and their associates who dominated New York City's government from 1866 to 1871 and who pilfered uncalculated millions of dollars from that city's treasury when many workers earned only a dollar or two per day. By portraying powerful men as buffoons, Nast's cartoons in *Harper's Weekly* from 1869 through 1871 were forceful in deflating the ring and helping to bring about its defeat in the 1871 city and state elections. In *Tweed's New York: Another Look* (1977) Leo Hershkowitz contends that much of the notoriety surrounding Tweed is a myth perpetrated in part by these caricatures and exemplified in them. However, Tweed himself admitted to the cartoons' effectiveness when he complained that he did not care a straw about what was written about him; his constituents did not know how to read, but they could not help seeing "them damned pictures." He reportedly clipped and saved every Nast cartoon lampooning him.

Tammany Hall was a social and patriotic club in New York City founded in 1786 and named after Tamanend, a legendary, wise Delaware Indian chief. The society's use of pseudo-Indian costumes and motifs provided imagery for a few of Nast's cartoons. Tammany soon grew into an important force in New York politics; it also became noted for corruption. In the early nineteenth century it became associated with the Democratic Party. Eventually its membership was extended to white males without property, including those of Irish and German background, and thus to Roman Catholics. Tammany established a system of political patronage—"spoils"—and charity through the purchase of votes and fraudulent naturalization procedures. Instead of attacking the problems of poverty, inadequate housing, and nonexistent sanitation, its leaders appealed to the underprivileged by offering jobs on the city's payroll, housing at usurious rates, or other amenities. In return they received straight-ticket, Tammany-sponsored Democrat votes, the power to name their candidates, and kickbacks on padded city contracts. At election time they stuffed ballot boxes and employed "repeaters" to vote several times under fictitious names and neighborhood toughs to police the polls. Nast ridiculed this voting process in "Going through the Form of Universal Suffrage" (*Harper's Weekly,* 11 November 1871), in which the gloating, cigar-smoking "Boss" Tweed (actually a nonsmoker) and "Brains" Sweeny grin at a long line of voters while the dapper Mayor Hall looks on. Such dishonesty was flagrant, but at the same time Tammany's opponents were equally corrupt, and more-idealistic statesmen were disinclined to go politicking among the poor. The insidiousness of Tammany's operations stemmed from the involvement of many of New York's politicians at that time. Although Tweed is acknowledged as the first Tammany "boss," his predecessor, Fernando Wood, had

already practically bought New York City's government. Tammany's strong Democratic focus; "foreign" elements in its constituency, especially Irish and Catholic ones; its control of much of the middle- and lower-class vote; and its venality were all anathema to the Republicans, the anti-immigrant Know-Nothings, and the established upper class. As ardent Republicans both Nast and Fletcher Harper shared this anti-Tammany sentiment.

At five feet eleven inches tall and about 280 pounds, Tweed was a big, swaggering man with a long, ruddy, bearded face; a high forehead made higher by balding; a banana-like nose; and a taste for ostentation that increased along with his ill-gotten wealth. He became the very image of greed in Nast's cartoons: fat, grinning, lecherous, arrogant, and vulgar. In her textbook *Cartooning* (1992) Polly Keener likens Nast's Boss to "a pear-shaped moneybag." He is shown towering over his associates in both size and cupidity. Nast drew Tweed's eyes smaller and gave them an avaricious leer. He lampooned Tweed's liking for showy jewelry by exaggerating the size and brilliance of his costly diamond stickpin, which radiated like a light bulb from his ample chest; the diamond was as much a part of its owner's image as his nose. Tweed's girth and coarse humor invited renderings of him as Falstaff. He had New York City "under his thumb" in a cartoon in the 10 June 1871 issue of *Harper's Weekly,* one of many captioned with the callous snarl, "Well, what are you going to do about it?," that Tweed ostensibly shouted to a reporter for *The New York Times.* These caricatures did not show Tweed's lively, sociable, and sometimes even charitable nature; any indication of his better qualities would have diminished the cartoons' impact.

The other ringleaders had little in common with Tweed except avarice and self-centeredness plus the fact that they and their misdeeds provided ideal targets for Nast. The most colorful character among them was Abraham Oakey Hall, a slender and sprightly attorney, mayor, public speaker, author, socialite, playwright, actor, and man of many other talents. Sporting a well-groomed beard and pince-nez, "the Elegant Oakey" wore expensive, flamboyant clothes and laced his speeches and writings with puns, jokes, and Latin quotes. He was a district attorney and from 1869 to 1872 the mayor of New York City. He changed political and religious affiliations several times; writers disagree whether his mutability and theatricality were indications of political shrewdness or emotional instability or both. Nast capitalized on Hall's beard and especially his glasses, enlarging them and turning them downward so that they drooped. Many authors em-

A Nast cartoon from the 11 November 1871 Harper's Weekly, *at the height of the "Tweed Ring" scandal—"Boss" William M. Tweed is seated at left, above the medallion*

phasize the importance of Nast's relentless caricature of Hall in implicating him as part of the Tweed Ring. As a respectable, well-bred man of New York society, Hall would have maintained a certain social distance from men such as Tweed who came up through the ranks. He denied any involvement with the scandals taking place during his term as mayor, and eventually he was acquitted. Yet Nast often pictured him keeping company with those involved in the ring, at times holding a broom as if to "keep things clean" in city government.

The city comptroller and the ring's financial wizard was a tall, portly Irishman, Richard Barrett Connolly, nicknamed Slippery Dick owing to his ingratiating but shifty, smooth-tongued manner, his facility in manipulating numbers and people, and his habit of feigning innocence. An important power in Tammany Hall for years because of his popularity with Irish-American voters, this former bank clerk and onetime state senator was a venal person who would do almost anything for money or to save his own neck. His neat penmanship and untrustworthiness in counting votes were both noted early in his political career. He looked slightly different in portraits than in Nast's cartoons and at times even from one picture to another. In some cartoons he was merely a background or shadow figure. Nast made Slippery Dick recognizable by the shape of his broad, clean-shaven face with prominent cheekbones; his hairline; and the deep creases from his

nose to his thin, unattractive mouth. The artist twisted that mouth into a smug, crooked sneer instead of the comptroller's usual smile. Perhaps Connolly got hot easily, for he is portrayed holding a fan in two *Harper's Weekly* cartoons. In one of these, "The Tammany Lords and Their Constituents" (2 September 1871), he sits across from his friends under a statue of a golden calf in a park, enjoying a leisure acquired at the expense of the poor who pay high rents; in the other, "Not a Bailable Case" (12 August 1871), he cools a sick mare (mayor) Hall with a "city fan—cost $10,000" while Horace Greeley tearfully complains of the abuse the press has been heaping on the ring.

Peter Barr Sweeny resembled an operatic or movie villain with his dark and intense features, deep voice, wild hair, and secretive, brooding disposition. This remarkably cunning lawyer and politician, designated city chamberlain in 1866, was seen as the adviser and counselor behind the ring; thus Nast called him Peter Brains Sweeny (or $weeny), among other nicknames, and in "Something That Did Blow Over" (alluding to a phrase in one of Mayor Hall's speeches), illustrating Tammany Hall's defeat in November 1871, Sweeny is shown walking away from the ruins carrying a moneybag labeled "Brains." The thickset, mustached Sweeny cared little for outward display or even about his personal appearance, for Nast drew him with tousled hair and sometimes with his coat misbuttoned.

He is frequently shown in poses that could variously imply reserve, deviousness, cowardice, or treachery: standing with his toes pointed inward, with one hand in a coat pocket, or with his arms folded. To loosen Sweeny's reticence when networking among fellow Irish-Americans, Connolly supposedly gave him a lesson in shaking hands, backslapping, and friendly small talk, according to Denis Tilden Lynch in *"Boss" Tweed: The Story of a Grim Generation* (1927). Sweeny is unsmiling, however, in "The Greek Slave" (*Harper's Weekly,* 16 April 1870), satirizing how Tammany Hall garnered Irish support: he glowers at a cringing, ape-faced Irishman chained to a post labeled "Tammany" and "Democrat" with a ballot box and bottles of rum and whisky on top of it. The picture's title probably refers to the noted sculpture by Hiram Powers. Both Sweeny and Connolly had opposed former mayor Fernando Wood in favor of Tweed within Tammany Hall, thus being instrumental in bringing the ring to power. Nast's *Harper's Weekly* cartoon for 4 December 1869, "The Foot Print on the Land of Peace," shows President Grant as Robinson Crusoe discovering a footprint belonging to the savage Tammany Tribe, whose chief is Peter the Great. The picture and the Peter the Great appellation gain resonance in light of Tammany's Indian trappings and Sweeny's admiration for Louis Napoleon of France respectively.

Though John T. Hoffman was not a ringleader, his lean, mustached face was a regular sight in Nast's anti-Tammany cartoons as a portrait on a wall if not as a main character. The artist first applied his mare-mayor pun to Hoffman in 1866 in his highly successful portrait exhibition for an opera ball given at the Academy of Music, reduced to a double-page feature, "Grand Masquerade Ball" (*Harper's Weekly,* 14 April 1866). Because Hoffman had Tammany Hall's backing first as mayor of New York City, then as governor, and even when he had presidential aspirations, Nast characterized him as a figurehead behind whose throne Tweed and Sweeny lurked as the real power in "The Tammany Ring-dom" (29 October 1870). The cartoonist jabbed at both Catholicism and Tammany's taxation methods in his earliest picture displaying the elements of the Tweed Ring scandal, "The Economical Council, Albany, New York" (25 December 1869), in which he cast Hoffman as Pope Pius IX, Sweeny as Cardinal Giacomo Antonelli (the Pope's adviser), and the other ring members as bishops in a parody of the First Vatican Council, *economical* punning with *ecumenical*.

Such distinctive characters hardly needed captions. However, the phonetic similarity between the Scottish surname Tweed and the Irish surname Sweeny invited a deliberate spoonerism Nast used in several cartoons. Alluding to Lewis Carroll's nonsense characters, he modified their names to Tweedledee and Sweedledum in a *Harper's Weekly* cartoon of 14 January 1871 showing Tweed and Sweeny dressed as clowns and looting the public treasury. Incensed, Tweed ordered the board of education to destroy schoolbooks published by Harper and to reject all Harper bids. This action caused much consternation for the publisher since Harper furnished most of the textbooks used in the city. After meetings and deliberations, Fletcher Harper determined to stand firm. Nast agreed, responding in the 13 May 1871 issue with "The New Board of Education," depicting Hall as a teacher presenting Tammany propaganda, Sweeny throwing Harper's books out the window, and Tweed punishing a boy using *Willson's Readers.* His titles for the ring-sponsored books are amusing: *Honest Government* and *Geography* by "Sweed" and *Arithmetic* by Connolly. The textbook episode and an anti-Catholic variant of this picture recur in *Miss Columbia's Private School.* The ring tried to stop Nast by offering to pay handsomely for him to study art in Europe, but the artist refused, stating that he intended to put his subjects behind bars. However, he decided to move his family from their cottage in Harlem to a larger home in Morristown, New Jersey, shortly thereafter.

As incisive as the individual characterizations are, the pictures featuring Tweed, Sweeny, Hall, and Connolly together, especially those drawn in the fall of 1871 as the fateful election neared, are the best known and most trenchant of the Tweed Ring cartoons. They are often reproduced and hailed as models of Nast's art. They include "Who Stole the People's Money?," a timeless illustration of passing the buck showing the Tammany Ring in a circle, each member pointing to the man next to him; "A Group of Vultures Waiting for the Storm to Blow Over—Let Us *Prey*"; and "The Only Thing They Respect or Fear," revealing the shadows of four nooses awaiting the cringing figures below, Connolly being represented only by his hat. Incidents involving the comptroller and the mayor, the burglary of Connolly's office, and the theft of certain vouchers not only precipitated the fall of the ring but also inspired Nast to anticipate Salvador Dalí's sense of distortion in his cartoon for 30 September 1871. He drew the four shrugging men, three of whom were actually fat, as emaciated, elongated ghosts that were, like their lame explanations of recent events, "too thin." The cartoonist's masterpiece was a fierce double-page spread made just before the November 1871 election, "The Tammany Tiger Loose—What Are

You Going to Do About It?" Nast included the tiger in most of his anti-Tammany drawings, but here it rages in the center of a Roman arena, mauling the figures of the Republic, Liberty, and Justice while the toga-clad Tweed and his friends gloat in the stands. A good deal of this picture's power lies in its synthesis of previously used images.

A country still reeling from the Civil War sought to resolve an issue resulting from the conflict. During the war the Confederacy used British-built cruisers, one of them named the *Alabama,* to destroy vessels of the Union merchant marine and was helped by British interests. The United States claimed damages; the suit was finally settled in 1872. Nast had hoped for a settlement favorable to the United States as early as 1 August 1868, when *Harper's Weekly* showed "The British Lion Disarmed" by Columbia, who trimmed its claws with scissors labeled "Alabama Claims."

Most of the artist's work during 1872 dealt with the upcoming presidential election and the issue of civil reform. The Republican Party was split between the radical wing, which supported Grant and favored a hard-line Reconstruction policy, and those who took a more conciliatory posture toward the South and who were critical of the corrupt Grant administration, demanding a system of civil service based on merit. Their ideas allied the liberal Republicans with the Democrats who accepted their platform. At the Cincinnati convention the liberal Republicans, led by Sens. Charles Sumner, Carl Schurz, Lyman Trumbull, and Reuben Fenton, selected a compromise candidate, Horace Greeley, with Missouri senator Gratz Brown for vice president. Using imagery from William Shakespeare's *Julius Caesar,* Nast pictured "The 'Liberal' Conspirators (Who, You Know, Are Honorable Men)" plotting to purchase Greeley to overthrow Grant. Harper's managing editor, George William Curtis, was a friend of the liberal Republicans, and although he allowed this cartoon to be printed in the 16 March 1872 issue, he berated Nast for attacking them. Today many agree that the cartoonist was needlessly vicious in this campaign; nevertheless, these accomplished men, especially Schurz and Greeley, made superb models for pictorial satire.

Like Nast, Schurz came from Germany; he spoke and wrote eloquently in both English and German and was a powerful influence on German-American voters. However, in the 2 November 1872 *Harper's Weekly* Nast's "The German Vote" informed readers and a chastened Schurz that "The Germans will vote as they please—they have no dictator," underscoring the political gulf between himself and the senator.

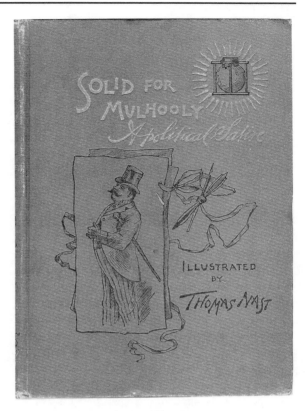

Cover for an 1889 book by Rufus E. Shapley, with illustrations by Nast (courtesy of Cushing Memorial Library, Texas A&M University)

self and the senator. Schurz's long and illustrious military, political, and literary career included a brief term as a U.S. ambassador to Spain in 1861, after which he fought in the Civil War. From 1869 to 1875 he served as a U.S. senator from Missouri. He was tall and gaunt with sharp features, an abundant beard, and pince-nez; in caricaturing him Nast exaggerated only his thinness and long legs. The senator's musical talent encouraged Nast to picture him at the piano. In "Played Out!" (*Harper's Weekly,* 15 June 1872) an exhausted Schurz is surrounded by his compositions on the themes of liberal Republicanism: "Grant is not honest about amnesty and civil service reform," "The administration is corrupt," "Down with Grant," "French arms for sale," "The Germans will vote for H. G.," "Military Ring at Washington," and "The heart that never quails." A selection titled "Liberal Reform" offers "music without words." The paths of the two German-Americans would cross many times. Schurz became secretary of the interior under President Rutherford B. Hayes, bringing Native American affairs under that domain and thus prompting cartoons on American Indian rights from Nast. In 1884 both men left the Republican Party in favor of the Democratic

An 18 April 1876 cartoon in which Nast attacks the Democratic support of "soft" money (the issuing of "greenback" paper currency) and inflation after the depression of 1873–1875

candidate. By an ironic quirk of fate Schurz became managing editor of *Harper's Weekly* after Curtis's death in 1892, but by that time Nast had left.

Greeley was practically a caricature in real life, with his pale, benign face; wire-rimmed glasses; thin white hair and mutton-chop whiskers; white coat and hat; shrill voice; and eccentric manner. He was the editor of the *New York Tribune* and had been an influential voice in American politics for years. He was inconsistent in his opinions yet dogmatic in his assertion of them. His self-contradiction in print was used against him in his campaign. In many cartoons Nast showed Greeley carrying copies of the *Tribune* on which were written a pet phrase of his, "What I know about ___." Because Greeley was slow to rebuke Tammany Hall and the Tweed Ring in the *Tribune,* especially Hall, Nast constantly accused him of cooperating with the ring. Because Nast could not get a photograph of Greeley's running mate, Gratz Brown, in time to meet a deadline, he resorted to simply writing "& Gratz Brown" on a tag

attached to Greeley's white coat. The makeshift proved so successful that the cartoonist used it throughout the campaign. Greeley had been a long-time presidential hopeful and was elated at his nomination. Thus, in caricature he was pictured shaking anybody's hand or doing almost "Anything to get in," as a *Harper's Weekly* cartoon of 10 August 1872 was captioned. In this caricature Greeley's head and Brown's tail tag appear on a Trojan horse driven by Schurz to Washington, D.C.; the horse resembles a child's toy with its wheels and cheerful spots. Ku Klux Klan members climb inside while the Tweed Ring and other disreputable politicians watch.

Such merciless derision, while ingenious, caused Greeley to exclaim that he did not know whether he was running for the presidency or the penitentiary. It also had unforeseen consequences. By a tragic coincidence, "We Are on the Home Stretch," showing a defeated Greeley being carried on a stretcher, was printed in the 6 November 1872 *Harper's Weekly,* only days after the death of Greeley's wife. Nast had not even been aware that she was critically ill. A few weeks later the election took place. Greeley lost miserably, as Nast had predicted. The strain of the campaign, his sleepless vigil at his wife's bedside and his bereavement at her death, and his crushing defeat at the polls were too much for Greeley, who himself became physically and mentally sick and died on 29 November 1872. It is widely agreed today that he succumbed to years of overwork, overambition, and stress rather than to Nast's ferocious ridicule. Nonetheless, Nast was denounced for his attacks and charged with contributing to Greeley's misfortune. The artist was a kinder person than his cartoons indicated, seldom intending personal malice toward his subjects, and Greeley's death distressed him.

Nast received accolades from Grant and other Republicans for his work in helping them achieve victory. Secretary of State Hamilton Fish offered Nast an appointment as U.S. commissioner for the Vienna Exposition, but the artist declined. Instead, Nast set sail for a European vacation. On board the same boat was James Redpath of the Bostom Lyceum Bureau, who urged him to undertake a lecture tour. Nast was unenthusiastic at first, but eventually he agreed. While abroad the artist visited W. L. Thomas, the engraver for the *London News,* and Col. J. W. Peard, whom he had befriended during the Garibaldi campaign. Upon his return Nast found himself in great demand as a public speaker, an activity for which he felt himself ill suited. His first engagement was at

Peabody Hall in Boston. The famous cartoonist suffered badly from stage fright, but he regained his composure once he started sketching. His tour extended as far west as Nebraska and brought in $40,000. These lectures contributed to the popularity of *Nast's Illustrated Almanac*, which Harper published from 1871 to 1874. Humorists such as Petroleum V. Nasby, Josh Billings, and Mark Twain contributed to the *Almanac*.

Between the 1872 election and the nation's centennial Tweed, Hall, and some of their accomplices (not Sweeny or Connolly, however) came to trial through the instigation of Samuel J. Tilden, New York's state Democratic chairman and an exceptionally astute politician. Tweed was sentenced to prison in 1873, but the other ringleaders were never convicted. Tilden's important role in bringing down the Tweed Ring and reforming Tammany Hall was a strong factor in his winning the New York gubernatorial election in 1874 and the Democratic presidential nomination in 1876. In spite of Tilden's accomplishments Nast never warmed up to him; to the artist he was another wily Tammany Hall Democrat. In the 7 November 1874 *Harper's Weekly* Nast pictured Tilden as "A Tammany Rat" protected by Tammany Hall "when it [the Tweed scandal] was blowing over," who turned into the "rat-catcher." *Tweedle-dee and Tilden-dee* (1 July 1876) is credited with helping in the identification and capture of Tweed, who had escaped from prison.

From 1873 to 1875 the nation experienced an economic depression followed by inflation. The issue of hard versus soft currency was a volatile one in the 1876 campaign, and it led to the Greenback movement. Generally speaking, hard currency or the resumption of specie payment was favored by business and industrial interests in the East and by Republicans, including Grant and Nast, whereas soft money and inflation–the issuing of greenbacks–was supported by debt-ridden western farmers and Benjamin Butler of Massachusetts, a complex politician and another of Nast's favorite subjects for caricature. The artist strongly upheld the "hard" cause, portraying inflation as a "Rag baby" in many cartoons and providing illustrations for *Robinson Crusoe's Money: or Remarkable Financial Fortunes of Remote Island Community* (1876), an allegorical explanation of capitalistic theory by economist David Ames Wells. Tilden's skillful advocacy of soft money in the West and hard money in the East inspired Nast to place Tilden's head at both ends of an elastic Democratic-Tammany tiger. The 1876 election was extremely close, and electoral votes from four

states were contested. Those votes were eventually given to the Republican Rutherford B. Hayes, whom Nast supported, but Tilden in fact claimed the popular vote. A victorious but injured Republican elephant illustrated the result in "Another Such Victory, and I Am Undone" (*Harper's Weekly*, 24 March 1877).

No American election since Nast's lifetime would be complete without the Republican elephant and Democratic donkey symbols the artist created. The elephant first appeared in "The Third Term Panic" (*Harper's Weekly*, 7 November 1874). The artist had long used the donkey in its popular connection with stupidity. It first acquired Democratic associations in "A Live Jackass Kicking a Dead Lion" (15 January 1870), the jackass representing the "Copperhead" press and the lion Edwin M. Stanton, who had just died. Since Tammany Hall was a Democratic stronghold, the tiger symbolized that party through 1876. The two political animals did not come together explicitly labeled until "Stranger Things Have Happened" (27 December 1879).

For all his sagacity in assessing other people's political character, Nast was surprisingly inept in handling his own investments. He lost money in an ill-fated western mining venture. Grant offered him an opportunity to invest in Grant and Ward. As his presidential career showed, Grant had no more foresight in his financial dealings than the artist. Ward proved an unscrupulous partner. In 1884 the company, which paid dividends from principal investments, went bankrupt. Both the cartoonist and the former president were ruined financially. Nast suffered another reversal in 1893 with the demise of the short-lived *Nast's Weekly*, a paper he established with Republican support the previous year. Following the fame and fortune of the 1870s, the last years of Nast's life were spent in relative poverty.

The 1884 election, the last one influenced by Nast's work, was also the one in which Nast, Curtis, and *Harper's Weekly*–plus Curtis's friend and Nast's old nemesis Schurz–withdrew their long-time support of the Republican Party in favor of the lackluster but honest Democratic candidate, Grover Cleveland, thus joining the picturesquely named mugwumps. The mugwumps would not back the Republican nominee, James Gillespie Blaine, because of his past record of rivalry with other Republicans loyal to Grant, his involvement in a movement to curtail Chinese immigration, and allegations that he used high office for personal gain. Nast declared that he would not vote for Blaine even if the Democrats nominated the

Nast's cartoon for the 27 December 1879 issue of Harper's Weekly, *the first to label both political-party mascots*

devil. Taking a cue from Robert Ingersoll's brilliant speech dubbing the handsome nominee a "plumed knight," the artist drew "Blaine of Maine" (as he was sometimes called) wearing a hat with three wilted feathers. Capitalizing on his subject's rather prominent nose, Nast characterized him as a thick-skinned rhinoceros. Blaine was shown carrying a bag marked, "Twenty years of _____" in reference to Blaine's just-published book, *Twenty Years of Congress* (1884). On 8 May 1880 Nast had pictured "the 'magnetic' Blaine; or, a very heavy 'load'-stone for the Republican Party to carry" as a magnet attracting the dross of numerous scandals to himself. He returned to this theme in "Too Heavy to Carry" (14 June 1884), this time with Blaine as a magnet overloading the Republican elephant. A Republican supporter made a remark equating the Democrats with "rum, Romanism and rebellion." That statement and Nast's cartoons probably cost Blaine the election—the results were that close.

After that election Nast's career declined even though the artist was only in his forties. Several cir-

cumstances contributed to his descent. He developed hand cramps brought on by his relentless work during the previous two decades; in modern terminology he suffered from repetitive-motion injuries. About 1880 the art of woodblock engraving gave way to a photochemical process that took Nast a while to master and was less suited to his style than the older technique. Other artists and magazines were coming to the fore, for example William Allen Rogers, Nast's successor at *Harper's Weekly*, and Joseph Keppler of *Puck*, giving Nast unprecedented competition. The tension between Nast and Curtis increased after Fletcher Harper's death on 29 May 1877; after that date Nast contributed fewer pictures for the magazine. However, the strongest factor in his decline was change in the overall political climate. Much of Nast's outlook reflected the issues of the Civil War and Reconstruction eras. After the Hayes administration, which in effect ended Reconstruction, these issues became less relevant to an increasingly complacent American public. Their shift in party affiliation, though based on principle, cost Nast, Curtis, and *Harper's Weekly* dearly, for their reputations were tied to their Republican bearings. As a result the artist had more difficulty getting his work published. Finally the leaders arising from the new political milieu were rather bland and lacking in the distinctive or eccentric qualities that made people such as Greeley, Schurz, Tilden, Butler, and Blaine irresistible to Nast as subjects for caricature. Even "Honest John" Kelly and Richard Croker, Tweed's successors in the perennially corrupt Tammany Hall, were no match for Tweed or his ring as objects of derision.

The last cartoon Nast drew for *Harper's Weekly* was the Christmas picture for 1886, captioned with the first two lines of Clement Clarke Moore's familiar poem, "'Twas the night before Christmas, and all through the house / Not a creature was stirring, *not even a mouse*," showing two mice cozily asleep in tiny beds, a picture of a smiling Santa Claus in the background. Aware of the appeal of Nast's work and of the artist's financial difficulties, the editors of Harper's agreed to pay him a retainer for another year to prepare collections of his Christmas drawings and the Tweed pictures. Only the first-named collection, *Christmas Drawings for the Human Race* (1890), was published; it contained all of Nast's Christmas pictures printed over the years plus a few new ones. A reprint with text by Thomas Nast St. Hill, the artist's grandson, was published by Dover in 1978. A generation of readers looked forward to the Christmas issues of *Harper's Weekly*, and many people collected them. These endearing illustrations reveal a gentler side of Nast than his political car-

Two of Nast's Christmas illustrations, which became a popular annual feature in Harper's Weekly

toons. In them he indulged his childlike love of home, family, and Yuletide celebration. Moore had made Saint Nicholas a pipe-smoking, "jolly old elf"; evidently under Dutch influence his name became Santa Claus. It was Nast, however, who gave the fat, fun-loving, generous saint his modern form, making a home for him at the North Pole, which was far enough away to be almost imaginary and, incidentally, politically neutral. The children in the pictures were modeled after those of the artist, and the fireplace decorated with images from Mother Goose rhymes was an actual fixture in Nast's home in Morristown, New Jersey. The appearance of nursery rhymes in some of the Christmas drawings, while apt, was an apparent coincidence; both Mother Goose and Santa Claus inhabit the worlds of childhood and fantasy. It is curious that Nast's plump, bearded, and smiling Santa Claus looks like the good-natured artist himself in his later portraits.

Nast's last published drawings were of a happy and an unhappy Santa Claus, the latter not sure whether his present to the nation's capital—the Hay-Pauncefote treaty with Great Britain establishing U.S. authority to build what would become the Panama Canal—would be appreciated. These appeared in the 19 December 1901 supplement to *Leslie's Weekly,* the paper to which Nast had first submitted his work forty-five years earlier. His artistic career had come full cycle.

During the last years of his life Nast did paintings, usually on Civil War themes and sometimes on commission. They did not bring enough income to pay off his debts. In March 1902 President Theodore Roosevelt, an admirer of Nast's art, offered him the position of U.S. consul in Guayaquil, Ecuador. Nast accepted, though he would have preferred a European assignment, and disembarked on 1 July. During his miserable stay there he contracted yellow fever and died on 7 December 1902 at the age of sixty-two. Over fifty years later his house in Morristown, New Jersey, was declared a national historic landmark, and in 1956 the U.S. government placed a plaque commemorating Thomas Nast in the barracks in Landau-Pfalz, Germany, where he was born.

Nast was rather short, with brown hair and beard and a somewhat long nose—though not bent as in his self-portraits, in which he usually chided himself and pictured himself as plump. He was meticulous in his dress. The most-reproduced portraits of Nast are a solemn photograph taken by Mathew Brady when the artist was a young man, a painting of himself contemplating the bust of Ward, and another photograph taken shortly before he sailed for Guayaquil. It should be noted that the word *nasty* is derived from Middle English and predates the artist even though it has been applied to some of his cartoons.

In the thousands of drawings Nast produced in his career, he promoted rights for laborers, defense spending, and temperance; commented on foreign affairs; denigrated woman suffrage (Curtis supported it); poked fun at social foibles; exposed scandals; and warned of the dangers of communism, anarchy, industrial pollution, and train travel. His art was one-sided in that it starkly delineated individuals, parties, and issues as either good or bad, but he could not have hinted at opposing viewpoints in his work without weakening its effectiveness. A study of Nast's drawings helps one to gain greater insight into the events and everyday life of America from the Civil War through the 1880s. The pictures become more amusing and insightful the more one knows about the situations and the people portrayed. No other cartoonist so powerfully captured and expressed the spirit of an age.

Biography:

Albert Bigelow Paine, *Th. Nast, His Period and His Pictures* (Gloucester, Mass.: Peter Smith, 1967).

References:

Albert Boime, "Thomas Nast and French Art," *American Art Journal,* 4 (1972): 43–65;

Alexander B. Callow Jr., "What are You Going to Do about It? The Crusade against the Tweed Ring," *New-York Historical Society Quarterly,* 49 (1965): 117–142;

Morton Keller, *The Art and Politics of Thomas Nast* (New York: Oxford University Press, 1968);

Wendy Wiek Reaves, "Thomas Nast and the President," *American Art Journal,* 19 (1987): 60–71;

Thomas Nast St. Hill, "His Grandson Recalls the Life and Death of Thomas Nast," *American Heritage,* 22, no. 6 (1971): 81–96;

"Thomas Nast in the Age of Grant," *Hayes Historical Journal,* 8 (1989): 52–60.

Papers:

The main collections of Thomas Nast's works, papers, scrapbooks, and memorabilia are housed in two institutions in the artist's adopted city of Morristown, New Jersey: the MacCulloch Hall Historical Museum and the Joint Free Public Library of Morristown/Morris Township. Together these institutions established the Thomas Nast Society, which publishes the annual *Journal of the Thomas Nast Society,* and a semiannual newsletter, *The Nasthead.* The Rutherford B. Hayes Presidential Center in Fremount, Ohio, houses a collection of notes, photocopies, and sale catalogues related to Nast. Several of Nast's original cartoons are located in the Peter Mayo Collection at the State Historical Society in Columbia, Missouri.

Violet Oakley

(10 June 1874 – 25 February 1961)

Susan Hamburger
Pennsylvania State University

BOOKS: *Cathedral of Compassion: Dramatic Outline of the Life of Jane Addams, 1860–1935* (Philadelphia: Press of Lyon & Armor, 1915);

The Holy Experiment: A Message to the World from Pennsylvania (Philadelphia: Privately printed, 1922);

International Supplement and Key to the Holy Experiment in French, German, Italian, Spanish and Japanese (Philadelphia: Privately printed, circa 1922);

Law Triumphant: Containing the Opening of the Book of the Law and the Miracle of Geneva (Philadelphia: Privately printed, 1933);

La Présence Divine à la Société des Nations (Geneva: Kundig, 1937);

Samuel F. B. Morse: A Dramatic Outline of the Life of the Father of Telegraphy & the Founder of the National Academy of Design (Philadelphia: Cogslea Studio Publications, 1939);

Great Women of the Bible: A Series of Paintings in the Room of the Pastoral Aid Society: First Presbyterian Church, Germantown, Philadelphia (Philadelphia: Eldon, 1949);

The Holy Experiment: Our Heritage from William Penn (Philadelphia: Cogslea Studio Publications, 1950).

SELECTED BOOKS ILLUSTRATED: Longfellow, Henry Wadsworth, *Evangeline: A Tale of Acadie,* illustrated by Oakley and Jessie Willcox Smith (Boston: Houghton, Mifflin, 1897);

Train, Elizabeth Phipps, *A Marital Liability* (Philadelphia: Lippincott, 1897);

Troubetzkoy, Amélie Rives, *A Damsel Errant* (Philadelphia: Lippincott, 1898);

King, Charles, *From School to Battle-field: A Story of the War Days* (Philadelphia: Lippincott, 1899);

Skinner, Charles Montgomery, *Do-nothing Days* (Philadelphia: Lippincott, 1899);

Skinner, *With Feet to the Earth* (Philadelphia & London: Lippincott, 1899);

Walford, Lucy Bethia, *A Little Legacy, and Other Stories* (Chicago: Herbert S. Stone, 1899).

Violet Oakley (photograph by Florence Maynard)

PERIODICALS: *Ladies' Home Journal,* 1897–1898;
McClure's, 1898;
Harper's, 1898;
Collier's, 1898–1908;
Woman's Home Companion, 1899;
Philadelphia Press, 1901;
Everybody's, 1901–1902;
Book Buyer, 1902;
St. Nicholas, 1902;
Century, 1902–1912;
Scribner's Magazine, 1907;

Architectural League Yearbook, 1914–1916;
American Magazine of Art, 1922;
International Studio, 1926;
Mentor, 1926;
Christian Science Monitor, 1929–1934;
New York Herald Tribune, 1930;
National Geographic, 1935;
Survey Graphic, 1935;
Philadelphia Forum, 1944;
Philadelphia Inquirer, 1948.

Violet Oakley–a versatile portraitist, illustrator, stained-glass artisan, and muralist–earned a reputation as the first American woman artist to succeed in the predominantly male architectural field of mural decoration. She began her career as a magazine and book illustrator, and while her peak period of creating for the literary and popular periodicals lasted from 1897 to 1908, Oakley continued to contribute illustrations while working on her murals. Her strong commitment to her religion and world peace influenced her art as well as her life.

Oakley was born in Bergen Heights, New Jersey, to the artistic family of Arthur Edmund Oakley and Cornelia Swain Oakley. Both of her grandfathers, George Oakley and William Swain, belonged to the National Academy of Design, and two of her aunts studied painting in Munich with Frank Duveneck. Oakley believed that her compulsion to draw was "hereditary and chronic." In an interview with the *Baltimore Sun* (20 August 1922) she commented that she must have been "a monk in some earlier state of existence. . . . The abbesses and sisters were too busy nursing the sick and doing fine needleworks. I never heard of them illuminating manuscripts. I am quite sure I was a monk."

The youngest of three children, Violet followed her sisters, Cornelia and Hester, in learning the acceptable feminine skills of poetry writing, piano playing, and sketching. While Hester attended Vassar College, Violet's asthma prevented her from obtaining a college education. Her parents thought attending college would be too rigorous for Violet's physical condition, but she never let the asthma impede her artistic education or career.

In 1892, at the age of eighteen, Oakley commuted to New York City to study at the Art Students League with Irving R. Wiles and Carroll Beckwith. Violet and Hester joined their parents on a European trip from 1895 to 1896, and Violet took art lessons in Paris from the symbolist painters Edmond Aman-Jean and Raphaël Colin at the Académie Montparnasse and in England from Charles Lazar. From Aman-Jean she learned the art nouveau style of elegant curving lines that she used in her illustrations.

When the family returned to the United States, Violet enrolled in classes taught by Henry Thouron at the Pennsylvania Academy of the Fine Arts in Philadelphia. At the academy she studied portraiture under Cecelia Beaux and took Joseph De Camp's life class. The family relocated from South Orange, New Jersey, to Philadelphia the same year. The father's ill health and the family's declining income prompted Hester and Violet to focus their artistic pursuits on the lucrative magazine-illustration field. The sisters collaborated on illustrated stories and poems that they published in *McClure's, Harper's,* and *The Woman's Home Companion.* Violet sketched scenes in charcoal for Hester's romantic fiction and poetry. Seeking the instruction of America's foremost illustrator, Howard Pyle, Violet Oakley enrolled in his classes at the Drexel Institute for one semester. Pyle taught Oakley practical illustration and technique, illustrative treatment of historical subjects, and drawing from the costumed model. More important, he instilled in his students the need to paint thoughts and ideas, to use light and shadow, to be historically accurate in costume and setting, and to use imagination. She assimilated his belief that illustration was "teaching under an aesthetic form" and applied his techniques first to book illustration and then to stained-glass and mural decoration.

From 1897 to 1902 Oakley's work appeared as book and magazine illustrations. She received commissions from magazines to illustrate stories and create covers with spiritual or religious themes, usually centered on a holiday such as Easter or Christmas. Pyle's stylistic influence is readily apparent in Oakley's large, expressive figures in a shallow space; broad, flat areas; draftsmanship; and design sense. For the Lenten cover of *Collier's Weekly* (20 May 1899) Oakley depicts a young girl seated in front of a Gothic cathedral doorway offering a devotional candle to a woman in medieval robes. The woman's downcast eyes and the girl's upturned face suggest a solemn, pious moment. On the June 1902 cover of *Everybody's Magazine* Oakley depicts a contemporary scene of a woman reading a letter to Henrietta Cozens, who is picking a bloom from a cascading bower of pink roses. The dichotomy between the secular and sacred images of Christmas appears in Oakley's December 1902 cover of *St. Nicholas.* Two adolescents sit in front of Saint Nick leaning over an oversized illuminated book opened to facing pages of a religious scene and a secular celebration. Saint Nick appears to be instructing the children in the different meanings of Christmas.

Illustration by Violet Oakley for the January 1908 issue of
Century Magazine

In the December 1902 issue of *Everybody's Magazine* Oakley's seven illustrations and unique caption lettering greatly enhance George M. Baxter's "The Story of Vashti," the biblical Persian queen. Framing each panel with a decorative frieze of rosettes and a winged disk at the top and the oriental block-letter caption on the bottom, Oakley's people and animals extended above the frame to give the images a three-dimensional quality. The historical accuracy of the costumes and decorative details antedate and indicate the directions she would take with her murals. Pyle recognized the similarities in the decorative styles of Oakley and another student, Jessie Willcox Smith, and obtained a commission for the classmates to collaborate on the illustrations for Henry Wadsworth Longfellow's *Evangeline: A Tale of Acadie* (1897). When Oakley

and Smith showed their original illustrations for *Evangeline* at the Pennsylvania Academy of the Fine Arts annual exhibition in January 1898, the artwork earned a favorable reception. The classmates never collaborated again but pursued their art in different directions.

Between 1897 and 1899 Oakley's work appeared in at least six books as frontispieces and interior illustrations. She contributed romantic drawings for Elizabeth Phipps Train's *A Marital Liability* (1897) and Civil War scenes for Charles King's *From School to Battle-field: A Story of the War Days* (1899). In *A Marital Liability* Oakley captures an emotional moment, employing intricate detailing of the room furnishings (clock on mantle, upholstery pattern on the woman's chair) to make a personal connection to the characters. Following Pyle's mental-projection technique, she visualizes the most exciting moments in *From School to Battle-field* to create dramatic scenes using various styles. In one image Oakley's softened lines and the dramatic use of light and dark suggest movement. Soldiers gathered around a mounted trooper are drawn in bold outline with an upward perspective toward the frightened horse. For these early illustrations Oakley used charcoal for black-and-white works, heavily outlining the principal forms. For color reproduction she overlaid transparent watercolor on the fixatif-sprayed charcoal.

Oakley's signature style, reminiscent of illuminated manuscripts, executed on a grand scale in her murals, appeared early in her book-illustration work, particularly in Amélie Rives Troubetzkoy's *A Damsel Errant* (1898). She created three illustrations as if they were woodcuts surrounded by a scrollwork border and continuing a gothic script caption. These pieces compare favorably with the woodcuts of Edward Burne-Jones and the lettering of William Morris at the Kelmscott Press. In her later book illustrations, particularly the frontispiece of *Samuel F. B. Morse: A Dramatic Outline of the Life of the Father of Telegraphy & the Founder of the National Academy of Design* (1939), Oakley abandoned the elaborate drawing for a simple crayon rendering of her subject, similar to her sketches of the League of Nations ambassadors.

Oakley (encouraged by Pyle) concentrated on producing stained-glass windows and murals. By 1899 Oakley produced the Epiphany Window for the Church Glass and Decorating Company in New York. She received her first major mural commission in 1900 to decorate All Angels' Church in New York City with two large murals, one glass mosaic altarpiece, and five stained-glass lancet windows. Prior to her completing the project, leading art critic Sadakichi Hartmann commented in *A History of American Art* (1903) that Oakley's work in All Angels' Church "promises to be well drawn, and interesting in its line, space, and colour composition with a delightful parallelism and repetition of figures. The religious feeling, which is generally missing in such works, is quite pronounced in Violet Oakley's art." In all, she produced eight stained-glass windows between 1900 and 1911 for private and public buildings.

Oakley depended on narrative and/or a moral stance to convey her art. Using her experience as an illustrator, she imbued her murals with subjects from popular culture as well as from an idealistic, updated traditional background. In 1898 Oakley and Smith rented studio and living space with another Pyle student, Jessie H. Dowd. When Dowd became ill and returned home to Ohio in 1899, Oakley and Smith designed and produced a Friendship Calendar for 1900 as a going-away gift. Another art-school colleague, Elizabeth Shippen Green, replaced Dowd in the household. When the three artists needed more working space, they first moved to the Red Rose Inn in Villanova, where they were joined by Henrietta Cozens, who became their gardener and household manager. Oakley enjoyed reciting poetry as she walked across the peaceful grounds. Although a cooperative venture for the women, Oakley declared in the *Philadelphia Press* for 24 October 1901, "This is not going to be an artists' colony at all. We have grown tired of working in the midst of trolley cars, drays, and all the noise of heavy traffic, so we three are going out where green trees grow, where the cows roam and where the air is pure, and quietness prevails."

When a new owner purchased the inn in 1905, the artists turned to Dr. and Mrs. George Woodward, their benefactors, to secure other living-studio space in the country. The Woodwards rented to the artists part of their Germantown property, which the women named Cogslea (for Cozens, Oakley, Green, and Smith), where Oakley had a spacious area to work on her murals. To the extended household Oakley, the youngest, brought her aging mother. The three friends pooled their resources to afford a grander lifestyle than any one of them could provide on her own, maintaining this living arrangement with a multitude of relatives for fourteen years until Green married. Smith built Cogshill nearby. Oakley and Edith Emerson, a student of Oakley's at the Pennsylvania Academy of Fine Arts, continued to live at Cogslea. Emerson later turned Cogslea, on St. George's Road above Allen's Lane in the Mount Airy section of Philadelphia, into the Violet Oakley Memorial Foundation to house Oakley's artwork. After Emerson died in 1986, the foundation dispersed the contents, sold the house, and disbanded.

Religion played an important role in Oakley's personal and professional life. She converted to Christian Scientist from Episcopalian; her faith helped cure her of her debilitating asthma and allowed her to tackle the physically exhausting mural work. She believed an artist should inspire and instruct. The slender woman with blue eyes and a delicate face had tremendous stamina. Oakley's strong personality also vaulted her to the position of matriarchal head of the household.

On 21 July 1902 architect Joseph Miller Huston awarded Oakley a prestigious commission to paint eighteen murals in the Governor's Reception Room in the Pennsylvania State Capitol in Harrisburg, which she titled *The Founding of the State of Lib-*

Illustrations by Oakley for Amélie Rives Troubetzkoy's A Damsel Errant *(1898)*

erty Spiritual (completed in 1906). It was the largest public commission given to a woman artist in the United States at that time.

Oakley's method of working included extensive research. After receiving Huston's commission, she left with her mother in 1903 for a six-month trip to study in Europe. She began her trip in England, where she researched seventeenth-century costumes and interiors, the life of William Penn, his philosophy of universal brotherhood, and ancient law. Oakley was determined to understand Penn's Quaker beliefs, and as Malcolm Vaughan stated in the *New York Herald Tribune* for 16 February 1930, to "express the religious feeling behind the founding of Pennsylvania." She wrote in "The Vision of William Penn," in *Pennsylvania History* for October 1953, "Thus the paintings in the Governor's Room were so planned as to deal exclusively with the founding of the state of Pennsylvania and stopped just short of recording any event within the life of the state itself—bringing Penn, in the prow of the ship *Welcome,* only within sight of his promised land."

In Italy, Oakley and her mother spent two months in Florence and toured Perugia, Venice, and Assisi. Oakley studied the old masters' fresco- and wall-painting techniques and discovered the Florentine Trecento (the fourteenth century in Italian literature and art), which she later incorporated into her own home and into the Vassar College Alumnae House Living Room commission, *The Great Wonder: A Vision of the Apocalypse,* in 1924. Throughout her travels Oakley drew bits and pieces of landscapes, architecture, and ethnic costumes into sketchbooks for later reference. As part of her research for the Penn mural, she copied the works of the Quattrocento masters, modeling her work after Vittore Carpaccio's mural paintings. Oakley returned to Italy in 1909 to study wall painting.

Not content to work on one project at a time, Oakley juggled several commissions—books, portrait drawings and paintings, posters, illuminated manuscripts, medals, and awards—while she created the capitol murals. Oakley, unlike many of her colleagues, did not use assistants to paint her large-scale murals, preferring to complete the entire project herself. Between 1913 and 1917 Oakley also taught design and a special class in mural decoration for advanced students at the Pennsylvania Academy of the Fine Arts. During this time she met Edith Emerson, who joined the Cogslea household in 1913.

Although the mural commission paid well ($20,000 for the Governor's Reception Room), Oakley had to spread the money over four years. Near the end of the project, her finances were low, but Oakley was too proud to ask for help. Jessie Willcox

Smith, noticing Oakley's need for money, gave her a check for $1,000. When Oakley began to cry, Smith, nicknamed The Mint by her friends, responded, "That's all right, Violet, I can do an Ivory soap ad anytime and make that up right away" (S. Michael Schnessel interview with Edith Emerson on 7 September 1976).

Her work on the Governor's Reception Room garnered Oakley much publicity. She won the Gold Medal of Honor from the Pennsylvania Academy of the Fine Arts in 1905 and a Medal of Honor from the Architectural League of New York in 1916, both firsts for a woman artist. Edwin Austin Abbey, commissioned to decorate the rotunda, House and Senate chambers, and the Supreme and Superior Court Room of the Pennsylvania State Capitol, died suddenly in 1911 before completing the last two rooms. While working on a mural for the Cuyahoga County Courthouse in Cleveland, Ohio, Oakley received the commission to complete the contract for the Senate chamber and Supreme and Superior Court Room in the Pennsylvania State Capitol, for which she was paid $100,000. As she stated in "The Vision of William Penn": "I was asked by the Board of Commissioners to undertake that part of his contract with the State which at the time of his death he had not even begun. I was not asked, as has been mistakenly reported, to finish any of the Paintings which he had begun or planned. That was done by his own Assistant in his Studio in England." Oakley did suggest, however, that one mural, *The Camp of the American Army at Valley Forge, February 1778,* which Abbey had finished for the Senate chamber, be moved to the House of Representatives chamber to keep all of his work in one room.

Oakley began a sixteen-year project to create nine murals for the Senate chamber titled *The Creation and Preservation of the Union* (completed in 1920) and sixteen murals in the Supreme and Superior Court Room titled *The Opening of the Book of Law* (finished in 1927). These last sixteen, the history of citizens' legal rights designed to resemble an illuminated manuscript scroll unrolled, are mounted on wooden stretchers and do not adhere directly to the walls. In all, Oakley painted forty-three murals for the Pennsylvania State Capitol in which she expressed her desire and hope for "world peace, equal rights, and faith in the work of unification of the Peoples of the Earth." In creating additional murals, Oakley recognized the opportunity to express her deep feelings about the spiritual liberty upon which Pennsylvania was founded. She wrote in "The Vision of William Penn" that she "burned to build a great Monument, not only as its Memorial, but that it might *live again*." Oakley included her equal passion for world peace in the panel *International Understanding and Unity* in the Senate chamber, conceived in 1912 when the Paris Peace Conference discussed forming the League of Nations. The first paintings in the Senate chamber, unveiled in 1917, and the final paintings in the Supreme and Superior Court Room, unveiled ten years later, Oakley dedicated to the cause of peace.

In 1922 Oakley published the three-hundred-copy limited edition *The Holy Experiment: A Message to the World from Pennsylvania,* reproducing the murals from the governor's reception room and Senate chamber. The favorable publicity Oakley received for the book gratified her. In a letter dated 1 March 1924 to Stanley R. Yarnall she thanked him for his "beautiful tribute to the spirit of The Holy Experiment. What you have said comes as the greatest encouragement and at a time when I needed it most—for many different reasons" (Charles Roberts Autograph Collection, Haverford College Library). Jessie Willcox Smith nicknamed Oakley Elaborate Violet for the talent in illumination and calligraphy with which she decorated the book.

Oakley's beliefs manifested themselves in her art and in her social activism for woman suffrage, world peace, and international government. She went to Geneva, Switzerland, in June 1927, one month after completing the paintings in the Supreme and Superior Court Room, as a self-appointed ambassador when the United States refused to join the League of Nations; she "wished to observe the development of International Law." Oakley stayed three years, drawing sixty portraits of the ambassadors and dignitaries. In September 1929 she attended the laying of the cornerstone for the library of the League of Nations and planned "to go to Geneva in time for the September [1936] session of the Assembly and make the presentation [of her original drawings] in person" (Violet Oakley letter to Harrison Streeter Hires, 8 June 1936, Hires Collection, Haverford College Library). An American committee of donors, headed by Oakley, presented the drawings to the secretary general and librarian in October 1936.

When the League of Nations adjourned, Oakley rented an Italian villa outside Florence to work on a commission to design an altarpiece for the Graphic Sketch Club's sanctuary in a former church. For *The Life of Moses* Oakley studied Egyptian motifs and imagery, combining them with medieval format and Christian religious symbolism. She spent 1927 to 1929 working with local craftsmen who were experienced in constructing artwork for churches.

Frontispiece for Cathedral of Compassion *(1915), Oakley's biography of the social reformer who founded Hull House in Chicago*

In order to publish the privately printed books *The Holy Experiment: A Message to the World from Pennsylvania* (1922), *Law Triumphant: Containing the Opening of the Book of the Law and the Miracle of Geneva* (1933), and *Samuel F. B. Morse,* Oakley solicited sponsorships from subscribers to the signed, limited editions. She had a keen sense of self-promotion and sent out typed and, later, calligraphic letters to potential supporters. For her October 1950 publication of *The Holy Experiment* Oakley also gave "a brief reading from the text to which all the advance subscribers will be invited—and [I] will present their special copies" (Violet Oakley letter to Amy Post, 31 July 1950, Charles Roberts Autograph Collection, Haverford College Library).

The art world, taken with surrealism and abstraction, bypassed Violet Oakley's religious symbolism in the 1930s. Art critic and editor of *The Arts* Forbes Watson in his article "In the Galleries: '33 Moderns' and Violet Oakley" harshly evaluated an exhibit of her League of Nations sketches, drawings from Florence, and reproductions from the Pennsylvania State Capitol murals in juxtaposition to thirty-three moderns at the Grand Central Galleries in New York City. He thought she represented "completely the wearisome, prayerful academic art against which the brighter spirits of today stand" and her pictures reeked of "conventional lifelessness." A critic for the 8 February 1930 issue of *The Art News* thought the "drawings display all the conventional virtues. Her line is crisp and incisive and although the gallery of celebrities is almost appallingly large, a certain degree of character is found in most of her work." In London the previous summer the same exhibit had drawn a different reaction from a British art critic for the *London Morning Post.* He compared her work to Abbey's and Pyle's and found "she conveys to her mural paintings much of the spirit and technical distinction which characterized the compositions of those brilliant men. She has thought out her designs with considerable care and breadth, and they form a stirring and withal dignified commentary on Penn's conceptions of Liberty, Justice, and Union." In 1942 an exhibit at the Woodmere Gallery drew a good review in the 15 March 1942 issue of the *Art Digest:* "Always astonishing in its virtuosity and variety, her art has the great common denominator of an idealism that can be read into an army altar triptych defined for the battlefield a message of peace. . . . If at times, her idealism of character robs it of personal punch, it also goes behind personality to what Miss Oakley herself believes—that there is a noble idealism in human nature."

Despite criticism from American art critics, Oakley continued to work and win awards. In 1940 she received the three-hundred-dollar Walter Lippincott Prize for the best figure in oil from the Pennsylvania Academy of the Fine Arts, and one year later she received the Emily Drayton Taylor Medal "for distinguished service in art" from the Society of Miniature Painters. Oakley began winning awards in 1904 when she won two medals at the Saint Louis Exposition—a gold for the watercolor illustrations for "The Story of Vashti" in *Everybody's Magazine* and a silver for the mural decoration of All Angels' Church. And in 1915 she won the medal of honor at the Panama-Pacific Exposition in San Francisco. The Pennsylvania Academy of the Fine Arts awarded Oakley several more awards: in 1922 the Philadelphia Prize for a portrait of Lt. Howard Henry Houston Woodward; in 1932 the Joseph Pennell Memorial Medal, by the Philadelphia Water Color Club, for distinguished work in the graphic arts; and in 1948 the Mary Smith Prize for a panel from *Great*

Women of the Bible in the First Presbyterian Church, Germantown, Philadelphia. Oakley also received the Woodmere Prize from the Woodmere Gallery, Philadelphia, in 1947, a gold medal from the Springside School, Chestnut Hill, Philadelphia, and a gold medal in 1950 as one of the twelve "distinguished daughters of Pennsylvania." One of her most impressive awards was an honorary doctor of laws degree which she received from the Drexel Institute in 1948 for her "portrayal of that which is noblest in mankind . . . in her paintings where love of mankind prevails over hatred and prejudice, spiritual aspiration over material ambition, and respect for Law and Order over those base emotions which would degrade mankind and destroy civilization."

Throughout her long career Oakley exhibited her drawings, portraits, studies for her murals, and watercolors at the Pennsylvania Academy of the Fine Arts. Between 1924 and 1953 she hung eighty-eight pieces ranging from hard pastels, sanguine, red and white chalk, crayon, and charcoal to watercolor in juried shows at the academy. In 1973 the academy mounted an exhibit of "The Pennsylvania Academy and Its Women," including an early charcoal-and-pencil drawing, *June,* purchased from Oakley in 1903 for the academy's permanent collection. Later additions to the permanent collection include Oakley's oils on canvas *Tragic Muse* (1912) and *Henry Howard Houston Woodward* (1921).

Even though murals went out of fashion and commissions dried up, Oakley continued her large-scale work. She completed twenty-five portable triptychs during World War II for the Citizens' Committee for the Army and Navy chapels. Oakley organized the Cogslea Academy at Lake George in the 1940s for summer art courses. She also continued illustrating books. Oakley wrote and illustrated biographies of Samuel F. B. Morse in 1939 and Jane Addams in 1955. The latter biography arose from Oakley's active membership in the Women's International League for Peace and Freedom, founded by Addams in 1915. Oakley received one last major mural project for the Jennings Room in the First Presbyterian Church of Germantown. Oakley completed this *Great Women of the Bible* series between 1945 and 1949, the year she turned seventy-five. The room resembles the Governor's Reception Room in proportion and design, and Oakley used her usual style of dramatic presentation with scriptural text bordering the historically accurate paintings. Oakley continued painting and working at her Cogslea studio until her death in 1961.

References:

Helen Goodman, "Violet Oakley," *Arts Magazine,* 54 (October 1979): 7;

Charlotte Herzog, "A Rose by Any Other Name; Violet Oakley, Jessie Willcox Smith, and Elizabeth Shippen Green," *Woman's Art Journal,* 14 (Fall/Winter 1993–1994): 11–16;

Patricia Likos, "Violet Oakley," *Philadelphia Museum of Art Bulletin,* 75 (June 1979): 2–27;

Likos, "Violet Oakley, Lady Mural Painter," *Pennsylvania Heritage,* 14 (Fall 1988): 14–21;

Clara R. Mason, "Violet Oakley's Latest Work," *America Magazine of Art,* 21 (March 1930): 130–138;

Sally Mills, *Violet Oakley; The Decoration of the Alumnae House Living Room* (Poughkeepsie, N.Y.: Vassar College Art Gallery, 1984);

Harrison S. Morris, "Miss Violet Oakley's Mural Decorations," *Century,* 70 (May–October 1905): 265–268;

Preserving a Palace of Art: A Guide to the Projects of the Pennsylvania Capitol Preservation Committee (Harrisburg, Pa.: Capitol Preservation Committee, 1993);

S. Michael Schnessel, *Jessie Willcox Smith* (New York: Crowell, 1977);

Catherine Connell Stryker, *The Studios at Cogslea, Delaware Art Museum, February 20–March 28, 1976* (Wilmington: Delaware Art Museum, 1976);

Malcolm Vaughan, "Violet Oakley: Painter of Peace," *New York Herald Tribune,* 16 February 1930, XIII: 16–17, 29;

"Violet Oakley on Visit Here Talks of Work," *Baltimore Sun,* 20 August 1922, IV: 6;

Forbes Watson, "In the Galleries: '33 Moderns' and Violet Oakley," *Arts,* 16 (February 1930): 423–424, 432;

Mahonri Sharp Young, "Violet Oakley: A Message for the World," *American Art & Antiques,* 1 (July–August 1978): 50–57.

Archives:

Violet Oakley papers and preliminary sketches are found at the Archives of American Art, Smithsonian Institution, Washington, D.C. Violet Oakley Correspondence, 1924–1950, is located in the Charles Roberts Autograph Collection, and the collection of the Harrison Streeter Hires Letters, 1916–1955, is located at Haverford College, Haverford, Pennsylvania. Additional correspondence is housed in the Violet Oakley Collection, 1933–1979, of the Swarthmore College Peace Collection and in the Friends Historical Library, Swarthmore, Pennsylvania. The bulk of artwork from the Violet Oakley Foundation is housed at the Pennsylvania Academy of the Fine Arts, Philadelphia; some pieces are in the Woodmere Art Gallery, Philadelphia.

Maxfield Parrish
(25 July 1870 – 30 March 1966)

Michael Scott Joseph
Rutgers University Libraries

SELECTED BOOKS ILLUSTRATED: Baum, L. Frank, *Mother Goose in Prose* (Chicago: Way & Williams, 1897);

Read, Opie, *Bolanyo: A Novel* (Chicago: Way & Williams, 1897);

Rayner, Emma, *Free to Serve* (Boston: Copeland & Day, 1897);

Lee, Albert, *The Knave of Hearts: A Fourth of July Comedietta* (New York: Russell, 1897);

Butler, William Mill, *Whist Reference Book* (Philadelphia: Yorkston, 1898);

Grahame, Kenneth, *The Golden Age* (London & New York: John Lane at Bodley Head, 1899);

Irving, Washington, *A History of New York from the Beginning of the World to the End of the Dutch Dynasty* . . . (New York: Russell, 1900);

Grahame, Kenneth, *Dream Days* (London & New York: John Lane at Bodley Head, 1902);

Smith, Arthur Cosslett, *The Turquoise Cup and The Desert* (New York: Scribners, 1903);

Field, Eugene, *Poems of Childhood* (New York: Scribners, 1904);

Wharton, Edith, *Italian Villas and Their Gardens* (New York: Century, 1904);

Carryl, Guy Wetmore, *The Garden of Years and Other Poems* (New York & London: Putnam, 1904);

Wiggin, Kate Douglas, and Nora A. Smith, eds., *The Arabian Nights, Their Best-Known Tales* (New York & London: Scribners, 1909);

Scudder, Horace Elisha, ed., *The Children's Book* (Boston & New York: Houghton Mifflin, 1910);

Hawthorne, Nathaniel, *A Wonder Book and Tanglewood Tales for Girls and Boys* (New York: Duffield, 1910);

Hawthorne, Hildegarde, *Lure of the Garden* (New York: Century, 1911);

Palgrave, Francis Turner, ed., *The Golden Treasury of Songs and Lyrics* (New York: Duffield, 1911);

Caine, Thomas H. H., ed., *King Albert's Book* (London: Daily Telegraph, 1914);

Saunders, Louise, *The Knave of Hearts* (New York: Scribners, 1925);

Maxfield Parrish

Stein, Ealeen, *Troubador Tales* (Indianapolis: Bobbs-Merrill, 1929).

PERIODICALS: *Harper's Weekly,* 1895–1906; *Ladies' Home Journal,* 1896–1915, 1920, 1930–1931; *Scribner's Magazine,* 1897–1905, 1923; *Century,* 1898–1917; *Life,* 1899–1924; *Collier's,* 1904–1913, 1929, 1936.

No American artist gained greater popularity or commercial success during the first three decades of the twentieth century than Maxfield Parrish. His combination of ethereal colors, exotic characters, and fanciful castles became a feature of American popular culture through his work for the major mass-circulation illustrated magazines, including *Scribner's Magazine, Century, Life,* and *Collier's.* His advertising posters for a multitude of products, ranging from Jell-o to Fisk tires; his children's book illustrations; and his art prints made the Parrish name known throughout the country. The latter work, begun in the early 1920s, became the avenue by which Parrish achieved his widest acclaim; by 1936 his rocky landscapes and idealized maidens were nearly unrivaled in popularity. The 17 February 1936 issue of *Time* reported that "as far as the sale of expensive color reproductions is concerned, the three most popular artists in the world are van Gogh, Cezanne, and Maxfield Parrish."

Maxfield Parrish was born 25 July 1870 to affluent Quaker parents, Stephen and Elizabeth Bancroft Parrish, of 324 North Tenth Street, Philadelphia. Although christened Frederick, as a young man he adopted his paternal grandmother's maiden name, Maxfield, signing his earliest works "Frederick Maxfield Parrish." Professionally, he dropped his first name entirely after 1896–signing his works "Maxfield Parrish," or "M. P."–but to his friends and family he preferred to be known as Fred.

Parrish applied himself to drawing at age five under the tutelage of his father–a competent painter and draftsman and an expert etcher–whom Maxfield would come to regard as his most influential teacher. In his early teens Parrish accompanied his parents on a trip to Europe; he illustrated many of the letters he sent home to friends and relatives with the kinds of caricatures that would resurface later in his decorations for the University of Pennsylvania's Mask and Wig Club.

In 1888 Parrish enrolled at Haverford College and went on to graduate, a member of Phi Kappa Sigma, in 1892. While a student he accepted many commissions from the colleges in the Philadelphia area and sold his first picture, a drawing of clowns, to the architect Walter Cape. After graduation Parrish sought a job in an architect's office but was advised to get an art education first. He entered the Pennsylvania Academy of Fine Arts, where he studied under Robert W. Vonnoh and Thomas P. Anschutz. His predilection for architectural design would later find distinctive expression in The Oaks, the artist's magnificent and idiosyncratic estate in New Hampshire.

After leaving the academy Parrish continued to enjoy a close, collegial relationship with his father. In 1892 and 1893 they shared a seaside studio at Annisquam, Massachusetts, where in August 1893 Parrish produced his first oil painting, *Moon-*

rise. Later that year the young artist exhibited *Moonrise* at the Philadelphia Art Club. With hopes of placing his son in the Drexel Institute where he could study under the distinguished painter and illustrator Howard Pyle, Stephen Parrish put together a portfolio of his son's drawings. He was surprised to be told his son had already advanced beyond the rudimentary level at which the classes were taught. Although Pyle raised no objection to young Parrish's auditing his classes if he wished to, after a brief while Parrish withdrew from the institute, finding the classes to be as Pyle had described them.

In the 1890s Americans did not view the division between fine and commercial art to be as significant as it came to seem following the Armory Show and the evolution of diverse styles of abstract art. Trained as an artist, Parrish regarded commercial art as the natural and inevitable field for earning his livelihood, and accordingly, with expectations of increasing the kind of employment he had undertaken as a student, he opened a studio at the southeast corner of Thirteenth and Walnut Streets in Philadelphia. Among his first commissions were the proscenium decorations for the clubhouse and theater of the Mask and Wig Club. These compare stylistically to the illustrations of Walter Crane. Not only was Crane a decided influence upon Parrish, but the young Philadelphian also shared the older artist's fascination with medievalism and Pre-Raphaelite imagery.

Additional commissions for the Mask and Wig Club included a five-foot-by-twelve-foot oil painting of the beloved nursery-rhyme figure Old King Cole for the grillroom. (*Old King Cole* reappeared in 1906 as the subject of one of Parrish's most admired murals in John Jacob Astor's Knickerbocker Hotel. Later in 1935, having outlasted the hotel, *Old King Cole* was removed to another of Astor's hotels, the Saint Regis, where it now presides over the King Cole Bar and Lounge.)

On 1 June 1895 Parrish married Lydia Austin. A talented painter in her own right, Austin also had been brought up a Quaker, in Woodstown, Salem County, New Jersey. She met Parrish when he attended one of her painting classes at Drexel Institute. After the wedding Parrish embarked on a solitary trip–a tour he had long planned for himself, to visit the museums and salons of Brussels, Paris, and London–about which he kept his bride informed through daily, enthusiastic letters. Upon the groom's return the reunited couple moved into an apartment on Twelfth and Spruce Streets. Meanwhile, a cover Parrish had designed for the 1895 Easter number of *Harper's Bazar* had found a warm reception, exposing the artist for the first time to na-

"Baa Baa Black Sheep," a Parrish illlustration for L. Frank Baum's
Mother Goose in Prose *(1897)*

tional attention. Over the next five years Parrish's strong posterlike covers combining bold lines and broad areas of color regularly appeared in at least five different Harper publications as well as in *Scribner's Magazine, Century, Life,* and *St. Nicholas.*

Parrish employed a variety of techniques in this early magazine work. He sometimes drew with a lithographic crayon on Steinbach paper and sometimes used wash, ink, and lithographic crayon. Afterward, he photographed his illustrations and colored the prints. He then varnished them and finished them in oil glazes when they were dry.

With each new issue his reputation increased. By the end of the century Parrish had es-

tablished himself, along with Edward Penfield, Will Bradley, and Louis Rhead, as one of America's most sought-after magazine illustrators. During the latter part of the 1890s the vivid storytelling element in Parrish's designs elicited opportunities for book work. Parrish's first book, *Mother Goose in Prose* (1897), paired the artist with an unknown author, L. Frank Baum, who would later achieve fame for his series of Oz books. The amiable originality of Parrish's fifteen black-and-white stipple and line drawings confirmed his reputation as an illustrator of charm and ability. Ingeniously, the landscape of *Mother Goose in Prose* evokes a bygone era that actually never was. Like

Title page by Parrish for a book by the author of
The Wind in the Willows *(1908)*

the imaginary worlds of the late-Victorian illustrators such as Edmund Dulac and Arthur Rackham, the world of Parrish's *Mother Goose in Prose* fancifully conflates elements of divergent periods and milieus: its castled towns synthesize Gothic and Dutch architectural motifs that invite a mood of nostalgic longing for a moment in history when, one imagines, medieval grandeur might have been wedded to bourgeois civility. Parrish's goblinlike, large-headed characters are also amalgamative, uniting the physical characteristics of child and adult; their awkward, commonplace congeniality reveals the artist at his comical best.

In 1898 Parrish began to construct a new home, which he dubbed "The Oaks," across the valley from his father's home in Cornish, New Hampshire. Many prominent artists and writers—led by the sculptor Augustus Saint-Gaudens and including Paul Manship, Kenyon Cox, Hamlin Garland, Stephen Parrish, and Maxwell Perkins—had colonized Cornish for their summer residences. Parrish and his wife moved into The Oaks before the roof was on, but with the aid of a friend, a local carpenter named George Ruggles, they added to the house as time went on. Eventually The Oaks encompassed fifteen rooms, including a music room where Lydia,

Illustrations by Parrish for Edith Wharton's Italian Villas and Their Gardens *(1904)*

an accomplished pianist, gave concerts. Magnificently and somewhat eccentrically designed, Parrish's home commanded public attention through articles written about it in many architectural journals. Parrish himself often borrowed some of the architectural features from The Oaks for his book and magazine illustrations; its latches and intricate hinges, for example, appear in the castle setting of his illustrations for *The Knave of Hearts* (1925), written by Parrish's neighbor Louise Sanders.

The impressive success of *Mother Goose in Prose* drew other book commissions in its wake, among them Washington Irving's *A History of New York from the Beginning of the World to the End of the Dutch Dynasty* (1900) and Kenneth Grahame's *The Golden Age* (1899) and *Dream Days* (1902). Their timely arrival enabled Parrish to continue to add on to his house, eluding the financial disaster that threatened to dispossess him of The Oaks.

Parrish began the series of nine drawings to *A History of New York* in the spring of 1898, finishing the last of them in September 1899, a year and a half

before publication. Rendered in lithographic crayon, his canny, tongue-in-cheek illustrations are well matched to Irving's satiric history yet make no attempt to reproduce the flavor of the period in which Irving wrote. In his depiction of Olaffe Van Kortlandt's dream of the future New York, Parrish takes the liberty of displaying the puffy Dutchman against the sweeping city skyline–which the artist imagined as turn of the century–thus extending the author's own idea of telescoping eras while absurdly intensifying the contrast. In other drawings as well, such as his illustration of a Native American sampling the colonists' dubious gift of alcohol, Parrish endeavors to give the book a contemporary polish while highlighting its original character. In this illustration a demijohn rearing up as an architectural monument within a row of buildings in the background anticipates Maurice Sendak's architectural milk bottles in *The Night Kitchen*.

Kenneth Grahame's *Golden Age* and *Dream Days* were the last books in which Parrish's illustrations were rendered fully in black and white. Sometimes listed among children's books, Grahame's nostalgic but emotionally reserved volumes about childhood were really intended to attract adults. Parrish's warm and energetic illustrations enliven the works considerably. Drawn from the perspective of a child, a technique to which the artist would occasionally return in the advertising posters of the 1900s, the photographically realistic pictures in *Dream Days* were praised by Sendak in *Caldecott & Co.* as a "meticulously depicted dream world." In *Mutabile Semper* Parrish invented identical chocolatiers, modeling them, as he did for many illustrations, upon himself. They stand upon plinths built on a level five stairs above a boy who gazes upward at the rectangular area between them. While the chocolatiers delimit the sides of the rectangle by which he is framed, the boy's own long, slender boat and its vertical prow and stern imply, in turn, another rectangle embracing the chocolatiers. Similar geometric designs recur throughout Parrish's work and reflect the artist's adherence to Jay Hambridge's neoclassical theory of Dynamic Symmetry, which involves laying out designs and compositions as a series of divisions based upon the rectangle.

In *A Saga of the Seas,* one of the most romantic drawings in *Dream Days,* a gigantic, half-naked pirate looms menacingly above a small, ordinary boy. So huge is the pirate that his head protrudes beyond the upper border even though he stands in a crouch. The boy, gripping a flimsy sword as he would a baseball bat, cannot help but seem weak and insignificant pitted against this paragon of homicidal intent. Parrish adroitly employs a jib pole as a diagonal line to suggest the roll and pitch of the sailing ship upon which they stand, thus further emphasizing the inequality of their mortal combat. The pirate's crouch conveys a sense of balanced weight, of coiled and carefully directed energy, whereas the boy's erect posture implies weightlessness, lack of sea experience, and puniness. The many disparities between the two figures are slyly humorous and dramatically underscore the magical strength of dreams in which such ominous phantoms can effortlessly be dispatched.

Parrish's own life at this time mirrored a similar struggle to the one depicted in *A Saga of the Seas.* At the turn of the century, when Parrish was approaching thirty, he was diagnosed with tuberculosis. Advised that a cold, dry climate could aid his recovery, Parrish retreated to an asylum on Saranac Lake, New York, to spend the winter of 1900–1901. As was his settled routine, he persisted in working despite ill health. While attempting to draw out-of-doors (sitting on one hand to keep it warm while he

"Concerning Witchcraft," an illustration by Parrish for Washington Irving's A History of New York . . . *(1900)*

worked with the other), the temperature dropped so low that his ink froze. Undeterred, Parrish resorted to unfreezable colored glazes. He had worked in colored glazes before coming to Saranac; they now became and would remain his preferred medium. With glazes Parrish could layer color upon color without mixing them and thus imbue his paintings with the limpid, ethereal quality he desired. Critics maintained they seemed to gaze through his colors, like Tiffany glass, rather than at them.

Parrish's accomplishments in color sometimes tend to eclipse his mastery of black-and-white shading and his fine draftsmanship. These skills can be seen to particularly good advantage in the 1902 editions of *Dream Days* and *The Golden Age,* in which the pictures were reproduced as photogravures.

In the spring Parrish left Saranac for Castle Creek, Arizona, where he continued to convalesce and paint. The Century Company financed the excursion for both him and his wife in order to secure the artist's scenic paintings of the mountains, the desert, and the Grand Canyon for the *Century* magazine. Parrish gained an additional $125 for each of the nineteen illustrations he produced for their series *The Great Southwest.* Although he of necessity returned immediately to figural illustration, Parrish's Arizona experience deepened a fascination with landscape painting that he had absorbed from his father and influenced his eventual decision to commit himself to it exclusively.

Upon his return to Cornish, Parrish accepted a commission from the *Ladies' Home Journal* to paint five large illustrations of his favorite lines from the poems of Eugene Field. He finished the first illustration, *The Sugar-Plum Tree* (one of two illustrations reproduced in color), in time for the 1902 Christmas issue, while the remaining four appeared the following year. Typically the paintings elaborate upon the artist's own feelings about specific features within Field's texts rather than engaging the underlying meanings of the poems. That characteristic prompted Edward W. Bok, the *Ladies' Home Journal* editor, to remark that there was perhaps more of Parrish in them than of Field. Nonetheless, among the many contented *Ladies' Home Journal* readers was the publisher, Arthur Scribner, who approached Bok and Parrish to inquire about the possibility of obtaining the illustrated poems for a book. The following year Scribners published a single volume of Field's poetry, augmented by the five commissioned pictures, three additional ones, a cover design, endpapers, and title page. Published in September, *Poems of Childhood* (1904) became one of the better, if not the best, known of all the books Parrish illustrated. It is largely distinguished by including the artist's picture of *The Dinkey-Bird,* which depicts a naked youth riding a swing; it deeply impressed the popular imagination as a symbol of the innocence and freedom of childhood.

When he had shipped off to Scribners the last of the Field paintings, Parrish embarked on a trip to Italy for the Century Company. His mission was to make notes and take photographs to aid him with his illustrations for Edith Wharton's *Italian Villas and Their Gardens* (1904), another series in which the artist would further cultivate his eye for landscape and architecture. Parrish did not meet the author to discuss the project before their separate departures for Italy, nor did he meet her overseas. Wharton always managed to keep one or two steps ahead, or perhaps the artist always managed to keep one or two steps behind. It was the last European trip Parrish and his wife would make together.

During the summer and fall of 1903 Parrish remained at The Oaks and executed the paintings for *Italian Villas and Their Gardens* while simultaneously the author prepared the text in Lenox, Massachusetts. The twenty-six paintings, some of which are reproduced in color, disclose the artist's careful study of form and shadow, subtleties of mood, id-

iom, and lyrical inspiration. These previously unsuspected talents delighted the greater part of the public, who had grown accustomed to his flair for comedy and fantasy. (Parrish would later merge the fanciful and the scenic in two series of paintings for *Collier's, The Arabian Nights* and *Greek Mythology*.) Although his admirers may have expected something else from Parrish, *Italian Villas and Their Gardens* met with favorable critical review. As a reviewer for *The Critic* noted in the February 1905 issue, "Mr. Parrish has performed his part of the task in a delightful and satisfactory way. He has put the best of his art into the subject, and has succeeded in depicting the beauties of the Italian gardens as they have never been depicted before."

The Century Company was pleased enough with *Italian Villas and Their Gardens* to offer Parrish free passage to whatever location he felt inclined to paint, but the artist chose to remain in Cornish, perhaps for personal reasons. In December 1904 Lydia Parrish had given birth—at home, as was the custom of the day—to John Dillwyn Parrish. Before the decade ended, she would bear two more sons: Maxfield Jr., born in August 1906, and Stephen, born in October 1909. Their only daughter, Jean, was born in June 1911. The delighted father often used his mechanical and artistic skills to invent toys and games for the children. As his father had done for him, Parrish encouraged his children to draw and paint, often making cartoons and caricatures for their amusement and instruction. The youngest Parrish, Jean, forged her own style and technique, ultimately carrying the family tradition of painting into the third generation.

The pleasures of fatherhood notwithstanding, Parrish remained steadfast in his primary devotion to his work. As spacious as The Oaks was, he gradually found he craved additional privacy and freedom from the noisy demands of a large family. Consequently, he spent much of his day in a fifteen-room studio he had erected a short walk across the lawn.

As Parrish approached forty, commissions for large paintings and murals began to absorb more of his attention. Having pleased the public with his thirty-foot-by-eight-foot mural, *Old King Cole,* Parrish created the *Pied Piper* in the same comic spirit for the Sheraton Palace of San Francisco in 1906 and *Sing a Song of Sixpence* for the Sherman Hotel in Chicago in 1909. Conceived to be funny, colorful, and graphic, these designs epitomize the commonplace, popular aspect of Parrish's vision and are reminiscent of his boyish caricatures. Other murals executed during the same period, such as his lunette-shaped overmantel panel, *Dream Castle in the Sky*

"Tramp's Thanksgiving," cover design by Parrish for the 18 November 1905 issue of Collier's
magazine (The Delaware Art Museum, Wilmington)

(1908), and his design for *Dream Garden* (1916), constructed in Fabrile glass by the Tiffany studios, demonstrate the private and sentimental side of the artist's imagination. This latter aspect received fuller treatment in Parrish's work during the 1920s and 1930s in the paintings the artist rendered for General Electric and for Brown and Bigelow.

His commission to decorate the Curtis Publishing Company Building in 1911 stands as the most ambitious and extended project Parrish ever accomplished. Consisting primarily of an eighteen-paneled mural for the girls' dining room, the work required five years to complete. When he

accepted the project, Parrish decided to make the studio his permanent residence. The artist's young model, Sue Lewin, who would pose for all but two of the more than two hundred figures of the men and women depicted in the Curtis panels, accompanied Parrish and remained his companion until 1953. As the artist's primary model, her face and figure inspired many of Parrish's most celebrated paintings, including *The Lantern Bearers* (1910), *Rubaiyat* (1915), *Djer Kiss* (1916), *Garden of Allah* (1918), and *Daybreak* (1922). Lewin also modeled for three of the characters in the paintings for Parrish's last and most lavish book, *The Knave of Hearts*.

"Snow White," cover design by Parrish for the August 1912 issue of Hearst's Magazine
*(Fine Arts Museums of San Francisco, lent by the William G. Irwin Charity Foundation,
on permanent loan)*

Although work on the larger panel required an additional three years, Parrish finished the seventeen smaller ones by March 1913. In 1912 the *Ladies' Home Journal* enthusiastically touted the mural as one of Parrish's major achievements, announcing, "All is happiness and beauty. Everyone is young. It seems to be a land where nobody is old. The whole will be a wonderfully successful result of the artist's idea to present a series of paintings that will refresh and 'youthen' the spirit and yet will not tire the eye."

When unveiled, *The Florentine Fête*—the name by which the untitled mural became best known—met a cordial reception. The officials of the Curtis Publishing Company reproduced several panels as

cover designs in the *Ladies' Home Journal,* and every week hundreds of visitors converged upon Independence Square to admire the subtle tans of Tuscan walls, the lush verdure of the Italian gardens, the Veronese-like arches, the colorful costumes, and the exuberant beauty and vivacity of the Florentine youths.

The beginning of Parrish's work on the Curtis mural coincided with the termination of another remarkable arrangement between the artist and *Collier's* magazine. In 1904 Parrish had agreed to allow *Collier's* exclusive rights to his magazine illustrations. Against the obvious argument that by eliminating competition for his services at a time when the public held him in high regard he was needlessly placing a limit on his income, Parrish asserted that the large format and high production values of *Collier's* made it the most desirable magazine for his work. Moreover, he felt that the princely fee of $1,250 per month *Collier's* had offered him was entirely satisfactory, well exceeding all previous arrangements.

In fact, *Collier's* printed many splendid illustrations during this period, some of which later appeared in books, including *The Arabian Nights, Their Best-Known Tales* (1909), edited by Kate Douglas Wiggin and Nora A. Smith, and Nathaniel Hawthorne's *A Wonder Book and Tanglewood Tales for Girls and Boys* (1910). Though he refused to extend the term of the contract, Parrish continued to publish illustrations in *Collier's* for another quarter of a century, including several illustrations from *The Knave of Hearts* in 1929.

Parrish's faculty for comic narration, improvisation, design, and decoration are amply exhibited in the advertising posters he created prolifically during his forties and fifties. His well-known designs for Fisk tires—*Magic Show* (1917); *Fit for a King* (1917); *Mother Goose* (1919); *The Magic Circle* (1919); and a fifth design (never published), *There Was an Old Woman Who Lived in a Shoe*—evince the artist's characteristic habit of finding advertising ideas from the conventional imagery of children's literature. *Fit for a King* imitates the classical composition, theme, and whimsical flourishes of *Old King Cole,* his Knickerbocker mural of 1906, while it also anticipates his portrayal of King Pompdebile for *The Knave of Hearts.* Parrish again betrays his penchant for ludicrous self-caricature by representing the nursery muse with his own features in *Mother Goose.*

Between 1916 and 1923 Parrish painted a series of four advertisements for the D. M. Ferry Seed Company—*Peter, Peter, Pumpkin Eater; Peter Piper; Mary, Mary;* and *Jack and the Beanstalk.* Another conventional nursery image, Jack Spratt and his wife, adorned a 1919 advertisement for Swift's Premium Ham, a likeness Parrish recycled from a design he had published in the 1897 Christmas issue of *Harper's Weekly.* In the ham advertisement both Jack and his wife appear to be the figures of robust good health, neither too lean nor too fat—no doubt the result, in an ideal world, of dining on a Swift's Premium Ham. Clearly Parrish not only placed his skill as a draftsman at the service of his clients but also provided his generous imagination, sympathy, persuasion, and ironic wit as well—exhibiting all the qualities of a superb adman. As modest as it is, and perhaps because it is modest, the Swift design perfectly reveals the essence of Parrish's appeal; that is,

he could put a captivating flash of bravado within a thoroughly prosaic context. This quality distinguishes Parrish's most impressive illustrations and places him among the few great American fantasists of the early twentieth century.

In the 1920s Parrish happened upon a way to capitalize on his wide popularity to achieve lasting wealth. By engaging the House of Art, a New York art publisher, to manufacture and distribute color reproductions of his work, Parrish was able to amass enough money to withdraw from the field of commercial art and focus exclusively on painting landscapes.

Although color reproductions of his paintings had occasionally been made available as early as 1904, these were secondary to the purposes for which the paintings had been created, and they were marketed without much regard for their sales potential. In 1918 hearty sales of the print *Garden of Allah* encouraged a reverse tack. *Garden of Allah,* the artist's third cover design for the gift boxes of chocolate manufactured by Clarence Crane, became an object of such enormous public demand that Crane appealed to the House of Art to assume the task of distribution. If the extravagant royalties he earned from the sales of *Garden of Allah* came as a windfall to Parrish, he nonetheless retained a certain presence of mind. When the House of Art offered to distribute carefully reproduced prints of whatever subject he pleased to paint next (no more superfluous product), Parrish accepted and severed relations with Crane, even though the disappointed chocolatier offered him $5,000 for one more design.

With the House of Art primed to distribute hundreds of thousands of copies of an image whose subject was left entirely to him, Parrish went about his next painting with great deliberation, not finishing it until December 1922. *Daybreak,* with its palpable symmetries; gentle, luminous light; much Parrish blue paint; and pleasant nudes dazzled a public eager to be dazzled. The painting became the decorating sensation of the decade as hotels exhibited it in their lobbies; housewives used it to brighten their kitchens or dining rooms; and collegians accorded it pride of place among their pennants, crew oars, fencing foils, and moose heads. Scott and Fowles, Parrish's New York gallery, used the popularity of *Daybreak* by scheduling a major exhibition of the artist's original paintings in November and December of 1925. Six thousand visitors to the gallery viewed fifty paintings. Twenty-eight were sold; the highest prices, $10,000 each, were paid for *Daybreak* and *Romance.*

Parrish's next two paintings for the art-print market, *Stars* (1926) and *Dreaming* (1929), did not

"Lobsters and Chef," a Parrish illustration for Louise Saunders's The Knave of Hearts *(1925)*

fare nearly as well, partly because, at the price asked for them by the House of Art, they could not compete with the inferior imitations being sold at the five-and-ten-cent stores. Parrish convinced himself, perhaps rightly, that all the vast public craved from him was Parrish blue and "girls having a pleasant chat," and that they ignored paintings of artistic quality, which he knew *Dreaming* to have, despite its public reception. At sixty, determined to continue to paint subjects without a care for their sales appeal, Parrish abandoned the art-print market and largely withdrew from the field of business art.

The yearly paintings he had been selling to General Electric to use on calendars advertising Edison Mazda lamps formed the one major exception although in 1923 that arrangement almost ended. Parrish agreed to continue relations with General Electric, providing the firm acquiesced to some restrictions—namely, that they purchase merely the reproduction rights to his yearly painting, rather than the painting itself; that they drop their demand that he affix the Edison Mazda symbol to the painting; and that they grant him freedom to select his own themes.

Despite Parrish's avowed need for thematic freedom, *Dream Light* (1924), his first painting to be produced under the terms of his new agreement with General Electric, reproduced essentially the identical theme depicted in *Dawn* (1918), Parrish's first General Electric painting. He repeated the same theme—one or two beautiful young maidens in a

rocky or wooded landscape—in every General Electric painting that followed. With the exception of 1926, for which he assigned to General Electric the use of an earlier painting he had done, Parrish created his formulaic paintings for Edison Mazda lamps for the next eight years.

In spite of the artist's earlier misgivings about his loss of popularity, demand for his calendars reached unprecedented heights. In 1931 General Electric estimated that if each of the regular calendars caught the eye of just one person each day in the year that it was current, Parrish's calendars had delivered about seven billion advertising messages for Edison Mazda lamps since 1918.

Critics regard Parrish's last illustrated book, a play for children titled *The Knave of Hearts,* as his unquestionable masterpiece. Offered the text the year he finished *Daybreak,* the artist completed twenty-six paintings for it in only three years, enthusiastically seizing the opportunity once again to jumble romantic, medieval, and classical themes to create a unique fantasyland. Printed in rich colors on heavy, coated stock, the bold, rectangular compositions; deep and luminous landscapes; elaborate costumes; droll improvisations; tender Pre-Raphaelite youths; and the vigorous old monarch coalesce to give *The Knave of Hearts* a singular visual opulence. While the text provided by Louise Sanders, the wife of Maxwell Perkins, appears ephemeral and pale by comparison, the illustrations constitute a celebration of the artist's best qualities.

Illustration by Parrish for Louise Saunders's The Knave of Hearts

In 1934 Parrish ended his relationship with Edison Mazda lamps, explaining that as an artist he was weary of painting girls on rocks. Approaching sixty-five, the artist wanted to paint landscapes unadorned by any figures at all. While he expressed a wish to be clear of commercial art altogether, the Minnesota greeting card company Brown and Bigelow offered to remunerate Parrish for the reproduction rights to any landscape he cared to paint. Settling himself within the hills of New Hampshire, Parrish agreed to the company's liberal terms and pursued no additional contracts thereafter. Parrish continued to paint meticulously detailed landscapes

until early 1962 when his arthritis made him put down his brushes at the age of ninety-one. While at home at The Oaks, surrounded by the New England landscapes he had used in his work for more than seventy years, Maxfield Parrish died on 30 March 1966.

Having established himself during the Golden Age of Illustration, a time when the monthly illustrated magazine occupied a position as lofty as that of television today, Parrish enjoyed a celebrity status attained by few American artists. Although the late 1930s witnessed a decline in his reputation, Parrish lived long enough to see a revival of interest in his art. This was galvanized in part by the re-evaluation of representational art brought about by the Pop Art movement of the 1960s; its proponents saw his naive landscapes as an American innocence untouched by the pretensions of the Abstractionists. Lawrence Alloway, cosponsor of a large Parrish exhibition, "Maxfield Parrish, A Second Look," which opened at Bennington College in May 1964 and then moved to the Gallery of Modern Art in New York, wrote in "The Return of Maxfield Parrish": "Behind a screen of high technique, Parrish is a master of the cliche, of the image of the moment." John Canaday, art critic of *The New York Times,* pronounced Parrish in his obituary in *The New York Times* (31 March 1966) "a superb technician and a considerable wit as well as a first rate storyteller." Alone among contemporary illustrators to single him out as an influence, Maurice Sendak has discovered in Parrish's remarkable draftsmanship and lucid fantasy-worlds grounds for comparison with the work of Winsor McCay, the creator of the comic-strip series *Little Nemo in Slumberland* for the *New York Herald.* Regarding Parrish's great celebrity, Sendak wrote in *Caldecott & Co.: Notes on Books & Pictures* (1990) that Parrish "was a popular artist in the best sense of the word. Supremely capable of meeting the demands of art for mass consumption, he never sacrificed his personal standards."

Biography:

Coy Ludwig, *Maxfield Parrish* (Atglen, Pa.: Schiffer, 1973).

References:

Lawrence Alloway, *Show IV,* 5 (May 1964): 62–67;

Laurence C. Cutler and Judy Goffman Cutler, *Maxfield Parrish: A Retrospective* (San Francisco: Pomegranate Books, 1995);

Alma M. Gilbert, *The Make Believe World of Maxfield Parrish and Sue Lewin* (San Francisco: Pomegranate Artbooks, 1990);

Gilbert, *Maxfield Parrish, The Masterworks* (Berkeley, Cal.: Ten Speed Press, 1992);

Gilbert, Introduction to *The Maxfield Parrish Poster Book* (San Francisco: Pomegranate Calendars and Books, 1989);

Maurice Sendak, *Caldecott & Co.: Notes on Books & Pictures* (New York: Noonday, 1990).

Archives:

Most of Parrish's personal papers and correspondence are housed in the library of Dartmouth College. Scrapbooks, correspondence, and photographs are held in the Smithsonian Institution's Archives of American Art and the Haverford College Library.

Edward Penfield

(2 June 1866 – 8 February 1925)

Margaret A. Irwin
Houston Academy of Medicine – Texas Medical Center Library

BOOKS: *Poster Calendar 1897* (New York: Russell, 1896);

Golf Calendar 1899 (New York: Russell, 1898);

Golf Calendar 1900 (New York: Russell, 1899);

The Big Book of Horses and Goats (New York: Russell, 1901);

Automobile Calendar for 1906 (New York: Moffat, Yard, 1905);

Holland Sketches (New York: Scribners, 1907);

Spanish Sketches (New York: Scribners, 1911);

Almanack for the Year of Our Lord 1919 (Philadelphia & New York: Beck Engraving, 1918);

Almanack for the Year of Our Lord 1920 (Philadelphia & New York: Beck Engraving, 1919).

SELECTED BOOKS ILLUSTRATED: King, Charles, *Cadet Days: A Story of Westpoint* (New York: Harper, 1894);

Davis, Richard Harding, *Three Gringos in Venezuela and Central America* (New York: Harper, 1896);

Pollard, Percival, *Posters in Miniature* (New York: Russell, 1896);

Bangs, John Kendrick, *The Dreamers: A Club* (New York: Harper, 1899);

Bangs, *Peeps at People: Being Certain Papers from the Writings of Anne Warrington Witherup* (New York: Harper, 1899).

PERIODICALS: *Harper's Weekly, Harper's Monthly, Harper's Bazar,* 1891–1901;

Collier's, 1900–1915;

Ladies' Home Journal, 1900–1915;

Life, 1900–1915;

The Saturday Evening Post, 1900–1915;

Scribner's Magazine, 1900–1915.

Edward Penfield (courtesy of the American Antiquarian Society)

Elegant is a word closely associated with the art of Edward Penfield. The hallmarks of his illustrations are simplified silhouettes, minimal detail, and clean lines. Penfield created designs for magazines, books, and calendars, but his most important work was his posters. A master craftsman, through the elimination of detail and extensive refinement Penfield produced some of America's finest posters. He was one of a vanguard of American image makers who fundamentally altered the practice of graphic art. Critics and fellow artists of his day recognized his influence, and historians continue to credit his contributions today. Penfield helped establish "Americanism" in graphic art.

Edward Penfield was born on 2 June 1866 in Brooklyn, New York. He was the son of Ellen Lock

Harper's Monthly *poster by Penfield, 1890s*

Moore, a native of England, and Josiah Penfield, a resident of Rye, New York. Penfield studied intermittently at the Art Students League from 1889 to 1895. There, under the tutelage of George de Forest Brush, he became enamored with Impressionism in America and France. A trip to Paris in 1892 reinforced his interest. Penfield's mentor, Brush, who studied in France, was a tremendous influence in the spread of Impressionism in America during the 1880s and the 1890s. Ukiyo-e, the Japanese prints of the late seventeenth through the early nineteenth centuries, influenced Penfield and his contemporaries. The abstract shapes, casually posed subjects, and flat colors of ukiyo-e provided an exciting artistic model. The influence from the 1880s and 1890s European Impressionist poster makers, the quiet, refreshing compositions of eighteenth-century Japanese prints, the hands-on approach of the Arts and Crafts movement, and even the outlined figures painted on Egyptian stone coffins can be seen in Penfield's work.

While still a student Penfield created his first design for Harper. In 1891, at the age of twenty-four, he was appointed art editor and illustrator for *Harper's Monthly.* Shortly thereafter he was assigned to direct the artwork for other Harper periodicals, *Harper's Weekly* and *Harper's Bazar.* Penfield pio-

neered his Art Nouveau style during his ten years with these magazines.

His exquisite illustrations and posters emphasized dignity and style. The images he most often depicted were handsome, vital, young American male collegians. He depicted American females with a delicate, ethereal quality in fashionable dress and elegant surroundings. Penfield had a great affection for animals and used the family's pets in many illustrations. Cats were a favorite subject for him. Penfield also had a keen interest in horse-drawn equipment. He enjoyed researching the history and design of coaches and eventually collected many of them. He wrote on the subject for *Outing* magazine (July 1901) and at one point contemplated a book.

The beginning of the American poster movement is usually dated from the beginning of the appearance of Penfield's advertising posters for Harper. He designed his first poster for Harper in March 1893. His mastery of design and composition spurred a craze. The posters were of small dimensions, generally seventeen inches by eleven inches. Each possessed brilliant designs that reflected meticulous draftsmanship and used spatter techniques and flat patterns of color. Penfield's son Walker, in a passage quoted by David Gibson in *Designed to Persuade: The Graphic Art of Edward Penfield* (1984), described his father's working method:

> After preliminary sketches had fixed the subject and layout of the poster, he would make a master drawing in black ink with pen and brush, mostly the latter. He would then color this in with watercolor. The next step would be to lay tracing paper over the master drawing, using a different piece for each color and painting in the appropriate areas in black ink. Each of these pieces of tracing paper became the diagram for one or another of the zinc plates. He made considerable use of "spatter"; often that on one plate would cover some of the areas of another. Thus green would be produced from the blue and yellow plates. . . . He . . . went into the pressroom until the presses settled down and the poster prints were coming out just as . . . [he] desired them.

The printing process used by Penfield enabled him to produce prints with rich, multiple colors and fine painterly strokes. Over the ten years with Harper, Penfield explored new techniques and styles. His discipline and fine workmanship remained constant.

The series of monthly images won quick approval. A critic for the 22 December 1894 issue of the *Publishers' Weekly* said he had moved the advertising poster into the "regions of art." *Century, Scribner's, Lippincott's,* and other journals capitalized on the popularity of the Harper posters and began issuing their own. Penfield was the sole artist

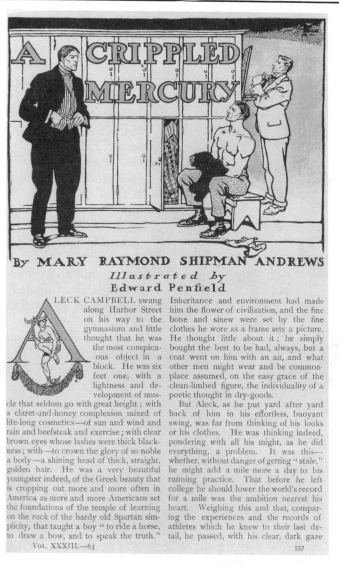

First page of a story Penfield illustrated for Scribner's Magazine
(May 1903)

Harper used for this poster series; thus it established his reputation.

Penfield used familiar objects and animals as models—cats, old uniforms, horses, and coaches. The human subjects of his posters mirror the upper-middle-class and middle-class readership of *Harper's Monthly*. Writing in the introduction to Percival Pollard's *Posters in Miniature* (1896), Penfield stated: "We are a bit tired of the very serious nowadays, a little frivolity is refreshing; and yet frivolity to be successful must be most thoroughly studied." His subjects were young, tall, robust men accompanied by lovely, fair ladies. Most often his posters portrayed only two people. Frequently, the figures were depicted holding or reading a copy of the magazine. The men were drawn to appear confident and strong. The women were portrayed as delicate

and composed. The settings were simple and familiar, often conveying a sense of home and family. The seasons were used as reference for backgrounds.

Over the years subtle changes became visible in Penfield's posters. Eye-catching, bold compositions were the hallmark of his early posters in 1893 and 1894. Abstracted shapes began to surface in 1895. The clothing on the figures became flattened, and large areas of color replaced detailed backgrounds (detail returned in his later work, however). Beautiful people in heavy black outline are portrayed with a detached quality in tranquil surroundings. Penfield's approach to design was straightforward, and his concept of posters clearcut. He believed, as he stated in *Posters in Miniature,* that "a poster should tell a story at once—a design

"The Morning Stroll," a Penfield cover design for Collier's *(10 November 1906)*

that needs study is not a poster no matter how well executed."

The changes in commercial activity in the nineteenth century, especially during the last decade, helped to establish the modern definition of the advertising poster. Direct visual communication became paramount; thus the pictures emphasized bold, simplified images. But this increased clarity often belied the amount of work that went into a composition. For Penfield many posters required a dozen or more sketches before work on the final product could begin.

Lithography was used extensively for commercial designs during the mid nineteenth century. American lithographers used chromolithography from the 1850s and 1860s forward to create bold, multicolored posters. The advances in chromolithography enabled Penfield to produce graphically pleasing posters displaying bold masses of color. The Arts and Crafts movement and the requirement of mixing ink on the press influenced the prominence of the artist's hand. While art editor at Harper, Penfield supervised the mixing of the inks. He also designed the lettering for his posters. This

direct involvement with the process and the finished product assured readability and uniformity.

Although Penfield left the editorship at Harper after ten years, and his poster series stopped in 1899, he did continue to illustrate books published by Harper and designed publicity posters for authors' books. In 1899 he provided pictures for John Kendrick Bangs's *The Dreamers: A Club* and *Peeps At People: Being Certain Papers from the Writings of Anne Warrington Witherup*. These black-and-white pictures were small, with detailed facial expressions. He also illustrated his own books for children. In addition, Penfield took on freelance clients and designed advertising posters for them, though these differed from the posters he produced for Harper. They are large and dramatic with expressive subjects relating to a product or activity. Penfield's inspiration came from many sources. The critic Royal Cortissoz in an article on Penfield in the 28 May 1926 *New York Herald Tribune* stated: "When he made his Dutch and Spanish drawings [published by Scribners in book form in 1907 and 1911] he thoroughly entered into the spirit of his themes and did some of his best work. . . . He was never the technical virtuoso alone. Humanity was always breaking into his world."

Penfield and Jennie Judd Walker were married on 27 April 1897. Jennie was the daughter of a railroad executive and veteran of the Civil War, Maj. Charles A. Walker. Major Walker was a domineering father-in-law, accompanying the Penfields on their honeymoon to Europe. Penfield and his bride lived with Major Walker in his large house in Pelham Manor, New York. Penfield used his wife as the subject of many of his drawings.

Penfield maintained two studios: one on the upper floors of the house in Pelham Manor and the other on West Twenty-third Street in New York City. His Manhattan studio was in the heart of the retail district, a neighborhood that had many large department stores and other commercial establishments. From 1908 to the 1920s Penfield produced large, colorful posters of male sportsmen and later calendars for the Beck Engraving Company of New York. Penfield's skill as a letterer is visible in the numbers and words of the calendars.

The influence of Jean-François Millet and Winslow Homer can be seen in the *1919 Almanac* he designed for the Beck Engraving Company of Philadelphia. The calendar was based on the *Farmer's Almanac of 1843*. Penfield's black-and-white drawings for the almanac are clean and sharp. This commitment to detail and sharp design is carried out in all of Penfield's calendars. The pictorial images on the calendars are primary and the date information

Frontispiece by Penfield for his travel book Holland Sketches *(1907)*

downplayed. Usually, several months were printed on one page. The calendars had themes, including golf, automobiles, and events. The subjects depicted involved activities related to the themes. The posters for *Golf Calendar 1900* are among Penfield's most beautifully colored. His composition brought spirit to the shapes.

Penfield continued to illustrate interiors and covers for prominent magazines. These publications include *Scribners, The Saturday Evening Post, Ladies' Home Journal, Collier's,* and *Metropolitan Magazine.* The Franklin Printing Company of Philadelphia retained Penfield for many years. He produced a handsome series of holiday announcements for them. Penfield's commercial-client list is impressive:

Aetna Dynamite, Orient and Northampton Bicycles, Nabisco, Galakton Baby Foods, R. R. Donnelly Printers, Kodak, Heinz, Adler Clothiers of Milwaukee, Arrow shirts, Pierce Arrow automobiles, and the clothiers Hart, Schaffner and Marx. His marvelous Pierce-Arrow Automobile posters brought him great attention. The visual vocabulary was outstanding—with a minimum of detail he created a dynamic and complex scene. The surviving advertisements show Penfield continuing to experiment with the quantity of details, techniques, complexity of background settings, and compositions. Hart, Schaffner and Marx provided steady work for Penfield. In his freelance practice he produced a variety of promotional and advertising pieces. In-

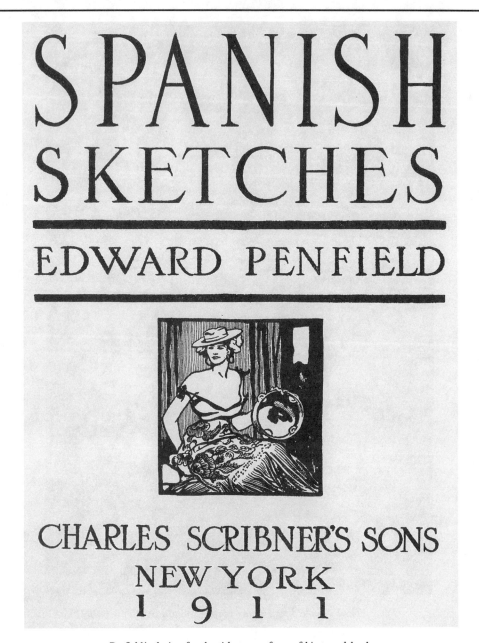

SPANISH SKETCHES

EDWARD PENFIELD

CHARLES SCRIBNER'S SONS
NEW YORK
1911

Penfield's design for the title page of one of his travel books

cluded were large-scale posters, small-style books, and pictorial cards. He produced scenes of the American Revolution for Hart, Schaffner and Marx. He also designed a small-poster series featuring clothes against the backdrops of various American cities. Penfield was one of the first American graphic artists to establish a distinctive artistic style and gain commercial success.

During World War I the federal government, through the Division of Pictorial Publicity, enlisted Penfield and other illustrators to create promotional material for the war effort. They helped to sell the idea of United States intervention to the American people. Their large posters presented handsome female figures laboring mightily on the home front for the welfare of the Allies, as for example the *Will You Help the Women of France?/SAVE WHEAT* poster in 1918. The women in Penfield's war posters display a strength not seen in the women depicted twenty years earlier.

Penfield was a member and officer of many professional art associations, including the American Watercolor Society, the Salmagundi Club, the Guild of Freelance Artists, and the New Rochelle Art Association. The Society of Illustrators elected him president from 1921 to 1923. He cofounded the

Art Center in New York City, an organization instrumental in helping exhibiting artists. Penfield was also involved with municipal affairs. He served as commissioner of streets in Pelham, New York.

Penfield graciously shared his knowledge with others. He returned to the Art Students League to teach where almost thirty years before he had been a student. In the academic year 1915–1916 he taught commercial draftsmanship and posters and lettering. With Frederic W. Goudy he taught a popular course on design. The *Art Students League Course Catalogue* for 1920–1921 says that "Mr. Penfield and Mr. Goudy will teach a class of immense value to young artists seeking to put their work to practical use. Mr. Penfield, the leading poster artist of America, and Mr. Goudy, the well-known designer and originator of the Goudy type, will offer invaluable direction in such branches of commercial art as poster work, lettering, design, layout, etc."

Penfield's work appeared in many exhibitions, including the annual shows held by the American Watercolor Society and the 1904 Saint Louis World's Fair. In 1921 Penfield helped organize the Hart, Schaffner and Marx exhibition of advertising art, and he had pieces displayed at the first annual show of the Art Directors' Club of New York.

On 8 February 1925 Edward Penfield died in Beacon, New York, from internal complications caused by a fall. The Society of Illustrators honored him the following year with an exhibition in New York. The vision and principles Penfield established in his work are extraordinary and admirable. He was a pioneer among graphic designers and illustrators, and his posters launched an American art movement. Through experimentation in technique, keen observation, and devotion to his craft Penfield achieved a visual vocabulary followed by generations of graphic artists.

References:

David Gibson, text for the Exhibition Catalogue for the Hudson River Museum, 20 May–15 July 1984, *Designed to Persuade: The Graphic Art of Edward Penfield* (Yonkers, N.Y.: Hudson River Museum, 1984);

Victor Margolin, *American Poster Renaissance* (New York: Watson-Guptill, 1975);

Henry C. Pitz, *200 Years of American Illustration* (New York: Random House, 1979);

Charles M. Price, *Posters: A Critical Study of Development of Poster Design in Continental Europe, England and America* (New York: Bricka, 1913);

Roger and Walt Reed, *The Illustrator in America 1880–1980: A Century of Illustration* (New York: Madison Square, 1984);

Peggy and Harold Samuels, *The Illustrated Biographical Encyclopedia of Artists of the American West* (Garden City, N.Y.: Doubleday, 1976).

Archives:

Collections of Penfield's works are found in the Children's Collection, the Library of Congress, Washington, D.C.; Engel Collection, Rare Book and Manuscript Library, Columbia University; Prints and Photographs Division, the Library of Congress, Washington, D.C.; the Metropolitan Museum of Art; the New York Historical Society; Hays Penfield Print Collection, The New York Public Library; Astor, Lenox, and Tilden Foundations; the Sinclair Hamilton Collection, Early American Book Illustrators and Wood Engravers, Princeton University, Princeton, New Jersey; Museum of American Illustration, New York; and Rare Book and Special Collections Division, the Library of Congress, Washington, D.C.

Joseph Pennell
(4 July 1857 – 23 April 1926)

Michael Scott Joseph
Rutgers University Libraries

and

Constance Vidor
Cathedral School, Cathedral Saint John the Divine

BOOKS: *A Canterbury Pilgrimage,* by Pennell and Elizabeth Robins Pennell (London: Seeley / New York: Scribners, 1885);

An Italian Pilgrimage, by Pennell and Elizabeth Robins Pennell (London: Seeley, 1887);

Two Pilgrims' Progress, by Pennell and Elizabeth Robins Pennell (Boston: Roberts, 1887);

Our Sentimental Journey through France and Italy, by Pennell and Elizabeth Robins Pennell (London & New York: Longmans, Green, 1888);

Our Journey to the Hebrides, by Pennell and Elizabeth Robins Pennell (New York: Harper, 1889);

Pen Drawing and Pen Draughtsmen, Their Work and Their Methods (London & New York: Macmillan, 1889);

The Stream of Pleasure: A Narrative of a Journey on the Thames, from Oxford to London, by Pennell and Elizabeth Robins Pennell (London: Unwin / New York: Macmillan, 1891);

The Jew at Home: Impressions of a Summer and Autumn Spent with Him in Russia and Austria (London: Heinemann / New York: Appleton, 1892);

Play in Provence, by Pennell and Elizabeth Robins Pennell (New York: Century, 1892);

Concerning the Etchings of Mr. Whistler (New York: Keppel, 1895);

The Illustration of Books: A Manual for the Use of Students (New York: Century, 1895);

Modern Illustration (London & New York: Bell, 1895);

The Work of Charles Keene, with an Introduction & Comments on the Drawings Illustrating the Artist's Methods (London: Unwin / New York: Russell, 1897);

Lithography & Lithographers: Some Chapters in the His-

Joseph Pennell (photograph by Heath Haviland)

tory of the Art, by Pennell and Elizabeth Robins Pennell (London: Unwin, 1898);

The Life of James McNeill Whistler, by Pennell and Elizabeth Robins Pennell (London: Heinemann, 1903);

Mr. Pennell's Etchings of New York "Sky Scrapers" (New York: Keppel, 1905);

A Little Book of London (London & Edinburgh: Foulis, 1911; Boston: Phillips, 1912);

Joseph Pennell's Pictures of the Panama Canal (London: Heinemann / Philadelphia & London: Lippincott, 1912);

Venice, the City of the Sea: Being Twenty-Five Reproductions in Photogravure, from Drawings & Etchings, Accompanied by Notes from the Writings of John Ruskin, Lord Houghton, John Addington Symonds . . . (Boston: Phillips, 1912);

San Francisco, the City of the Golden Gate: Being Twenty-Five Reproductions in Photogravure from Etchings & Drawings (Boston: Phillips, 1913);

Haunts of Old London: Being Twenty-Five Etchings of Literary and Historical London in Photogravure (Boston: Phillips, 1914);

Cantor Lectures on Artistic Lithography (London: Clowes, 1914);

Joseph Pennell's Pictures in the Land of Temples (London: Heinemann / Philadelphia: Lippincott, 1915);

Joseph Pennell's Pictures of the Wonder of Work (London: Heinemann / Philadelphia & London: Lippincott, 1916);

Joseph Pennell's Pictures of War Work in England (London: Heinemann / Philadelphia: Lippincott, 1917);

Lithographs of War Work (Saint Louis: City Art Museum, 1917);

Joseph Pennell's Liberty-Loan Poster: A Text-Book for Artists and Amateurs, Governments and Teachers and Printers, with Notes, and Introduction and Essay on the Poster by the Artist (Philadelphia: Lippincott, 1918);

Joseph Pennell's Pictures of War Work in America (Philadelphia & London: Lippincott, 1918);

Etchers and Etching (New York: Macmillan, 1919);

The Graphic Arts, Modern Men and Modern Methods: The Scammon Lectures for 1920 (Chicago: University of Chicago Press, 1921);

The Whistler Journal, Pennell and Elizabeth Robins Pennell (Philadelphia: Lippincott, 1921);

The Senefelder Club, by Pennell and Campbell Dodgson (London: Morland, 1922);

Series of Colored Drawings by F. Walter Taylor (New York: Knoedler Gallery, 1922);

Aubrey Beardsley and Other Men of the Nineties (Philadelphia: Privately printed for the Pennell Club, 1924);

Joseph Pennell's Pictures of Philadelphia (Philadelphia & London: Lippincott, 1924);

The Adventures of an Illustrator: Mostly in Following His Authors in America and Europe (Boston: Little, Brown, 1925);

The Glory of New York (New York: Rudge, 1926);

A London Reverie, J. C. Squire, ed. (London: Macmillan, 1928).

SELECTED BOOKS ILLUSTRATED: Bucke, Richard Maurice, *Walt Whitman* (Philadelphia: McKay, 1883);

A Sylvan City; or, Quaint Corners in Philadelphia (Philadelphia: Our Continent, 1883);

Cable, George Washington, *The Creoles of Louisiana* (New York: Scribners, 1884);

Howells, William Dean, *Tuscan Cities* (Boston: Ticknor, 1886);

Keppel, William Coutts, *Cycling* (London: Longmans, Green, 1887);

Scott, Leader, *Tuscan Studies and Sketches* (London: Unwin, 1887);

Hamerton, Philip Gilbert, *The Saône: A Summer Voyage* (London: Seeley, 1887);

De Vinne, Theodore Low, *Christopher Plantin, and the Plantin-Moretus Museum at Antwerp* (New York: Privately printed for the Grolier Club, 1888);

Martin, Benjamin Ellis, *Old Chelsea; A Summer-Day's Stroll* (London: Unwin, 1889);

Stockton, Frank Richard, *Personally Conducted* (New York: Scribners, 1889);

McCarthy, Justin, *Charing Cross to St. Paul's* (London: Seeley / New York, Macmillan, 1891);

Van Rensselaer, Mariana Griswold, as Mrs. Schuyler Van Rensselaer, *English Cathedrals: Canterbury, Peterborough . . .* (New York: Century, 1892);

Van Rensselaer, *Handbook of English Cathedrals* (New York: Century, 1893);

Pennell, Elizabeth Robins, *To Gipsyland* (London: Unwin / New York: Century, 1893);

Stevenson, R. A. M., *The Devils of Notre Dame: A Series of Eighteen Illustrations* (London: Pall Mall Gazette, 1894);

Oliphant, Margaret Wilson, *The Makers of Modern Rome,* illustrated by Pennell and Henry P. Riviere (New York & London: Macmillan, 1895);

Dodd, Anna Bowman Blake, *On the Broads* (London & New York: Macmillan, 1896);

Irving, Washington, *The Alhambra* (London: Macmillan, 1896);

Flower, Wickham, *Aquitane: A Traveller's Tales* (London: Chapmann & Hall, 1897);

Norway, Arthur Hamilton, *Highways and Byways in Devon and Cornwall,* illustrated by Pennell and Hugh Thomson (London: Macmillan, 1897);

Pennell, Elizabeth Robins, *Over the Alps on a Bicycle* (London: Unwin, 1898);

Norway, Arthur Hamilton, *Highways and Byways in Yorkshire,* illustrated by Pennell and Thomson (London & New York: Macmillan, 1899);

Dearmer, Percy, *Highways and Byways in Normandy* (New York: Macmillan, 1900);

Hooper, William, *The Stock Exchange in the Year 1900, a Souvenir,* illustrated by Pennell, Dudley Hardy, and others (London: Spottiswoode, 1900);

James, Henry, *A Little Tour in France* (Boston: Houghton, Mifflin / London: Heinemann, 1900);

Besant, Walter, *East London,* illustrated by Pennell, Phil May, and L. Rauch-Hill (New York: Century, 1901);

Dutt, William Alfred, *Highways and Byways in East Anglia* (London & New York: Macmillian, 1901);

Howells, William Dean, *Italian Journeys* (London: Heinemann / Boston & New York: Houghton, Mifflin, 1901);

Bradley, Arthur Granville, *Highways and Byways in the Lake District* (London: Macmillan, 1901);

Tennyson, Alfred, *Some Poems by Alfred, Lord Tennyson* (London: Freemantle, 1901);

Duguid, Charles, *The Story of the Stock Exchange* (London: Richards, 1901);

Hay, John, *Castilian Days* (London: Heinemann, 1903);

Hewlett, Maurice Henry, *The Road in Tuscany,* 2 volumes (London: Macmillan, 1904);

Crockett, Samuel Rutherford, *Raiderland: All About Grey Galloway, Its Stories, Traditions, Characters, Humours* (New York: Dodd, Mead, 1904);

James, Henry, *English Hours* (London: Heinemann / Boston & New York: Houghton, Mifflin, 1905);

Crawford, Francis Marion, *Salve Venetia; Gleanings from Venetian History* (London: Macmillan, 1905);

Arensberg, Walter Conrad, *Mr. Pennell's Etchings of London* (New York: Keppel, 1906);

Treves, Frederick, *Highways and Byways in Dorset* (London & New York: Macmillan, 1906);

James, Henry, *Italian Hours* (Boston & New York: Houghton Mifflin, 1909);

Van Dyke, John Charles, *The New New York* (New York: Macmillan, 1909);

Pennell, Elizabeth Robins, *French Cathedrals, Monasteries and Abbeys, and Sacred Sites of France* (New York: Century / London & Leipzig: Unwin, 1909);

Pennell, *Our House* (London: Unwin, 1910);

Pennell, *Our House and the People in It* (Boston & New York: Houghton Mifflin, 1910);

Singer, Hans Wolfgang, *Some New American Etchings by Mr. Joseph Pennell* (New York: Keppel, 1910);

Pennell, Elizabeth Robins, *Our House and London out of Our Windows* (Boston & New York: Houghton Mifflin, 1912);

Pennell, *Our Philadelphia* (Philadelphia & London: Lippincott, 1914);

Pepperman, Walter Leon, *Who Built the Panama Canal?* (New York: Dutton, 1915);

Pennell, Elizabeth Robins, *Nights: Rome, Venice in the Aesthetic Eighties; London, Paris in the Fighting Nineties* (Philadelphia: Lippincott, 1916);

Pennell, *The Lovers* (Philadelphia: Lippincott, 1917);

Sabbe, Maurits, *Christopher Plantin* (Antwerp: Buschmann, 1923);

Gissing, George, *An Heiress on Condition* (Philadelphia: Privately printed for the Pennell Club, 1923);

Dark, Sidney, *London* (London: Macmillan, 1924).

PERIODICALS: *Century,* 1881–1914;
Harper's Monthly, 1881–1914;
Harper's Weekly, 1881–1890;
Portfolio, 1881–1911;
Our Continent, 1882;
St. Nicholas, 1884–1911;
Bicycling World, 1885–1886;
Daily Graphic (New York), 1886–1911;
Illustrated London News, 1891–1913;
Studio, 1893;
Daily Chronicle, 1895–1911;
Yellow Book, 1896.

Joseph Pennell considered that all art was illustration and that he was a born illustrator. In a career that spanned more than half a century Pennell relentlessly, perhaps obsessively, but always elegantly illustrated what he termed the "Wonder of Work." His oeuvre includes more than nine hundred etchings, six hundred lithographs, and uncounted pen drawings, charcoals, watercolors, and pastels of architectural views as varied as the locks of the Panama Canal, the Alhambra, the stockyards of Chicago, the temples of Greece, the great munitions plants of wartime England, Federalist houses in Philadelphia, French cathedrals, and the first skyscrapers of New York City.

As well as being an extraordinary draftsman, Pennell was a gifted writer with a big, forceful voice and a colorful, incisive wit. As an art critic in London during the 1890s, his bluntly opinionated columns earned him many enemies yet also helped to establish the careers of several young artists, including Aubrey Beardsley. His long advocacy and sup-

Illustration by Pennell for George Washington Cable's series on New Orleans in Century Magazine *(1883)*

port of the graphic arts through his columns, his public-speaking engagements, his classes at the Art Students League, and his books on etching, lithography, and drawing continue to influence generations of artists who may be unfamiliar with his illustrations. Although contemporary critics, acknowledging the lapse of interest in Pennell's prints, have noted that Pennell's posthumous career was a failure, the vitality of graphic arts in America is an eloquent reminder of his fertile presence in art history.

Joseph Pennell was born on 4 July 1857 (not 1860 as he supposed) in Philadelphia. His parents, Larkin Pennell and Rebecca A. Barton, married in 1855, two years to the day before Joseph was born. Devout Quakers, they instilled an admiration of humility, self-reliance, and candor in their son but did nothing to encourage his artistic potential. His father, uncommonly quiet and withdrawn (opposite traits to those of the excitable and combative Pennell), allowed his son to draw as a child and so pro-

vided at least tacit encouragement. Pennell claimed that his liking for rendering views from a slightly elevated angle came from the days that his father would let him draw while looking out the window from the office of Cope Brothers, where his father worked as a clerk in the shipping business.

A sensitive boy, Pennell enjoyed solitary play most, particularly illustrating stories he would make up. By age thirteen he already liked going on solitary tramps, drawing the woods and streams as well as the old houses and mills around Germantown. He became left-handed after breaking his right arm in a sledding mishap and wrote and drew left-handed thereafter despite the persistent efforts of his teachers to retrain him. He broke his nose as well, thus acquiring the fierce, pugilistic countenance that so fit his nature in adult life.

Pennell's parents enrolled him in the Germantown Friends' Select School, where drawing classes were provided for mental discipline. Although his emerging aesthetic predilection met institutional resistance, Pennell received technical guidance from a succession of drawing instructors, of whom James R. Lambdin proved the most influential. Lambdin exhorted his pupils to draw from memory, a skill Pennell boasted of in later life, writing in his *Adventures of an Illustrator* (1925) that an artist thus enabled would make an ideal spy.

Upon graduation in 1876 Pennell applied, unsuccessfully, to the Pennsylvania Academy of Fine Arts. This rejection forced him to seek a clerkship in the Philadelphia and Reading Coal and Iron Company. The bleak prospect of a career in coal was eased somewhat by his acceptance into the Pennsylvania School of Industrial Art, which had recently opened. His daily routine was rigorous. After a day in the office, which would begin at 7:00 A.M., Pennell would hasten home for supper at 6:30 P.M., then walk the several miles to the Pennsylvania School of Industrial Art to attend night class. After class he would wait for more than an hour for an 11:45 P.M. bus to return home.

Charles Marquedant Burns, a noted architect whose brash individualism may have restricted the number of commissions he received but endeared him to his students, developed a loyal band who followed him on sketching walks through town. Pennell received time off from the coal and iron company to join these excursions, and the few cartoons in his oeuvre come from this period. As well as drawing with chalk, usually on brown paper in black and white, Pennell made etchings on glass, a technique he had learned from Joseph Ropes, the last of his Germantown drawing instructors. In 1879 Pennell's glass etching *Dingman's Ferry* appeared in a Pennsylvania Academy of Fine Arts exhibition; this was the first public acknowledgment of Pennell's talent.

Pennell unhesitatingly severed his association with the Philadelphia and Reading Coal and Iron Company when, partly owing to Burns's influence, he finally gained admission to the Pennsylvania Academy of Fine Arts. Through its president, James L. Claghorn, who possessed a sizable collection of etchings, Pennell came into contact with the work of accomplished masters of the idiom, Seymour Haden and James McNeill Whistler, whose style he studied and imitated. Claghorn also introduced Pennell to Frederick Keppel—a print seller, publisher, and gallery owner—whose sponsorship would help to establish him in the public eye. Pennell's association with Keppel's gallery lasted for the rest of his life.

Although Pennell learned much at the Pennsylvania Academy of Fine Arts, he withdrew only a year after being admitted, partly in response to a confrontation with the painting master, Thomas Eakins. Eakins intended to encourage Pennell but one day too bluntly criticized a large pen-and-ink drawing for being too original. Unable to tolerate criticism, Pennell withdrew from the school—a decision he regretted but could not change.

At this time Pennell made the acquaintance of Stephen Ferris, who had helped to found the New York Etching Club and the Philadelphia Society of Etchers. Ferris showed Pennell how to etch on copper, perhaps the single most important lesson in Pennell's life, and ushered him into the Philadelphia Society of Etchers in 1881. Ferris also acquainted Pennell with the work of modern Spanish artists, such as Mariano Fortuny and Martin Rico, whose realistic treatment of sunlight as a pictorial element stimulated Pennell's imagination, as it did a generation of American illustrators active during the 1890s.

Another factor in Pennell's decision to leave the Pennsylvania Academy of Fine Arts was his rising reputation as a commercial artist. By the end of 1880 an increasing number of private commissions allowed him to rent a studio in the Presbyterian Board of Publication Building at 1334 Chestnut Street, which he shared with the painter Harry Poore. Among his neighbors were Stephen Parrish, an able etcher (and the father of Maxfield Parrish), and the painter Cecelia Baux.

While Pennell applied himself diligently to drawing, he also relaxed by skating during the winter and riding the tall bicycle—the only kind available at the time—joining the League of American Wheelmen and the Germantown Bicycle Club. Pennell's fondness for cycling persisted (as did his fondness for clubs), enabling him to travel extensively during an era when the automobile was of greater novelty than utility. The bicycle even served as a source of inspiration, as Pennell's many bicycle illustrations, including those published in the magazine *Bicycling World* and the books *Cycling* (1887) and *Over the Alps on a Bicycle* (1898), attest.

During the last quarter of the nineteenth century success in illustration rested heavily on gaining entry into the large illustrated American periodicals such as *Scribner's Magazine* (then *Century*), *Harper's Weekly,* and *Harper's Monthly*. In 1881 Pennell traveled by train to New York, where his portfolio favorably impressed Alexander W. Drake, the powerful and innovative art director at *Century*. In July *Century* published Pennell's drawings of The Mash, a marshy terrain in southern Philadelphia that included an oil refinery. Pennell's eye for city views and picturesque structures, his tireless industry, and his gifted draftsmanship quickly made him indispensable; in the specialized world of American magazine illustration Pennell carved a place for himself as the preeminent architectural illustrator in America.

Through *Century* Pennell made the acquaintance of his future wife, the author Elizabeth Robins. In her 1929 biography of Pennell, *The Life and Letters of Joseph Pennell,* she describes her first impression of him: "young, tall, exceedingly thin, with brown hair, brown moustache and shortish brown beard, deep-set grey-green eyes, intent and serious beyond his years, holding one's attention at once."

In January 1882 *Century* dispatched Pennell to New Orleans to illustrate a series of articles by George Washington Cable. This dual assault on the picturesque was the first of Pennell's "adventures"; it set a precedent that would often be repeated, usually at the behest of *Century.* Pennell liked Cable, whom he described as "the tiny little man with a black beard and bright eyes," and their collaboration succeeded. When Pennell returned to Philadelphia in May, the magazines were waiting with additional commissions. In the following year many of Pennell's local drawings for *Our Continent* were included in *A Sylvan City; or, Quaint Corners in Philadelphia* (1883). Encouraged by public response to Pennell's etchings of New Orleans, *Century* published them in 1884 as *The Creoles of Louisiana;* they made, to Cable's appreciative eye, "a handsome parlour table book."

After the triumph of his Creole illustrations there was no more peripatetic illustrator in America than Pennell. In 1883, as soon as Pennell returned to Philadelphia *Century* commissioned him to accompany William Dean Howells, then at the height of his popularity, on a tour of Italy, making drawings and etchings to illustrate a series of Howells's articles. His Tuscany prints, finished by July, may have comprised the twenty-one pieces shown at the Walker Art Gallery, Liverpool, in 1884. While relations with the patrician Howells were awkward, Pennell enjoyed the congenial company of other artists such as Frank Duveneck and W. Gedney Bunce. From Italy, Pennell traveled to Scotland, where his drawings for the author and collector of fairy tales Andrew Lang began an affectionate, although combative, friendship.

In June 1884 Pennell and Elizabeth Robins married and soon afterward sailed for Liverpool so that Pennell could begin making drawings and etchings of English cathedrals for *Century.* In *The Life and Letters of Joseph Pennell* Elizabeth characterizes their marriage as Pennell's idea for furthering their partnership without compromising her reputation. As a collaboration the marriage was highly successful, resulting in ten books and many periodical pieces. It

also served as the linchpin of Pennell's emotional equilibrium. While allowing Pennell to pursue his livelihood across the globe without the burdens of a conventional home and family, marriage to the dignified, articulate, and wellborn Elizabeth Robins (the niece of author Charles Godfrey Leland) eased their way into social circles and attracted prominent artists and writers to their home.

When an outbreak of cholera prevented the Pennells from continuing to Italy, their ultimate destination, they cycled from London to Canterbury, where Pennell made drawings for the *Portfolio* and completed a piece on the public schools for *St. Nicholas,* the children's periodical owned by the Century Company. Once they were able to enter Italy, Pennell turned out illustrations for *St. Nicholas, Harper's Monthly, Harper's Weekly,* and *Century* and consorted with local English artists such as Elihu Vedder, then obsessed with his illustrations for Edward Fitzgerald's translation of Omar Khayyám's *Rubáiyat* (1884), and Duveneck, who by night presided over noisy, inebriated gatherings and by day invited Pennell to print his copperplates on an etching press reputed to have belonged to Canaletto.

But he had not printed all of his Italian plates before *Century* editors, impatient for his *Cathedral* series, summoned Pennell to London. Mindful of the abundant opportunities for artistic and literary exploration and the close proximity to Europe, Pennell and his wife elected to make London their adopted home.

Work on English cathedrals dictated the tempo of Pennell's life for the next two years. Each spring Elizabeth would remain in London (sometimes joining her husband in transit) while he made a slow circuit of cathedral towns, drawing and recording in letters his colorful impressions: Salisbury was "too perfect," resembling "an overgrown toy.... You feel as if you would like to pick it up and put it away in its box." Winchester was "a sad place" with a bland exterior as "inspiring as a New England barn." Wells was the "most lovely of all the English cathedrals," although the gentle beauty of Peterborough and its environs stirred feelings of awe. Pennell wrote with uncharacteristic religious sentiment of a yearning for an eternal state infused with everlasting sensations of its beauty. Although he had intended to make etchings of the cathedrals, Pennell found the pen more suitable, his control over architectural complexities not being sure enough yet to make direct impressions upon a sensitive and unforgiving plate.

In 1885 *A Canterbury Pilgrimage,* which the Pennells co-authored, appeared in an English edition published by Richard Seeley and an American edi-

"Up and Down in Siena," an 1883 illustration by Pennell for an unsigned article by William Dean Howells in Century Magazine

tion published by Scribners. Andrew Lang cordially saluted it in a *London Daily News* headline as "the most wonderful shilling's worth modern literature has to offer," thus ensuring lusty sales of the book. The Pennells enjoyed a rising popularity with the public, as well as with their fellow artists and writers. Their acquaintance with English poet and critic Edmund Gosse drew them into the privileged company of writers Thomas Hardy, Henry James, Brander Matthews, Walter Pater, and Alice Meynell. The Pennells also socialized with a Hammersmith neighbor, poet and artist William Morris, who in turn introduced them to printer and engraver Emery Walker, artist Walter Crane, and young playwright Bernard Shaw (the only one of this crowd, they wrote, capable of fluent conversation).

While discussing book ideas with various publishers, Pennell made illustrations for *Bicycling World*

magazine to go with an article written by William Albemarle and etched plates occasionally, which he took to T. Brooker to print. The lordly arrogance of Frederick Goulding, the widely regarded and feared London printer, disgusted Pennell, and, averse to letting Goulding determine the ultimate appearance of his work, he turned away from etching. In the 1890s Pennell purchased a press and resumed etching with greater intensity and skill; however, for the time being, he concentrated on drawing.

In 1886 *Century* interrupted Pennell's work on Canterbury Cathedral, dispatching him to Antwerp to render illustrations of the Plantin Museum. While in Antwerp, Philip Gilbert Hamerton, admired English critic, author, and editor of *Portfolio,* asked Pennell to accompany him through the south of France on a boat to work on a book about its rivers and canals in the spirit of *The Creoles of Louisiana* and *Tuscan Cities* (1886).

Unlike his earlier collaborations and contrary to his expectations, teaming up with Hamerton proved disagreeable. Not only did Hamerton's earnest and fastidious personality exasperate Pennell, but also he found camping out under a tent unpleasant, not least of all when it rained, as it frequently did. In addition, the French police became alarmed at the sight of a foreigner making drawings near the German border and arrested Pennell at Pontaillier. Out of sorts, he walked away from the project (before Hamerton thought it was concluded) and vowed he would never again be tempted into another such picturesque excursion—a vow he would not keep. Pennell returned to England and the serenity of his cathedral work in late July.

Together once more, the Pennells meandered around England in 1887, continuing the round of the lesser cathedrals. That same year Seeley and Company published *An Italian Pilgrimage* and *The Saône: A Summer Voyage,* bringing the Hamerton episode to a satisfactory conclusion; Roberts Brothers published *Two Pilgrims' Progress;* and Longmans, Green published *Cycling.*

While Pennell considered himself a loyal "*Century* man," one journal alone could not include his prolific output. *Harper's Weekly* gladly published an account of the Pennells' tour of the Hebrides, for which the Pennells followed the route traveled by Samuel Johnson, but in reverse.

An afternoon paper, *The Star,* began publication at this time, and Shaw persuaded Pennell to write on art for it. Pennell's critiques, written under the pseudonym U. A. (Unknown Artist), proved unsettling for artists who thought his uninhibited criticism a form of betrayal. Although Pennell knew from experience what it was to be lambasted by a powerful critic, he could never persuade himself to soften or blur his opinion. Quick to take offense, Pennell was also quick to give offense although he successfully kept his personal feelings separate from his critical judgments. While he made enemies, artists he supported profited by his reputation for integrity.

Pennell's irrepressible candor also outraged members of the lofty Royal Academy, who regarded him as an outsider and an irritatingly opinionated gadfly. Illustrators were to painters as journalists were to serious authors, in their view. Since they were the most venerated of painters and Pennell was flatly uninterested in painting, they considered his slashing and self-confident attacks as presumptuous.

In 1888 Pennell began work on a book about drawing that effectively combined his critical acumen with a love of technique. Late in the year he and Elizabeth dashed to Paris, soliciting examples of work by the European artists he admired, such as Daniel Vierge, Enrique Casanova, and Martin Rico. Finding the illustrators who had inspired him as a young student glad to be included in his book intensified Pennell's excitement, and he went on to collect work from Charles Keene; from the Dalziels, a firm of wood engravers who had preserved the drawings they had copied onto woodblocks during the 1860s; and from the editors of *Century.*

Macmillan published *Pen Drawing and Pen Draughtsmen, Their Work and Their Methods* in 1889, engendering spirited, controversial debate. Morris and the architects of the typographic renaissance deemed it a cardinal sin for illustration to ignore the printed page and protested that wash drawings should not have been included as book illustration. That the Venetian masters had omitted wash drawings from their early books furnished proof, in their view, of the inherent unsuitability of the technique. Pennell countered by extolling the virtue of experimentation without which illustration would never have progressed beyond the famous Saint Christopher block. Had the early masters and engravers possessed the necessary technique for making and reproducing wash, he argued, they would certainly have employed it, for they were no less adventuresome than the makers of American magazines.

Other controversies spilled over into the newspapers. Royal Academician Hubert von Herkomer published a set of photogravures which he advertised as etchings. Pennell challenged Herkomer's conflation of techniques but quickly found himself out on a limb; save for William Ernest Henley, the venerable editor of the *Scots Observer,* few men were hardy enough to challenge a member of the Royal Academy. But Henley encouraged Pennell to write

an "Open Letter," which he published, and Whistler joined his scorn of Herkomer's carelessness to Pennell's. Herkomer finally surrendered in a letter he wrote to the London *Times,* explaining that he had used the photogravure process to save time and complaining he saw no harm in it. Pennell's successful brief had made sure that photogravures would be called by their right name (as would etchings) and fortified his reputation as an astute iconoclast.

Century once again eased Pennell out of London in the spring of 1890 with the idea of following its series on English cathedrals with one on French cathedrals. Although his relationship with Mariana Griswold Van Rensselaer, the author of *English Cathedrals: Canterbury, Peterborough . . .* (1892), had been cordial, during the next few years it would unravel beneath Pennell's unwillingness to compromise his artistic judgment. Van Rensselaer dictated specific subjects and vantage points, and Pennell refused them. At Périgueux he discovered that the restorer appointed by the French government had ruined Périgueux Cathedral, stripping it bare in the interests of returning it to his own notion of Romanesque perfection. Van Rensselaer nevertheless insisted that he render details of its former appearance. When Pennell demurred, she sent a note of complaint to Richard Watson Gilder, the editor of the Century Company. Pennell's reply to Gilder's inquiry was polite but hardly intended to convey repentance; it concluded, "I never should think of criticizing Mrs. Van Rensselaer's scheme or methods, but I cannot help repeating that she ought to bear in mind that I cannot draw the ideas of the old men when their work is not visible." Seeing that Gilder could be of no help, Van Rensselaer left the text of the French cathedrals series unfinished.

In 1890 the south of France offered the Pennells additional scope. Their study of Provençal sports appeared in *Century* in 1891, and *Play in Provence,* published by the Century Company, followed in 1892. The year did not end well for the artist, however. In late fall Larkin Pennell's health collapsed, and in November he died. Pennell had been intensely attached to this taciturn man who, for several years, had made his home with the Pennells in London, and he grieved the loss of his father deeply.

In the spring of 1891 the Pennells again took to the road, cycling through Belgium, Prussia, Saxony, Bohemia, Bavaria, Austria, and finally Hungary, stopping for a month in Budapest. Pennell continued alone to Russia, where he united with Harold Frederic to make a journalistic study of Russian Jews. Despite getting arrested yet again and getting expelled from the country, Pennell succeeded in producing enough material for a series of articles,

Title page designed by Pennell for an 1885 travel book

which appeared during December 1891 in *The Illustrated London News* and in a book published by the young William Heinemann in 1892 as *The Jew at Home: Impressions of a Summer and Autumn Spent with Him in Russia and Austria.*

Having determined at Larkin Pennell's death that they needed new quarters, in February 1892 the Pennells moved into 14 Buckingham Street, where their windows overlooked an exquisite stretch of the Thames. From here they could see the Embankment wending toward Waterloo Bridge and, beyond, toward Saint Paul's dome. During this year Pennell spent more time with Whistler, whose affection perhaps filled the gap in his life left by the passing of Pennell's father. Also during this period Pennell bought a secondhand etching press from An-

thony Henley, brother of editor and author William Ernest Henley, and with the newfound ability to control the finished product of his labors, devoted himself once more to etching. Pennell saw printing as a means to develop and improve the etched image and studied each proof for new expressive possibilities. Pennell's etchings of the cathedrals that summer exemplify his ripening interest and expertise.

When cool autumn weather sent Pennell back to London, his Buckingham Street apartment offered the kind of heady social atmosphere that, in the early years, had characterized his Barton Street address. W. E. Henley, a lion among English men of letters, regularly adjourned there after work with his retinue of newspaper writers. Members of the Arts and Crafts movement, such as Walter Crane, also gathered at the Pennells', as did members of the New English Art Club, such as Walter Sickert and Arthur Tomson. There Phil May, quiet and pleasant, became the center of a large circle of worshipful illustrators, and there members of the Art Workers' Guild, occasional visitors from *Century* staff who happened to be passing through town, and architects who descended in "herds" also found a warm welcome. A young and unknown Beardsley appeared there as well one day, a portfolio tucked under his arm. Pennell wrote admiringly of Beardsley for the first volume of *The Studio* in April 1893, praising his "use of the single line, with which he weaves his drawings into an harmonious whole, joining extremes and reconciling what might be oppositions—leading, but not forcing, you properly to regard the concentration of his motive." Beardsley ingenuously accepted the older man's appreciation as unstinting praise. Indeed, posterity has tended as well to ignore the secondary aim of Pennell's article, which was to observe the superiority of process engraving over wood engraving. In praising Beardsley's line, Pennell intended to praise the accuracy of its reproduction: process engraving "gives Mr. Beardsley's actual handiwork, and not the interpretation of it by some one else." Pennell developed a greater enthusiasm for Beardsley as the young man developed a more adventurous style, and he remained one of Beardsley's staunchest advocates.

Pennell set out again in early May 1893, sojourning in Paris with Elizabeth and spending most of the spring and summer sketching Parisian cathedrals. He then continued to Laon and Rheims, where he worked alone. During 1893 and early 1894 Pennell busied himself selecting new specimens of drawing for a second, expanded edition of *Pen Drawing;* acquiring old paper, which he preferred to modern; and making etchings of London views. He also assisted in the birth of the magazine *Yellow Book,* dispensing advice to Beardsley and his literary editor, Henry Harland, and graciously allowing them to reproduce his etching of *Le Puy* in Auvergne, which he thought "the most picturesque place in the world." But Pennell had to abandon London on the eve of the publication of the first volume of the *Yellow Book* because *Century* had arranged another picturesque excursion for him to Dalmatia with Harriet Waters Preston and her niece, Louise Dodge. After Dalmatia, Pennell alighted in Rome to make drawings for Margaret Wilson Oliphant's *The Makers of Modern Rome* (1895), a Macmillan publication, and there he happily renewed his acquaintance with Vedder and James. Elizabeth joined them in Siena, and together the Pennells braved the blistering, midsummer heat of southern Spain, where Pennell could both see and feel the source of the brilliant light that bathed the drawings of Fortuny y Carbó, Vierge, and Rico.

Returning to London, Pennell spent that fall and winter preparing a series of lectures for the Slade School of Fine Art at University College, London, eventually published as *The Illustration of Books: A Manual for the Use of Students* (1895). Pennell's writing had always revealed a strong pedagogical element. Delivering the Slade lectures inspired him with a desire to teach classes, which, however, University College could not satisfy. Not content with halfway measures, Pennell resigned the lectureship.

During this period Pennell also served the short-lived Society of Illustrators, presided over by Sir James D. Linton. Despite raising funds by arranging formal dinners and by publishing a book of poetry about London, *The London Garland* (1895), in which an original illustration accompanied each poem, the society failed to ignite public enthusiasm and dissolved. Another commission from *Century* sent Pennell to Norfolk to illustrate Anna Bowman Blake Dodd's *On the Broads* (1896), which Macmillan made into a book that same year.

Pennell spent part of that year writing introductions: first for an exhibition of Edwin Austin Abbey's pastels at the Fine Art Society, then for Whistler's lithographs. While Pennell thought highly of Abbey's work, Whistler, as he did for many younger English artists, stood at the pinnacle of Pennell's esteem. In his *Adventures of an Illustrator* Pennell writes, "from the beginning, I was able to . . . recognize, . . . that he was a great man, the greatest I have known, the greatest artist of his day." In Paris an exhibition of lithography marking the approaching centenary of its invention excited Pennell, who immediately planned with Fisher Unwin to publish a history of the craft to appear in 1898—the actual centennial year. In December, Pennell eagerly raced to Düsseldorf to see another exhibition of lithographs, and when Macmillan contracted with him to illustrate Washington Irving's *Alhambra* in March 1896, Pennell chose lithography for his medium.

Twelve lithographs appeared in the book; competent as they are, they clearly reflect Pennell's nascent understanding of the medium's potential and betray his habit of pen drawing in their reliance on line over tone. He exhibited the full series of Alhambra lithographs in the autumn at the Fine Art Society but sold only a few. Not only did the public reject Pennell's lithographs, but also Sickert attacked them in *The Saturday Review*. In accusations comparable to those Pennell previously leveled at Herkomer, Sickert said that by advertising his copies of illustrations made on transfer paper as origi-

*"Gloucester on the River," an illustration by Pennell for
Mariana Griswold Van Rensselaer's series
on English cathedrals*

nal lithographs, Pennell had engaged in deception. Some accounts of this episode state that Sickert's attack arose out of his feud with Whistler, who also used transfer paper, and at whom he meant to strike through Pennell. Nevertheless, Pennell felt his own livelihood imperiled, and rather than launching a campaign in the press, which he deemed at best an insufficient remedy, he sued Sickert. The result was one of the most famous trials in art history—in part due to Whistler's coloratura testimony—and Pennell's absolute vindication.

Pennell showed that the inventor of lithography, Alois Senefelder, had himself invented transfer paper as a means of making lithographs. How else could he manage to work away from home, he asked, being no Hercules to drag stones along on his journeys? For the defense, Frank Harris, the editor of *The Saturday Review,* was forced to admit that he routinely used transfer paper to print what he called lithographs, and Will Rothenstein, another of Sickert's witnesses, also confessed under cross-examination that he too used transfer paper to make what he also called lithographs.

While Harris good-heartedly paid Sickert's legal expenses, Pennell celebrated his victory by racing off to Holland to make a series of lithographs and by throwing himself into a slew of projects, including his book on lithography, for which he scoured London's libraries and bookshops for appropriate illustrations. Another of Pennell's projects for 1897 was a book of appreciation for artist Charles Keene, whom Pennell regarded as "the greatest English artist since [William] Hogarth." *The Work of Charles Keene* (1897) helped to bolster Keene's reputation.

Pennell's most consuming and physically arduous project took him and Elizabeth through Switzerland, Italy, France, Belgium, Luxembourg, Germany, and Austria, where they climbed and coasted through the Alps on bicycle. *Century* subsidized some of the expense by publishing several articles that captured in word and picture the intoxicating pastoral beauty and soon-to-be-lost serenity of pre–World War I Europe. While *The Work of Charles Keene* appeared in print before the year's end, *Over the Alps on a Bicycle* and *Lithography & Lithographers* appeared a year later (1898).

In that year a group of English artists formed the International Society for the purpose of exhibiting artists of different nationalities in cities throughout Europe and America. The International, as it was called, savored of a *salon de refusés* since its guiding principle opposed the Royal Academy's Anglophilic attitudes about art and elected Whistler, the paradigmatic iconoclast, as president. Whistler brought Pennell into the executive committee of the society, and for many years Pennell worked zealously on its behalf, involving himself with selecting committees and helping with hanging for the International's frequent exhibitions. While his friendship with Whistler grew (in spite of both men's dominating personalities), the Pennells entertained a wide circle of friends, including author John Charles Van Dyke—who would collaborate with Pennell on *The New New York* (1909).

Pennell continued to illustrate Macmillan's popular series of guidebooks, which followed in an almost perfect parade of one a year: *Highways and Byways in Devon and Cornwall* by Arthur Hamilton Norway in 1897, *Highways and Byways in Yorkshire* by Norway in 1899, *Highways and Byways in Normandy* by Percy Dearmer in 1900, and *Highways and Byways in East Anglia* by William Alfred Dutt and *Highways and Byways in the Lake District* by Arthur Granville Bradley in 1901.

On the strength of the continued popularity of the travel book, Macmillan commissioned Pennell to undertake a travel book of greater proportions. He spent eight months of 1901 in Italy traveling with, or following after, Maurice Hewlett and his wife, a trip for which Pennell utilized the newly invented motorized bicycle. Although he loved returning to Italy, Pennell disliked Hewlett, whom he called "as nervous and sensitive as I am," and disliked Hewlett's writing style. "I know that very superior people and very inferior people pretended to like his writing," he recalled, but he dismissed it as pretentious "and not really anything." Hewlett reciprocated Pennell's dislike. Nevertheless, *The Road in Tuscany* was published to favorable notices in

"The Market, Kiev, Jews and Russians Bargaining," illustration by Pennell for his
The Jew at Home *(1891)*

1904, and the director of the Uffizi asked Pennell to contribute the Florentine drawings. Pennell recalled the invitation years later with both a sense of honor and, recalling Hewlett's envy, a sense of amusement.

Between two excursions with the Hewletts, Pennell passed the summer and autumn of 1901 reviving old friendships in Venice, enjoying the warm Italian nights at the Piazza with Bunce and Duveneck; Howells's brother-in-law, sculptor Larkin Mead; and even Burns, Pennell's old instructor from the Pennsylvania School of Industrial Art. In 1905 Pennell produced a Venetian book for Macmillan with author Francis Marion Crawford. Pennell found Crawford alternately remote and overbearing (although Pennell respected Crawford's writing skill). Crawford prescribed scenes for Pennell to draw, as had Van Rensselaer, which Pennell blithely ignored, choosing to draw what he liked. Fortunately, roistering evenings at the Piazza kept his spirits high.

During the early years of the twentieth century Pennell made repeated use of Russian charcoal, adopting it for his work in Italy with Crawford and Hewlett. He also illustrated *Castilian Days* (1903) with charcoal, evidently preferring it for its ability to evoke the brilliant light of the sunny Mediterranean countries. Having temporarily set down his pen in Italy, Pennell also composed many impressions in pastel—lightning-quick sketches that Elizabeth characterizes as "retaining the exaltation of the moment."

Pennell's involvement in the International Society carried him back to the United States in 1904, where he won a grand prize at the Saint Louis Exposition. In March of that year, eight months after Whistler's death, the council of the International Society proposed a Whistler Memorial Exhibition, and Pennell devoted himself to the cause. The Memorial Exhibition occupied him up to the day it opened on 19 February 1905 and beyond as he continued to supervise every detail relevant to its complete success. Although the International Society proposed a small exhibition of Pennell's work in Dresden in May, and although a simultaneous exhibition in Liège bestowed a Gold Medal on him, Pennell continued to devote his complete attention to the Whistler exhibition. His correspondence suggests he recognized the toll it was taking. "The Whistler was a great artistic and—luckily for us—a financial success and thank heaven it is over," he wrote to Hans Singer; "and I will never get mixed up in such an affair again."

After 1906 without Whistler's leadership and with the new president, Auguste Rodin, unable to provide a new vision, the attention of the International Society began to wander, and Pennell gradually distanced himself from it. His work, too, began to change. He now concentrated more on etching, and perhaps having wearied of the temperaments of authors, he restricted his serial contributions to sets of illustrations unaccompanied by text. However, he did make a series of charcoal studies of London—designed to illustrate a book by Henry James, but one James never would write. Some of these appeared in Sidney Dark's *London,* published in 1924, and *A London Reverie,* with text by J. C. Squire, the Georgian poet and editor of *The London Mercury,* published in 1928 (two years after Pennell's death).

In 1906 and 1907 Pennell returned to France in order to complete his work on the French cathedrals, long interrupted. Elizabeth had agreed to assume the burden of authorship laid down by Van Rensselaer. Pennell's ability to etch the difficult features of the cathedrals at Amiens, Rouen, and Beauvais demonstrates the technical virtuosity he commanded in his late forties and signifies his growth as an etcher since his first attempts to create illustrations of these cathedrals a decade earlier. While the overall effect of the view dominates the experience of any of Pennell's etchings as it does with Whis-

tler's, the calligraphic details of Pennell's later French cathedrals glimmer with jewel-like clarity.

When in 1900 Whistler had expressed a desire to have Pennell and his wife write his biography, they began immediately to gather material. However, with Whistler's subsequent illness and death, they laid aside the project until 1906 when they could at last dedicate themselves to it completely. In November a lawsuit brought by Whistler's executrix, Rosalind Birnie Philip—who felt, for some reason, the Pennells had not obtained Whistler's authorization—slowed progress somewhat. By January 1908, however, five months after the court had dismissed the suit, the project was finished—"finished half an hour ago—as I write"—Pennell noted exultingly to Van Dyke in a letter dated the nineteenth, "and then, if you still want me in New York, *Voilà.*"

Before sailing for New York in June to work with Van Dyke on *The New New York,* Pennell moved from Buckingham Street, which had become cramped, to Adelphi Terrace, relishing the new view and the greater space he had for his work. Arriving in New York, Pennell christened it the "Unbelievable City" in dumbstruck admiration of the climbing "sky scrapers." In *Joseph Pennell's Pictures of the Wonder of Work* (1916) he describes New York, with what strikes contemporary readers as credulous hyperbole, as "more shimmering than Venice," "more magical than London," "more noble than Seville," "finer than any [city] in any world that ever existed, finer than Claude ever imagined, or [Charles] Turner ever dreamed." The skyscrapers confirmed Pennell's belief in the importance of the overarching theme of his life, the Wonder of Work: the astonishing and varied evidence of industry and bold intelligence that dominated the landscape, asserting everywhere the human presence. Pennell's plain, bold language intends to place him within a tradition of landscape artists that included Joseph Mallord William Turner, Claude Lorrain, and Canaletto. In her introduction to *Catalogue of the Lithographs of Joseph Pennell* (1991) by Louis A. Wuerth, Elizabeth notes that for her husband "the huge power houses, refineries and mills, bridges, coal breakers, and furnaces were as truly the Castles of Work of to-day as the great cathedrals were the Temples of Religion in the past."

After returning home to Adelphi Terrace, Pennell experimented with the intaglio processes of mezzotint and aquatint and arranged the American representation at the Venice Exhibition. Although Pennell was ultimately displeased with the exhibition, American artists were pleased, and his New York etchings found ready buyers. Toward the end of 1909 Pennell's thoughts returned to lithography, which he deemed more effective than other media for treating the larger compositions he envisioned. In 1909 he helped to found the Senefelder Club, named after the inventor of lithography, which held its first exhibition the following January. The club held exhibitions annually thereafter, relying heavily upon the industry of Pennell.

In September, Pennell returned to the United States, partly to seek more Wonder of Work material among the western and midwestern cities, including Chicago. He recoiled at the changes immigration had brought upon the American scene, and his letters to Elizabeth henceforth registered his loathing for the European immigrants of the early twentieth century. As did many Americans, Pennell shrank from the immigrant minorities, blaming them for the ugliness of their impoverished lives in America, their unfamiliar appearances, and their alien habits. Having suffered the jeers directed at Quaker children and having dwelled as an outsider in London for so many years, as well as having traveled in many of the countries these unwilling travelers had once called home, Pennell showed them remarkably little sympathy.

In London, Pennell busied himself with various matters, including the publication of twenty-five of his etchings in *A Little Book of London* (1911), published in London and Edinburgh by T. N. Foulis and in Boston the following year by Le Roy Phillips. He also wrote letters in a resounding defense of Whistler, who had come under attack for reputedly having filched the idea for his *Nocturnes* from a neighbor, Harry Greaves—part of a Whistler backlash that had gained ferocity since the artist's death. Pennell also continued to work with the International Society to raise funds for a Whistler Monument. The Senefelder Club occupied him as well, and between illustrating the ceremonies surrounding the death of one English monarch and the coronation of another, he pushed himself to prepare the Barcelona International Exhibition for the Senefelder Club.

The immensity of constructing the Panama Canal allured Pennell. Early in the year he had written to R. U. Johnson (who had recently succeeded Gilder as editor of *Century*), "What I Want Is To Go To Panama NOW." The business of arranging for the next Senefelder Club exhibition and the next International Exhibition restrained him; however, he soon freed himself to travel, and for the next eight months he labored upon one of the most extraordinary enterprises of his career. The Panama Canal challenged him as the most colossal work of modern times, and Pennell made thirty lithographs of it,

"A Chimera of Notre Dame," illustration by Pennell published in the Pall Mall Gazette *(1893) and later in R. A. M. Stevenson's* The Devils of Notre Dame *(1894)*

each drawing done on the spot with no preliminary sketches or photographs to rely upon. Pennell's mastery of lithographic technique was expert now, far excelling his first serious efforts of 1896. With the help of a skillful printer at the Ketterlinus Lithographic Company in Philadelphia, whose work he superintended, Pennell was able to forward finished lithographs to Lippincott and Heinemann for publication as *Joseph Pennell's Pictures of the Panama Canal,* released before the end of 1912. Elated with his Panama triumph, Pennell remained in Philadelphia and, accompanied by Elizabeth, wandered his native town making lithographs. If he was saddened by the destruction of the beloved landmarks of his youth, Pennell drew what had survived with added vigor and affection, and with Elizabeth's text Lippincott published *Our Philadelphia* in 1914. It reproduces 105 of Pennell's most accomplished and sensitive lithographs.

Having depicted in Panama what he considered the crest of the Modern Age, Pennell next determined to return to the Classical Age, and he set out for the "Land of Temples." Pennell docked in

"Civita Vecchia," illustration by Pennell for Henry James's Italian Days *(1905)*

Athens and slowly wended his way home by way of Taormina and Girgenti. He considered the resulting lithographs "as good as any I ever made," and both Heinemann and Lippincott were pleased to publish them as *Joseph Pennell's Pictures in the Land of Temples* (1915).

With a change of ownership in 1914, *Century* and Pennell parted company, ending a thirty-three-year association. Without foreign commissions, Pennell found much to do with the administrative details of his many clubs in London although in June he traveled to Berlin and then continued to other parts of Germany. He was still in Germany when the Austrian archduke was assassinated in Sarajevo and still there when, soon afterward, Germany and Russia entered into war. By the time Pennell found his precipitous way home, England had already joined the Allies, and war was everywhere.

Pennell's anguish was terrible; he grieved over the terrible slaughter of men as well as the devastation of many beautiful parts of the world he had spent endless contented hours drawing. The destruction of Germany appalled him no less than that of Belgium and France, for he knew Germany well. Writing to an American friend, he lamented, "All that is too awful—everything smashed up—all the people I knew—disappeared—my work in the country—and I had work and shows there for near a year—stopped and all for this cursed, damnable military doctrine."

The war left no part of his life undisturbed. In 1915 Pennell found himself on a committee organized by the Royal Academy—"one of the most extraordinary things the war has accomplished," he wrote ironically. As president of the Senefelder Club he was asked to help bring about a War Relief Exhibition, to which English artists were to contribute works of art with half the profits earmarked for war funds. By 1916, two years into World War I, the English people tended to exhibit a wariness of the foreign born, and Pennell felt ostracized. He began to contemplate resettling in America. Yet while he made preparations, including the painstaking boxing and shipping of his immense collection of Whistleriana to the Library of Congress, he also began to regard the war in terms of his own great theme, the Wonder of Work. Reflecting in his autobiography, he wrote, "I do not believe in war. I abominate it. It wrecked my life; it ruined my plans; it smashed my ideals and beliefs. But it was the cause of my seeing, in their greatest activity, those phases in the Wonder of Work which for years I had been trying to draw, for there never was such industrial energy in the world as during the War."

By July, Pennell had begun his circuit of English war works at an airplane factory at Farnham. From there he traveled to Leeds to the munitions works, where he was mistaken for a spy and chased out of town by an enraged mob that might have killed him had it caught him. From there he went to

Newcastle to draw the Tyne shipyards, where a nervous policeman arrested him. Crossing the Tyne, Pennell journeyed through Wales, drawing munitions works where he could before crossing back into England. Before the end of the year his war lithographs were exhibited with great fanfare at Guildhall Art Gallery in London. That the novelist H. G. Wells thought well enough of the work to compose an introduction to the Guildhall catalogue pleased Pennell. Heinemann found the war depictions irresistible and enthusiastically arranged to make them into another book in his Joseph Pennell's Pictures Series, published the following year as *Joseph Pennell's Pictures of War Work in England* (1917).

Although the Guildhall opening was a triumph, Pennell remembered years later that critical notices coolly pondered why he, an American, had been permitted to make pictures of sights that English people were not permitted to see. A sense of estrangement pervaded other aspects of Pennell's life. He resigned as the president of the Senefelder Club, discovering himself out of sympathy with some of the council members. While England gradually rejected the man, his war lithographs found enthusiastic audiences. Exhibitions were held throughout England and Scotland and in February 1917 even in New York at Keppel's Gallery. M. Henry Davray entreated Pennell to cross the English Channel and make similar drawings of French war work. Already dismayed by the jumble of his life in London, Pennell's decision to accept Davray's invitation and face the war at close quarters led him perilously close to collapse.

In May, having redrawn his will, Pennell departed for France but quickly returned, stunned by the carnage he had witnessed, railing at the French for dragging him to the front; his interest lay in engineering and construction, not in war horrors. Against his better judgment, Pennell allowed himself to be talked into returning to France, his pride at never having failed a commission at stake. He found Paris unbearable, the buildings shattered and ruined, men unspeakably crippled—"heroes for a moment, junk for the rest of their lives," he recounted in the most powerful chapter of his autobiography—and bombs forever exploding in the distance, providing ominous punctuation. His mental state deteriorated so that when he finally arrived in Verdun he found work nearly impossible. What drawings he made he quickly disowned. He could not slip into the artist's trance that since his student days had enabled him to stand in the street, oblivious to the noise and movements of the assembled crowds, and to make exacting drawings with a pen or an etching needle. Defeated, unable to conceive that art could convey the war's loathsome reality, he gave up trying. Retreating to Paris, he discovered that his passport restrictions prohibited him from crossing the English Channel into London and that he would have to return by the tortuous route of Bordeaux and America. After long delays in Paris and Bordeaux, which would have been nerve-wracking under ideal circumstances, he departed for America, arriving in New York just after his sixty-third birthday. Far from the haven of Adelphi Terrace, in bad mental shape, believing that he had no work to pursue and berating himself severely for having failed his French assignment, Pennell saw his career as an illustrator as over.

Lacking incentive to continue to London, he returned to Philadelphia. Elizabeth began to conclude her own professional duties, attended to the colossal, heartbreaking task of packaging their vast art collections—including a copy of every print Pennell had ever made and many of his unique etched plates—carefully arranged for their safekeeping, and closed their home at Adelphi Terrace, bringing their thirty-six-year London residency to an end.

Pennell had not been forgotten in America. By August invitations to speak in Chicago and New York invigorated him, and a plan to illustrate American war work—an American counterpart to his *Pictures of War Work in England*—restored his sense of purpose. The many exhibitions accorded his subsequent American lithography also pleased him greatly. In 1918 Lippincott published a collection under the title *Joseph Pennell's Pictures of War Work in America*. In the introduction Pennell gratefully thanks America, "his country," for having snatched him from "the mouth of hell, the jaws of death." Interestingly, his war work was to be his farewell to lithography. "The world offered him no motives that would not have come as an anticlimax," Elizabeth explained in her introduction to Wuerth's *Catalogue of the Lithographs of Joseph Pennell*.

When Elizabeth arrived in Philadelphia, Pennell was already enmeshed in a furious schedule of work, lecturing in art schools and museums from Boston to Philadelphia to Chicago and donating time to the Division of Pictorial Publicity, Committee on Public Information, presided over by illustrator Charles Dana Gibson. The chief purpose of the committee was to create posters in support of the war effort. Having sheared his associations with the International Society and the Senefelder Club, Pennell found the shared dedication and collegiality of his fellow committee members heartening. He extended his patriotic efforts further, serving on a government committee to select eight artists to send to the front and visiting the School for Disabled Sol-

An illustration by Joseph Pennell for French Cathedrals
*(1909), text by Elizabeth
Robins Pennell*

diers in New York run by W. A. Rogers, another illustrator he admired. Pennell also lectured for the War Emergency Fund and offered proceeds from the sale of fifty sets of his war lithographs to various war charities. Although Pennell and Elizabeth were reunited, they could not immediately locate large enough quarters and for a while resided in a hotel.

But Pennell by no means had eluded the shadow of the war. His despairing vision that the war had savaged civilization never wholly left him. He felt it keenly when he and Elizabeth learned that their priceless collection of Whistleriana had been carelessly opened in transit; exposed to dampness, the beauty of the material had been lost, and many of the pieces were ruined entirely. Just as it had disturbed his cozy, useful life at Adelphi Terrace, the war now seemed bent on extirpating his past.

Pennell's trip to the South, which on his way had led to his gloomy discovery at the Library of Congress, took him to West Virginia, where his spirits descended further, and on to Chicago. Pennell's Chicago scenes, rendered in Russian charcoal, include eighteen telling views of the Chicago Union Stock Yards, comprising what the *Art Digest* later termed "a document in eccentricity." They feature cattle trains arriving, acres of cattle pens, slaughterhouses, the dressing of meat, and similarly morbid sights, evoking Pennell's morbid psychological state. From there Pennell continued to Detroit and Cleveland for similarly odd work.

During this period the U.S. government ordered a large edition of Pennell's one war poster. Although certainly a minor work for someone who had drawn the great cathedrals of England and France, written the biography of "the greatest artist of the nineteenth century," and recently witnessed the awesome and anomalous creations of the English war engine, Pennell's *Liberty Poster* is nonetheless significant for several reasons. Steve Baker writes that the World War I posters signaled "the emergence of modern graphic design," in which artists sought to create images that spoke to the common man. Pennell's imagery is stark and immediate, reflecting his experiences in Paris as well as the scarred state of his psyche. The poster, according to Pennell, shows "New York City bombed, shot down, burning, blown up by an enemy. A fleet of aeroplanes fly over Lower Manhattan, flames and smoke envelop the burning skyscrapers, in the foreground Liberty, from a pile of ruins, rises headless on her pedestal, her torch shattered." Just as the English war poets—such as Robert Graves, Siegfried Sassoon, and Isaac Rosenberg—exposed both the horror of the war and their own psychological vulnerabilities in simple, straightforward language, Pennell exposed his in the graphic language New Yorkers could best understand.

But as ghastly as it was, Pennell avoided self-revelation in discussions of technique. "The idea is nothing," he wrote, effecting his familiar mandarin role; it "is a hindrance, and a drag to an artist, if he cannot carry it out, if he has not command of his tools and his trade." If Pennell meant to elude his darker reflections, issues of technique offered him an ideal asylum, as did the finicky details of printing. He concluded, "Technically [the War project] was in the printing one of the most interesting of the experiments and experiences of my life." Elizabeth put the matter more succinctly, saying "working for his own country alone saved" her husband's life.

The Armistice contributed to Pennell's recovery. Reconciled to Philadelphia, he renewed his interest in club life while he maintained an active schedule as a lecturer. His itinerary stretched to include Memphis among his more-usual stops in Washington, D.C.; New York; and New Jersey. The American railroad loomed as his new Wonder of Work project. In his introduction to Keppel's *Catalogue of an Exhibition by Joseph Pennell* (1919) in the

A Pennell lithograph for his War Work in England *(1916)*

autumn, he declares Grand Central Station in New York to be "the Temple of Travel," while the Pennsylvania Station in Philadelphia resonates with "the dignity of usefulness." Having had publication of *Etchers and Etching* (1919), ultimately to be one of his most enduring books, sidetracked by the war, Pennell now arranged for its publication in both America and England. The subtle parallel between the book's having outlasted the war and his own artistic survival did not elude him; his "Postscript to Preface" conveys the passionate hope that the graphic tradition the book represents, and in which Pennell had long toiled, might also continue to flourish. It also conveys a new sense of hopefulness that all might yet end well. "The world is now made up mostly of prigs and prohibitionists; they will venture on the suppression of art as they have ventured on the suppression of wine and song. . . . But art will arise again, and laziness, hypocrisy, and sentiment, which crush and cumber the earth, again will be swept away." Indeed, by 1920 new editions of his *Lithography & Lithographers* and *Pen Drawing,* minor

monuments to technical virtuosity, gave Pennell additional reasons for optimism. In 1921 in order to be closer to New York, "the Unbelievable City," but sufficiently removed from it to see and draw it properly, Pennell and Elizabeth moved to Brooklyn, New York, taking residence at the Hotel Margaret on the northernmost tip of Brooklyn Heights. They soon adopted an old French restaurant, Mouquin, as their dining room, for it was only fifteen minutes away by subway and allowed friends to collect in a manner reminiscent of times at Adelphi Terrace and Buckingham Street, and even Venice and Paris. There Pennell seriously began to write his *Adventures of an Illustrator* (published in 1925, although he had conceived of it as early as 1886), serializing it with his old employer *Century.* In the autumn Lippincott published Elizabeth's *Whistler Journal* (1921), a supplement to the biography, and the Art Institute of Chicago published a selection of Pennell's Chicago lectures titled *The Graphic Arts, Modern Men and Modern Methods* (1921). Although now limiting his speaking engagements, Pennell ventured on another speaking tour of the South and took pleasure in discovering that New Orleans had remained virtually unchanged. He was also highly gratified to be elected to the American Academy of Arts and Letters, an honor that Paul Bartlett convinced him he must accept to "represent the Graphic Arts." (His old friend Timothy Cole was the only wood engraver in the academy.) Pennell added the responsibility of writing art criticism for the *Brooklyn Eagle* to his schedule of arranging exhibitions of his work and for the academy although the appointment proved short-lived.

To his surprise Pennell found himself representing the American Academy of Arts and Letters at a celebration of the 150th anniversary of the Royal Belgian Academy in 1922. It was with great pleasure and curiosity that he renewed his acquaintance with European art. An enemy of abstract expressionism, Pennell was nevertheless intrigued and challenged by it and took every opportunity to seek it out. His trip to Europe also gave him a chance to visit art schools in Leipzig and London. He had been solicited to teach at the Art Students League in New York, and nearing the realization of his cherished dream of teaching a class, he wanted to observe how art was currently taught.

Charmed by Belgium and hopeful about the immediate future, Pennell returned to Philadelphia to Elizabeth's harrowing news that their complete collection of books, prints, drawings, plates, oil paintings, and detailed notes—which had been so carefully boxed, marked, and stored in an English warehouse—had been exposed to flood. It was again the war. The government had commandeered space for army blankets and uniforms; Pennell's possessions had been haphazardly exiled to the cellar. Five years of sopping up water had spared no more than a third of their collection; the rest were muck. To his wife's anxious and devastating post, Pennell weakly replied, "It is only what I expected . . . a wasted life. I knew it was coming."

Pennell's long-awaited tenure at the Art Students League proved a success, stimulating for teacher and student alike. He overhauled the poor facilities and constructed workable studio spaces for teaching etching and lithography. He brought in a lithographer when he found he could not allow adequate time to both techniques, and he took his students to museum openings and to his home so that they might experience the Manhattan skyline from his hotel rooftop. His correspondence reflects his concern for students and his pride in their accomplishments.

But 1923 brought a decline in Pennell's stamina and health. In June he fell seriously ill but refused medical advice to undergo surgery. His surgery-free convalescence, seemingly successful, was protracted and incomplete. Newly confronted with his mortality, he retreated to the dubious comfort of asserting that all had been lost in the war and slipped into a state of affectlessness. When a fire at the Margaret Hotel drove the Pennells to relocate at the nearby Hotel Bossert, he brought with him little beyond a watercolor box and paper.

Pennell rallied in 1924 when consulted about a newly discovered canvas whose owner claimed it as an authentic Whistler. Pennell had been repeatedly asked since coming to New York about ostensible Whistlers, invariably dismissing them as impostors. This time he was not so sure and corresponded with many Whistler scholars, including David Croal Thomson, who had managed the 1892 Whistler Exhibition. But the matter never reached a conclusion, and the painting mysteriously vanished—at least from Pennell's life. Nevertheless, during his correspondence with Thomson, Pennell seized the opportunity to purchase a collection of Whistler's letters. These confirmed Whistler's artistic seriousness at a period of his life when detractors derided him as a mountebank. The letters gave Pennell immense satisfaction, and he donated them to the Library of Congress, proudly adding them to "the Pennell Whistler collection, already far the finest and most complete in the world."

In 1925 Pennell rewrote an introduction for a new edition of *Etchers and Etching,* gave various lectures, and saw the next publication of the Pennell Club, *A Book of Drawings* by William Makepeace Thackeray, through publication. Begun in Philadelphia in 1923 with George Gissing's *An Heiress on Condition,* the Pennell Club flourished until 1927, outliving its namesake by one year and concluding with the publication of *Italy's Garden of Eden* by Elizabeth. Pennell reserved his clearest and strongest energies for completing and designing his autobiography. The book appeared on 23 November 1925; its conclusion reads, as it was intended, as the conclusion of a life: "The view from our windows is the last of our world, for all else has gone—we have seen it go—and we are going and it is going. But it is good to have lived, to have adventured, to have known, and to remember." Five months later to the day, Pennell died of pneumonia. He was buried in the Friends' Graveyard in Philadelphia beside his mother and his aunt Martha.

Biography:

Elizabeth Robins Pennell, *The Life and Letters of Joseph Pennell* (Boston: Little, Brown, 1929).

Pennell's World War I poster

References:

Steve Baker, "Describing Images of the National Self: Popular Accounts of the Construction of Pictorial Identity in the First World War Poster," *The Oxford Art Journal*, 13, 2 (1990): 24–30;

Frederick Keppel, *Joseph Pennell, Etcher, Illustrator, Author* (New York: Keppel, 1907);

Malcolm C. Salaman, ed., *Joseph Pennell: Modern Masters of Etching No. 28* (New York: Rudge / London: The Studio, 1931);

William Makepeace Thackeray, *A Book of Drawings* (Philadelphia: Privately printed for the Pennell Club, 1925);

Louis A. Wuerth, *Catalogue of the Etchings of Joseph Pennell* (San Francisco: Alan Wofsky Fine Arts, 1988);

Wuerth, *Catalogue of the Lithographs of Joseph Pennell* (San Francisco: Alan Wofsky Fine Arts, 1991).

Archives:

The Library of Congress holds a large collection of Pennell's archives and prints; the Archives of American Art at the Smithsonian Institution holds a collection of Pennell's letters and papers; and the Van Pelt Library at the University of Pennsylvania holds a collection of Pennell's manuscripts.

May Wilson Preston

(11 August 1873 – 18 May 1949)

Nancy Allyn Jarzombek

SELECTED BOOKS ILLUSTRATED: French, Anne Warner, *Seeing France with Uncle John* (New York: Century, 1906);

Henry, O. [William Sydney Porter], *The Gentle Grafter* (New York: McClure, 1908);

Butler, Ellis Parker, *The Cheerful Smugglers* (New York: Century, 1908);

Wells, Carolyn, *The Rubáiyát of Bridge* (New York: Harper, 1909);

Johnson, Owen, *The Prodigious Hickey: A Lawrenceville Story* (New York: Baker & Taylor, 1910);

Street, Julian Leonard, *Paris a la carte* (New York: John Lane, 1912);

Woods, Alice, *Fame Seekers* (New York: Doran, 1912);

Cameron, Margaret, *The Golden Rule Dollivers* (New York: Harper, 1913);

Rinehart, Mary Roberts, *The After House* (Boston: Houghton Mifflin, 1914);

Shaw, George Bernard, *Pygmalion, a Romance in Five Acts* (London: Constable, 1914);

Ford, James L., *The Great Mirage* (New York: Harper, 1915);

McLaurin, Kate L., *The Least Resistance* (New York: Doran, 1916);

Rinehart, Mary Roberts, *Tish* (Boston: Houghton Mifflin, 1916);

Lardner, Ring, *Gullible's Travels* (Indianapolis: Bobbs-Merrill, 1917);

Rinehart, Mary Roberts, *Bab: a Sub-deb* (New York: Doran, 1917);

McCutcheon, George Barr, *The City of Masks* (New York: Dodd, Mead, 1918);

Putnam, Nina Wilcox, *Esmerelda* (Philadelphia: Lippincott, 1918);

Rinehart, Mary Roberts, *Twenty-Three and a Half Hours' Leave* (Toronto: McClelland, Goodchild & Stewart, 1918);

Sterrett, Frances R., *Jimmie the Sixth* (New York: Appleton, 1918);

Wallace, Irwin, *Venus in the East* (New York: Doran, 1918);

May Wilson Preston

Lardner, Ring, *The Real Dope* (Indianapolis: Bobbs-Merrill, 1919);

Lardner, *The Big Town* (Indianapolis: Bobbs-Merrill, 1921).

PERIODICALS: *Cosmopolitan,* 1903, 1905;

The Saturday Evening Post, 1903–1938;

Scribner's Magazine, 1903–1908, 1910, 1914–1916, 1918;

Collier's, 1904–1916, 1919;

McClure's, 1904–1907, 1910, 1913–1920;
Harper's Monthly, 1905–1918, 1920;
Outing, 1906–1908;
Everybody's, 1907–1920;
Redbook, 1908–1909;
Harper's Weekly, 1908–1909, 1913–1914;
Life, 1912–1913, 1920;
Vanity Fair, 1915;
Ladies' Home Journal, 1928, 1930–1935.

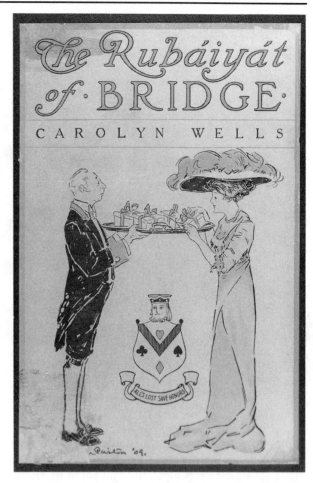

Cover for a book of humorous verse illustrated by Preston

May Wilson Preston was an insightful illustrator best remembered for her humorous drawings of upper-class life. In 1915 *Vanity Fair* named her one of a dozen of the most distinguished illustrators in the world. Success came slowly for Preston, after years of hard work and determination. From the start of her career in 1901 she experimented with different types of stories and styles of drawings until she developed a successful formula that she used well into the 1930s.

May Wilson was born in New York City on 11 August 1873. She was the only child of John J. and Ann Taylor Wilson, and she enjoyed, in the words of an anonymous critic writing in the July 1910 *Craftsman,* "the sympathetic appreciation of finely intelligent parents." She showed an interest in art early, and in 1889 she was one of the founding members of the Women's Art Club (later renamed the National Association of Women Artists). She attended Oberlin College in Ohio. In 1892 she returned to New York and enrolled in the Art Students' League, where she studied for five years, probably under William Merritt Chase and John H. Twachtman. Although documentation of Preston's life is scarce—few of her letters or other papers exist—anecdotes survive that suggest an energetic and determined woman with a lively sense of humor.

In 1898 Wilson married Thomas Henry Watkins, and the following year she went to Paris to study under James McNeill Whistler. Her husband does not appear to have accompanied her. Their marriage was brief—Watkins died in 1900—and few details of their relationship are known. Wilson did not thrive under Whistler's tutelage. She found the studio disappointing and the monthly critiques terrifying. She soon left the studio to work independently. After a year abroad she returned to New York, and a short time later her husband died.

In 1901 Watkins sold her first drawings to *Harper's Bazaar* for a story titled "The Bright Side of Hospital Life." Also at this time she enrolled in the New York School of Art to study with Chase. With two other art students, Edith Dimock and Lou Seyme, she shared an apartment at the Sherwood Studio Building at 58 West Fifty-seventh Street. The

three women were called the "Sherwood Sisters," and their apartment became a convivial meeting place for young artists, one of them being James Moore Preston, whom Watkins had met in Paris in 1899. Preston introduced his friend William Glackens to Edith Dimock. Preston and Wilson were married in December of 1903; Glackens and Dimock soon followed suit, and the two couples remained lifelong friends.

Preston was probably his wife's connection to Robert Henri, who also had a studio in the Sherwood Building, and a circle of artists who studied with Henri in Philadelphia and who had recently moved to New York. Preston knew Glackens, John Sloan, Everett Shinn, and George Luks when they worked as artists-reporters for Philadelphia newspapers. By 1900 they had moved to New York, where they worked as illustrators, and their rough, sketchy style set them apart from the more refined illustrators of the time. Henri introduced the young artists to French realist writers and artists. He encouraged them to pursue a realist approach in their paintings,

"Listen!" I said. "What did them two girdles cost?"

Illustration by Preston for Ring Lardner's The Big Town *(1921)*

looking to the city streets around them for subject matter. Preston embraced the artistic philosophy of these artists. She was especially influenced by Glackens's sketchy style. While her earliest illustrations are delicately modeled and squared off in a self-consciously artistic manner, by 1904 she had adapted a coarser style, modeling with heavy diagonal strokes and capturing the characters with only a few accurately drawn lines. Like Glackens, Preston exaggerated the features and poses of her characters for comic effect.

For two years Preston tried to sell her drawings to the major magazines, with no success. In 1903, however, her big break came. Not only did she sell stories to *Scribner's, Harper's Monthly,* and *Cosmopolitan,* but she also sold her first illustrations to *The Saturday Evening Post,* for "The Making of a Sport" by Emery Pottle. The following year she illustrated eight stories for the *Post,* and from then on her drawings appeared steadily until she stopped illustrating in 1938.

Altogether she illustrated hundreds of stories and articles in *The Saturday Evening Post* by such authors as Robert W. Chambers, Grace Ellery Channing, Richard Washburn Child, Alice Duer Miller, Owen Johnson, Mary Roberts Rinehart, and P. G. Wodehouse. During her busiest years—between 1908 and 1925—Preston worked most frequently for *The Saturday Evening Post, Harper's Monthly, McClure's, Every-*

body's, and *Collier's.* In December 1909 *The Craftsman* identified her as one of "the foremost American illustrators" and placed her work "on a scale between that of [William] Glackens and [John] Sloan." She was praised for her "fine freedom of technique" and her "intimate sympathies with the tragedies in life." The same magazine featured Preston in the July 1910 issue, describing her as energetic, determined, and talented. Her work, it was reported, was "inevitably out of life, implicit with the realities of our present civilization."

Preston's seemingly effortless technique belies the amount of work each drawing demanded. She was thorough and meticulous in researching her subject to make sure the details of her pictures would be accurate. She made many preliminary sketches for each final drawing and, as one of the steps toward reaching the final composition, would fit sketches onto pages of text to approximate the final layout. Once satisfied with a composition she would lay a piece of transparent paper over her drawing and make another drawing using only those lines that were essential. At this point, having distilled the sketch to its essential lines, she made the final drawing on cardboard, continuing to refine and start over until the deadline arrived.

In addition to working as an illustrator, Preston was a painter, producing interior scenes and landscapes in a realist mode. Between 1906 and

1911 she exhibited work at the Pennsylvania Academy of the Fine Arts and the National Academy of Design in New York. She participated in two exhibitions that helped launch American modernism: the Independent Artists' Exhibition in 1910 and the Armory Show in 1913. In 1915 she won a bronze medal at the Pan-Pacific Exposition at San Francisco.

In 1935 the Prestons moved to East Hampton, Long Island. May Wilson Preston continued to illustrate stories for *The Saturday Evening Post* until 1938 when, wearied by a serious skin infection, she retired. She died of a heart attack in 1949.

References:

"A Dozen of the Best Illustrators in the World and Every One of Them American," *Vanity Fair,* 4 (August 1915): 28–29;

Rowland Elzea and Iris Snyder, "May Wilson (Watkins) (Preston) 1873–1949," in their *American Illustration: The Collection of the Delaware Art Museum* (Wilmington: Delaware Art Museum, 1991);

"Foremost American Illustrators: Vital Significance of their Work," *Craftsman,* 17 (December 1909): 266–280;

Ira Glackens, *William Glackens and The Eight* (New York: Horizon, 1957), pp. 148–154;

Jane Grant, "May Wilson Preston," in *Notable American Women 1607–1950: A Biographical Dictionary,* volume 3, edited by Edward T. James (Cambridge, Mass.: Harvard University Press, 1971);

Elizabeth H. Hawkes, "May Wilson Preston, 1873–1949," in her *City Life Illustrated: 1890–1940* (Wilmington: Delaware Art Museum, 1980), pp. 76–79;

"People Who Interest Us: May Wilson Preston, Illustrator of Real Life," *Craftsman,* 18 (July 1910): 472–473;

Wesley Stout, "Yes, We Read the Story," *Saturday Evening Post* (25 June 1932): 8–9.

Howard Pyle

(5 March 1853 – 9 November 1911)

Elizabeth H. Hawkes

See also the Pyle entries in *DLB 42: American Writers for Children Before 1900* and *DS 13: The House of Scribner, 1846–1904.*

BOOKS: *The Merry Adventures of Robin Hood* (New York: Scribners, 1883);

Within the Capes (New York: Scribners, 1885);

Pepper and Salt, or Seasoning for Young Folk (New York: Harper, 1886);

The Wonder Clock, by Pyle and Katharine Pyle (New York: Harper, 1888);

The Rose of Paradise (New York: Harper, 1888);

Otto of the Silver Hand (New York: Scribners, 1888);

Men of Iron (New York: Harper, 1892);

A Modern Aladdin (New York: Harper, 1892);

The Garden Behind the Moon (New York: Scribners, 1895);

The Story of Jack Ballister's Fortunes (New York: Century, 1895);

Twilight Land (New York: Harper, 1895);

The Ghost of Captain Brand (Wilmington, Del.: John M. Rogers, 1896);

The Price of Blood (Boston: Richard G. Badger, 1899);

Rejected of Men (New York: Harper, 1903);

The Story of King Arthur and His Knights (New York: Scribners, 1903);

The Story of the Champions of the Round Table (New York: Scribners, 1905);

Stolen Treasure (New York: Harper, 1907);

The Story of Sir Launcelot and His Companions (New York: Scribners, 1907);

The Ruby of Kishmoor (New York: Harper, 1908);

The Story of the Grail and the Passing of Arthur (New York: Scribners, 1910).

SELECTED BOOKS ILLUSTRATED: *Yankee Doodle: An Old Friend in a New Dress* (New York: Dodd, Mead, 1881);

Tennyson, Alfred, *The Lady of Shalott* (New York: Dodd, Mead, 1881);

Carleton, Will, *Farm Ballads* (New York: Harper, 1882);

Howard Pyle

Baldwin, James, *The Story of Siegfried* (New York: Scribners, 1882);

Read, Thomas Buchanan, *The Closing Scene* (Philadelphia: Lippincott, 1887);

Baldwin, James, *A Story of the Golden Age* (New York: Scribners, 1887);

Frederic, Harold, *In the Valley* (New York: Scribners, 1890);

Holmes, Oliver Wendell, *The One Hoss Shay* (Boston: Houghton, Mifflin, 1892);

Holmes, *Dorothy Q with a Ballad of the Boston Tea Party and Grandmother's Story of Bunker Hill Battle* (Boston: Houghton, Mifflin, 1893);

Wilkins, Mary E., *Giles Corey, Yeoman* (New York: Harper, 1893);

Holmes, Oliver Wendell, *The Autocrat of the Breakfast-Table* (Boston: Houghton, Mifflin, 1894);

Janvier, Thomas A., *In Old New York* (New York: Harper, 1894);

Stevenson, Robert Louis, *David Balfour* (New York: Scribners, 1895);

Stevenson, *Kidnapped* (New York: Scribners, 1895);

Stevenson, *The Merry Men and Other Tales and Fables, and the Strange Case of Dr. Jekyll and Mr. Hyde* (New York: Scribners, 1895);

Doyle, Arthur Conan, *The Parasite* (New York: Harper, 1895);

Howells, William Dean, *Stops of Various Quills* (New York: Harper, 1895);

Andrews, E. Benjamin, *The History of the Last Quarter-Century* (New York: Scribners, 1896);

Page, Thomas Nelson, *In Ole Virginia* (New York: Scribners, 1896);

Dyke, Henry Van, *The First Christmas Tree* (New York: Scribners, 1897);

Wilson, Woodrow, *George Washington* (New York: Harper, 1897);

Mitchell, S. Weir, *Hugh Wynne, Free Quaker* (New York: Century, 1897);

Sienkiewicz, Henry, *Quo Vadis* (Boston: Little, Brown, 1897);

Lodge, Henry Cabot, *The Story of the Revolution* (New York: Scribners, 1898);

Ford, Paul Leicester, *Janice Meredith* (New York: Dodd, Mead, 1899);

Deland, Margaret, *Old Chester Tales* (New York: Harper, 1899);

Johnston, Mary, *To Have and to Hold* (Boston: Houghton, Mifflin, 1900);

Markham, Edwin, *The Man with the Hoe and Other Poems* (New York: Doubleday, McClure, 1900);

Goodwin, Maud Wilder, *Sir Christopher* (Boston: Little, Brown, 1901);

Van Dyke, Henry, *The Blue Flower* (New York: Scribners, 1902);

Wilson, Woodrow, *A History of the American People* (New York: Harper, 1902);

Dibdin, Thomas Frognall, *The Bibliomania or Book-Madness* (Boston: Bibliophile Society, 1903);

Forman, Justus Miles, *The Island of Enchantment* (New York: Harper, 1905);

Cabell, James Branch, *The Line of Love* (New York: Harper, 1905);

Cabell, *Gallantry, an Eighteenth Century Dizain* (New York: Harper, 1907);

Cabell, *Chivalry* (New York: Harper, 1909);

Seitz, Don C., *The Buccaneers* (New York: Harper, 1912);

Beymer, William Gilmore, *On Hazardous Service* (New York: Harper, 1912);

Cabell, James Branch, *The Soul of Melicent* (New York: Stokes, 1913).

PERIODICALS: *Scribner's Monthly,* 1876–1881; *St. Nicholas,* 1877–1903; *Harper's Weekly,* 1877–1904; *Harper's Monthly,* 1878–1913; *Harper's Young People,* 1880–1894; *Our Continent,* 1882; *Harper's Bazar,* 1882–1891; *Wide Awake,* 1885–1889; *Scribner's Magazine,* 1887–1903; *Northwestern Miller,* 1890–1900; *Cosmopolitan,* 1892–1894; *Century,* 1893–1902; *Harper's Round Table,* 1896–1897; *Ladies' Home Journal,* 1896–1899; *Collier's,* 1898–1906; *McClure's,* 1899–1906; *Everybody's,* 1902–1913.

During his thirty-five-year career Howard Pyle became one of America's most prominent illustrators. Moreover, he achieved recognition as a writer, teacher, and mural painter. For him the purpose of art was to entertain and to inspire. He argued that artists should not simply make beautiful pictures or pleasing decorations but should also convey ideas about the past and present in pictorial form. More than three thousand of his illustrations were reproduced in leading magazines and books of the day. In addition he wrote twenty books, of which half were for children, and many short stories. Near the end of his life he worked on four mural projects, as well as large easel paintings. He also made an important contribution as a gifted teacher of more than one hundred students.

Howard Pyle was born on 5 March 1853 in Wilmington, Delaware, the first child of William Pyle, a Quaker who operated a leather business, and Margaret Churchman Painter Pyle, who had literary aspirations. His ancestors were Quaker settlers from England who in the eighteenth century had come seeking religious freedom and a new life farming in the Brandywine Valley.

Pyle grew up in a fieldstone farmhouse now known as Goodstay. When his father's business fell on hard times, the family moved to a smaller dwelling in the city. He studied at the Friends School and later at T. Clarkson Taylor's Scientific and Commercial Academy in Wilmington. Though birthright Quakers, the Pyle family joined the Swedenborgian church in Wilmington in 1866. Pyle's

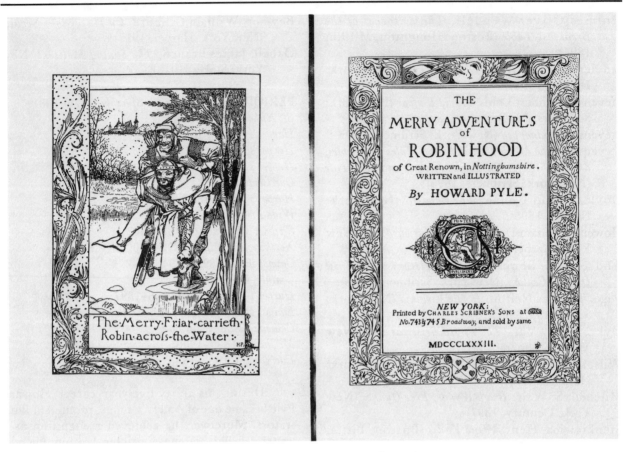

Frontispiece and title page for Pyle's first book

younger sister Katharine (1863–1938) became an artist and writer of children's books.

Pyle's mother observed his artistic talents and encouraged him to draw at a young age. He read German and English folktales, Daniel Defoe's *Robinson Crusoe* (1719), novels by Charles Dickens and William Makepeace Thackeray, and illustrated English periodicals—*Punch, Illustrated London News, Once a Week,* and the *Churchman's Family Magazine.* He became familiar with drawings by the English artists Arthur Boyd Houghton, Charles Keene, John Leech, and the Pre-Raphaelites.

In 1869 Pyle studied art in Philadelphia with Adolph van der Wielen, a Belgian painter who established an art school that existed only a few years. The curriculum followed academic precepts of making meticulous copies from plaster casts, still lifes, and posed models. Pyle learned technique, but years later, when he began to teach, he complained that the curriculum had not stimulated his imagination.

After almost three years of art study, Pyle returned to Wilmington to work for the family leather business—drawing and writing in his spare time. He designed a masthead for the local Wilmington news-

paper, the *Every Evening,* and even gave art lessons. For Pyle the year 1876 marked a turning point in his fledgling career. *Scribner's Monthly* published his humorous poem about a magic pill and an illustrated article on Chincoteague Island's annual wild pony roundup in Virginia. *St. Nicholas,* a children's magazine, accepted one of his fairy tales for publication.

Roswell Smith, an editor at *Scribner's,* told Pyle's father that New York publishing companies needed talented artists and writers and encouraged Pyle in his pursuit of an illustration career. That fall Pyle moved to New York, staying at a boardinghouse on Forty-eighth Street. He entered night classes at the Art Students League, taking life drawing and sketch classes. While working for *Harper's Weekly,* Pyle met the influential art editor Charles Parsons and staff artists Charles Stanley Reinhart, Edwin Austin Abbey, and A. B. Frost. He learned firsthand how Harper produced the magazine—with illustrators creating pictures and wood engravers translating the pictorial image on engraved blocks for printing. At first Pyle sold Harper "idea-sketches" that were redrawn by more-experienced artists. Then in 1878 he submitted a drawing of a contemporary subject titled *A Wreck in the Offing* that was not redrawn by another artist, signifying the end of his apprenticeship status. Later that year *Harper's Monthly* published Pyle's first American historical subject, *Carnival, Philadelphia, 1778.* Thus, Pyle developed contacts with the two rival New York publishing houses—Harper and Scribners.

In 1879 Pyle returned to Wilmington. His closest friend, Frost, had already left New York to work near Philadelphia, and Abbey had moved to England. Pyle briefly considered studying in Europe, but this idea never materialized. After arranging for Harper to send him articles, Pyle set up a studio in the third floor of his parents' house to work as a freelance artist and writer. Pyle eagerly entered the social life of Wilmington. He joined the lyceum's chorus, where he met Anne Poole, the daughter of a successful manufacturer of milling machinery. In 1881 they married in a Quaker ceremony, with Frost serving as best man. They reared a family of two daughters and five sons though their first child, Sellers, died tragically at the age of seven. While his wife managed the household, Pyle continued to submit drawings and articles to New York publishers. By 1883 he felt financially secure enough to build a studio in a quasi-Tudor cottage style on what was then the edge of town; the studio at 1305 North Franklin Street still stands and is on the National Register of Historic Places.

The decade following Pyle's return to Wilmington marked a period of artistic maturation for him. Harper regularly sent manuscripts of travel pieces and children's stories as well as ideas for full-page drawings for *Harper's Weekly.* Combining his dual talents of drawing and writing, Pyle sent his own illustrated articles for publication. He prepared text and drawings for articles on John Bartram's garden in Philadelphia, Quaker life in Wilmington, and descriptive travel pieces on the Pocono Mountains and the Lancaster County farmland in nearby Pennsylvania. He also sent amusing poems and stories with lively drawings to *Harper's Young People,* a children's magazine.

Pyle's first opportunity to illustrate a book came in 1879. He made several gouache drawings, still youthful and not distinguished, to accompany stories by Nathaniel Hawthorne and Charles Dickens in *McGuffey's Fifth Eclectic Reader.* Two years later the Dodd, Mead publishing company commissioned watercolor drawings for two children's books: *Yankee Doodle: An Old Friend in a New Dress* (the nursery-rhyme song) and Alfred Tennyson's *The Lady of Shalott.* Pyle designed the covers and color decorations for both books. Dodd, Mead hoped to capture the American nursery-book market by imitating the style of English artists Walter Crane, Kate Green-

away, and Randolph Caldecott, whose children's books were popular in America. The quality of the color printing disappointed Pyle, but this experience gave him insight into the nature of children's book publication, which served him well as he tackled more-complex book assignments.

Pyle's *The Merry Adventures of Robin Hood,* published by Scribners in 1883, was his first serious effort at providing both text and pictures for a book. While still in New York he thought about reworking the Robin Hood legend and had perused his childhood copy of Thomas Percy's *Reliques of Ancient English Poetry* (1765). For his modern version Pyle retold Percy's classic tales and added old English ballads to appeal to children. He embellished the stories with drawings of the characters and episodes. In a style reminiscent of Walter Crane's book design, Pyle added hand-lettered captions and floral borders. To create authentic settings Pyle turned to books in his own library on knighthood and armor, period costumes and furniture, and architecture. In particular he consulted Georg Hirth's *Bilderbuch* (1881–1890), a compendium of fifteenth- and sixteenth-century Old Master prints, to find objects that were typical of the period. For example, in his drawing of Robin Hood's death at a nunnery, Pyle enhanced the setting with bottle-glass windows, a shelf with a curved bracket, and an hourglass adapted from Albrecht Dürer's engraving *St. Jerome in His Cell* (1514).

Robin Hood, richly illustrated with drawings, chapter headings, initial letters, and tailpieces, became a landmark in American publishing. Reflecting the impact of the English Arts and Crafts movement, Pyle designed his book as an aesthetic whole, with illustrations, text, typeface, and binding unified in concept and style. The line drawings were photographed onto metal plates and mechanically engraved—this new printing technology eliminated the middle step of wood engravers redrawing designs. The book set new standards in American book production. Even William Morris, a leader of the English Arts and Crafts movement, admired Pyle's *Robin Hood.*

Throughout his career Pyle alternated between child and adult audiences. He reached out to a broad spectrum of educated readers with light-hearted fairy tales for young children, tales of adventure for youth, and historical nonfiction or romance stories for adults.

In the 1880s Pyle wrote and illustrated fairy tales, fables, and poems based on English and German folk legends for *Harper's Young People.* Harper published these stories about princesses and kings, talking animals, and trolls in two books marketed

Pyle (seated) and some of his students at Chadds Ford. N. C. Wyeth is standing second from right.

for the Christmas trade—*Pepper and Salt, or Seasoning for Young Folk* (1886) and *The Wonder Clock* (1888). The *Pepper and Salt* stories, interspersed with hand-lettered poems and drawings, reveal Pyle's close study of Crane and Greenaway. On the frontispiece a jester (who looks remarkably like Pyle as a young man) entertains and invites children to have a "little pinch of seasoning in this dull, heavy life of ours."

In *The Wonder Clock* old Father Time and his grandmother tell twenty-four tales—one for each hour of the day. Pyle's sister Katharine, an aspiring artist and writer, decorated a page introducing each story. Stock fairy-tale characters enliven the tales: handsome princes, old bearded kings, long-haired princesses dressed in richly ornamented costumes, the evil and ugly stepmother, the fumbling soldier, and a host of magical, otherworldly figures such as bird-men, giants, and ogres. In the same year Scribners published Pyle's *Otto of the Silver Hand,* a tale about a young boy's adventures growing up in medieval Germany. These four books—*The Merry Adventures of Robin Hood, Pepper

and Salt, The Wonder Clock,* and *Otto of the Silver Hand* —established Pyle's reputation as a writer and illustrator for children.

Pyle's contemporaries admired his woodcut-style drawings for the children's books though a few criticized his ample borrowings from Dürer. Joseph Pennell, in his book *Pen Drawing and Draughtsmen* (1889), comments on Pyle's ability to "saturate himself with the spirit of the age in which the scenes are laid, and to give his work the color and character of the biggest man [Dürer] of that age." In his essay on American pen drawings in *Modern Pen Drawings: European and American* (1901) Ernest Knaufft calls *Robin Hood* "a pleasant revival of the antique." Sadakichi Hartmann, in *A History of American Art* (1901), asserts that Pyle was "one of the few great masters of linear composition of the day." The clear outlines and patterns of short parallel lines of his woodcut style conformed to the requirements of the new photomechanical printing process used by American publishers.

While he was producing the four children's books, Pyle continued submitting American historical subjects geared to an adult audience. He earned a reputation as a skilled delineator of American history in articles by Charles Carleton Coffin, Benson J. Lossing, and Thomas Wentworth Higginson. For full-page reproductions in *Harper's Weekly* Pyle painted meticulous scenes of historic events such as William Penn's first visit to America and women voting in New Jersey. Wood engravers copied these paintings until photomechanical halftones gradually replaced this intermediate step in the mid 1890s. To ensure historical accuracy in his work Pyle researched topics and located genuine artifacts. He was an avid collector of Americana and amassed a collection of antique furniture, decorative arts, and costumes.

An outgrowth of Pyle's interest in the past was his fascination with pirates, which became a dominant theme in his work. Pyle's "The Rose of Paradise," a pirate tale serialized in the summer 1887 issues of *Harper's Weekly,* was followed by "Buccaneers and Marooners of the Spanish Main" in *Harper's Monthly*. Pyle became linked in the public's mind with pirates, as Frederic Remington had with cowboys. During summer weekends on the Delaware coast at Rehoboth Beach—an area once inhabited by pirates—Pyle searched for vestiges of pirate yore. The incongruity remained that Pyle, born to Quaker parents, romanticized these rough, thieving individuals who led solitary but violent lives.

Pyle returned to the pirate subject throughout his career. In 1890 he adapted excerpts from Charles Johnson's *The Lifes and Adventures of the Most Famous Highwaymen, Pyrates, Etc.* (1742) for *Harper's Monthly*. In 1905 Pyle's dramatic illustrations of pirate scenes for his story "Fate of a Treasure Town" created a sensation when they were published in full color in *Harper's*. For *Marooned* (1909) Pyle transformed the subject of a stranded pirate from a black-and-white illustration into a large, full-color oil painting, now in the Delaware Art Museum collection, which he intended for exhibition, not publication.

While Pyle was on assignment in Jamaica in 1889, his seven-year-old son, Sellers, died suddenly at home. This tragedy devastated Pyle, and he turned to the Swedenborgian faith for support. In 1890 he began a cordial correspondence with William Dean Howells discussing theology as well as literary matters. Howells read Pyle's manuscripts dealing with mystical themes and encouraged him to publish a religious novel, *Rejected of Men* (1903), and two short stories about life and death, "To the Soil of the Earth" and "In Tenebras."

By the 1890s Pyle gained stature as one of America's leading illustrators. A prolific draughts-

man, Pyle averaged more than 150 illustrations each year from 1890 to 1895. He frequently sent work to exhibitions, including the World's Columbian Exposition in Chicago (1893), the Society of Arts and Crafts in Boston (1899), the Exposition Universelle in Paris (1900), and the Pan-American Exposition in Buffalo (1901). He had one-person exhibits in Philadelphia and Boston in 1897 and at the Macbeth Gallery in New York in 1908.

Though living in Wilmington, Pyle commuted regularly to meet with New York publishers and engaged in social activities there. He became active in literary and choral groups as well as organizations devoted to book collecting and the theater. He was a founding member of a bibliophile group, the Grolier Club, and made drawings for their edition of Diedrich Knickerbocker's *A History of New York* (1886). He joined the Players Club and the Salmagundi Club in New York, the Bibliophile Society in Boston, and the Franklin Inn Club in Philadelphia. In Wilmington, besides being active in the Church of the New Jerusalem (Swedenborgian), he was a member of an amateur choral society called the Tuesday Club and a literary supper club, the Quill and Grill Club.

During the 1890s Pyle published four children's books. Two of the books were for older children—*Men of Iron* (1892), set in fifteenth-century England, and *The Story of Jack Ballister's Fortunes* (1895), the exploits of a kidnapped English lad who meets the pirate Blackbeard in Virginia. For a younger audience Pyle wrote *The Garden Behind the Moon* (1895), a touching allegory written after the death of his son.

Twilight Land (1895), a collection of folktales, marked a striking change in Pyle's repertoire for children. First of all, he drew quasi-Mediterranean settings instead of the northern European locale of his earlier stories. Also, thin, delicate line work replaced the familiar woodcut style. The "scratchy" line, as Pyle called it, reflected his interest in Daniel Vierge, a contemporary Spanish Impressionist who captured transitory effects of sunlight and motion in his drawings. Likewise, Pyle conveyed the impression of atmospheric effects by contrasting black shadows with complex patterns of flickering lines and by leaving some portions of the white paper blank.

Pyle adapted his new Impressionist drawing style for book illustrations geared to adults, in particular for poems and essays by Oliver Wendell Holmes published from 1892 to 1894. In "Grandmother's Story of Bunker Hill Battle" from Holmes's *Dorothy Q* (1893), billowing clouds of smoke convey the atmosphere and drama of the

Illustration for Pyle's Pepper and Salt, or Seasoning
for Young Folks *(1886)*

scene. By contrast, the ink-wash drawings for *The Autocrat of the Breakfast-Table* (1894) are allegorical in nature, echoing the content of Holmes's writing.

Mystical content was new for Pyle but compatible with his Swedenborgian faith. Allegorical figures adorned poems by his friend William Dean Howells in *Harper's Magazine* (1893–1894) and in the book *Stops of Various Quills* (1895). Typical images were angels with graceful wings, the grim reaper in black hood, and a brooding man holding an hourglass and empty goblet symbolizing approaching death. Pyle's use of symbolism allied him with other artists—notably, Kenyon Cox, Augustus Saint-Gaudens, and Daniel Chester French.

In 1894 James MacAlister, president of Drexel Institute of Art, Science, and Technology in Philadelphia, invited Pyle to teach illustration. At that time there were few schools offering programs for training illustrators. Over the years Pyle developed a curriculum based on what illustrators needed to know to produce work for reproduction in magazines and books. His first class at Drexel, "Practical Illustration in Black and

White," focused on composition, drawing from costumed models, and historical subjects. He encouraged students to compile scrapbooks with pictures of costumes, architecture, and other reference material. To give an illustration an authenticity of historical detail, he recommended examining paintings and prints from the period.

Pyle's primary objective, however, was to nurture a student's imagination. He inspired students to imagine a scene so vividly that they projected themselves into the picture. While painting a battle scene, for example, Pyle reported that he could smell the gun smoke. One of Pyle's quarrels with traditional academic instruction was that it stressed copying from nude models and plaster casts of classical sculpture instead of cultivating the imagination. According to Henry Pitz's 1975 Pyle biography, when students drew from a model, Pyle counseled them to "find [the model's] proportions, how his weight is supported, how each joint is functioning. Watch for the presence of the body under the clothes, how the folds and wrinkles tell the story. Look for the color and tone and texture of the garments. See how the light falls on the figure especially on the face. But above all, this is an opportunity to make a picture—a picture more than a copy!" Furthermore, Pyle believed that an illustration did not necessarily have to picture a specific scene mentioned in the text as long as it captured the feeling the author wished to convey. In an interview in *Pearson's Magazine* for September 1907 he explained: "Of course, I don't mean by illustration, the making of diagrams of the text. A work of true art must be independent and superior to the text."

Pyle's illustration classes at Drexel attracted many students. In 1895 the Pennsylvania Academy of Fine Arts, the leading art school in Philadelphia, invited him to teach there, but he turned them down in favor of remaining at Drexel. Pyle extended his commitment to Drexel in 1896 by increasing his teaching schedule to two days each week. Drexel held annual exhibitions of students' work showcasing the early efforts of artists such as Elizabeth Shippen Green, Violet Oakley, Frank Schoonover, and Jessie Willcox Smith. For the summers of 1898 and 1899 Drexel offered scholarships to ten gifted students to study with Pyle at Chadds Ford, Pennsylvania, a small town in the historic Brandywine Valley, not far from Wilmington. An abandoned gristmill, converted into studios, housed the classes; students also painted out-of-doors. Pyle's class shared a productive period of work and camaraderie.

Frustrated with large classes at Drexel, Pyle resigned in 1900 to open a small, private art school in Wilmington. He selected serious students to work in three large studios he built next to his own. There was no tuition, and fees for studio expenses, models, and art supplies were modest. Students worked independently, and Pyle visited them several times a day to offer criticism. He held a weekly composition lecture to discuss students' work and an evening sketch class, where everyone drew from an assigned theme entirely from imagination. The Chadds Ford summer classes continued to thrive from 1901 to 1903.

Pyle inspired a generation of illustrators. One of his most accomplished students was N. C. Wyeth, whose illustrated editions of *Treasure Island* (1911) and *Robinson Crusoe* (1920) remain classic children's books today. Like Pyle, Wyeth did independent work as well as book and periodical illustration. Wyeth's vivid recollection of meeting Pyle underscores the importance of his teacher's influence: "But here was I at last, seated before him [Pyle] in the very room in which were born so many of the pictures I had breathlessly admired from boyhood. Paintings and drawings that had long since become a living and indispensable part of my own life." Pyle's Drexel alumnae included Violet Oakley, a mural artist and painter, as well as Smith and Green, known for their scenes of children and family life. Among Pyle's most devoted followers were Schoonover and Stanley Arthurs, who attended both the Drexel and Wilmington classes. Schoonover produced many illustrations for adventure stories, while Arthurs specialized in American historical subjects. Harvey Dunn and Thornton Oakley became important teachers of illustration in New York and Philadelphia, respectively, passing along Pyle's ideas to still another generation of artists. Edward Wilson, Douglas Duer, and Gayle Hoskins moved to Wilmington to become part of the art colony growing up around Pyle. More than one hundred artists studied with Pyle at either Drexel or his Wilmington school.

Pyle encouraged his students and often acted as an intermediary, helping them get publishing assignments. During the 1899 summer school session, several students illustrated Paul Leicester Ford's "Janice Meredith," a historical drama serialized in *Collier's*. Within a few months of joining Pyle's class, Wyeth sold work to *Success* and *The Saturday Evening Post*. That magazines eagerly published the students' illustrations demonstrated the success of Pyle's teaching method. In 1904–1905 Pyle expanded his educational effort by giving biweekly lectures at the Art Students League in New York and on several occasions at the Art Institute of Chicago. A 1907 article in *Outlook* reported that young professional illustrators who were not students of Pyle set up studios in Wilmington to at-

Illustration by Pyle for J. Bacon's "The Castle on the Dune," published in Harper's Monthly *(September 1909)*

tend his Saturday afternoon lecture, which was open to the public. Other artists from Philadelphia and New York frequently attended. Wilmington became an enclave for illustrators seeking Pyle's advice. He found the daily contact with students stimulating and willingly looked at compositions that artists brought.

In the years he actively taught this upcoming generation of illustrators, Pyle produced some of his most revered illustrations. His vision of the American past matured in illustrations for Woodrow Wilson's *George Washington* (1897) and *A History of the American People* (1902) and for Henry Cabot Lodge's *The Story of the Revolution* (1898).

Alternating from one genre to another, Pyle reached out to a broad spectrum of readers. Shortly after Robert Louis Stevenson's death in 1894, Scribners commissioned illustrations for *Kidnapped, Dr. Jekyll and Mr. Hyde,* and *David Balfour,* all published in 1895. Pyle also illustrated spine-tingling stories by Arthur Conan Doyle, Rudyard Kipling, and Arthur Quiller-Couch. There was an occasional allegorical piece, such as the "Travels of the Soul" series in *Century* (1902) and Erik Bogh's "Pilgrimage of Truth" (1900). The popularity of Pyle's illustrations for Thomas Frognall Dibdin's *The Bibliomania or Book-Madness* (1903) led to a limited-edition portfolio of the pictures. New periodicals—*Collier's, McClure's,* and *Everybody's*—published his literary and pictorial work.

In 1902 Pyle proposed to Scribners the idea of publishing the legends of King Arthur following the general format of his Robin Hood book, which was still popular after twenty years. After first serializing the King Arthur story in the children's magazine *St. Nicholas,* Scribners published the book in 1903 and launched a plan for three additional volumes: *The Story of the Champions of the Round Table* (1905), *The Story of the Sir Launcelot and His Companions* (1907), and *The Story of the Grail and the Passing of Arthur* (1910). Pyle drew his stories from Sir Thomas Malory's King Arthur legends, compiled in the fifteenth century, but altered the story by deleting some violent passages that might offend children.

Of the quartet, *The Story of King Arthur and His Knights* is the masterpiece. The last book in the cycle, *The Story of the Grail and the Passing of Arthur,* completed only a year before Pyle's death, lacks vigor and is repetitive. Pyle generously embellished the books with illustrations, hand-lettered titles, illuminated initials, and decorative headings. Complex textures and patterns of delicate lines replace the woodcutlike black outlines of the *Robin Hood* drawings. The silken garb of the Lady of the Lake and Enchanter Merlin's fur collar and heavy cloak have rich, tactile qualities. Though in black and white, the portrait of King Arthur pulses with a sensation of color tonality. In *Two Knights Do Battle Before Camilard,* a bloodless joust in an enchanting landscape of castle and moat, Pyle contrasted stippled brushstrokes with the gleaming whiteness of the paper. He experimented with stylistic devices evident in the Art Nouveau drawings of contemporary artists Aubrey Beardsley and Maxfield Parrish.

While engaged in the King Arthur project for Scribners, Pyle negotiated a contract with Harper to provide three illustrations a month for their magazines. He became known for his colorful renditions of medieval subjects, ranging from "Saint Joan of Arc" by Mark Twain to historical romance by James Branch Cabell. After a few years Pyle grew discontented with the quality of conventional magazine stories, which lacked any permanent literary value. Though he was at the top of his profession, he yearned to paint independent subjects without the constraints of text and flirted with the idea of attempting mural decoration.

Pyle's earliest works for *Harper's Weekly,* beginning with *Wreck in the Offing* (1878), were full-page illustrations without any accompanying text. A few years later *Harper's Weekly* offered paintings of pirates and highwaymen in full-page reproduction, such as *How the Buccaneers Kept Christmas* (1899). *Collier's* reproduced independent paintings by Pyle, Frederic Remington, Parrish, and others. *The Flying Dutchman* (1900) and *The Nation Makers* (1906), now both in museum collections, first appeared in the pages of *Collier's.* In 1906 *Harper's Monthly* added a twist by publishing independent pictures of favorite characters from William Makepeace Thackeray's novels. American readers already knew these stories and did not need explanatory text.

In 1905 Pyle expanded his endeavors from illustrating, writing, and teaching to mural painting, which was enjoying a renewed interest among painters such as Kenyon Cox, Edwin Blashfield, and John La Farge. In 1902 Violet Oakley, one of Pyle's most successful students, and his friend Abbey received commissions to paint murals for the Pennsylvania Capitol Building. All this stimulated Pyle to consider mural painting as an alternative to magazine illustration.

To celebrate his daughter's coming-out party in 1905, Pyle decorated his house with several murals. He exhibited the largest one, *The Genus of Art,* at the Society of Architects in New York. Soon afterward Cass Gilbert, architect of the Minnesota State Capitol Building in Saint Paul, selected Pyle to do a large-scale painting of a Civil War battle in which Minnesota soldiers played a significant role. *The Battle of Nashville,* though usually referred to as a mural, was actually a large, framed painting for the governor's reception room. This was no heroic, romanticized view of war, but a stark scene of determined soldiers, some wounded and some dying, carrying tattered flags as they marched across a bleak winter landscape. Having interviewed survivors of the battle, Pyle captured both the horror and the valor of war. His rendering of the experience of war, foreshadowed in *The Battle of Bunker Hill* (1897) and *The Nation Makers* (1906), reached a culmination in this work.

In 1906 S. S. McClure invited Pyle to become art director of *McClure's.* At first Pyle, not wanting to move to New York City, declined the offer, but when McClure offered a generous salary for a three-day workweek, Pyle accepted the position. At the beginning he saw the job as an opportunity to free himself from illustration commitments and to allow time for mural projects, but from all accounts the *McClure's* hiatus was a mistake. He alienated his students Wyeth and Schoonover by pressing them to work exclusively for *McClure's.* Apparently Pyle was impractical and lacked business skills.

"So the Treasure Was Divided"; illustration by Pyle for the December 1905 issue of Harper's Monthly

Pyle returned to illustration, working primarily for Harper with intermittent commissions from other publishers. He continued to advise students as well as young professional illustrators. In 1906 Gilbert commissioned a mural, *The Landing of Carteret,* for the Essex County Court House in Newark, New Jersey. Pyle also painted several large independent paintings, such as *Marooned* (1909), a beach scene of a stranded pirate, and *Mermaid* (begun in 1910 and unfinished at his death). These works were twice the size of Pyle's standard illustrations.

In 1910 Pyle completed several murals on the subject of the Dutch and English settlement of Manhattan Island for the Hudson County Court House in Jersey City. Though the project's architect, Hugh Roberts, disliked Pyle's efforts, the local newspaper called them the most popular decorations in the courthouse. Apparently Pyle, a latecomer to mural painting, had some misgivings about the project and resolved to study the Renaissance masters in Italy. He sailed with his family for Italy in November 1910, and he died there on 9 November 1911 at the age of fifty-eight.

Pyle's death stunned the Wilmington community. America's reading public at large and, in particular, his former students felt the loss. In a 14 November 1911 letter Wyeth wrote his mother of his resolve "to carry on the honest impulses he [Pyle] awakened within us—to perpetuate his *beginning*." To promote the Pyle legacy in Wilmington, the artist's friends and former students raised funds to buy a collection of paintings and drawings from his widow. The organization they founded became the forerunner of the present-day Delaware Art Museum, now housing the largest holdings of Pyle's work.

Pyle's students organized a memorial exhibition in 1912 at Wilmington's Hotel du Pont that attracted thousands of visitors. Organizers of the Pan-Pacific Exhibition in San Francisco (1915) honored Pyle's distinguished contribution to American illustration by exhibiting a collection of his work. In 1923, to celebrate the seventieth anniversary of his birth, Pyle's former students held a special tribute at the Philadelphia Art Alliance. Meanwhile, in Wilmington the tradition of holding annual exhibitions

Pyle and his wife, Anne, in 1910

of paintings by Pyle's students commenced.

The first book documenting Pyle's career was a bibliography (1921) of his illustrations and writings by Willard S. Morse, a Pyle bibliophile, and Gertrude Brincklé, Pyle's former secretary and a family friend. Two years later Morse donated his Pyle collection of nearly two hundred drawings and paintings as well as a full set of published illustrations and autographed books to the Wilmington Society of the Fine Arts. In 1925 Harper published Charles D. Abbott's biography of Pyle, which has remained a classic in the field of illustration study. Fifty years later Henry C. Pitz, himself an accomplished writer and illustrator, reexamined Pyle's contribution to the Brandywine tradition of illustration in his Pyle biography (1975). Both the Brandywine River Museum and the Delaware Art Museum have held exhibitions devoted to Pyle and his circle.

From modest beginnings Howard Pyle developed into one of America's most influential illustrators and teachers. His career spanned a period of momentous changes in image-making in America, from wood engravers meticulously copying pictures to advances in photomechanical printing and the use of color. He embraced these innovations and used them to his advantage. As a writer Pyle

reached out to a broad spectrum of readers with lighthearted fairy tales for young children, adventure stories for youth, and history and allegory for adults. His King Arthur and Robin Hood books are still in print. As a teacher he launched the careers of Violet Oakley, Schoonover, Smith, and Wyeth, among others. Today Pyle remains a respected figure in the field of American illustration, and his work continues to inspire new generations of artists and readers.

Bibliography:

Willard S. Morse and Gertrude Brincklé, *Howard Pyle: A Record of His Illustrations and Writings* (Wilmington, Del.: Wilmington Society of the Fine Arts, 1921).

Biographies:

Charles D. Abbott, *Howard Pyle, A Chronicle* (New York: Harper, 1925);

Henry C. Pitz, *Howard Pyle: Writer, Illustrator, Founder of the Brandywine School* (New York: Clarkson N. Potter, 1975).

References:

Lucien Agosta, *Howard Pyle* (New York: Macmillan, 1987);

Michele H. Bogart, "Artistic Ideals and Commercial Practices: The Problem of Status for American Illustrators," *Prospects,* 15 (1990): 225–281;

The Brandywine Heritage: Howard Pyle, N. C. Wyeth, Andrew Wyeth, James Wyeth (Greenwich, Conn.: New York Graphic Society, 1971);

Howard Pyle Brokaw, *The Howard Pyle Studio: A History* (Wilmington, Del.: Studio Group, 1983);

Ann Barton Brown, *Howard Pyle, A Teacher: The Formal Years, 1894–1905* (Chadds Ford, Pa.: Brandywine River Museum, 1980);

Elizabeth H. Hawkes, "Drawn in Ink: Book Illustrations by Howard Pyle," in *The American Illustrated Book in the Nineteenth Century,* edited by Gerald W. R. Ward (Winterthur, Del.: Henry Francis du Pont Winterthur Museum, 1987), pp. 201–231;

Hawkes, "Howard Pyle and His School of Art," in *Artists in Wilmington* (Wilmington: Delaware Art Museum, 1980), pp. 23–30;

Howard Pyle: The Artist & His Legacy (Wilmington: Delaware Art Museum, 1987);

Howard Pyle: Diversity in Depth (Wilmington: Delaware Art Museum, 1973);

Robert Lawson, "Howard Pyle and His Times," in *Illustrators of Children's Books: 1744–1945,* edited by Bertha E. Mahoney, Louise Payson Latimer, and Beulah Folmsbee (Boston: Horn Book, 1947), pp. 105–122;

Richard Wayne Lykes, "Howard Pyle: Teacher of Illustration," thesis, University of Pennsylvania, 1947;

Jill P. May, ed., *Children's Literature Association Quarterly,* 8, special issue on Pyle (Summer 1983);

Elizabeth Nesbitt, *Howard Pyle* (New York: Walek, 1966);

Henry C. Pitz, *The Brandywine Tradition* (Boston: Houghton Mifflin, 1969);

Pitz, *Illustrating Children's Books: History, Technique, Production* (New York: Watson-Guptill, 1963);

Howard Pyle, "A Small School of Art," *Harper's Weekly,* 41 (17 July 1897): 710–711;

Jessie Trimble, "The Founder of an American School of Art," *Outlook,* 85 (23 February 1907): 453–460;

John W. Vandercook, "Howard Pyle: Artist, Author, Founder of a School of Illustration," *Mentor* (June 1927): 1–14;

N. C. Wyeth, "Howard Pyle as I Knew Him," *Mentor* (June 1927): 15–17.

Archives:

There are collections of Howard Pyle's papers at the Historical Society of Delaware; the Delaware Art Museum; the Pierpont Morgan Library; and the libraries of Harvard University, Princeton University, and the University of Virginia. The major collections of Pyle illustrations are at the Brandywine River Museum and the Delaware Art Museum. Among other institutions owning illustrations are the Boston Public Library; the Brown County Library in Wisconsin; the Library of Congress; the Metropolitan Museum of Art; and the New York Public Library.

Frederic Remington

(4 October 1861 – 26 December 1909)

Melissa J. Webster

See also the Remington entries in *DLB 12: American Realists and Naturalists* and *DLB 186: Nineteenth-Century American Western Writers.*

BOOKS: *Pony Tracks* (New York: Harper, 1895);
Drawings (New York: R. H. Russell, 1897);
A Rogers Ranger in the French and Indian War (New York: Harper, 1897);
Crooked Trails (New York: Harper, 1898);
Remington's Frontier Sketches (Chicago: Werner, 1898);
Stories of Peace and War (New York & London: Harper, 1899);
Sundown Leflare (New York & London: Harper, 1899);
Men with the Bark On (New York & London: Harper, 1900);
A Bunch of Buckskins (New York: R. H. Russell, 1901);
Done in the Open, with text by Owen Wister (New York: R. H. Russell, 1902);
John Ermine of the Yellowstone (New York & London: Macmillan, 1902);
Western Types (New York: Scribners, 1902);
Remington Portfolio of Drawings (New York: Collier, 1904);
The Way of an Indian (New York: Fox, Duffield, 1906; London: Gay & Bird, 1906);
Remington Portfolio: Eight New Remington Prints (New York: Collier, 1908–1909).
Editions: *Frederic Remington's Own West,* edited by Harold McCracken (New York: Dial, 1960);
Frederic Remington's Own Outdoors, edited by Douglas Allen (New York: Dial, 1964);
The Collected Works of Frederic Remington, edited by Peggy Samuels and Harold Samuels (Garden City, N.Y.: Doubleday, 1979).

SELECTED BOOKS ILLUSTRATED: Custer, Elizabeth B., *Tenting on the Plains* (New York: Charles L. Webster, 1887);
Eggleston, Edward, *The Household History of the United States* (New York: Appleton, 1888);

Frederic Remington

Muir, John, *Picturesque California* (San Francisco: J. Dewing, 1888);

Roosevelt, Theodore, *Ranch Life and the Hunting Trail* (New York: Century, 1888);

Janvier, Thomas A., *The Aztec Treasure House* (New York: Harper, 1890);

Longfellow, Henry Wadsworth, *The Song of Hiawatha* (Boston: Houghton, Mifflin, 1890);

Davis, Richard Harding, *The West from a Car Window* (New York: R. H. Russell, 1892);

Parkman, Francis, *The Oregon Trail* (Boston: Little, Brown, 1892);

Dodge, Theodore Ayrault, *Riders of Many Lands* (New York: Harper, 1893);

Gunnison, Almon, *Wayside and Fireside Rambles* (Boston: Universalist Publishing, 1893);

Bigelow, Poultney, *The Borderland of the Czar and Kaiser* (New York: Harper, 1894);

Miles, Nelson A., *Personal Recollections of General Nelson A. Miles* (Chicago: Werner, 1896);

Davis, Richard Harding, *Cuba in War Time* (New York: R. H. Russell, 1897);

Inman, Henry, *The Old Santa Fe Trail* (New York: Macmillan, 1897);

Lewis, Alfred Henry, *Wolfville* (New York: Stokes, 1897);

Bigelow, Poultney, *White Man's Africa* (New York: Harper, 1898);

King, Charles, *An Apache Princess* (New York: Hobart, 1903);

King, *A Daughter of the Sioux* (New York: Hobart, 1903);

Hough, Emerson, *The Way to the West* (Indianapolis: Bobbs-Merrill, 1903);

Garland, Hamlin, *The Book of the American Indian* (New York: Harper, 1923).

PERIODICALS: *Harper's Weekly,* 1882, 1885, 1886–1901;
Outing, 1886–1903;
St. Nicholas, 1886–1890;
Harper's Bazar, 1887, 1893, 1899;
London Graphic, 1887, 1889;
Century Magazine, 1888–1894;
Youth's Companion, 1888–1889;
Harper's Monthly, 1889–1901;
Scribner's Magazine, 1889, 1892–1893, 1899, 1901–1902, 1910;
Cosmopolitan, 1891–1906;
Harper's Round Table, 1896–1898;
Metropolitan Magazine, 1896, 1906, 1908;
New York Journal and Advertiser, 1897–1898;
Collier's, 1898–1909;
McClure's, 1899–1901;
Everybody's Magazine, 1901–1905;
The Saturday Evening Post, 1901, 1903.

Frederic Remington enjoyed a highly productive and successful career as illustrator and fine artist. Between 1882 and 1913 people across the United States saw his drawings and paintings appear frequently in books and popular publications. He was known especially for his renderings of nineteenth-century Western frontier life. His contemporaries believed that he was recording for posterity a vanishing segment of American history, and they lauded his scenes for their realism, accuracy, and verve. Remington's work as painter, sculptor, illustrator, and writer remains ardently sought today and to many represents the true Old West.

Frederic Sackrider Remington was born on 4 October 1861 in Canton, New York. He was the only child of Clara Sackrider and Seth Pierre Remington. As a child Remington identified strongly with his father, who was a journalist, politician, soldier, and horse-racing enthusiast. Seth Remington founded Canton's only weekly newspaper, the *St. Lawrence Plaindealer,* and served as a volunteer in the Union Army during the Civil War. In 1873 he was appointed U.S. Customs Collector for the Port of Ogdensburg, New York, and he sold his newspaper and moved his family to this small town on the Saint Lawrence River, near the border between the United States and Canada. While in Ogdensburg, Seth Remington began to raise thoroughbreds for racing at the Saint Lawrence County fairgrounds, a hobby he pursued for the rest of his life. Joining a friend, trainer Walter Van Valkenberg, Seth bought the horses, and his partner trained them for harness racing.

Frederic Remington grew up in an atmosphere of news publications, soldiers, horses, and the outdoors. Canton and Ogdensburg, small towns in upstate New York, were rural, surrounded by farms, lakes, mountains, and streams. Happiest in the open air, Remington spent as much time as he could hunting the woods, fishing the streams, and swimming the lakes. He began drawing at a young age and is said to have passed hours on his grandparents' kitchen floor sketching. A favorite spot was the Saint Lawrence fairgrounds, where his father's horses were stabled. There Remington would spend time watching Van Valkenberg work out and train the thoroughbreds, making endless sketches of the horses.

Remington was an energetic child. He reveled to hear his father's exploits as a cavalry officer and stories of military life, a favorite topic of his early drawings. In 1875, at age thirteen, he went to a preparatory school, the Vermont Episcopal Institute, in Burlington, Vermont. Remington disliked this school, and the following year his parents transferred him to the Highland Military Academy in Worcester, Massachusetts. He attended Highland for two years.

For his university work Remington had contemplated going to Cornell to study journalism, after which he would follow in his father's career. He also planned to study art. Cornell did not offer art courses, however, and Remington chose to attend

Remington's "An Ox Train in the Mountains," published in the 26 May 1888 Harper's Weekly

Yale instead, entering their art program in the fall of 1878 and remaining three semesters.

Remington had little interest in schoolwork. He won his reputation at Yale through athletics—in boxing and football—not through his artistic talent or academic achievements. John Fergueson Weir, the director of the art program, said that the often-bruised Remington was the most unusual looking art student he ever had. Remington left Yale in December 1879 when his father became ill, and he did not return. Seth Remington died on 18 February 1880.

For three years after his father's death the young man moved from one job or diversion to another. He had moved to Albany, New York, to live near his uncles, who attempted to find him work and settle him on a career. In the summer of 1881 Remington decided to take a vacation and to travel west—a trip that was to have a lasting impression on him, for it helped to focus his ideas on a career as an illustrator and artist of Western subjects. For two months he explored the Montana Territory, where the Old West still thrived. In an autobiographical essay published in *Collier's* (18 March 1905) Reming-

ton recalled that one evening he came upon the camp of an old man who told him stories about the West that once had been. Remington claimed that it was this wagon freighter who inspired him to record on canvas the Old West before it completely disappeared: "Without knowing exactly how to do it, I began to try to record some facts around me, and the more I looked the more the panorama unfolded."

Remington came into an inheritance from his father on 4 October 1882, and the following March he moved to Peabody, Kansas, and bought a sheep ranch. He soon discovered that he detested ranching. In the summer of 1883 he traveled to the New Mexico territory to vacation, and by February 1884 he had sold his ranch and moved back to Canton, New York. In March he returned west to Kansas City, Missouri, to invest in a hardware store. When this failed, he became a silent partner in a saloon.

During the autumn of 1884 Remington returned for a brief period to Gloversville, New York, where he married Eva Caten, whom he had met some years earlier. They went to Kansas City, but soon after their arrival she returned to Gloversville to live with her parents. Remington stayed on in Kansas City alone until July 1885 when he lost his share in the saloon. In August he wandered through the Southwest to the New Mexico and Arizona Territories, taking in what he saw and making sketches. Upon his return to Kansas City he headed east to New York City to concentrate on a career as an illustrator and artist.

Illustrating for journals and popular taste was a natural direction for Remington. His art had been reportorial and detailed from his earliest work. His childhood drawings were of horses at his father's stables, Civil War battle scenes, and Indians. At grade school he paid little attention to his lessons but was known for his caricatures of classmates and instructors. While at Highland Military Academy, Remington illustrated his cadet manual, filling the margins with drawings of military exploits. The drawings, simple and lucid, showed soldiers with detailed equipment on military maneuvers. Though stiff and lacking three-dimensionality, the illustrations were convincing and filled with energy and imagination.

During his years at Highland, Remington corresponded with another young man, Scott Turner, who also drew and was enthusiastic over cavalry and Indian pictures. Remington admired his skill as an artist and wrote to him in 1877 requesting drawings, but only those with fighting and action: "Don't send me any more women or any more dudes. Send me Indians, cowboys, villains or toughs. These are what I want."

Remington made his first published illustration in college. Through Poultney Bigelow, a classmate in Yale's art program and the editor of the school's newspaper, Remington became the first illustrator of the *Yale Courant*. His subjects were narrative scenes of student life, complete with captions. The drawings were competent, though stiffly rendered.

At Yale first-year art students had classes in drawing, perspective, form, and proportion. Live-figure drawing was not undertaken until the second year; first-year students drew from casts of Greek sculpture. Remington is said to have been bored and impatient with his art lessons. He did not like drawing the reproductions of classical Greek art assigned by their drawing instructor, John Henry Niemeyer. Bigelow, in recalling these years in his book *Seventy Summers* (1925), wrote:

We were by ourselves in the dingy cellar or basement spaces, whose only decoration consisted of casts from the antique. . . . No studio was better designed if its object was to damp the ardor of a budding Michel Angelo. . . . The Yale of 1879 saw nothing of genius or even talent

in the big, burly blond undergraduate who played in the football eleven, cursed Praxiteles and left Yale disgusted with art and its New Haven exponents.

After Remington left Yale he did not study art formally for several years, although his uncles were willing to send him back to Yale to finish his program. While moving from job to job in Albany he perpetuated his reputation for drawing. At work, just as at school, he was heedless of his responsibilities and sketched during the day, making narrative drawings and caricatures.

Shortly after his return to Albany in 1881, inspired by his summer trip to Montana and a desire to record life in the West, Remington submitted an illustration to Charles Parsons, the art director of *Harper's Weekly*, based on sketches he had made on this first trip. Parsons published the sketch (redrawn by staff artist W. A. Rogers) in the 25 February 1882 issue. Although Remington's inspiration had come from Montana, the illustration appeared with the title *Cow-boys of Arizona: Roused by a Scout*. The scene depicts five alarmed cowboys emerging from their bedrolls in the mountains as they listen to a mounted scout anxiously pointing to an unseen danger beyond the borders of the composition. The viewpoint is low, placing the observer on the same plane as the awakening cowboys, three of which are close to the foreground, giving the impression that the viewer is right behind them and reinforcing the immediacy of the scene.

When Remington moved to Peabody, Kansas, in 1883 to raise sheep, he spent hours sketching, covering the walls of his ranch house with drawings. In Kansas City he passed time in his saloon watching and sketching people. He began to paint in watercolor and oil and sold his first three paintings at W. W. Findlay's art-supply store in Kansas City. *Harper's Weekly* published another of his sketches on 28 March 1885, titled *Ejecting an "Oklahoma Boomer,"* once again redrawn by a staff artist, this time Thure de Thulstrup. In the drawing soldiers escort a family of homesteaders who sit dejectedly in their mule-drawn wagon or walk alongside it. The figures loom large and the picture's edge crops the two outside soldiers. As in Remington's first published sketch, the placement of the figures so close to the foreground lends a sense of immediacy to the scene.

Remington returned to New York in the fall of 1885 loaded with sketches that he had made while living in the West. His portfolio in hand, he showed up at Harper in the fall of 1885 to present his material to the director, J. Henry Harper. Harper and the art editors found Remington's sketches compelling. They were caught up by his subject, the West,

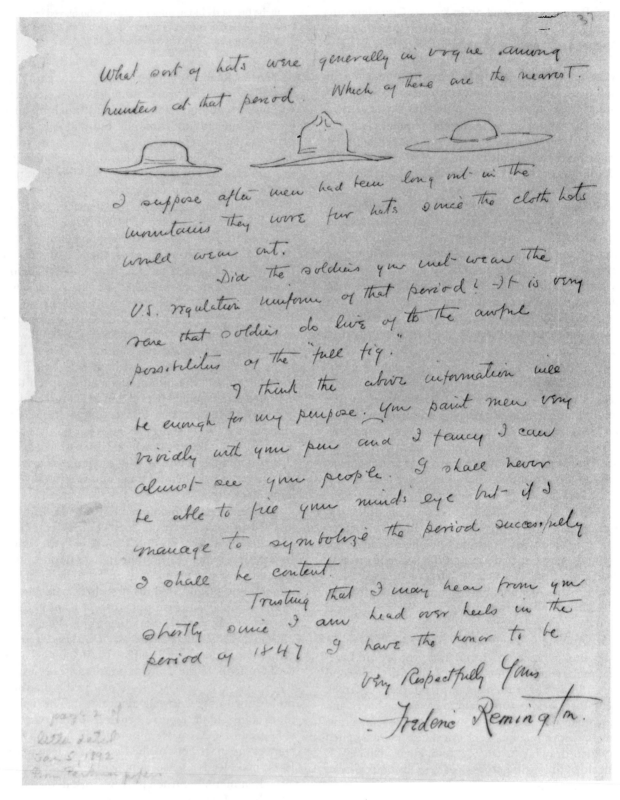

What sort of hats were generally in vogue among hunters at that period. Which of these are the nearest.

I suppose after men had been long out in the mountains they wore fur hats once the cloth hats would wear out.

Did the soldiers you met wear the U.S. regulation uniform of that period? It is very rare that soldiers do live up to the awful possibilities of the "full fig."

I think the above information will be enough for my purpose. You paint men very vividly with your pen and I fancy I can almost see your people. I shall never be able to fill your minds eye but if I manage to symbolize the period successfully I shall be content.

Trusting that I may hear from you shortly since I am head over heels in the period of 1847 I have the honor to be

Very Respectfully Yours

— Frederic Remington.

Page from a 5 January 1892 letter to Francis Parkman, discussing illustrations for Parkman's 1892 book, The Oregon Trail
(Remington Art Memorial and the Massachusetts Historical Society)

which during the nineteenth century gripped the popular imagination. The push to settle the area was culminating, and the territory elicited deep romantic visions as the last frontier, where opportunity, adventure, and individualism supposedly still thrived. Because Remington had been there and was drawing from his own experiences, his pictures had an authenticity that added to their appeal, and it was felt by his contemporaries that they were records of a place and life that were fast disappearing.

Harper's Weekly published four of Remington's illustrations in the winter and spring of 1886. In June, Remington left for the Southwest with Gen. Nelson A. Miles to cover a story on the search for Geronimo. Five illustrations for *Harper's Weekly* resulted from this extensive trip to the New Mexico and Arizona Territories and Mexico.

Three of the first six drawings that Remington submitted to the magazine had to be redrawn by staff artists. In March 1886 Remington enrolled at the Art Students League in New York City, where he practiced his art and learned the technique of ink-wash drawing. His painting instructor was Julian Alden Weir, an influential American impressionist painter whose loose brushwork and dissolution of form would not be seen in Remington's art for another fifteen years. Although Remington's earlier sketches were flawed in perspective and proportion, editors found his art compelling. Equally alluring was his novel approach to the subject matter. Art editors appreciated the boldness and force of the drawings.

Influenced by the French military painters and illustrators Alphonse Marie de Neuville and Jean-Baptist-Edouard Detaille and the Russian military painter Vasili Verestchagin, Remington adopted a style in the 1880s and most of the 1890s that was detailed, realistic, and forcible, as it had been from his earliest days. He wanted to be accurate about the physical details of his subject matter to the degree that viewers could identify a type of saddle or wagon or count the number of bullets in a cartridge belt. He was a documentary, visual reporter in his rendering of uniforms, equipment, and costumes.

His scenes were also romantic. He believed that imagination was important in art, and his illustrations were a harmonious combination of personal experiences, objective information, and fantasy. That creativity was primary with Remington is revealed in a 5 November 1899 letter that he wrote to Howard Pyle: "Color is great—it isn't so great as drawing and neither are in it with Imagination. Without that a fellow is out of luck."

The year 1886 marked the advancement of Remington's career as an illustrator, a career that blossomed quickly and grew steadily thereafter. *Harper's Weekly* published a total of fourteen of his illustrations that year, and his work also appeared in *Harper's Young People* and *St. Nicholas*. His Yale classmate Bigelow was the editor of *Outing* and commissioned Remington to illustrate the final articles in a series by Lt. John Bigelow titled "After Geronimo." Based on his southwestern experiences in the summer of 1886, Remington produced thirty-four illustrations for this series. In 1887 he added *Harper's Bazar* and the *London Graphic* to the list of publications seeking his work, and he received the prestigious commission to illustrate Theodore Roosevelt's book, *Ranch Life and the Hunting Trail,* which was published in 1888 by Century Company and which appeared serially in *Century* that same year.

The magazine medium imposed certain limitations on Remington's art. The technology required to print an image with text using a mechanical screened halftone process was not developed until 1889 and not perfected until 1892. Until 1889 illustrations with text in magazines and books had to be engraved on woodblocks, and the engraver always came between the illustrator's original depiction and what the public saw. Even after halftones came into use, the meticulous Remington complained in a 15 January 1892 letter to the photo engraver at *Harper's Weekly,* a man named Kurtz, that definition was being lost, obstructing his original intentions.

At the end of the 1870s photography-on-the-block reproduction was invented, enabling the engraver to copy the original more accurately. In addition, by the early 1880s wood engraving had developed into a refined craft, and there were highly skilled engravers translating images onto wood for reproduction. Unfortunately for Remington, however, the finest engravers worked for distinguished artists, and lesser craftsmen reproduced his work.

Remington made concessions for the sake of the engraver. The first was to draw in pen and ink. Through the process of line engraving the engraver could then simply copy Remington's lines, an easier process than trying to reproduce the tonal values of paintings. When Remington did paint, he worked in black and white, whether it be watercolor, oil, or ink wash, to help the engraver reproduce tonal values. He essentially translated color into gradations of black and white, which the engraver then reproduced with hatchings.

Illustrations in popular magazines continued to be published only in black and white until the turn of the century, when color photolithography was invented. Throughout the 1890s, then, Remington frequently painted in monochrome for publication. He became increasingly adept at discriminat-

Illustration by Remington for his first book of stories, Pony Tracks *(1895)*

ing subtle nuances in tone, reproducing the effects of color. This skill was to have major influences on the nocturnal pictures that he painted at the end of his career.

Other artists who worked for publishers were also faced with these concerns. Remington developed friendships with several of the leading illustrators of his day, such as E. W. Kemble, Charles Dana Gibson, and Howard Pyle. They, too, had their specialties. Kemble was known for his depictions of black Americans, Gibson for his idealized beauties, and Pyle for his pirates and medieval romance scenes. Over the years these men encouraged each other, praised one another's art, exchanged artwork, and shared their thoughts and frustrations.

In 1887 Remington embarked upon another successful venture: writing a text that he would illustrate. His first article, "Coursing Rabbits on the Plains," appeared in *Outing* in May. From 1887 to 1906 Remington authored and illustrated approximately 109 articles and stories. The majority appeared in *Harper's Monthly* and *Harper's Weekly*, but other magazines such as *Century, Collier's, Cosmopolitan,* and *McClure's* featured his writing. Remington also wrote extended captions to his Spanish-American War illustrations that were published

during 1897 and 1898 in William Randolph Hearst's newspaper, *The New York Journal and Advertiser.*

Remington published in book form previously printed articles and stories: *Pony Tracks* (1895); *A Rogers Ranger in the French and Indian War* (1897); *Crooked Trails* (1898); *Sundown Leflare* (1899); *Stories of Peace and War* (1899); and *Men with the Bark On* (1900). He also wrote and illustrated two novels, *John Ermine of the Yellowstone* (1902) and *The Way of an Indian* (1906). The former was made into a stage play in 1903 by Louis Shipman, and the latter also appeared serially in *Cosmopolitan* in 1905–1906. After 1906, other than letters, one hears from Remington only through his diaries, which he kept from 1907 to 1909. His writing, like his art, was realistic, vivid, and full of life.

Many of Remington's travels to gather illustrating material were commissioned by Harper, *Century,* or *The New York Journal and Advertiser.* Between 1881 and 1909 Remington made major annual trips. A dozen of these trips were to the Southwest: Texas, the New Mexico and Arizona Territories, and Mexico. Around thirteen trips were to the West: Wyoming, Montana, and the Dakotas. Six were to Canada, and four were to Florida and Cuba. Remington also made excursions to Europe and Africa. During the 1880s and 1890s there were smaller trips as well to cover specific events for *Harper's Weekly,* such as the earthquake in South Carolina in 1886, the Wounded Knee crisis in South Dakota in 1890, and the railroad strikes in Chicago in 1896. Closer to home he illustrated dozens of articles, quite often using his favorite subjects—the military and horses—covering events such as the New York National Guard's skirmishing drills, practice at the American Cavalry School, races at the Fleetwood Trotting Track, and horse shows at Madison Square Garden. In all Remington produced more than twenty-eight hundred illustrations during his career.

In the spring of 1887 *Harper's Weekly* sent him to Montana to sketch on the Crow Reservation and to Calgary and Alberta to visit the Blackfeet Indian Reservation. The trip resulted in several illustrations published in 1887 and 1888, such as *In the Lodges of the Blackfeet* (23 July 1887), *Crow Indians Firing into the Agency* (5 November 1887), and *Canadian Mounted Police on a "Musical Ride"* (24 December 1887).

In June and July of 1888 *Century* commissioned Remington to go to Fort Grant in Arizona to follow along with Lt. Powhatan Clarke and his command of black cavalrymen, the Buffalo Soldiers. After completing this assignment Remington continued to Fort Sill, the Comanche Agency, and finally to Fort Reno, the Cheyenne Agency, where he made notes and sketches of the Cheyenne and Kiowa Indians. Several *Century* articles written and illustrated by Remington resulted from this trip, including "A Scout with the Buffalo Soldiers" (April 1889), "On the Indian Reservations" (July 1889), and "Artist Wanderings Among the Cheyennes" (August 1889). In the July article Remington gives an idea of how he sketched the Apaches at San Carlos who were reluctant to have their likenesses recorded. In the illustration, *Method of Sketching at San Carlos,* he depicts himself standing behind an officer, his sketch pad resting discreetly on the officer's back, as he peeks over the officer's shoulder to make his drawing of an Indian covertly.

From Houghton, Mifflin and Company, Remington received his largest commission in 1888, the illustrating of Henry Wadsworth Longfellow's *The Song of Hiawatha* (1890). The assignment took six months to finish. In all, he produced 379 pen-and-ink drawings and 22 oil paintings for the book.

Remington illustrated for seven magazines in 1889, including for the first time *Scribner's Magazine.* In February he was en route to Mexico, working for Harper to gather material to illustrate articles by Thomas A. Janvier, specifically, *The Aztec Treasure House,* which appeared serially in *Harper's Weekly* in 1889 and 1890 and in book form in 1890. Other articles of the Mexican genre by Janvier that Remington illustrated were "Bull-Fighting in Mexico" (1 June 1889), "Silver Mining at Zacatecas" (19 October 1889), and "Mexican Burros" (30 November 1889), all published in *Harper's Weekly,* and "The Mexican Army" (November 1889), published in *Harper's Monthly.* In December, Remington linked up with his friend Julian Ralph, a popular writer, and the two traveled to Canada to hunt moose. Their adventure was written up by Ralph in "Antoine's Moose-Yard," illustrated by Remington and published in the October 1890 issue of *Harper's Monthly.*

By 1890 Remington's reputation as an illustrator, particularly of the military and the West, was secure, and his schedule was filled with illustrating commissions, traveling, and deadlines. The summer of 1890 found him in Canada again with Ralph, and this time Remington's wife, Eva, was along with them. They visited Montreal and Victoria, British Columbia, producing six articles for *Harper's Monthly* printed in 1890 and 1891. In March 1891 Remington and his wife traveled to Mexico, guests of General Miles, to sketch the Mexican army for *Harper's Weekly.* The resulting illustrations appeared during 1890 and 1892 and depicted both military and tourist topics.

Remington had developed into a superb draftsman. His work was respected for its truth and dash and was in demand. Eager to have Remington illustrate his account of his 1847 trip to Wyoming titled *The Oregon Trail* (1892), Francis Parkman wrote to the artist on 7 January 1892: "I am very glad that you are to illustrate the 'Oregon Trail,' for I have long admired your rendering of Western life, as superior to that of any other artist. You have seen as much and observed so closely that you have no rival in this department." Remington made seventy-five illustrations for the book, including eight full-page pictures.

Remington produced approximately 210 illustrations in 1892, making it one of his most prolific years as an illustrator. His art appeared in *Century, Cosmopolitan, Harper's Monthly, Harper's Weekly, Outing,* and *Scribner's Magazine.* In May he and Bigelow left for Europe. Commissioned by Harper, Bigelow was to write articles about the German and Russian militaries, and Remington was to illustrate them. Their route included stops in London, Berlin, Saint Petersburg, Tilsit, Prussia, and Paris. One of Remington's goals was to illustrate the military forces of the world. He had already depicted the U.S. cavalry and infantry and the Mexican army. This trip enabled him to add German, Prussian, and Russian soldiers. The two travelers had planned a trip down the Volga River in Russia, but, suspecting them as

Remington at his studio in New Rochelle, New York, circa 1895

spies, the Russians escorted them from their country prematurely. Bigelow wrote about this experience in "Why We Left Russia," and it was published in *Harper's Monthly* in January 1893. A total of six articles and sixty-nine illustrations appeared in *Harper's Monthly* based on their trip, and Remington's illustrations with and without text were printed in four issues of *Harper's Weekly* in 1892 and 1893. The subjects varied, from Buffalo Bill's show in London to highlights of the German army to the Russian cossacks in the field to Emperor William's stud farm in Trakehnen, Germany.

In 1893 Remington traveled to Bavicora, Mexico, in February with Will Harper to visit his friend Jack Follansbee at his ranch, to Yellowstone National Park in August where he met Owen Wister for the first time, and to Fort Wingate in the New Mexico Territory in October to bear hunt with General Miles and his comrades. In Mexico he sequestered material for several articles that he wrote and illustrated for *Harper's Monthly,* such as "An Outpost of Civilization" (December 1893), "In the Sierra Madre with the Punchers" (February 1894), and "A Rodeo at Los Ojos" (March 1894). After their meeting in Yellowstone, Wister and Remington began a long friendship.

Remington illustrated many of Wister's stories for *Harper's Monthly,* and Wister wrote the introductions to *Drawings* (1897), *A Bunch of Buckskins* (1901), and *Done in the Open* (1902), collections of Remington's pictures. For *Done in the Open* Wister also wrote poems to accompany each scene. Remington described and depicted his hunt with General Miles in "Bear-Chasing in the Rocky Mountains," published in *Harper's Monthly* in July 1895.

In 1894 Remington and Bigelow again became traveling companions; this time the destination was Africa. Poultney was to write articles about the Algerian and French armies, and Remington was to illustrate them. Two articles resulted, both printed in *Harper's Monthly:* "An Arabian Day and Night" (December 1894) and "French Fighters in Algiers" (February 1895). Remington and Eva vacationed in January 1895 in Punta Gorda, Florida, where he hunted birds and produced six drawings for "Winter Shooting on the Gulf Coast of Florida" for *Harper's Weekly* (11 May 1895). Another article, "Cracker Cowboys of Florida" (*Harper's Monthly,* August 1895), was also published shortly after this trip.

In February 1896 Remington traveled to Texas and Mexico. He wrote and illustrated several articles for *Harper's Monthly* based on this trip, including "The Blue Quail of the Cactus" (October 1896) and "How the Law Got into the Chaparral" (December 1896). Invited by Lt. Carter Johnson, Remington traveled to Montana in September to observe Johnson's troops and sketch military scenes. He wrote of his experiences and illustrated them in "Vagabonding with the Tenth Horse," published in *Cosmopolitan* (February 1897). A second article, "A Sergeant of the Orphan Troop," also written and illustrated by Remington, was published in the August 1897 issue of *Harper's Monthly* and recounts a heroic incident in Carter's military career.

At the end of 1896 Remington set off again to find heroes in battle, this time to Cuba. Hearst hired Remington to illustrate scenes of the Spanish-American War to accompany stories by Richard Harding Davis for *The New York Journal and Advertiser*. Between December 1896 and June 1898 Remington made three trips to Cuba to observe the developments of the war. His illustrations also appeared in *Harper's Weekly* and *Harper's Monthly*; *Collier's* commissioned him to return to Cuba in February 1899 so that he could sketch scenes of the aftermath of the war.

Remington spent the summer of 1899 in Wyoming, and the following February he was in Yellowstone National Park sketching for *Outing* and *Collier's* articles. In October 1900 he traveled to the Ute Reservation in Ignacio, Colorado, and then on to New Mexico to Espagnola, Santa Fe, and Taos. He made figure and landscape oil sketches to use in final compositions, such as *The Monte Game at Southern Ute Agency* published in *Done in the Open*.

In 1901 Remington's illustrations appeared in ten magazines, the largest number in any one year, although the actual number of his illustrations had been slowly decreasing since 1892; the number of articles that he both wrote and illustrated, however, increased until 1898. Throughout the 1880s and 1890s Harper had been Remington's largest and most steady client, but because of financial problems they dropped him as an illustrator in 1901. His last illustration for *Harper's Weekly* appeared in the 2 March 1901 issue, and the last for *Harper's Monthly* was in the June 1901 issue.

In 1902 Remington spent the summer in Ingleneuk, his island on Chippewa Bay in the Saint Lawrence River, finishing his first novel, *John Ermine of the Yellowstone*. He made no major trips in 1901 or 1902, but December 1903 found him again in Mexico, where he stayed until the middle of January 1904. Although Remington's illustrating load had lightened, in May 1903 he received an exclusive four-year contract with *Collier's,* under which he

would produce at least twelve pictures a year. It was a lucrative deal and an important arrangement for Remington because the paintings were to be of topics that Remington chose and were featured pictures, examples of fine art that would stand alone. In addition, *Collier's* sold the illustrations individually as prints and in groups as portfolios, where they were touted as "artist's proofs." Remington's relationship with *Collier's* went well until 1908, when changes in their administration and image forced Remington out in January 1909.

Since the 1880s Remington's illustrating career had been intertwined with his career as a fine artist, and the two had been incompatible in the minds of most art critics; hence it had been a struggle for Remington to be both, despite his successes. Although the conflict between fine artist and commercial artist pursued him his entire life, the two aspects of his art grew in tandem.

Early in his career Remington made steps toward establishing himself as a fine artist. He began exhibiting his work in 1887, showing with the American Water-Color Society, the National Academy of Design, and the American Art Association. Every year thereafter, except for 1900 and 1902, he exhibited his work several times a year in art academies or galleries.

In 1888, when his illustrations were increasingly in demand, he evinced stirrings to disassociate himself from illustration. In a 3 January letter to Lieutenant Clarke, just before embarking on a trip west for *Century,* he wrote: "I want to do 'US soldiers'–some Pueblo Indians–some Apaches–and then Mexico–I am not going to fool with any d–– illustrating but make finished studies for painting." Despite this remark, Remington continued to illustrate.

In 1889 Remington won second place at the Paris International Exposition for his painting *Last Lull in the Fight*. Another mark of distinction as a painter came in 1891 when he was elected an associate member of the National Academy of Design. Full membership was limited, however, and Remington never made it to that status; he stopped exhibiting with them after 1899.

In 1893 he held his first one-man exhibition and sale, exhibiting ninety-seven works with the American Art Association. He collected Western artifacts–such as Indian and cowboy clothing, weapons, pottery, and baskets–to refer to when painting (along with his sketches and photographs). In the style of George Catlin sixty years earlier Remington displayed a sampling of these items with the artworks, enhancing the aura of authenticity of the Western scenes. There were a

Remington in 1896 with some of his collection of Southwestern artifacts, which he used as source materials for his paintings

whites." At both sales the praise was for Remington as illustrator, not fine artist.

In 1894 Remington ventured into a new medium: bronze. Like his paintings and drawings, these sculptures were honest and direct. Many were filled with the Western action found in his first piece, *The Bronco Buster* (1895), where a rank horse bucks fiercely to free himself of his rider. Between 1895 and 1909 Remington created twenty-one different compositions, including *The Cowboy* (1908) and variations of the original models plus small and large versions of *The Bronco Buster* and *The Rattlesnake* (1905). Remington was an innovator in subject matter and technique. He worked closely with the Italian founder of the Roman Bronze Works in New York City, Ricardo Bertelli, to reintroduce the lost wax process of bronze casting. Remington's bronzes sold well and were profitable. That they helped toward establishing him as a fine artist is evidenced not only by the prestigious art gallery M. Knoedler and Company giving him a one-man exhibition of nine of his statuettes in January 1905 but also by two museums, the Corcoran Gallery and The Metropolitan Museum of Art, purchasing six bronzes during his lifetime.

As Remington's desire to be accepted as a painter and not just an illustrator grew, he started to focus on painting and color. In 1895 and 1896 Remington retreated to his beloved north country to relax and sketch and experiment with color and pastels. In 1901, with the invention of color photolithography, his illustrations began to appear in color. After years of working in black and white for publication, however, Remington felt he had lost his sense of color. Art reviewers' critical remarks underscored this sentiment, as did comments made about his 1897 Hart and Watson exhibition in Boston. One reviewer referred to his artwork as "illustrative paintings." Writing for the 8 December 1897 *Boston Evening Transcript,* the reviewer extolled Remington's keen eye and intimate knowledge of his subject but then went on to say that "his indifference to beauty of form, his unfeeling realism, and his poverty of color, are formidable handicaps."

Remington began to study the work of artists painting in an impressionist style because of their use of color. He socialized with American impressionists Childe Hassam, Robert Reid, Edmund Tarbell, and his former teacher at the Art Students League, Julian Alden Weir, who also became his neighbor when Remington moved to Ridgefield, Connecticut, in May 1909. Remington was interested in the effects of light, studying its

few oils in the exhibition, but the majority of artworks were previously published illustrations. There was standing room only as swarms of people showed up to view the art and make bids, and it was Remington's illustrations that the buyers sought. As the art critic writing for the 14 January 1893 *New York Sun* noted, "Mr. Remington's preeminence as the artist of the far West was readily recognized in the prices paid for his illustrations, while some of his paintings failed to reach the expected figures."

Two years later Remington held another one-man show and auction of 114 artworks with the American Art Association, and again his illustrations drew eager buyers. A reviewer for *The New York Times* writing in the 21 November 1895 issue noted: "Anxiety to secure black and white sketches by this popular man made bidding lively." The reviewer for the 17 November 1895 *New York Daily Tribune* wrote: "Mr. Remington's work in color is always a trifle hard and opaque. His gifts declare themselves in his black and

chromatic and atmospheric appearances. After he bought Ingleneuk in 1900, he spent his summers at his studio there working on illustrating commissions and painting landscapes en plein air, noting how light changed throughout the day and capturing not only midday light but also twilight, dawn, and night scenes such as those by contemporary American color-mood painters. He was also influenced by the night paintings of the tonalist painter Charles Rollo Peters and viewed an exhibition of Peters's nocturnes in 1899.

Sometimes Remington would make a charcoal sketch on the canvas and paint the composition directly on the canvas. At other times he would use a more deliberate method that began by painting a landscape out of doors. He was not strictly a plein air painter, however, because he finished the oils in the studio. In this latter method, back in his studio, he would draw the figures on paper and then transfer the figures to the landscape by tracing them onto a red Conte-crayoned tissue laid on top of the canvas, leaving a red drawing of the figures behind; he would then paint the composition.

While looking at impressionist and tonalist works, Remington became aware not only of their color but also of the looseness of their brushwork compared to his own tight, more linear style. Seeking to "let go" of form, he began to develop a looser, more fluid style. During the last decade of his life he experimented with his technique as he struggled to become a fine artist. In 1908 and 1909, disappointed with his progress, he destroyed many of the canvases from these years.

Remington's last exhibit of black-and-white illustrations was in 1904 at the Detroit Institute of Art. In 1905 and 1906 he began exhibiting small oils alongside his standard 27-by-40-inch canvases, in tonalist values, such as *Against the Sunset,* in which a cowboy races before the orange sky of evening and muted mountains; or quieter scenes, such as *Stormy Morning in the Badlands,* which depicts a solitary tepee in gray, cloudy morning light; or *A Dangerous Country,* a nocturne in which a mounted Indian rides alone alongside his packhorse in the gloom of night. He continued to paint action Western scenes in bright sunlight, such as *Downing the Nigh Leader* (1907), in which Indians have shot the lead horse of a team thundering across the plains pulling a stagecoach, and *The Buffalo Episode* (1909), a brightly lit composition of spiraling action as a bison charges a horse who throws his rider.

Between 1906 and 1909 M. Knoedler held annual one-man exhibitions of Remington's paintings. Of the sixty-six artworks exhibited, thirty-three had never been published, and twenty-nine of the remaining paintings had appeared in *Collier's* or *Scribner's Magazine* as works of fine art, not as illustrations of text. Of the ones never published, twelve were pure landscapes, exhibited for the first time in 1908 and 1909. The reviews of these exhibitions show that the critics were aware of Remington's efforts to be a fine painter. Of the 1907 exhibition the *American Art News* critic wrote in the 7 December 1907 issue: "The artist has not yet ceased to be an illustrator while becoming a painter" and goes on to write that Remington portrays the West "with an intensity that thrills us as no other American artist has done or can do." Of the 1908 show the reviewer for the January 1909 *Craftsman* wrote that Remington "has grown to think through his paint so freely and fluently that in some of his more recent work he seems to have used his medium unconsciously." Art critic Royal Cortissoz wrote in the 7 December 1909 *New York Daily Tribune,* "In the last few years he has been making tremendous strides. There is something positively exciting about the rapidity with which he passes one milestone after another."

Aside from a few scattered commissions, after 1903 *Collier's* was Remington's primary client. Although the magazine continued to publish their backlog of Remington's art until 1913, his severance with them in 1909 marked the end of his twenty-seven years of illustrating. Free of commercial commitments, he wrote in his diary on 1 January 1909, "I am no longer on a salary and fully embarqued on the uncertain career of a painter." Unfortunately, Remington's opportunities to explore further sculpting, landscape painting, tonalism, impressionism, and even symbolism were cut short when his appendix ruptured just before Christmas, and he died of peritonitis on 26 December 1909.

Remington's Western compositions have influenced generations of artists, writers, and (more recently) filmmakers. His art is still sought today and demands high prices, and reproductions of his sculptures and paintings remain popular items. In his day he was the best-known artist of the Old West; he is still so today.

Letters:

Frederic Remington: Selected Letters, edited by Allen P. Splete and Marilyn D. Splete (New York: Abbeville, 1988).

Biography:

Peggy Samuels and Harold Samuels, *Frederic Remington: A Biography* (Garden City, N.Y.: Doubleday, 1982).

References:

James K. Ballinger, *Frederic Remington* (New York: Abrams, 1989);

Peter Hassrick, *Frederic Remington: Paintings, Drawings, and Sculpture in the Amon Carter Museum and the Sid W. Richardson Foundation Collections* (New York: Abrams, 1973);

Hassrick, "Remington: The Painter," in his *Frederic Remington: The Masterworks* (New York: Abrams, 1988);

Hassrick and Melissa J. Webster, *Frederic Remington: A Catalogue Raisonne of Paintings, Watercolors, and Drawings* (Cody, Wyo.: Buffalo Bill Historical Center / Seattle: University of Washington Press, 1996);

Harold McCracken, *Frederic Remington: Artist of the Old West* (New York: Lippincott, 1947);

Michael Shapiro, *Cast and Recast: The Sculpture of Frederic Remington* (Washington, D.C.: Smithsonian Institution, 1981).

Archives:

The Remington Art Museum in Ogdensburg, New York, has the largest deposit of archival material about Frederic Remington, including his diaries, scrapbooks, photo albums, sketches, tear sheets, proofs, and a large collection of original art. The Buffalo Bill Historical Center in Cody, Wyoming, has a collection of original art along with artifacts and 108 small oil sketches and paintings from Remington's New Rochelle Studio; it also has an electronic catalogue raisonne with bibliography and exhibition databases.

Norman Perceval Rockwell

(3 February 1894 – 8 November 1978)

Kimberly Kizer and Donald H. Dyal
Texas A&M University

BOOKS: *My Adventures as an Illustrator,* as told to Thomas Rockwell (Garden City, N.Y.: Doubleday, 1960);

The Norman Rockwell Album (Garden City, N.Y.: Doubleday, 1961);

102 Favorite Paintings (New York: Crown, 1978).

SELECTED BOOKS ILLUSTRATED: Jackson, Gabrielle E., *The Maid of Middies' Haven* (New York: McBride, Nast, 1912);

Claudy, C. H., *Tell-Me-Why Stories about Mother Nature* (New York: McBride, Nast, 1912);

Cave, Edward, *The Boy Scout Camp Book* (New York: Doubleday, Page, 1913);

Cave, *The Boy Scout Camp Book* (New York: Doubleday, Page, 1914);

Tomlinson, Everett T., *Scouting with Daniel Boone* (New York: Doubleday, Page, 1914);

Lewis, Sinclair, *The Trail of the Hawk* (New York: Harper, 1915);

Dawson, A. J., *Jan a Dog and a Romance* (New York: Harper, 1915);

Gregor, Elmer Russell, *The Red Arrow* (New York: Harper, 1915);

Camp, Walter, *Danny the Freshman* (New York: Appleton, 1915);

Barbour, Ralph Henry, *The Secret Play* (New York: Appleton, 1915);

Barbour, *The Lucky Seventh* (New York: Appleton, 1915);

Barbour, *The Purple Pennants* (New York: Appleton, 1916);

Heyliger, William, *Don Strong of the Wolf Patrol* (New York: Grosset & Dunlap, 1916);

Hill, Grace Livingston, *A Voice in the Wilderness* (New York: Harper, 1916);

Sawyer, Ruth, *This Way to Christmas* (New York: Harper, 1916);

Stanwood, Arthur, *The Plattsburgers* (Boston: Houghton Mifflin, 1917);

Cheyney, Edward G., *Scott Burton, Forester* (New York: Appleton, 1917);

Barbour, Ralph Henry, *Hitting the Line* (New York: Appleton, 1917);

Barbour, *Keeping His Course* (New York: Appleton, 1918);

Wilson, John Fleming, *Tad Sheldon's Fourth of July* (New York: Macmillan, 1919);

Jackson, Gabrielle E., *Peggy Stuart, Navy Girl* (New York: Knickerbocker, 1920);

Twain, Mark, *The Adventures of Tom Sawyer* (New York: Heritage, 1936);

Twain, *The Adventures of Huckleberry Finn* (New York: Heritage, 1940);

Saunders, Richard, *Poor Richard's Almanacks* (New York: Heritage, 1964);

Coles, Robert, *Dead End School* (Boston: Little, Brown, 1968).

PERIODICALS: *Everyland,* 1913–1916;
Boy's Life, 1913–1921, 1924–1976;
Youth's Companion, 1915–1917;
Leslie's Weekly, 1916–1917;
St. Nicholas, 1916–1919;
American Boy, 1916–1920;
The Saturday Evening Post, 1916–1963;
Afloat and Ashore, 1917–1918;
Judge, 1917–1919;
Country Gentleman, 1917–1922;
Life, 1917–1924;
McCall's, 1917–1969;
Farm and Fireside, 1918–1922;
Red Cross Magazine, 1918–1922;
Literary Digest, 1918–1923;
American Magazine, 1918–1923, 1934–1942;
Collier's, 1919;
Ladies' Home Journal, 1921–1945;
Woman's Home Companion, 1933–1941;
This Week, 1935–1937;
Look, 1964–1971.

Norman Rockwell's preeminence as an illustrator in the public mind springs from a variety of sources, but leading them all was Rockwell's su-

Norman Rockwell, 1919

premacy as a cover artist for *The Saturday Evening Post* and other magazines. Rockwell's illustrations transcended the illustrator's role as provider of graphic adjuncts to some already-written story and achieved another dimension. At the height of his powers his illustrations breathed an atmosphere and a life of their own. Rockwell's artistic eloquence labored with the clay of the prosaic. While from time to time such comforting and cheering appraisals of the American scene as Rockwell mastered are out of critical or artistic fashion, Rockwell's honest portrayals of American life, values, and ideals present an almost unique aspect of truth. Just as Rockwell eschewed painting the sordid, malicious, or squalid in American society, he also eschewed glamorous art, elitist art, and the landscapes made popular by Romanticists. Commenting on his own work in a 1976 interview with David H. Wood, Rockwell observed: "I was showing the America I knew and observed to others who might not have noticed. And perhaps, therefore, this is one function of the illustrator. He can show what has become so familiar that it is no longer noticed." Thus Rockwell's explo-

ration of the everyday and obvious was deliberate and democratic, yet potentially profound and moving. This artist depicted life in middle America, where he was at home, and in so doing made a home for middle America in art.

Born on 3 February 1894 in New York City, Norman Perceval Rockwell was named after an obscure English nobleman of Rockwell relation. His middle name resonated so weakly with Rockwell that initially he signed his work Norman P. Rockwell. Soon, however, he dropped the middle initial and during his most productive decades was known simply as Norman Rockwell. The second son of Jarvis Waring Rockwell and Nancy Hill Rockwell, Rockwell spent his early years in the city as the family moved from one apartment to another. When he was nine years old, the family moved to Mamaroneck, New York.

Rockwell inherited artistic skills, interests, and examples from both sides of his family. His father was an avid sketch artist and amateur painter. His mother, who possessed a personal aversion to artists and art as a livelihood, nevertheless also possessed artistic skill. Rockwell's maternal grandfather, a borderline alcoholic, enlisted the aid of his sizable family to mass-produce paintings that were sold door to door. The experience soured Rockwell's mother on art as a vocation. It is perhaps revealing, however, that despite her prejudice, she married a man with artistic proclivities.

Rockwell's father enjoyed trying to reproduce illustrations from magazines, and his most avid fan was young Norman. Jarvis Rockwell taught his son the rudiments of drawing, and Norman proved an apt pupil. His father also stimulated Norman's imagination in other ways. One of Rockwell's fondly remembered childhood traditions was father Rockwell's nightly reading to his family from the works of such authors as Charles Dickens, Mark Twain, and O. Henry. Rockwell's later work would echo many of the ideals and sentiments impressed during these childhood readings.

Thin, pigeon-toed, and unathletic, the young Rockwell turned to drawing for recognition. Even as a young boy he entertained friends with sidewalk drawings and with sketches on cardboard of naval vessels, which his companions cut out as toys. At age fourteen Rockwell enrolled in part-time study at the Chase Art School, using odd jobs (such as mail delivery) to finance his art education. When Rockwell received a request for some custom Christmas scenes, for which he was paid, he realized that it was possible to make money while pursuing his avocation.

Within two years Rockwell left high school and dedicated himself wholly to his studies at the Chase Art School. There he came under the influence of George Bridgeman, who drilled him in the fundamentals of anatomy, perspective, composition, and drawing. Bridgeman rooted Rockwell solidly in the work of the masters. A perfectionist himself, Rockwell absorbed everything Bridgeman could give him.

Another early scholastic influence was artist-instructor Thomas Fogarty. Fogarty awakened in his pupil a desire to "step over the frame . . . and live in the picture," as Rockwell later recounted in his autobiography. Rockwell also cited as mentors Howard Pyle, Edwin Austin Abbey, J. C. Leyendecker, A. B. Frost, and N. C. Wyeth. Rockwell considered Pyle his ideal, once stating that he considered Pyle the greatest American illustrator.

While Rockwell's acknowledgment of these artists' influences is noteworthy, the foundations vouchsafed by Bridgeman and Fogarty sustained the young artist as he began to develop his own unmistakable style. This style, a twentieth-century artistic antinode, became not just a defining style for

its creator but a defining and stylistic statement on American life, love, and ideals. "Rockwellian"—for good or ill—came to embody a generic set of positive values. Rockwell consistently sought creative ways to present human ideals and foibles without descending into treacly nostalgia.

Rockwell made his start as an illustrator with children's stories. In 1912 Fogarty helped him obtain his first professional assignments: illustrating C. H. Claudy's *Tell-Me-Why Stories about Mother Nature* and Gabrielle E. Jackson's *Maid of Middies' Haven*. Rockwell continued to illustrate children's books through 1960, with more than twenty-five such titles to his credit, including many by Ralph Henry Barbour, an author widely read by young boys. In 1913 he illustrated *The Boy Scout Camp Book*. Like Rockwell's other early illustrations, these were mainly crude and unsophisticated line drawings. Nevertheless, he progressed and became art editor of *Boy's Life* and illustrated for the children's magazines *St. Nicholas* and *Youth's Companion*.

Book and story illustration played a significant role throughout Rockwell's career. His earliest work lacks the character that made his magazine-cover art and other illustrations recognizable. Initially Rockwell was keen to derive his inspiration from author descriptions in the books or stories he illustrated. With experience, all-important success, and consequent confidence he defined his own style. There is a gap in his book and story illustration record between 1920 and 1935, and in the late 1940s he virtually halted book illustrations altogether in order to focus on covers for *The Saturday Evening Post*. His career as a story and book illustrator was long but sporadic and ended in 1968 with Robert Coles's *Dead End School*.

Magazine covers allowed Rockwell more freedom of expression—a plus for a natural storyteller—and it was in this market that his artistic and composition skills achieved new heights. Rockwell's uncanny sensitivity to the unstated emotional bonds of middle-class America operated in the harsh environment of work done on commission, mechanical and artistic challenges to overcome, and deadlines to meet. Authenticity, composition, graphic excellence in work that would never be seen except in photographic reproduction, and a prodigious lifetime production all bespeak more than commitment; this artist's professionalism was driven by his unyielding compulsiveness about his work. Oft-repeated stories of Rockwell personally delivering canvases with the paint still wet reinforce these impressions. In addition, the artist's self-criticism led to constant revision and repainting. While in his six-

MISSOURI DARK MULE—By JACK ALEXANDER

Magazine cover featuring one of Rockwell's humorous self-portraits

ties Rockwell enrolled as a student in a sketch class to improve his spontaneity.

Beginning with the 20 June 1916 issue of *The Saturday Evening Post,* Rockwell produced 323 covers in forty-seven years with that periodical—a career average of about seven covers per annum. His covers were so well received that the *Post* could increase print orders by 250,000 when it featured a Rockwell cover.

Rockwell's first *Post* cover portrays two boys obviously on their way to a baseball game. They pass an unfortunate playmate pushing a baby carriage, and the boys make faces and tease the disappointed and exasperated unfortunate, who must miss the game because of a babysitting assignment. The subject of the cover is such a common and

down-to-earth occurrence that it needs no explanation. Showing the viewer the banal, the artist opens anew the beholder's eyes. The illustration is meticulous: the wicker of the baby carriage is photographic in detail, and the reflections of the baby bottle mirror the surroundings. Rockwell's labor to be authentic is evident.

After a tenacious pursuit Rockwell married Irene O'Connor on 1 July 1916, just a few months after he published his first cover for the *Post.* Although his relationship with the *Post* became a long and fruitful one, the same could not be said of his first marriage. Ill-suited to each other, the Rockwells' married life quickly became stale. Rockwell's commercial success after World War I further estranged the couple, until eventually Rockwell

"Freedom from Want," the third of Rockwell's 1943 series, The Four Freedoms

moved to a separate studio. The marriage lasted thirteen years, until his wife fell in love with another man. She divorced Rockwell in 1929 while he was abroad.

Shortly after the divorce friends Clyde Forsythe and his wife encouraged Rockwell to spend some time in California. Forsythe introduced the eligible Rockwell to Mary Barstow. The two were married on 17 April 1930, within three months of their meeting. The couple moved to New Rochelle, where Rockwell had previously lived. They eventually had three sons: Jarvis, Tom, and Peter. All of Rockwell's sons inherited artistic talent. Norman and Mary Rockwell lived happily together until her death in 1959.

Rockwell's ability to wring poignancy from everyday situations served him well in many of his covers for the *Post*. World War II plunged the world into a conflict that slew and uprooted millions and reconfigured geography. Amidst this turmoil Rockwell also labored. He had served in the U.S. Navy during World War I doing artistic work. Too old for active duty in World War II, Rockwell performed patriotic service in his art. He did a series of covers following the life of one young man, Willie Gillis, from enlistment through his eventual discharge. Willie Gillis became the American Everyman of World War II.

Two out of three *Post* covers published during World War II were in some way related to the war effort. Wanting to match his art with the spirit of the time, Rockwell conceived *The Four Freedoms,* a concept inspired by President Franklin D. Roosevelt's address to Congress in 1941. The paintings *Freedom of Speech, Freedom of Worship, Freedom from Want,* and *Freedom from Fear* were published as posters in 1943, a trying period of the war. Done in an American idiom (Roosevelt's four freedoms were intended to be universal in application), Rockwell plunged into his self-appointed crusade with enthusiasm. The results are mixed. Rockwell misses the mark with the *Speech* and *Worship* images. *Worship,* a collage of adherents to differing faiths looking toward a divine light, falls flat. Its style does not marry with the other three. *Speech* employs a good idea, but the thrust (a leathery blue-collar worker rising in a town meeting to make a point) is spoiled by the beatific visage of the worker and the almost worshipful admiration of his listeners; the work is almost a cartoon of the freedoms of speech it espouses. With the remaining two, *Freedom from Want* and *Freedom from Fear,* Rockwell succeeds marvelously. *Want* presents a snapshot of a large family apparently at Thanksgiving dinner. Animated eyes, hands, and faces punctuate the cheery anticipation as Grandmother places a sumptuously sized roast turkey on the table. Grandfather, ceremoniously standing at the table's head with carving implements at his right hand, presides. The power of this composition flows from the recognizability of the event: it is replicated annually by millions of middle-class Americans. Because it is almost taken for granted, the Thanksgiving feast propels Rockwell's otherwise trite composition into an understated yet potent commentary on American bounty.

The last of the series, *Freedom from Fear,* is perhaps the most powerful. In it Rockwell juxtaposes two incongruous images: Wartime tumult, terror, and tragedy with the tranquility and domesticity of parental care. Rockwell again paints an ordinary event, instantly recognizable to millions. Two small children asleep in their bed, toys and clothes discarded where they left them, are being tucked in by solicitous parents. The children and parents, in typical Rockwell fashion, are unremarkable in appearance; therefore, the viewer relates to them easily. It is a homely scene made powerful by the emotions of the war, which intrudes into the composition via shrieking headlines on the newspaper in the father's hand. Rockwell, in painting this most ordinary yet tender domestic scene—at odds with a roiling world at war—lifts the work from a wishful hope to a patriotic affirmation of humble American values. It is

still powerful more than fifty years later; in the midst of war-torn 1943 it moved many viewers to tears.

The innate drama of war provided Rockwell with one of his most potent palettes, but he never glamorized the conflict. *War News, Norman Rockwell Visits a Ration Board, A Night on a Troop Train,* the Willie Gillis series, and other wartime paintings invested a nobility into the ordinary lives and work of Americans. Rockwell only painted one battle scene: a lone, beleaguered marine firing a water-cooled machine gun. His face is in shadow, his fatigues in tatters. As he fires his weapon, spent brass cartridges pile up around his feet. Rockwell portrays him not as a hero, but instead as a soldier with a sense of grim and desperate duty. The painting was intended to encourage war-plant workers by forging a relationship between what the workers were producing and the needs of those who used the product. *Home for Thanksgiving,* the *Post* cover of November 1945, is particularly poignant. A recently returned soldier, still in uniform, peels potatoes (a task he doubtless loathed on KP) with his grateful mother. Again, a simple domestic scene is made eloquent in its emotional impact and context.

Shortly after the publication of Rockwell's *The Four Freedoms,* his studio in Arlington, Vermont, burned. He lost everything, including thirty original paintings, sketches, and a lifetime collection of props and costumes that could not readily be replaced. The loss impacted his methodology: Rockwell began his illustration career using live models, but while doing the Willie Gillis series it became necessary to utilize photography. He later remarked that he felt using this technology somehow made him a traitor to his profession. Nevertheless, the obvious advantages of photography—particularly for action poses—was undeniable. While Rockwell had little or no interest in mechanical innovations in painting, he was willing to experiment.

Some of his experiments were stylistic, but others reflected an expansion or evolution of Rockwell's native humor. *The Game* (1943), *Fire!* (1944), and *April Fool* (1945) are examples of Rockwell's visual humor. Surprisingly, one of Rockwell's favorite paintings was *The Game*—the artist's version of the theme of "what's wrong with this picture?" It is full of intentional mistakes and artful inappropriateness. A painting on the wall has the subject's hands coming out of the picture and resting on the frame; ducks fly through the parlor; a trout swims up the staircase; and a deer lies contentedly like a spaniel under a man's chair. The painting was placed on exhibit, but Rockwell did not wish to sell it, so he instructed that it carry a $500 price tag. The gallery

"*Saying Grace,*" *Rockwell's cover design for the 24 November 1951 Thanksgiving issue of*
The Saturday Evening Post *(private collection)*

priced it at $1,000–just to be safe. A customer nevertheless purchased it. Rockwell attempted to buy it back, but the purchaser adamantly refused to sell. Rockwell never quite understood why his cover painting would be worth such a price.

During Rockwell's half-century relationship with the *Post,* perhaps his best-known and most cherished cover illustration was the Thanksgiving cover of 1951, *Saying Grace.* Often reprinted, the painting represents the Rockwell skill at its height. Like almost all of his work, it represents a simple idea: in this case, a young boy and his grandmother saying a prayer before partaking of a meal. What lifts this idea beyond the banal is Rockwell's canny staging and composition. The artist utilized a snapshot approach that freezes the action. More important, Rockwell deliberately chose to portray this quiet moment of prayer and contemplation not in a church or even at home around a dining table. Instead he deliberately explores the theme of reverence in an inhospitable environment–a bustling railroad station. The praying pair appear in high relief, as others, initially surprised or even stunned by the apparent incongruity of the prayer in that environment, are left alone with their thoughts about what they see. Rockwell's sympathies are clearly drawn–light from the window bathes the pair in a divine glow. So potent was Rockwell's idea and composition that the viewer identifies with the other diners and idlers pondering the praying woman and boy.

Rockwell, like filmmaker Alfred Hitchcock, enjoyed making cameo appearances in his work. He frequently painted himself into crowd scenes or as a bystander in some scene. Combining a self-deprecating humor with self-portraiture, Rockwell also became the subject of more than one magazine-cover illustration. The best known of these is *Triple Self-Portrait* (*Post,* 13 February 1960), while *The Gossips* (*Post,* 6 March 1948) presents at least eight cameos.

Rockwell married once again in October 1961. His third wife was Mary "Molly" L. Punderson, a retired spinster schoolteacher whom he met in

Stockbridge, Massachusetts. They lived contentedly until Rockwell's death in 1978.

In 1963 Rockwell stopped painting for the *Post* because of a disagreement over the journalistic direction of the magazine: the editors of the *Post* wanted to present a more sophisticated image and felt that Rockwell's art would not fit with the new direction. Working for *Look* magazine instead, the artist became more journalistic and documentary, expanding his focus to include astronauts, politicians, and election coverage. While he avoided such controversial topics as Prohibition, the Depression, and the Korean and Vietnam Wars during his career, Rockwell chose to address the highly controversial issue of desegregation in *The Problem We All Live With* (14 January 1964). The painting received mixed reviews, although over time it has gained greater acceptance. Rockwell did not feel he was on solid ground in taking up moral and political issues. He enjoyed popularity rather than critical acclaim; but popularity can be far more fragile. In his autobiography Rockwell wryly observes that his worst enemies were "world-shaking ideas."

In the twilight of his career Rockwell focused on painting portraits of famous Americans and branched out to do illustrative work for the advertising campaign of the 1966 remake of the film *Stagecoach*. He also designed a 1972 postage stamp commemorating the centennial of Mark Twain's novel *Tom Sawyer*.

In 1973 Rockwell established an art trust to preserve his work. Administered through the Old Corner House of Stockbridge, Massachusetts, the museum maintains Rockwell's art and memory. Norman Perceval Rockwell died on 8 November 1978 at age eighty-four in Stockbridge.

He entered the business of illustration during its Golden Age; he outlived, outworked, and extended that Golden Age. Best known as a cover artist and an artistic storyteller, Rockwell eventually became the complete illustrator–adept in several formats. Despite the fact that critical acclaim largely eluded his art during his lifetime, he became one of the most popular and significant American illustrators, and he made unique contributions to American

social history. A sixty-year retrospective opened in New York in the 1970s and toured the country for a year. While the critics still disparaged his work, the American public cherished it. In the end, that is what mattered most to Rockwell anyway.

Biography:

Donald Walton, *A Rockwell Portrait: An Intimate Biography* (Kansas City, Kans.: Sheed Andrews & McMeel, 1978).

References:

Thomas S. Buechner, *Norman Rockwell: Artist and Illustrator* (New York: Abradale Press, 1983);

Christopher Finch, *Norman Rockwell's America* (New York: H. N. Abrams, 1975);

Finch, *332 Magazine Covers* (New York: Abbeville Press, 1979);

Arthur Leighton Guptill, *Norman Rockwell: Illustrator* (New York: Watson-Guptill, 1946);

William Hillcourt, *Norman Rockwell's World of Scouting* (New York: H. N. Abrams, 1977);

Laurie Norton Moffatt, *Norman Rockwell: A Definitive Catalogue* (Stockbridge, Mass.: The Norman Rockwell Museum at Stockbridge, 1986);

Mary Moline, *Norman Rockwell Encyclopedia: A Chronological Catalog of the Artist's Work, 1918–1978* (Indianapolis: Curtis, 1979);

Donald Robert Stoltz, *The Advertising World of Norman Rockwell* (New York: Madison Square Press, 1985).

Archives:

The most important collections reside in the Norman Rockwell Museum, Stockbridge, Massachusetts, and the Norman Rockwell Museum, Philadelphia, Pennsylvania. The first, located in Rockwell's hometown, includes paintings, drawings, sketches, correspondence, papers, and the artist's studio, with working materials and memorabilia. The second, housed in the Curtis Publishing Building, where Rockwell sold his first magazine cover, contains the entire collection of cover illustrations for *The Saturday Evening Post,* lithographs, collotypes, prints, sketches, and a replica of Rockwell's studio.

Charles M. Russell
(19 March 1864 – 24 October 1926)

Donald A. Barclay
New Mexico State University Library

BOOKS: *Studies of Western Life* (New York: Albertype, 1890);

Pen Sketches (Great Falls, Mont.: W. T. Ridgely, 1899);

Rawhide Rawlins Stories (Great Falls: Montana Newspaper Association, 1921);

Back Trailing on the Old Frontiers (Great Falls: Cheely-Raban Syndicate, 1922);

More Rawhides (Great Falls, Mont.: Montana Newspaper Association, 1925);

Trails Plowed Under (Garden City, N.Y.: Doubleday, Page, 1927);

Good Medicine: The Illustrated Letters of Charles M. Russell (Garden City, N.Y.: Doubleday, Doran, 1929).

SELECTED BOOKS ILLUSTRATED: Beacom, John H., *How the Buffalo Lost His Crown* (New York: Forest & Stream, 1894);

Wallace, Charles, *Cattle Queen of Montana* (Saint James, Minn.: C. W. Foote, 1894);

Hough, E., *Story of the Cowboy* (New York: Appleton, 1897);

Coburn, Wallace D., *Rhymes from a Round-Up Camp* (Great Falls, Mont.: W. T. Ridgely, 1899);

Vaughn, Robert, *Then and Now: or, Thirty-Six Years in the Rockies* (Minneapolis: Tribune, 1900);

Freeman, Harry C., *Brief History of Butte, Montana* (Chicago: Henry O. Shepard, 1900);

Allen, William A., *Adventures with Indians and Game, or Twenty Years in the Rocky Mountains* (Chicago: A. W. Bowen, 1903);

Parker, Frances, *Hope Hathaway: A Story of Western Ranch Life* (Boston: C. M. Clark, 1904);

Wheeler, Olin D., *Trail of Lewis and Clark* (New York: Putnam, 1904);

Steedman, Charles J., *Bucking the Sagebrush: or, The Oregon Trail in the Seventies* (New York: Putnam, 1904);

Hamilton, W. T., *My Sixty Years on the Plains Trapping, Trading, and Indian Fighting* (New York: Forest & Stream, 1905);

Bower, B. M., *Chip of the Flying U* (New York & London: Street & Smith, 1906);

Bower, *The Range Dwellers* (New York & London: Street & Smith, 1907);

Bower, *The Lure of the Dim Trails* (New York: G. W. Dillingham, 1907);

Harriman-Browne, Alice, *Chaperoning Adrienne: A Tale of Yellowstone National Park* (Seattle: Metropolitan, 1907);

Strahorn, Carrie Adell, *Fifteen Thousand Miles by Stage* (New York: Putnam, 1911);

Wister, Owen, *The Virginian* (New York: Macmillan, 1911);

Bower, B. M., *The Uphill Climb* (Boston: Little, Brown, 1913);

Harte, Bret, *Trent's Trust and Other Tales* (Boston & New York: Houghton Mifflin, 1914);

Linderman, Frank B., *Indian Why Stories* (New York: Scribners, 1915);

Linderman, *Indian Lodge-Fire Stories* (New York: Scribners, 1918);

Linderman, *Indian Old-Man Stories* (New York: Scribners, 1920);

Laut, Agnes C., *Blazed Trail of the Old Frontier* (New York: McBride, 1926).

PERIODICALS: *Northwest Magazine*, 1888–1901;
Helena Journal, 1890–1891;
Great Falls Weekly Tribune, 1891–1893;
Western Field and Stream, 1897–1898;
Field and Stream, 1898–1907;
Rocky Mountain Magazine, 1900–1902;
Great Falls Tribune, 1900–1925;
Butte Miner, 1903–1919;
Frank Leslie's Illustrated Newspaper, 1904–1907;
Outing, 1904–1909;
Scribner's Magazine, 1905–1921;
Popular Magazine, 1906–1907;
McClure's, 1906–1910;
Great Falls Leader, 1907–1909;
Treasure State, 1908–1912;
American Magazine, 1909–1919;

American Art News, 1911–1915;
Literary Digest, 1911–1917;
Saturday Evening Post, 1913;
St. Nicholas, 1915;
Montana Magazine, 1915–1916.

Charles M. Russell stands with Frederic Remington as one of the two great painters of America's frontier West. Though best known for his paintings and bronzes, Russell was also an illustrator of books, magazines, and newspapers. In all mediums he strove to depict accurately the peoples, animals, and landscapes of the West, but his view of the West was so nostalgic that his artist's eye remained focused always on the West that no longer was.

Despite his close association with the West, Charles Marion Russell was not born on the frontier; he entered the world on 19 March 1864 in the well-settled vicinity of Saint Louis, Missouri. Russell's Yale-educated father was a well-to-do manufacturer of firebricks who could afford to give his son a good education—a gift in which Charlie had little interest. Russell was such a poor scholar that he never mastered more than the basics of spelling and grammar, a fact that makes his adult writing colorfully colloquial but which thoroughly vexed his teachers and parents and brought frequent punishments to the boy. That he learned to read at all was perhaps due to his interest in the Western dime novels that featured the highly fictionalized deeds of William "Buffalo Bill" Cody, Kit Carson, and other Western heroes. The root of Russell's problems with school lay in the fact that he was interested in drawing pictures and making clay models to the exclusion of all other subjects. Not even a family-enforced stint at a New Jersey military school could divert young Charlie's one-track mind from the subject of art.

Russell grew up fascinated with the frontier West and filled his boyhood sketchbooks with drawings of horses and Indians, the latter figures modeled on the Indians drawn by such artists as George Catlin, Karl Bodmer, and Carl Wimar. Russell's attraction to things western came naturally as he was the grand nephew of the Bent brothers—prominent Missouri fur traders and the builders of the famous Bent's Fort on the Arkansas River. For his sixteenth birthday Russell's parents gave in and allowed him to take a trip to the West, possibly in hopes that the roughness of the frontier would send their boy scurrying back to the comfort and safety of Saint Louis. Fortunately for the future of Western art, nothing of the sort happened. Under the guidance of family friend Wallis Miller, Russell made his way to the wild Judith Basin of Montana, where he took a job herding sheep. Something of a dilettante, young "Kid Russell" was easily distracted by the natural beauty of his surroundings and quickly lost his sheepherding job for dereliction of duty. Although the Russell legend has the former sheepherder spending the next two years of his life under the tutelage of Jake Hoover, a Judith Basin hunter and trapper who would make a perfect figure for educating a raw boy from Saint Louis in the ways of the West, the truth is that Russell was more a frequent houseguest than Hoover's full-time apprentice. Still, Russell was deeply influenced by the older man, though not so much that he ever became keen on killing animals. The adult Russell would go hunting for the camaraderie of it—to be with his friends, out of doors and telling campfire stories—but he was not known to shoot any animals during these trips. He apparently enjoyed watching, sketching, and modeling animals more than shooting them. In 1881 Russell made a trip back east to see his family, who had been sending him money to help take care of his meager wants. Back in Montana in 1882, young Russell took a job as a night herder for a Montana cattle outfit—Russell had at last embarked on a cowboy career that would last eleven years. He soon adopted the red "half-breed" sash and boots that would constitute his trademark outfit for the rest of his life.

To understand Russell's artwork fully it is important to understand the West he knew and the role he played in it. The frontier West was in its final decade in 1880; there were still a few good-sized herds of buffalo and a few bands of "wild" Indians, but both would be wiped out forever by 1890. Russell himself never witnessed Indian warfare or saw buffalo hunted from horseback though he eventually did become acquainted with several old-timers—Indians as well as whites—who had witnessed or participated in both of these quintessentially western pursuits. Similarly, Russell witnessed only the last stages of the open-range era. By beginning work as a night herder in 1882, Russell just managed to take part in some of the last large round-ups in Montana history, but within six years of the start of his cowboy career a combination of shifting economic conditions, summer droughts, and winter blizzards had finished off open-range grazing as surely as the coming of the whites had finished off the buffalo and the free-roaming Indian.

Because Russell experienced only the final days of the frontier period, his work must be seen as a nostalgic attempt to re-create a vanished past instead of as a series of documentaries based on the artist's personal experience although Russell is of-

Charles Russell and his wife, Nancy, at their summer cabin on Lake McDonald, 1903

ten hailed as a documentarian on the basis of his avid pursuit of accuracy in his art. So that his art would show western life as it really was, Russell filled his studio with genuine artifacts, such as saddles, headdresses, guns, and blankets. He often used photographs of western scenes and people and occasionally would hire local cowboys and Native Americans to serve as models. Russell was an expert model maker who would sometimes make beeswax figures of people and animals to assist his painting and drawing. This keen eye for three-dimensional form no doubt contributed to Russell's celebrated ability to draw humans and animals accurately in motion as well as at rest.

Russell also called on his own cowboy experience to lend accuracy to his work and, unlike Remington, would never make so glaring an error as depicting a cowboy throwing a lasso while wearing a quirt on his throwing wrist (as Russell well knew, any cowboy who tried such a trick would most likely end up quirting himself in the face). However, what keeps Russell from becoming a documentarian of the life he actually knew—the final decade of the frontier and the early days of the twentieth-century West—is his deep nostalgia for the era he had just missed. Although there were plenty

of genuine cowboys and Indians as well as miles of unspoiled country in the Montana that Russell knew, the artist did not earn his fame by painting cowboys behind the wheels of Model T's or reservation Blackfeet visiting the movie houses of Great Falls. It was the sweet, departed past—the age of Meriwether Lewis and William Clark on the Missouri, Blackfeet warring against the Crows, vast herds of buffalo, cowboys on horseback—that was always the setting and subject of Russell's art. The buffalo skull that Russell eventually incorporated into his distinctive signature was more than a decorative device: it was the symbol of the artist's deep yearning for a West that had vanished with the buffalo and which was just as unlikely to return.

Along with understanding the nostalgia that guided Russell's hand, it is also important to understand the nature of the artist's celebrated and occasionally overstated career as a cowboy. By his own admission Russell was "neither a good roper nor rider," and he spent much of his cowboy career working as a night herder, one of the lowliest jobs. Such work may have suited Russell better than more-prestigious jobs, however, as it allowed him to spend a good part of his daylight hours observing men and animals. During his free days the young

Illustrations by Russell and J. H. Smith for the 18 May 1889 issue of Frank Leslie's Illustrated Newspaper

artist sketched everything he saw and in this way began to develop his ability to draw men and horses in motion, one of the trademarks of his mature work.

Russell's art also benefited from the seasonal, transient nature of the cowboy's life, which left him time to draw and travel. Besides frequent trips back to Saint Louis to visit his family, in May 1887 Russell was able to take an impulsive, three-month trip to Canada. The Russell legend would eventually inflate the length of the trip to Canada to an entire winter, during which time the artist was supposed to have been adopted by the Blood Indians and was wedded to an Indian woman. Though his experiences with the Bloods were exaggerated, Russell had a great deal of respect for Indian people and Indian culture. Throughout his life Russell had many Indian friends, and when Young Boy's band of Cree refugees was seeking land for a reservation outside of Great Falls, Russell was one of their strongest supporters even though most Montanans were disgusted by the unfortunate Crees and held them in total contempt. That Russell preferred to depict Indians in their own element—hunting buffalo, traveling on horseback, practicing native customs—rather than in the fighting scenes so favored by his contemporaries Remington and Charles Schreyvogel, may have been in part due to his respect for Indians. Rus-

sell was not entirely free of the prejudices of his time, however: he did execute an obligatory painting of Custer's Last Stand, and the few surviving examples of his erotica depict cowboys having sex with Indian women.

After 1885 Russell began developing a local reputation as an artistic cowboy who would give away his drawings to anyone who admired them (or who would buy the artist a drink in trade). In 1886 Russell successfully entered his oil painting *Breaking Camp* in a Saint Louis art show, and by 1887 he was occasionally being written up in the local newspapers. Greater exposure came with the wide circulation of his *Waiting for a Chinook* (also known as *The Last of 5,000*). This small watercolor of a dying steer, emaciated by the terrible blizzards of 1886–1887 and surrounded by equally emaciated wolves, was one of the first eyewitness depictions of the severe winter that all but destroyed the western cattle business as it was known in the nineteenth century. If the exposure that resulted from *Waiting for a Chinook* did not turn Russell into an instant national celebrity, then it made him a local one. He had established himself as Montana's favorite painter and would always remain so.

In 1890 Russell published *Studies of Western Life,* a portfolio that reproduced twelve of his oils.

Still, he continued to work off and on as a cowboy until the fall of 1893, when he devoted himself full-time to making his living as an artist. By that time he had already had a few works reproduced nationally, but what really convinced Russell he could make a living as an artist was a commission to execute several paintings for William Niedringhaus, the wealthy owner of the N Bar N ranch, where Russell had once worked as a cowboy. While working on the commission Russell also did eight illustrations for *How the Buffalo Lost His Crown* (1894) by John H. Beacom, an army officer stationed at Fort Shaw. Russell continued to eke out a living as an artist until 1896, the year he married seventeen-year-old Nancy Cooper and irrevocably changed his fortunes. Though only half Russell's age, Nancy Cooper Russell was a strong-willed woman who saw her new husband as something more than a saddle bum with a knack for drawing horses. Almost before the honeymoon was over Nancy set about putting Russell's career on a more profitable track.

Her first move was to cut back on the amount of time Russell spent hanging around the saloons of Great Falls, drinking and telling stories with his legion of cronies. Though his friends at The Mint saloon may have resented the intrusion, regular hours in front of the easel and Nancy's insistence on a two-drink-per-day limit increased Russell's output. These changes of habit, coupled with Nancy's head for business, paved the way for Russell's career to take off. As her husband's agent, Nancy had no qualms about demanding more money for a painting than the artist would have dared to ask. Shortly after Russell's career began to prosper, Nancy sold a painting for $400, a sum Russell referred to as a "dead man's price." By Russell's final years Nancy was getting thousands per painting. In 1920 Russell's *Salute of the Robe Trade* fetched $10,000. Two large paintings done for the E. L. Doheny mansion just months before the artist's death fetched $30,000.

Another evidence of Nancy Russell's genius for the business of art was that she realized that provincial Montana was not the best place from which to market paintings. Nostalgia for the western frontier had spread beyond the borders of Montana and into the eastern cities, where the real art money was. The local saloon owners, ranchers, and merchants who had been Russell's chief patrons would never be able to pay the eastern prices Nancy had in mind. In 1903 Charlie and Nancy made their first trip to New York City to test the waters. There Russell became acquainted with many of the most successful illustrators of the day. The fresh, vibrant, but unschooled artist would come to learn a great deal about artistic technique from his new, academy-trained friends—who had no idea that the westerner they had taken under their wings would eventually eclipse them in fame and fortune. In particular John N. Marchand, a successful illustrator originally from Kansas, took a liking to Russell, introducing him to editors at *Scribner's Magazine, Leslie's, Outing,* and *McClure's.* As a result Russell came to publish illustrations in all four magazines. Also, offers to illustrate W. T. Hamilton's *My Sixty Years on the Plains Trapping, Trading, and Indian Fighting* (1905) and B. M. Bower's *Chip of the Flying U* (1906) came in the wake of the New York visit. In both of these books Russell's role as illustrator was given more prominence than ever before in his career. During 1903 and 1904 three of the four books to which Russell contributed illustrations—*Adventures with Indians and Game* (1903), *Hope Hathaway* (1904), and *Trail of Lewis and Clark* (1904)—did not include the artist's name on their title pages; after Russell's New York fame, no savvy publisher would ever again make such an omission.

The Russells came to make regular trips to the city Charlie called, somewhat derisively, the "Big Camp." In 1911 Russell mounted his first one-man New York show, which was billed as "The West That Has Passed." The show, which featured oils, watercolors, and bronzes, was held in a prestigious Fifth Avenue gallery and drew a great deal of attention from the press—as did the artist. Dressed in his Stetson, his boots, and his red sash, the publicly soft-spoken Russell perfectly conformed to the popular idea of what a real cowboy should be. *The New York Times* and the *World* both ran full-page profiles of the artist. If he did not know it when he first came to town, Russell soon discovered that dressing and acting the part of a cowboy did nothing to hurt the sales of his Western paintings.

In playing the part of the unlettered, unschooled cowboy, Russell was to an extent pulling a fast one on the public. Though he never studied in any of the great art schools, Russell was a deliberate, purposeful artist who did not spring up full grown from the cattle camps of Montana. Though he refused to talk publicly about the fine points of art, disparaging it as a rather sissified subject, in private he was eager to learn what he could from master artists. Russell's work after his contact with New York illustrators such as Marchand shows improvement in technique when compared to his earlier efforts. Also, the development of his drawing and painting clearly shows that he was a good student who paid careful attention to what other artists were doing. In addition to being influenced by early Western artists such as Bodmer, Russell was greatly

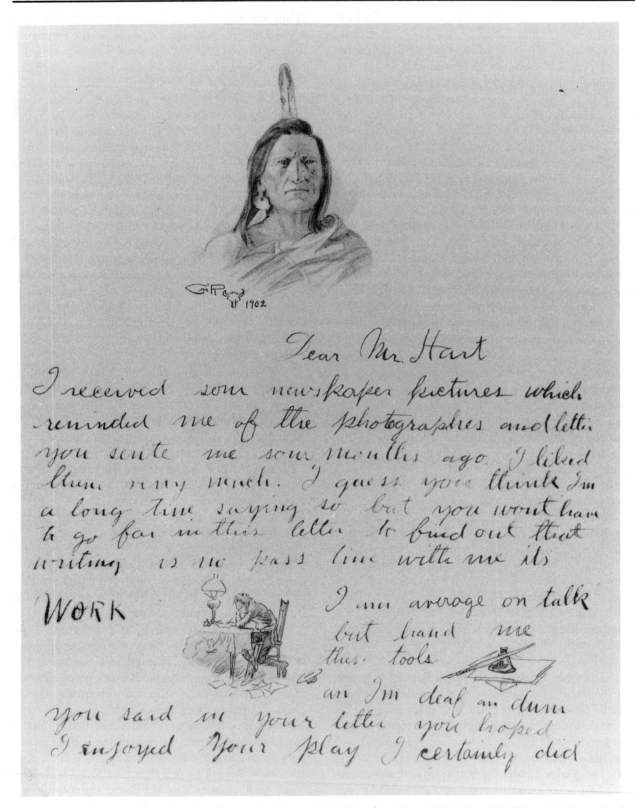

Letter from Russell to cowboy film star W. S. Hart (from Good Medicine: The Illustrated Letters of
Charles M. Russell, *1929)*

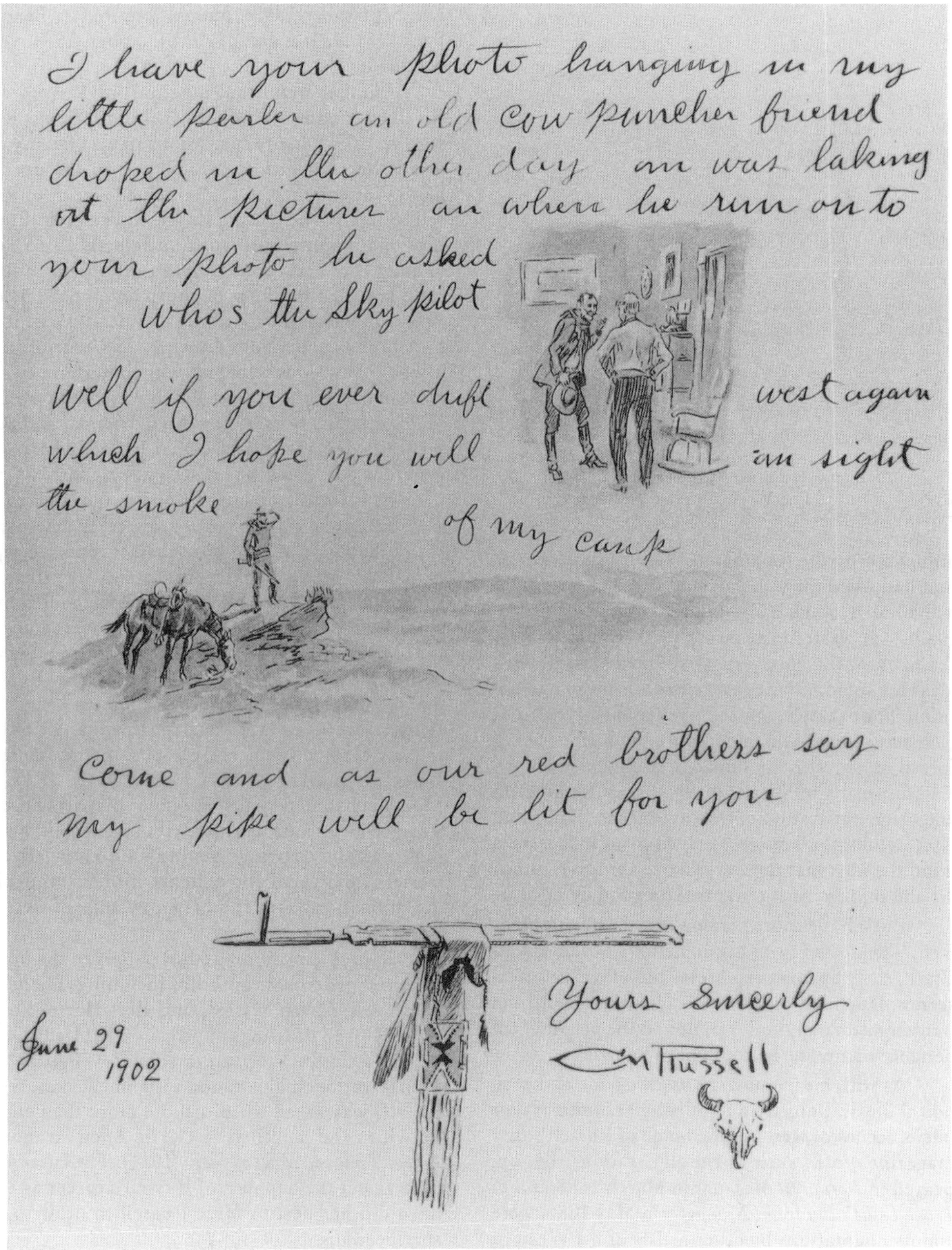

I have your photo hanging in my little parlor an old cow puncher friend droped in the other day an was lakeing at the picture an when he run on to your photo he asked whos the Sky pilot

well if you ever drift west agan which I hope you will an sight the smoke of my camp

Come and as our red brothers say my pipe will be lit for you

June 29 1902

Yours Sincerly

CM Russell

Illustration by Russell for Owen Wister's novel
The Virginian *(1911)*

influenced by the Remington Western illustrations that had filled the popular magazines of his young manhood. Though Russell never became the propagandist for western expansion that Remington was, the work of the older artist provided Russell with ideas for subject matter as well as lessons in composition. For example, Russell's watercolor *Dance, You Shorthorn, Dance,* which depicts a tenderfoot being forced to dance to the tune of a drunken cowboy's six-gun, owes its origin to an earlier Remington magazine illustration of the same scene. If nothing else, Remington's success helped plant in Russell's mind the idea that there was a market for Western art and that an artist could make a good living at it.

Russell did more reading than he admitted, as well. The accuracy of his depictions of Lewis and Clark, early Spanish explorers, and other historical scenes depended on Russell's familiarity with the written history of the West, not on the personal experience of anyone he could have known.

As with his paintings, Russell's book and periodical illustrations tried to portray accurate, if nostalgic, scenes of western life. Some of Russell's first magazine work, such as the illustrations that appeared in *Northwest Magazine* in March 1888 and in *Frank Leslie's Illustrated Newspaper* in May 1889, were simply adaptations by other artists of his Western paintings. Later on, Russell executed original drawings for magazine pieces, as can be seen in his illustrations for such magazine stories as Stewart Edward White's "Arizona Nights" (*McClure's,* January–February 1906), Edgar Beecher Bronson's "The Evolution of a Train Robber" (*American Maga-*

zine, September 1909), and Al Jennings's "Beating Back" (*Saturday Evening Post,* 4 October–15 November 1913).

Another important medium for Russell was the illustrated letter. When writing to friends Russell typically added illustrations to accompany the words he managed to scratch out in his uneven hand. For example, a 1902 one-page letter to Russell's Cree friend Young Boy includes color drawings of a mounted Indian, a buffalo skull, a shield (Young Boy had recently given the shield to Russell), and a bounding pronghorn antelope. The envelope in which the letter was sent features another buffalo skull and a color drawing of a Cree village as it would have looked before white interference and alcohol had reduced the tribe to wretched poverty. Wild animals, horses, cowboys, friends, and self-portraits decorate hundreds of Russell letters, all generous gifts from the artist to his friends.

In 1915 Russell created fifty-two drawings for *Back Trailing on the Old Frontiers,* a weekly newspaper series that appeared in more than seventy newspapers. Each weekly installment featured an article on some incident of western history accompanied by a Russell drawing. Because the series covered nearly four hundred years of western history–from the expedition of Coronado to the cowboy era–Russell had to paint scenes that were beyond his own experiences. But whether it was depicting Juan de Oñate in New Mexico in the early 1600s, the massacre of Blackfeet Indians at Fort McKenzie in 1844, or Montana badman Henry Plummer preparing to rob a stagecoach, Russell acquitted himself well, bringing to all the drawings his intimate knowledge of western landscapes and animals, his flair for depicting dramatic action, and his knowledge of western history.

Russell contributed illustrations to the books of many prominent authors, including Theodore Roosevelt, Owen Wister, and Bret Harte. Forty-three Russell drawings appear in a 1911 edition of Wister's classic Western novel, *The Virginian.* An even larger book-illustration assignment came when Russell was asked to contribute more than eighty drawings and paintings to Carrie Adell Strahorn's *Fifteen Thousand Miles by Stage* (1911). The latter project was not the happiest of Russell's career as Strahorn did her best to force Russell to draw to her specifications.

Although he did good work illustrating the writings of others, some of Russell's best book and magazine work was done for his own first-person stories of western life. Never a good hand at spelling or grammar, Russell was nevertheless a master storyteller. He was so gifted, in fact, that it is often said that when Russell and his friend Will Rogers were together in a roomful of people, it was Rogers who took a back seat to listen while Russell amused the crowd with his droll tales of cowpunching and western life. When telling stories in person Russell would illustrate them with movements of his graceful hands, sometimes casting shadow pictures of people and animals on the wall as he spoke. It was only natural for Russell to illustrate his stories when he eventually took on the laborious task of writing them. Like his paintings, Russell's oral and written stories were based in part on his own experience, in part on stories he had heard, and in part on his nostalgia for the frontier. Whatever the subject of the story, Russell's ear for dialogue and his sense of humor came through. In the story "A Gift Horse," Russell's alter ego and narrator, Rawhide Rawlins, tells of an outlaw horse that had thrown him and run away: "How am I going to catch him? If I had a Winchester, I'd catch him just over the eye." The accompanying illustration shows an arch-backed horse, the stirrups on its empty saddle bouncing high. The rider is shown piling in head first, both feet in the air and hat flying out of the picture. Russell's illustrated tales were published in such magazines as *Recreation* (April 1897) and *Outing* (1907–1908). In book form Russell's stories and accompanying illustrations appeared as *Rawhide Rawlins Stories* (1921), *More Rawhides* (1925), and *Trails Plowed Under* (1927).

Besides appearing as accompaniments to stories and articles, Russell's illustrations were frequently published in magazines and newspapers for their own sake, without any text at all. An early example of this is the 18 May 1889 issue of *Frank Leslie's Illustrated Newspaper,* which includes seven Russell pen-and-ink sketches published on a single page. The use of Russell drawings in advertisements was another means by which his work made its way into the periodicals of his day.

Russell's career as a book and periodical illustrator did not end with the heart attack that took his life on 24 October 1926. Since his death Russell's works have appeared in periodicals more often than they did in his lifetime. Over the years magazines ranging from *American Rifleman* to *Connoisseur* have featured his work. *Montana: The Magazine of Western History* has published several hundred reproductions of Russell paintings and drawings since 1955. It seems that as the frontier West fades further into the past, Charles M. Russell's nostalgic vision of the era he almost knew becomes more popular with a public that never knew that era at all.

References:

Brian W. Dippie, *Charles M. Russell, Word Painter: Letters 1887–1926* (Fort Worth: Amon Carter Museum, 1993);

Dippie, *Looking at Russell* (Fort Worth: Amon Carter Museum, 1987);

Dippie, *Remington and Russell* (Austin: University of Texas Press, 1982);

Frederic G. Renner, *Charles Marion Russell: Greatest of All Western Artists* (Washington, D.C.: Potomac Corral of the Westerners, 1968);

John Taliaferro, *Charles M. Russell: The Life And Legend of America's Cowboy Artist* (Boston: Little, Brown, 1996);

Dan L. Thrapp, *Encyclopedia of Frontier Biography* (Glendale, Cal.: Arthur H. Clark, 1988);

Karl Yost and Frederic G. Renner, *A Bibliography of the Published Works of Charles M. Russell* (Lincoln: University of Nebraska Press, 1971).

Archives:

Significant collections of Charles M. Russell's work are held by the Amon Carter Museum in Fort Worth, Texas; the Buffalo Bill Historical Center in Cody, Wyoming; the Colorado Springs Fine Art Center in Colorado Springs, Colorado; the C. M. Russell Museum in Great Falls, Montana; and the National Cowboy Hall of Fame and Western Heritage Center in Oklahoma City, Oklahoma.

J. Allen St. John
(1 October 1872 – 23 May 1957)

Richard Bleiler
University of Connecticut

BOOK: *The Face in the Pool* (Chicago: McClurg, 1905).

SELECTED BOOKS ILLUSTRATED: De Balzac, Honoré, *The Complete Works of Honoré De Balzac*, Colonial Press Edition, 36 volumes, illustrated by St. John and others (Boston: Colonial, 1899–1901);

Twain, Mark, *The Works of Mark Twain,* Hillcrest Edition, 24 volumes, illustrated by St. John and others (Hartford, Conn.: American, 1899);

Harrison, Edith Ogden, *The Lady of the Snows* (Chicago: McClurg, 1912);

Morton, L. Curry, *The Hero and the Man* (Chicago: McClurg, 1912);

Mason, Edith Huntington, *The Great Plan* (Chicago: McClurg, 1913);

Perry, Lawrence, *Holton of the Navy: A Story of the Freeing of Cuba* (Chicago: McClurg, 1913);

Wells, H. G., *The Wife of Sir Isaac Harman* (New York: Donohue, 1914);

Burroughs, Edgar Rice, *The Return of Tarzan* (Chicago: McClurg, 1915);

McCarter, Margaret Hill, *The Corner Stone* (Chicago: McClurg, 1915);

Burroughs, Edgar Rice, *The Beasts of Tarzan* (Chicago: McClurg, 1916);

Kipling, Rudyard, *Kipling Boy Stories* (Chicago: Rand, McNally, 1916);

Burroughs, Edgar Rice, *The Son of Tarzan* (Chicago: McClurg, 1917);

McCarter, Margaret Hill, *Cuddy's Baby* (Chicago: McClurg, 1917);

Brady, Cyrus Townsend, *Waif-o-the-Sea* (Chicago: McClurg, 1918);

Burroughs, Edgar Rice, *Jungle Tales of Tarzan* (Chicago: McClurg, 1919);

Burroughs, *The Warlord of Mars* (Chicago: McClurg, 1919);

Parrish, Randall, *Comrades of Peril* (Chicago: McClurg, 1919);

J. Allen St. John

Guest, Edgar, *A Heap o' Livin* (Chicago: Reilly & Lee, 1919);

Guest, *The Paths to Home* (Chicago: Reilly & Lee, 1919);

Burroughs, Edgar Rice, *Tarzan the Untamed* (Chicago: McClurg, 1920);

Burroughs, *Thuvia, Maid of Mars* (Chicago: McClurg, 1920);

Guest, Edgar, *When Day Is Done* (Chicago: Reilly & Lee, 1921);

Burroughs, Edgar Rice, *Tarzan the Terrible* (Chicago: McClurg, 1921);

Ogden, George W., *The Bondboy* (Chicago: McClurg, 1922);

Mulford, Clarence E., *Bring Me His Ears* (Chicago: McClurg, 1922);

Burroughs, Edgar Rice, *The Chessmen of Mars* (Chicago: McClurg, 1922);

Ogden, George W., *Claim Number One* (Chicago: McClurg, 1922);

Parrish, Randall, *Gift of the Desert* (Chicago: McClurg, 1922);

Mulford, Clarence E., *Tex* (Chicago: McClurg, 1922);

Burroughs, Edgar Rice, *At Earth's Core* (Chicago: McClurg, 1922);

Burroughs, *Pellucidar* (Chicago: McClurg, 1923);

Burroughs, *Tarzan and the Golden Lion* (Chicago: McClurg, 1923);

Bennet, Robert Ames, *Tyrrell of the Cow Country* (Chicago: McClurg, 1923);

Cummings, Ray, *The Man Who Mastered Time* (Chicago: McClurg, 1923);

Dana, Marvin, *The Lake Mystery* (Chicago: McClurg, 1923);

Guest, Edgar, *The Passing Throng* (Chicago: Reilly & Lee, 1923);

Ogden, George W., *The Baron of Diamond Tail* (Chicago: McClurg, 1923);

Bennet, Robert Ames, *Branded* (Chicago: McClurg, 1924);

Bennet, *The Two Gun Man* (Chicago: McClurg, 1924);

Burroughs, Edgar Rice, *Tarzan and the Ant Men* (Chicago: McClurg, 1924);

Guest, Edgar, *Rhymes of Childhood* (Chicago: Reilly & Lee, 1924);

Marvin, Dana, *The Mystery of the Third Parrot* (Chicago: McClurg, 1924);

Mulford, Clarence E., *The Orphan* (Chicago: McClurg, 1924);

Bennett, Robert Ames, *The Rough Rider* (Chicago: McClurg, 1925);

McCarter, Margaret Hill, *The Candle in the Window* (Chicago: McClurg, 1925);

Ogden, George W., *The Road to Monterey* (Chicago: McClurg, 1925);

Perkins, Kenneth, *Queen of the Night* (Chicago: McClurg, 1925);

Hoffman, W. D., *Gun Gospel* (Chicago: McClurg, 1926);

Ogden, George W., *The Valley of Adventure* (Chicago: McClurg, 1926);

Hoffman, W. D., *Knights of the Desert* (Chicago: McClurg, 1927);

Burroughs, Edgar Rice, *The Master Mind of Mars* (Chicago: McClurg, 1928);

Burroughs, *Tarzan, Lord of the Jungle* (Chicago: McClurg, 1928);

Guest, Edgar, *Harbor Lights of Home* (Chicago: Reilly & Lee, 1928);

Hoffman, W. D., *Bravo Jim* (Chicago: McClurg, 1928);

Hoffman, *The Saddle Wolf* (Chicago: McClurg, 1928);

Hoffman, *Santone* (Chicago: McClurg, 1929);

Burroughs, Edgar Rice, *Tarzan at the Earth's Core* (New York: Metropolitan Books, 1930);

Hoffman, W. D., *The Boss of Thunder Butte* (Chicago: McClurg, 1930);

Buchanan, Madeleine Sharps, *The Black Pearl Murders* (Chicago: McClurg, 1930);

Worts, George, *The Silver Fang* (Chicago: McClurg, 1930);

Cummings, Ray, *Brigands of the Moon* (Chicago: McClurg, 1931);

Guest, Edgar, *The Friendly Way* (Chicago: Reilly & Lee, 1931);

Hoffman, W. D., *Termaine of Texas* (Chicago: McClurg, 1931);

Hoffman, *The Canyon of No Return* (Chicago: McClurg, 1932);

Burroughs, Edgar Rice, *Tarzan and the City of Gold* (Tarzana, Cal.: Edgar Rice Burroughs, 1933);

Burroughs, *Tarzan and the Lion Man* (Tarzana, Cal.: Edgar Rice Burroughs, 1934);

Burroughs, *Tarzan and the Leopard Men* (Tarzana, Cal.: Burroughs, 1935);

Burroughs, *Swords of Mars* (Tarzana, Cal.: Burroughs, 1936);

Burroughs, *Tarzan's Quest* (Tarzana, Cal.: Burroughs, 1936).

PERIODICALS: *Delineator,* 1900–1901;
Woman's World, 1912–1915, 1920, 1925;
Green Book Magazine, 1919–1921;
Red Book Magazine, 1919–1925;
Blue Book Magazine, 1919–1928;
Child Life, 1926–1937;
Weird Tales, 1932–1936;
Young People's Weekly, 1933–1937;
Boy's World, 1933–1940;
Fantastic Adventures, 1940–1950;
Amazing Stories, 1941–1950;
Other Worlds Science Stories, 1950–1953.

For the first half of the twentieth century J. Allen St. John (as he often signed himself) was generally considered one of the finest illustrators of the fantastic adventure, but to remember him solely for his commercial artwork in this area of popular literature is to limit him unfairly. St. John began his ar-

Dust jacket by St. John for a novel (1923) in a popular adventure series

tistic career as a capable painter of portraits for the socially prominent, and although later in his life he would provide artwork (pictorial dust jackets and internal illustrations in pencil) for writers as popular and ephemeral as Robert Ames Bennet, Madeleine Sharps Buchanan, Cyrus Townsend Brady, W. D. Hoffman, and George F. Worts, it should not be forgotten that he was once considered respectable enough to paint the portrait of noted artist, engineer, and author F. Hopkinson Smith. Nevertheless, in spite of his apparent artistic versatility, St. John's illustrations are surprisingly traditional, consistently old-fashioned, and unprogressive in their uses of lines and spaces and representations of events. Contemporary artists such as Joseph Clement Coll frequently experimented with perspectives, styles, and differing treatments of similar subjects, but St. John never did, and he remains in essence a late-nineteenth-century narrative painter apparently unaware of modern illustrative techniques. His artworks are technically capable and precisely detailed, but even when they are intended to depict violent life-and-death situations, they remain carefully posed tableaux reminiscent of stills from a stage play, an impression heightened by backgrounds that frequently resemble canvas backdrops.

Furthermore, St. John was rarely able to portray the weird and ineffable: his illustrations of the fantastic bring it into realism, thereby diminishing it. Paradoxically, when St. John is remembered at all, it is for his fantastic illustrations of the works of Edgar Rice Burroughs and for the nine covers he painted during the 1930s to illustrate stories published in *Weird Tales,* a shaky, low-budget, fantasy-oriented pulp magazine that is currently popular.

James Allen St. John was born of moderately well-to-do parents in Chicago. His maternal grandfather, Hilliard Hely, enjoyed painting and was a minor painter, and his mother, Susan Hely St. John, studied with noted American painter George Peter Alexander Healy and later traveled to Paris before opening a studio in Boston. The young St. John accompanied his mother on her European trips, and his interest in art began to manifest itself at an early age. Reflecting on his childhood in an article published in the *Metropolitan Magazine* of November 1898, St. John recalled that "My first recollections are my mother's studio, and the eyes of her portraits following me about the place. . . . Even as a child I found delight in the society of the so-called bohemians my mother gathered around her, and one of my greatest pleasures was to ramble at will through the Louvre, the Luxembourg and the countless quaint and charming corners of the unfashionable parts of the city, so dear to all dreamers. But I unconsciously imitated those with whom I was brought in contact, and began to sketch and paint before I could read and write."

However, St. John's father, Josephus, intended for his son to become a businessman and, when St. John was sixteen, bought him a partnership with an experienced businessman. St. John rebelled and was sent to California to live in the San Joaquin Valley on a ranch owned by his uncle. While traveling to Los Angeles, St. John befriended Western artist Eugene Torrey and spent the next three years traveling and sketching landscapes. He returned east for his formal schooling, enrolling at the Art Students League of New York and studying under H. Siddons Mowbray, William Merritt Chase, Carroll Beckwith, and F. V. Du Mond; in Paris and Belgium he studied with Jean-Paul Laurens and Henri Vierin.

St. John emerged from his schooling a capable painter of portraits, his style combining aspects of John Singer Sargent, Howard Chandler Christy, and the German realistic school of the mid nineteenth century. He rapidly became known as a society painter, providing portraits of such socialites as Caroline Miskel Hoyt, F. Luis Mora, and F. Hopkinson Smith and exhibiting with the Society of American Artists. In the *Metropolitan Magazine* of November 1898 St. John offered his interviewer his philosophy of art:

Portrait painting . . . appeals to me as one of the highest branches of the painter's craft. So commonplace when stiffly and uninterestingly treated, but, on the other hand, presenting infinite possibilities when the idea of making it a work of art holds equal place with that of truthfully rendering the features. For instance, one should look at a portrait as . . . not merely a likeness or photographic copy of the face alone, but a thing that is the sitter himself, his personality, to the tips of his fingers, the wrinkle of his clothes; and the artist should draw all these in so broad and sympathetic a way that those who do not know the person may yet find pleasure in the counterfeit, the lighting and the harmony of the colors.

Early in the twentieth century St. John returned to Chicago, married, and opened a studio (The Tree Studio). He found employment as instructor of painting and illustration at the prestigious Chicago Art Institute, eventually moving to Chicago's American Academy of Art, where he served as professor of life drawing and illustration. Although he never ceased to paint portraits, he began to publish more of his work in magazines, taking advantage of the market offered by the pulp magazines.

Though widely used, and often in a pejorative sense, the term *pulp* is somewhat misleading since virtually all paper contains wood pulp, but when it is applied to magazines, *pulp* has a dual meaning. It refers first to a particular sort of paper made cheaply out of partially processed groundwood: pulp paper was thick, rough in texture, occasionally spotted with wood fragments, frequently brittle, and sometimes slightly brownish or yellowish in tint, with an uncorrected acidity that caused rapid deterioration of the stock. The second meaning of *pulp* is adjectival, a reference to the fiction that appeared in the magazines printed on wood-pulp paper. In general, the pulp magazines offered stories in which things happened, not necessarily stories of violent action, but stories in which events or plot—as opposed to stories offering exhaustive analyses of character, personal relationships, or social situations—were important. The pulps (with few exceptions) stressed sensation, with the intent of arousing emotion in the reader, and they concentrated on the physical resolutions of problems.

Operating in semirivalry with the pulp magazines were the "slicks," the magazines printed on paper that had been treated with sizing and thus had glossy pages slick to the touch. Although the quality of material in the best pulps and the slicks might be identical, the general critical perception during the first half of the twentieth century was that the majority of the pulps were somewhat disreputable, as were those who wrote and illustrated for them. Pulp magazines nevertheless needed artists, and a fast, versatile, and moderately talented artist could earn

St. John's cover design for a 1926 novel

a living or additional income providing artwork for them. St. John ultimately became a pulp artist, painting not only cover art and interior illustrations for the pulp magazines but also providing dust-jacket artwork for the books that reprinted the stories initially published in the pulp magazines.

St. John's first illustrations for a magazine appear to be those in the March 1898 issue of *Harper's New Monthly Magazine,* a prestigious literary magazine that during the 1890s was regularly publishing most of the notable American writers. St. John (and several others) illustrated an article by Henry S. Williams titled "The Century's Progress in Anatomy and Physiology." St. John's portraits of the dis-

tinguished physicians-scientists Matthias Jakob Schleiden and William Hyde Wollaston are technically competent.

St. John's artistic career began to change its direction more noticeably at the turn of the century when he provided illustrations for *The Complete Works of Honoré de Balzac* (Colonial Press Edition, 1899–1901) and *The Works of Mark Twain* (Hillcrest Edition, 1899). In 1900 he provided illustrations for many poems published in *Delineator,* a well-regarded women's periodical later to be edited by Theodore Dreiser. These illustrations are capable depictions of the dramatic moments described in the texts, but more significantly they mark the beginning of St.

John's transition from a society painter to a commercial artist, one whose talents were used to excite interest in and sell products.

Within five years St. John was no longer working as a society portraitist. In addition to teaching classes and illustrating magazines, he had started a professional relationship with Chicago publisher A. C. McClurg, which in 1905 published *The Face in the Pool,* St. John's only work of fiction. *The Face in the Pool* is a late-Victorian fairy tale, the story of the star-eyed Princess Astrella and the gallant prince who repeatedly rescues her and other maidens. The book is lavishly illustrated with pictures of knights in armor, castles, gnomes, fairies, witches, dragons, and monsters, but although it received generally favorable reviews, it does not appear to have sold well. St. John never wrote another book.

During the next three decades St. John provided McClurg with dust jackets and interior illustrations, beginning with books as diverse, unmemorable, and ephemeral as Edith Ogden Harrison's *The Lady of the Snows* (1912), L. Morton Curry's *The Hero and the Man* (1912), Edith Huntington Mason's *The Great Plan* (1913), and Lawrence Perry's *Holton of the Navy: A Story of the Freeing of Cuba* (1913). St. John's dust jackets for these books generally consist of depictions of the characters posed against a romantic backdrop; they are as unmemorable and ephemeral as the books themselves.

St. John's association with Edgar Rice Burroughs began in 1915 when McClurg (then Burroughs's publisher) asked him to illustrate *The Return of Tarzan,* the second of Burroughs's Tarzan books. Though the dust jacket of *The Return of Tarzan* was by N. C. Wyeth and reproduced Wyeth's cover for the August 1913 *New Story Magazine,* each of the novel's twenty-six chapters began with a small sketch by St. John. Successive Tarzan novels had dust jackets and internal illustrations by St. John, as did the first books in Burroughs's John Carter of Mars series and Burroughs's Pellucidar series.

During the next twenty-one years St. John provided original illustrations for thirty-two of Burroughs's novels, producing some of his finest artwork in the process. St. John's dust jacket for *Tarzan and the Golden Lion* (1923), for example, is a study of intense muscular tension. The figures of Tarzan and Jad-bal-ja (the golden lion) are standing in partial profile on a small, grassy rise in the painting's foreground; nothing in the painting distracts from their figures, which hold identical poses and are painted in identical shades of brown and black: their concentration is almost palpable. St. John's illustrations for *Tarzan the Untamed* (1920) depict equally dramatic moments, including an intensely visualized

scene (painted in tan, black, and gray-blue) in which Tarzan seizes an attacking vulture. His interior illustrations for *At Earth's Core* (1922) and *Pellucidar* (1923) are similarly imaginative and include well-imagined renditions of vicious dinosaurs. St. John's drawings of cats—lions, tigers, leopards, and saber-toothed tigers—are always excellent and appear in many of his illustrations.

On the debit side, St. John was highly uneven as a commercial artist, and his best illustrations from this time are those that do not reveal facial features but instead depict scenes in which action occurs. Those illustrations in which facial features are visible are curiously static, the postures and features of the characters betraying their studio origins and often demonstrating a surprising amount of artistic weakness. This fault is especially noteworthy in St. John's dust jacket for *Pellucidar,* in which a menacingly poised saber-toothed tiger stares up at a woman casually holding a spear by her side: not even the tension and threat in the tiger's posture can overcome the weaknesses in the depiction of the woman's limp posture and vapid expression. The entire illustration is disappointingly anticlimactic.

It is also unfortunate and ironic that St. John, despite a growing reputation as the foremost illustrator of Burroughs's African adventures, was rarely able to depict women, apes, or Africans with any conviction or accuracy. The features of St. John's women invariably resemble those of the Gibson Girl, and their vacuousness and general lack of vitality and personality almost invariably destroy scenes that could otherwise be exotic. St. John's apes are unintentionally comical, their musculature and proportions the work of a man who apparently never saw a living ape. And the pictures of St. John's Africans rely heavily and unpleasantly on the cultural stereotype of Africans as bestial, spear-wielding savages. St. John may nevertheless be partially excused for these illustrative shortcomings, for as a commercial artist he was merely providing what the market (that is, Burroughs and Burroughs's readers) wanted, and Burroughs could not characterize women, had never been to Africa, and was demanding.

Disappointing though some of St. John's illustrations for Burroughs are, the majority of them remain exciting and vividly memorable, and the book-buying public of the first quarter of the twentieth century rapidly identified St. John's paintings with Burroughs's characters. Burroughs himself recognized St. John's importance and on 18 May 1920 wrote to St. John, stating, "If I could do the sort of work you do I would not change a line in any of the drawings. I think your work for *Tarzan The*

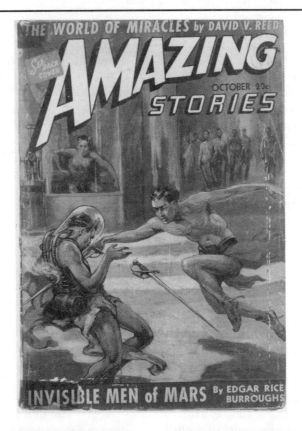

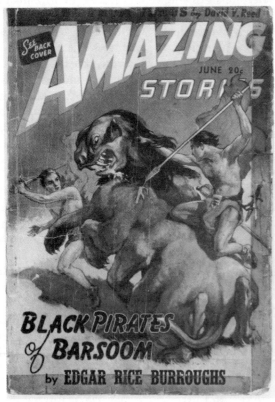

Three 1941 magazine covers by St. John

Untamed is the finest I have ever seen in any book. Each picture reflects the thought and interest and labor that were expended in it." Indeed, when Burroughs left McClurg in 1929, having decided to publish his books himself, he hired St. John as his illustrator.

Although the relationship between Burroughs and St. John remained outwardly amicable, literary success ultimately spoiled Burroughs, who became quite vain. Burroughs did not like to be reminded that he owed at least some of his success to St. John or that his fictional creations were identified with St. John's artwork. During the early 1930s Burroughs quietly attempted to replace St. John with other artists, beginning with his nephew Studley O. Burroughs. On 24 May 1932 Burroughs wrote a peevish letter of complaint to Studley, unintentionally revealing that St. John's artwork was superior to the books it surrounded:

> If you have any of my former books I wish you would note the almost total loss of outstanding sales value in St. John's jackets. As works of art they seem to me about all that could be desired, but as outstanding, compelling attention attracters they are not so hot. With all the thousands of books on display in a book shop we must bend every effort to have our covers not only artistic but at the same time demanding the attention of the passerby with a loud shriek.

Studley, however, was not successful as an artist; his Tarzan is paunchy rather than the poised, trimly muscular figure provided by St. John, and his additional illustrations are also poor. Studley's defects were readily commented upon by contemporary reviewers such as C. A. Brandt, whose review of *Tarzan Triumphant* (1932) appeared in the December 1932 *Amazing Stories:* "Mr. Burroughs is probably the only author who does his own publishing and makes money at it, and it is of course creditable to keep all the profits in the family, but I think he overstepped his limit, by having a member of his clan do the illustrations. They are awful." Burroughs grudgingly rehired St. John and wrote to him in March 1933, stating: "I am delighted with the Tarzan cover and illustrations. . . . I am sure that my readers are going to be glad to see you back again."

In 1936 Burroughs finally succeeded in replacing St. John by hiring his son John Coleman Burroughs to illustrate his fiction. On 28 September 1936, shortly after St. John provided the dust jacket and five interior illustrations for *Tarzan's Quest* (1936), Burroughs wrote dismissively to him: "It has always been the ambition of my son, Jack, and myself that one day he would illustrate one of my books. He is doing very excellent work, and I am

having him illustrate the Spring book for us. However, he stands in the same position that any artist must; and if the work is not satisfactory, I shall have to have it done elsewhere."

The artwork for *Tarzan's Quest* ranks among St. John's poorest: the figures on the dust jacket are clumsy, awkwardly posed, and unconvincingly drawn, and the interior illustrations are equally lacking in dramatic tension and artistic conviction. Perhaps St. John, knowing that his long and lucrative association with Burroughs was finally at its end, deliberately submitted second-rate material.

St. John's relationship with Burroughs lasted from 1915 until 1936, but during this time Burroughs was merely St. John's most notable client, and St. John continued to illustrate for McClurg. Thus, in addition to providing artwork for Burroughs, St. John illustrated such McClurg publications as the poems of Edgar Guest; the Westerns of Robert Ames Bennet, W. D. Hoffman, Clarence E. Mulford, George W. Ogden, Randall Parrish, and Kenneth Perkins; the romances of Margaret Hill McCarter; and the mysteries of Madeleine Sharps Buchanan and Marvin Dana. He drew propaganda posters for World War I and illustrations for two of Ray Cummings's scientific romances, *The Man Who Mastered Time* (1923) and *Brigands of the Moon* (1931).

During this time St. John was also selling artwork to such magazines as *The Blue Book Magazine, Boy's World, Young People's Weekly, Green Book Magazine, Red Book Magazine,* and *Weird Tales.* This art, the majority of which appeared in the pulp magazines, marks the direction taken by the final phase of St. John's career, that of an illustrator for the science-fiction pulp magazines. Thus, from 1940 until 1950 St. John provided frequent illustrations (covers and interior artwork) for *Fantastic Adventures* and *Amazing Stories,* science-fiction magazines published by the Ziff-Davis Publishing Company of Chicago. Though St. John was by now elderly, his illustrations for these magazines reveal no loss of technique and are in some respects markedly superior to his earlier artwork; when they are shown, the facial features of his characters are frequently quite convincing.

During this last phase of St. John's career the editors of *Fantastic Adventures* and *Amazing Stories* often called upon St. John to illustrate the stories of the elderly Edgar Rice Burroughs, whose work was frequently serialized in these magazines. St. John's illustrations for the magazine versions of Burroughs's *John Carter and the Giant of Mars* (*Amazing Stories,* January 1941), *The City of Mummies* (*Amazing Stories,* March 1941), and *Yellow Men of Mars* (*Amazing Stories,* August 1941) rank among his finest work, and when Burroughs died in 1950, St. John wrote to his friend Darrell C. Richardson on 1 May: "In the passing of Edgar Rice Burroughs the fantastic literature has sustained a great loss, as evidenced by the many letters I have received from his fans. Personally, I owed him a lot for the opportunity his work afforded me to illustrate the type of story he was a master at, and I recall many happy discussions I had with him."

St. John's last original artwork appeared in February 1954 in the short-lived (and low-budget) pulp magazine *Science Stories*. He died quietly in Chicago in 1957. His passing received absolutely no national attention, perhaps because he was so strongly identified with fantastic fiction, a field whose practitioners have until recently received virtually no critical attention. Had St. John remained an artist in the classical tradition, painting portraits of wealthy men and women, he probably would be remembered as one of the more capable traditional portraitists of the twentieth century.

Few originals of St. John's paintings survive, and most of them are held by private collectors. Pulp magazines having artwork by him are in perilous shape; many are no longer accessible and exist only on microfilm. Those interested in learning of St. John's life and in seeing color reproductions of his art must rely on the books and pamphlets published by St. John's fans, and these are frequently produced in small numbers and are invariably poorly distributed. Nevertheless, although St.

John's work is hard to obtain, it often repays the effort spent in locating it. It is unlikely that he will ever be completely forgotten. Although his illustrations of the fantastic are old-fashioned and only rarely rise above their subject matter, at his best he remains one of the twentieth century's finest illustrators of adventure.

References:

James J. Best, *American Popular Illustration: A Reference Guide* (Westport, Conn.: Greenwood Press, 1984);

Arthur B. Estes, "J. Allen St. John," *Metropolitan Magazine* (November 1898): 502–506;

Bertha E. Miller, Louise Payson Latimer, and Beulah Folmsbee, *Illustrators of Children's Books, 1744–1945* (Boston: Horn Book, 1947);

Irwin Porges, *Edgar Rice Burroughs: The Man Who Created Tarzan* (Provo, Utah: Brigham Young University Press, 1975);

Walt Reed, comp., *The Illustrator in America, 1900–1960s* (New York: Reinhold, 1990);

Darrell C. Richardson, "J. Allen St. John," *The Edgar Rice Burroughs Library of Illustration,* volume 1 (West Plains, Mo.: Russ Cochran, 1976);

Richardson, *J. Allen St. John: An Illustrated Bibliography* (Memphis, Tenn.: Mid-America, 1991);

John I. Tucker, "Tarzan Was Born in Chicago," *Chicago History: The Magazine of the Chicago Historical Society,* new series 1 (1970): 18–31.

John Sloan

(2 August 1871 – 7 September 1951)

Elizabeth H. Hawkes

SELECTED BOOKS ILLUSTRATED: Keely, Robert N. Jr., and Gwilym George Davis, *In Arctic Seas: The Voyage of the "Kite" with the Peary Expedition* (Philadelphia: Hartranft, 1893);

Pollard, Percival, *Cape of Storms* (Chicago: Echo, 1895);

Wayne, Charles Stokes, *The Lady and Her Tree: A Story of Society* (Philadelphia: Vortex, 1895);

Lindsey, William, *Cinder-Path Tales* (Boston: Copeland & Day, 1896);

Snyder, Charles M., *Comic History of Greece: From the Earliest Times to the Death of Alexander the Great* (Philadelphia: Lippincott, 1898);

Corelli, Marie, *Boy: A Sketch* (Philadelphia: Lippincott, 1900);

Crane, Stephen, *Great Battles of the World* (Philadelphia: Lippincott, 1901);

Kock, Charles Paul de, *Monsieur Dupont,* St. Gervais Edition, 2 volumes (Boston: Quinby, 1902);

Edwards, Louise Betts, *The Tu-Tze's Tower* (Philadelphia: Coates, 1903);

Kock, Charles Paul de, *The Barber of Paris,* St. Gervais Edition, 2 volumes (Boston: Quinby, 1903);

Kock, *Frère Jacques,* St. Gervais Edition, 2 volumes (Boston: Quinby, 1903);

Kock, *The Gogo Family,* St. Gervais Edition, 2 volumes (Boston: Quinby, 1903);

Kock, *The Memoirs of Charles Paul de Kock,* St. Gervais Edition (Boston: Quinby, 1903);

Kock, *Adhémar,* St. Gervais Edition (Boston: Quinby, 1904);

Kock, *André the Savoyard,* St. Gervais Edition, 2 volumes (Boston: Quinby, 1904);

Kock, *Jean,* St. Gervais Edition, volume 2 (Boston: Quinby, 1904);

Kock, *Madame Pantalon,* St. Gervais Edition (Boston: Quinby, 1904);

Kock, *Cherami,* St. Gervais Edition, 2 volumes (Boston: Quinby, 1905);

Kock, *The Flower Girl,* St. Gervais Edition, 2 volumes (Boston: Quinby, 1905);

John Sloan, 1908 (photograph by Gertrude Käsebier)

Daly, Thomas A., *Canzoni* (Philadelphia: Catholic Standard and Times Publishing, 1906);

Collins, Wilkie, *The Moonstone* (New York: Scribners, 1908);

Collins, *The New Magdalen* (New York: Scribners, 1908);

Kirkpatrick, George R., *War—What For?* (West La Fayette, Ohio: The author, 1910);

Daly, Thomas A., *Madrigali* (Philadelphia: McKay, 1912);

Gaboriau, Émile, *The Count's Millions* (New York: Scribners, 1913);

Gaboriau, *Baron Trigault's Vengeance: A Sequel to "The Count's Millions"* (New York: Scribners, 1913);

Gaboriau, *Caught in the Net* (New York: Scribners, 1913);

Gaboriau, *The Champdoce Mystery: A Sequel to "Caught in the Net"* (New York: Scribners, 1913);

Gaboriau, *The Clique of Gold* (New York: Scribners, 1913);

Gaboriau, *Within an Inch of His Life* (New York: Scribners, 1913);

England, George Allan, *The Air Trust* (Saint Louis: Wagner, 1915);

England, *The Golden Blight* (New York: Fly, 1916);

Masters, Edgar Lee, *Mitch Miller* (New York: Macmillan, 1920);

Bergengren, Ralph, *Gentlemen All and Merry Companions* (Boston: Brimmer, 1922);

Raison, Milton, *Spindrift* (New York: Doran, 1922);

Miller, Max, *The Beginning of a Mortal* (New York: Dutton, 1933);

Maugham, Somerset, *Of Human Bondage,* 2 volumes (New Haven: Yale University Press, 1938).

PERIODICALS: *Chap-Book,* 1894;

Gil Blas, 1895;

Inland Printer, 1895;

Moods, 1895;

Echo, 1895–1996;

John-a-Dreams, 1896;

Red Letter, 1896;

Ainslee's Magazine, 1899–1901;

Leslie's Monthly, 1904;

Success, 1904;

Century Magazine, 1904–1905, 1908–1909, 1914–1915, 1922–1923;

Collier's, 1904, 1906, 1908–1913;

Good Housekeeping, 1904–1905, 1909;

McClure's, 1905–1906;

The Saturday Evening Post, 1905–1907;

Scribner's Magazine, 1905, 1908, 1911;

Gunter's Magazine, 1906;

Appleton's Booklovers' Magazine, 1906–1907;

Sunday Magazine, 1906–1908;

Woman, 1907;

Everybody's, 1907, 1911–1913, 1915;

Coming Nation, 1910–1913;

Masses, 1911–1916;

Harper's Weekly, 1913–1915;

Metropolitan Magazine, 1914–1915, 1917;

Hearst's International Magazine, 1922–1923;

Dial, 1925;

New Masses, 1926;

Vanity Fair, 1926;

New Freeman, 1930–1931;

Americana, 1932;

New Mexico Quarterly Review, 1949;

Seventeen, 1950.

A prominent figure in American art history, John Sloan was a distinguished painter and etcher in the first half of the twentieth century. Early in his career he worked as an illustrator for the thriving publishing business, contributing drawings to newspapers, magazines, and books. Though he considered his illustration work ancillary to his painting and largely as a source of income, he produced a significant body of illustrations numbering more than 950 drawings and etchings. His sympathetic portrayals of immigrants and working-class people, as well as his humorous renditions, were enjoyed by the popular-magazine readership.

John Sloan was born in Lock Haven, a small lumber town in the central Pennsylvania mountains. His father, John Dixon Sloan, worked in the family cabinetmaking and undertaker business and then as a portrait photographer. Sloan's mother, Henrietta Ireland, a schoolteacher, grew up in Philadelphia, where her father worked as a bookbinder. Sloan's paternal forebears had come to America from Scotland in the eighteenth century, while his maternal relatives, who had emigrated from Belfast in the early nineteenth century, were of English and Irish background.

Around 1877 the family moved to Philadelphia, where Sloan's father worked for the company belonging to Marcus Ward, a greeting-card and book publisher. Sloan remembered his family as poor but not underprivileged. He and his two younger sisters, Marianna and Elizabeth, always had books to read. As a child Sloan perused folios of prints by William Hogarth and Thomas Rowlandson, books illustrated by George Cruikshank and Gustave Doré, and illustrated magazines such as *Punch* and *Harper's Monthly.*

Though a precocious student, Sloan had to leave Philadelphia's prestigious Central High School in 1888 at the age of sixteen to help support his family. For a time he worked as a cashier for a bookstore and made copies of Rembrandts for sale. Next he worked as a designer and illustrator for A. Edward Newton's fancy-goods business designing greeting cards and making etchings for calendars and pamphlets. When he left Newton in 1891, Sloan worked briefly as a freelance artist, designing streetcar ads and illustrations.

Sloan had little formal art training. He taught himself how to etch from Philip Gilbert Hamerton's *The Etcher's Handbook* and in 1890 painted his first oil painting after studying *A Manual of Painting* by John Collier. He enrolled in a night course on freehand drawing at the Spring Garden Institute in Philadelphia. Later Sloan took night courses at the Pennsylvania Academy of the Fine Arts, but he became frustrated by drawing from plaster casts and did not continue.

In 1892, at the age of twenty, Sloan embarked on a twelve-year career as a newspaper artist. His first newspaper job was with the *Philadelphia Inquirer,* which, following the successful strategy of Joseph Pulitzer's *New York World,* was attracting new readers by using pictures of news events as well as more-sensational headlines and human-interest stories. Pictures sold papers, so newspapers added artists to their staff. The newspapers looked for young men (they rarely employed women as artists) with basic drawing skills and trained them on the job.

Some of Sloan's early assignments for the newspaper involved copying photographs of debutantes and brides for the society page. He also made action drawings of accidents, fires, and other catastrophes. He drew people in the street, in courtrooms, at sports events, and at concerts and balls. Learning to rely on his memory, he made a quick sketch at the scene and then composed the drawing back at the *Inquirer* studio.

In 1894, inspired by contemporary poster design and Japanese prints, Sloan developed a style new to newspaper illustration but well suited to the linecut printing process. His poster style incorporated asymmetrical black-and-white compositions with bold outlines and contrasting surface patterns. Sloan drew with ink and brush (and sometimes pen), a technique he learned from a Japanese artist-reporter. The *Inquirer* published his first poster-style drawing, a scene of young men and women attending a tennis match, on the sports page in June 1894. Sloan became identified with this style and often used it for his newspaper drawings.

Sloan's first serious notice as an artist came in October 1894 when the *Inland Printer* published a short article noting that his poster-style drawings were in the Aubrey Beardsley manner but had "an individuality of their own." His work was reproduced in several avant-garde "little magazines" (modeled after Beardsley's *The Yellow Book*)–*The Chap-Book, The Echo, John-a-Dreams,* and *The Red Letter* in 1895–1896.

In addition Sloan designed book and magazine covers adapting the poster style of his newspaper work. The covers for *Moods* (July 1895), a short-lived Philadelphia magazine, and *The Echo* (15 February 1896), reveal the full blossoming of his Art Nouveau style. *The Echo,* published by Chicago author and critic Percival Pollard, championed some of the finest American poster designers–among them Will Bradley, E. B. Bird, and Sloan. The *Moods* and *Echo* covers show women in flowing garb in a landscape setting. For *Moods* a woman fol-

Magazine cover by Sloan (1895)

lows a fluttering butterfly through a wood of sinuous trees. The red and black cover for *The Echo,* which also served as the poster design, features a woman blowing an alpine horn toward a rocky cliff in a scene representing the echo of the magazine's title. The *Philadelphia Ledger* commended Sloan as a poster artist of the first rank for this work.

The most important influence in Sloan's early career in Philadelphia was Robert Henri, a young, dynamic artist who encouraged him to paint the familiar scenes of everyday life. When he met Henri, Sloan was only interested in becoming a good illustrator. It was Henri who motivated him to become serious about painting. Though Sloan observed and listened to Henri's criticism classes, Sloan never studied with Henri formally. They remained close friends until Henri's death in 1928.

After four years at the *Inquirer* Sloan moved to the rival *Philadelphia Press,* where his friend William

"Bliss," an Art Nouveau drawing by Sloan for Echo Magazine *(1 July 1895)*

Glackens and other former *Inquirer* artists worked. Then, in the summer of 1898, Sloan worked for a few months at the *New York Herald,* replacing artists sent to Cuba to cover the Spanish-American War. At the *New York Herald* Sloan based his drawings on photographs and descriptions from reporters' news stories about the war.

When Sloan returned to the *Philadelphia Press* in the fall, he worked on the new Sunday magazine making full-page picture puzzles printed on new color presses by the Benday photoengraving process. In addition, he illustrated short stories and features, designed decorative borders, and accepted an occasional book or magazine commission. He illustrated stories for *Ainslee's Magazine* when his friend Everett Shinn was art editor. Sloan also worked for two Philadelphia publishing companies, the Joseph Lippincott and Henry T. Coates firms, on four quite different books: a comic history of Greece, two maudlin adventure tales, and Stephen Crane's *Great Battles of the World* (1901). Sloan married Anna Marie "Dolly" Wall, daughter of an Irish immigrant, in Philadelphia on 5 August 1901.

In 1902 Glackens, who was illustrating works by mid-nineteenth-century French novelist Charles Paul de Kock, recommended Sloan to work on the project. The publisher, Frederick J. Quinby Com-

pany, planned to publish special limited editions of the ribald, sentimental novels. Sloan produced more than one hundred illustrations, of which fifty-three were etchings, for eighteen volumes. Though he had furnished etchings for A. Edward Newton's booklets in the early 1890s, Sloan's work on the Kock series renewed his interest in the medium. When the Kock project ended in 1905, Sloan made a set of ten *New York City Life* etchings of scenes he observed in the city. He continued to make etchings throughout his career.

While illustrating the Kock work, Sloan mastered the technical skills of etching, making bolder compositions and creating an ample cast of humorous characters for the books. He immersed himself in the life and customs of mid-nineteenth-century France, studying books on French costume and architecture as well as old maps of Paris streets. He studied John Leech's scenes of middle-class life in *Punch,* Honoré Daumier's caricatures in *Le Charivari,* and contemporary French magazine illustrations by Théophile Alexandre Steinlen and Jean-Louis Forain for details that provided an authentic feeling and texture of the period. The facial contortions of several Kock characters—Dodichet, Rossignol, and Cherami—reveal Sloan's careful study of Daumier's character types. Sloan sometimes used facial features of friends and family for subjects, with his wife Dolly posing as a plump dancing partner and Henri as a dignified artist.

By 1904 Sloan's Kock illustrations for *André the Savoyard* and *Madame Pantalon* exhibited an adroitness and humor that distinguished them as his best work to date. At the beginning of the project the publisher had hired several illustrators to work on each volume. However, by 1904 this policy changed, enabling Sloan to illustrate an entire volume with a unified style and sensibility. His illustrations began to outshine Kock's pedestrian text. Proud of his Kock work, Sloan sent etchings and drawings to exhibitions at the Pennsylvania Academy of the Fine Arts, where critics for the *Philadelphia Inquirer* praised them. This critical attention helped propel Sloan into a career as an inventive illustrator and etcher.

In 1903 Sloan's workload at the *Philadelphia Press* was reduced to only three days a week; meanwhile, he concentrated on the Kock project and painted. He finally lost his job at the *Philadelphia Press* in December 1903 when the newspaper subscribed to a syndicated magazine instead of producing its own. Sloan arranged with the editor to continue supplying the *Philadelphia Press* with "word charade" puzzles, which remained a Sunday feature in the paper until 1910. These puzzles provided Sloan with a small but guaranteed source of income.

Newspaper illustration had blossomed in the 1890s but ended abruptly when it became economically feasible to reproduce halftone photographs on newsprint. Photographers steadily replaced illustrators. Sloan hung on to his job longer than most because his skills as a designer and illustrator remained essential as long as the *Philadelphia Press* published a Sunday magazine. Spending his young adulthood years working for newspapers, Sloan gained an artistic foundation in the pressroom instead of the more conventional classroom.

Taking along proofs of his Kock work, Sloan made an exploratory trip to New York City, the center of the magazine- and book-publishing business, to look for work as an illustrator. Having procured jobs designing a *Collier's* cover and illustrating stories for *Century* and *Leslie's Monthly,* he moved to New York in April 1904 with his wife Dolly. They joined their old friends—Henri, Glackens, Shinn, and George Luks—who were either teaching or illustrating as well as painting.

Sloan's first year in New York was financially successful. In 1904 he earned an adequate income of about $3,000 for his Kock work, his magazine illustrations, and the *Philadelphia Press* puzzles. However, when the Kock commission ended, he earned sub-

stantially less. By 1907 his earnings dropped to $1,640, and he regularly visited publishers, seeking work. In 1908 he supplemented his income with a teaching stint in Pittsburgh and by sales of etchings.

Sloan never achieved the financial success of magazine illustrators who had exclusive contracts with publishers, but his ambition was not an affluent lifestyle. By working as a freelance illustrator, he earned enough money to pay his bills and still had the time and independence to paint, etch, organize exhibits, and get involved with politics. Sloan viewed himself as an artist, not as an illustrator. Though he joined the Society of Illustrators in 1907, he resigned the next year because he could not afford the dues. He did not enjoy any particular benefits or association with the members, even lampooning them in his diary.

Sloan sometimes griped about making drawings for stories he considered trite or for editors whose taste he did not respect. On the other hand, he enjoyed working with Will Bradley, art editor for *Collier's,* in 1908, developing humorous characters and a distinctive woodcut style for a series about comic pirates. And while making the rounds of the magazine offices, he took time to observe incidents in the life of city dwellers that formed the basis for subsequent paintings. Years later his second wife, Helen Farr, recorded his recollections: "I started to see the life of the city and to study the neighborhood streets and rooftops. It was a new world to me."

Sloan received occasional jobs from the high-toned *Century* and *Scribner's Magazine,* but he mainly sent drawings to the newer, inexpensive magazines—*Collier's, Everybody's,* and *McClure's*—as well as the short-lived *Gunter's Magazine, Success,* and *Woman.* Magazine editors tended to earmark him for humorous or melancholy urban-life stories often dealing with immigrants accommodating to life in American cities and scenes of lower-middle-class working people. On occasion he illustrated stories focusing on childhood foibles, life in the theater, and the newspaper business.

Sloan's diaries record that he regularly visited magazine offices with portfolio in hand. On 4 March 1907 he made the rounds, visiting several publishing houses with no success. The next day he secured an article about court and prison reform from *Everybody's.* After reading the article by Brand Whitlock, Sloan toured a courtroom and prison, meeting with a judge and a probation officer. Next he watched proceedings at the Jefferson Market Court before talking to the art editor at *Everybody's* about his ideas for the illustrations. That evening he completed four crayon drawings of figures, downcast and forlorn, that he had observed in the courtroom. After

Illustration by Sloan for Charles Paul de Kock's Flower Girl *(1905)*

completing this and two other illustration assignments, Sloan concentrated on painting for several weeks, working on *Wake of the Ferry, Easter Eve,* and *Throbbing Fountain, Madison Square.*

By 1908 Sloan's career as a painter reached a new height when he joined his friends Henri, Glackens, Luks, Shinn, Arthur B. Davies, Maurice Prendergast, and Ernest Lawson in the exhibition of "The Eight," held at the Macbeth Gallery in New York City. This controversial exhibit challenged the conservative leadership of the National Academy of Design. The exhibit was widely covered by the press, and large numbers flocked to see the paintings. Though Sloan did not sell any works, this exhibit raised him to the leadership ranks of the current American art scene and claimed for him a position in the history of American art. His paintings presented ordinary people observed from his studio window or while on walks through Chelsea and Greenwich Village or the Lower East Side, recording warmhearted, humorous, or melancholy anecdotes of his adopted New York. Many National Academy of Art members objected to the subject matter and the dark tonality of his work while others found them refreshing and daring in concept by focusing on ordinary, sometimes uncouth, subjects.

"Battle of Bunker Hill," an illustration by Sloan for Stephen Crane's
Great Battles of the World *(1901)*

In 1909 Sloan became sympathetic to socialist causes. Charles Wisner Barrell, who wrote an article about Sloan's etchings for *The Craftsman,* explained to him the general principles of socialism, and before long Sloan began attending meetings and donating cartoons to the socialist newspaper *The Call.* In 1910 he and Dolly joined the Socialist Party, and Sloan ran for a New York State Assembly seat on the party ticket.

Sloan began contributing drawings to *The Coming Nation,* a socialist weekly published in Girard, Kansas, in 1910. He illustrated articles about humanitarian causes, the working class, the labor movement, and the Mexican Revolution of 1910, as well as serialized fiction. One of his early contributions was a drawing of seven Christmas vignettes that *Collier's* had rejected. Sloan received only $30 for the piece, whereas *Collier's* would have paid $150 for a comparable work. However, he recorded in his diary (18 November 1910) that he enjoyed making the drawing because he felt "free from the dry as dust restrictions of the magazine 'art depts.'" Sloan used one of the subjects—a young woman visiting a pawnshop—for the Christmas etching he and Dolly sent to friends that year.

To support the pacifist views of his book

War—What For? (1910), fellow socialist George R. Kirkpatrick commissioned a series of caustic drawings condemning the brutality of war. Other socialist publications, such as *The Coming Nation,* reprinted some of the drawings.

For years Sloan had contemplated producing a magazine devoted to pictorial art that was free from the constraints of commercialism. Therefore, he enthusiastically joined editor Max Eastman and a small band of artists and writers in reviving *The Masses,* a magazine founded in 1911 and devoted to the socialist cause. In the December 1912 issue the new editorial leadership announced their goals: "We are going to make *The Masses* a popular socialist magazine—a magazine of pictures and lively writing . . . with entertainment, education, and the livelier kinds of propaganda." The magazine appealed to an audience of both socialist and nonsocialist readers in part by using "humorous, serious, illustrative and decorative pictures of a stimulating kind."

Sloan joined Art Young, George Bellows, Stuart Davis, Maurice Becker, and others in contributing drawings for no pay. *The Masses* was unique in American publishing at the time because it provided a forum for art that was expressive, not just illustrative, in the spirit of European satiric journals, such as *Simplicissimus* and *L'Assiette au Beurre*. While acting informally as art editor, Sloan redesigned the magazine's format, introducing a clean, simplified layout with bold, easy-to-read typography. The drawings were in ink or crayon and had a strong visual impact when reproduced by the linecut process. As Rebecca Zurier points out in her pivotal study *Art for The Masses: A Radical Magazine and Its Graphics, 1911–1917* (1988), the drawings were presented as independent works, not subordinate to text as in most magazines of the period.

Sloan's experience working on *The Masses* differed from his commercial magazine work. At weekly meetings artists and writers reviewed material submitted for the next issue and heatedly debated opinions about what to include. "To do as it pleases and conciliate nobody, not even its readers" was the defiant editorial policy declared in the December 1912 issue. By contrast, publishers of commercial magazines maintained tight control of editorial content and style to avoid offending their readership.

Sloan contributed seven cover designs and fifty-six drawings that assaulted moral and political injustice, ridiculed fashion, and recorded scenes of New York City's parks, streets, and rooftops. He supported striking workers and woman's rights while attacking big business, military power, the

privileged, and the wealthy. These drawings were stronger and more direct than his work for commercial magazines. He worked from his own ideas, not those imposed on him by a story or an editor. As Lloyd Goodrich observed in his 1952 essay for an exhibition catalogue, Sloan was doing "the kind of illustration he believed in."

After contributing several drawings to nearly every issue for two years, Sloan began to have some fundamental differences with editorial policies for *The Masses*. He and some of the other artists felt the magazine was becoming too doctrinaire. In particular, he resented writers adding captions to artists' drawings without their approval. In April 1916 he submitted his resignation and in a few years left the Socialist Party.

While working for *The Masses,* Sloan still received commissions from the commercial press. When Norman Hapgood (formerly of *Collier's*) became editor of *Harper's Weekly* in 1913, he hired Sloan to liven up the magazine with full-page drawings of lighthearted city-life subjects—tango dancers, flirtatious teenagers carousing on a street corner, and the regulars at McSorley's ale house. Sloan's painting of McSorley's, done in 1912, was already widely appreciated; he based another painting, *McSorley's Cats* (1928–1929), on this drawing. Sloan also sent some political drawings to *Harper's Weekly*. One work criticized American policy toward Mexico, and two accompanied Lincoln Steffens's article about free speech. In all he did twenty-one drawings and two covers for *Harper's* during 1913 and 1914.

Between 1908 and 1913 Sloan illustrated about six stories per year for *Collier's*. His work followed two distinctive stylistic approaches: humorous woodcut-style drawings for Ralph Bergengren's pirate stories and crayon drawings with hatching (parallel and crossed lines for shading) for muckraking pieces about loan sharks and assorted business cheats. In 1913 Sloan sent *Collier's* fifteen drawings, including illustrations for a story about suffragettes and for a humorous piece by P. G. Wodehouse. The Bergengren pirate stories by then had moved from *Collier's* to *Everybody's* and were eventually published in a book titled *Gentlemen All and Merry Companions* (1922). Also in 1913 *The Coming Nation* published eleven drawings before ending their operation that year, and *The Masses* used thirty-six. Inspired by the modernist European painting in the Armory Show of 1913 (where Sloan exhibited two paintings and five etchings) and by his first sale of a painting to Albert C. Barnes, Sloan decided to spend the next summer at Gloucester, Massachusetts, painting landscapes, uninterrupted by illustration assignments.

By 1916 Sloan's illustration career had dwindled. He had two exhibitions of his paintings that year and began a long association with the Kraushaar Gallery. He accepted a teaching position at the Art Students League in New York that, along with periodic sales of his work, freed him from doing illustration as a primary source of income. Aside from making a set of woodcut-style drawings for his friend and fellow contributor to *The Masses,* John Reed (published in *Metropolitan Magazine* in 1917), Sloan did not work for the commercial magazines again until 1922 when he sent drawings to *Century* and *Hearst's International Magazine.* In 1923 *Century* commissioned two lithographs of city subjects—a Washington Square scene and one based on his painting *Sunday, Girls Drying Their Hair* (1912). He occasionally contributed drawings and prints to small-circulation literary magazines—*Americana, Dial, New Mexico Quarterly Review, Pagan,* and *Vanity Fair*—and political ones, such as *New Freeman* and *New Masses.*

After the Kock commission ended in 1905, book illustration occupied Sloan only sporadically during his career. He illustrated two books for Philadelphia poet and journalist Thomas A. Daly, *Canzoni* (1906) and *Madrigali* (1912), with frontispiece etchings and crayon drawings to accompany poems about Irish and Italian immigrants. Scribners commissioned illustrations for American editions of suspense novels by Wilkie Collins in 1908 and French writer Émile Gaboriau in 1913. After that, the book assignments were even more infrequent. For George Allan England, a fellow contributor to *The Masses,* he illustrated two science-fiction novels, one published in 1915 and one in 1916. Later, Sloan made ink drawings for two coming-of-age novels about boys growing up in the Midwest: Edgar Lee Masters's *Mitch Miller* (1920) and Max Miller's *The Beginning of a Mortal* (1933). The size and quality of the reproductions in *Mitch Miller* disappointed Sloan. His last book commission was sixteen etchings for Somerset Maugham's novel *Of Human Bondage* (1938), published for the Limited Editions Club. Pleased with the etchings, Maugham complimented Sloan for capturing the "tang" of the period and arousing the reader's interest in the characters.

After Sloan's wife Dolly died on 4 May 1943, he married Helen Farr, a former student and editor of his book *Gist of Art* (1939), on 5 February 1944 in Santa Fe, New Mexico. In 1949 Sloan undertook a rare illustration assignment for the *New Mexico Quarterly Review,* embellishing the journal of essays with decorative headings and several full-page drawings in ink. He drew a self-portrait to ac-

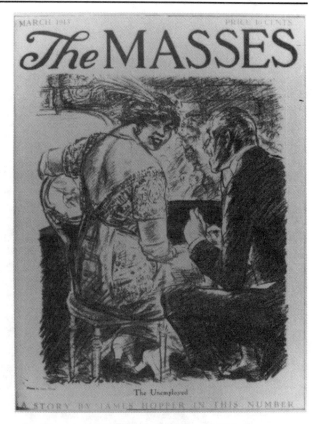

Sloan's cover for the March 1913 issue of the leftist magazine edited by Max Eastman

company an article about him by friend and fellow artist Walter Pach.

Sloan's last commercial assignment, done in 1950 at the age of seventy-one, was for *Seventeen,* a magazine for teenage girls. Because Sloan refused to alter his illustration for a short story, the editor chose to reproduce only the top portion of the picture. Relating this episode in his diary, Sloan expressed annoyance and reiterated his difficulty in doing his best work for the commercial press.

The Philadelphia Museum of Art had organized an exhibit titled *Artists of the Philadelphia Press* in 1945 that included drawings by Sloan. After his death in 1951, the Whitney Museum of American Art presented a retrospective exhibition of more than two hundred paintings, drawings, and prints. Of these, fifty-four were illustrations, posters, and pages from magazines and newspapers. In his catalogue essay Goodrich characterizes Sloan's illustrations as "genuine, good in character, solid, with a true graphic touch." He further observes that in his better moments Sloan was "one of the best magazine artists of his day."

While attention to Sloan's paintings, in particular the city pictures, grew in the following years, interest in his illustrations waned. How-

"Circumstances Alter Cases," a Sloan illustration for The Masses *(May 1913). The caption read: "Positively Disgusting! It's an Outrage to Public Decency to Allow Such Exposure on the Streets!"*

ever, John Bullard's 1971 catalogue essay on Sloan's illustrations for the John Sloan retrospective exhibition, organized by the National Gallery of Art, and Rebecca Zurier's 1988 book on the magazine *The Masses* stimulated a renewed interest in Sloan's contribution to American illustration, as did two exhibitions at the Delaware Art Museum in 1980 and 1988. Elizabeth Hawkes's 1993 illustrated catalogue of Sloan's book and magazine illustration further documents his career as an illustrator.

After working as a newspaper illustrator in Philadelphia in the 1890s and the competitive field of freelance magazine and book illustration in New York City, Sloan turned to part-time illustration as a way to support his painting career until he began to teach. Admittedly, the quality of his illustrations varied, depending on his interest in the story and the freedom he was allowed in developing the pictures. In *Gist of Art* Sloan encouraged students to observe the commonplace details of a scene as an illustrator does. He advised them: "Do illustrations for a while. It won't hurt you.

Get out of the art school and studio. Go out into the streets and look at life."

References:

Michele H. Bogart, "Artistic Ideals and Commercial Practices: The Problem of Status for American Illustrators," *Prospects,* 15 (1990): 225–281;

Van Wyck Brooks, *John Sloan: A Painter's Life* (New York: Dutton, 1955);

Edgar John Bullard III, "John Sloan and the Philadelphia Realists as Illustrators, 1890–1940," M.A. thesis, University of California, Los Angeles, 1968;

Bullard, "John Sloan as an Illustrator," *American Artist,* 35 (October 1971): 52–59;

Rowland Elzea, *John Sloan's Oil Paintings: A Catalogue Raisonné* (Newark: University of Delaware Press, 1991);

Elzea and Elizabeth Hawkes, *John Sloan: Spectator of Life,* exhibition catalogue (Wilmington: Delaware Art Museum, 1988);

Lloyd Goodrich, *John Sloan,* exhibition catalogue (New York: Macmillan, 1952);

Elizabeth Hawkes, "John Sloan, 1871–1951," *City Life Illustrated, 1890–1940,* exhibition catalogue (Wilmington: Delaware Art Museum, 1980);

Hawkes, *John Sloan's Illustrations in Magazines and Books* (Wilmington: Delaware Art Museum, 1993);

Hawkes, "John Sloan's Newspaper Career: An Alternative to Art School," *The Cultivation of Artists in Nineteenth-Century America* (Worcester, Mass.: American Antiquarian Society, 1997);

Patricia Hills, "John Sloan's Images of Working-Class Women: A Case Study of the Roles and Interrelationships of Politics, Personality, and Patrons in the Development of Sloan's Art, 1905–16," *Prospects,* 5 (1980): 157–196;

John Loughery, *John Sloan: Painter and Rebel* (New York: Holt, 1995);

Peter Morse, *John Sloan's Prints: A Catalogue Raisonné of the Etchings, Lithographs and Posters* (New Haven: Yale University Press, 1969);

F. Penn, "Newspaper Artists—John Sloan," *Inland Printer,* 14 (October 1894): 50;

Bruce St. John, *John Sloan* (New York: Praeger, 1971);

St. John, ed., *John Sloan's New York Scene: From the Diaries, Notes and Correspondence, 1906–13* (New York: Harper & Row, 1965);

Charles H. Sawyer, "John Sloan, Draughtsman," *University of Michigan: Bulletin, Museums of Art and Archaeology,* 2 (1979): 46–55;

David Scott, *John Sloan* (New York: Watson-Guptill, 1975);

Scott and Bullard, *John Sloan, 1871–1951,* exhibition catalogue (Washington, D.C.: National Gallery of Art, 1971);

Helen Farr Sloan, comp., *American Art Nouveau: The Poster Period of John Sloan* (Lock Haven, Pa.: Hammermill Paper, 1967);

John Sloan, "Artists of The Press," *Artists of the Philadelphia Press: William Glackens, George Luks, Everett Shinn, John Sloan,* exhibition catalogue (Philadelphia: Philadelphia Museum of Art, 1945);

Rebecca Zurier, *Art for The Masses: A Radical Magazine and Its Graphics, 1911–1917,* introduction by Leslie Fishbein (Philadelphia: Temple University Press, 1988);

Zurier, Robert W. Snyder, and Virginia M. Mecklenburg, *Picturing the City: New York in the Press and the Art of the Ashcan School, 1890–1917,* 2 volumes (Ann Arbor, Mich.: University Microfilms, 1990);

Zurier, *Metropolitan Lives; The Ashcan Artists and Their New York* (New York: National Museum of American Art, 1995).

Archives:

The major collection of Sloan illustrations is at the Delaware Art Museum, Wilmington. Among other collections owning illustrations are the Addison Gallery of American Art, Phillips Academy; Brandywine River Museum; Georgia Museum of Art, University of Georgia; Harvard University Art Museums (Fogg Art Museum); Hood Museum of Art, Dartmouth College; University of Michigan Museum of Art; Sheldon Memorial Art Gallery, University of Nebraska; Whitney Museum of American Art; and the Yale University Art Gallery. The primary collection of Sloan correspondence and manuscripts is at the Helen Farr Sloan Library, Delaware Art Museum, Wilmington.

Jessie Willcox Smith

(6 September 1863 – 3 May 1935)

Susan Hamburger

Pennsylvania State University

BOOKS: *A Child's Book of Old Verses* (New York: Duffield, 1910);

Dickens's Children, Ten Drawings by Jessie Willcox Smith (New York: Scribners, 1912);

The Jessie Willcox Smith Mother Goose (New York: Dodd, Mead, 1914);

A Child's Stamp Book of Old Verses (New York: Duffield, 1915);

The Little Mother Goose (New York: Dodd, Mead, 1918).

SELECTED BOOKS ILLUSTRATED: Staver, Mary Wiley, *New and True* (Boston: Lee & Shepard, 1892);

Longfellow, Henry Wadsworth, *Evangeline: A Tale of Acadie,* illustrated by Smith and Violet Oakley (New York & Boston: Houghton, Mifflin, 1897);

Goodwin, Maude Wilder, *The Head of a Hundred* (Boston: Little, Brown, 1897);

Smith, Mary P. Wells, *The Young Puritans in Captivity* (Boston: Little, Brown, 1899);

Hawthorne, Nathaniel, *Mosses from an Old Manse,* volume 5 of the Old Manse Edition, *The Complete Writings of Nathaniel Hawthorne* (Boston: Houghton, Mifflin, 1900);

Hawthorne, *Tales and Sketches,* volume 16 of the Old Manse Edition, *The Complete Writings of Nathaniel Hawthorne* (Boston: Houghton, Mifflin, 1900);

Sill, Sarah Cauffman, *Reminiscences of the Old Chest of Drawers* (Philadelphia: Lippincott, 1900);

Reed, Helen Leah, *Brenda, Her School and Her Club* (Boston: Little, Brown, 1900);

Reed, *Brenda's Summer at Rockley* (Boston: Little, Brown, 1901);

Alcott, Louisa May, *An Old Fashioned Girl* (Boston: Little, Brown, 1902);

Humphrey, Mabel, *The Book of the Child,* illustrated by Smith and Elizabeth Shippen Green (New York: Stokes, 1903);

Goodwin, Elizabeth Sage, *Rhymes of Real Children* (New York: Fox, Duffield, 1903);

Jessie Willcox Smith

Burnett, Frances Hodgson, *In the Closed Room* (New York: McClure, Phillips, 1904);

Stevenson, Robert Louis, *A Child's Garden of Verses* (New York: Scribners / London: Longmans, Green, 1905);

Long, John Luther, *Billy Boy* (New York: Dodd, Mead, 1906);

Whitney, Helen Hay, *The Bed Time Book* (New York: Duffield, 1907);

Higgins, Aileen C., *Dream Blocks* (New York: Duffield, 1908);

Thirty Favorite Paintings by Leading American Artists
(New York: Collier, 1908);

Wells, Carolyn, *The Seven Ages of Childhood* (New
York: Moffat, Yard, 1909);

Stuart, Ruth McEnery, *Sonny's Father* (New York:
Century, 1910);

Keyes, Angela M., *The Five Senses* (New York: Moffat, Yard, 1911);

Chapin, Anna Alice, *The Now-A-Days Fairy Book*
(New York: Dodd, 1911);

Coussens, Penrhyn Wingfield, *A Child's Book of Stories* (New York: Duffield, 1911);

Moore, Clement C., *'Twas the Night Before Christmas*
(Boston & New York: Houghton Mifflin,
1912);

American Art by American Artists (New York: Collier,
1914);

Alcott, Louisa May, *Little Women; or Meg, Jo, Beth,
and Amy* (Boston: Little, Brown, 1915);

Chapin, Anna Alice, *The Everyday Fairy Book* (New
York: Dodd, Mead, 1915);

Underwood, Priscilla, *When Christmas Comes Around*
(New York: Duffield, 1915);

Kingsley, Charles, *The Water-Babies* (New York:
Dodd, Mead, 1916);

Sheldon, Mary Stewart, *The Way to Wonderful* (New
York: Dodd, Mead, 1917);

MacDonald, George, *At the Back of the North Wind*
(Philadelphia: McKay, 1920);

Skinner, Ada M., and Eleanor Skinner, comps., *A
Child's Book of Modern Stories* (New York: Duffield, 1920);

MacDonald, George, *The Princess and the Goblin*
(Philadelphia: McKay, 1921);

Spyri, Johanna, *Heidi* (Philadelphia: McKay, 1922);

Skinner, Ada M., and Eleanor L. Skinner, comps., *A
Little Child's Book of Stories* (New York: Duffield, 1922);

Smith, Nora Archibald, *Boys and Girls of Bookland*
(New York: Cosmopolitan, 1923);

Skinner, Ada M., and Eleanor L. Skinner, comps., *A
Very Little Child's Book of Stories* (New York:
Duffield, 1923);

Crothers, Samuel McChord, comp., *The Children of
Dickens* (New York: Scribner, 1925);

Toogood, Cora Cassard, *A Child's Prayer* (Philadelphia: McKay, 1925);

Skinner, Ada Marie, and Eleanor Skinner, *A Child's
Book of Country Stories* (New York: Duffield,
1925);

Bell, Louise Price, *Kitchen Fun: A Cookbook for Children*
(Cleveland: Harter, 1932).

PERIODICALS: *St. Nicholas,* 1888–1905;
Harper's Round Table, 1891;

Harper's Young People, 1892;
Ladies' Home Journal, 1896, 1904–1915, 1926;
Woman's Home Companion, 1896–1920;
Collier's, 1899–1916;
Scribner's, 1900–1915;
Century, 1902, 1904;
Harper's Bazar, 1902–1912;
Harper's Weekly, 1902–1903;
Frank Leslie's Popular Monthly, 1903;
Harper's Monthly, 1903;
McClure's, 1903–1909;
Brush and Pencil, 1906;
National Weekly, 1907;
Appletons' Journal, 1908;
Good Housekeeping, 1912–1933;
Delineator, 1915;
Independent, 1915;
Red Cross, 1918;
Southern Woman's Magazine, 1918;
Publishers' Weekly, 1923;
House and Garden, 1931;
Literary Digest International Book Review, 1932.

Jessie Willcox Smith revolutionized the illustration of children in books and magazines at the beginning of the twentieth century. She realistically captured children as individuals, portraying them in the context of a romantic, serene, and maternal world. A generation of mothers measured their children against Smith's ideal portrayed on the covers of *Good Housekeeping.*

Smith was born in Philadelphia, Pennsylvania, to Charles Henry Smith, an investment broker, and Katherine DeWitt Willcox Smith. The Smiths had two sons and two daughters. Jessie was the younger of the two girls. The Smiths, newcomers to Philadelphia from New York, earned a comfortable enough living to send Jessie to private elementary schools in Philadelphia and, at age sixteen, to live with cousins in Cincinnati, Ohio, to finish her education.

Smith, who dedicated her life to creative pursuits, chose to live simply. As a young woman and throughout her life, Smith preferred to wear plain, floor-length gowns on her tall, graceful frame. She eschewed jewelry and wore her long black hair either in a bun or tied loosely in a Victorian style of ponytail. Although not actively religious, Smith accepted the Swedenborgian faith. When she did attend church services, she went to an Episcopal church because it was closer to home. She exercised by walking briskly to retain her youthful vigor and relaxed by reading, especially books by Henry James. Smith never married, but not for lack of suitors. She devoted her life to art; derived pleasure from friends' children, whom she used for models;

An illustration by Smith for Louisa May Alcott's An Old-Fashioned Girl *(1902)*

and financially and emotionally supported an extended family.

Smith trained to become a teacher and secured a kindergarten position in 1883. Because of her height, she found herself physically unsuited to the backbreaking bending and stooping required to work with little children. On two fateful evenings Smith accompanied a cousin who gave art lessons to a young professor and discovered she had a talent for drawing. Encouraged by her friends, Smith gladly relinquished her teaching position to go to art school.

In 1884 Smith enrolled in Philadelphia's School of Design for Women. Society accepted art school as a proper avenue for young women to travel on their way to marriage—gathering musical,

literary, and artistic skills along the way. Female illustrators began publishing their work in national popular periodicals in the late nineteenth century, and Smith, aware of their success, focused her studies on commercial illustration. Dissatisfied with all but William Sartain's portrait-painting classes, she transferred in the fall of 1885 to the Pennsylvania Academy of the Fine Arts, where she studied with Thomas Eakins and Thomas Anschutz, her first major artistic influences. Smith likely developed her interest in photography as an aid for illustrating from Eakins, a skilled photographer. Smith eventually became an accomplished photographer, and she used photographs to capture fleeting images to which she later referred for settings, positioning of subjects, and props.

HOUGH YE HAVE LAIN AMONG THE POTS,
YET SHALL YE BE AS THE WINGS OF A DOVE

Drawn by Jessie Willcox Smith.

An illustration by Smith for Scribner's Magazine *(May 1903)*

In 1888 she hung a painting, *An Idle Moment,* in her first of over fifty exhibitions at the Pennsylvania Academy of the Fine Arts. Soon afterward *St. Nicholas* published her first magazine illustration, *Three Little Maidens All in a Row.*

After graduation in June 1888, Smith secured her first assignment with the Dreka Stationers notions firm to design place cards with a Japanese theme for a performance of *The Mikado.* Seeking regular employment in her field, Smith signed on with the advertising department of *The Ladies' Home Journal* in 1888. Her entry-level work consisted of finishing rough sketches, drawing borders and de-

signs, and preparing advertising art. In her spare time Smith illustrated Mary Wiley Staver's poems; the publication of Staver's *New and True* in 1892 marked the first appearance of Smith's work in a book. Aware that she needed more experience in illustration, Smith enrolled part-time from 1894 through 1897 in the Drexel Institute of Arts and Sciences. When Drexel offered the first class in illustration taught by Howard Pyle, Smith applied for admission, passed Pyle's required drawing examination, and became one of his first thirty-nine students. Participating in his Saturday-afternoon class changed her life and her art.

"The Land of Counterpane," an illustration by Smith for Robert Louis Stevenson's A Child's Garden of Verses *(1905)*

Pyle, founder of the Brandywine School of American illustration, profoundly influenced many artists, including N. C. Wyeth, Maxfield Parrish, Violet Oakley, and Smith. He encouraged his students to compete for the privilege of illustrating books for major publishers and obtained commissions for the most talented students. Of Howard Pyle, Smith wrote in the *Report of the Private View of the Exhibition of Works by Howard Pyle at the Art Alliance* in 1923 that he "simply blew away all that depressed atmosphere and made of art an entirely different thing." Smith also wrote of Pyle's influence on her art: "At the Academy we had to think about compositions as an abstract thing, whether we needed a spot here or a break over here to balance, and there was nothing to get hold of. With Mr. Pyle it was absolutely changed. There was your story, and you knew your characters, and you imagined what they were doing, and in consequence you were bound to get the right composition because you lived these things." Pyle recognized Smith's talent and sug-

gested she select subjects and topics that were comfortable to her. He imparted to her a love and appreciation for color and encouraged her to paint her illustrations rather than draw them.

At the Drexel Institute of Arts and Sciences, Smith also met two other women artists with whom she would share talent, mutual interests, and a lifelong friendship and artistic working relationship—Elizabeth Shippen Green in 1895 and Violet Oakley in 1896. Pyle paired the similar decorative artistries of Smith and Oakley for their first commissioned work, Longfellow's *Evangeline: A Tale of Acadie* (1897). Writing in the preface to the book, Pyle praised their illustrations for "grace and beauty." Pyle also secured Smith's first major project, Maude Wilder Goodwin's *The Head of a Hundred* (1897). Immediately following came a request from the publisher Little, Brown and Company for Smith to provide six illustrations for another one of their books, *The Young Puritans in Captivity* (1899). Unfortunately, both books dealt with Indians, not a familiar and thus not a comfortable subject for Smith; after extensive research, however, she executed both commissions so well that the publisher offered a third book about Indians.

About this commission she commented in the October 1917 *Good Housekeeping,*

> I received it with none too good grace, but in those days I was not declining any work, and I appreciated that my future hinged on how I fulfilled my early commissions. So, unpleasant though I found the work, I took infinite pains to make it both attractive and accurate in detail. When the third Indian story came in quick succession, I said to myself, "This must cease." And so, I wrote to the publisher that I did not know much about Indians and that if they had just an every-day book about children, I thought I could do it better. I was immediately rewarded with one of Louisa M. Alcott's stories, and a letter saying they were glad to know I did other things as they had supposed Indians were my specialty.

After completing Pyle's courses in 1897, Smith turned down a teaching position at the School of Design for Women. Although she never taught art classes or accepted private pupils, Smith advised young illustrators and visited classes at the precursor of the Philadelphia College of Art.

Because of Pyle's assistance with commissions, Smith had ample assignments to complete while on her journey to financial and artistic independence. In 1898 Smith felt confident enough that she could earn her living from freelance illustration to quit her job at *The Ladies' Home Journal.* As her career developed, the artist often had ten to twelve projects in process at the same time.

An illustration by Smith for The Seven Ages of Childhood *(1909), a series by*
Carolyn Wells

The friendships Smith developed with Green and Oakley at Drexel brought the three together to share living and studio quarters. Smith had left her parents' home in 1895 for a small studio in downtown Philadelphia within walking distance of her job at *The Ladies' Home Journal.* Oakley lived far enough away from Smith that they could not easily consult on their collaborative efforts outside the classroom. Since Smith did not have enough space to work, she and Oakley sought larger studio space to share. Joined by another Pyle student, Jessie H. Dowd, the women found a three-room studio with living quarters for the modest rent of eighteen dollars per month per person. They decorated their new home with drawings, sculptures, and their own work amid an eclectic mix of patterned pillows, chintz, and oriental rugs. When Dowd returned to Ohio in 1899, Green took her place in the household.

The busy artists realized a country studio would provide a spacious, quiet, and relaxed atmosphere in which to live and work. They found the Red Rose Inn outside Bryn Mawr during the summer of 1900 and fell in love with the house and its surroundings. Since the property was for sale at a price even their combined incomes could not meet, they returned to their cramped Philadelphia quarters. When they heard in early 1901 that the Red Rose Inn had a new owner, Anthony J. Drexel, they approached him with the proposition that they rent the inn and the studio buildings. Drexel accepted, and the women lived there until Drexel sold the

Smith's illustration for "Jack and the Beanstalk" in A Child's Book of Stories *(1911) by Penrhyn Wingfield Coussens*

place in 1905. During their four-year residency the artists increased the size of their household considerably. A friend of Green, Henrietta Cozens, joined the Red Rose Inn as their gardener, household manager, and model. Green's parents also joined them, and Oakley brought her ailing mother.

Around this time Smith's success escalated dramatically, as did her workload. In 1901 and 1902 alone Smith's work appeared in four magazines, two books, a calendar, and advertisements for Ivory soap. Other work included advertisements for Quaker cereal and Kodak cameras, illustrated posters, postcards, and calendars. She achieved national recognition in the Charleston (S.C.) Exposition when she won the bronze medal for paintings. The Pennsylvania Academy of the Fine Arts awarded its prestigious Mary Smith Prize to her in 1903. The Society of Illustrators Exhibit displayed her work at the Waldorf Astoria Hotel in New York in 1907. In 1911 the American pavilion at the Rome Exhibition hung her works before an international audience. The same year she won the prestigious Philadelphia Water Color Club's Beck Prize.

Smith collaborated with her new studio-mate, Green, on several projects. For the 1902 Bryn Mawr

College calendar they produced two-toned drawings of young women engaged in various activities, including horseback riding, traveling, and studying. Inspired by this success, they created their own calendar, *The Child,* which the New York publisher Stokes reprinted as a book with poems by Mabel Humphrey to accompany the pictures. Their images of children solidified the artists' reputations and insured they would have ample assignments for the rest of their careers.

With the loss of the Red Rose Inn in 1905 the artists turned to their wealthy neighbors, Mr. and Mrs. George Woodward, for a solution. The Woodwards agreed to lease part of their own property—a farmhouse and carriage house/studio—in Chestnut Hill. The women combined the first initials of their last names—COGS—and added LEA to name their new home Cogslea. The household grew to include four servants, Smith's brother Dewitt, and later, one of her elderly aunts. Nicknamed "The Mint," Smith generously supported up to eleven relatives at one time.

With her increasing income and fame, Smith approached the Woodwards to sell her one acre for her own studio where she could have more space and privacy in which to work. Smith purchased the land on Allen Lane in 1913 and built her new sixteen-room house, Cogshill, which offered enough room for her, Henrietta Cozens, Dewitt Smith, and her aunt. Smith continued winning awards and in 1915 completed the illustrations for one of her most successful books, Charles Kingsley's *The Water-Babies* (1916). She also accepted a contract to produce the monthly covers of *Good Housekeeping;* for fifteen years she earned between $1,500 and $1,800 per cover.

In the 1920s Smith concentrated more on portrait painting and cut back on book illustrating. *Heidi* (1922) became the last major children's story that Smith illustrated although she occasionally contributed a frontispiece or dust jacket and previously published magazine illustrations did appear in later books. Edith Emerson described Smith's portrait style in the introduction to an exhibition catalogue The Art Alliance of Philadelphia titled *Portraits, Drawings, and Illustrations by Jessie Willcox Smith* (4–28 December 1924) as "well-mannered, clean, and graceful, and a generous dash of common sense gives it savor and freshness." Smith's subjects consisted of the children of Philadelphia—well-bred and well-dressed—whose poses bespoke their position in life. If milk and cookies did not keep the child still while she sketched the preliminaries, Smith resorted to telling fairy stories. In her October 1917 *Good Housekeeping* article Smith said, "A child will always look directly at anyone who is telling a story; so while I paint, I tell tales marvelous to hear."

Never a travel enthusiast, Smith finally agreed to tour Europe in 1933 with Cozens's niece and a nurse. Failing health—difficulty walking and seeing—made the trip more taxing than relaxing, and her condition deteriorated severely upon her return home. She died in her sleep two years later at age seventy-one.

Smith's illustrations initially appeared in black and white in the books and magazines up to 1900. The three calendars—two for Bryn Mawr in 1901 and 1902 using tinted colors and the self-published one that became *The Book of the Child* (1903), with its hand-lettered text, bold capitals, and bright-orange chapter headings—marked a publishing turning point for Smith. Her use of design and color shone through and defined the style for which she became known. Influenced by Japanese prints, Mary Cassatt aquatints, and the static art of French illustrator Louis-Maurice Boutet de Monvel, Smith and Green created decorative and visually appealing illustrations for *The Book of the Child.* As publishers sought Smith's work, they reproduced her illustrations in large formats best suited to her images. *Dream Blocks* (1908) included the largest number of color illustrations ever to appear in Smith's books; it included an illustrated dust jacket, color cover insert, and fifteen color plates.

One mark of Smith's renown is the commission she received from Joseph H. Chapin for a series for Charles Scribner's Sons, *Scribner's Illustrated Classics.* Chapin sought out America's greatest illustrators, including Maxfield Parrish, to illustrate popular juvenile fiction. He asked Smith in 1904 to illustrate *A Child's Garden of Verses* (1905) for $3,600. Her execution of the drawings for this volume drew rave reviews from critics, the public, and her editor. One illustration, *The Land of Counterpane,* is a compositional masterpiece in which Smith used foreshortened perspective, realistic color, and minute detail to give an impression of soldiers marching through the pass and over the mountain of rumpled blanket.

By 1909, her reputation established, Smith no longer waited for commissions and suggestions. She actively participated in planning and preparing ideas for books by seeking authors to write word pictures to accompany her drawings and at other times illustrating their words. These illustrations for series accompanied compilations of discrete poems or stories. Smith's work often stood alone without text or captions, just as Parrish's did.

Smith's artistic style gradually changed. In the beginning she used dark-lined borders to delineate brightly colored objects and people. In her later work she muted the colors and softened the lines until they nearly disappeared. Smith worked in mixed media—oil, pastels, charcoal—whatever would give her the desired effect. She often overlaid oils over charcoal on paper whose grain or texture added an important element to the work. This use of color lends an impressionistic tone to her work, an influence of the French impressionist painters. Smith adapted and evolved her style to suit the situation. She employed a sympathetic, sometimes humorous, approach in her imaginative compositions of brilliant colors. Her portraits include children in relaxed poses, painted with affection, not cloying sentiment. For *Water-Babies* she painted the canvas with watercolor and oil overlaid on charcoal. Knowing these were her best work, Smith bequeathed the entire set of twelve originals to the Library of Congress.

For her early magazine covers Smith needed to create visually exciting images in charcoal that did not rely on subtle tones, which might not reproduce well on the monotone or duotone covers. For her *Good Housekeeping* color covers Smith enjoyed more latitude to work with bold colors and contrasts.

Smith disdained using professional child models. In her October 1917 *Good Housekeeping* article she wrote, "Such a thing as a paid and trained child model is an abomination and a travesty on childhood—a poor little crushed and scared unnatural atom automatically taking the pose and keeping it in a spiritless lifeless manner. The professional child model is usually a horribly self-conscious overdressed child whose fond parents proudly insist that he or she is just what you want and give a list of the people for whom he or she has posed." Smith instead preferred to invite friends' children to Cogslea or Cogshill and observe them investigating their surroundings, "and while they were playing at having a perfect time, I would watch and study them, and try to get them to take unconsciously the positions that I happened to be wanting for a picture."

While she gained substantial financial independence from her art—retaining the reproduction rights to magazine illustrations for reprinting in books and collecting portrait fees and reproduction fees for the same work—Smith as an artist preferred children and maternal scenes. Either through her affirmed love of children or bowing to the established belief of her time that only certain subjects were appropriate for women to paint—children, maternal scenes, still lifes, and landscapes—leaving challenging mythological, historical, and allegorical scenes to male artists, Smith rarely ventured beyond these traditional bounds for her subjects. Although she preferred children, Smith expertly depicted a young

Union soldier for the December 1900 *Scribner's Magazine*. It was not that she could not illustrate other topics but rather that she consciously chose childhood themes. As the audience clamored for more images of children, Smith happily obliged. Between 1916 and 1920 she developed an expertise in illustrating fantasy and fairy tales.

Despite critics' opinions that Smith's illustrations were too sentimental, her strongest appeal lay with the *ideal* of childhood: what an adult remembers of the best times, what a parent wishes to see in a child, and what a carefree childhood should be. That book and magazine publishers continued contracting with Smith and paying handsomely for her work attests to the attraction her work held for millions of readers. As an artist she reached more people through her magazine and book illustrations than any museum or gallery exhibitor could hope to attract. Gritty reality could be laid bare for the world by other artists; Smith concentrated on the pleasures of childhood—adulthood would come soon enough.

References:

Gene Mitchell, *The Subject Was Children: The Art of Jessie Willcox Smith* (New York: Dutton, 1979);

Edward D. Nudelman, *Jessie Willcox Smith; A Bibliography* (Gretna, La.: Pelican, 1989);

Nudelman, *Jessie Willcox Smith: American Illustrator* (Gretna, La.: Pelican, 1990);

Marilyn Nuhn, "The Lady Artist of Allen Lane, Jessie Willcox Smith," *Hobbies,* 88 (January 1984): 54–58;

Report of the Private View of the Exhibition of Works by Howard Pyle at the Art Alliance: Philadelphia, January 22, 1923 (Philadelphia: Ad Service Printing, 1923);

S. Michael Schnessel, *Jessie Willcox Smith* (New York: Crowell, 1977);

Catherine Connell Stryker, *The Studios at Cogslea* (Wilmington: Delaware Art Museum, 1976);

Jessie Willcox Smith, "Jessie Willcox Smith," *Good Housekeeping,* 60 (October 1917): 24–25, 190, 193.

Archives:

Jessie Willcox Smith's papers are located in the Archives Department, Pennsylvania Academy of the Fine Arts. The Jessie Willcox Smith Photograph Collection, 1916–1926, of fourteen hundred study photographs used to create illustrations and portraits is located in the Print Department, Library Company of Philadelphia. A Jessie Willcox Smith Collection is in the Cabinet of American Illustration, Division of Prints and Photographs, Library of Congress.

Alice Barber Stephens
(1 July 1858 – 14 July 1932)

Phyllis Peet
Monterey Peninsula College

SELECTED BOOKS ILLUSTRATED: Eliot, George, *Middlemarch* (New York: Crowell, 1899);

Hawthorne, Nathaniel, *The Marble Faun; or The Romance of Monte Beni,* 2 volumes (Boston: Houghton, Mifflin, 1900);

Murfree, Mary Noailles, as Charles Egbert Craddock, *The Champion* (Boston: Houghton, Mifflin, 1902);

Harte, Bret, *Poems, and Two Men of Sandy Bar* (Boston: Houghton, Mifflin, 1902);

Cutting, Mary Stewart, *Little Stories of Married Life* (New York: McClure, Phillips, 1902);

Gilson, Roy Rolfe, *Mother and Father* (New York: Harper, 1903);

Craik, Dinah Maria Mulock, *John Halifax, Gentleman* (London: Walter Scott, 1903);

Slosson, Annie Trumbull, *Fishin' Jimmy* (New York: Scribners, 1903);

Ray, Anna Chapin, *By the Good Sainte Anne: A Story of Modern Quebec* (Boston: Little, Brown, 1904);

Alcott, Louisa May, *Little Women* (Boston: Little, Brown, 1904);

Ray, Anna Chapin, *Nathalie's Sister: The Last of the McAlister Records* (Boston: Little, Brown, 1904);

Wiggin, Kate Douglas, *Homespun Tales; Rose O' the River, The Old Peabody Pew; and Susanna and Sue,* illustrated by Stephens and George Wright (Boston: Houghton, Mifflin, 1905);

Ray, Anna Chapin, *On the Firing Line: A Romance of South Africa* (Boston: Little, Brown, 1905);

Walcott, Earle Ashley, *Blindfolded* (New York: Bobbs-Merrill, 1906);

Ray, Anna Chapin, *Hearts and Creeds* (Boston: Little, Brown, 1906);

Gilson, Roy Rolfe, *Katrina: A Story* (New York: Baker & Taylor, 1906);

Roach, Abby Meguire, *Some Successful Marriages* (New York: Harper, 1906);

Walcott, Earle Ashley, *The Apple of Discord* (New York: Bobbs-Merrill, 1907);

Alice Barber Stephens

Laughlin, Clara Elizabeth, *Felicity: The Making of a Comedienne* (New York: Scribners, 1907);

Martin (Reimensnyder), Helen, *His Courtship* (New York: McClure, Phillips, 1907);

Wiggin, Kate Douglas, *The Old Peabody Pew: A Christmas Romance of a Country Church* (Boston: Houghton, Mifflin, 1907);

Litchfield, Grace Denio, *The Supreme Gift* (Boston: Little, Brown, 1908);

Cutting, Mary Stewart, *The Wayfayers* (New York: McClure, 1908);

Howells, W. D., Mary E. Wilkins Freeman, Mary Heaton Vorse, Mary Stewart Cutting, Elizabeth Jordan, J. Kendrick Bangs, Henry James,

Elizabeth Stuart Phelps, Edith Wyatt, Mary R. Shipman Andrews, Alice Brown, and Henry Van Dyke, *The Whole Family: A Novel by Twelve Authors* (New York: Harper, 1908);

Taylor, Sophie C., *A Daughter of the Manse: A Novel* (Philadelphia: Winston, 1909);

Wiggin, Kate Douglas, *Susanna and Sue,* illustrated by Stephens and N. C. Wyeth (Boston: Houghton Mifflin, 1909);

Deland, Margaret, *The Way to Peace* (New York: Harper, 1910);

Wiggin, Kate Douglas, *Mother Carey's Chickens* (New York: Grosset & Dunlap, 1910);

Tompkins, Juliet Wilbor, *Mothers and Fathers* (New York: Baker & Taylor, 1910);

Demarest, Virginia, *Nobody's* (New York: Harper, 1911);

Alcott, Louisa May, *Under the Lilacs* (Boston: Little, Brown, 1911);

Richmond, Grace Louise [Smith], *Under the Christmas Stars* (New York: Doubleday, Page, 1913);

Lothrop, Harriet M., *The Commodore* (Boston: Lothrop, Lee, 1914);

Lothrop, *Our Davie Pepper* (Boston: Lothrop, Lee, 1920).

PERIODICALS: *Woman's Words,* 1877–1879;
Scribner's Monthly, 1878–1881;
Our Continent, 1882–1884;
Century Magazine, 1882–1905;
Harper's Young People, 1884–1896;
Ladies' Home Journal, 1887, 1891–1910;
Harper's Weekly, 1889–1896;
Harper's Monthly, 1890–1906;
Harper's Bazar, 1890–1909;
Leslie's Weekly, 1892–1898;
St. Nicholas, 1893;
McClure's, 1894–1906;
Harper's Round Table, 1897–1900;
Collier's, 1899–1910;
Woman's Home Companion, 1904–1909.

Alice Barber Stephens was among the first generation of American women artists to acquire professional training independent of family connections. Through newly opened institutional opportunities for women she acquired skills in drawing the human figure from life, which gave her the skills necessary for an active illustration career. Stephens started her career as a wood engraver, a profession which women were encouraged to enter because there was a shortage of engravers, and went on to become one of the best-known American illustrators at the turn of the century.

Alice Barber was born on 1 July 1858 near Salem, New Jersey, one of nine children of farmers Mary Owen and Samuel Clayton Barber. Her mother's family had emigrated from Wales before 1775 and had settled on Long Island, New York. Her father's parents were Quakers who had come from England to Princeton, New Jersey. Barber's family moved to Philadelphia when she was seven.

Barber loved to draw and, supported by her liberal Quaker father, studied one day a week at the Philadelphia School of Design for Women (now Moore College of Art) while she was finishing high school. The first art school open to women, the School of Design was planned to meet two of America's pressing needs. It won public support because its fundamental goal was to train commercial artists to meet the demands of industrial growth. It also was designed to provide training for women who, displaced from traditional home manufacture by industrialization, now needed to work outside the home. The School of Design had offered drawing, wood engraving, and other arts considered appropriate for women since its founding in 1848.

School of Design records show Barber as a student in 1869. By 1872–1873 she was attending full-time, taking wood engraving from a Mrs. Williams. During her third year in wood engraving, 1874–1875, Barber studied with John Sanderson Dalziel, the son of Sir Robert Dalziel of the well-known Dalziel Brothers wood-engraving workshop and publishing house of London. Joseph H. Byram, a Philadelphia wood engraver since 1853 who joined the faculty of the School of Design around 1877, was probably Barber's last wood-engraving teacher. She graduated from the School of Design in 1879.

Barber earned her first commission at age fifteen through the School of Design's student work-study program. During the 1870s she engraved illustrations for *Scribner's Monthly* and Philadelphia's *Woman's Words*. In 1877 the publisher of *Woman's Words*, Mrs. Juan Lewis, announced that she was commissioning the School of Design wood-engraving class to engrave all of the paper's illustrations. The paper credited the School of Design for the work and featured the school in a couple of articles. The only student identified by name under her wood engravings was Alice Barber, who was probably the most advanced student in the wood-engraving class. Barber's signature appears in wood engravings for several examples of the series Eminent Women of the Past. In April 1878 the magazine hired her as its staff wood engraver. The series on eminent women continued in 1879, the year Barber graduated from the school.

An illustration by Stephens for Josephine Daskam Bacon's "Where Thieves Break In," published in
Collier's *(May 1909)*

Eager for additional training in drawing and painting to enable her to leave behind what she considered to be "the confining work at the block," Barber entered evening classes at the Pennsylvania Academy of the Fine Arts in 1876, enrolling in the antique class. While she is listed in the academy's student register as a member of the life class for each year from 1877–1878 through 1880–1881, she reportedly took the fall of 1877 off, and in the spring of 1878 she entered the ladies' life class. Thomas Eakins, who had just been employed to teach evening classes at the academy, was her instructor. In 1878 he introduced to his students modern French

methods of painting directly from nature. During her years at the academy Barber learned his "radical" naturalistic techniques by painting, rather than drawing, directly from the nude model. Barber probably learned photography, which she used as a tool for composition and studying light effects, from Eakins.

Frequently published is a black-and-white painting of the *Female Life Class* in 1879, in which Barber documented her participation as an advanced student in the eleven-year-old ladies' life class. Included in the painting are portraits of her fellow students in the class, including Susan

McDowell (later to marry Thomas Eakins) and Margaret White Leslie (Bush-Brown). Eakins selected Barber to paint this illustration for "The Art Schools of Philadelphia" by William Brownell, published in the September 1879 issue of *Scribner's Monthly*. Barber engraved her painting for reproduction in the magazine. Eakins introduced her to Scribner's art editor Alexander Drake and asked her to engrave his own paintings for the magazine. In 1879 she engraved his watercolor *Thar's Such a Thing as Calls in this World* to illustrate Richard M. Johnson's "Mr. Neelus Peeler's Conditions" for the June *Scribner's Monthly*. Barber also engraved Eakins's paintings *The Chess Players* and *On the Harlem (The Biglin Brothers Turning the Stake)* for the May and June 1880 issues, respectively.

Determined to establish herself professionally among the artists' community in Philadelphia, Barber established a studio on Arch Street. There Barber taught wood engraving, executed illustration commissions for the magazines, and painted. For several years during her transition from wood engraver to illustrator Barber continued to seek work in both media. Her Philadelphia art-world ties led to work for a new but short-lived general-interest periodical, *Our Continent,* which was being published in Philadelphia. The first issue featured a story on the wood engraving class at the School of Design. The story, written by John Sartain, a prominent Philadelphia artist who was president of the board of directors of the school, was illustrated with wood engravings by the students. Sartain's daughter Emily, a painter and steel engraver, was the art editor for the magazine. She saw that each issue was well illustrated with wood engravings and commissioned a variety of illustrations by Barber from 1882 to 1884. Barber's first commission was for "Quaker and Tory," an article on Philadelphia history in the 25 October 1882 edition, for which she drew and engraved illustrations of Philadelphia's historic architecture. Over the next year and a half she illustrated landscapes and genre scenes as well as architectural views. It appears that she also engraved most of her illustrations for the magazine.

Encouraged by her work for *Our Continent,* Barber was anxious to build her career as an illustrator. She took her work to Charles Parsons, the art director for Harper and Brothers publications, who placed her on his list of illustrators. Her detailed pen-and-ink illustrations began to appear in *Harper's Young People* in 1884. Assigned special editions at first, her popularity increased, and her position as one of the publisher's best illustrators was soon established. Early illustrations include those for "Story of Babette" by Ruth McEnery Stuart and "The Stark Monro Letters" by Sir Arthur Conan Doyle. Her reputation grew as an illustrator of children's fiction by well-known authors Louisa May Alcott and Kate Douglas Wiggin. Over the years she gradually added other Harper publications to her list of clients.

Barber began to exhibit her work annually at the Boston Art Club in 1880 and the next year at the Pennsylvania Academy. Her proofs for engravings of Greek Tanagra figures published in the April 1881 issue of *Scribner's Monthly* to illustrate Edward Strahan's "Greek Terra-Cottas from Tanagra and Elsewhere" won her recognition from critics. The Library of Congress holds one titled *Terra-Cotta Heads Found in Cyprus,* which she annotated: "I consider this and other plates engraved of the Tanagra Figurines among my best work in wood engraving." She exhibited oil paintings in the academy each year from 1884 to 1890, the year she won the academy's Mary Smith Prize for *Portrait of a Boy*. During the 1880s she also exhibited illustrations regularly at New York's Salmagundi Club and the Philadelphia Society of Artists. The 1886 Southern Exposition in Louisville, Kentucky, showed four of her oil paintings, two narrative scenes, and two flower paintings.

In 1886 she went to London, where American illustrator Edwin Austin Abbey introduced her to the Pre-Raphaelite artist Lawrence Alma-Tadema. Barber then continued to Paris. Shut out of the prestigious Ecole des Beaux Arts because it did not admit women, she sought such additional training opportunities as were open to her. She studied for about a year at the Académie Julien with Tony Robert-Fleury and at the Académie Colarossi, each of which had separate studios for women students. A pastel drawing and a wood engraving of a drawing by Charles W. Hawthorne that she submitted to the jury of the Paris Salon were accepted for exhibition in 1887. Barber traveled in Holland, Belgium, and Italy before returning to Philadelphia with her new knowledge of contemporary European art—the decorative styles related to the Arts and Crafts movement and the paintings of light that were coming to be called Impressionism.

Barber reestablished her studio on "artist's row": Chestnut Street in Philadelphia. The street also held the studios of other artists as well as the all-male Artists' Fund Society and other opportunities for male artists to socialize. In March 1897 she and other women, excluded from the full camaraderie of art life in Philadelphia, formed the Plastic Club to support women artists by providing a clubhouse, a lecture program, and regular exhibitions.

Soon after Barber's return Emily Sartain, the new principal of the School of Design, asked her to teach at the school. Sartain was modernizing the curriculum, and she wanted to adopt France's progressive approach of teaching students to draw directly from nature, which Eakins had employed at the Pennsylvania Academy. When Sartain established the first life-drawing class at the school, she approached Barber because she was seeking teachers sympathetic to these modern ideas. Barber taught drawing and painting from life, the crayon portrait class, and pen drawing for illustrating.

In June 1890 Barber married portrait painter Charles Hallowell Stephens, who had been a fellow student at the Pennsylvania Academy and was teaching painting there. They maintained separate studios and heavy schedules balanced between teaching and producing art. Their son, Daniel Owen Stephens, born in 1893, became an architect and oil painter.

During her first years as a mother Stephens reinforced her professional life through friendships with other artists. She was particularly close to her former student at the School of Design, Charlotte Harding, a young illustrator who had gone on to study with Howard Pyle at the Drexel Institute. Stephens also developed a working relationship with Pyle, who acted as a mentor. In 1899 Stephens invited Harding to share her studio at 1004 Chestnut Street. Stephens's time was fully committed between her personal and professional activities. She was active with the Plastic Club and the fellowship of the academy and was fully employed as an illustrator. She turned down an invitation to teach at the Pennsylvania Academy.

Stephens continued to exhibit her illustrations, entering them in shows at the Union League Club; the 1893 World's Columbian Exposition in Chicago; the Cotton States and International Exposition in Atlanta, 1895; the Tennessee Centennial and International Exposition in Nashville, 1897; the Great American Exposition, Omaha, 1899; and the Louisiana Purchase Exposition, Saint Louis, 1904. She was also included in an 1899 exhibition of women's work at Earl's Court, London, and in the Exposition Universelle et Internationale, Paris.

Harding remained in the Chestnut Street studio when Stephens went to Europe in 1901 for fifteen months. While she reportedly went to Europe in order to take a break from her busy life and restore her health, she continued to work, perhaps at a slower pace and certainly without the routine of her domestic responsibilities. During this period she continued to exhibit her paintings, and her illustrations appeared regularly in the magazines.

Soon after Stephens returned to Philadelphia, she executed her first of two advertising projects for Proctor and Gamble. In 1902 her Ivory Soap ads were published in *Ladies' Home Journal.* Her drawing *Fast Asleep* was published for Cream of Wheat in

Cover for the 1907 novel illustrated by Stephens

1909. Her book- and magazine-illustrating career flourished in the early 1900s. She had completed and published two major book commissions before she went to Europe. The first, an illustrated edition of George Eliot's *Middlemarch,* was published by Thomas Y. Crowell in 1899. Her second, *The Marble Faun* by Nathaniel Hawthorne, was published by Houghton, Mifflin in 1900. These drawings about the life of an artist in Florence may have inspired her trip. Also directing her attention toward Europe was the display of her *Middlemarch* drawings in the exhibition at Earl's Court in London and of one of her illustrations for *Century* at the 1900 Exposition Universelle in Paris.

Stephens's early illustrations for books include those for Bret Harte's *Poems, and Two Men of Sandy Bar* (1902), which the author reportedly requested before he died; *John Halifax, Gentleman* by Dinah Maria Mulock Craik (1903), with drawings dated 1897; and *Little Women* by Louisa May Alcott (1904). Many of the serialized stories she illustrated for magazines such as *Collier's* or *Ladies' Home Journal* were later published in books. Beginning in 1902 she illustrated at least three or four books a year until 1913 when her pace slowed.

In 1904 the Stephens family moved to Rose Valley at Moylan, Pennsylvania. Near Philadelphia, Rose Valley was founded as a rural arts community, where people who were involved in the city's cultural life could retreat. She and her husband each had a studio adjacent to their home, a barn remodeled by their architect friend William L. Price. Their life in the community was featured in two magazine articles, one in the January 1908 *Suburban Life* and the other in the March 1909 issue of *American Homes.*

Stephens produced little art between 1914 and 1920. At the request of illustrator Charles Dana Gibson, who volunteered as the director of the Office of Pictorial Publicity for the U.S. Office of Information during World War I, she produced a poster for the war effort, *War Gardens: Somebody Has to Raise Everything You Eat, Do Your Share,* depicting a woman using a hoe in a garden. It was reproduced in the November 1917 *Red Cross Magazine.* Stephens retired from her illustration career in 1926 but continued to paint portraits of neighboring Quakers and Pennsylvania Germans and landscapes of rural Pennsylvania. The Plastic Club, which held a solo exhibition of her paintings, pastels, and illustrations in February 1898, organized a retrospective of her work in 1929. A year after her husband's death in 1931, Stephens died at her home on 14 July 1932 following a stroke.

Active in professional activities, Stephens served on the jury for the Philadelphia Photographic Society's first salon in 1898 and on the fine-arts jury for the Louisiana Purchase Exposition in Saint Louis in 1904. She was a member of the Society of American Wood Engravers and a founder in 1897 of both the Plastic Club of Philadelphia, where she served as vice president from 1897 to 1912, and of the Fellowship of the Pennsylvania Academy, where she served on the board of managers. The fellowship served as an alumni association for the academy, supporting current students and programs and holding exhibitions. She also was a member of the New Century Club of Philadelphia and the Women's Club of Media, Pennsylvania.

Stephens won several prizes for her illustrations. She was awarded a bronze medal for her watercolor illustration *I Will Drink It All* at the Cotton States International Exposition, Atlanta, in 1895. In London she received a gold medal for *The Love Feast of the Manheim Drunkards* from George Eliot's *Middlemarch* (which she illustrated in 1899, although the piece was not included in the published book) in the exhibition of women's work at Earl's Court, London. In 1900 she won a bronze medal for her illustration for *Century, Pierre Was Mother as Well as Father,* at the Exposition Universelle in Paris.

Her early reputation as an illustrator was built on her illustrations for *Harper's Young People* and *St. Nicholas.* Much admired are her illustrations for Louisa May Alcott's *Little Women,* first published in 1904 and reprinted several times, and *Under the Lilacs,* which she illustrated seven years later. Her illustrations for Kate Douglas Wiggin's "The Old Peabody Pew" and "Susanna and Sue" were published in *Homespun Tales* in 1905. Houghton, Mifflin reprinted *The Old Peabody Pew* with Stephens's illustrations in 1907 and *Susanna and Sue* with illustrations by Stephens and N. C. Wyeth in 1909. Her drawings for mysteries include those for Earle Ashley Walcott's *Blindfolded* (1906). Adventure and romance stories include those for Hawthorne's *The Marble Faun,* Anna Chapin Ray's *By the Good Sainte Anne* (1904) and *On the Firing Line* (1905), and Craik's *John Halifax, Gentleman.*

Stylistically, Stephens's illustrations reflect the technology of reproducing images and its changes as well as the influences of what she saw as she worked and traveled. Her illustrations of the 1870s and 1880s, like those of her contemporaries, are in pen and ink and closely resemble wood engraving. Even after 1890, when the photographic halftone process enabled any drawing or painting medium to be reproduced quickly and economically, she occasionally used pen and ink. Her 1897 drawings for Craik's *John Halifax, Gentleman* are in the old pen-and-ink style, perhaps because Stephens wanted to create an historical mood for the drawings to go with the period of the novel.

Barber's 1877–1879 illustrations for *Woman's Words* demonstrate both her wood engraving and her pen-and-ink drawing styles. Portraits for the Eminent Women of the Past series are mostly busts in a tight, detailed style similar to traditional engraving on copper. Most of each image is constructed with varying parallel lines. In her more ambitious, half-length portrait of German writer Wihelmine von Hillern for the July 1877 illustration, Barber experimented with more-fluid lines and some cross-hatching.

In reproducing Eakins's paintings for *Scribner's Monthly* in 1879 and 1880, Barber used a more painterly, naturalistic approach to wood engraving, in part inspired by the original works. Her black-and-white painting of the women's life class, which she also engraved on wood, for the September 1879 *Scribner's* reflects a more painterly approach to both drawing and wood engraving as a result of her training under Eakins at the Pennsylvania Academy. She applied this naturalistic, sketchy, dot-and-line technique which had enabled her to capture the sparkling light on the water in her engraving of Eakins's

On the Harlem in her work (both drawing and engraving) for *Our Continent* in the early 1880s.

Stephens strengthened her naturalistic style by using the shading capabilities of charcoal, color crayon, oil, gouache, and watercolor for illustrations done after 1889, when these media could be reproduced through photogravure. Her illustrations of the 1890s are influenced not only by her training under Eakins but also by her having viewed the new Impressionism during her European travels.

Stephens used the naturalistic light effects made possible with painterly materials to create stronger, more dramatic images, which particularly attracted viewers' attention in the magazines. She especially favored washes, which created a luminous feeling of color even when reproduced in black and white. A fine example of this style, used to depict indoor light, is *Buying Christmas Presents* (1895), which she painted in watercolor and gouache for *Harper's Weekly.*

Stephens had also seen English Arts and Crafts movement work when she was abroad. Artists who were part of her Philadelphia circle, including Harding, worked in a decorative style related to the Arts and Crafts movement and to turn-of-the-century Art Nouveau. For a brief time around 1904 and 1905 Stephens adopted the strong, sinuous line used by these artists as the basis of her illustration style. For these more decorative drawings she outlined her forms and then filled them in using oil, watercolor, or charcoal. Many of them have a beautiful linear quality through her strongly delineated forms and well articulated areas of light and dark. However, when illustrator Howard Pyle was art director for *McClure's,* he wrote to Stephens in 1906 congratulating her for moving away from this decorative work and returning to her older style of work, which he thought more serious.

Later drawings, such as those for Kate Douglas Wiggin's *Susanna and Sue,* Margaret Deland's *The Way to Peace* (1910; first published in *Ladies' Home Journal* in 1909), and Wiggin's *Mother Carey's Chickens* (1910), retain some of the linear quality of the decorative style. While she acknowledged that she had come in contact with many artists whose ideas had influenced her work, she felt that "direct contact with nature" was her greatest teacher.

As was typical of nineteenth- and early-twentieth-century criticism, Stephens's work and career were usually evaluated in the context of women's work, although she was also frequently referred to broadly as one of America's leading illustrators. Her engravings also were highly regarded and were characterized as possessing a painterly quality. She was consistently praised by contemporaneous reviewers for the high quality of her work and frequently singled out by art professionals as an exemplary "woman artist." By the early 1900s she was considered by many to be the equal of such artists as E. A. Abbey, Frank Smedley, and A. B. Frost.

Even women authors of the period generalized about and disparaged women's work. Esther Singleton in the August 1895 *Book Buyer* wrote that Stephens was "one of the most successful and capable women now practicing in the art of book illustration in America. . . . [She] is one of the few women who knows how to draw and who recognizes the intense importance of form and line and shading." Elizabeth Lore North in "Women Illustrators of Child Life" for *Outlook* in 1904 compared her work to the stereotype of women's work and said that Stephens's was "entirely free from prettiness or sentimentality."

In 1897, after years of frequently having her work segregated by sex in exhibitions, Stephens, in responding to questioning by newspaper critic and former student Aimee Tourgee, objected to being separated by sex: "Why woman?. . . If I do clever work, why not let it go at that? Can't they judge me as an artist, not as a woman?"

Stephens was honored with a solo exhibition by the Plastic Club in 1929, but as there was less interest in illustration after the 1920s, she received little attention until the surge of publications on American art for the bicentennial of 1976, when the history of women artists also began to be uncovered. She was included in several exhibitions and catalogues on American illustration. The Brandywine River Museum in Chadds Ford, Pennsylvania, held a solo exhibition of her work and produced a catalogue in 1984.

References:

Ann Bartin Brown, *Alice Barber Stephens, a Pioneer Woman Illustrator* (Chadds Ford, Pa.: Brandywine River Museum, 1984);

Helen Goodman, "Alice Barber Stephens," *American Artist,* 48 (April 1984): 46–49;

Goodman, "Alice Barber Stephens, Illustrator," *Arts,* 58 (January 1984): 126–129.

Archives:

The Library of Congress and the Brandywine River Museum (Chadds Ford, Pennsylvania) have collections of Alice Barber Stephens's work. Her papers are in the New York Public Library and the Archives of American Art, Smithsonian Institution; the latter includes unpublished correspondence. A scrapbook of her illustrations is held by the Art Division of the New York Public Library.

Thure de Thulstrup

(5 April 1848 – 9 June 1930)

Steven E. Smith
Texas A&M University

BOOKS: *Grant From West Point to Appomattox,* by Thulstrup and J. O. Davidson (Boston: Prang, 1885);

Drawings, by Thulstrup and Others (New York: E. R. Herrick, 1898);

Outdoor Pictures (New York: F. A. Stokes, 1899).

SELECTED BOOKS ILLUSTRATED: Longfellow, Henry Wadsworth, *Michael Angelo* (Boston: Houghton, Mifflin, 1884);

Munroe, Kirk, *Flamingo Feather* (New York: Harper, 1887);

Battles and Leaders of the Civil War, 4 volumes (New York: Century, 1888);

Haggard, H. Rider, *Maiwa's Revenge* (New York: Harper, 1888);

Smith, F. Hopkinson, *American Illustrators* (New York: Scribners, 1892);

Doyle, Arthur Conan, *The Refugees: A Tale of Two Continents* (New York: Harper, 1893);

Fuller, Henry B., *The Cliff Dwellers* (New York: Harper, 1893);

Davis, Richard Harding, *The Exiles and Other Stories* (New York: Harper, 1894);

Matthews, Brander, *His Father's Son: A Novel of New York* (New York: Harper, 1896);

Davis, Rebecca Harding, *Frances Waldeaux* (New York: Harper, 1897);

Seawell, Molly Elliot, *The History of Lady Betty Stair* (New York: Scribners, 1897);

Davis, Richard Harding, *A Year from a Reporter's Notebook* (New York: Harper, 1898);

Wyeth, John Allen, *The Life of General Nathan Bedford Forrest* (New York: Harper, 1899);

Lodge, Henry Cabot, *The War with Spain* (New York: Harper, 1899);

Sage, William, *The Claybornes: A Romance of the Civil War* (Boston: Houghton, Mifflin, 1902);

Seawell, Molly Elliot, *The Fortunes of Fifi* (Indianapolis: Bobbs-Merrill, 1903).

PERIODICALS: *New York Daily Graphic,* 1875–1879;

Thure de Thulstrup, circa 1895

Frank Leslie's Illustrated Newspaper, 1878–1880;

Harper's Weekly, 1880–1913;

Harper's Young People, 1881–1893;

Century Magazine, 1882–1900;

Harper's Monthly, 1883–1905;

St. Nicolas, 1884–1885;

Outing, 1885–1895;

Scribner's Magazine, 1887–1899;

Truth, 1891–1898;

Cosmopolitan, 1895–1902;

McClure's, 1897–1900;

Collier's, 1898–1902, 1915.

Though all but forgotten by the end of his life and now generally unknown, Thure de Thulstrup was one of the leading illustrators of the last quarter of the nineteenth century. His contemporaries were such artists as A. B. Frost, Charles Dana Gibson, W. T. Smedley, Rufus Zoagbaum, Charles Graham, and W. A. Rogers. His illustrations appeared in *Harper's Weekly* for more than three decades, and he also did work for many other popular periodicals, including *Scribner's Magazine, Century, Outing,* and *Harper's Monthly.* He was praised for his versatility and dependability as well as his ability to work twelve to fifteen hours at a stretch. Because of these characteristics and a special knack for depicting crowd scenes, he was often assigned to cover presidential inaugurations and other important public events. Thulstrup was also considered a specialist in the area of military illustrations, for which he was particularly well suited due to his own experience in the French and Swedish armies.

Born Bror Thure Thulstrup to a prominent family in Stockholm, Sweden, on 5 April 1848, Thulstrup changed his name sometime after arriving in America. In later years he was called "Thully" by friends. His father was a soldier, a member of the Swedish ministry, the secretary of the navy, and for eleven years the minister of defense. Nothing is known of Thulstrup's childhood though he must have enjoyed an education suitable to his family's standing. At the age of twenty he graduated from the National Military Academy in Stockholm and was commissioned in the Swedish army as an artillery officer. Shortly thereafter he left his native land and went to Paris, where he joined the French Foreign Legion and eventually saw service in the Franco-Prussian War. By the war's end he had risen to the rank of captain.

What occasioned Thulstrup's move to France and his becoming a legionnaire is not known; he left no heirs and no papers. Thulstrup said in an 1895 interview: "I was more fond of fighting than of drawing in those days, and so, lacking a war at home, I joined the French army." As a young officer he could simply have been seeking some experience under fire. On the other hand, he could merely have been a restless youth looking for adventure.

Whatever his motives for going to France, the direction of his life and career changed drastically after the war, again for reasons unknown. In 1872 he studied topographical drawing for a short time in Paris and then immigrated to Canada to work as a civil engineer. From Canada he was hired by the Prang Lithographic Company in Boston to prepare maps for an atlas. There he began sending illustrations to the *New York Daily Graphic* and was soon hired to the staff and moved to New York. His work there was limited exclusively to stories of local or passing interest—"fires and funerals," as he described it. His first signed illustration was of an ice gorge in the Delaware River for the 6 March 1875 issue, but it was his second signed work, which appeared in the 1 June issue and showed the Decoration Day ceremony at the grave of Adm. David Farragut in Woodlawn Cemetery, that presaged what would become a specialty for him—crowd scenes. Though the size of the crowd is fairly modest compared to later assignments, this picture shows that Thulstrup was learning the basic skills of his trade, one of which, as he said in an 1895 interview, is the ability to give the "salient feature of a . . . group and nothing more . . . with a dozen lines, in a space an inch or two square." His next illustration was of the presentation of the colors by the Maryland Fifth National Guard Regiment on 22 June, and it also shows the artist's impressive ability to deal with a great amount of detail in a small space and with minimal lines.

In the late 1870s Thulstrup was hired by *Frank Leslie's Illustrated Newspaper.* Though for the most part still limited to fires and funerals, he slowly began to take on more-ambitious work. On 9 March 1878 he contributed an impressive full-page illustration of a miner "picking ore" in the Consolidated Virginia Silver Mine in Virginia City, Nevada. His first cover illustration, *The Latest Marvel of Science,* appeared in the 20 April issue, showing a "Prima Donna warbling a *scena* from an opera" into the microphone of a new phonograph machine.

The two newspapers provided Thulstrup with an invaluable apprenticeship. While in their employ he learned the fundamentals of his trade, and by the time he left he had expanded his portfolio beyond inner-page illustrations of mundane news events. These periodicals also introduced him to such illustrators as Joseph Keppler, A. B. Frost, Charles S. Reinhart, and E. W. Kemble. But *Frank Leslie's Illustrated Newspaper* and the *Daily Graphic* were not the only places where he would have come in contact with other artists. From his earliest days in New York, Thulstrup was an avid joiner of clubs and societies. One of his first acts on arriving in the city was to enroll in the newly organized Art Students League. Over the next few years he became a member of the American Water Color Society, the Society of Illustrators, the John Ericsson Society, the Century Club, and the Players Club. In addition to club activities Thulstrup also regularly participated in exhibits and other events, both as a contributor and as an organizer.

In 1879 Thulstrup married Lucie Bavoillot. To this point the defining characteristic of his life had been change. In the space of ten years he went from being an officer in the Swedish army to a staff artist at *Frank Leslie's Illustrated Newspaper.* He had

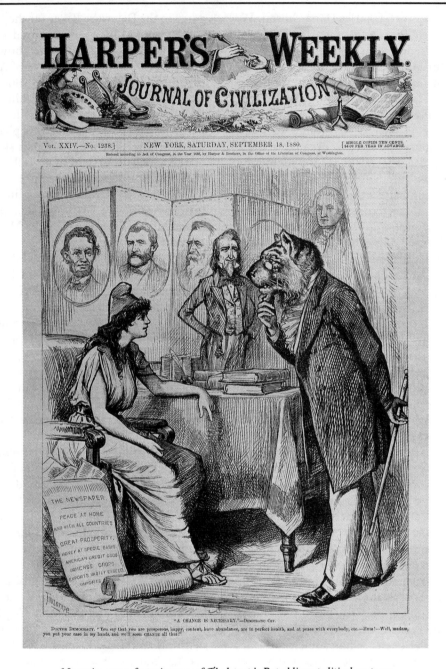

Magazine cover featuring one of Thulstrup's Republican political cartoons

jumped careers three times, countries four times, and jobs six times. Constancy did not seem to be one of Thulstrup's better qualities, but after his marriage his career assumed a much steadier course. In 1880 he joined *Harper's Weekly,* where he stayed on the full-time staff for at least ten years. For another twenty-five years after that he published freelance illustrations in the periodical.

His first appearance in *Harper's Weekly* was on 14 February 1880; it was not a commissioned illustration but rather a sketch by a staff artist of a paint-

ing that Thulstrup had placed in the Thirteenth Annual Exhibition of the American Watercolor Society. This small picture shows something of Thulstrup's lighthearted side. The scene is set in the eighteenth century and depicts a maid dusting a cabinet and a gentleman in a powdered wig eying her from behind. The gentleman is closely inspecting either her housekeeping skills or other traits. This penchant for mocking the upper classes continued throughout the artist's career. In 1899 *Outdoor Pictures,* a portfolio book of his works in color, was

THE TRAGEDY AT WASHINGTON—THE NIGHT-WATCH BEFORE THE EXECUTIVE MANSION.—DRAWN BY T. DE THULSTRUP, FROM A SKETCH BY W. A. ROGERS.

Thulstrup's illustration of the crowds outside the White House gates after the shooting of President Garfield
*(*Harper's Weekly, *special edition, 8 July 1881)*

published by F. A. Stokes. One of the paintings included is *Charge of the 400,* which features a group of well-dressed young people "charging" down Riverside Drive on bicycles.

Humor is apparently what gave Thulstrup his start at *Harper's Weekly.* His earliest illustrations there were political cartoons in the manner of Thomas Nast. On 7 August 1880 he contributed a cover illustration featuring Miss Columbia reviewing the public debt. The caption, alluding to the upcoming national elections, reads: "Which party will you trust, the one that made this debt, or the one that has so far paid it?" His next illustration, which appeared in the 4 September issue, is even more pointed. Titled *Up-Hill Work,* it shows Winfield Scott Hancock, the Democratic presidential nominee, toiling uphill under the burden of the Tweed and other Democratic scandals. Perhaps the most Nast-like of Thulstrup's cartoons came on 18 September: the Tammany tiger, in conference with Columbia, is saying, "You say that you are prosperous, happy, content, have abundance, are in perfect health, and at peace with everybody, etc.—Hum!—Well, madam, you put your case in my hands, and we'll

soon CHANGE all that!" These illustrations not only show that humor was an important part of Thulstrup's early work, but they also indicate that he had quickly acclimated himself to his adopted homeland. Thulstrup was also turning out work of high quality by this time. He had become a master of line and composition, capable of producing illustrations that rivaled the best of Nast's work.

It was Nast's liking of the Democratic candidate Hancock during the 1880 campaign that opened the door for Thulstrup. Although *Harper's Weekly* claimed to be nonpartisan, it had always favored the Republican Party, and Nast's vitriolic attacks on past Democratic candidates, as well as his staunch support of Ulysses S. Grant in the presidential campaigns of 1868 and 1872, had done much to increase the magazine's circulation. It used cartoons by Thulstrup as well as Rogers and J. Bernard Gillam to compensate for Nast's comparatively sympathetic treatment of Hancock.

In 1881 Thulstrup began to move away from political topics and from Nast. After the presidential elections of 1880 and President James Garfield's assassination, he seems to have lost all interest in the satiric side of politics. Around this time Thulstrup began to share assignments with Rogers, and an improvement in his style is apparent. The illustration titled *The Tragedy at Washington—The Night Watch Before the Executive Mansion* appeared in the special edition of 8 July 1881 and shows the scene outside the White House after the shooting of President Garfield; it was drawn by Thulstrup from a sketch by Rogers. The characters are rendered more capably than in his earlier work. He is also able for the first time to inject a sense of emotion into a news-based illustration.

Another artist with whom Thulstrup worked closely was Charles Graham. In 1883 the two men began sharing assignments, signing their work "T&G," and they continued to illustrate together for several years. In 1885 they covered the inauguration of President Grover Cleveland. For the 14 March issue they executed two full-page illustrations. Thulstrup also drew the cover illustration and a double-page depiction of the inaugural ball for the same issue. In 1889 they were teamed again for the inauguration of President Benjamin Harrison. For this event they produced a massive foldout illustration of the presidential procession returning from the capital.

Thulstrup's reputation as a master of the crowd scene was well established by the middle of the decade, and this talent made him the magazine's lead illustrator of important public events. His ability to complete such assignments depended in part on his "Viking constitution"; however, an ingenuity worthy of a native-born Yankee also played a role. When assigned to cover President Grant's funeral procession, for example, the short deadline required Thulstrup to make background sketches ahead of time. To fill space, he dotted the crowd with umbrellas, knowing that they offer protection against both the rain and the sun.

Such resourcefulness was also necessary in other respects since Thulstrup was often not a witness to the events he was assigned to draw. James Barnes, writing in the 15 June 1930 Players Club *Bulletin,* recalled Thulstrup receiving such an assignment from the magazine's editor:

> The first time I met "Thully" was down in the old Harper donjon in Pearl Street. I had just joined the staff of "the Weekly." The editor decided suddenly that he wanted a double page drawing of a national convention then going on. Who was to do it?
>
> Some one said that de Thulstrup was in the building, and in a few minutes a short, thick set, military figure came into the editor's office. When told what was required, he stroked his blond beard and his light blue

eyes took on a thoughtful expression. "How many figures?" he asked.

> About a thousand," said the editor, and then he mentioned who were the well known characters that were to appear in the foreground. That was simple enough. Thully was familiar with their appearance and there were some photographs to help him.
>
> "How long have I got?" asked he, still pondering.
>
> "Two days," said the editor. "It must be here on Thursday by noon."
>
> Hastily the assistant editor, who had a knack of drawing, sketched what he thought the Convention Hall looked like—galleries, walls, and rafters. The artist walked out with the data thrust into a side pocket. On Thursday the drawing was done: without sleep and almost without food, the big job had been accomplished.

The conference in question was a political gathering at Madison Square Garden for the purpose of presenting Cleveland and A. E. Stevenson as the Democratic presidential and vice-presidential candidates, respectively. The illustration appeared in the 30 July 1892 issue. Because Thulstrup was not at the meeting, he had to make certain accommodations in his drawing. The scene is pictured from behind the delegation stand, looking out over the audience. Thus, most of the dignitaries are shown with their backs to the viewer. This relieved Thulstrup of the time-consuming burden of rendering accurate likenesses. Cleveland is turned so that only the side of his face is shown. Another trick Thulstrup used when he was not at an event or he was unsure of someone's appearance was to place the subject of the picture in the far distance. This is evident in his 11 June 1892 illustration of the Republican convention. The scene is set inside Minneapolis's "great auditorium." The focal point is the speaker's platform on which the party leaders are seated. The platform, however, is so far away that only the barest outlines of the dignitaries are visible.

In 1888 ten of Thulstrup's illustrations appeared in the four-volume *Battles and Leaders of the Civil War,* published by the Century Company. All of these illustrations had previously appeared in a series of the same name published in *Century* magazine from 1884 to 1888. Most of Thulstrup's illustrations depict crowded battlefield scenes. Two of the illustrations, *Capture of a Confederate Battery* and *Repulse of the Confederates on the Slope of Crew's Hill,* show cannon batteries in action, drawing on the artist's experience as an artillery officer. His illustration of the Union field hospital at Savage's Station is his only contribution credited after a photograph,

THE INAUGURATION BALL IN THE ROTUNDA OF THE PENSION BUILDING, WASHINGTON. Drawn by T. de Thulstrup.

Inauguration ball for Grover Cleveland, one of Thulstrup's crowd scenes for Harper's Weekly *(18 March 1893)*

though other of his pictures bear the same harsh contrasts typical of drawings done from photographs. Thulstrup was not the only illustrator to rely on secondary information for his pictures, however. Few of the participating artists experienced the war firsthand, so most had no choice but to rely on old photographs or drawings. This project was one of the Century Company's most successful publishing ventures, and although other artists contributed many more illustrations than did Thulstrup (indeed, volume four of the book version contains no work by him), his participation helped establish his reputation as a specialist in the area of military scenes.

Since Thulstrup often did not witness the events he drew, he relied heavily on information provided by others. His first signed illustration, in fact, was drawn from sketches by "E. Brodhead" and a photograph by "E. P. Masterson." In addition to photographs, sketches, and his own imagination, Thulstrup also relied heavily on props. In the September 1895 *Book Buyer* Philip Hubert wrote that

Thulstrup's studio at Broadway and Forty-fourth Streets "is so much of an arsenal, with its half a hundred army rifles of every sort, its piles of military clothes and trappings, that when the artist sits down at his easel you fully expect him, when he gets up again, to don a uniform as his legitimate dress."

Thulstrup was a stay-at-home illustrator. It has been reported that he was a special artist for *Harper's Weekly* and *Collier's* during the Spanish-American War, but though he executed many illustrations for these magazines on the subject, he does not appear to have left New York to do so since his sources are almost always acknowledged as photographs or sketches by witnesses or other artists. Throughout his career his assignments rarely took him north of Boston or west of Philadelphia, and he only traveled east of Long Island and south of Washington, D.C., on one occasion—his only tour abroad as an illustrator. In 1888 Thulstrup traveled through South America and then Europe with the correspondent Theodore Child. He recalled this experience as one of the most pleasant of his life. A

Illustration by Thulstrup for Molly Elliot Seawell's novel
The Fortunes of Fifi *(1903)*

highlight of the trip was the opportunity to sketch the czar in Russia. Thulstrup culled material from this tour for articles in *Harper's Monthly* over the next few years. His sketch of the czar appeared with an article titled "Social Life in Russia," by the Vicomte Eugène Melchior de Vogüé, in the May 1889 issue. He also provided pictures for the series *The Armies of Europe.* Beginning in 1890, each installment was written by a different expert. As a veteran of the Franco-Prussian War, Thulstrup must have felt at least a bit strange returning to face old friends and foes in the capacity of illustrator. He also provided pictures for articles on the Russian, Austro-Hungarian, and Italian military establishments. Illustrations for several articles on the peoples and social conditions in Russia, Norway, Peru, Uruguay, and Argentina also resulted from this trip, many of which were later reused as Harper published books from these articles.

In the 1890s Thulstrup began to produce portraits of notable figures, which *Harper's Weekly* published as double- or full-page illustrations. The series began with a full-length portrait of Joseph H. Choate in the 10 July 1890 issue and ended with Woodrow Wilson in Thulstrup's last illustration for the magazine on 8 March 1913. In between he also did portraits of noteworthy military figures, for example Gen. Nelson A. Miles on 9 July 1898. These portraits, reproduced from Thulstrup's original

gouaches by the halftone process, gave the public a better view of his skills as a painter. His early art education in Paris in topographical drawing would have involved the use of ink washes and watercolors. On his arrival in this country Thulstrup continued working with brush and palette, both through classes at the Art Students League and on his own. Around the turn of the century he produced a popular series of paintings on American colonial life, a few of which were *A Meet in Old Virginia, When Quality Goes to Town, Gossip after Church, The Morning Ride,* and *The Cession of Louisiana.* This last work was exhibited in the Saint Louis Exposition in 1904 and was reproduced for many years in basic history textbooks. Much less successful were two portfolio books of his paintings. *Drawings, by Thulstrup and Others* was published by E. R. Herrick in 1898 as part of a series featuring the work of one well-known artist along with others of presumably lesser rank. The second, *Outdoor Pictures,* was published by F. A. Stokes in 1899. By all indications these books fell stillborn from the press.

While Thulstrup's involvement with the periodical press was long and prolific, his book-illustration career was much less successful. His book career peaked, in fact, with his first assignment. He was one of several artists who contributed original work to the Houghton, Mifflin edition of Henry Wadsworth Longfellow's *Michael Angelo* (1884). The book was well reviewed, and both the *Nation* and the *Dial* singled out Thulstrup's work for praise. His next most noteworthy book project came ten years later–Arthur Conan Doyle's *The Refugees: A Tale of Two Continents,* published by Harper and Brothers in 1893. However, all of these illustrations were recycled from the serialized version of the novel that first ran in *Harper's Monthly* from January to June 1893. What makes this book important is that for the first time Thulstrup is given credit on the title page as the illustrator, indicating that the publishers thought him well known enough to merit such treatment. That same year three of his watercolors and eighteen of his pen-and-ink sketches were shown in the World's Columbian Exhibition in Chicago, and a year earlier F. Hopkinson Smith had included Thulstrup, along with the likes of Frederic Remington, Charles Dana Gibson, Howard Pyle, and Winslow Homer, in his portfolio book, *American Illustrators.* No doubt Harper intended to take advantage of such exposure.

Although the high point of Thulstrup's career in book illustration was *Michael Angelo,* he illustrated Kirk Munroe's *Flamingo Feather* (1887), H. Rider Haggard's *Maiwa's Revenge* (1888), and Rebecca Harding Davis's *Frances Waldeaux* (1897). Unfortunately these did nothing to further his career. After the turn of the century he did illustrations for two more books, William Sage's *The Clayborness: A Romance of the Civil War* (1902) and Molly Elliot Seawell's *The Fortunes of Fifi* (1903), but these also were greeted by less than widespread notice.

After 1900 Thulstrup's output steadily declined. Failing eyesight seems to have been a factor, though at the end of his life he claimed it was the camera that sent him into oblivion. As early as 1895 he was worrying about the impact of photography on the profession:

> Like all illustrators who began work twenty years ago, I have seen a revolution brought about by the use of the camera, and by the tremendous demand for pictures from the daily press. . . . Just at present the danger is that the camera will make young draughtsman careless; it does so much for them, and so easily. A photograph is a good servant for an artist but a poor master. Just now, when the newspapers seem to aim at quantity rather than quality in their pictures, the temptation is to rely too much upon the camera. Some "artists" think that with a few photographs they can do anything with a subject.

The comment is somewhat disingenuous given that Thulstrup had used photographs throughout his career. However, what drove him out of the market was not carelessness or any dropping-off in quality but simply the decrease in demand for illustrators as the periodical press began to rely more on photographs. Thulstrup was precisely the kind of illustrator who was most vulnerable to displacement by the camera. His main strength was in fact-based, news-oriented subjects—military scenes, inaugurations, coronations, parades, public speeches, weddings, fires, and funerals. Thus, as photographs became cheaper and easier to reproduce, there was less need for his kind of reportorial illustration. In 1910 Charles Dana Gibson threw what appears to be a retirement party for Thulstrup. Five years later Thulstrup's wife died, and this event, coupled with failing eyesight, seems to have taken some of the fire out of the old soldier.

In 1921 Thulstrup entered the Episcopal Home for Old Men and Aged Couples in New York. Having given up drawing and painting some years earlier, he told an interviewer for *The New York Times* in 1928 that he spent his time reading "trashy" novels, watching the slow construction of the Cathedral of Saint John the Divine across the street, and making an occasional foray to the Century or the Player's Club. At the end of the interview Thulstrup declares: "I never felt finer in my life . . . I suppose it's because we don't get any drinks here." Two years later the paper reported Thulstrup's death. The obituary states that Thulstrup had suffered a fall and died later of complications in Saint Luke's Hospital.

In his 1892 portfolio book, *American Illustrators,* Smith wrote of Thulstrup: "Give [him] any known subject under the heavens, from the deck of a yacht crowded with pretty girls to a gang of convicts off to Siberia, and in forty-eight hours he will give you a double page that will have all the elements of a Salon line picture. It will exactly express the subject, tell the story, illustrate it. It will be correctly drawn, fine in its mass, and have that nameless quality which comes only when a man's brush obeys him instantly." In an 1893 issue of the *Quarterly Illustrator* Perriton Maxwell called Thulstrup a "painter of pictures for the press," and as early as 1883 the *Nation* had declared him one of the country's leading illustrators. Today, if he is remembered at all, it is as one of many minor illustrators who were active in the late nineteeth century. In his own day, however, he stood in the front rank of his profession and was held in high esteem by his colleagues. He was amazingly prolific and produced an impressive variety of work. In addition to his art, Thulstrup also gave his time as an active member of many art societies and clubs and as a frequent contributor to and organizer of exhibitions. He was indeed a workhorse, but he was also a resourceful and accomplished artist who deserves to be better known for the important role he played in the first half of the golden age of American illustration.

References:

James Barnes, "Thulstrup in 1892," *Players Bulletin* (15 June 1892), n.p.;

Philip G. Hubert Jr., "Book Illustrators XVI: Thure de Thulstrup," *Book Buyer,* 12 (September 1895): 439–441;

Perriton Maxwell, "A Painter in Black and Whate," *Quarterly Illustrator,* 1 (January–March, 1893): 48–55;

F. Hopkinson Smith, *American Illustrators,* part 2 (New York: Scribners, 1892), p. 27;

Steven E. Smith, "Thure de Thulstrup: Harper's Workhorse," *Imprint,* 21 (Autumn 1996): 2–11;

Frederic Dorr Steele, "Thully," *Players Bulletin* (15 June 1930): n.p.

Archives:

There is no major repository of Thure de Thulstrup's work. His paintings, watercolors, and sketches are scattered among many museums and institutions, primarily in the eastern United States. Some of these institutions include the Library of Congress, the New-York Historical Society, the Museum of the City of New York, and the Delaware Art Museum.

Alfred Rudolph Waud
(2 October 1828 – 6 April 1891)

Jackie R. Esposito
Pennsylvania State University

SELECTED BOOKS ILLUSTRATED: Hunter, William S. Jr., *Hunter's Panoramic Guide from Niagara to Quebec* (Boston: Jewett, 1857);

Gunn, Thomas Butler, *Physiology of New York Boarding Houses* (New York: Mason, 1857);

Abbott, Jacob, *Rollo in Rome* (Boston: Brown, Taggard & Chase, 1858);

Moore, James, *Kilpatrick and Our Cavalry* (New York: Widdleton, 1865);

Goodrich, Frank B., *The Tribute Book* (New York: Derby & Miller, 1865);

Nichols, George Ward, *The Sanctuary: A Story of the Civil War* (New York: Harper, 1866);

Guernsey, Alfred H., and Henry M. Alden, *Harper's Pictorial History of the Great Rebellion,* 2 volumes (Chicago: McDonnell, 1866–1868);

Longfellow, Henry Wadsworth, *Flower de Luce* (Boston: Ticknor & Fields, 1867);

Stowe, Harriet Beecher, *Queer Little People,* illustrated by Waud and others (Boston: Ticknor & Fields, 1868);

Adams, F. Colburn, *The Von Toodleburgs; or The History of a Very Distinguished Family* (Philadelphia: Claxton, Remsen & Haffelfinger, 1868);

Richardson, Albert D., *Beyond the Mississippi* (Hartford, Conn.: American Publishing Co., 1869);

Cooke, John Esten, *A Life of General Robert E. Lee* (New York: Appleton, 1871);

Hinton, Howard, *School Days at Mount Pleasant* (New York: Hinton, 1871);

Bryant, William Cullen, ed., *Picturesque America,* 2 volumes (New York: Appleton, 1872–1874);

Whittaker, Frederick, *A Complete Life of Gen. George A. Custer* (New York: Sheldon, 1876);

Whittier, John Greenleaf, *Mabel Martin; a Harvest Idyl* (Boston: Osgood, 1876);

Crafts, William A., *Pioneers in the Settlement of America,* 2 volumes (Boston: Walker, 1876–1877);

Holland, Josiah G., *The Mistress of the Manse* (New York: Scribner, Armstrong, 1877);

Taylor, Bayard, *The National Ode,* illustrated by Waud and others (Boston: Gill, 1877);

Adams, William T., as Oliver Optic, *Out West; or Roughing It on the Great Lakes* (Boston: Lee & Shepard, 1877);

Longfellow, Henry Wadsworth, *Excelsior* (Boston: Osgood, 1878);

Lowell, James Russell, *The Rose* (Boston: Osgood, 1878);

Young, John Russell, *Around the World with General Grant,* illustrated by Waud and others (New York: American News, 1879);

Williams, Henry T., ed., *The Pacific Tourist, Williams' Illustrated Transcontinental Guide of Travel,* illustrated by Waud and others (New York: H. T. Williams, 1879);

Longfellow, Henry Wadsworth, *The Poetical Works of Henry Wadsworth Longfellow,* 2 volumes (Boston: Houghton, Osgood, 1879);

Adams, William T., as Oliver Optic, *Going South; or, Yachting on the Atlantic Coast* (Boston: Lee & Shepard, 1880);

Twain, Mark, *A Tramp Abroad* (Hartford, Conn.: American Publishing Co., 1880);

Bryant, William Cullen, and Sydney Howard Gay, *Bryant's Popular History of the United States,* 4 volumes (New York: Scribners, 1881);

Hall, Eugene J., *Lyrics of the Homeland* (Chicago: Griggs, 1881);

Johnson, R. U., and C. C. Buel, eds., *Battles and Leaders of the Civil War,* 4 volumes (New York: Century, 1884–1888);

Art-Printing Works of Matthews, *Mountain Campaigns in Georgia or War Scenes on the Western & Atlantic* (New York: Northrup, 1886);

McClellan, George B., *McClellan's Own Story* (New York: Webster, 1887);

Pictorial History of the Civil War (Chicago & New York: New York Illustrated News, 1899).

PERIODICALS: *Weekly Novelette,* 1857–1862;
New York Illustrated News, 1859–1862;
Harper's Weekly, 1862–1876;
Harper's Monthly, 1866–1890;

*Alfred Rudolph Waud at Gettysburg, 4 July 1863 (stereograph by
Alexander Gardner)*

Riverside Magazine for Young People, 1867–1868;
Every Saturday, 1871;
Century Magazine, 1883–1886.

Considered the greatest Civil War combat artist, Alfred Rudolph Waud provided an inestimable service to modern war historians with his detailed drawings of Civil War battle scenes. One of the most prolific illustrators of this period, Waud is also one of the few combat artists whose original work survives today. During his lifetime he was so acclaimed as a reliable and accurate illustrator of wartime that even long after the war he was still sought out by biographers and historians for his realistic portrayals of the landscape of war.

Alfred Waud (pronounced "Wode") was born in London, England, on 2 October 1828. The family name—originally Swiss and spelled *Vaud*—had a long history in the county of Yorkshire. As a young

man Waud was apprenticed by his parents to a decorator, but the situation was not good for him, and he left as soon as he was of age. He decided to pursue an art career and enrolled at the School of Design at Somerset House and later at the Royal Academy Schools. When not in school, Waud got some experience working in theaters as a scene painter.

Early in his career Waud thought he would pursue the profession of marine painter, and he devoted much time to study in that area. His later work reflects this interest. According to a critic in *American Artists and Their Work* (1889), "Waud's versatile and skillful hand has drawn many hundreds . . . of illustrations, but is never surer or more satisfactorily employed . . . than when portraying some subject where ships and water make up the scene. . . ."

Described as a genial and sociable fellow by nature, with a striking appearance, Waud was also

A Waud drawing for Harper's Weekly *(11 October 1862) and the engraving based on it by a staff engraver at the magazine, who hid the missing leg of the man on the stretcher and the amputation the doctors are performing (top: Library of Congress)*

ambitious. Finding few opportunities in London, he decided to set out for America to make his fortune. Landing in New York, he soon found that despite his theater credentials, there was no work for him, so he made his way to Boston. There he was able to secure work in an engraver's shop, where he learned the detailed procedures involved in producing illustrations and, most particularly, how to draw on woodblocks. He discovered he had a talent for this kind of work, and he used it, along with his knowledge of printing procedures, extensively in his later career.

Also while in Boston, Waud met and married Mary Gertrude Jewett, and in 1856 their first child, Mary, was born. Later three other children, Selina, Alfred, and Edith, would enlarge the Waud family.

The earliest documented examples of Waud's illustrations appear in Barnum and Beach's *Illustrated Weekly* in the early 1850s. Critics praised his considerable ability for architectural delineation, his versatility, and his prolific production. The latter, however, may not have been driven so much by aesthetics as by economics, for illustrators were paid per image. With pay generally ranging from five dollars to twenty-five dollars for an illustration, depending on the publication, an artist's livelihood depended on a quick hand.

By 1857 Waud was working steadily. He was contributing drawings not only to *The Illustrated Weekly* but also to *The Weekly Novelette,* where his work would continue to appear until 1862. Waud also completed his first book commission in 1857. Written by William S. Hunter Jr. and published in Boston, *Hunter's Panoramic Guide from Niagara to Quebec* enabled Waud to explore landscape drawing. The book included among the many drawings a 7½-inch-wide-by-12-foot-long folded panorama that traced the length of the Niagara River. Such detailed, on-the-spot drawings foreshadowed the work he so ably undertook during the Civil War.

In 1859 he began creating illustrations for the *New York Illustrated News.* In the three years he drew for the weekly, more than 129 of his illustrations appeared within its pages. The variety of images he was called upon to illustrate, coupled with the speed with which he was forced to produce them, compelled Waud to absorb and synthesize the elements of perspective, composition, and design so that they were second nature to him. So impressed were the publishers with Waud's results that they commissioned him to design for the publication a new masthead that first appeared in 1861.

As the Civil War began in earnest, Waud became a "Special Artist" with *Harper's Weekly.* "Special artists," or "specials," were trained draftsmen who went wherever the battles were taking place to create on-the-spot sketches for the pictorial press. The specials sketched the battles and skirmishes in rough and hasty detail and sent them back to the illustrated weekly to be engraved and printed. Their implements, besides the pencil, were the crayon, the brush, and the sketchbook. They followed the armies and depicted the battles as they occurred, often at considerable peril to their own lives.

Waud's illustrations have been immensely valuable to modern Civil War historians due to the often lengthy descriptions of the battles that he attached to his drawings. Although Waud knew a great deal about the various campaigns he sketched, he never made editorial comments about them or the officers involved; in this way he developed a great friendship with the commanders. He was well liked by all who knew him, but despite several offers of staff appointments in federal service, he maintained his independence, even going so far as to keep his British passport on him at all times in case of capture by the enemy.

In addition to sniper fire, the specials were subject to the illnesses and hardships of the battlefield. Often they were forced to move so hastily with the army that they lost their equipment and supplies. Conditions were as harsh for artists as for the soldiers, and under battlefield conditions the specials often resorted to sketchbook shorthand, using a line or two to fix the horizon or a series of pencil strokes to represent the men on the line. These early sketches were later embellished with the details supplied from the artists' memories and their reference notebooks. Waud seldom used photographs for his illustrations, although the engravers back at the publishing house sometimes relied on them to fill in details of landscape.

Artists' sketches were often scrawled with advice to the engraver. Waud, in particular, made many notes to the engraver, since he had acquired engraving skills earlier in his professional life. It is no surprise then that Waud would have little tolerance for those who substantially altered his work. Thomas Nast, who had joined the staff at Harper soon after Waud in 1862 and who would later go on to become that publication's most famous political cartoonist, was employed to convert Waud's field sketches into finished drawings. Unfortunately, he had a habit of tampering with Waud's drawings and then signing his own name to them, acts which infuriated Waud.

Occasionally Waud worked with other artists, such as Winslow Homer and Edwin Forbes, and even at times with his brother William, who had followed his brother Alfred to America in the mid

Waud's on-site drawing of General Lee leaving the McLean house at Appomattox, a more complete sketch made later, and the final engraving for Battles and Leaders of the Civil War *(1884–1888); from Frederic E. Ray,* Alfred R. Waud: Civil War Artist *(1974)*

1850s. William Waud was a combat artist for *Frank Leslie's Illustrated Magazine* but spent the majority of his time in Alabama, Georgia, and South Carolina.

The illustrations submitted by field artists were traced on a block of smooth-surfaced boxwood. A large block was made up of many rectangular sections held together by sunken nuts and bolts. After the guide-drawing was completed, a wood engraver cut in all the lines that crossed from one individual section to another. The entire block was then taken apart so each section could be given to a separate engraver. In this way many engravers could work on a single illustration at one time. (The number of engravers involved in the process sometimes led to changes in the details transferred from the original illustration.) Some of these engravers were highly specialized and would work on only one type of drawing within the whole.

When all the engravings were finished, the separate pieces were reunited. The engraved block was then locked up in a form with handset type from which a wax-mold electrotype was created. These electrotypes were printed as flat-beveled plates on Taylor Cylinder Presses or were cast as curved plates to be used on the Hoe Rotary Press, which could produce five thousand sheets an hour. After being engraved and printed, the original sketches were often discarded. Alfred Waud is one of a small number of Civil War field illustrators whose work has been preserved. A collection of twenty-three hundred of his and his brother William's illustrations were presented in 1918 to the Library of Congress as part of the J. Pierpont Morgan Collection.

Artists' sketches were often edited by the weeklies to support a specific story or editorial opinion. Sometimes the horrors of war were softened for the reading public. In *Citizen Volunteers Assisting the Wounded on the Field of Antietam,* sketched by Waud on 18 September 1862, the artist showed the amputation of limbs that was the common response of the field doctors to the horrible wounds inflicted by shelling. The finished engraving, published in *Harper's Weekly* on 11 October 1862, shows one amputee discreetly turned around to hide his severed limb while another nonchalantly crosses his good leg over the truncated one as he is carried off. Not only did the engravers alter his drawings, but they also dimmed the vitality of Waud's work. As Pat Hodgson wrote in *The War Illustrators* (1977), Waud's sketches have a "freshness and ferocity which the engravers never caught."

The most stringent critics of the illustrations were the troops, who compared them against their own memories. For his accuracy and unromantic portrayals of the battlefield, Waud was praised as a "truthful draughtsman" by the soldiers. He was so popular that *Harper's Weekly* eventually published 215 of his illustrations, more pictures than for any other special.

Of all the combat artists, only two, Waud and Theodore R. Davis, remained on duty for the entire war. Waud spent almost his entire time during the war with the Army of the Potomac in Virginia and was well acquainted with Generals George McClellan, George Meade, Ambrose Burnside, and George Custer. He was present at many of the major battles of the war–including Antietam, Bull Run, and Gettysburg–and is reputed to have been the only special to witness the surrender of Gen. Robert E. Lee at Appomattox. His close working relations with the Union army and his affiliation in the Virginia theater of operations led to his own strong pro-Union sentiments during and after the war.

Waud's visual portrayals were comprehensive. He sketched on any paper at hand, although his finished works were generally on colored paper with pencil outlines, Chinese white, and an ink wash. The toned paper allowed the Chinese white to add considerable drama to the drawings. In *Wounded Soldiers Escaping from the Burning Woods, May 6, 1864,* Waud's use of white for the leaping flames brings an immediacy to the image. The wounded soldiers stagger along past the dead and dying at their feet while others raise their arms, piteously crying for help to get away from the fire. The image is an unflinching look at the suffering that occurred during the war and was a topic that Waud returned to time and time again.

Another illustration that shows Waud's talent for composition is *The Mud March, January 21, 1863.* The sketch shows the fruitless attempt of Burnside's army to move through impassable mud in the midst of a miserable wind- and rainstorm. Through the repeated pattern of diagonal lines in the marching columns of men to indicate the direction the wind is blowing, Waud intensifies the moment. Trees are almost blown over in the gale, and wagons are tipped precariously as their wheels become buried in the mud. The drawing immediately arouses the viewers' sympathies for the army.

Waud's talents were recognized after the war as well. Following the Confederate surrender, *Harper's Weekly* assigned Waud to travel through the South to depict the Reconstruction. In 1866 Waud set out for the Mississippi by way of the Ohio River, eventually going farther south and west. His first group of illustrations from this trip featured Cincinnati, Ohio; Louisville, Kentucky; and Nashville, Tennessee. He commented in his notes from this trip on the differences between easterners and west-

"A Herd of Texas Cattle Crossing a Stream," an illustration by Waud for Harper's
Weekly *(1867)*

erners, particularly concerning their attitudes toward liquor and business, which in all Southern cities seemed lethargic.

On these travels Waud got his first view of New Orleans, a city he loved for its picturesque beauty. Waud returned to New Orleans several times, including an 1871 trip on which he was accompanied by writer Ralph Keeler to create a series on the lower Mississippi for *Every Saturday,* a short-lived illustrated weekly.

In 1868 Charles Parsons, the art editor for Harper, recommended Waud to prospective publishers, and commissions soon followed this pronouncement. In 1869 Waud produced forty illustrations for Albert D. Richardson's *Beyond the Mississippi.* That same year he was commissioned to design the invitation for President Ulysses Grant's inaugural ball.

The demise in 1871 of *Every Saturday,* which carried more than 470 of his drawings during its tenure, was a blow to Waud, who had hoped to have another steady source of income. Soon after, he agreed to produce a series of drawings for the two-volume *Picturesque America,* published by Appleton from 1872 to 1874. The drawings in these volumes underline Waud's talents for architectural rendering as well as his love of nautical subjects.

Waud also served as one of a few artists who headed west across the plains to the Rocky Mountains between 1865 and 1867 to record the westward expansion. His contribution to the field of Western illustration draws upon his skill in depicting the movement of people and civilization honed through years of direct observation during the Civil War.

For his Western sketches he was allowed to publish descriptive and signed notes in addition to his illustrations. These notes contribute information on his activities and offer insights into his choice of subjects for illustrations.

Waud's Western travels feature illustrations of cattle drives credited as among the earliest printed in the national illustrated press. He continued down the Ohio to Cairo, Memphis, and Little Rock, through central and western Louisiana, and possibly as far west as Texas. The most interesting of these illustrations concentrate on early Western railroad construction, including his sketches *Building the Union Pacific Railroad in Nebraska* and *Railroad Building on the Great Plains* for Richardson's *Beyond the Mississippi.*

In 1883 *Century* asked Waud to be one of the contributing artists for their Civil War series. So popular was the series that it was later published as a four-volume set titled *Battles and Leaders of the Civil War* (1884–1888). Waud's skill in depicting war scenes brought him many commissions to depict other historical eras, including the American Revolution, the War of 1812, and the Battle of the Alamo. General McClellan respected Waud's drawings so intensely that he utilized the artist's talents to illustrate his biography, *McClellan's Own Story,* published in 1887.

Despite his proclivity for combat art, Waud was not limited to it. During the late 1880s he also illustrated books for Henry Wadsworth Longfellow, James Russell Lowell, John Greenleaf Whittier, Harriet Beecher Stowe, and other writers located in and around Boston and Philadelphia.

"Custer's Last Fight," the first known picture of Custer's last stand, an illustration by Waud for
Frederick Whittaker's A Complete Life of Gen. George A. Custer *(1876)*

After 1882 Waud's illustrations in Harper publications almost disappear, and the last years of his life are largely undocumented. It is believed he spent them trying to regain his failing health. He died of heart disease in Marietta, Georgia, on 6 April 1891 while on a sketching tour of Southern battlefields. His family never claimed his body, and he was buried by friends in Georgia.

After his death the work of Alfred Rudolph Waud lapsed into obscurity. In 1937 J. C. Randall's *The Civil War and Reconstruction* published for the first time in more than four decades some of Waud's remarkable original drawings. His reputation has grown since then through the countless reproductions of his work. The historical record he left of this period remains an unequaled source of information and secures Waud's place as the premier combat artist of the Civil War.

References:

The Album of American Battle Art. 1755–1918 (Washington, D.C.: Library of Congress, 1947);

Alfred R. Waud, Special Artist on Assignment: Profiles of American Towns and Cities. 1850–1880 (New Orleans: Historic New Orleans Collection, 1979);

American Artists and Their Work (Boston: Houghton, Mifflin, 1889);

The Civil War: A Centennial Exhibition of Eyewitness Drawings (Washington, D.C.: National Gallery of Art, Smithsonian Institution, 1961);

Pat Hodgson, comp., *The War Illustrators* (New York: Macmillan, 1977);

Paul Hogarth, *The Artist as Reporter* (London: Fraser, 1986);

Frederic E. Ray, *Alfred R. Waud: Civil War Artist* (New York: Viking, 1974);

Philip Van Doren Stern, *They Were There: The Civil War in Action as Seen by Its Combat Artists* (New York: Crown, 1959);

Robert Taft, *Artists and Illustrators of the Old West 1850–1900* (New York: Scribners, 1953);

Frank Weitenkampf, *American Graphic Art* (New York: Holt, 1924);

Hermann Warner Williams Jr., *The Civil War: The Artist's Record* (Boston: Beacon, 1961).

Archives:

Notable collections of original art by Waud are found at the American Heritage Publishing Company, the Chicago Historical Society, the Historic New Orleans Collection, the Library of Congress, the Missouri Historical Society, and the Boston Museum of Fine Arts.

N. C. Wyeth

(22 October 1882 – 19 October 1945)

Christine B. Podmaniczky
Brandywine River Museum

See also the Wyeth entry in *DS 16: The House of Scribner, 1905–1930.*

SELECTED BOOKS ILLUSTRATED: Johnston, Mary, *The Long Roll* (Boston: Houghton Mifflin, 1911);

Stevenson, Robert Louis, *Treasure Island* (New York: Scribners, 1911);

Johnston, Mary, *Cease Firing* (Boston: Houghton Mifflin, 1912);

Stevenson, Robert Louis, *Kidnapped: Being Memoirs of the Adventures of David Balfour in the Year 1751 . . .* (New York: Scribners, 1913);

Stevenson, *The Black Arrow: A Tale of the Two Roses* (New York: Scribners, 1916);

Twain, Mark, *The Mysterious Stranger: A Romance* (New York: Harper, 1916);

Lanier, Sidney, ed., *The Boy's King Arthur: Sir Thomas Malory's History of King Arthur and His Knights of the Round Table* (New York: Scribners, 1917);

Creswick, Paul, *Robin Hood* (Philadelphia: McKay, 1917);

Verne, Jules, *The Mysterious Island* (New York: Scribners, 1918);

Cooper, James Fenimore, *The Last of the Mohicans: A Narrative of 1757* (New York: Scribners, 1919);

Kingsley, Charles, *Westward Ho!; or, The Voyages and Adventures of Sir Amyas Leigh . . .* (New York: Scribners, 1920);

Defoe, Daniel, *Robinson Crusoe* (New York: Cosmopolitan, 1920);

Longfellow, Henry Wadsworth, *The Courtship of Miles Standish* (Boston: Houghton Mifflin, 1920);

Porter, Jane, *The Scottish Chiefs* (New York: Scribners, 1921);

Irving, Washington, *Rip Van Winkle* (Philadelphia: McKay, 1921);

Matthews, Brander, comp., *Poems of American Patriotism* (New York: Scribners, 1922);

Doyle, Arthur Conan, *The White Company* (New York: Cosmopolitan, 1922);

Stevenson, Robert Louis, *David Balfour: Being the Memoirs of the Further Adventures of David Balfour* (New York: Scribners, 1924);

Bulfinch, Thomas, *Legends of Charlemagne* (New York: Cosmopolitan, 1924);

Cooper, James Fenimore, *The Deerslayer; or The First War-Path* (New York: Scribners, 1925);

Parkman, Francis, *The Oregon Trail: Sketches of Prairie and Rocky-Mountain Life* (Boston: Little, Brown, 1925);

Verne, Jules, *Michael Strogoff: A Courier of the Czar* (New York: Scribners, 1927);

Boyd, James, *Drums* (New York: Scribners, 1928);

Palmer, Charles Herbert, trans., *The Odyssey of Homer* (Boston: Houghton Mifflin, 1929);

Fox, John Jr., *The Little Shepherd of Kingdom Come* (New York: Scribners, 1931);

Allen, Francis H., ed., *Men of Concord . . . As Portrayed in the Journal of Henry David Thoreau* (Boston: Houghton Mifflin, 1936);

Roberts, Kenneth, *Trending into Maine* (Boston: Little, Brown, 1938);

Rawlings, Marjorie Kinnan, *The Yearling* (New York: Scribners, 1939);

Johnson, Edna, and Carrie E. Scott, comps., *Anthology of Children's Literature* (Boston: Houghton Mifflin, 1940).

PERIODICALS: *The Saturday Evening Post,* 1903–1917;

Success, 1903–1904;

Collier's Weekly, 1904–1920;

Scribner's Magazine, 1904–1920;

Harper's Monthly, 1905–1916;

Ladies' Home Journal, 1906–1931;

McClure's, 1906–1916;

Outing, 1906, 1907;

Century Magazine, 1907–1915;

Popular Magazine, 1909–1923;

New Story Magazine, 1912–1915;

Country Gentleman, 1918–1946;

McCall's, 1923–1931;

Progressive Farmer, 1936–1945.

N. C. Wyeth in his studio

For more than a quarter century N. C. Wyeth was the country's most prestigious illustrator of books and magazines. His pictures for the classic tales of romance and adventure are now classic illustrations, familiar to generations of readers. Some of the best-known characters in literature have become nearly inseparable from the images he created.

Born in Needham, Massachusetts, Newell Convers Wyeth was the first son of Andrew Newell Wyeth, owner of a grain business in Charlestown, Massachusetts, and Henriette Zirngiebel Wyeth, granddaughter of the Swiss-born head of the Harvard Botanical Gardens. The Wyeths descended from Welsh stock (transplanted to North America in 1645) and were witness to every important event in American history. With the Zirngiebels came hardy French-Swiss blood fresh from the great immigrant experience of the nineteenth century. Convers, as he was called, grew up in a family that revered and nourished this rich and colorful heritage; throughout his life the bonds of history and family exerted considerable influence on his work. The small Needham farm where Wyeth spent his boyhood sharpened his appreciation of nature and provided the animals and scenes he sketched as a child. With some resistance from his father but encour-

aged by his mother, he entered Mechanic Arts High School in Boston to study drafting and then attended Massachusetts Normal Arts School where an instructor suggested that he consider illustration as a career. Wyeth studied briefly with artist and illustrator Eric Pape before spending the winter and spring of 1902 under the tutelage of Charles W. Reed, a book illustrator with vivid memories of the Civil War. Wyeth had yet to meet his true master, but for the rest of his life he acknowledged in biographical sketches his studies with Pape and Reed.

Encouraged by fellow student Clifford Ashley, Wyeth arrived in Wilmington, Delaware, in October 1902 to join the Howard Pyle School of Art founded in 1900 by Howard Pyle, America's foremost illustrator of the period. The reputation of the school rested on Pyle's impressive list of former and aspiring pupils, including Jessie Willcox Smith, Harvey Dunn, Violet Oakley, and Frank Schoonover. Pyle, firm in his belief that illustrators were artists first, stressed the principle of sound, personal knowledge of one's subject. He emphasized realism and authenticity tempered with appropriate drama based on imagination and emotional response. His curriculum for entering students consisted of figure drawing from plaster cast and live models; weekly composition

Drawn by N. C. Wyeth. Half-tone plate engraved by R. Varley

"'KEEP YOUR ARMS FOLDED!'"

Illustration by Wyeth for Century Magazine *(May 1907)*

classes with criticism from the master; and, during the summer months, landscape study in the countryside surrounding Wilmington. His insistence on a solid art education ran contrary to the most prevalent practice of training students solely for illustrative work.

On 3 November 1902, after less than a week in Wilmington, Wyeth wrote to his mother, "The composition lecture lasted 2 hours and it opened my eyes more than any talk I ever heard." He made swift progress under Pyle's direction, benefiting also from the stimulation provided by other stu-

dents. By January 1903 he had commissions from *Success* magazine and the Curtis Publishing Company of Philadelphia—his first cover illustration, one for *The Saturday Evening Post* (21 February 1903). The following month Pyle accepted Wyeth as a full student at the school. Wyeth's letters document an almost legendary enthusiasm and tenacity for his studies and a growing devotion to the master. He worked diligently for eighteen months, a pupil of recognized talent who supported himself with a growing number of commissions. He completed Pyle's course in August 1904, choosing to remain in

Wilmington within the circle of students and former students who gathered around Pyle. Wyeth's natural zest for life translated into subjects of great action and vitality; he found himself increasingly drawn toward Western themes, and so he readily accepted Pyle's suggestion that his work would improve with personal knowledge of the American West.

Wyeth made three Western trips between autumn of 1904 and autumn of 1906, collecting visual images that would serve to place him among the top illustrators of the day. His letters suggest that he spent the greatest portion of his time not sketching but absorbing the Western experience in a wide variety of adventures. From these trips he drew inspiration for the frontispieces and illustrations that appeared in *Century, McClure's, Outing, The Saturday Evening Post,* and *Scribner's Magazine.* Among the best of this early work one finds "A Day with the Round-Up," an article illustrated and written by Wyeth for *Scribner's Magazine* of March 1906. The article included seven illustrations, four reproduced in full color. These scenes from life on the range, predominantly in the blue and purple hues of the Western shadows, utilize a daring foreshortening to create the excitement of a roundup. The thunder of hooves and swirling dust seem to emanate from the very pages of the magazine. The following year the January issue of *Outing* magazine included four illustrations by Wyeth for "How They Opened the Snow Road," by W. M. Raine and W. H. Eader. These images, with their crisp colors and stark designs, capture the cold, bleak Colorado snowscape. Expanding his interest in Native Americans to include Eastern tribes, Wyeth painted five subtle and sensitive portraits titled *The Indian in His Solitude* for the June 1907 issue of *Outing. Outing* offered to its readers larger reproductions of these illustrations, collected in a portfolio and heralded as "choice pictures by a master painter." The advertisement named Wyeth "one of our greatest, if not our greatest, painter of American outdoor life" and stated that his appeal lay in his ability to "get at the soul" of his subjects. Another series of four Native American portraits appeared in *Scribner's Magazine* (December 1909) to illustrate George T. Marsh's poem "The Moods." In these pictures of solitary figures at one with nature Wyeth found the essence of the poetry in images apart from the text. *Winter,* which accompanied the poem titled "Death," is a masterful exegesis.

By 1906 Wyeth's relationship with Pyle had suffered major strain, due in part to forceful personalities and Pyle's attempt as art editor of *McClure's* magazine to secure Wyeth's illustrations exclusively for that publication. Eschewing Pyle's advice, Wyeth worked increasingly by himself with great success, and in March 1908 he completed the break with Pyle by moving to the nearby Pennsylvania countryside. Already secure in his association with Charles Scribner's Sons, Wyeth had commissions also from *Century, Ladies' Home Journal, McClure's,* and several advertising firms, all lucrative enough to allow him to purchase farmland in nearby Chadds Ford, Pennsylvania. He and his wife, Carolyn Brenneman Bockius of Wilmington, whom he had married in April 1906, already had the first of their extraordinarily talented offspring, Henriette, born in October 1907.

By 1910 Wyeth's ardor for Western themes had abated considerably, especially under the hypnotic influence of the picturesque hills and pastures of Chadds Ford. On the recommendation of Edwin Austin Abbey, art editors at Charles Scribner's Sons offered Wyeth a commission to illustrate an edition of Robert Louis Stevenson's adventure *Treasure Island* in March 1911. Wyeth's letters testify to his enthusiasm for the project ("I can see my pirates passing before me in almost real flesh and blood–mostly blood!") and to the effort that went into each of the seventeen canvases during the summer of that year. When he completed the series by July he wrote to his mother, "I've turned out a set of pictures, without doubt far better in every quality than anything I ever did. . . . I was . . . able, throughout the series, to keep my pictures fresh and brilliant and striking in their variety of composition and color, dramatic incident and emotional quality." This personal assessment was prophetic, for the *Treasure Island* pictures still rank among his best work.

Treasure Island appeared in September 1911, with high critical praise for the illustrations. Each image, enveloped in a warm, golden light or a stark, shimmery silver, depicts an episode of high action or focuses intensely on a particular character. Wyeth distilled Stevenson's characters above and beyond the textual description, creating such unforgettable images as the figures of Old Pew, blindly tapping his way along the road to his death, and Bill Bones, brooding, expectant, atop the cliff. By illuminating the focal point of many scenes in intense light, Wyeth underscored the increasing emotional tension of the tale, heightening the dramatic effect with a strong ray of sunlight or a figure silhouetted against a fire. Sales for the book were brisk, and by the end of 1912 the paintings had been exhibited in Boston, New York, and Philadelphia, adding to Wyeth's increasing reputation. Scribners published reprintings of the volume through at least 1956. So many generations of readers came to identify Stevenson's characters with Wyeth's images that in

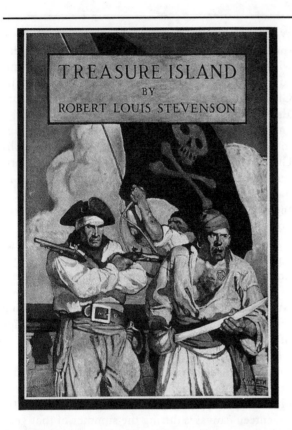

Dust jacket and illustrations by Wyeth for a 1911 edition of Stevenson's classic adventure novel

1981 Scribners celebrated the one-hundredth anniversary of the publication of *Treasure Island* with a new issue of the Wyeth volume.

Shortly after the appearance of *Treasure Island,* Wyeth learned of the death in Italy of Pyle. Wyeth wrote to his family on 14 November 1911 that in his grief he could see "the man in all his power, goodness and glory, shorn entirely of the many petty matters" he had held against his former teacher. The success of *Treasure Island* and a posthumous peace with Pyle marked the beginning of the most important period in Wyeth's career as an illustrator.

During the decade following the publication of *Treasure Island* Wyeth produced nearly 450 illustrations for various magazines and books. His association with Charles Scribner's Sons, begun in 1904 under the astute eye of editor Joseph Chapin and strengthened by the success of *Treasure Island,* became a major source of commissions. By November 1912 Scribners again had offered him the opportunity to illustrate a Stevenson text, scheduling *Kidnapped: Being Memoirs of the Adventures of David Balfour in the Year 1751* . . . for publication the following October. In March 1913 Wyeth wrote to a friend that he had begun the work; by August he had completed the set of seventeen paintings and had worked with the engravers on the plates and proofs. As in *Treasure Island,* Wyeth created figures of realistic substance and intense characterization through his handling of color and light. Broadly brushed, with areas of impasto to weight the figures, the *Kidnapped* pictures as a group are a tour de force in atmospheric effects.

The comfortable and profitable relationship between Scribners and Wyeth continued. For Scribners, Wyeth illustrated Stevenson's *The Black Arrow: A Tale of the Two Roses* in 1916; *The Boy's King Arthur: Sir Thomas Malory's History of King Arthur and His Knights of the Round Table,* edited by Sidney Lanier, in 1917; Jules Verne's *The Mysterious Island* in 1918; and James Fenimore Cooper's *The Last of the Mohicans: A Narrative of 1757* in 1919. His work also appeared regularly in *Scribner's Magazine,* illustrating stories by authors such as James B. Connolly ("The Rakish Brigantine"), Arthur Conan Doyle ("Through the Mists"), and Stevenson ("The Waif Woman"). Scribners alone among Wyeth's publishers paid promptly, records indicating a lump sum of between $3,500 and $5,000 per book. The agreement to illustrate *The Last of the Mohicans* characterizes Wyeth's association with Scribners; it occurs in a postscript to a letter to Chapin, more gentlemen's agreement than contract. The publisher even displayed and sold much of Wyeth's original artwork in its Fifth

Avenue bookstore until 1919 when Wyeth insisted that all originals remain his property.

Scribners did not monopolize Wyeth's talents. Harper and Brothers commissioned him to illustrate Mark Twain's *The Mysterious Stranger* in 1916, serializing the story first in *Harper's Monthly,* then publishing it in hardcover. David McKay of Philadelphia brought out Paul Creswick's *Robin Hood* in 1917 with Wyeth illustrations. Readers clamoring for more were rewarded in 1920 with the publication of three "Wyeth" classics: *Westward Ho!; or, The Voyages and Adventures of Sir Amyas Leigh . . .* (Scribners), *Robinson Crusoe* (Cosmopolitan), and *The Courtship of Miles Standish* (Houghton Mifflin). By this time Wyeth had worked for five different publishers in the field of year-end gift books and commanded a reputation as the preeminent illustrator of juvenile literature. Exhibitions of the paintings for the three books of 1920 attracted favorable reviews in many cities; by 1921 Wyeth had shown the canvases in Boston, Brooklyn, Cleveland, New York, and Philadelphia. As critic John Black reflected, writing in *The Book Review* of November 1921, Wyeth's name had become as important as the author's on the cover of a book.

The Wyeth family had expanded over the years, with Carolyn (1909), Nathaniel (1911), Ann (1915), and Andrew (1917) joining Henriette. Concurrently with his work as an illustrator, Wyeth had established a national reputation as a muralist; he also supplemented his income with advertising art. In 1921 the Wyeths moved to Needham, Massachusetts, to satisfy N. C.'s intense longing for the family homestead and his native New England. But two years later, homesick for the Brandywine Valley, Wyeth, his wife, and the five children returned to Chadds Ford. There the family stayed, bound by new roots that grew deep and strong. Three of the children—Henriette, Carolyn, and Andrew—chose to study seriously with their father. Wyeth continued to illustrate books, magazine stories, and textbooks, including two juvenile gift books in 1924 (*David Balfour: Being the Memoirs of the Further Adventures of David Balfour* and *Legends of Charlemagne*) and two in 1925 (*The Deerslayer; or The First War-Path* and *The Oregon Trail: Sketches of Prairie and Rocky-Mountain Life*). Thereafter, however, Wyeth's enthusiasm for illustration diminished.

Despite quick fame and financial success, Wyeth had always felt keenly the distinction between painter and illustrator. As early as 1909 he wrote to his father that illustration obscured the path to higher achievement in art. Later, financial obligations associated with a large family prevented him from giving up illustration, but he searched for

"Robin Hood and His Companions Lend Aid from Ambush," illustration by Wyeth for Paul
Creswick's Robin Hood *(1917)*

ways to combine illustration and pure painting. By the 1930s, despairing of the quality of illustration in general and disappointed in his own efforts to fuse the arts of illustration and painting, he concentrated on still lifes and landscapes. He accepted fewer book and magazine commissions, largely limiting his magazine work during that decade to occasional covers for *Country Gentleman* and *Progressive Farmer,* and his book work to four major titles. Of these four, *Men of Concord . . . As Portrayed in the Journal of Henry David Thoreau* (1936), edited by Francis H. Allen, and *Trending into Maine* (1938), by Kenneth Roberts, presented him with unique opportunities to create images based on his emotional response to

texts that mined the rich relationship between history and nature.

Since Wyeth had been a lifelong admirer of Henry David Thoreau and had made several pilgrimages to Walden, he eagerly undertook the commission to illustrate a selection of Thoreau's writings. Wyeth's maternal grandfather had moved easily among the men who figured in Thoreau's journals, and Wyeth felt himself bound to his subject by family stories he had heard since boyhood. The twelve pictures and many pen-and-ink drawings gathered much critical acclaim. Henry Canby, writing in *The Saturday Review* (5 December 1936), asserted that Wyeth had captured "the very contour

"Sir Mador's spear brake all to pieces, but the other's spear held," a Wyeth illustration for Sidney Lanier's The Boy's King Arthur *(1917)*

and color of the Concord fields, woods, and waters"; Canby found the pictures "the first interesting illustrations of Thoreau that caught the poetry inherent in the text."

"The Maine book" also came from the heart. As a young art student Wyeth had discovered the appeal of the Maine coast. In 1920 he purchased property in the midcoast fishing village of Port Clyde, establishing a summer residence that satisfied his desire for New England roots. When presented with the opportunity to illustrate Roberts's book, Wyeth insisted that if he were to contribute meaningfully to the book, the illustrations should embrace his own feelings about the Maine coast. Roberts agreed that Wyeth should choose his own subjects. Among the fifteen paintings delivered, at least two had been done as easel paintings some three or four years earlier. These lyric, painterly images do not correspond to specific episodes in the text; they portray instead the essence of the Maine coast. Wyeth judged this series his "tops in illustrative painting."

The Anthology of Children's Literature appeared in 1940, the last book to include a series of illustrations by N. C. Wyeth. Five years later Wyeth prepared an entry for *Who's Who in American Art,* recording a lengthy list of mural commissions and art awards. At the end of the biography he chose to summarize his career as an illustrator with a terse "has illustrated 20 juvenile classics." Unfortunately, he did not live to revise his assessment. He died near his home in October 1945 when a train struck his car at a railroad crossing exactly forty-three years to the day after his arrival in Wilmington as a young art student.

Although Wyeth considered the option at several points in his career, he never taught students in the formal manner of Pyle. A few students did journey to Chadds Ford, but Wyeth focused his major teaching efforts on his daughters Carolyn and Henriette, his son Andrew, and later his son-in-law Peter Hurd. At the height of his career, however, he advised many prospective illustrators through articles, speeches, and letters. Writing in *The New York Times* in October 1912, he accused authors and publishers of hastening the decline of illustration. Neither the publisher, who viewed illustration as a commercial asset, nor the author, who accepted "the pictorial contributions to his book as a necessary evil to be tolerated" for its advertising potential, fully understood, he felt, the requirements and capabilities of illustrative art. Wyeth insisted that "illustration be supplementary to the author's creation," that the illustrator be given the same creative freedom accorded the author. Rather than remain bound to explicit renderings of details in the text, Wyeth contended that the illustrator increased his chance of producing a work of merit by exercising his own emotional and technical powers.

In a 1916 article published in *The American Art Student,* Wyeth characterized the state of illustration as one of "slothful carelessness." He then turned his salvos against the system that produced illustrators, asserting that the training course for an illustrator should be no different and no less thorough than that for a painter. Concentration on "the technical methods, style and the restrictions of the publishing process" would ensure failure, Wyeth wrote. Instead, all art students should acquire a "thorough working knowledge of nature" in her simplest forms: "none would succeed until they had occupied their senses with nature's truths." "You must know that all great work is based on *Nature,* that there is no master ever lived who did not follow in her footsteps," he exhorted the illustrator Gayle Hoskins in an undated letter in the collection of the Helen Farr Sloan Library, Delaware Art Museum. In "For Better Illustration," an article that appeared in *Scribner's Magazine* (November 1919), Wyeth linked growth in artistic power to character development. These precepts occur over and over in Wyeth's letters to friends, to students seeking advice, and in his own work.

In an interview published in *American Artist* (January 1945), Wyeth stated that before beginning work he would search first for "something that echoes within me . . . something that has come within the range of my experience . . . a common denominator." With an unerring sense he accepted those commissions to which his personality was most suited. A forceful man of legendary physical strength, Wyeth was well matched to the Western yarn or the classic adventure tale. Larger than life himself, he infused his characters with his own sense of virility and power. "Power and conviction in dramatic expression," he wrote, "lie fundamentally in its autobiographical nature." He refused to illustrate *Gulliver's Travels* by Jonathan Swift and *Twenty Thousand Leagues Under the Sea* by Jules Verne because neither story spoke directly to him.

Guided by a profound and lifelong respect for history, Wyeth always prepared earnestly for each commission. During his Western trips he amassed a remarkable collection of props—such as guns, saddles, and costumes—that grew larger and more varied as the years passed. As late as about 1934 he added a one-hundred-year-old silver birch–bark canoe to his studio collection. He often traveled to the site of a story in preparation for illustrations, and letters chronicle his visits to, among many places, the Adirondacks for *The Last of the Mohicans,* to Cape Cod for *The Courtship of Miles Standish,* and to Florida's "Scrub" for *The Yearling* (1939). On most of these trips Wyeth strove to experience the essence of a place rather than record an actual location. While in Edenton, North Carolina, the site of James Boyd's *Drums* (1928), he wrote Boyd in December 1927 of the "mute romance" he had found among relics of eighteenth-century docks and warehouses. And while Wyeth photographed the extant buildings, scene of several episodes in the story, he did not copy the prints for any of the illustrations. Despite a newspaper report that he was readying for a trip to Scotland in preparation for *The Scottish Chiefs* (1921), he never traveled abroad, feeling that the universality of nature made the Chadds Ford woodlands as appropriate a setting for Sir William Wallace or Robin Hood as the Highlands or Sherwood Forest. Similarly, the ocean scenes from *Robinson Crusoe* and *Westward Ho!* were adaptations of careful studies made on the Massachusetts or New Jersey coast. He corresponded with many of the authors whose work he illustrated, seeking a clarification of dramatic intention or the verification of a fact from such authors as Mary Johnston, Marjorie Kinnan Rawlings, or Roberts. Wyeth was a familiar figure at the Wilmington Public Library, where he would research Scottish costumes of the twelfth century or medieval English armor. "I have spent almost two months now absorbing data of all descriptions, embracing most of the authentic history of the early middle ages in Scotland, and renewing and augmenting my knowledge and dreams of the 'Hielands,'" he wrote to his father in early 1921, before beginning the paintings for *The Scottish Chiefs.* Yet he never became a slave to history, depending on his

"The Battle at Glens Falls," a Wyeth illustration for James Fenimore Cooper's The
Last of the Mohicans *(1919)*

keen imagination to impart vivid reality to a scene of long ago or far away.

Wyeth began his work with many charcoal studies, sometimes using family members or friends as models. He usually chose a large canvas and oil paint for his work. The size of the canvas and the ease of the oil lent themselves to his quick, broad strokes; one can sense his energy in the handling of the paint. Later in his career, beginning with the *Men of Concord* series, he preferred to use oil paint on commercially prepared gessoed panels. His palette varied, ranging from subtle, natural colors for the Indian stories to the more Fauve colors appropriate to the fantastic illustrations for *Legends of Charlemagne*. Even in the reproductions one senses the various applications of paint, a heavy impasto that defines and weights an object in several strokes or thin glazes applied in translucent layers to achieve a

tempera-like effect. His compositions often lead the reader into a scene from an oblique path, a technique that heightened the dramatic intensity by its unexpectedness. His control of light, refined after lessons well learned from Pyle, was exceptional, and his penchant for illuminating even the deepest shadows with a shaft of brilliant light contributed to the tension of the unfolding drama. On the large canvas and with the fluidity of the medium, Wyeth could infuse his own energy and enthusiasm into his heroes and villains. He created monumental characters, and despite the fact that his paintings could be reduced by 98 percent for publication, the illustrations retain that sense of size and power that grips the original artwork. Stylistically, Wyeth was the master of a great range of illustrative techniques, from the painterly, golden atmospheres that permeate the *Treasure Island* paintings to the interplay of basic shapes and colors that dominates his work for *The Last of the Mohicans* to the expressionistic movement and color of his images for *The Odyssey of Homer* (1929). Even within a story one finds the artist adopting stylistic variations without losing coherency. This versatility permitted Wyeth to capture each dramatic situation in a style appropriate to the mood of the narrative.

Throughout his career Wyeth remained conscious of the technical limitations of the reproduction processes. Unhappy with a reproduction early in his career, he admonished a publisher to use a better-quality process and charge him personally for the expense. While he thought the *Treasure Island* reproductions stood in great distinction to "those miserable smudges" printed elsewhere, the reproduced image generally disappointed and often frustrated him. His mastery of color and his handling of light suffered most often. When confronted with the canvases for the *Snow Road* series, for example, the viewer stands before a snowscape of subtle coloration that shapes the mass of snow, tingling with the physicality of the driven ice. The reproduction process effaced these effects, and the resulting illustrations appear flat and less realistic than the painted image. Proofs for *The Last of the Mohicans* illustrations Wyeth assessed as failures and bitterly blamed the engravers for ruining the color plates. His frustration with color reproduction grew over the years, and his constant disappointment increased his disaffection with illustration.

In 1912 an anonymous reviewer labeled an exhibition of Wyeth's work "a new school of illustrative art." Seventy-five years later Andrew Wyeth reiterated that his father had transformed the field of illustration. This unique accomplishment becomes apparent when one considers other contemporary work. Through a scheduling error Wyeth and fellow Pyle student Thornton Oakley illustrated *Westward Ho!* in the same year, Wyeth for Scribners and Oakley for the Macrae Smith Company. Wyeth's realistic scenes reinforce the credibility of the narrative while Oakley's illustrations create a fairy-tale aura inconsistent with the text. Particularly succinct is the comparison between the images each artist made to illustrate Rose Salterne's meeting with the White Witch. Wyeth chose to illustrate a moment in the narrative prior to the most dramatic point in the episode; his picture of the two women on a beach, bathed in stark moonlight, contributes greatly to the reader's sense of mounting suspense. Oakley selected the most important moment in the narrative as the subject of his illustration, but the weakly drawn figure of Rose in the surf, the insignificant scale, and the unnatural seascape diminish the textual drama of the story. N. C. Wyeth brought to illustration a power, an emotion, and a dramatic intensity unequaled by other artists of the period.

Wyeth's reputation waned after his death, and he left no distinct group of students. His son Andrew turned away from illustration early in his career; while he acknowledges the debt he owes his father, he has forged his own way in art. Two exhibitions, one in Harrisburg, Pennsylvania, in 1965, and one in Chadds Ford, Pennsylvania, in 1972, renewed appreciation for Wyeth's illustrations by focusing on the original artwork. Excerpts from his extensive correspondence, edited by his daughter-in-law Betsy James Wyeth, appeared in 1971, chronicling the passions of his life and career as no biography could. In 1981 Charles Scribner's Sons began to republish many of the Wyeth-illustrated titles to excite new generations of readers. And many of the paintings for these tales of adventure and romance belong now to museums and libraries, icons of what Pyle called America's own art form.

Letters:

Betsy James Wyeth, ed., *The Wyeths: The Letters of N. C. Wyeth* (Boston: Gambit, 1971).

References:

Douglas Allen and Douglas Allen Jr., *N. C. Wyeth: The Collected Paintings, Illustrations and Murals* (New York: Bonanza, 1972);

James H. Duff, "An American Vision," in *An American Vision: Three Generations of Wyeth Art* (Boston: Little, Brown, 1987);

Duff, *The Western World of N. C. Wyeth,* exhibition catalogue (Cody, Wyo.: Buffalo Bill Historical Center, 1980), pp. 2–75;

Ernest W. Watson, "Giant on a Hilltop," *American Artist Magazine,* 9, (January 1945): 16–22, 28;

Andrew Wyeth, "N. C. Wyeth," in *An American Vision: Three Generations of Wyeth Art* (Boston: Little, Brown, 1987), pp. 78–87.

Archives:

The Brandywine River Museum, Chadds Ford, Pennsylvania, holds the largest collection of original art and reference material, including tear sheets and proofs, illustrated books, and an electronic catalogue raisonné and bibliography. Other notable collections include the Buffalo Bill Historical Center in Cody, Wyoming; the Delaware Art Museum in Wilmington; the New York Public Library; the Philadelphia Public Library; and the Wilmington Public Library in Delaware. The unpublished letters between N. C. Wyeth and editors at Charles Scribner's Sons are located at Princeton University Library, Princeton, New Jersey.

Books for Further Reading

Best, James J. *American Popular Illustration: A Reference Guide.* Westport, Conn.: Greenwood Press, 1984.

Bland, David. *A History of Book Illustration, the Illuminated Manuscript and the Printed Book.* Cleveland: World, 1958.

Bolton, Theodore. *American Book Illustrators: Bibliographic Checklists of 123 Artists.* New York: R. R. Bowker, 1938.

Brenni, Joseph Vito. *Book Illustration and Decoration: A Guide to Research.* Westport, Conn.: Greenwood Press, 1980.

Dykes, Jeff. *Fifty Great Western Illustrators, A Bibliographic Checklist.* Flagstaff, Ariz.: Northland, 1975.

Ellis, Richard Williamson. *Book Illustration: A Survey of Its History and Development Shown by the Work of Various Artists, Together with Critical Comments.* Kingsport, Tenn.: Kingsport Press, 1952.

Feaver, William. *When We Were Young: Two Centuries of Children's Book Illustration.* New York: Holt, Rinehart & Winston, 1977.

Goodrum, Charles, and Dalrymple, Helen. *Advertising in America: The First 200 Years.* New York: Abrams, 1990.

Grunwald Center for the Graphic Arts. *The American Personality: The Artist Illustrator of Life in the U.S., 1860–1930.* Los Angeles: Grunwald Center, 1976.

Hogarth, Paul. *Artists on Horseback: The Old West in Illustrated Journalism 1857–1900.* New York: Watson-Guptill, 1972.

Horwitt, Nathan G. *A Book of Notable American Illustrators.* New York: Walker, 1926.

Larson, Judy L. *American Illustration 1890–1925: Romance, Adventure and Suspense.* Calgary, Alberta, Canada: Glenbow Museum, 1986.

Meyer, Susan E. *America's Great Illustrators.* New York: Abrams, 1978.

Miller, Bertha E. Mahony. *Illustrators of Children's Books, 1744–1945.* Boston: Horn Book, 1947.

Murrell, William. *A History of American Graphic Humor.* New York: Cooper Square, 1967.

Museum of Fine Arts, Boston, and the Harvard College Library. *The Artist and the Book 1860–1960.* Boston: Museum of Fine Arts, 1972.

North American Print Conference. *The American Illustrated Book in the Nineteenth Century.* Winterthur, Del.: Winterthur Museum, 1987.

Pennell, Joseph. *Pen Drawing and Pen Draughtsmen. Their Work and Their Methods: A Study of the Art Today with Technical Suggestions.* London & New York: Macmillan, 1889.

Pierpont Morgan Library. *Early Children's Books and Their Illustration.* Boston: Godine, 1975.

Pitz, Henry C. *The Practice of Illustration*. New York: Watson-Guptill, 1947.

Pitz. *A Treasury of American Book Illustration*. New York: Watson-Guptill, 1947.

Princeton University. *Early American Book Illustrators and Wood Engravers, 1670–1870; a Catalogue of a Collection of American Books*. Princeton, N.J.: Princeton University Press, 1958.

Reed, Walt. *Great American Illustrators*. New York: Crown, 1979.

Schwarcz, Joseph H. *Ways of the Illustrator: Visual Communication in Children's Literature*. Chicago: American Library Association, 1982.

Smith, F. Hopkinson. *American Illustrators*. New York: Scribners, 1892.

Society of Illustrators. *America's Great Women Illustrators, 1850–1950*. New York: Madison Square, 1985.

Taft, Robert. *Artists and Illustrators of the Old West 1850–1900*. New York: Scribners, 1953.

Watson, Ernest William. *Forty Illustrators and How They Work*. New York: Watson-Guptill, 1946.

Contributors

Donald A. Barclay ....*New Mexico State University Library*

Georgia B. Barnhill ....*American Antiquarian Society*

Richard Bleiler ....*University of Connecticut*

Susan Thach Dean ....*University of Colorado at Boulder Libraries*

Donald H. Dyal...*Texas A&M University*

Jackie R. Esposito ....*Pennsylvania State University*

Laura S. Fuderer ....*University of Notre Dame*

Michael R. Grauer...*Panhandle-Plains Historical Museum*

Douglas G. Greene ....*Old Dominion University*

Susan Hamburger ....*Pennsylvania State University*

Catherine A. Hastedt ....*Texas A&M University*

Elizabeth H. Hawkes...*West Chester, Pennsylvania*

John Neal Hoover..*Saint Louis Mercantile Library Association*

Margaret A. Irwin......................*Houston Academy of Medicine–Texas Medical Center Library*

Nancy Allyn Jarzombeck ....*Ithaca, New York*

Michael Scott Joseph ....*Rutgers University Libraries*

Kenneth Kempcke ....*Montana State University*

Kimberly Kizer ....*Texas A&M University*

Katherine Kominis ....*Boston University*

Carrie L. Marsh..*Claremont Colleges*

Francis Martin Jr. ....*University of Central Florida*

Phyllis Peet ....*Monterey Peninsula College*

Felicia A. Piscitelli..*Texas A&M University*

Christine B. Podmaniczky ....*Brandywine River Museum*

Jane R. Pomeroy..*Limington, Maine*

Sue Rainey ....*Charlottesville, Virginia*

Steven E. Smith...*Texas A&M University Library*

Carole Sims Tabor...*Louisiana Tech University*

David Tatham..*Syracuse University*

Constance Vidor ....*Cathedral School, Cathedral Saint John the Divine*

Melissa J. Webster...*Powell, Wyoming*

Stephen Zimmer ....*Philmont Museum*

Cumulative Index

Dictionary of Literary Biography, Volumes 1-188
Dictionary of Literary Biography Yearbook, 1980-1996
Dictionary of Literary Biography Documentary Series, Volumes 1-16

Cumulative Index

DLB before number: *Dictionary of Literary Biography,* Volumes 1-188
Y before number: *Dictionary of Literary Biography Yearbook,* 1980-1996
DS before number: *Dictionary of Literary Biography Documentary Series,* Volumes 1-16

G

O

Pro